What They Said
in 1974

What They Said In 1974

The Yearbook of Spoken Opinion

●

Compiled and Edited by

ALAN F. PATER

and

JASON R. PATER

MONITOR BOOK COMPANY, INC.

SIXTH ANNUAL EDITION

Printed in the United States of America

Library of Congress catalogue card number: 74-111080

ISBN number: 0-9600252-7-8

WHAT THEY SAID is published annually by
Monitor Book Company, Inc.
Beverly Hills, Calif.

To

The Newsmakers of the World . . .

May they never be at a loss for words

Preface to the First Edition (1969)

Words can be powerful or subtle, humorous or maddening. They can be vigorous or feeble, lucid or obscure, inspiring or despairing, wise or foolish, hopeful or pessimistic . . . they can be fearful or confident, timid or articulate, persuasive or perverse, honest or deceitful. As tools at a speaker's command, words can be used to reason, argue, discuss, cajole, plead, debate, declaim, threaten, infuriate, or appease; they can harangue, flourish, recite, preach, discourse, stab to the quick, or gently sermonize.

When casually spoken by a stage or film star, words can go beyond the press-agentry and make-up facade and reveal the inner man or woman. When purposefully uttered in the considered phrasing of a head of state, words can determine the destiny of millions of people, resolve peace or war, or chart the course of a nation on whose direction the fate of the entire world may depend.

Until now, the *copia verborum* of well-known and renowned public figures—the doctors and diplomats, the governors and generals, the potentates and presidents, the entertainers and educators, the bishops and baseball players, the jurists and journalists, the authors and attorneys, the congressmen and chairmen-of-the-board—whether enunciated in speeches, lectures, interviews, radio and television addresses, news conferences, forums, symposiums, town meetings, committee hearings, random remarks to the press, or delivered on the floors of the United States Senate and House of Representatives or in the parliaments and palaces of the world—have been dutifully reported in the media, then filed away and, for the most part, forgotten.

The editors of *WHAT THEY SAID* believe that consigning such a wealth of thoughts, ideas, doctrines, opinions and philosophies to interment in the morgues and archives of the Fourth Estate is lamentable and unnecessary. Yet the media, in all their forms, are constantly engulfing us in a profusion of endless and increasingly voluminous news reports. One is easily disposed to disregard or forget the stimulating discussion of critical issues embodied in so many of the utterances of those who make the news and, in their respective fields, shape the events throughout the world. The conclusion is therefore a natural and compelling one: the educator, the public official, the business executive, the statesman, the philosopher—everyone who has a stake in the complex, often confusing trends of our times—should have material of this kind readily available.

These, then, are the circumstances under which *WHAT THEY SAID* was conceived. It is the culmination of a year of listening to the people in the public eye; a year of scrutinizing, monitoring, reviewing, judging, deciding—a year during which the editors resurrected from almost certain oblivion those quintessential elements of the year's *spoken* opinion which, in their judgment, demanded preservation in book form.

WHAT THEY SAID is a pioneer in its field. Its *raison d'etre* is the firm conviction that presenting, each year, the highlights of vital and interesting views from the lips of prominent people on virtually every aspect of contemporary civilization fulfills the need to give the *spoken* word the permanence and lasting value of the *written* word. For, if it is true that a picture is worth 10,000 words, it is equally true that a verbal conclusion, an apt quote or a candid comment by a person of fame or influence can have more significance and can provide more understanding than an entire page of summary in a standard work of reference.

The editors of *WHAT THEY SAID* did not, however, design their book for researchers and scholars alone. One of the failings of the conventional reference work is that it is blandly written and referred to primarily for facts and figures, lacking inherent "interest value." *WHAT THEY SAID,* on the other hand, was planned for sheer enjoyment and pleasure, for searching glimpses into the lives and thoughts of the world's celebrities, as well as for serious study, intellectual reflection and the philosophical contemplation of our multifaceted life and mores. Furthermore, those pressed for time, yet anxious to know what the newsmakers have been saying, will welcome the short excerpts which will make for quick, intermittent reading—and rereading. And, of course, the topical classifications, the speakers' index, the subject index, the place and date information—documented and authenticated and easily located—will supply a rich fund of hitherto not readily obtainable reference and statistical material.

Finally, the reader will find that the editors have eschewed trite comments and cliches, tedious and boring. The selected quotations, each standing on its own, are pertinent, significant, stimulating—above all, relevant to today's world, expressed in the speakers' own words. And they will, the editors feel, be even more relevant tomorrow. They will be re-examined and reflected upon in the future by men and women eager to learn from the past. The prophecies, the promises, the "golden dreams," the boastings and rantings, the bluster, the bravado, the pleadings and representations of those whose voices echo in these pages (and in those to come) should provide a rare and unique history lesson. The positions held by these luminaries, in their respective callings, are such that what they say today may profoundly affect the future as well as the present, and so will be of lasting importance and meaning.

ALAN F. PATER
JASON R. PATER

Beverly Hills, California

Table of Contents

About the 1974 Edition . . .

A sizeable part of this edition of *WHAT THEY SAID* is, necessarily, devoted to the Watergate affair, and indeed that scandal occupied much of the national and world-wide media throughout the year. We believe our Watergate section is the single most comprehensive collection of spoken opinion on this subject available.

But the United States was not the only nation to experience shake-ups in government in 1974. The year saw sudden, and sometimes unexpected, changes at the top in such countries as Greece, West Germany, Japan, Cyprus, Portugal, France and Britain.

Despite these governmental comings and goings, however, most would agree that the Number One topic of concern, generally everywhere in the world, was more monetary than political. Inflation (especially the ever-higher cost of oil and its derivatives) made 1974 an economic year more than anything else.

The current volume in the *WHAT THEY SAID* series documents these and virtually all other significant happenings of 1974 in its customary distinctive style, detail and depth. Over the years we have incorporated many new features and improvements in the series, and as always we sincerely invite suggestions for continued betterment of any phase of *WHAT THEY SAID*.

With no intention of being a complete news summary of 1974, following are some of the happenings reflected in many of this year's quotations . . .

Commerce:

With continuing increases in the retail prices of oil products, oil-company profits attracted the criticism of many. Indeed, profits in general were under fire from varied sources. The pros and cons will be found in this year's *WHAT THEY SAID*.

Environment:

The continuing debate over conservation and pollution was joined by the energy crisis, oil shortage and other energy-related phenomena.

Foreign Affairs:

Foreign aid was a controversial issue in the U.S. Congress, as were allegedly illegal activities of the Central Intelligence Agency, both domestically and internationally.

Labor/The Economy:

One of the most talked-about issues, certainly the one of most concern to the individual, was the economy—with inflation leading to talk of recession and even depression. The value of wage/price controls was frequently debated.

ABOUT THE 1974 EDITION

Politics:

Watergate heads the list of the most-discussed issues of 1974. A Congressional impeachment inquiry eventually led to Richard Nixon's resignation, the first ever by a U.S. President. Gerald Ford took over as Chief Executive, with Nelson Rockefeller becoming Vice President several months later. The November general election saw the Democrats win decisively, despite President Ford's warning of a "veto-proof" Congress.

Africa:

South Africa was suspended from the United Nations General Assembly because of its racial practices. A coup in Portugal set the stage for eventual independence of its colonies on this continent.

Americas:

Alleged U.S. Central Intelligence Agency involvement in the 1973 coup overthrowing Chilean President Salvador Allende emerged. The Organization of American States failed to attain the needed two-thirds majority in a vote to end the economic and political isolation of Cuba.

Asia:

Japanese Prime Minister Kakuei Tanaka resigned amidst scandal of alleged financial inequities, and was succeeded by Takeo Miki. India detonated its first nuclear device. Martial law continued in the Philippines.

Indochina:

U.S. President Ford promulgated a leniency program for U.S. Vietnam draft-dodgers and deserters; by year's end its success was not certain. Debate in the U.S. Congress was heated on the subject of continued aid to South Vietnam. Fighting continued in Vietnam and Cambodia.

Middle East:

Petroleum export prices from this oil-rich area continued going up as the world pondered what to do about it. U.S. President Nixon was warmly received during a visit that included Egypt and Saudi Arabia. Arab guerrilla leader Yasir Arafat was invited to speak before the United Nations in a move that sparked much controversy.

Journalism:

Veteran NBC news commentator Chet Huntley died.

Sports:

The National Football League staged a player strike near the beginning of the season.

Europe:

A coup on Cyprus ousted President Makarios, temporarily installed Nikos Sampson, who was succeeded by Glafkos Clerides, who relinquished the office back to Archbishop Makarios. Meanwhile, Turkey invaded the island on behalf of Turkish Cypriots; and, by the end of the year, the situation was more or less in a state of flux. As a possible result of the Cyprus crisis, the ruling Greek junta resigned, to be replaced by Constantine Caramanlis as Premier, who won heavily in a national election which followed his takeover. In Portugal, Prime Minister Marcelo Caetano was ousted in a coup. West German Chancellor Willy Brandt resigned as a result of a Communist spy being discovered on his staff. The French elected Valery Giscard d'Estaing President after the death of Georges Pompidou. In Britain, Conservative Prime Minister Edward Heath lost to Labor's Harold Wilson in a fall election. And the Soviets exiled dissident author Alexander Solzhenitsyn, who thereafter settled in Switzerland.

Editorial Treatment

ORGANIZATION OF MATERIAL

Special attention has been given to the arrangement of the book—from the major divisions down to the individual categories and speakers—the objective being a logical progression of related material, as follows:

(A) The categories are arranged alphabetically within each of three major sections—

Part One: "National Affairs"
Part Two: "International Affairs"
Part Three: "General"

In this manner, the reader can quickly locate quotations pertaining to particular fields of interest (see also *Indexing*). It should be noted that some quotations contain a number of thoughts or ideas—sometimes on different subjects—while some are vague as to exact subject matter and thus do not fit clearly into a specific topic classification. In such cases, the judgment of the Editors has determined the most appropriate category.

(B) Within each category, the speakers are in alphabetical order by surname.

1. Surnames of which "de," "du," "da," "van," "von," "St.," etc., are a part are usually alphabetized by these prefixes. Example: Simone de Beauvoir is alphabetized under "de Beauvoir." This does not apply to prefixes "el" or "al," as used in some Middle Eastern names.
2. Compound surnames (whether or not hyphenated) are alphabetized by the first part of the compound. Example: Alec Douglas-Home is alphabetized under "Douglas-Home."
3. Compound surnames, principally Spanish, in which the last part of the compound is frequently dropped, are alphabetized by the first part of the compound, while the second is shown in parantheses. Example: Luis Echeverria Alvarez is alphabetized under "Echeverria (Alvarez)."
4. Those names, principally Asian, in which the family name is customarily shown first, are alphabetized in that manner. Example: Chou En-lai is alphabetized under "Chou."

(C) Where there are two or more quotations by one speaker within the same category, they appear chronologically by date spoken or date of source.

SPEAKER IDENTIFICATION

(A) The occupation, profession, rank, position or title of the speaker is given as it was *at the time the statement was made*. Thus, due to possible changes in status during the year, a speaker may be shown with different identifications in various portions of the book, or even within the same category.

(B) In the case of speakers who hold more than one position or occupation simultaneously (or who held relevant positions in the past), the judgment of the Editors has determined the most appropriate identification to use with a specific quotation.

(C) Nationality of speakers is normally not given unless this information is of interest or relative to the quotation(s).

THE QUOTATIONS

The quoted material selected for inclusion in this book is shown as it appeared in the source, except as follows:

(A) *Ellipses* have been inserted wherever the Editors have deleted extraneous or overly long words or passages within the quoted material. In no way has the meaning or intention of any quotation been altered. *Ellipses* are also used where they appeared in the source.

(B) *Punctuation and spelling* have been altered by the Editors where they were obviously incorrect in the source, or to make the quotations more intelligible, or to conform to the general style used throughout this book. Again, meaning or intention of the quotations has not been changed.

(C) *Brackets* ([ ]) indicate material inserted by the Editors or by the source to either correct obvious errors or to explain and/or clarify what the speaker is saying.

(D) *Italics* have sometimes been added by the Editors where emphasis is clearly desirable.

Except for the above instances, the quoted material used has been printed verbatim, as reported by the source (even if the speaker made factual errors or was awkward in his choice of words).

Special care has been exercised to make certain that each quotation stands on its own merits and is not taken "out of context." The Editors, however, cannot be responsible for errors made by the original newspaper, periodical or other source, i.e., incorrect reporting, mis-quotations or errors in interpretation.

DOCUMENTATION AND SOURCES

Documentation (circumstance, place, date) of each quotation is provided as fully as could be obtained, and the sources are furnished for all quotations. In some instances no documentation details were available; in those cases only the source is given. Following are the sequence and style used for this information:

> Circumstance of quotation, place, date/Name of source, date: section (if applicable), page number.
>
> Example: *Before the Senate, Washington, Dec. 4/The Washington Post, 12-6:(A)13.*

The above example indicates that the quotation was delivered before the Senate in Washington on December 4. It was taken for *WHAT THEY SAID* from *The Washington Post,* issue of December 6, section A, page 13. (When a newspaper publishes more than one edition on the same date, it should be noted that page numbers may vary from edition to edition.)

(A) When the source is a television or radio broadcast, the name of the network or local station is indicated, along with the date of the broadcast (obviously, page and/or section information does not apply).

(B) One asterisk (*) used before the slash-mark (/) in the documentation indicates that the quoted material was written rather than spoken. Although the basic policy of *WHAT THEY SAID* is to use only *spoken* statements, there are occasions when written statements are considered by the Editors to be important enough to be included. These occasions are rare and usually involve Presidential messages, Presidential statements released to the press and other such documents attributed to a person in high governmental office.

(C) Two asterisks (**) after the slash-mark indicate the speaker supplied the quotation to *WHAT THEY SAID* directly.

INDEXING

(A) The *Index to Speakers* is keyed to the page number. (For alphabetization practices, see *Organization of Material,* paragraph B.)

(B) The *Index to Subjects* is keyed to both the page number and the quotation number on the page (thus, 210:3 indicates quotation number 3 on page 210); the quotation number appears at the upper right-hand corner of each quotation.

(C) To locate quotations on a particular subject, regardless of speaker, turn to the appropriate category (see *Table of Contents*) or use the detailed *Index to Subjects.*

(D) To locate all quotations by a particular speaker, regardless of subject, use the *Index to Speakers.*

(E) To locate quotations by a particular speaker on a particular subject, turn to the appropriate category and then to that person's quotations within that category.

(F) The reader will find that the basic categorization format of *WHAT THEY SAID* is itself a useful subject index, inasmuch as related quotations are grouped together by their respective categories. All aspects of journalism, for example, are relevant to each other; thus, the section *Journalism* embraces all phases of the news media. Similarly, quotations pertaining to the U.S. Presidency, Congress, revenue-sharing, etc., are together in the section *Government.*

MISCELLANEOUS

(A) Except where otherwise indicated or obviously to the contrary, all universities, colleges, organizations and business firms mentioned in this book are located or based in the United States; similarly, references to "national," "Federal," "this country," "the nation," etc., refer to the United States.

(B) In most cases, organizations whose titles end with "of the United States" are Federal government agencies.

SELECTION OF CATEGORIES

The selected categories reflect, in the Editors' opinion, the most widely-discussed public-interest subjects, those which readily fall into the over-all sphere of "current events." They represent topics continuously covered by the mass media because of their inherent relevance to the changing world scene. Most of the categories are permanent; they appear in each annual edition of *WHAT THEY*

EDITORIAL TREATMENT

SAID. However, because of the transient character of some subjects, there may be categories which appear one year and are not repeated.

SELECTION OF SPEAKERS

The following persons are *always* considered eligible for inclusion in *WHAT THEY SAID:* top-level officials of all branches of national, state and major local governments (both U.S. and foreign), including all United States Senators and Representatives; top-echelon military officers; college and university presidents, chancellors and professors; chairmen and presidents of major corporations; heads of national public-oriented organizations and associations; national and internationally known diplomats; recognized celebrities from the entertainment and literary spheres and the arts generally; sports figures of national stature; commentators on the world scene who are recognized as such and who command the attention of the mass media.

The determination of what and who are "major" and "recognized" must, necessarily, be made by the Editors of *WHAT THEY SAID* based on objective personal judgment.

Also, some persons, while not recognized as prominent in a particular professional area, have nevertheless attracted an unusual amount of attention in connection with a specific issue or event. These people, too, are considered for inclusion, depending upon the circumstances involved.

SELECTION OF QUOTATIONS

The quotations selected for inclusion in *WHAT THEY SAID* obviously represent a decided minority of the seemingly endless volume of quoted material appearing in the media each year. The process of selection is scrupulously objective insofar as the partisan views of the Editors are concerned (see *About Fairness,* below). However, it is clear that the Editors must decide which quotations *per se* are suitable for inclusion, and in doing so look for comments that are aptly stated, offer insight into the subject being discussed, or into the speaker, and provide—for today as well as for future reference—a thought which readers will find useful for understanding the issues and the personalities that make up a year on this planet.

ABOUT FAIRNESS

The Editors of *WHAT THEY SAID* understand the necessity of being impartial when compiling a book of this kind. As a result, there has been no bias in the selection of the quotations, the choice of speakers or the manner of editing. Relevance of the statements and the status of the speakers are the exclusive criteria for inclusion, without any regard whatsoever to the personal beliefs and views of the Editors. Furthermore, every effort has been made to include a multiplicity of opinions and ideas from a wide cross-section of speakers on each topic. Nevertheless, should there appear to be, on some controversial issues, a majority of material favoring one point of view over another, it is simply the result of there having been more of those views expressed during the year, reported by the media and objectively considered suitable by the Editors of *WHAT THEY SAID* (see *Selection of Quotations*). Also, since persons in politics and government account for a large percentage of the speakers in *WHAT THEY SAID,* there may exist a heavier weight of opinion favoring the political philosophy of those in office at the time, whether in the United States Congress, the Administration, or in foreign capitals. This is natural and to be expected and should not be construed as a reflection of agreement or disagreement with that philosophy on the part of the Editors of *WHAT THEY SAID.*

Abbreviations

The following are abbreviations used by the speakers in this volume. Rather than defining them each time they appear in the quotations, this list will facilitate reading and avoid unnecessary repetition.

ABA:	American Basketball Association
ABM:	antiballistic missile
ACLU:	American Civil Liberties Union
ACT:	American Conservatory Theatre (San Francisco)
AFL-CIO:	American Federation of Labor-Congress of Industrial Organizations
AMA:	American Medical Association
AT&T:	American Telephone & Telegraph Company
BART:	Bay Area Rapid Transit (San Francisco)
BBB:	Better Business Bureaus
CBS:	Columbia Broadcasting System
CIA:	Central Intelligence Agency
CREEP:	Committee to Re-elect the President
DNC:	Democratic National Committee
FBI:	Federal Bureau of Investigation
FCC:	Federal Communications Commission
FTC:	Federal Trade Commission
GM:	General Motors Corporation
GNP:	gross national product
HEW:	Department of Health, Education and Welfare
IBM:	International Business Machines Corporation
ICC:	Interstate Commerce Commission
IMF:	International Monetary Fund
IRS:	Internal Revenue Service
ITT:	International Telephone & Telegraph Corporation
MIA:	missing in action
NAACP:	National Association for the Advancement of Colored People
NATO:	North Atlantic Treaty Organization
NBA:	National Basketball Association
NBC:	National Broadcasting Company
NFL:	National Football League
NHI:	national health insurance
NHL:	National Hockey League
NYSE:	New York Stock Exchange
OAS:	Organization of American States
OEO:	Office of Economic Opportunity
OMB:	Office of Management and Budget

ABBREVIATIONS

OPEC: Organization of Petroleum Exporting Countries
PBS: Public Broadcasting Service
PGA: Professional Golfers Association
PLO: Palestine Liberation Organization
POW: prisoner of war
SALT: strategic arms limitation talks
SDS: Students for a Democratic Society
SEC: Securities and Exchange Commission
TV: television
UN: United Nations
U.S.:   United States
U.S.A.: United States of America
USIA: United States Information Agency
U.S.S.R.: Union of Soviet Socialist Republics
WFL: World Football League
WHA: World Hockey Association

Party affiliation of United States Senators and Congressmen—
C: Conservative-Republican
D: Democratic
I: Independent
R: Republican

The Quote of the Year

"We are given to the cult of personality; when things go badly we look to some messiah to save us. But in our day there are no messiahs! And if by chance we think we have found one, it will not be long before we destroy him."

—CONSTANTINE CARAMANLIS
Premier of Greece

PART ONE

National Affairs

The State of the Union Address

Delivered by Richard M. Nixon, President of the United States, to a joint session of Congress, House of Representatives, Washington, January 30, 1974.

Mr. Speaker, Mr. President, my colleagues in the Congress, our distinguished guests, my fellow Americans:

We meet here tonight at a time of great challenge and great opportunities for America. We meet at a time when we face great problems at home and abroad that will test the strength of our fiber as a nation. But we also meet at a time when that fiber has been tested, and it has proved strong.

America is a great and good land, and we are a great and good land because we are a strong, free, creative people and because America is the single greatest force for peace anywhere in the world. Today, as always in our history, we can base our confidence in what the American people will achieve in the future on the record of what the American people have achieved in the past.

America at Peace

Tonight, for the first time in 12 years, a President of the United States can report to the Congress on the state of a union at peace with every nation of the world. Because of this, in the 22,000-word message on the state of the union that I have just handed to the Speaker of the House and the President of the Senate, I have been able to deal primarily with the problems of peace—with what we can do here at home in America for the American people—rather than with the problems of war.

The measures I have outlined in this message set an agenda for truly significant progress for this nation and the world in 1974. Before we chart where we are going, let us see how far we have come.

It was five years ago on the steps of this Capitol that I took the oath of office as your President. In those five years, because of the initiatives undertaken by this Administration, the world has changed.

Change in America

America has changed. As a result of those changes, America is safer today, more prosperous today, with greater opportunity for more of its people than ever before in our history.

Five years ago, America was at war in Southeast Asia. We were locked in confrontation with the Soviet Union. We were in hostile isolation from a quarter of the world's people who lived in mainland China.

Five years ago, our cities were burning and besieged.

Five years ago, our college campuses were a battleground.

Five years ago, crime was increasing at a rate that struck fear across the nation.

Five years ago, the spiraling rise in drug addiction was threatening human and social tragedy of massive proportion, and there was no program to deal with it.

Five years ago—as young Americans had done for a generation before that—America's youth still lived under the shadow of the military draft.

Five years ago, there was no national program to preserve our environment. Day by day our air was getting dirtier, our water was getting more foul.

And five years ago, American agriculture was practically a depressed industry, with 100,000 farm families abandoning the farm every year.

RICHARD M. NIXON

Meeting the Challenges

As we look at America today we find ourselves challenged by new problems. But we also find a record of progress to confound the professional criers of doom and prophets of despair. We met the challenges we faced five years ago, and we will be equally confident of meeting those that we face today.

Let us see for a moment how we have met them:

After more than 10 years of military involvement, all of our troops have returned from Southeast Asia, and they have returned with honor. And we can be proud of the fact that our courageous prisoners of war—for whom a dinner was held in Washington tonight—that they came home with their heads high, on their feet and not on their knees.

In our relations with the Soviet Union, we have turned away from a policy of confrontation to one of negotiation. For the first time since World War II, the world's two strongest powers are working together toward peace in the world. With the People's Republic of China, after a generation of hostile isolation, we have begun a period of peaceful exchange and expanding trade.

Peace has returned to our cities, to our campuses. The 17-year rise in crime has been stopped. We can confidently say today that we are finally beginning to win the war against crime. Right here in this nation's capital, which a few years ago was threatening to become the crime capital of the world, the rate of crime has been cut in half. A massive campaign against drug abuse has been organized. And the rate of new heroin addiction, the most vicious threat of all, is decreasing rather than increasing.

For the first time in a generation, no young Americans are being drafted into the armed services of the United States. And for the first time ever, we have organized a massive national effort to protect the environment. Our air is getting cleaner, our water is getting purer, and our agriculture, which was depressed, is prospering. Farm income is up 70 per cent, farm production is setting all-time records, and the billions of dollars the taxpayers were paying in subsidies has been cut to nearly zero.

Standard of Living

Over all, Americans are living more abundantly than ever before, today. More than 2½ million new jobs were created in the past year alone. That is the biggest percentage increase in nearly 20 years. People are earning more. What they earn buys more, more than ever before in history. In the past five years, the average American's real, spendable income—that is, what you really can buy with your income even after allowing for taxes and inflation—has increased by 16 per cent.

Despite this record of achievement, as we turn to the year ahead we hear once again the familiar voice of the perennial prophets of gloom telling us now that because of the need to fight inflation, because of the energy shortage, America may be headed for a recession.

Well, let me speak to that issue head on. There will be no recession in the United States of America. Primarily due to our energy crisis, our economy is passing through a difficult period. But I pledge to you tonight that the full powers of this Government will be used to keep America's economy producing and to protect the jobs of America's workers.

We are engaged in a long and hard fight against inflation. There have been—and there will be in the future—ups and downs in that fight. But if this Congress co-operates in our efforts to hold down the cost of Government, we shall win our fight to hold down the cost of living for the American people.

As we look back over our history, the years that stand out as the ones of signal achievement are those in which the Administration and the Congress, whether of one party or the other, working together, had the wisdom and the foresight to select those particular initiatives for which the nation was ready and the moment was right—and in which they seized the moment and acted.

Goals for 1974

Looking at the year 1974, which lies before us, there are 10 key areas in which landmark accomplishments are possible this year in America. If we make these our national agenda, this is what we will achieve in 1974:

We will break the back of the energy crisis; we will lay the foundation for our future capacity to meet America's energy needs from America's own resources.

And we will take another giant stride toward lasting peace in the world—not only by continuing our policy of negotiation rather than confrontation where the great powers are concerned, but also by helping toward the achievement of a just and lasting settlement in the Middle East.

We will check the rise in prices without administering the harsh medicine of recession, and we will move the economy into a steady period of growth at a sustainable level.

We will establish a new system that makes high-quality health care available to every American in a dignified manner and at a price he can afford.

We will make our States and localities more responsive to the needs of their own citizens.

We will make a crucial breakthrough toward better transportation in our towns and in our cities across America.

We will reform our system of federal aid to education—to provide it when it is needed, where it is needed—so that it will do the most for those who need it the most.

We will make an historic beginning on the task of defining and protecting the right of personal privacy for every American.

And we will start on a new road toward reform of a welfare system that bleeds the taxpayer, corrodes the community and demeans those it is intended to assist.

And, together with the other nations of the world, we will establish the economic framework within which Americans will share more fully in an expanding worldwide trade and prosperity in the years ahead, with more open access to both markets and supplies.

In all of the 186 state-of-the-union messages delivered from this place in our history, this is the first in which the one priority, the first priority, is energy. Let me begin by reporting a new development which I know will be welcome news to every American.

Oil, Energy, Environment

As you know, we have committed ourselves to an active role in helping to achieve a just and durable peace in the Middle East on the basis of full implementation of Security Council Resolutions 242 and 338. The first step in the process is the disengagement of Egyptian and Israeli forces, which is now taking place.

Because of this hopeful development, I can announce tonight that I have been assured, through my personal contacts with friendly leaders in the Middle Eastern area, that an urgent meeting will be called in the immediate future to discuss the lifting of the oil embargo. This is an encouraging sign. However, it should be clearly understood by our friends in the Middle East that the United States will not be coerced on this issue.

Regardless of the outcome of this meeting, the co-operation of the American people in our energy-conservation program has already gone a long way toward achieving a goal to which I am deeply dedicated. Let us do everything we can to avoid gasoline rationing in the United States of America.

Last week I sent to the Congress a comprehensive special message setting forth our energy situation, recommending the legislative measures which are necessary to a program for meeting our needs. If the embargo is lifted, this will ease the crisis, but it will not mean an end to the energy shortage in America. Voluntary conservation will continue to be necessary, and let me take this occasion to pay tribute once again to the splendid spirit of co-operation the American people have shown which has made possible our success in meeting this emergency up to this time.

The new legislation I have requested will also remain necessary. Therefore, I urge again that the energy measures that I have proposed be made the first priority of this session of the Congress. These measures will require the oil companies and other energy producers to provide the public with the necessary information on their supplies. They will prevent the injustice of "windfall" profits for a few as a result of the sacrifices of the millions of Americans, and they will give us the organization, the incentives, the authorities needed to deal with the short-term emergency and to move toward meeting our long-term needs.

Just as 1970 was the year in which we began

a full-scale effort to protect the environment, 1974 must be the year in which we organize a full-scale effort to provide for our energy needs not only in this decade but through the 21st century.

As we move toward the celebration two years from now of the 200th anniversary of this nation's independence, let us press vigorously on toward the goal that I announced last November for Project Independence. Let this be our national goal: At the end of this decade, in the year 1980, the United States will not be dependent on any other country for the energy we need to provide our jobs, to heat our homes and to keep our transportation moving.

To indicate the size of the Government commitment to spur energy research and development, we plan to spend 10 billion in federal funds over the next five years. That is an enormous amount. But during the same five years, private enterprise will be investing as much as 200 billion dollars—and in 10 years, 500 billion dollars—to develop the new resources, the new technology, the new capacity America will require for its energy needs in the 1980s. That's just a measure of the magnitude of the project we are undertaking.

But America performs best when called to its biggest tasks. It can truly be said that only in America could a task so tremendous be achieved so quickly, and achieved not by regimentation, but through the effort and ingenuity of a free people working in a free system.

Health Care

Turning now to the rest of the agenda for 1974, the time is at hand this year to bring comprehensive, high-quality health care within the reach of every American. I shall propose a sweeping new program that will assure comprehensive health-insurance protection to millions of Americans who cannot now obtain it or afford it, with vastly improved protection against catastrophic illnesses. This will be a plan that maintains the high standards of quality in America's health care. And it will not require additional taxes.

Now, I recognize that other plans have been put forward that would cost 80 billions or even 100 billion dollars and that would put our whole health-care system under the heavy hand of the Federal Government. This is the wrong approach. This has been tried abroad, and it has failed; it is not the way we do things here in America. This kind of plan would threaten the quality of care provided by our whole health-care system.

The right way is one that builds on the strengths of the present system and one that does not destroy those strengths—one based on partnership, not paternalism. Most important of all, let us keep this as the guiding principle of our health programs: Government has a great role to play, but we must always make sure that our doctors will be working for their patients and not for the Federal Government.

Federal vs. State and Local Government

Many of you will recall that in my state-of-the-union address three years ago I commented that most Americans today are simply fed up with government at all levels, and I recommended a sweeping set of proposals to revitalize State and local government, to make them more responsive to the people they serve.

I can report to you today that, as a result of revenue sharing—passed by the Congress—and other measures, we have made progress toward that goal. After 40 years of moving power from the States and the communities to Washington, D.C., we have begun moving power back from Washington to the States and communities and, most important, to the people of America.

In this session of the Congress, I believe we are near the breakthrough point on efforts which I have suggested, proposals to let people themselves make their own decisions for their own communities, and in particular on those to provide broad new flexibility in federal aid for community development, for economic development, for education. And I look forward to working with the Congress, with members of both parties, in resolving whatever remaining differences we have in this legislation so that we can make available nearly 5½ billion dollars to our States and localities to use not for what a federal bureaucrat may want but for what their own people in those communities want. The decision should be theirs.

Transportation

I think all of us recognize that the energy crisis has given new urgency to the need to improve public transportation, not only in our cities but in rural areas as well. The program I have proposed this year will give communities not only more money, but also more freedom to balance their own transportation needs. It will mark the strongest federal commitment ever to the improvement of mass transit as an essential element of the improvement of life in our towns and cities.

Education

One goal on which all Americans agree is that our children should have the very best education this great nation can provide. In a special message last week, I recommended a number of important new measures that can make 1974 a year of truly significant advances for our schools and for the children they serve.

If the Congress will act on these proposals, more-flexible funding will enable each federal dollar to meet better the particular need of each particular school district. Advance funding will give school authorities a chance to make each year's plans, knowing ahead of time what federal funds they are going to receive. Special targeting will give special help to the truly disadvantaged among our people. College students, faced with rising costs for their education, will be able to draw on an expanded program of loans and grants.

These advances are a needed investment in America's most precious resource, our next generation, and I urge the Congress to act on this legislation in 1974.

Privacy Rights

One measure of a truly free society is the vigor with which it protects the liberties of its individual citizens. As technology has advanced in America, it has increasingly encroached on one of those liberties—what I term the right of personal privacy. Modern information systems, data banks, credit records, mailing-list abuses, electronic snooping, the collection of personal data for one purpose that may be used for another—all these have left millions of Americans deeply concerned by the privacy they cherish.

And the time has come, therefore, for a major initiative to define the nature and extent of the basic rights of privacy and to erect new safeguards to ensure that those rights are respected. I shall launch such an effort this year at the highest levels of the Administration, and I look forward again to working with this Congress in establishing a new set of standards that respect the legitimate needs of society, but that also recognize personal privacy as a cardinal principle of American liberty.

Welfare

Many of those in this chamber tonight will recall that it was three years ago that I termed the nation's welfare system "a monstrous, consuming outrage—an outrage against the community, against the taxpayer, and particularly against the children that it is supposed to help."

That system is still an outrage. By improving its administration, we have been able to reduce some of the abuses. As a result, last year, for the first time in 18 years, there has been a halt in the growth of the welfare case load. But, as a system, our welfare program still needs reform as urgently today as it did when I first proposed in 1969 that we completely replace it with a different system.

In these final three years of my Administration, I urge the Congress to join me in mounting a major new effort to replace the discredited present welfare system with one that works, one that is fair to those who need help or cannot help themselves, fair to the community and fair to the taxpayers. And let us have as our goal that there will be no Government program which makes it more profitable to go on welfare than to go to work.

I recognize that from the debates that have taken place within the Congress over the past three years on this program that we cannot expect enactment overnight of a new reform, but I do propose that the Congress and the Administration together make this the year in which we discuss, debate and shape such a reform so that it can be enacted as quickly as possible.

Foreign Trade

America's own prosperity in the years ahead depends on our sharing fully and equitably in an expanding world prosperity. Historic negotiations will take place this year that will enable us to ensure fair treatment in international markets for American workers, American farmers, American investors and American consumers.

It is vital that the authorities contained in the trade bill I submitted to the Congress be enacted so that the United States can negotiate flexibly and vigorously on behalf of American interests. These negotiations can usher in a new era of international trade that not only increases the prosperity of all nations but also strengthens the peace among all nations.

Defense

In the past five years, we have made more progress toward a lasting structure of peace in the world than in any comparable time in the nation's history. We could not have made that progress if we had not maintained the military strength of America. Thomas Jefferson once observed that "the price of liberty is eternal vigilance." By the same token and for the same reason, in today's world the price of peace is a strong defense as far as the United States is concerned.

In the past five years, we have steadily reduced the burden of national defense as a share of the budget, bringing it down from 44 per cent in 1969 to 29 per cent in the current year. We have cut our military manpower over the past five years by more than a third, from 3½ million to 2.2 million.

In the coming year, however, increased expenditures will be needed. They will be needed to assure the continued readiness of our military forces, to preserve present force levels in the face of rising costs and to give us the military strength we must have if our security is to be maintained and if our initiatives for peace are to succeed.

The question is not whether we can afford to maintain the necessary strength of our defense; the question is whether we can afford not to maintain it. And the answer to that question is "No." We must never allow America to become the second-strongest nation in the world.

I do not say this with any sense of belligerence, because I recognize the fact that is recognized around the world: America's military strength has always been maintained to keep the peace—never to break it. It has always been used to defend freedom—never to destroy it. The world's peace as well as our own depends on our remaining as strong as we need to be as long as we need to be.

In this year, 1974, we will be negotiating with the Soviet Union to place further limits on strategic nuclear arms. Together with our allies, we will be negotiating with the nations of the Warsaw Pact on mutual and balanced reduction of forces in Europe. And we will continue our efforts to promote peaceful economic development in Latin America, in Africa, in Asia. We will press for full compliance with the peace accords that brought an end to American fighting in Indo-China, including particularly a provision that promised the fullest possible accounting for those Americans who are missing in action.

And, having in mind the energy crisis to which I have referred to earlier, we will be working with the other nations of the world toward agreement on means by which oil supplies can be assured at reasonable prices on a stable basis in a fair way to the consuming and producing nations alike.

All of these are steps toward a future in which the world's peace and prosperity—and ours as well—as a result are made more secure.

Priority for Peace

Throughout the five years that I have served as your President, I have had one overriding aim, and that was to establish a new structure of peace in the world that can free future generations of the scourge of war. I can understand that others may have different priorities. This has been and this will remain my first priority and the chief legacy I hope to leave from the eight years of my Presidency.

This does not mean that we shall not have other priorities, because as we strengthen the peace we must also continue each year a steady strengthening of our society here at home. Our conscience requires it, our interests require it, and we must insist upon it.

As we create more jobs, as we build a better health-care system, as we improve our education, as we develop new sources of energy, as we provide more abundantly for the elderly and the poor, as we strengthen the system of private enterprise that produces our prosperity, as we do all of this and even more, we solidify those essential bonds that hold us together as a nation.

Even more importantly we advance what, in the final analysis, government in America is all about. What it is all about is more freedom, more security, a better life for each one of the 211 million people that live in this land. We cannot afford to neglect progress at home while pursuing peace abroad. But neither can we afford to neglect peace abroad while pursuing progress at home. With a stable peace all is possible, but without peace nothing is possible.

In the written message that I have just delivered to the Speaker and to the President of the Senate, I commented that one of the continuing challenges facing us in the legislative process is that of the timing and pacing of our initiatives, selecting each year among many worthy projects those that are ripe for action at that time.

What is true in terms of our domestic initiatives is true also in the world. This period we now are in in the world—and I say this as one who has seen so much of the world, not only in these past five years but going back over many years—we are in a period which presents a juncture of historic forces unique in this century. They provide an opportunity we may never have again to create a structure of peace solid enough to last a lifetime and more: not just peace in our time but peace in our children's time as well. It is on the way we respond to this opportunity more than anything else that history will judge whether we in America have met our responsibility, and I am confident we will meet that great historic responsibility which is ours today.

It was 27 years ago that John F. Kennedy and I sat in this chamber as freshmen Congressmen, hearing our first state-of-the-union address delivered by Harry Truman. I know from my talks with him, as members of the Labor Committee on which we both served, that neither of us then even dreamed that either one or both might eventually be standing in this place that I now stand in now and that he once stood in before me. It may well be that one of the freshmen members of the 93rd Congress—one of you out there—will deliver his own state-of-the-union message 27 years from now, in the year 2001.

Well, whichever one it is, I want you to be able to look back with pride and to say that your first years here were great years and to recall that you were here in this 93rd Congress when America ended its longest war and began its longest peace.

Watergate

Mr. Speaker and Mr. President and my distinguished colleagues and our guests, I would like to add a personal word with regard to an issue that has been of great concern to all Americans over the past year. I refer, of course, to the investigations of the so-called Watergate affair.

As you know, I have provided to the Special Prosecutor voluntarily a great deal of material. I believe that I have provided all the material that he needs to conclude his investigations and to proceed to prosecute the guilty and to clear the innocent.

I believe the time has come to bring that investigation and the other investigations of this matter to an end. One year of Watergate is enough. And the time has come, my colleagues, for not only the Executive, the President, but the members of Congress—for all of us to join together in devoting our full energies to these great issues that I have discussed tonight which involve the welfare of all of the American people in so many different ways as well as the peace of the world.

I recognize that the House Judiciary Committee has a special responsibility in this area, and I want to indicate on this occasion that I will co-operate with the Judiciary Committee in its investigation. I will co-operate so that it can conclude its investigation, make its decision, and I will co-operate in any way that I consider consistent with my responsibilities to the office of the Presidency of the United States.

There is only one limitation: I will follow the precedent that has been followed by and defended by every President from George Washington to Lyndon B. Johnson of never doing anything that weakens the office of the President of the United States or impairs the ability of the Presidents of the future to make the great decisions that are so essential to this nation and the world.

Another point I should like to make very briefly: Like every member of the House and Senate assembled here tonight, I was elected to the office that I hold. And like every member of the House and Senate, when I was elected to that office, I knew that I was elected for the purpose of doing a job and doing it as well as I possibly can. And I want you to know that I have no intention whatever of ever walking away from the job that the people elected me to do for the people of the United States.

Now, needless to say, it would be understatement if I were not to admit that the year 1973 was not a very easy year for me personally or for my family. And, as I have already indicated, the year 1974 presents very great and serious problems, as very great and serious opportunities are also presented.

But, my colleagues, this I believe: With the help of God—who has blessed this land so richly—with the co-operation of the Congress and with the support of the American people, we can and we will make the year 1974 a year of unprecedented progress toward our goal of building a structure of lasting peace in the world and a new prosperity, without war, in the United States of America.

After succeeding to the Presidency upon Richard Nixon's resignation, Gerald R. Ford delivered his first address before a joint session of Congress, August 12, 1974. In effect a State of the Union report, the address follows in full:

Mr. Speaker, Mr. President, distinguished guests and dear friends:

My fellow Americans, we have a lot of work to do.

My former colleagues, you and I have a lot of work to do. Let's get on with it.

I am grateful for your very warm welcome.

I am not here to make an inaugural address. The nation needs action, not words.

Nor will this be a formal report on the state of the Union. God willing, I will have at least three more chances to do that.

It's good to be back in the People's House.

But this cannot be a real homecoming. Under the Constitution, I now belong to the executive branch. The Supreme Court has even ruled that I am the executive branch, head, heart, and hand.

With due respect to the learned justices—and I greatly respect the judiciary—part of my heart will always be here on Capitol Hill. I know well the co-equal role of the Congress in our constitutional process. I love the House of Representatives. I revere the traditions of the Senate despite my too-short internship there. As President, within the limits of basic principles, my motto towards the Congress is communication, conciliation, compromise and cooperation.

This Congress will, I am confident, be my working partner as well as my most constructive critic. I am not asking for conformity. I am dedicated to the two-party system, and you know which party is mine.

I do not want a honeymoon with you. I want a good marriage.

I want progress and a problem-solving which requires my best efforts, and also your best efforts.

I have no need to learn how Congress speaks for the people. As President, I intend to listen. But I also intend to listen to the people themselves—all the people—as I promised them last Friday. I want to be sure we are all tuned in to the real voice of America.

My Administration starts off by seeking unity in diversity. My office door has always been open and that is how it is going to be at the White House. Yes, Congressmen will be welcome—if you don't overdo it.

The first seven words of the Constitution, and the most important, are these: "We, the people of the United States." We, the people, ordained and established the Constitution and reserved to themselves all powers not granted to Federal and state governments. I respect and will always be conscious of that fundamental rule of freedom.

Only eight months ago, when I last stood here, I told you I was a Ford, not a Lincoln. Tonight I say I am still a Ford, but I am not a Model T.

I do have some old-fashioned ideas. I believe in the basic decency and fairness of America. I believe in the integrity and the patriotism of the Congress. And while I am aware of the House rule that one never speaks to the galleries, I believe in the First Amendment and the absolute necessity of a free press.

But I also believe that over two centuries since the first Continental Congress was convened, the direction of our nation's movement has been forward. I am here to confess that in my first campaign for president—of my senior class in South High School in Grand Rapids—I headed the Progressive party ticket.

Now I ask you to join with me in getting this country revved up and moving.

My instinctive judgment is that the State of the Union is excellent. But the state of our economy is not so good.

Everywhere I have been as Vice President, some 118,000 miles into 40 states and through 55 news conferences, the unanimous concern of Americans is inflation. For once all the polls agree. They also suggest that people blame Government far more than either management or labor or the high cost of everything.

Federal Budget

You who come from 50 states, three territories and the District of Columbia know this better than I. That is why you have created since I left here your new budget reform committee. I welcome it and will work with its

members to bring the Federal budget into balance by fiscal 1976.

The fact is that for the past 25 years that I served here, the Federal budget has been balanced in only six.

Mr. Speaker, I am a little late getting around to it, but confession is good for the soul. I have sometimes voted to spend more taxpayers' money for worthy Federal projects in Grand Rapids while vigorously opposing wasteful Federal boondoggles in Oklahoma.

Be that as it may, Mr. Speaker, you and I have always stood together against unwarranted cuts in national defense. This is no time to change that nonpartisan policy.

Just as escalating Federal spending has been a prime cause of higher prices over the years, it may take some time to stop inflation.

But we must begin now.

For a start, before your Labor Day recess, Congress should reactivate the Cost of Living Council through passage of a clean bill, without reimposing controls, that will let us monitor wages and prices to expose abuses.

The American wage earner and the American housewife are a lot better economists than most economists care to admit.

They know that a Government big enough to give you everything you want, is a Government big enough to take from you everything you have.

If we want to restore confidence in ourselves as working politicians, the first thing we all have to do is learn how to say "no."

The first specific request by the Ford Administration is not to Congress but to the voters in the upcoming November elections. It is this: Support your candidates, Congressmen and Senators, Democrats or Republicans, conservative or liberal, who consistently vote for tough decisions to cut the cost of government, restrain Federal spending and bring inflation under control.

I applaud the initiatives the Congress has already taken. The only fault I find with the joint economic committee inflation study authorized last week is that we need its expert findings in six weeks instead of six months.

A month ago the distinguished majority leader of the Senate asked the White House to convene an economic conference of members of Congress, the President's economic consultants, and some of the best economic brains from labor, industry and agriculture.

Later, this was perfected by a resolution to assemble a domestic summit meeting to devise a bipartisan action later for stability and growth in the American economy. Neither I nor my staff have much time just now for letter-writing. So I will respond in person. I accept your suggestion and I will personally preside.

Furthermore, I propose that this summit meeting be held at an early date and in full view of the American public. They are anxious to get the right answers as we are.

My first priority is to work with you to bring inflation under control. Inflation is our domestic public enemy No. 1. To restore economic confidence, the Government in Washington must provide leadership. It does no good to blame the public for spending too much when the Government is spending too much.

I began to put my Administration's own economic house in order, starting last Friday.

I instructed my Cabinet officers and counsellors and my White House staff to make fiscal restraint their first order of business, and to save every taxpayer's dollar the safety and genuine welfare of the country will permit. Some economic activities will be affected more by monetary and fiscal restraints than other activities. Good government clearly requires that we tend to the economic problems facing our country in a spirit of equity to all our citizens.

Tonight is no time to threaten you with vetos. But I do have that last recourse and I am a veteran of many a veto fight in this very chamber. Can't we do the job better by reasonable compromise?

Minutes after I took the Presidential oath, the joint leadership of Congress told me at the White House that they would go more than halfway to meet me. This was confirmed in your unanimous concurrent resolution of cooperation, for which I am deeply grateful. If for my part I go more than halfway to meet the Congress, maybe we will find a much larger area of national agreement.

I bring no legislative shopping list tonight. I will deal with specifics in future messages and

talks with you. But here are a few examples of my seriousness.

Education

Last week the Congress passed the elementary and secondary education bill and I found it on my desk. Any reservations I might have about some of its provisions—and I do have—fade in comparison to the urgent needs of America for quality education. I will sign it in a few days. I must be frank. In implementing its provisions, I will oppose excessive funding during this inflationary crisis.

Health Care

As Vice President, I have studied various proposals for better health-care financing. I saw them coming closer together, and urged my friends in Congress and in the Administration to sit down and sweat out a sound compromise. The comprehensive health insurance plan goes a long way toward providing early relief to people who are sick.

Why don't we write a good health bill on the statute books before this Congress adjourns?

The economy of our country is critically dependent on how we interact with the economics of other countries. It is little comfort that our inflation is only part of a worldwide problem, or that American families need less of their paychecks for groceries than most of our foreign friends.

Foreign Trade

As one of the building blocks of peace, we have taken the lead in working toward a more open and equitable world economic system. A new round of international trade negotiations started last September among 105 nations in Tokyo. The others are waiting for the United States Congress to grant the necessary authority to proceed.

With modification, the trade reform bill passed by the House last year would do that. I understand good progress has been made in the Senate committee. But I am optimistic, as always, that the Senate will pass an acceptable bill quickly as a key part of our joint prosperity campaign.

I am determined to expedite other international economic plans. We will be working together with other nations to find better ways to prevent shortages of food and fuel. We must not let last winter's energy crisis happen again. I will push Project Independence for our own good and the good of others. In that, too, I will need your help.

Foreign Policy

Successful foreign policy is an extension of the hopes of the whole American people for a world of peace and orderly freedom. So I would say a few words to our distinguished guests from the governments of other nations where, as at home, it is my determination to deal openly with allies and adversaries.

Over the past five and a half years, in Congress and as Vice President, I have fully supported the outstanding foreign policy of President Nixon. This I intend to continue.

Throughout my public service, starting with wartime naval duty under the command of President Franklin D. Roosevelt, I have upheld all our Presidents when they spoke for my country to the world. I believe the Constitution commands this. I know that in this crucial area of international policy I can count on your firm support.

Let there be no doubt or misunderstanding anywhere. There are no opportunities to exploit, should anyone so desire. There will be no change of course, no relaxation of vigilance, no abandonment of the helm of our ship of state as the watch changes. We stand by our commitments and will live up to our responsibilities, in our formal alliances, in our friendships and in our improving relations with any potential adversaries.

On this, Americans are united and strong. Under my term of leadership I hope we will become more united. I am certain we will remain strong.

Defense

A strong defense is the surest way to peace. Strength makes detente attainable. Weakness invites war, as my generation knows from four bitter experiences.

Just as America's will for peace is second to none, so will America's strength be second to none.

We cannot rely on the forebearance of others to protect this nation. The power and diversity of the armed forces, the resolve of our fellow citizens, the flexibility in our command to navigate international waters that remain troubled—all are essential to our security.

I shall continue to insist on civilian control of our superb military establishment. The Constitution plainly requires the President to be the Commander in Chief, and I will be.

Continuity

Our job will not be easy. In promising continuity, I cannot promise simplicity. The problems and challenges of the world remain complex and difficult. But we have set out upon a path of reason and fairness, and we will continue on it.

As guideposts on that path, I can offer the following:

● To our allies of a generation, in the Atlantic community and Japan, I pledge continuity in the loyal collaboration on our many mutual endeavors.

● To our friends and allies in this hemisphere, I pledge continuity in the deepening dialogue to define renewed relationships of equality and justice.

● To our allies and friends in Asia, I pledge a continuity in our support for their security, independence and economic development. In Indochina, we are determined to see the observance of the Paris agreement on Vietnam and the cease-fire and negotiated settlement in Laos. We hope to see an early compromise settlement in Cambodia.

● To the Soviet Union, I pledge continuity in our commitment to the course of the past three years. To our two peoples, and to all mankind, we owe a continued effort to live and, where possible, to work together in peace; for, in a thermo-nuclear age, there can be no alternative to a positive and peaceful relationship between our nations.

• To the People's Republic of China, whose legendary hospitality I enjoyed, I pledge continuity in our commitment to the principles of the Shanghai communiqué. The new relationship built on those principles has demonstrated that it serves serious and objective mutual interests and has become an enduring feature of the world scene.

• To the nations of the Middle East, I pledge continuity in our vigorous efforts to advance the process which has brought hopes of peace to that region after 25 long years as a hotbed of war. We shall carry out our promise to promote continuing negotiation among all parties for a complete, just and lasting settlement.

• To all nations, I pledge continuity in seeking a common global goal: a stable international structure of trade and finance which reflects the interdependence of all peoples.

• To the entire international community— to the United Nations, to the world's non-aligned nations, and to all others—I pledge a continuity in our dedication to the humane goals which throughout our history have been so much a part of our contribution to mankind.

So long as the peoples of the world have confidence in our purposes and faith in our word, the age-old vision of peace on earth will continue to grow brighter.

I pledge myself unreservedly to that goal. I say to you in words that cannot be improved upon: Let us never negotiate out of fear, but let us never fear to negotiate.

Privacy

As Vice President, I addressed myself to the individual rights of Americans in the area of privacy. There will be no illegal tapings, eavesdropping, buggings or break-ins by my Administration. There will be hot pursuit of tough laws to prevent illegal invasions of privacy in both government and private activities.

Morality

On the higher plane of public morality there is no need for me to preach tonight. We have thousands of far better preachers and millions of sacred scriptures to guide us on the path of personal right-living and exemplary official conduct. If we can make effective and earlier use of the moral and ethical wisdom of the centuries in today's complex society, we will prevent more crime and corruption than all the policemen and prosecutors governments can ever deter. This is a job that must begin at home, not in Washington.

People's Man

I once told you that I am not a saint, and hope never to see the day that I cannot admit having made a mistake. So I will close with another confession.

Frequently, along the tortuous road of recent months, from this chamber to the President's house, I protested that I was my own man.

Now I realize that I was wrong.

I am your man, for it was your carefully weighed confirmation that changed my occupation.

I am the people's man, for you acted in their name, and I accepted and began my new solemn trust with a promise to serve all the people, and to do the best I can for America.

When I say all the people, I mean exactly that.

To the limits of my strength and ability, I will be the President of the black, brown, red and white Americans, of old and young, of women's liberationists and male chauvinists and all the rest of us in between, of the poor and the rich, of native sons and new refugees, of those who work at lathes or at desks or in mines or in the fields, and of Christians, Jews, Moslems, Buddhists and atheists, if there really are any atheists after what we have all been through.

Fellow-Americans, a final word:

I want to be a good President.

I need your help.

We all need God's sure guidance.

With it, nothing can stop the United States of America.

George D. Aiken
United States Senator, R—Vermont
1

The individual is almost freer now than he ever was before. Thirty years ago people would not have dared to get together and knock the hell out of the government, as they do now. Some people get away with things today that they probably would have been hanged for a generation or two ago. I'm thinking of that fellow, Daniel Ellsberg. In practically no other country could he have gotten away with what he did here [releasing secret government papers on Vietnam to the news media]. And people are living better now than they ever did before. They never had the educational opportunities, the health benefits, the standard of living, the clothes to wear. If my mother got one new dress a year, she was lucky; and they were gingham dresses at that. I went barefoot beginning the first of May until it got too cold.

Interview, Washington/
Los Angeles Times, 4-15:(2)7.

Anne L. Armstrong
Counsellor to President of the
United States Richard M. Nixon
2

Our gross national product has doubled over the last few years, but are Americans twice as happy as they were? New technology leaps at us with such fierceness as to startle the human mind, but has it contributed fundamentally to our stature as a people? We have gone to the moon and back, but have we gone to the well of life? These are the questions which will haunt the future of America. Let us remember: Our cities may gleam with tall buildings; our farms may overflow with the abundance of our soil; our backyards may be strewn with the prerequisites of affluence; our children may never suffer the illnesses that we know now; and our leisure hours may expand with a suddenness which would shock our parents and

their parents. We can have all this and more; but if we don't join this progress with a renewal of our spirit and an enrichment of our soul, we may have nothing. That is why, as we enter our third century of independence, we will be searching for more. We will be looking for the anchors of life which perpetuate the truths which Jefferson wrote of as being self-evident. We will look for the moorings which fasten freedom not only as a word written into our national charter, but as a condition which is brought to life in the way we go forward. We will be seeking new values, to be sure; but we must do so in a way which gives new meaning and sustenance to the values which have preserved our civilization through the stresses of war and domestic conflict.

At Alfred M. Landon Lectures,
Kansas State University, Feb. 12/
Vital Speeches, 3-15:343.

Irving Berlin
Composer
3

I wouldn't worry about patriotism being dead. It is only suffering from sleeping sickness. I tell you this: If America was a stock, I'd buy all I could of it, and put it in storage for the long pull. Patriotism is easily forced out of style in our land, and it even becomes fashionable to be unpatriotic, because nobody is forcing you to be otherwise. But it always will come bouncing back.

Interview/
Los Angeles Herald-Examiner, 7-6:(A)11.

Tore Browaldh
Deputy chairman, Nobel Foundation; Chairman,
Svenska Handelsbanken, Stockholm
4

[Saying the U.S. should not lose faith in itself]: You are pulling out of your troubles, and admittedly they have been big ones. You have quieted your university students, while we

(TORE BROWALDH)

Europeans haven't quieted ours. Your racial problems are diminished. You have a leadership problem, but that will be solved, too. You have a solid economy; your industry is a world leader; your managerial skills are far ahead of anyone else's. The dollar is sound. Your Secretary of State [Henry Kissinger] is a wonder, and you have improved relations with [Communist] China and the Soviets.

Interview, Stockholm/
Nation's Business, April:60.

Patrick J. Buchanan
Special Consultant to President of
the United States Richard M. Nixon 1

If they [the news media] emphasize our troubles while ignoring our achievements, if they disregard our successes while elevating our failures, if they insist upon holding the United States up against Utopian standards no nation has ever achieved—instead of comparing our enormous progress with that of other lands and other peoples—they can weaken that traditional American confidence and pride . . .

At seminar, Sangamon State University,
Springfield, Ill., Jan. 7/
Los Angeles Times, 1-8:(1)18.

Earl L. Butz
Secretary of Agriculture of the United States 2

Three times in the last 11 years we've seen an abrupt change of leadership forced in this land, but each time the transition has been orderly. We have survived the assassination of President Kennedy, the soul-searching decision of Lyndon Johnson not to seek a second term as President, and two weeks ago the resignation of President Nixon. Through all of this, the single tragic shot in Dallas has been the only one fired. The military has stayed in its barracks; the government has kept working. Our world defense posture has remained strong, no businesses have been forced to close, no markets have collapsed, no publications have been burned and no presses have been destroyed. Men and women have maintained their right to speak freely, to pursue liberty and happiness as

they see fit. That would not have been the case in many countries of the world. We're all aware of that sobering fact; that's why we're Americans. All of us in this room are immigrants or from immigrant stock. Even the American Indians probably came over the Bering Strait 25- or 50,000 years ago. Our mothers, our fathers, our brothers and sisters—we all live in America because we chose to do so. No one holds us here. We are in this country because we believe it has something special to offer. That something special is freedom; the right of every man, woman and child to live in peace and individual dignity, the right of every human being to pursue a livelihood and life-style of his or her own choice. This is our system. It is a system that works.

At Polish Legion Veterans convention,
Miami Beach, Aug. 24/
Vital Speeches, 9-15:710.

Robert C. Byrd
United States Senator, D—West Virginia 3

One of the most prevalent and frightening attitudes in America today is that of being complacent, apathetic and noncommittal—the absence of deep convictions on anything. We can condemn—and we do—the intellectual shortcomings of television and newspapers; we can decry—as we should—those who abuse the protection of the Fifth Amendment; we can deplore—as we do—the vicious and senseless criminality that pervades our social structure. But how often do we hear our leading citizens, in all walks of life, stand up in public and declare themselves unequivocally on matters of real principle and consequence? Ethics cannot thrive in a neutral mind. And the most dangerous enemies to our way of life are not only those who loudly threaten to overthrow the system; equally dangerous to our freedoms are those who say they don't much care, one way or the other.

Quote, 2-24:181.

Stewart S. Cort
Chairman, Bethlehem Steel Corporation 4

According to what I read, there's been a definite change in the attitudes of today's student population. They're more conservative and traditional in their outlook and behavior . . . Unfortunately, some people see this return to conservatism as proof that our nation has turned its back on social and humanitarian progress. I don't see it that way at all. The majority of people in this nation haven't rejected social progress. To my way of thinking, what they rejected were the revolutionary tactics that endangered the very fabric of our society, extreme and often violent tactics that were seen as doing more harm than good. And I hope we've learned the lesson that our people are willing to change—if and when the proponents of change go about it the right way—by working within the system rather than attacking it from outside.

At Honors Convocation,
Oklahoma Christian College/
Newsweek, 5-20:13.

Walter Cronkite
News commentator,
Columbia Broadcasting System
1

What promise this nation could realize if we all believed, without hint of doubt, that the words of the Constitution and the Bill of Rights mean precisely what they say and apply equally to every man of us, rich or poor, peasant or president, black or white, Northerner or Southerner—no matter how contemptible, untidy or non-conformist either his thoughts or his appearance. This is the law of our land, and in its great fundamentals is the foundation of our past and our future.

Before the Dallas Assembly, Vail, Colo./
The Dallas Times Herald, 4-14:(B)3.

Rene Dubos
Environmentalist; Professor Emeritus of
Microbiology, Rockefeller University
2

[A] thing I think is going to happen is that urban agglomeration will break up into subunits. Los Angeles will be several sub-units—it already is. Sub-units will become more self-sufficient. They will have their own life, which they are already beginning to have, their own centers of interest, their own gathering places and transportation. In the development of New York since the war, old neighborhoods were absolutely destroyed. But here and in other cities where the same thing has happened, there has begun to take place a gut response from the people. In New York, people are rebuilding neighborhoods. You see block parties, local newspapers like *The Village Voice,* banks catering to local interest and decentralization of the school system. We must re-create smaller groups with which we can identify.

Interview, New York/
Los Angeles Times, 11-28:(2)7.

Harold L. Enarson
President, Ohio State University
3

The energy shortage is the least important of the shortages in our national life. The American society is now short of those attributes that, mattering the most, undergird all else: integrity, high purpose, confidence in one another, faith in a brighter future.

Quote, 5-19:457.

Gerald R. Ford
Vice President of the United States
4

It's the quality of the ordinary, the straight, the square that accounts for the great stability and success of our nation. It's a quality to be proud of. But it's a quality that many people seem to have neglected.

Jan. 28/Time, 8-19:27.

5

A [football] team is doomed if it attributes insurmountable power to its opponents. A nation is in serious trouble at home or abroad if it gives in to pessimism or to a psychological complex of defeat . . . The time has come for the nation, the Congress and the Administration to unite to move America forward. Let us restore harmony to our national team . . . I only wish that I could take the entire United States into the locker room at halftime. It would be an opportunity to say that we have lost yards against the line drives of inflation and the end runs of energy shortages, and that we are not using all our players as well as we might because there is too much unemployment. There would be no excuses about previous

WHAT THEY SAID IN 1974

(GERALD R. FORD)

coaches and previous seasons. I would simply say that we must not look at the points we have lost but at the points we can gain. We have a winner. Americans are winners.

At Frank Leahy awards dinner, Chicago,
Feb. 14/Los Angeles Times, 2-15:(1)6.

1

Some are saying today that we in America are over-indulging ourselves in exaggeration—particularly the over-exaggeration of our problems . . . I do not come before you today as the Vice President of a nation suffering from the plagues of slavery, pestilence, famine, revolution or war. If you were to inventory today everything that is right in the world, America's contributions would head the list.

Before the Louisiana Legislature,
Baton Rouge, May 13/
Los Angeles Herald-Examiner, 5-14:(A)7.

2

I think they [the American people] want reassurance that the United States is the great country they really believe in. And I think they realize that in foreign policy we have been spectacularly successful. But they do have some doubts about our capability to handle such problems as inflation; and they want reassurance that we are going to solve these domestic problems in particular. I think they will get that reassurance; but they are hungering for that reassurance. They believe America is great, but skeptics and cynics and some of our problems lead them to an opposite conclusion. They want reassurance through leadership that America is everything they've read about and believed in.

Interview, Washington/
The Christian Science Monitor, 7-25:1.

Gerald R. Ford
President of the United States

3

As one of the great nations of the world—spiritually, militarily, diplomatically and economically—we in America have the best of many worlds. We have nearly all the natural resources we need. We have the technological resources. We have the human resources. Now

we need the will to solve our problems, the will to win. And win we will . . . I see the Bicentennial of 1976 as a rebirth as well as a birthday—a rediscovery of our strength and our potential. It will strengthen our resolve to fulfill the promises of our forefathers. It will fortify our determination to continue to build a freer, more just, more human society.

At American Freedom Train ceremony,
Alexandria, Va., Dec. 19/
Los Angeles Herald-Examiner, 12-19:(A)3.

George Foreman
Heavyweight boxing champion of the world

4

Don't talk down the American system to me. I know what men go through to make it run. I know also some of its rewards can be there for anybody, if he will make up his mind, bend his back, lean hard into his chores and refuse to allow anything to defeat him. I'll wave the flag in every public place I can.

San Francisco Examiner & Chronicle,
10-13:(This World)2.

J. William Fulbright
United States Senator, D—Arkansas

5

For all the ingeniousness of our system of checks and balances, our ultimate protection against tyranny is the fact that we are a people who have not wished to tyrannize one another. "The republican form of government," wrote Herbert Spencer in 1891, "is the highest form of government; but because of this it requires the highest type of human nature—a type nowhere at present existing." We have shown in times of adversity in the past that we are capable of this "highest type of human nature." Let us call it into existence once again; we have never needed it more.

At National Press Club, Washington, Dec. 19/
The Washington Post, 12-26:(A)24.

Barry M. Goldwater
United States Senator, R—Arizona

6

I am the most optimistic guy in the world about America. I think if the Congress would get off the backs of America and let America go, let the enterprise system work, encourage young people, not try to bribe them; I think if we would find schools teaching Americanism and extolling patriotism and teaching the Constitution; if we would find families willing to devote time with their kids—there is nothing that would stop this country.

TV-radio interview, Washington/
"Meet the Press,"
National Broadcasting Company, 1-13.

Billy Graham
Evangelist

1

I am often asked, "Is America at the cross-roads?" My answer is an emphatic "no!" I do not think that America is at a crossroads today. You see, the image of the crossroad implies that we are at a place where we can choose one or more roads to follow. I think we have already made a choice at a crossroads some time ago. I doubt that anyone can specify the exact time when this choice was made ... but it has been made. We are well along the dead-end road we deliberately chose to follow. In a nation which will pay an actor $3 million to play in a pornographic film or make a hero-ine of an actress who displays her talents of sexual perversion on the screen; who not only makes heroes of people who are calling for the overthrow of the government, but pays them high fees for their speeches—then we are in deep trouble. America reminds me of a mental institution where the patients have taken over and have locked up the doctors. Our values are upside-down. We are not thinking straight. The choice was made when America as a nation abandoned obedience to God and to His moral Law. We chose the road of secularism, hedo-nism, materialism and moral permissiveness.

At Kansas State University, March 4/
Vital Speeches, 4-15:387.

Louis Harris
Public-opinion analyst

2

In 1967, substantial majorities of our [poll] sample—60 to 75 per cent—thought the follow-ing people were "dangerous or harmful to the country": people who didn't believe in God, black militants, student demonstrators, prosti-tutes, homosexuals. In the fall of [1973], we couldn't find a majority to say that any one of those groups was dangerous. Today, the people considered "dangerous" by a majority of Americans are these: people who hire political spies, 52 per cent; Generals who conduct secret bombing raids, 67 per cent; politicians who engage in secret wiretapping, 71 per cent; busi-nessmen who make illegal political contribu-tions, 81 per cent; and politicians who try to use the Central Intelligence Agency, the Federal Bureau of Investigation and the Secret Service for political purposes or to try to restrict free-dom, 88 per cent. That is what has happened in America.

Interview/The New York Times, 1-21:16.

Paul Harvey
News commentator,
American Broadcasting Company

3

If we'd given up and run for cover every time it rained, we'd still be 13 colonies. Our Americanism is made of very durable stuff. In the 200 years since we weaned ourselves, every other nation in the world had been turned upside down, and ours is still right side up. Two hundred years ago, England and France were absolute monarchies and kings ruled both. Italy and Germany didn't even exist. Our Latin American neighbors were still colonies. China was ruled by the Manchus, Japan by the shoguns, Russia by tyrannical czars. Only that which we built here was built so well that it has endured intact.

July 28/Quote, 9-1:195.

4

Our country is not over the hill. It's barely a beardless, post-puberty adolescent. What's messing up Page One is not senility; it's acne.

Quote, 8-18:145.

Gabriel Hauge
Chairman, Manufacturers Hanover
Trust Company, New York

5

America's ultimate reserves are not the glis-tening little bars at Fort Knox. Rather, they are a consensus of values, agreement on goals, a superb mechanism for transforming resources into products, tested institutions for compro-

WHAT THEY SAID IN 1974

mising conflicts, individuals who are inventive, energetic and imbued with a hopeful outlook. The need for a reaffirmation of these values is greatest when the times are most out of joint, when the world seems to retreat . . . The autonomy of America derives from its vast human and natural resources and their superb organization. The capacity of America to change itself, and to influence the world, in turn derives from its autonomy. Responsibility falls to us because of our power to help shape events. Our freedom requires us to direct that power to good ends, for we do believe this "is still the fairest, richest and freest land of all."

At National Foreign Trade Convention,
New York, Nov. 19/
Vital Speeches, 12-15:146.

Woody Hayes
Football coach, Ohio State University   1

Football is about the only unifying force left in America today. It's certainly one of the few places in our society where teamwork, mental discipline and the value of hard work still mean anything . . . You can see the pattern just as clear as day. We're tearing down all our heroes in America. And I can tell you, a society that's always tearing down its heroes is a *suicidal* society. A civilization without heroes isn't going to be a civilization much longer.

Interview, Columbus, Ohio/
The New York Times, 10-5:31.

Jesse A. Helms
United States Senator,
R—North Carolina   2

The fundamental verities of the defense of liberty, the attainment of knowledge, the worship of God and the practice of private enterprise are still the American goals. I would say that the priorities of the American people are in good order.

At testimonial dinner for Clarence Manion,
former dean of the Notre Dame Law School,
Washington/Human Events, 5-25:4.

Bob Hope
Actor, Comedian   3

Patriotism is a lot like loving your wife: You don't run around the streets saying, "I love my wife, I love my wife," but you do.

News conference, Saratoga Springs, N.Y.,
July 4/The Dallas Times Herald, 7-5:(A)2.

Leon Jaworski
Lawyer; Special government
prosecutor for Watergate   4

The French scholar and philosopher, de Tocqueville, in his prolonged studies of American democracy and our institutions, referred with unbounded admiration to the greatness and genius of our country. He concluded that America was great because America was good— especially in a sense of morality and in respecting laws and the rights of fellow-man. But this greatness is not self-perpetuating. It can vanish much faster than the time that it took to win it. Are these not truisms that need to be imparted to our young? . . . indoctrinations in good citizenship at an early age will enable oncoming generations to carry forward the work that must be done to assure that America will continue to be great. If this obligation is not discharged, history will surely record our failure. Inasmuch as we will celebrate soon the Bicentennial of our nation, whose constitutional form of government through law is recognized to be a triumph over the despotism and individual repression of authoritarian forms, the time to foster this program seems especially propitious. And let us ever remember the words of the English Prime Minister Disraeli: "The youth of a nation are the trustees of posterity."

Before International Platform Association/
The Washington Post, 8-13:(A)18.

Walter Laqueur
Director, Institute of
Contemporary Affairs, London   5

American confidence is not yet broken. The country has so many resources. The economy, for all its ups and downs, does not face a major crisis. If the President [Nixon] is impeached, there will be a new President. America is better off than Europe or Japan. It may not be wonderful, but everything is comparative.

Interview, Washington/
Los Angeles Times, 4-3:(2)7.

Clare Boothe Luce
Former American diplomat and playwright
1

There's been an enormous change, in my lifetime, in American attitudes. Traditionally, Americans are an optimistic and Utopian-minded people. This is because they've lived for 200 years in marvelously fortunate conditions. They've lived on a vast and bountiful land which has produced an endless quantity of material goods. They've lived under a form of government originally designed to encourage competition and personal initiative. They've lived in a country where the average American has always been better off—richer, freer, better educated—than his parents, and where he has always expected his children to be better off than himself. Up to now, Americans have always believed that, despite national ups and downs, they were making progress toward the American Utopia, in which poverty—and even work—would be abolished, and all men would live equally free to pursue their own ideas of happiness. Call it "the American dream." Well, we are waking up from it. We are beginning to face the realities of the world we live in. And it's a traumatic experience. Consider that only 25 years ago we had won the greatest war in history, and we stood at the highest pinnacle of wealth and power any nation had ever attained ... The violent changes that have since taken place in the world, and that have adversely affected America, have come on us so suddenly. Nothing in our national experience has prepared us to deal with them. We are—at least for the moment—demoralized by them.

Interview/
U.S. News & World Report, 6-24:52.

Shirley MacLaine
Actress
2

I've traveled a lot in my life, and whenever I'm away from them very long, I miss Americans—especially the sense of humor here. There's nowhere else on earth a human being will tell you the truth as they see it more directly than in the United States. I think this says that we—above all other nations—have the ability to solve our problems if we can just trust one another more, if we can have the feeling as individuals that we're worth something.

Interview, Las Vegas, Nev./
The Christian Science Monitor, 10-3:7.

Edgar F. Magnin
Rabbi, Wilshire Boulevard Temple,
Los Angeles
3

Today many people have lost faith in America, and this is foolish. In the first place, corruption is nothing new to those who read history. This does not justify it, but we should realize that the majority of Americans are honest, decent people, and this is true also of most political leaders. There is nothing wrong with our form of government. The weakness lies in human nature. We are still better off than most people in other parts of the world. We are free to believe what we want, to attend any church or synagogue we choose, to say what we please and to elect or reject our political leaders. Our duty as Americans is not to pull down the political structure because it doesn't function 100 per cent, but to correct its weaknesses as far as possible. We must never lose faith in ourselves and in our form of government. It took a long time before the American dream came into fruition. It must never be permitted to fade out. We owe this to ourselves and to those who will come after us.

Los Angeles Times, 6-29:(1)26.

Abner V. McCall
President, Baylor University
4

The general morality of our people is on the decline. The divorce rate and illegitimacy continue to climb, and the family, the basic social unit, is threatened with dissolution. Self-restraint and self-discipline are becoming rare as personal virtues ... We have more liberty than our morality will support. We have more liberty than our self-discipline will support.

At Texas Police Association Conference,
Dallas, June 17/
The Dallas Times Herald, 6-18:(B)1.

WHAT THEY SAID IN 1974

Daniel P. Moynihan
United States Ambassador to India **1**

President [John] Kennedy had this sense of the fragility of the society. He and his brother [the late Attorney General Robert Kennedy] had the sense of the extreme tensions in American life, the thin skin of stability stretched over the complex ethnic and class and regional structures in the country. To keep it going is the great achievement. Not to know how hard it is to keep it going is the disastrous innocence.

Interview, New Delhi/
The New York Times Magazine, 3-31:68.

Richard M. Nixon
President of the United States **2**

Those of us who work [in Washington] . . . may get a distorted view of what is America and what it is really like. It is there that you hear, more than any place in the world, that America is sick, that there is something wrong with this country that cannot be corrected . . .

At Honor America Day rally, Huntsville, Ala.,
Feb. 18/Los Angeles Times, 2-19:(1)19.

3

The [U.S.] Bicentennial [in 1976] is not going to be invented in Washington, printed in triplicate by the Government Printing Office, mailed to you by the U.S. Postal Service and filed away in your private library. Instead, we shall seek to trigger a chain reaction of tens of thousands of individual celebrations—large and small—planned and carried out by citizens in every part of America . . . We must use the opportunity the Bicentennial offers us to develop new institutions and new ideas to help determine America's course in the coming century. We face great challenges, of course; but in our laws, in our ideals and in the character of the American people, we hold the keys to all the problems that confront us.

Radio address to the nation,
Key Biscayne, Fla., March 10/
Los Angeles Herald-Examiner, 3-11:(A)2.

4

[America] needs character because today . . . the peace of the world for generations, maybe centuries, to come will depend not just on America's military might, which is the greatest in the world, or our wealth, which is the greatest in the world, but it is going to depend on our character, our belief in ourselves, our love of our country, our willingness to not only wear the flag but to stand up for the flag . . .

Nashville, Tenn., March 25/
The Christian Science Monitor, 4-19:4.

Olof Palme
Prime Minister of Sweden **5**

America will never be weak, but it cannot be strong unless it solves its internal divisiveness. Any country that can put a man on the moon, produce the Marshall Plan and solve problems of World War II has the power to solve its own problems. That is a matter of political will.

Interview/Nation's Business, April:62.

Norman Podhoretz
Editor, "Commentary" magazine **6**

. . . neither the political nor the intellectual leaders of America are worthy today of the people they presume and offer to lead. And if we ask how such a situation came to pass, I think we will find a good part of the answer in the attitude of the American elites toward the American people. To put the matter bluntly, the American people are neither respected by nor beloved of the American elites. On the left, among liberals and radicals, the people are thought of and spoken of in the most contemptuous terms. They are constantly being denounced as selfish, as materialistic, as crude, as bigoted, as dolts who are easily manipulated by public relations and advertising. The contempt of the right for the people is more discreet, less openly expressed. Among conservatives, the people are not so much sneered at as patronized: They are children— innocent, naive, soft, unable to look after themselves properly, and in need of protection from the dangers which surround them but to which they are persistently blind. Well, the American people are neither selfish barbarians nor helpless children. They are, however, guilty of liking and wanting to preserve and improve the kind of society they already have—the kind of society that used to be called a bourgeois democracy. This is their true crime in the eyes of the American elites. For the American elites have no love for the bourgeois democratic order.

On Far East tour sponsored by U.S. State Department's Bureau of Educational and Cultural Affairs/ The National Observer, 3-9:10.

Lewis F. Powell, Jr.
Associate Justice, Supreme Court of the United States

1

Whatever the faults and problems of our country and system may be, the essential structure of our democracy and freedom under the rule of law gives hope for the future and is worth struggling to preserve. If one has doubts, let him reflect upon the most likely alternative: the Fascist or Communist type of totalitarian regime, where—as [exiled Soviet author Alexander] Solzhenitsyn has written so poignantly—repression is always a brooding omnipresence and not just a slogan.

At convocation, Washington and Lee University/ The National Observer, 2-9:12.

William Proxmire
United States Senator, D—Wisconsin

2

There's a pervasive feeling of public cynicism about the nation and the Federal government. Much of it is justified, but it overlooks the fact that the last 15 years have been the most productive time in our history. Someone has to point out the good side . . . We are infected with a man-bites-dog syndrome. If we do something right, it tends to pass unnoticed. It's the unusual, the wrong, that we dwell on. As one of the most critical members of Congress, I'm probably as guilty as anyone else in this regard. So now I'm trying to point out that, while it's healthy to look at the problems, we also shouldn't forget the degree of solution we have achieved.

Interview/The National Observer, 5-4:3.

3

People are beginning to feel that something is terribly wrong [in the U.S.]. Watergate, with all the word implies, has become a focal point for our national anxieties. Lest we in Congress start to preen our feathers at these sorry estimates of the Executive Branch's performance, let us remind ourselves that, over the past year, public approval of Congressional efforts has plummeted by 17 per cent . . . It would be foolish to try to change this cloud-drenched landscape into a rosy sunset. Pollyanna would probably strike out at a similar task. On the other hand, it is just as dangerous to lose our national will by underestimating our virtues as it is to lull ourselves into a collective nirvana by making light of our serious problems.

Los Angeles Times, 5-8:(1)8.

Hyman G. Rickover
Admiral, United States Navy

4

A declining sense of morals touches every aspect of society. The decline in public confidence in government, business, labor and other institutions, for example, is due in part to the slow but subtle elevation of craftiness, slickness, toughness and pragmatism as desirable leadership characteristics. There has even been a disturbing increase in the value attributed to dishonesty and violence. These traits are made to appear as being efficient, which is often considered important and even virtuous in this technological age . . . Too much today we find our lives and times motivated by slogans, 30-second commercials, headlines and the instant mass culture of superficiality. Much of this is due to the abundance of material wealth with which this country has been blessed. Because of our wealth, life has become too easy for us. We have tended to squander and waste not only our material abundance, but our spiritual and moral heritage as well. We find ourselves a people whose bellies are full, but whose spirits are empty. I do not believe we will continue this way. The coming age of scarcity is going to make things tougher for all. Society will go back to the notion of individual responsibility, so that blame for crime will fall squarely on the criminal, not on society at large. The scarcity of material wealth will again make spiritual and moral values important, and people will lead more ethical lives motivated

WHAT THEY SAID IN 1974

(HYMAN G. RICKOVER)

not by commercials, but by the virtues of honesty, integrity, compassion and cooperation.

Before House Appropriations Subcommittee,
Washington/The National Observer, 8-24:18.

R. A. Riley
President, Firestone Tire and
Rubber Company   1

I am much more concerned today about the things America is doing to herself than I am about the dangers from outside. I am ready to sound the alarm against self-inflicted wounds. Nothing good can come from a constant repetition of our faults. We begin to believe them and we begin to despair. We lose faith and abandon hope. Our children inherit our beliefs and our degree of confidence, whatever it may be. If all they hear is what is wrong with our way, how can we expect them to build something better on such a foundation? You build on what you believe in, and if there is no belief there is no building. I feel strongly that student demonstrations and student unrest of a few years back were built and nourished on our own criticisms of our own way of life. In recent years we have not adequately expressed, either in word or deed, our confidence in our American way of life and in its institutions. And this lack of confidence shows up in all the social, political, economic and industrial segments of our lives. In fact, we have frequently presented a very unhealthy picture for all to see—an image very much weakened by the severe wounds we are inflicting on ourselves. Does this mean stop all criticism? No, not at all. It simply means that we stop accepting the things that are wrong as a total evaluation. It means seeking out and emphasizing the good things with as much fervor as we embrace the bad, and then and only then drawing a balance sheet to get the over-all picture. No person would think of evaluating his actual worth by listing his liabilities only.

Before Downtown Rotary Club,
Akron, Ohio, April 16/
Vital Speeches, 6-1:492.

William P. Rogers
Former Secretary of State of
the United States   2

Our nation is not disintegrating; it is developing and progressing. It is not complacent and self-satisfied; it is still young and self-critical. We rarely get much satisfaction in solving problems because we are so busy searching out and confronting new problems. Our success in every field—science, technology, education, health, production of food, housing, transportation, communication, space, etc.—astounds people everywhere. The initiative and drive of this nation are the envy of the world. We are the strongest, most prosperous and successful nation the world has ever known. I am proud of our country and confident of its future.

At conference of Second Judicial Circuit
of the United States/
The New York Times, 9-29:(4)17.

Dean Rusk
Professor of International Law,
University of Georgia; Former
Secretary of State of the United States   3

I have great confidence in democracy. I raise the back of my hand to people who say democracy cannot survive. This is a bad time, but it reminds me of Secretary of State George Marshall, who was asked during the Berlin crisis of 1948, "How can you stay so calm?" He replied, "I've seen worse." I think it is fundamental that democracy and this country are going to endure. We do have major problems, but I believe our young people will write a unique chapter in the history of the human race. The human race has the capacity to be rational at the end of the day, even if they are crazy in the morning.

Interview, University of Georgia/
"W": a Fairchild publication, 11-1:8.

Howard K. Smith
News commentator,
American Broadcasting Company   4

I am as ill as others at the cynical Watergate tapes. But I know, from having lived there, that most other nations have Watergates. We [in the

U.S.] are blessed with an aggressive press, sure to get at them and stop them. Nowhere else can one be as certain of ultimate justice as in a court system which in one week acquitted [John] Mitchell and [Maurice] Stans, and disbarred [Spiro] Agnew, because it was right. The cure for our awful inflation is increasing supply, mainly of food and fuel. Nowhere else [but in the U.S.] can farming do that, as it will. No other nation has so much fuel, more than all Arabia, needing only technology to extract it from shale and atoms. What other nation can be as sure technology will do it as the country that leads the world in the newest big industry, computers, and the oldest big industry, agriculture? The nation's spirit is good. The spontaneous rise in recent years of the sturdiest consumer lobbies in the world, the steady movement of minorities into the American mainstream, the public's refusal to settle for lame White House explanations display a spirit it is hard to find with the same vigor elsewhere. Optimism is not always justified. But in a country like this, when in doubt, trust it.

ABC News commentary/
The Christian Science Monitor, 5-14:(F)10.

Gloria Swanson
Actress

1

The decline of manners [in America] is what bothers me . . . the rudeness . . . a young person sitting like a lump when an older person comes into the room. And when I go to Europe, who's making all the noise? Americans. And in Paris, who pinched my bottom? An American, of course. I'm not anti-American; it's not that at all. But we've lost so much. We were so beautiful. My father used to shake hands and that was his bond. Now I sign ironclad contracts, and they mean nothing. Nothing!

Interview, Napa Valley, Calif./
TV Guide, 2-23:13.

John W. Warner
Administrator, American Revolution Bicentennial Commission

2

I'm of the firm belief that out of all of the Bicentennial participation will grow a national consensus of opinion to the effect that the blueprint for our country, as laid down by the Founding Fathers in the Declaration of Independence, the Constitution and the Bill of Rights, is the proper blueprint and one which can carry the nation forward into the third century. It has withstood the test of time; and, in my judgment, each time this country has been faced with a serious issue such as Watergate, this blueprint has resolved the problem, and this country has emerged from that resolution stronger than it was before.

Interview, Washington/
Los Angeles Herald-Examiner, 7-21:(1)14.

Ben J. Wattenberg
Political analyst

3

What we have been through in recent years proves there are a bunch of strong people in the country. That is the root of my optimism. In these last dozen years we have lived through an unpopular war in Vietnam, racial violence, assassination, stark challenge to established values, a great political scandal [Watergate]. The people were challenged right up to their eyes with problems at least as great and probably greater than we are faced with now. That was about as tough a sequence of events as you can imagine; and on top of it we were being poor-mouthed to death—told that Americans were racists, imperialists and what-not. Yet throughout that time you will find that, in measurable fields like income, jobs, racial attitudes, we made in this country enormous progress . . . Americans are bright, creative, non-flappable, technologically minded. They are going to do what they have to do in the end. Despite inflation and the energy shortage, the overriding sense that I get in looking at the way Americans handled their problems the last dozen years is that these people can cope. In fact, they have become expert copers and are tougher, more sophisticated and charitable than their critics have suggested. They have learned—or they always knew—how to handle tough national problems.

Interview, Washington/
Los Angeles Times, 10-14:(2)7.

Lowell P. Weicker, Jr.
United States Senator, R—Connecticut 1

Democracy is bloody inefficient, especially when it comes to law and order. The motif of the Constitution and the Bill of Rights is the importance and dignity and liberty of the individual, the freedom to blossom and flower and develop and grow and experiment as a person. If law and order is the prime requisite of our society, then there are other forms of government which are far more efficient. Our Constitution does not guarantee a structured peace. In fact, it guarantees trouble, because it encourages a nation to strive, to seek out trouble, to find out where the raw spots are.

Interview, Washington/Parade, 7-14:5.

William H. Whyte
Land planner 2

What attracts people most in a city is other people. People are attracted to the very density they say they don't like. The physical amenities are an easy thing to come by . . . a place to sit, to eat, to girl-watch. They are the essence of the greatness of a city. And they're right under our nose.

Before Central Business District Association, Dallas, Jan. 31/ The Dallas Times Herald, 2-1:(A)24.

Jerome B. Wiesner
President, Massachusetts Institute of Technology 3

While correcting the things that are wrong in our system, we have to protect the things that are right. What really worries me is that people might get so discouraged that they will come to believe the solution lies in some form of autocratic management. Every autocratic management I have examined looks so much worse than what we have—not only in terms of limitations on the individual, which is inevitable, but in terms of ability to solve the basic problems we are talking about.

Interview, Cambridge, Mass./ Los Angeles Times, 12-12:(2)7.

Malcolm Wilson
Governor of New York 4

The wonder of America is not its great cities and swelling suburbs—but that once, and not so long ago, all this was an untamed wilderness. The wonder of America is not our endless ribbons of railways and roadways—but that a few centuries ago America had no roads at all. The wonder of America is not our great universities and famous capitals of research—but that a moment ago, as history is measured, America lacked even a schoolhouse. I have no fear for the American people in a time of adversity. We will learn anew that adversity brings out the true character of a people. There is within our national character a gene of toughness, of resourcefulness, of courage. It may have been blunted by years of prosperity. It may have been softened by easy living. It may have been dulled by an obsession with comforts and convenience. But the inner core of the American character remains strong. Let us never forget, we are people who conquered an untamed continent, surviving civil war, rode out the great Depression, saved the world from tyranny in two world wars. We are not going to be defeated by a 55 mile-an-hour speed limit, or a thermostat set at 68 degrees. The energy crisis and the other challenges we face will only force us to reach inside ourselves to find the strength that has been there all along. These challenges are pulling us closer together—making us see the need, the value, indeed the beauty of helping one another. They are reminding us of the sweet satisfaction that comes from knowing we can still do for ourselves.

State of the State address, Albany, N.Y., Jan. 9/The New York Times, 1-10:32.

Coleman A. Young
Mayor of Detroit 5

The crisis in the cities is the major crisis facing America today. America cannot live if its central cities die . . .

At National Urban League forum, San Francisco, July 30/ San Francisco Examiner, 7-31:17

Ralph D. Abernathy
*President, Southern Christian
Leadership Conference*

1

We've got to survive, and this is the most important question in the black community today. We want a piece of the pie. Black people are not going anywhere. This is our land. This is our home. Africa may be the home of our ancestors, but America is our home; and we love this land, because we helped develop this nation . . . First, there needs to be a dialogue. We must come together. There has to be a charted course that is clear. General Motors and Ford and ITT, all major companies, must forge ahead, actually issuing clear-cut statements against racism, against poverty and against injustice. We must then move ahead to create the jobs and income necessary for all to live as brothers in this society, enjoying our God-given and Constitutional rights.

Interview/San Francisco Examiner, 2-28:35.

James Baldwin
Author

2

. . . I think that almost unconsciously black people in the '70s in this country don't relate merely to this country, or merely to other black people in this country, but have a real sense, a very dim sense, but a real sense of the way in which the fate of black people [in the U.S.] is tied to the fate of non-white people all over the world. And I have a certain suspicion that the black experience which has created the present generation of black people is in the vanguard of a certain global struggle which is only beginning dimly to be felt by black people here and in other places. I suspect that because you can't go anywhere in the world without finding echoes of the civil-rights movement in the States, from Black Power to Indian Power, or Portuguese students, Latin American students and women. It created all kinds of children all over the world and they know their human problems. That changes the nature of the struggle in the sense that it is no longer purely a domestic struggle of American black people.

*Interview, Washington, June/
The Washington Post, 7-21:(C)4.*

Terrel H. Bell
*Commissioner of Education of
the United States*

3

. . . those who want massive, long-distance busing [of school children for racial balance] need to look at what happens after the bus ride: The youngster still goes back to a segregated neighborhood; he still spends 18 out of his 24 hours a day in that segregated neighborhood. The whole problem runs deeper than the schools and busing. I think it runs to zoning ordinances, the rehabilitation of our great urban centers, and the restoration of economic and social health to cities. As an educator, I've felt that the responsibility for solving the racial problem has been too heavily placed upon the schools and not enough on other agencies that have a responsibility, and that busing doesn't get at the root cause of racial problems.

*Interview/
U.S. News & World Report, 9-16:42.*

Edward W. Brooke
United States Senator, R—Massachusetts

4

The hope for an end to racial division lies in our education system. For each generation of segregation in our schools, we risk another generation of division in our nation.

*Before the Senate, Washington, May 15/
The Washington Post, 5-16:(A)4.*

Warren E. Burger
Chief Justice of the United States

5

[Ruling on cross-district busing of school children for racial balance between city and

(WARREN E. BURGER)

suburbs]: Before the boundaries of separate and autonomous school districts may be set aside by consolidating the separate units for remedial purposes or by imposing a cross-district remedy, it must first be shown that there has been a Constitutional violation within one district that produces a significant segregative effect in another district. Specifically, it must be shown that racially discriminatory acts of the state or local school districts, or of a single school district, have been a substantial cause of inter-district segregation. Thus an inter-district remedy might be in order where the racially discriminatory acts of one or more school districts caused racial segregation in an adjacent district, or where district lines have been deliberately drawn on the basis of race. In such circumstances an inter-district remedy would be appropriate to eliminate the inter-district segregation directly caused by the Constitutional violation. Conversely, without an inter-district violation and inter-district effect, there is no Constitutional wrong calling for an inter-district remedy.

Supreme Court ruling, Washington, July 25/ The Washington Post, 7-26:(A)8.

Kenneth B. Clark
Professor of Psychology,
City College of New York
1

Unlike Southern white supremacists, who make no bones about their feelings, the strongest supporters of institutional racism have an exactly contrary personal image. These proponents of invidious racism—as I call it—think they're free of it, or if they acknowledge it at all, they claim the distinctions they make are empirically based. They really think they're not like other whites. Therefore, given that self-image—a powerful defense mechanism—any attempt at discussing the subject evokes an emotional polemic, and probably an attack on the questioner for being a racist himself. That, of course, postpones coming to grips with reality or with facing the real issue, for you first have to deal with the question of who is a racist. Such people will trot out their liberal

credentials. Basically, this is all diversionary, and by the time you've dealt with the diversion, you're emotionally exhausted before you get at the real issue. The intensity of the delusion you're dealing with is really a deep unwillingness to change. The psychological devices that are used merely indicate the depth of the racism. For these people have invested so much of themselves in the emotional part of all this, that any significant change would make them admit much more than they can possibly admit about themselves.

The New York Times Magazine, 5-12:52.

John Doherty
President, Boston Teachers Union
2

[Arguing against busing of schoolchildren for racial balance]: I don't think any parent likes to be told that their children can't go to the closest school, especially when there is no concrete educational reason except for a philosophical, ideological argument that an integrated education is best.

The Washington Post, 11-10:(A)11.

Sam J. Ervin, Jr.
Former United States Senator,
D—North Carolina
3

. . . I think that when the court enters a school-busing decree for integration purposes, the court clearly violates the equal-protection clause in two respects. First, it treats groups of children in the same zone differently, thereby violating the equal-protection clause. And in the second place, when it buses children from their own districts to districts elsewhere, it does so in order to reduce the number of children of that particular race in their neighborhood schools, or they increase them in the schools elsewhere, and this is clearly denying those children the right to attend neighborhood schools on account of their race. Which is exactly what the school desegregation case said was un-Constitutional. In other words, I think the courts have perverted and distorted the Constitution, and thereby have made guinea pigs out of little children of both races.

Interview/The Washington Post, 12-29:(B)3.

Charles Evers
Mayor of Fayette, Mississippi
1

Getting a piece of the economic and political pie is what it's all about [in the civil-rights movement today]. I'm a capitalist all the way. Nothing else but. You can't have a voice [when you're] on welfare. Money and politics—that's the name of the game now. The civil-rights war is over—the marches and protests and fights, that phase of it. No one gives a damn about marches any more. If you marched from here to Washington, nobody would pay any attention. What we [blacks] care about is financial success and running for office—building an empire; and we've made a good start into the financial and political phase.

The Washington Post, 8-18:(C)3.

Gerald R. Ford
President of the United States
2

I believe that all school districts, North and South, East and West, should be able to adopt reasonable and just plans for desegregation which will not result in children being bused from their neighborhoods.

Washington, Aug. 21/
The Washington Post, 8-22:(A)12.

Edith Green
United States Representative, D—Oregon
3

[Arguing against forced busing of school-children for racial balance] : We are not talking about busing out of choice to achieve an educational purpose. We are not talking about a family with children who buy a farm and know when they purchase the farm that there is no school nearby and that they will necessarily have to bus their children. That was their decision, not a government decision. It was a decision based entirely on their choice. We are talking about a family who establishes residence in a particular area and where a major factor that entered into buying their home or establishing their residence there was the school in that area which they had every right to expect their children to attend. Let me repeat, what we are talking about is not voluntary busing but forced busing. I have for some time opposed

forced busing. It is not within the realm of possibility for us to go back 100 years to correct the errors of our ancestors. The only thing we can do is look at the present state of education in this country and decide what is happening to it. I oppose forced busing because I believe we have seen it is absolutely unworkable. I have seen no evidence that it has accomplished its objective. It has no educational value and dubious social value.

Before the House, Washington, Feb. 20/
Human Events, 4-13:15.

Richard G. Hatcher
Mayor of Gary, Indiana
4

[Saying more moderate black leaders should cooperate with black nationalists and other more radical blacks] : Everyone must be brought into the fold. In the name of all black Americans who have been abandoned, in the name of all the dispossessed and disenfranchised, I summon our leaders back to our ranks . . . We need [NAACP executive director] Roy Wilkins now; it's time that Mr. Wilkins stopped defending our grandfathers and started defending our children. We need [Urban League executive director] Vernon Jordan now; we need [U.S. Senator] Edward Brooke now; we need Charles Diggs and we need Floyd McKissick and we need [Los Angeles Mayor] Tom Bradley . . . we need every black man and woman who has risen from the ranks. If our leaders abandon us, we are lost.

At National Black Political Convention,
Little Rock, Ark./
San Francisco Examiner & Chronicle,
3-24:(This World)9.

Randolph A. Hearst
President and editor,
"San Francisco Examiner"
5

I think we've got too many problems. We talk about the black problem, the Chicano problem and the Indian problem. I think the problem is the white problem. I think it's about time we looked at our so-called minorities as assets instead of liabilities. I think until that

WHAT THEY SAID IN 1974

(RANDOLPH A. HEARST)

happens we're going to have a great deal of social troubles.

San Francisco Examiner & Chronicle,
4-14:(This World)2.

A. Leon Higginbotham, Jr.
Judge, United States District Court for
the Eastern District of Pennsylvania
1

I do not see the [the U.S. Supreme] Court of the 1970s or envision the Court of the 1980s as the major instrument for significant change and improvement in the quality of race relations in America. I am not suggesting a reversion back to the era of Plessy vs. Ferguson, but I do not see a steady march forward where the Supreme Court is the major catalyst for obtaining social justice for blacks and other Americans... We [blacks] must make major efforts in other forums without the exclusive reliance on the Federal legal process. So in some ways maybe it will be the laws of the city, the laws of the state, which must be major vehicles of the mechanisms for change. Of course, we must maximize our efforts in the political arena... Integration in itself will not solve many of the major problems in our society. We will have obtained very little... if we have only unfulfilled promises, unfulfilled hopes, unfulfilled attainments amidst substantial pockets of integrated unemployment, integrated malnutrition, integrated inferior housing and integrated poor educational systems.

Before Association for the Study
of Afro-American Life and History,
Philadelphia, Oct.2/
The Washington Post, 10-26:(A)4.

Jacquelyne J. Jackson
Associate Professor of Medical Sociology,
Duke University
2

It is ignorant to raise the idea that blacks aspiring for certain goals are aping white middle-class people. It is not white to speak English. It is not white to be clean. People were washing themselves in the Nile River centuries ago. It is not white to eat or to want the best possible education for your children. What these people are doing is conforming to standards—borrowed from other societies and customs and traditions—that are American. They are being American, not trying to be white.

U.S. News & World Report, 10-14:51.

Jesse L. Jackson
Civil-rights leader;
President, Operation PUSH
(People United to Save Humanity)
3

You cannot be against the rape of black women; you've got to be against rape. You cannot be against the murder of blacks; you have got to be against murder. You cannot be against robbery of black people; you have got to be against robbery. We've got to move from the ethnic to the ethics.

At National Urban League convention,
San Francisco, July 31/
The New York Times, 8-2:9.

Maynard H. Jackson, Jr.
Mayor of Atlanta
4

There's always a place for black candidates in a Presidential campaign. But if you're asking if a black candidate has a chance to be President in '76, the answer is no. The struggle is not won overnight. Those who are impatient are not serious about social revolution. When we get to the floor of the Democratic Convention... I believe the nominee will be white. But with a strong black coalition, we can make sure we get the candidate most sensitive to our needs.

At Bishop College, Dallas/
The Dallas Times Herald, 3-24:(I)3.

5

We [blacks] must seek allies regardless of color. Our protracted struggle must be one of good people against bad ideas. The struggle for black liberation is a battle for human rights, black and white. If we are to change our national policies, we must be a broad-based political force that can change the people who make the policies. So let black America be united, but let us also reach out as we did in the 1960s and include our white brothers and sisters of good heart.

At Congressional Black Caucus dinner, Washington, Sept. 28/ The Atlanta Journal and Constitution, 9-29:(A)16.

Daniel James, Jr.
Lieutenant General, United States Air Force; Principal Deputy Assistant Secretary for Public Affairs, Department of Defense of the United States

1

I say to many of the black militants to reach out. There are many hands reaching out toward you, in friendship and in help. Many of these hands are white, but they find it pretty hard to reach out in friendship or in help if your hand is curled tightly into a fist of hate ... And I say to the white majority in the same breath, don't you make me a liar.

Before Commonwealth Club of California/ The Wall Street Journal, 9-17:22.

John H. Johnson
Publisher, "Ebony" magazine

2

Obviously, we [blacks] have not gone as far as we would like. But we have made tremendous progress. Some of our young people look at certain situations and they are very disenchanted. But those of us who are older, who know how really far back we were at one time, can appreciate the progress that has been made. We have made it in education, in jobs, in politics, in all areas. One need only look at the number of black Mayors, the increasing number of black Congressmen and the great number of blacks in many official positions throughout the Deep South to recognize just how much progress has been achieved.

Interview, Chicago/ Nation's Business, April:49.

Barbara Jordan
United States Representative, D–Texas

3

In the future, I don't think we will see much in terms of legislation with regard to civil rights. I think blacks have begun to recognize that our future is in the political process and that the gains will be made there. It is very tough. It is not a very sexy way to proceed in civil rights; but it is now an accepted, legitimate way to achieve gains for black people, and I think this is what we are going to see more and more.

Interview, Washington/ The Christian Science Monitor, 3-18:6.

Vernon E. Jordan, Jr.
Executive director, National Urban League

4

The President has a hammer, but he's using it to save himself and not to save the people. The Congress has a hammer, but is using it to beat on busing as a way to stay in office and not using it to save the children. The media has a hammer in its influence and power over men's minds, but it uses it to sell papers, not to seek truth. So black people truly sing "If I had a hammer," for we had a hammer in the civil-rights movements of the 1960s and we hammered out a movement of mutual respect and social and economic progress. With the hammer in our hands, black people can rise above the selfishness and suspicion of these United States in this tortured year of 1974 and help to create a newer, better nation, more just, more humane, more free. Yes, black people are asking for the hammer of freedom, the hammer of justice, the hammer of decency; for with that hammer we can build wonders. We can hammer out love and peace, justice and fairness ... all over this great land of ours.

Before Capital Press Club, Washington, May 4/Vital Speeches, 6-15:544

5

When Southern sheriffs turned water hoses on black civil-rights demonstrators, the [news] cameras were rolling and the news columns full. When ghetto blacks rioted, the media decided it was time to add a little color to the newsroom and the editorial offices. But the heat is off now. Backlash has become respectable and the media has gone back to its traditional neglect of black people. We have a situation in which a black leader can get all the space he wants for an attack on other blacks, but none if he's got something to say about welfare, health policy, housing or a dozen other areas of life-and-death importance to all black people. The media has done a great job on the Watergate story; but it

WHAT THEY SAID IN 1974

(VERNON E. JORDAN, JR.)

has also "Watergated" black people in its treatment of us in the news columns. It has placed black folk under the hammer of the very media neglect that helps to validate the actions of the Administration and the Congress.

Before Captial Press Club,
Washington, May 4/
The Washington Post, 9-1:(K)5.

1

The biggest disappointment to me is that the vast majority of white Americans never really understood what we [blacks] were talking about. They thought we were just talking about defining elementary rights and responsibilities for black Americans. That was just a wedge in the big door. It's the big door we really need, and it's the big door they've turned their backs on—the full range of economic and political rights that they [whites] enjoy.

The New York Times Magazine, 5-12:46.

2

There is a great temptation for some Jewish people to turn to others [blacks] still engaged in [the civil-rights] struggle and suggest: "We made it by our bootstraps; we persevered in the face of brutal obstacles. You, too, must now do the same." [But] black people have paid their dues in the form of slavery, peonage and exclusion for nearly 400 years, and there is little justification to add another 50 or 100 years to our passage into equality. Times have changed, too. Our technological economy, the shrinking of traditional stepping-stone jobs, the over-credentialization in the workplace, all combine to make it impossible for today's deprived to duplicate the Jewish experience.

Before Atlanta chapter,
American Jewish Committee, June 2/
Los Angeles Times, 6-3:(1)5.

3

[President Nixon] has made it clear that our national government, once the rock of hope for minorities, is now, at best, indifferent to their needs and aspirations. There has been a massive failure of moral leadership from the White House, which has encouraged the negative forces in our society.

At National Urban League convention,
San Francisco, July 28/
The Washington Post, 7-29:(A)2.

Edward M. Kennedy
United States Senator, D—Massachusetts

4

We must realize that part of every effort must be the struggle to erase the shame of racism in the United States. [But instead of vision from the national leadership,] we have received the sound of fear. Instead of wisdom, we have received racist slogans. Instead of commitment and action, we have received empty promises.

Before meeting of Martin Luther King Jr.
Center for Social Change, New York, April 6/
The New York Times, 4-7:(1)49.

Peter MacDonald
Chairman, Navajo (Indian) Tribal Council

5

It is not bad to be old; it is a glorious thing. It is bad to be old and poor. It is worse to be old, poor and Indian. Suppose you lived as a member of a minority group in some foreign country ruled absolutely by people of another race. You do not speak their language. They have segregated you on the worst land in the country. Their concept of religion, family and tradition is alien to your own. You are born in squalor, and the infant-mortality rate is so high you are lucky to live at all. You are under-nourished. You are not educated in their ways. You do not learn their language. In the pretense of helping you, they create institutions that oppress you. The aid you receive is given in a manner calculated to shatter your dignity. You live a life that is a continual battle for simple existence. You grow old and sick, isolated from decent medical care by no communications system, bad roads and the language barrier. You are weary in body and spirit—the culmination of a lifetime of discrimination. If you can place yourself living out your life in these circumstances, you can begin to see what it means to be an elderly Indian.

Before regional meeting of
National Council on the Aging, April 24/
Los Angeles Times, 4-25:(2)1.

Lester G. Maddox
Former Governor of Georgia

1

When I was Governor and Lieutenant Governor, I paid no attention to whether a person was black or white. That's got nothing to do with it. So far as segregation is concerned, I believe that every person, black or white, who loves his race enough and other races enough to want to protect and defend them, or has enough racial pride and integrity to want to defend his race and other races, that person in my definition would be a segregationist. And the true integrationist is the one who has no love for his race or other races and no racial pride or integrity, and doesn't care what happens to his race or other races. I don't believe there's one per cent of the people in this nation that I would label as integrationists, and believe that 99 per cent of them are segregationists, whether they are black or white. They're proud of their race, they want to protect and defend it, and I stand with that crowd.

The Washington Post, 9-1:(A)6.

Floyd B. McKissick
Former director, Congress of Racial Equality

2

I was always an integrationist, still am, always will be . . . The black man has got to be part of the system. We've never been in it, so we don't know if it will work. I say, "Get in and see" . . . There are two concepts of black power. One of them, to tear down, burn down, destroy. The other is to get involved in economics, in politics, in government, in the whole fabric of life. Blacks now understand the second one. You *kick* down a door and then you find you're not able to do anything inside; you've got no skills, no knowledge, no expertise.

Interview, Soul City, N.C./
The New York Times, 12-22:(1)29.

Michael Novak
Educator, Philosopher

3

The trouble is that no one rewards integration. When a neighborhood integrates today, your garbage doesn't get picked up one more time a week—it probably gets picked up one less time. If a street light goes out, it isn't repaired more quickly—it's repaired more slowly. The school doesn't get better—it deteriorates. We want integration as a major national goal, so we should reward it. There isn't any policy for neighborhood redevelopment and neighborhood stability. Right now, there's little way to protect your investment in house and neighborhood—and for white ethnics, the home is their first and biggest investment.

Interview/
U.S. News & World Report, 10-14:48.

Alvin F. Poussaint
Associate Professor of Psychiatry and associate dean of students,
Harvard University Medical School

4

The black middle class probably is growing, but in my opinion there has been a lot of nonsense put forth on its extent—that half of all blacks now belong to the middle class, and so forth. If you stop and analyze, you find the situation is not at all as the media put it. They include blacks who would not be middle class if they were white. This country is so used to thinking of blacks as poverty-stricken that any black who isn't totally impoverished is considered to have joined the middle class.

U.S. News & World Report, 10-14:50.

Wilson Riles
California State Superintendent of
Public Instruction

5

The easiest way for schools to be integrated is to have quality schools all over; and if you expect parents to send their children to schools that are inadequate, you're going to have resistance. The basic answer to integration, again, is economic. You have to provide jobs and employment and lower barriers to where people might live. Then people can make a choice.

Interview, Sacramento/
San Francisco Examiner & Chronicle,
9-22:(California Living)6.

Bayard Rustin
Executive director,
A. Philip Randolph Institute
1

Those blacks who are educated are moving ahead rapidly. Those not educated, with no skills, are moving backward faster than anybody else. Blacks as well as whites are moving in two different directions at the same time.
U.S. News & World Report, 5-20:24.

William B. Saxbe
Attorney General of the United States
2

I don't think anybody's satisfied with the progress of integration [in schools]. It's our intent to firmly enforce the law. But the discouraging part of it is that school integration just hasn't worked too well. So much of it boils down to economic segregation, and we've never had a way to satisfactorily handle that problem. We have succeeded in integrating our schools legally, but I don't think it's been effective. Here in Washington you can walk 10 minutes from this building and find schools that are 95 per cent black; and you go 10 miles farther away and you find schools that are 95 per cent white—because of economic pressures and living patterns of people. One thing that has emerged as rather disturbing lately is black racism—when blacks don't want to go to school with whites. They don't want whites on their basketball team, and they don't want whites in the cafeteria. It's become a peacekeeping job at the highest level to run these schools.
Interview, Washington/
U.S. News & World Report, 2-4:29.

George C. Wallace
Governor of Alabama
3

I was for segregation because that was the law and that's what the people of Alabama wanted. Well, it's not the law any more. They may still want it, but we don't have it any more. Now it's time for all of us to go on together.
Quote, 5-12:434.

Earl Warren
Former Chief Justice of the United States
4

While race prejudice, like hatred, bigotry and cruelty, cannot be eliminated by law from the inner sanctums of the mind, the infliction of any of them upon others can be and must be eliminated if the plural society we have proudly established in America is to have the tranquility its high purpose justified.
Quote, 6-23:578.

Ben J. Wattenberg
Political analyst
5

Blacks are still well behind whites, but, for the first time in the history of the republic, 51 per cent of blacks are in the middle class. The gap is still a national disgrace, but there has been one hell of a lot of catching up going on. Real income for whites went up by 69 per cent during the 1960s, but black incomes doubled. In this area, I think a revealing study is one that shows that 81 per cent of white parents don't care if their child brings home a black child to play. Fifteen years earlier, more than half objected strongly. This shows that there are still racists, but fewer of them.
Interview/People, 10-28:53.

Caspar W. Weinberger
Secretary of Health, Education and
Welfare of the United States
6

I think we ... have to face the facts that we are dealing with very fierce public opposition to desegregation in many Northern cities, and that the bulk of segregated practices occurs in concentrated urban areas of the North where the opposition to [school] busing [for racial balance], and various forms of desegregation, is far stronger than it appears to be in the South.
Interview, Washington, Sept. 6/
The Washington Post, 9-7:(A)2.

John C. West
Governor of South Carolina
7

Segregation is dead. I think we have to avoid using past history to describe the present situation. I know of no Governor who espouses segregation openly. It's beating a dead horse. Let's go ahead and approach our goals and problems as an integrated society.
At meeting of Commission on the
Future of the South, Helen, Ga., Aug. 17/
The Atlanta Journal and Constitution,
8-18:(A)8.

Roy Wilkins
Executive director, National Association for the Advancement of Colored People

1

The '60s produced a change in the standard of behavior for whites. It is no longer right or appropriate to segregate or to discriminate. That is not to say that it's no longer done. It is to say that the whole thing has been flipped over. It used to be the right thing to do. Now it's wrong. That's no mean accomplishment.

Interview, New York/
The New York Times Magazine, 5-12:44.

Commerce · Industry · Finance

Georgi A. Arbatov
Director, U.S.A. Institute,
Soviet Academy of Sciences 1

[U.S.] Senator [Henry] Jackson claims that development of Soviet-American trade will indirectly help Soviet military programs. The mirror image of that is for us to ask: Should we [Soviets] help your domestic economic problems by trading with the U.S. and thus creating jobs there and supplying needed raw materials? By trade we do not mean mutual aid, but mutual profit.

Time, 7-1:26.

Daniel Bell
Professor of Sociology, Harvard University 2

The automobile industry . . . now finds itself highly regulated, yet it was the freest of free enterprises, with almost no government regulation. Now it is regulated from design through marketing. This didn't have to be. The smog problem, for example, came into view in California years ago. If the automobile people had taken the initiative in smog-control and highway safety, they wouldn't have had this regulation. But in neither case did they take the initiative and control over their own fate. And the oil industry may be facing the same problem. Business hasn't thought politically. If you are afraid of Washington and regulation, you have to take the initiative yourself. Be a good citizen. Be ahead of Washington. Among the consequences of business' failure is the rising distrust of corporations, the rising feeling among people that they are being swindled. Look at what's happened to the stock market. People don't have much faith. They have no confidence that business can make the right decisions.

Interview, Cambridge, Mass./
Los Angeles Times, 3-22:(2)5.

Norborne Berkeley, Jr.
President, Chemical Bank, New York 3

In the months to come, we [the banking industry] must be prepared to contribute our efforts in public affairs on a much broader scale than ever before. No longer should we raise our voices in the halls of government only when the question at hand directly affects the banking industry. In the future, we must be there in support of—or opposition to—legislation that affects not only banking but community affairs as well. We must demonstrate by our actions that our goal is not profit for profit's sake, but profit for the good of many. Only then will the confidence that has been so badly shattered be restored. The very nature of our business quite obviously makes it an economic force of major importance. What I think we must now recognize is that we cannot afford to restrict our activities solely to the world of business and finance. We must think in terms of banking as a significant social force in this country—and the world—for indeed we are. And this capability carries with it a responsibility to use our resources and talents to find solutions to more than purely financial matters. I do not think any other industry is so uniquely equipped to meet this challenge.

At Bank Marketing Association-American
Bankers Association Public Affairs Conference,
Atlanta, Feb. 11/Vital Speeches, 3-1:312.

William Black
Philanthropist; Founder,
Chock Full O'Nuts restaurants 4

[Arguing against learning business from textbooks]: Business education is a complete waste of time, because it just cannot be taught. It is not an exact science, and so you have to use common sense to succeed in it.

Interview, New York/
The New York Times, 3-24:(3)7.

Arch N. Booth
*President, Chamber of Commerce of
the United States*

1

The National Association of Food Chains says their industry made a net profit of less than one-half cent on the sales dollar in 1973, and a return on investment of less than six per cent. Their projections indicate that profit may improve to three-quarters of a cent for 1974. That's a 50 per cent gain, but is three-quarters of a cent much of a profit? Critics of our business system often use these unanalyzed percentage increases to make a case against business. But I would hope and trust that other business people would be more understanding. We should think long and hard before criticizing the other man's profit, if it's honestly earned. If we encourage and abet those who don't understand the function of profit—those who are trying hard to make it a four-letter word—then one day [we] will have the government arbitrarily deciding what's a "moral" profit, and enforcing that decision—for all of us. You know and I know what that would do to our economy. But I don't think most of the American people understand it yet. So the danger of adding to public confusion about profits is very, very great.

*Before Colorado Cattle Feeders Association,
Vail, Aug. 15/Vital Speeches, 9-15:720.*

Gene E. Bradley
*President, International Management and
Development Institute*

2

[The] fronts of international economic policy are interrelated. On not one of these fronts can government succeed without the understanding and cooperation of business. On not one of these fronts can business succeed without government understanding and favorable policies. America has long enjoyed, prospered from and jealously guarded its "balance of powers" within its own society. No believer in our system would suggest that government should dominate U.S. corporate affairs or that corporations should use their economic power to guide or misguide the affairs of State. On the contrary, business must continue to guard its inherent rights against government encroach-

ment, and, conversely, government should and must keep itself free from questionable persuasions of business. American society is based on a plurality of interests, on checks and balances, where each party guards against a take-over by another. But given this precaution, the "adversary concept" between U.S. government and business simply must be buried, or the U.S. government-industry team, so-called, will be buried under the avalanche of issues that we find before us.

*At International Management and Development
Institute State Department Workshop, January/
Vital Speeches, 3-1:313.*

Thornton F. Bradshaw
President, Atlantic Richfield Company

3

We [oil companies] have got to get some credibility with the public, or else the public might decide it doesn't need the private oil industry any more ... The public thinks all oil companies make much too much money. They read that Atlantic Richfield made $200 million last year, and they think that's too much. But in fact, it's only 9 per cent return on our capital investment, whereas the average for all other American industries is 12 per cent.

U.S. News & World Report, 1-14:15.

Harold Bridges
President, Shell Oil Company

4

[On criticism of oil companies' high profits when there is an oil shortage in the country]: ... you ask how we're going to explain this question of high profits. But ... you only compare the '73 results with a very low '72 performance. And if you look at this over an extended period of time, which I submit you must do in all fairness, then there is no bonanza in profits whatsoever.

*Before Senate Permanent Subcommittee on
Investigations, Washington, January/
U.S. News & World Report, 2-4:15.*

Carroll G. Brunthaver
*Assistant Secretary for International Affairs
and Commodity Programs, Department of
Agriculture of the United States*

5

I am bullish on America and its agriculture. We are learning now that our agriculture, in

WHAT THEY SAID IN 1974

(CARROLL G. BRUNTHAVER)

addition to being our largest industry, is also our most dynamic growth industry. Far from being a subsidized problem child, U.S. agriculture is literally bailing out our dollar and keeping the whole economy afloat. As I travel around this country and see our agriculture and its capability—and even more as I travel other countries and see their economic growth outstripping their agricultures—I get more and more enthusiastic about the future of agriculture in the United States . . . The world is continuing to grow richer—and it wants to eat better. I don't think the energy problem will stand in the way for long. We produce the raw materials for that better diet. We produce the feed grains, the soybeans and the meat itself that people increasingly want. Our agriculture is a national asset comparable to the oil that lies under the sands of the Middle East . . . and it is being increasingly recognized in that light.

At American Farm Bureau Federation Wheat, Feed Grains and Soybean Conference, Atlantic City, N.J., Jan. 15/ Vital Speeches, 3-1:309.

Arthur F. Burns
Chairman, Federal Reserve Board

1

Our foreign trade balance has moved into deficit this year, principally because of the huge increase in the bill for imported oil. The dollar value of our fuel imports rose from an annual rate of $8 billion in the second quarter of 1973 to a $28-billion rate in the second quarter of this year. The deterioration in the over-all trade account was much less than this, however, since our exports over the past year have risen much more than imports outside the petroleum category. Partly for these reasons, partly also because our money and capital markets have been attracting funds from oil-exporting nations, the high price of imported oil has not created a serious balance-of-payments problem for the United States.

Before Congressional Joint Economic Committee, Washington/ The New York Times, 8-16:29.

2

Only a very small number of banks can be justly described as being in trouble. Despite all the strains recently experienced in credit markets, the banking system remains strong and sound. There is no reason to doubt the ability of our banks to meet their commitments, even in these trying times . . . In the past year we have had the two largest bank failures in the nation's history. But it is equally important to recognize that these failures did not cause any loss to depositors. Nor did they have serious repercussions on other banks or businesses . . . The central role now played by American banks in international trade and finance imparts a new and global dimension to the need for confidence in our banking system.

Before American Bankers Association, Honolulu, Oct. 21/ Chicago Tribune, 10-22:(4)9.

3

This depressing picture of corporate profits has been largely ignored by the general public, but not by the stock exchanges—as the sorry price quotations for corporate shares testify. The recent inadequate level of corporate profits has forced corporations to borrow heavily, not only to finance their large and expanding capital expenditures, but often even to maintain their current production. The recent profit performance certainly provides too little incentive for investment in the new and more efficient capacity a growing economy will need.

Before Congressional Joint Economic Committee, Washington/ U.S. News & World Report, 11-4:55.

Earl L. Butz
Secretary of Agriculture of the United States

4

One of my goals, as a free-market economist, has been to get the government out of agriculture. A few years ago, we were spending $4 billion a year in payments to farmers for land diversion, which is an indirect form of price support. Last year this was reduced to approximately $2.5 billion. This year I think our payments will be less than one-half billion dollars, a total which includes some holdover from long-term contracts we had for conservation practices. Some programs still persist for selected commodities such as peanuts and rice. We're trying to change that, but it will not be easy since the South controls the Congress and these are Southern crops. Still, we're moving away from price supports. Our philosophy is full production for agriculture. We're encouraging farmers to produce fence row to fence row.

Interview/San Francisco Examiner, 2-22:35.

1

[Saying the U.S. government will no longer stockpile food]: Some [countries] feel that once again the United States will backstop the world's food supply while nations go elsewhere shopping for bargain prices—happy in the thought that the U.S. granaries will take care of any serious shortage that arises. Part of my mission here is to say as fully and as politely as I can, as a friend of Japan, that it's not going to work that way. The United States is not going to build unneeded government surpluses once again at great public expense . . . If U.S. farmers cannot market their farm products overseas, then these incentive-oriented farmers will reduce their production.

Before America-Japan Society and American Chamber of Commerce in Japan, Tokyo, April 18/ The Washington Post, 4-19:(F)8.

2

I think it's in America's interest to sell grain to anybody in reasonable quantities, including Russia. I know the Russian grain sale has been politicized in this country. It's an emotional issue. Russia is one of our customers. We want to maintain this relationship. The other day somebody asked me, "Isn't it evil to be trading with those Communists?" And my answer was, "Far better we exchange bushels with them than bullets."

Interview, Washington/ U.S. News & World Report, 1-6('75):26.

W. Sterling Cary
President, National Council of Churches

3

The profit motive has been shown not adequate for the system. Man was not created to amass dollars or wealth. The question is how we in the churches must address ourselves to a situation where profits seemingly always take priority over human needs.

News conference, Los Angeles, Feb. 25/ Los Angeles Times, 2-26:(2)6.

Robert A. Chadbourne
President, Associated Industries of Massachusetts

4

No business, industry or profession can stand alone. The problems they face are not only immense; they are incredibly complex. To make an impact, have a voice or just simply cope, a trade association has become a modern imperative.

Nation's Business, December:53.

George S. Cohan
Senior vice president, Bozell & Jacobs, Inc., advertising

5

Advertising as we know it today, certainly consumer advertising, will be severely restricted and controlled [by 1984]. Almost all advertising will be informational, factual and controlled to eliminate puffery or unsubstantiable claims . . . Part of the blame for this dreary state of affairs is the fault of some people in our industry who have fostered and harbored a style of writing in which cutesy-pie, adjective-ridden, superlative-abused, truth-bending, puffery-inflated language is a way of life . . . The copywriter of tomorrow will do well to read the columns of any major newspaper of today to find the copy style which he will be permitted in the future.

Before Association of Industrial Advertisers/ Los Angeles Times, 3-18:(3)10.

Edward N. Cole
President, General Motors Corporation

6

The happiest day of my [professional] life was the day I was accepted by GM, and the next-happiest will be the day I leave. The fun of trying to run a business and do an effective job is gone. If I were a young man, knowing what I know now, would I go again? No. I wouldn't go into the auto industry . . . It's gotten to be such a grind. Responsibilities today are so involved with Washington legislation and unrealistic pressures that a large industry or company such as

(EDWARD N. COLE)

GM finds itself trying to monitor the rest of the industry. The government puts the [price] squeeze on the larger industry, which then has to pass along the squeeze to smaller industries—and GM alone has 40,000 suppliers . . . There's no such thing as a free-enterprise system any more. There's a hell of a lot of enterprise, but little of it is free.

Interview/Newsweek, 9-9:67,68.

Donald C. Cook
Chairman, American Electric Power Company 1

It's sad but true that the further up you get in an organization, the less likely it is that people will tell you what you ought to hear. A lot of people are what I call "wet-finger people." They hold up a wet finger to see which way the breeze is blowing. They try to guess what you have in mind. They try to anticipate your view, then give you your own view. If that's the way matters are to be decided, you don't have to have a meeting of your executives. You just scribble out orders and issue them to the troops. If you know your executives' true views and how they support those views, if you hammer them out on the anvil, then you're going to get a better piece of steel. This gets more difficult the higher you go in an organization.

Interview, New York/
Nation's Business, September:54.

Norman A. Copeland
Senior vice president,
E. I. du Pont de Nemours & Company
2

The conflict of interest many young people envision between the enterprise system and building a world where all people can live in freedom and dignity is what the philosophers used to call a false dichotomy but what we engineers might call a red herring. Every responsible business leader knows that long-term business health requires the solution of a long list of social ills. What we lack at the moment is the know-how, the ability, in the economists' language, to manage the best trade-offs among scarce resources so that we can, for example,

provide better jobs, better health care, better tools for living, and at the same time wipe out illiteracy, poverty, unemployment, foul air and dirty water.

Before MIT Club of Delaware Valley,
May 16/Vital Speeches, 7-1:573.

Tony Dechant
National president, Farmers Union
3

Our country desperately needs a national food policy. The United States today is dangerously short of food. What is worse, we are dangerously short even of farmers. We are dangerously short of farming capacity—of machinery and breeding stock and production supplies. We are dangerously short, above all, of morale among our farm people . . . A careful search and review of the government's own reports on wheat production, wheat stocks, domestic consumption estimates, shipments already made overseas, and reports of overseas sales shows that the total wheat supply in the United States will be down to the vanishing point by the end of this marketing year . . . A short grain crop anywhere on earth—or a natural disaster anywhere on earth—or an international military crisis anywhere on earth—would catch America short of one of its most valuable resources. A world grain crop like that of 1972 would doom millions to starvation.

At national food policy conference,
Hershey, Pa./The New York Times, 1-21:27.

Lewis A. Engman
Chairman, Federal Trade Commission
4

The [TV] advertiser who chooses a child audience as the target for his selling message is subject not only to the standards of truthful advertising; he is, in my judgment, also bound to deal in complete fairness with his young viewers. In my opinion, advertising directed to or seen by children which is calculated to, or in effect does, exploit their known anxieties or capitalize on their propensity to confuse reality and fantasy is unfair within the meaning of Section 5 of the Federal Trade Commission Act.

Before American Advertising Federation,
Washington, June 3/
Los Angeles Herald-Examiner, 6-4:(A)9.

1

Most [government-] regulated industries have become Federal protectorates living in a cozy world of cost-plus, protected from the ugly specters of competition, efficiency and innovation . . . Our airlines, our truckers, our railroads, our electronic media, and countless others are on the dole. We get irate about welfare fraud, but our system of hidden regulatory subsidies makes welfare fraud look like petty larceny . . . If, after close examination, society decides subsidies to farmers, airlines, truckers and others are good and necessary, then perhaps we should make them directly and not hidden in a complicated rate structure imposed by the Federal government.

Before Financial Analysts Federation, Detroit, Oct. 7/Chicago Tribune, 10-8:(4)9.

2

The role of the Federal Trade Commission is to ensure that the economy remains open and free, and that consumers are not forced to pay tribute exacted by sellers insulated from competition . . . Government vigilance in enforcing competitive conditions can ensure that price increases attributable to excessive demand or short supply do not provide a cover for additional increases born of anti-competitive conduct or the abuse of market power.

Interview, Washington/ The National Observer, 10-26:3.

3

It has been said that businessmen love free enterprise but hate competition. I think there is some truth in that statement.

The National Observer, 10-26:3.

4

The FTC has a statutory obligation to look out for the interest of the consuming public. And I would be the last to suggest that he be stripped of protections against the occasional predator in the marketplace. I suggest, however, that we bear in mind that protecting the public from the cost of consumer abuse is not itself a costless process; and that there are occasions when the latter cost greatly exceeds the former cost. There is such a thing as over-regulation, and for it we all must pay a price. The issue of whether or not to regulate is not one which pits the consumer against someone else. It is an issue which pits the consumer's left pocket against his right. Government cannot protect everybody from everything. There will always be bears in the woods. It is wiser to accept that fact and to proceed with appropriate caution than to employ a scorched-earth regulatory policy which gets rid of the bears by getting rid of the woods and leaving everybody with a serious erosion problem. The record of state and Federal regulation in this country is by no means all bad. But, too often, the results of anti-competitive regulation have been to gouge the consumer, lock the doors to future employment by stifling the growth that comes with competition and distort our national economy in ways we have not even begun to measure. In my view, special-interest regulation is a luxury and it's time we followed the example of many individual citizens and cut luxuries in favor of necessities.

*Before National Association of Attorneys General, Hot Springs, Ark., Dec. 12/***

Sam J. Ervin, Jr.
United States Senator, D—North Carolina

5

The expression of ideas in advertising is a vital part of the total system of free expression of thought which the First Amendment was designed to protect. If government at any level ever assumes the authority to prohibit absolutely the advertisement of perfectly legal products, if it ever assumes the role of final arbiter as to what is truth in advertising, if it develops the power to dictate to the people what they should buy and for what reason, then not only will the dissemination and exchange of economic ideas be dead, but freedom in all its many facets will soon disappear from our land.

Quote, 1-27:75.

Peter M. Flanigan
Assistant to President of the United States Richard M. Nixon

6

[On foreign investment in the U.S.]: [U.S. policy is to] continue to grant foreign investors

WHAT THEY SAID IN 1974

(PETER M. FLANIGAN)

"national treatment"—that is, it will admit and treat foreign capital on a basis of equality with domestic capital. As in the past, the Federal government will offer foreign investors no special incentives to invest in the United States. And, with a few internationally recognizable exceptions, we will impose no special barriers to foreign investment . . . American restrictions on foreign investment in the United States would certainly invite retaliation against American investment abroad. As history has repeatedly shown, restrictive, overly nationalistic economic policies invariably lead to a breakdown of nearly all aspects of international relations. Given the current potential for such a breakdown, an irrational policy by the United States toward foreign investment—particularly at this time—would be exceedingly dangerous.

At symposium sponsored by Chamber of Commerce of the United States, Washington, Feb. 6/The Washington Post, 2-7:(F)3.

Gerald R. Ford
Vice President of the United States
1

Business must profit because profit is required—for research and development of new products, for exploration of new raw materials, for expansion of facilities that provide more jobs and lower prices through increased production and as a reward to investors who have risked their savings in an enterprise. [But] the propaganda that's abroad in the land on the subject of profit doesn't mention these things. Instead, profit is pictured as a rip-off. It's denounced as exploitation. It's held up as something the bad guys steal from the good guys. In my view, the people who are hammering these notions into the national consciousness are playing a dangerous game. Carried to its ultimate conclusion, it can lead only to a centrally planned economy. Instead of a free marketplace, we would have one dictated to by a monolithic bureaucracy.

At meeting sponsored by Chamber of Commerce of the United States and National Association of Manufacturers, Washington, Jan. 30/ Nation's Business, March:56.

John W. Gardner
Chairman, Common Cause
2

When a top executive is selecting his key associates, there are only two qualities for which he should be willing to pay almost any price: taste and judgment. Almost everything else can be bought by the yard.

Quote, 10-20:361.

Carl A. Gerstacker
Chairman, Dow Chemical Company
3

We are rapidly reaching the point where it must be asked of candidates for executive posts in our major corporations: "How does he come across on television?" . . . Too often, we who represent business are competing today in a situation where the opposition are pros and we are amateurs. The public, therefore, sees us in a bad light, doesn't understand and doesn't buy our point of view. Yet it is safe to assume that at some point in his career, the senior corporate executive might well have to cope with an audio-visual situation involving [AFL-CIO president] George Meany, [business critic] Evelyn Davis, [consumerist] Ralph Nader, Clergy and Laymen Concerned, [Senator] Philip Hart, or the Symbionese Liberation Army.

Before Society of the Chemical Industry/ The Wall Street Journal, 12-24:4.

J. Paul Getty
Industrialist
4

[Saying that, instead of setting up a foundation with his wealth, his money will remain in his companies]: It always works against the grain to see these foundations so opposed to what I know was the philosophy of the founder. You can't tell me that 90 per cent of what the Ford Foundation is doing would have been approved by Henry Ford. I thought I'd rather leave a company, an industrial organization, that would be well-run, probably better than a foundation. Because you have the Securities and Exchange Commission looking at you, you have the market analysts, you have Wall Street, you have stockholders, all of them keen for results. And I think a large industrial organization that employs thousands of people is doing more good than many a foundation does.

Interview, Woking, England/
The New York Times, 2-6:58.

Mills E. Godwin
Governor of Virginia

1

It is not very popular in many quarters to sing the praises of business and industry. It seems to be more popular to criticize the profit motive and to chastise our incomparable technology for violating our environment. And strangely enough, many who are singing this song of criticism are themselves the beneficiaries of the private-enterprise system in so many ways.

At Virginia State Chamber of Commerce
50th anniversary dinner, May/
The Washington Post, 8-26:(A)28.

Barry M. Goldwater
United States Senator, R—Arizona

2

... we are headed at this very moment toward a determined drive for more nationalization of our businesses, and it has a greater chance of success than at any time in our history. Now, you can ignore the fact, or you can pretend that nationalization is something other than what it really is; you can butter-up the term, sweeten it, pour syrup on it, do anything you want with it—but it turns out to be socialism, and that is the system that has never done anything for any people.

Before American Iron and Steel
Institute board of directors,
Washington, Feb. 5/Human Events, 4-6:14.

3

[There is a determined effort] by patriotic, well-intentioned idealists to replace the "evils of capitalism" and "big, bad" business corporations with government corporations operated "by and for the people" ... [Forces leading the attack on big business are employing] a series of nibbling, piecemeal tactics—what our old nemesis Nikita Khrushchev called salami-slicing tactics. Their weapons are the national electronic media networks and the well-coordinated

regiments of liberal politicians, intellectuals, journalists and educators.

Before American Iron and Steel Institute,
Washington, Feb. 6/
The Dallas Times Herald, 2-6:(G)8.

4

[On oil-company profits in face of the oil shortage] : I don't think there's been any undue profits in oil. But in my opinion, unless we allow profits we will have another problem—a high degree of unemployment. We have to be building more factories. We have to be putting more money into capital investment than we're doing. In fact, I would be very much in favor of increasing incentive allowances so people will drill more holes in the ground. This is the big objection I have to what we've been doing on Capitol Hill. All we've done [by criticizing the oil companies] hasn't put one gallon of gasoline in anybody's tank. Nobody's gone out and started drilling new holes. So far, all we've been arguing about in the Senate is how to impose regulations and create new staffs and new bureaus and add to the woes of people who are honestly trying to get more fuel for the American people ... government intervention in American business has been a history of the slow destruction of the free-enterprise system. And that's another problem: We're just on the verge of becoming a socialist economy. No, I think we have to let the oil companies or individuals operate freely. Let them explore; and if they lose their money, let them have a decent deduction on it.

Interview, Washington/
U.S. News & World Report, 2-11:41.

Stanley J. Goodman
Chairman, May Department Stores Company

5

With all its faults, the world has seen nothing to compare with the creative release of human energy produced by the free-market system manned by resourceful, energetic people. Profits are what keep it all in motion; and if profits dwindle to a marginal level, the economy will wither into atrophy. And high profits for the most efficient should never be thought of as going counter to the social needs of our society, because it is precisely the companies who are

(STANLEY J. GOODMAN)

good enough to achieve high profits in a competitive environment that will be good enough to get results on social problems. Don't expect much of a contribution to society from the business that is struggling for survival. And American business management has the energy and resourcefulness to do well for society without doing less well in their business.

Before National Retail Merchants
Association, St. Louis, Jan. 7/
U.S. News & World Report, 1-28:80.

Rodney C. Gott
Chairman and president, AMF, Inc.   1

[Multinational companies] are responding directly to the sameness in peoples and not the differences in their institutions. Multinationals are building bridges between nations and, in so doing, have done more for world peace and prosperity than all our political organizations have been able to achieve. To call all multinationals evil *now* would be to deny the real progress they have brought to the world. To throw up restrictions against their growth *now* would be to vote a step backward for those less-privileged countries who will never be able to pull themselves up by their own bootstraps. To blunt common economic incentives among peoples of all nations *now* would be to blunt their most effective incentive for mutual social and political progress. *Now* is not the time for any of these—not the time to cancel the future of many because a few would cling fearfully to the status quo. *Now*, in my opinion, is the time for businessmen such as ourselves to stand up and be counted on the side of the common future we are all trying to build.

Before Federation of Austrian
Industrialists, Vienna, March 27/
Vital Speeches, 5-1:447.

Bill Gunter
United States Representative, D—Florida   2

[On interlocking directorates]: If I were a stockholder, I would want to know how a director is fighting for my interest but sitting on the board of another company. A larger question that bothers me is whether or not in fact interlocking directorates stifle competition to one degree or another. If there is no meaningful competition in the oil and gas industry, then it follows there is inadequate incentive to provide the nation with the needed energy resources.

Interview/The New York Times, 3-12:26.

James T. Halverson
Director, Bureau of Competition,
Federal Trade Commission   3

There is a clear need for antitrust enforcement to tackle and solve the deeper economic problems of competition lest they become unsolvable by antitrust means and we are forced to abandon the benefits and economic freedoms of our competitive system in substantial sectors of the economy . . . restoring competition to markets which are artificially and anticompetitively controlled should be viewed as a rehabilitation program which is essential to the conservation of our competitive system. In effect, the antitrust laws serve not only as the policeman of the free economy, but as its conservator—the alternative to which may well be ever-increasing government regulation . . . Experience teaches us that competition is more likely than government regulation to lower costs, raise productivity, induce innovation, allocate scarce resources efficiently, and satisfy consumer wants and needs most effectively.

Before Harvard Business School Club, Houston/
The Washington Post, 11-12:(D)9.

W. Dow Hamm
Former executive vice president,
Atlantic Richfield Company   4

[On criticism of oil-company profits]: Oil companies make less profit than the manufacturing industries. Banks were up 20 to 25 per cent in their earnings last year. Let oil companies come out 25 per cent ahead and they are going to be investigated. Banks take some risks, but not the kind wildcatters take who think it is going to cost $200- or $300-million to develop a field and it ends up costing $600- or

$700-million. And the wildcatter is lucky at that.

Before Dallas Geological and
Geophysical Auxiliary, Jan. 17/
The Dallas Times Herald, 1-18:(C)2.

Alvin Hampel
Executive vice president and
director of creative services,
Benton & Bowles, Inc., advertising

1

[On "creative" advertising]: If you remember the joke in my commercial while forgetting my product, the joke is really on my client. If my star presenter grabs you but you ignore what she's trying to tell you, I've blown it. If you're struck by my cleverness but remain unsold by my ideas, I've bombed as a copywriter. If you award my commercial a sterling-silver bowl for excellence without asking how well it worked, you've given me an empty bowl . . . In the pursuit of creative advertising we must be very careful not to take our eye off what advertising must accomplish. The very things that are remembered most may contribute least to making the sale. They may even detract from the sale.

Before American Advertising
Federation, Washington/
Los Angeles Times, 6-17:(3)11,13.

C. Lowell Harriss
Professor of Economics, Columbia University

2

The American people have working for them a business structure of unparalleled strength and potential. The positive, ever-improving accomplishments of business produce most output, well over 80 per cent, and create most income. Most jobs are in business. Real earnings—including the benefits paid for by taxes which deplete take-home pay—have risen markedly. Most of the financing of government comes out of taxes on earnings in the private sector. The business system is a popular, a national, asset whose worth is beyond calculation. We do best in building for [the] economic future by strengthening competitive enterprise. Yet, as we see daily, the public gets minimal news about what [big] business firms do well and much about what is, or is said to be, done poorly. With hundreds of thousands of companies, and with billions of transactions each day, some deplorable actions will occur. Yet by reasonable standards, business firms—giant and tiny—do well. In a world of human beings, not everyone will be a St. Francis. And even the best of us will at times fail to meet our own highest standards.

At Columbia College, March 2/
Vital Speeches, 5-1:438.

Fred L. Hartley
President, Union Oil Company

3

[On criticism of oil-company profits]: . . . let me report on the earnings for the first three quarters of 1973—the latest period for which I have figures—of three of the loudest voices maligning the oil industry: *The Washington Post,* up 66 per cent; *The New York Times,* up 65 per cent; and our little *Los Angeles Times,* up 45 per cent. I've seen no crusade by them on exhorbitant media profits, even though their return on investment makes oilmen look like public benefactors.

At symposium sponsored by
Los Angeles Area Chamber of Commerce,
Feb. 6/Los Angeles Times, 2-7:(1)18.

S. I. Hayakawa
President emeritus,
San Francisco State University

4

[On advertising copywriting]: Cereal is not just corn flakes, but "the breakfast of champions." Toothpaste gives the mouth sex-appeal. That certain bourbon is for "the man of distinction." The purpose [of advertising] is not only to give us the facts about the product, but to cast an imaginative glow—whether it's corn flakes, tooth[paste] or snake-bite medicine . . . The interesting point is that advertising is a form of poetry. Poetry doesn't have a sponsor, but advertising does. Advertising copywriters, perhaps, are the highest paid poets in history.

Before California Newspaper
Advertising Executives Association,
San Francisco, June 21/
San Francisco Examiner, 6-21:64.

Alfred Hayes
President, Federal Reserve Bank of New York 1

The Federal Reserve always stands ready to fulfill its essential role as lender of last resort— not only to the member banks but, in a broader sense, to the economy at large. This does not mean that bankers and businessmen will necessarily be spared the consequences of their own misjudgment. It does mean the continuous functioning of the credit markets can be counted on.

Before New Jersey Bankers Association/
The New York Times, 5-28:57.

Hubert H. Humphrey
United States Senator, D–Minnesota 2

[Criticizing tax loopholes and government subsidies in the oil industry]: I'm not going to listen to all this bonanza talk about that poor little fellow who's going around with a corkscrew looking for oil [and needs a depletion allowance]. That's not the one we're talking about. When the price of wheat goes up, when the price of cotton goes up, we take off the subsidies. But when the price of oil goes up, they say, "Yummy, yummy, give us more."

Before the Senate, Washington, June 26/
The Washington Post, 6-27:(A)22.

Lee A. Iacocca
President, Ford Motor Company 3

[On charges that the Big Three automobile makers are too big]: Big Business and Big Labor pale in comparison to Big Brother in Washington. Who says how big is too big? Funny, during World War II they thought we might not be big enough to turn out the required number of tanks and aircraft engines— but we were, thank God. You reach a point where somebody looks up and says, "Those guys are too damn good." What if they broke us up? Then they'd have to have 10 presidents at my salary and that would be terrible. Yes, we are big. And because the industry is big, it accounts for 18-20 per cent of the GNP. The auto industry is also the biggest employer and the biggest taxpayer. When it comes to bigness, the public at large is the final arbiter. It votes every day by buying a product or not buying it.

Interview, Dearborn, Mich./People, 9-23:38.

Frank N. Ikard
President, American Petroleum Institute 4

[On criticism that oil companies' profits are excessive]: When you compare profits, say, for the third quarter of last year with the third quarter of 1972, it's very unfair because you're comparing a good year with a bad year. And then, you've got to look at any measure of profits—if you're going to be fair about it—as a return on investment. Using that measure, the oil industry is getting a return of about 10.8 per cent, if my memory serves me right, as against 12.2 per cent in manufacturing generally, in 1972. So I don't think that profits have been excessive. I certainly don't think anybody anywhere would agree that anybody should unduly profit by some scarce situation [such as the current oil shortage]. On the other hand, this is a highly capital-intensive industry. We're going to need in excess of $200 billion for capital investment in the next 10 years; and when we go out to get that money, we've got to compete for it in the market.

Interview, Washington/
Los Angeles Times, 2-15:(1)30.

Frederick G. Jaicks
Chairman, Inland Steel Company 5

There are still some in our society who are captivated by the myth that business does not pay its fair share of taxes, and the supposition that profits are too high ... What are the facts? Growth of personal income has exceeded the growth of business profits before taxes by a ratio of nearly 3-to-1 since 1965. And Federal taxes have outstripped the growth in industry's profits during the same period. And the question really should be: Hasn't industry been paying more than its fair share of taxes?

At American Iron and Steel
Institute Congressional Luncheon,
Washington, Feb. 6/Vital Speeches, 4-1:358.

J. K. Jamieson
Chairman, Exxon Corporation
1

I'm often asked the question: "All right, things are tight and for understandable reasons. But why should everybody hurt except the oil companies? What about those huge profit increases you people have been showing?" Let me say two things about these profits. First, they must be seen in perspective. In our own case, for instance, the comparison is against 1972 results which showed no gain over the previous year. In the larger perspective of the last decade, the profits of the petroleum industry, expressed as a return on investment, have been consistently exceeded by the average of all U.S. manufacturing. Even at today's relatively high profits for the industry, there would be no great difficulty in finding non-petroleum companies which as a matter of course have been making comparable or higher returns... The second point about profits which I want to make is that by being large or small they serve an economic function. They signal to the investor that not enough or too much is being invested in this or that direction. Surely, if there was ever a direction toward which investment resources needed to be channeled, energy investment in the coming years would seem to be that direction. Our own investment plans are expanding at an unprecedented rate. Over the next four years, we now foresee outlays in the neighborhood of $16 billion. It is still not clear where all this money is coming from. Certainly, if our profits were at 1972 levels, the problem would be all the greater.

Before Economic Club,
Detroit, Jan. 28/Vital Speeches, 4-1:364.

E. Douglas Kenna
President, National Association of Manufacturers
2

We favor freer trade with all of the non-market economies, including the Soviet Union. And I don't think the term "most-favored-nation treatment" really is an apt phrase to use in this particular thing; in fact, I regret very much it ever became the nomenclature we do use. What we are saying is that we should not discriminate against these countries; we should give them the same sort of trading treatment that we give all of the other people we trade with.

TV-radio interview/"Meet the Press,"
National Broadcasting Company, 3-10.

Henry A. Kissinger
Secretary of State of the United States
3

It is not in the long-term interest of even the [oil-] producer countries to pursue a policy of unrestrained [oil] price increases, because the producers, too, are living in the same world economy that the consumers are. And a worldwide depression produced by an imbalance in balance of payments and a complete over-emphasis on the energy side would have the inevitable consequence of depressing also the situation of the producer countries... In the short term, it is possible to see how particular producing countries can enrich themselves by an unrestrained use of their temporarily strong bargaining position. But in the long term, it is bound to lead to disaster for everybody. It is particularly a case where the common interest is also everybody's selfish interest.

News conference, San Clemente, Calif., Jan. 3/
The New York Times, 1-4:12.

Virginia H. Knauer
Director, Federal Office of Consumer Affairs
4

In 1975, business will emphasize value rather than gimmicks to sell the consumer. We will see great competition over quality, price and service rather than jingles and comic-strip characters. This will lead to a healthier relationship between business and the consumer and a more dynamic market place.

Los Angeles Times, 12-29:(4)14.

Ray Kroc
Chairman and president,
McDonald's Corporation
5

[On his competitors in the fast-food business]: Okay, I think they're great people, and if we were all at the bar I'd put my arm around them and wish them well and buy them a drink. But when it comes to competition—well, if they are drowning I'd put a hose in their mouth. I

(RAY KROC)

have a feeling about competitors that I've tried to get across in McDonald's. Competitors are somebody you learn to hate. There's no nice way of being in business and loving your competitors.

Interview, Fort Lauderdale, Fla./
Los Angeles Times, 2-8:(3)5.

Mary Wells Lawrence
Chairman, Wells, Rich, Greene advertising 1

... I've seen government's anti-business feeling grow in almost direct proportion to increased government spending. Yesterday some Congressmen and labor leaders spoke as though a socialized state and nationalization of business were their *goal*. This anti-business trend is surprising when you consider that over 80 per cent of all taxes are generated by business—through corporate profits, Social Security taxes, taxes paid by people employed by business, and other business taxes. It's also surprising when you consider that people need business to prosper so that they can work in confidence, increase their wages and improve their standard of living. It's surprising, too, when we can see the problems Italy has and England has as warnings. The United States' first national priority should be to help its businesses succeed in world markets and to nourish them so they can provide high employment and higher salaries. In this regard, I'll speak to the regulatory fever in government. It has created so many restrictions and controls that a great many businessmen operate defensively rather than aggressively.

Before President's council on inflation,
Washington/Human Events, 12-28:11.

Walter J. Levy
Energy economist 2

The high prices that the Organization of Petroleum Exporting Countries have been able to extract for their oil may result in disruptive trade and monetary policies, including currency restrictions as well as social and political upheavals, that will be most harmful to both oil-

producing and oil-consuming countries ... What would really be involved would be a massive transfer of wealth from oil-importing to oil-exporting countries. The oil-exporting countries would become owners of a rapidly increasing share of the economic resources of the rest of the world based on what is fundamentally a monopolist rent for their oil resources amounting to some 50 to 60 times the actual cost of producing their oil. Moreover, as revenues from oil production accrue largely to the governments of oil-exporting countries, investments made with these funds in oil-importing countries would be predominantly owned and controlled by foreign governments. It is unlikely that this state of affairs could provide a stable basis for the world economy or would prove acceptable to the industrialized countries.

Interview, New York/
The New York Times, 1-17:61.

John W. Macy, Jr.
President, Council of Better Business Bureaus 3

The expansion of consumerism and the evidence of corporate concern for the consumer necessitate the development of self-regulation. The instrument for that self-regulation is available in the business-supported objective programs pursued by the Better Business Bureaus. This style of self-regulation is an earnest business commitment to a marketplace governed by fair practices, truth and accuracy and concern for the individual buyer ... "There ought to be a law against it" is a natural enough reaction, even though instances of grievances are relatively limited in our massive and complex economy. But the avalanche of public reaction for the consumer has proliferated to the extent that the Federal government now has 1,000 consumer programs involving 57 agencies at an annual cost of $3 billion. But even with this growth, there is a continuing demand for improvement which makes self-regulation even more imperative than at any time in the long history of the BBB.

Before Better Business Bureau of
Metropolitan Dallas, March 20/
The Dallas Times Herald, 3-21:(C)12.

William J. McGill
President, Columbia University
1

I go out regularly in the business community downtown, and I see a tremendous ethical sensitivity . . . From what I have seen of the standards of ethics of three corporations on whose boards I sit [Texaco, AT&T and McGraw-Hill], I am extremely impressed. I know of a case in which the management of a large oil company was approached to pay off the political leaders of European countries in order to continue to sell oil. It could have been done easily; with the price rises, nobody would have known. To their everlasting credit, they said: No way. That is more common in the business community than people give credit for.

Interview, New York/
Los Angeles Times, 4-24:(2)7.

George Meany
President, American Federation of Labor-
Congress of Industrial Organizations
2

On behalf of American labor, I have a message for the capitalists and commissars. We are not buying the idea that we further the cause of peace with freedom by unilateral concessions to the Soviets with nice profits for American business. For us, human freedom and human dignity have always come before the dollar. That's what the labor movement is all about—by definition.

San Francisco Examiner & Chronicle,
3-31:(This World)2.

3

I think the most reckless people in America today are the money changers. They are the people who are going to bring this economy to a collapse. What's the motivation? It's very simple; it's a very simple word: greed. Yes, I mean the bankers.

News conference, Chicago, Aug. 5/
Chicago Tribune, 8-6:(1)4.

Bess Myerson
Former Commissioner of Consumer
Affairs of New York City
4

[The] seedbed of shoddy products and services and abuses is inevitably and inescapably related to shoddy morality. Consumer protection is economic justice based on moral law. Abuse . . . paves the way for abuse everywhere. Consumer abuses are dirty tricks and they are an assault on the truths that once [were] self-evident to us as a nation.

At consumerism luncheon organized by
The Women's Forum, New York, Oct. 8/
The New York Times, 10-9:38.

James J. Needham
Chairman, New York Stock Exchange
5

Yes, we are worried about the lack of small investors in the [stock] market. But the reason for the investor's lack of interest is inflation. Until the government comes to grips with this problem, we will continue to see limited participation in the market . . . We are not afraid of manipulation of the market by large investors or large funds; we have safeguards against these actions. We are only afraid that lack of government concern for the real causes of inflation, and attendant high interest rates, could keep investor participation down.

News conference, Los Angeles, April 30/
Los Angeles Herald-Examiner, 5-1:(B)5.

6

[On the Dow Jones industrial average]: . . . a lot of people look at it and behave because of it, and I accept that as a part of life. What amazes me is that so many people follow the Dow who don't even own stocks. It's as though they were taking their own temperature. When the Dow is down, they're down; when the Dow is up, they're up—it is an accepted barometer of American industry and economic activity. So if the American people look at the Dow Jones and become upset and write their Congressman and say, "Look, we want a better economy," I think that's good, that's good.

Interview/
The Atlanta Journal and Constitution,
11-10:(C)23.

Richard M. Nixon
President of the United States
7

. . . I pledge to you that I shall do everything in my power to prevent the big oil companies

WHAT THEY SAID IN 1974

(RICHARD M. NIXON)

and other major energy producers from making an unconscionable profit out of this [oil-shortage] crisis. Too many Americans have sacrificed too much to allow that to happen. That is why I shall urge the Congress . . . to act immediately on the windfall-profits tax that I requested last month. This tax would require that windfall profits either be turned over to the government or be invested in the development of new supplies, supplies that will be vitally needed in the years ahead. Private profiteering at the expense of public sacrifice must never be tolerated in a free country.

Radio address to the nation, Jan. 19/
The New York Times, 1-20:(1)36.

Don Paarlberg
Director of Agricultural Economics,
Department of Agriculture of
the United States　　　　　　　　　　*1*

[On criticism of 1972's U.S. wheat sale to the Soviet Union]: When those sales were made, wheat was in very heavy supply in this country, prices were depressed, storage costs were great, everybody was anxious to see these stocks reduced—and in that situation the Russians made their purchases. We could not foresee at that time, nor could anyone foresee, that the 1972 crop in many countries of the world would be a poor crop, and that many countries besides Russia would be in need of wheat. Indeed, our sales of wheat to countries other than the Soviet Union accounted for the bigger share by far of the exports. So that while in hindsight one might say that it would have been better to have sold less wheat to the Russians or to have obtained a higher price, this is Monday-morning quarterbacking, and we have responsibility to operate with regard to the current facts.

Interview, Washington/
U.S. News & World Report, 2-18:44.

Nikolai S. Patolichev
Minister of Foreign Trade of
the Soviet Union　　　　　　　　　　*2*

[On 1972's U.S. grain sale to his country which has been criticized by some Americans

for giving Russia too good of a deal]: Nineteen seventy-two was a very unfortunate year in agriculture for us, and therefore we had to buy somewhat larger quantities of grain. But the American side was very interested in closing the deal at the time . . . Don't say we outsmarted you—because the Americans are sea wolves on the ship of trade and we are just young sailors. What we did was to come to the United States and ask, "Do you have grain to sell to us?" And the Americans said, "Yes." Of course, we didn't sound trumpets. We approached the grain companies we had dealt with in the past. They told us their price, and we paid it. We bought wheat in Canada and Australia at the same price. Everything was done according to the classical pattern of trade. I don't know who is telling these fairy tales about outsmarting you.

Interview, Washington/
U.S. News & World Report, 3-18:59.

Jacob Rabinow
Chief, Office of Invention and
Innovation, National Bureau of
Standards of the United States　　　　*3*

There is change in the management of our large corporations. Originally, these companies were managed by their founders: Eastman ran Eastman Kodak, Watson ran IBM, Ford ran Ford, and so on. As the years go by, however, our corporations are more and more run by "professional managers." I use this in quotes with some disdain. In many corporations, these are people who do not care personally about the product they make. Their goal is to make a profit. Their salary and their stock options and their benefits will depend on how much profit they make *now*. The result is they don't really care what happens 20 years down the line. Chances are their business will not be inherited by their children. So their point of view is very much narrower than was that of the founding father of the business. He took pride in his product, pride in the new developments his company could pioneer. Few of these new, nameless professional managers would ever stick their necks out on some bold new invention.

Interview, Washington/
U.S. News & World Report, 12-23:46.

Simon Ramo
Vice chairman, TRW, Inc.
1

The most outstanding business firms of the future will be those whose leadership is skilled in the interface problems—technology with economics, marketing with social change, and business with government. The time has passed when good business management can narrowly focus merely on design, manufacture and attempts to sell products oblivious to the broader society. Such management will satisfy neither the individuals working in their companies nor the individual buyers in the marketplace. Those companies will have the wrong products or the wrong timing. The ability to put it all together will mean success.

At seminar, University of Southern California Business School, April 16/ Los Angeles Times, 4-17:(3)10.

Donald T. Regan
Chairman, Merrill Lynch, Pierce, Fenner & Smith, Inc.
2

The primary function of [the New York Stock Exchange] is to serve as the premier marketplace of the world. We are the envy of London, of Paris, of Tokyo. The Japanese, who carefully studied all methods of raising money for corporations and corporate ownership, came to the conclusion that the marketplace as exemplified by the New York Stock Exchange was by far the best. Besides providing a marketplace, the stock exchange has a self-regulatory role in which it supervises us brokers, who are its members. This gives the public an additional layer of protection that the SEC is not able to provide. If you did not have the New York Stock Exchange, you'd have to provide another layer of regulation for the securities business, either by government or by some other self-regulatory body.

Interview/U.S. News & World Report, 3-4:52.

3

A stock certificate is an archaic remnant of an era in which we did not have computers. It's a legal piece of paper with a lot of mumbo-jumbo on the front and some blank spaces on the back with some pretty Spencerian penman-

ship. Why an individual has to have that particular piece of evidence that he's an owner of a corporation, I don't know. If you have an account with a bank, all you get is a statement once a month that you have X dollars on deposit. That's all you need. The same thing can be done to show that you're an owner of IBM or U.S. Steel or General Motors or any other corporation. Today's stock certificates have attached to them other pieces of paper—legal opinions, dividend claims, proxies, all this type of stuff—and we get this horrible mess of paper going through our financial area. At times I think the lower part of Manhattan will damned near be inundated by a blizzard of this paper.

Interview/U.S. News & World Report, 3-4:54.

Abraham A. Ribicoff
United States Senator, D—Connecticut
4

You [the oil companies] are reaping the whirlwind of 30 years of arrogance . . . You have embarked on a program of redistributing the sale of oil, using the [oil-shortage] conditions we have, the shock and the fright, to squeeze out the independent dealers and smaller franchises throughout the nation. You have created a panic situation [and have formed] a conspiracy with the Middle Eastern states [to avoid U.S. taxes]. The time has come for Congress to move against the major oil companies.

At Senate Permanent Subcommittee on Investigations hearing, Washington, Jan. 21/ Los Angeles Times 1-22:(1)1.

Benjamin A. Rogge
Professor of Political Economy, Wabash College
5

We Americans talk a great deal about how inventive we are, yet most of the world's great ideas did not originate on this continent. They really didn't. They're European, most of them. Or Chinese or Arabian or who knows what? What American businessmen have been good at has been not invention but innovation—putting an idea to use. And that derives from the capitalist environment.

Lecture, Hillsdale (Mich.) College, May/ Vital Speeches, 7-1:566.

John W. Rollins
Chairman, Rollins International 1

I think businessmen should participate [in politics]. Some of them stay out to themselves and are always talking about the fact that politics is beneath them; but they play around with company politics in their respective companies seven days a week, so there is no reason for them to be pious. They need to have an understanding of government, because government is tied into so many phases of business today. And I think you should belong to one of the major parties and help elect its candidates. If you simply sit back and don't participate, you won't help the country, because people with other philosophies will be making the decisions. That brings us to another thing. Businessmen who go into politics have a tendency to run things in it the way they run a business. It's not the same. You have to work with people, to influence them; and it's a selling job all the time—not a telling job.
Interview, Wilmington, Del./
Nation's Business, February:50.

Robert D. Rowan
President, Fruehauf Corporation 2

[On the FTC]: I have never seen a group so anti-business. I would rather walk in with a problem to the Kremlin than I would to the Federal Trade Commission.
The National Observer, 10-26:3.

William B. Saxbe
Attorney General of the United States 3

Bigness per se is good for American companies when they have to deal with the combines of Japan and some of the big European corporations outside of this country. If we think that we're going to grab off chunks of business around the world, which return dollars and provide jobs, with nickel-and-dime corporations, we're making a big mistake. In this area, I don't think that we should be unnecessarily pressuring multinational corporations that are based here. They'll just base someplace else. They'll have to. But bigness in this country frightens me. It frightens me because it eliminates so much individual initiative. We only have real individual initiative in the service areas today, and even there the bigness is moving in. . . . It's frightening to think that we're down to four automobile manufacturers in this country, and that between them and the union there is no way that anybody else can enter this field in a significant way. That's happening in other businesses, too. The conglomerate can be in the aircraft business, housing, insurance companies, computer software and all of these things.
Interview, Washington/
U.S. News & World Report, 2-4:29.

4

Antitrust violations are not casual crimes. Business tycoons are not seized by a fit of passion that compels them to rig bids. Corporate executives do not gather in the boardroom to fix prices because they are in the throes of a joint, irresistible impulse. They violate the antitrust laws deliberately. Those in the business community who would break the laws had better face one hard fact of life: The day of the easy gouge, the fast ripoff is over. The Department of Justice will not look the other way when business imposes upon the public what are nothing more than totalitarian practices and totalitarian disdain for our democratic way of life.
Before legal committee of Grocery
Manufacturers of America, Washington,
Oct. 29/The New York Times, 10-30:67.

Donald V. Seibert
Chairman-designate, J. C. Penney Company 5

The overriding challenge with any company growth plan, whether it is for five years or for 15 and regardless of any astronomical numbers you put into it, is that it can only succeed if you are able to cope with the problems of today.
Interview/The New York Times, 9-22:(3)5.

Irving S. Shapiro
Chairman, E. I. du Pont de Nemours
& Company 6

The philosopher Alfred North Whitehead is remembered for saying that in a great society businessmen think greatly of their function. Today, that comment ought to be turned the other way: A society which thinks poorly of its businessmen and deeply distrusts their motives is not a great society but a society in trouble. We are in danger of demolishing our own house and hanging the carpenter.

At University of Richmond/
The Wall Street Journal, 3-19:20.

1

Throughout our history, antitrust policy has been shaped by adversary proceedings in which the men from government always wear white hats and the men from industry always wear black hats. For decades at a time only the white hats could win. In case you think I am exaggerating a bit, let me refer you to Justice Potter Stewart of the Supreme Court. In an opinion some years ago, he observed that the only thing certain about antitrust was that the government always wins. Some of that has changed in recent years, but the adversary policy—the system for making antitrust policy—has not changed. Let's look at the basics. The Sherman Act reads on restraint of trade and monopoly. It reads in broad, general language. Apart from a few actions that have been spelled out by the courts as "*per se* offenses"—price fixing, for example— the question of what the statute means depends on who pours meaning into it. Over the years, most of the pouring has been done by prosecuting attorneys who are charged with the duty of bringing lawsuits and trying to win them . . . it still remains that prosecutors ought to prosecute, and economic policy-making ought to be consigned to people skilled by education and experience to function in that area. There is no quarrel here with antitrust being used as a vigorous defense of competition in our economy; but those of us concerned with the operation of this economy are entitled to ask that Congress clarify its intent in the antitrust area by sharpening the legislative guidelines. And further, we have a right to ask that Congress delegate responsibility for administration of antitrust policy to people who understand the dynamics of the economic system, who have some accountability for its well-being—and

whose primary mission is not to win lawsuits.

Before Economic Club, Detroit, Oct. 7/
Vital Speeches, 11-15:88.

Richard P. Simmons
President,
Allegheny Ludlum Steel Corporation

2

We [the U.S.] really don't have a national economic policy. And until we have a rational policy, the businessman can't cope with some of the conditions he faces . . . Because of the incredible number of demands placed on business—ecology, energy, trade and all the others—the businessman often feels like Custer and all those Indians. The solution is a restatement at the highest levels that we indeed believe in the free market and that we try to develop a total, unified economic policy at the national level.

Interview, Dallas/
The Dallas Times Herald, 5-19:(I)1.

William E. Simon
Administrator, Federal Energy Office

3

[On criticism that oil companies are making too much profit]: I think that every company in this country is entitled to a reasonable profit. And what is a normal return? A normal return is a return at the lowest possible level to induce investment in that company; not excessive profits that come from an imbalance between supply and demand. And, in looking at the oil industry in particular over the last 15 years, our preliminary results of some of the numbers we've got right now on the net return on invested capital show them in the middle range of all manufacturing companies.

Interview, Jan. 18/
The New York Times, 1-19:14.

William E. Simon
Secretary of the Treasury of
the United States

4

Because of ever-increasing government regulations, many of which had their origin in the 1930s, banks, and particularly savings and loan institutions, have come to rely excessively on the Federal government to carry them through

WHAT THEY SAID IN 1974

(WILLIAM E. SIMON)

periods of monetary restraint. Additionally, consumer interests have been severely penalized. Consumer savers have not been allowed a fair return on their savings, and consumer borrowers have suffered through periods of credit unavailability.

Before Senate Subcommittee, Washington, May 13/The New York Times, 5-14:47.

1

To many Americans, profits are not the legitimate and honest return on investment. They are rather the immoral rewards of corporate greed, the conspicuous consumption of big business at the expense of the common man . . . If the nation doesn't understand that if through hasty or unwise legislation we restrict or diminish these profits further, some Americans will feel some short-term satisfaction at the distress of business; but the nation will pay for that temporary gratification in lost jobs, in diminished prosperity and in failure to achieve the grand goals we have set for ourselves as a people.

Before Conference Board, New York, Sept. 19/The Washington Post, 9-20:(D)9.

Charles H. Smith, Jr.
Chairman, SIFCO Industries; Chairman, Chamber of Commerce of the United States

2

The multinational corporation, as I see it, has done more to bring progress in developing countries than anything else that ever existed. All the government programs don't hold a candle to the real progress that comes when a multinational corporation goes into an underdeveloped country and starts to produce something. So those who are proposing legislation which would halt the progress multinational corporations have brought to developing countries are flirting with very real dangers for the American people and for the whole world. What I fear is that, over an extended period of time, if Americans say, "We don't care what happens to the rest of the world," the rest of the world won't care what happens to America, either. Then we are in real trouble.

Interview, Cleveland/ Nation's Business, May:46.

A. A. Sommer, Jr.
Commissioner, Securities and Exchange Commission of the United States

3

[Criticizing public companies that repurchase their own stock to "go private"]: When a corporation chooses to tap public sources of money, it makes a commitment that, absent the most compelling business justification, management and those in control will do nothing to interfere with the liquidity of the public investment or the protection afforded the public by the Federal securities laws. That liquidity is a benefit that the shareholder pays for and he should not be deprived of it by those who have fiduciary responsibilities to him. Further, absent such considerations, they must do nothing to deprive him of the value of his investment if he chooses to retain it . . . What is happening is, in my estimation, serious, unfair and sometimes disgraceful, a perversion of the whole process of public financing and a source that inevitably is going to make the individual shareholder even more hostile to American corporate mores.

Lecture, University of Notre Dame Law School, Nov. 15/The New York Times, 11-15:51,54.

Howard Stein
Chairman, Dreyfus Corporation

4

The investment community is in real transition and, if I were to be critical, it would only be to say that many members of the community are not willing to accept the changes rolling toward them. More energy is lost in defending past practices than in preparing for the future potentials. Over the next 10 years, we will see the introduction of fully negotiated commission rates and a lessening of the traditional importance of the major exchanges. Research—the service used to differentiate among firms in the days of fixed commission rates—will take on a new importance. Research will stand on its own two feet and it will sell on quality alone and become a far more exciting and profitable business. The underwriting business will become increasingly specialized and, hopefully, quite separate from money management; and the ability to execute orders in a much more competitive environment will prove to be just as rewarding for those remaining in the business as it was in the past for the many.

U.S. News & World Report, 4-1:30.

Jules C. Stein
Former chairman, MCA, Inc.

1

The sign of a great executive is a man who can find somebody to do his job better than he can. Most executives *control* power. They're afraid to delegate it, because those people may supplant them.

Interview, Los Angeles/
Los Angeles Times, 5-26:(Calendar)19.

O. E. Swain
President, Kraft Foods Corporation

2

The future of national brands has never been brighter. We have to earn our way because of the more questioning attitude among today's consumer; but there is an awareness of value and the consumer is still looking for a name she knows and trusts. Price is a factor with the struggle to make ends meet, but the consumer is looking for a quality beyond price. There is an awareness of nutritional value, and the consumer still relies on the brand name for dependability. The national brands will continue to do better than the cheaper brands. The cheaper brands have always been around.

Dallas/The Dallas Times Herald, 4-7:(J)1.

Steven D. Symms
United States Representative, R-Idaho

3

The American government began destroying the gold standard in 1913 with the creation of the Federal Reserve System, which, through its 12 regional offices, could supply member banks with paper currency not backed by any commodity whatsoever. Noting that mild recessions had taken place in the past whenever banks reached their lending limits, determined by the extent of their gold reserves, the Fed decided that if money could be made available at the right time, recession need never be experienced again. The fact that the Fed could not reliably predict when this money would be needed was proven over and over again through the 20th century, but its most spectacular failure was its

first. Rapid credit expansion led to the so-called "Roaring Twenties" and wild speculation in the stock market, culminating in its infamous crash in 1929, along with the crash of the American and world economies. With typical statist logic, the [Franklin] Roosevelt Administration argued that it was the gold standard that precipitated the 1929 crash and subsequent economic collapse. But we had been off a true gold standard since 1913. It was the paper printed by the government not backed by gold which led to the world-wide economic debacle.

Before the House, Washington, Nov. 20/
Human Events, 12-21:9.

John K. Tabor
Under Secretary of Commerce
of the United States

4

[Domestic inflation, world-wide shortages of raw materials and the Arab oil embargo] caused many people and many members of the Congress to react with a wave of isolationism and nationalism. A series of bills were introduced to impose export controls on a whole list of different products—ferrous scrap, soybeans, logs and others. But we believe there is a critical need to maintain our export position ... It is the [Nixon] Administration's purpose to keep the United States economy and the world economy as free as possible.

News conference, Seoul, South Korea/
The Washington Post, 3-24:(E)6.

O. Pendleton Thomas
Chairman, B. F. Goodrich Company

5

Increasingly, many important business decisions are not being made in corporate headquarters or in boardrooms. Rather, these decisions are being made in Washington, in state capitals, city halls, and in township halls. This is a fact of life. There will be no return to those simpler days. By itself, the fact that business is subject to more government regulation is neither good nor bad. Certainly, it does not signal the end of economic freedom in America, the demise of capitalism nor the impending nationalization of business, as some alarmists would have us believe. But we must recognize and adjust to an entirely new process of inter-

(O. PENDLETON THOMAS)

action between business and government. We must do so in order to preserve the balance of institutional power that is so critically important in a democratic society.

Before American Institute of Chemical Engineers, Southeast Texas section, Beaumont, Texas, Sept. 30/ Vital Speeches, 11-15:72.

Lynn A. Townsend
Chairman, Chrysler Corporation 1

Several financial forecasters have recently added up the total capital for plant and equipment that corporate America needs to stay healthy over the next 10 years. They came up with a figure of about $2 trillion, counting the effects of inflation. This is about three times what corporations needed in the past decade. Even if we eliminate the effects of inflation over the next 10 years, they need about twice that of the last 10. This huge need comes from all sides. Our industrial plant is old, while that of our competition overseas, rebuilt after the ravages of war, is relatively modern. If basic industry in the United States is going to survive as a first-class power in the face of that competition, it is imperative that outmoded, inefficient plant and equipment be replaced with the latest technology, and very soon.

Before Securities Industry Association, Greenbrier, W. Va., May 10/ Vital Speeches, 6-15:540.

Dow Votaw
Professor of Business Administration, University of California, Berkeley 2

Society has altered its expectations of higher education and corporations. In the case of businesses, society expects more than making as much money as possible for shareholders. In the case of higher education, businesses are the major conduit for upward social mobility.

At conference on urban involvement and higher education, San Francisco/ San Francisco Examiner & Chronicle, 3-17:(A)23.

George Wald
Professor of Biology, Harvard University 3

Profit is the evil. The incessant drive to maximize profit is spreading devastation. The whole planet is being sacrificed to that kind of obsessive activity that feeds on itself, while most of humanity, particularly the young, is going down the drain. Corporate wealth has reached unprecedented proportions. Where there were millionaires there are billionaires now in the United States. A billionaire is an obscenity ... We have become a giant banana republic in which everything is for sale.

Interview, University of California, Berkeley/San Francisco Examiner, 6-10:21.

Leslie H. Warner
Chairman, General Telephone and Electronics Corporation 4

In the short-run, the inflow of capital resulting from foreign investment in the U.S. is beneficial because of the positive effect it has upon the balance of payments. From the long-term viewpoint, the return of earnings made in the U.S. to the countries making the investments will lessen that positive effect. Although the size and diversity of the U.S. economy can support moderate levels of direct foreign investment, we would be opposed to significant foreign investments in key industries related to national security.

Interview, New York/ The Dallas Times Herald, 1-6:(E)8.

Harrison A. Williams, Jr.
United States Senator, D—New Jersey 5

[Criticizing a New York Stock Exchange proposal that Congress legislatively require all trades of listed securities to take place on an exchange]: The NYSE's proposal is a perfect illustration of a self-regulatory organization confusing the public interest, which it is licensed to serve, with its private interest, which it has an economic instinct to protect ... We need more—not less—competition among market-makers operating both on and off exchanges to enhance the over-all depth and liquidity of the market.

Before American Institute of Public Accountants, Jan. 9/ The Washington Post, 1-10:(H)10.

Leonard Woodcock
President, United Automobile Workers of America

1

The principal saboteur of the healthy growth of U.S. foreign trade was not tariffs, quotas, isolationism or what-have-you, but the appetite of U.S. corporations to buy and develop the assets of foreign corporations or to simply move abroad—lock, stock and barrel.

At world trade conference, Chicago, Feb. 28/Los Angeles Times, 3-1:(1)11.

Walter B. Wriston
Chairman, First National City Bank, New York

2

Over-regulation [of business by government] is partly our [business'] own fault. Our history sometimes reveals a cycle. We let something run wide open until the law of compensating forces operates. Businessmen sometimes fail to anticipate or even respond to the demands of the consumer. If this continues too long, the public becomes angry. Typically, then, the industry or the labor union that is perceived to be out of control forms a "self-regulating" group to set standards and police its own activity. These self-regulatory groups usually fail to respond quickly and strongly enough, so that pressure continues to mount and the government steps in . . . Failure to reform themselves and to perceive how rapidly our value systems change will create volumes of regulations we will all live to regret.

Before Economic Club, Detroit, Feb. 25/Vital Speeches, 4-1:377.

Clayton Yeutter
Assistant Secretary for Marketing and Consumer Services, Department of Agriculture of the United States

3

It's a good thing very few cattlemen live to be past 90. If the ranchers who worried about the passing of the open range in the last century were alive today, they'd feel positively strangled . . . It would be the growing maze of regulations that would get them. Almost every week, more rules, laws or regulations affecting the livestock industry issue forth from some state capital or Federal agency, including some under my jurisdiction. The good old days of sitting around the fire rubbing Neatsfoot oil into your saddle are gone forever. They have been replaced by paperwork. The cowman is becoming almost as deskbound as the rest of us.

Before Colorado Cattle Feeders Association/ Quote, 3-17:245.

Crime • Law Enforcement

John R. Bartels, Jr.
*Administrator, Drug Enforcement
Administration of the United States*   1

Nobody [in the general public] knows what a Federal narcotics agent does. Nobody knows the demands put on him. I think there are a great number of people who regard narcotics agents as corrupt Nazis who don't know how to open a door except with the heel of their right foot. Sure, there is a very small element of our people that we have a problem with. But all our men are college educated. They come on this job motivated by a sense of doing what they consider the toughest job in law enforcement. They run risks, and they work 80-hour weeks as a matter of course. Yet there have been very few serious mistakes compared with the number of arrests, and very few instances of corruption compared with the number of seizures.

*Interview, Washington/
U.S. News & World Report, 4-1:40.*

Abraham D. Beame
Mayor of New York   2

There are people who say I'm wrong to try and get more cops out on the street. They say that this is a simplistic solution to the crime problem. They say the real problem is clogged courts and revolving-door justice—district attorneys and more courts rather than more cops. There are two ways of looking at this crime problem. One, how do the people feel about it? And two, what is the solution? I agree that the solution is to revise the whole system. But like it or not, the man in the street doesn't see it that way; the revolving door means nothing to him; all he knows is that when he sees a cop he's got more confidence. So I'm trying to get about 2,500 more cops into the street.

The New York Times Magazine, 10-6:68.

Brendan F. Brown
*Professor of Law, Loyola University,
New Orleans*   3

The claim of society to protect itself by recourse to capital punishment is not unreasonable. While it is not certain that capital punishment protects society by deterrence, the conclusion that it does is not unreasonable. Life imprisonment may not be adequate as a punishment by society because it is common knowledge that sentences of life imprisonment are seldom, if ever, fully served, so that the offender is out in 10 or 15 years, threatening society again with a repetition of his actions. Whether capital punishment protects society by way of deterrence is a conclusion of fact, which cannot be resolved with certainty. But the conclusion of the members of the 40 legislatures in the respective states of the United States, who legislated the death penalty, is surely not less valid in this matter than that of the Justices of the Supreme Court [who ruled against capital punishment]. What superior wisdom do judges have to reach the factual conclusion with certainty that capital punishment is not necessary as a deterrent and as a definitive means of permanently preventing a repetition of the crime?

*At International Congress of Jurists,
University of Detroit, July 21/
Vital Speeches, 10-1:760.*

Thomas E. Bryant
President, Drug Abuse Council   4

[Saying he favors decriminalization of marijuana]:—in effect, getting state laws to reflect more adequately and more equitably the potential risk to the individual and to society with the use and possession of marijuana and put it in balance with the potential criminal sanction ... I think the price we are paying for criminalizing the millions of Americans who are using marijuana, each of whom is breaking the law when he does, each of whom I think is building up a storehouse of resentment and disrespect for the law . . . I think all of this, the price that society is paying for that, far outweighs any potential harm that would come with moving toward decriminalization.

Interview, Washington, Sept. 1/
Chicago Tribune, 9-2:(1)3.

1

[Saying the health and criminal aspects of marijuana use should be dealt with separately]: We have medical proof, for example, that alcohol—the abuse or misuse of it—can destroy the human liver, the brain, the kidney and the body's resistance to disease. But we do not jail those who simply use alcohol. We do not confuse potential health hazard with criminality.

Before Senate Subcommittee on Alcoholism
and Narcotics, Washington, Nov. 19/
The Christian Science Monitor, 11-20:6.

Warren E. Burger
Chief Justice of the United States

2

The percentage of [prison] inmates in all institutions who cannot read or write is staggering . . . The figures on literacy alone are enough to make one wish that every sentence imposed could include a provision that would grant release when the prisoner had learned to read and write.

U.S. News & World Report, 8-19:38.

Joseph P. Busch
District Attorney,
Los Angeles County, California

3

The juvenile court law, although revised in recent years, still clings to an outmoded philosophy of protection for the offender, which does not recognize that young people are, in fact, committing criminal offenses. We rarely find the hubcap stealer or the apple-off-the-pushcart thief today, but instead the murderer, robber, mugger, rapist and assaulter . . . Responsibility for one's own anti-social and criminal acts must be emphasized in the juvenile court law. This concept, in

my opinion, is totally lacking in the law as written today.

Before California Senate Subcommittee
on Violence, and Vandalism in Schools,
March 15/Los Angeles Times, 3-16:(3)14.

Don A. Byrd
Chief of Police of Dallas

4

We [police] have tried to deal with the causes of crime, and the causes appear to be so many and varied that they are beyond our grasp. We've become frustrated. Perhaps some sociologist understands the causes of crime; perhaps he can treat them. But I am satisfied that law-enforcement agencies can't treat all the causes of crime . . . We are treating only the symptoms, not the disease which is the cause, and for that we simply don't have the know-how.

The Dallas Times Herald, 3-17:(K)3.

Eugene J. Camp
Chief of Police of St. Louis

5

There are fewer criminals in prison now than in 1960, yet crime has risen 150 per cent. The word penitentiary stems from the word punitive, and we've got to restore "punitive" to the system . . . even at the cost of alienating some sociologists.

Interview, Chicago/
The Washington Post, 9-15:(E)12.

Charles F. Campbell
Warden, Fort Worth Federal
Correctional Institute

6

[On the open, less-rigid policy at his prison]: The way prisons are, they're characterized by criminal behavior, assaults, predatory homosexuality, drug traffic, strong-arm cliques, racial tension—all of the pathology that characterizes a typical prison. People who have to accommodate to that are naturally going to be diminished as people. We [at this prison] have a lot of problems; we have a bunch of troubled human beings. But we don't have *those* problems.

Interview, Fort Worth/
Los Angeles Times, 1-28:(1)15.

James S. Campbell
Former general counsel, National Commission on the Causes and Prevention of Violence
1

To the extent that we tried dealing with the crime problem by increasing the number of police, we were doing something that everybody knew wasn't going to work. It was superficial relief from some symptoms. It was not a case of getting at the over-all causes. We found that in all serious crimes that were committed only 1.5 per cent of the suspected criminals were imprisoned. Crime does pay. The odds were 99 to 1 that you could commit a serious crime and not go to jail for it. That hasn't changed very much, I am sure. This effort at beefing up the police and other factors may have slowed the rise in crime for a while; but if the forces that generate the crime are not dealt with, you would expect to see them break through again, as they have now. This little lull we seemed to have was nice, but there is no reason to think we have had a reversal of a longtime trend. We have done nothing about the conditions that caused the trend. Crime may go up and get a lot worse before people do something about it.

Interview/Los Angeles Times, 9-4:(2)5.

Gerald M. Caplan
Director, National Institute of Law Enforcement and Criminal Justice, Law Enforcement Assistance Administration of the United States
2

[To some extent, crime] is a characteristic of industrial society and urban life. If crime disappeared totally in a society, we would really be in trouble. In democratic societies where social controls are not imposed by government and tend to be more informal and customary, one can expect greater forms of deviation—more eccentricity, more spontaneity and, at the same time, more crime.

Interview, Washington/ Los Angeles Times, 11-24:(1)16.

Hugh L. Carey
United States Representative, D–New York
3

Look at the criminal-justice system. Everyone in this state [N.Y.] knows how much crime

goes unpunished. Less than a tenth of one per cent of all burglaries are punished by prison sentences. Fully 40 per cent of the most serious narcotics felony convictions are dealt with by sentences so mild they're supposed to be illegal under state laws. We know that, either through our laziness or incompetence or venality, too many of our judges will not enforce the law fairly or effectively. These people make a mockery of our efforts to create an effective criminal-justice system. They do not belong on the bench.

Before Bronx-Pelham Reform Democratic Club, New York, July 28/ The New York Times, 7-29:27.

Frank G. Carrington
Executive director, Americans for Effective Law Enforcement
4

The criminal-justice system just totally ignores the victims of crime. We are confounded with a bunch of rules, court decisions, a total preoccupation with the rights of the suspected criminal and the convicted criminal. I don't say concern about such rights is wrong. But I think there should be a balance.

U.S. News & World Report, 12-16:31.

Jimmy Carter
Governor of Georgia
5

There is a vast opportunity to improve the dispensing of justice to those who have no money, no influence and no voice. I don't think it's any accident that the prisons are filled with the poor. I don't think there's any big difference between the morality of the richer and poorer citizens.

Before Governor's Commission on Criminal Justice Standards and Goals, Atlanta, Oct. 12/ The Atlanta Journal and Constitution, 10-13:(B)7.

Milton S. Eisenhower
President emeritus, Johns Hopkins University; Former Chairman, National Commission on the Causes and Prevention of Violence
6

The crime rate in the cities today is eight times what it is in the country. In the city the crime rate is three times higher in the ghetto than elsewhere. The worst group of the criminally prone is 15 to 20 years [of age]. The second worst—and this will startle you—is 10 to 14, and it is getting worse all the time. These youngsters are spending more time before the TV than in school. What they watch is almost exclusively crime. They reach the point where they fail to distinguish between fact and fiction. In the 1960s, for political reasons, some of our politicians promised blacks the millenium, the moon. The millenium has not arrived, and whenever people have their expectations raised and then are made disappointed, it is a sure cause of violence. The way crime is rising today threatens the character of American society.

Interview/Los Angeles Times, 9-4:(2)5.

Sam J. Ervin, Jr.
United States Senator, D—North Carolina
1

[Saying the collection and dissemination of crime records should not be centralized in the Justice Department]: For one man [the Attorney General] to have control of crime data might be more efficient. But this country wasn't based on the idea of efficiency so much. It was based on the idea that power be diffused.

Before Senate Subcommittee on Constitutional Rights, Washington, March 7/ The Washington Post, 3-8:(A)6.

W. J. Estelle, Jr.
Director, Texas Department of Corrections
2

[On the new type of prison inmate such as the revolutionary]: The average prisoner now is younger, smarter, more violent and more difficult to manage. They are usually better educated and more aware of their rights, but they are not any more aware of their responsibility to democracy than the prisoners of 20 years ago. The problem in dealing with the revolutionary mind lies with you and me [in law enforcement]. Their reasoning is so far out that we just can't comprehend people really willing to give their lives and the lives of innocent bystanders to reach their goal.

Before East Texas Peace Officers Association, Nacogdoches, June 24/ The Dallas Times Herald, 6-25:(A)15.

Gerald R. Ford
President of the United States
3

We must take the criminal out of circulation. We must make crime hazardous and very costly. We must insure that swift and prolonged imprisonment will inevitably follow each and every offense. Only then will we deter others from pursuing careers of crime.

Before International Association of Chiefs of Police, Washington, Sept. 24/ Chicago Tribune, 9-25:(1)5.

Valery Giscard d'Estaing
President of France
4

. . . prison life should add no other sanctions to the detention. The penalty is the detention, and the other activities should be designed, with the aid of prison personnel, with an eye toward the readaptation and reinsertion of the prisoners into the larger . . . society.

News conference, Paris, July 25/ The Christian Science Monitor, 7-30:4.

James R. Hoffa
Former president, International Brotherhood of Teamsters
5

[Speaking from his experience in having served time in a Federal penitentiary]: . . . less than 2 per cent of the people in prison are really what you could call gangster-type individuals. Most of the people in there are people who, one way or the other, got in prison without really knowing what they were doing, such as kids who smoked marijuana, kids who passed checks or used credit cards, or somebody who did some white-collar crime without any violence attached to it. Now, when you take those kids—or grown-up people, adults—and you put them in with that 10 per cent who are the second-, third- and four-time offenders, the dedicated criminal, you contaminate everything that should be considered rehabilitation. So until they classify people at time of sentencing by birth, background, work habits, the whole bit, to determine should they be on parole, should they be on probation, or should they be put into a special institution to determine what was mentally or physically wrong with them

(JAMES R. HOFFA)

that caused the crime—until then, prisons are nothing but jokes.

Interview, Miami Beach/
The National Observer, 6-15:1.

Sidney Hook
Former Professor of Philosophy,
New York University   1

We have legitimately been concerned with the rights of criminals and of those charged with crime; but we have not been concerned to the same extent with the rights of victims and with the rights of potential victims of criminals. For good reasons we all must be concerned with the rights of criminals. Yet the likelihood of my committing a criminal act is far less than the likelihood these days of my becoming a victim of criminal violence. Consequently, I want to defend my rights not to become a victim. I don't believe there is a hard line or a soft line with respect to crime. There should be an intelligent line, which is as concerned with justice and compassion for the victim as with the rights of the criminal. I believe that in the last few decades there has been a disproportion in the concern for the rights of the criminal. I don't want to give the impression that criminals have no rights. But when there is a mounting crime wave, you have to ask yourself how we are going to prevent the increase in the number of victims.

Interview, Washington/
Los Angeles Times, 2-27:(2)7.

Harold E. Hughes
United States Senator, D–Iowa   2

Is the morbid trip back to the death penalty the right way to go to protect society from violence and to keep faith with our moral purpose as a people? Is ultimate violence the antidote for violence? For me, the answer must be no. I cannot be brought to believe that the way to conquer crime in America is to revert to institutional killings in the name of justice. It is true that I am one of those who, for deeply religious reasons, believes in the absolute sanctity of human life ... But I oppose the restitu-

tion of capital punishment for good and sufficient reasons in addition to my basic religious conviction. I oppose the death penalty because it demeans human society without protecting it. The weight of the evidence is that capital punishment does not deter serious crime. The weight of history is that judicial killing brutalizes the nations who practice it ... I oppose the death penalty because it cannot undo or rectify any crime that was committed, however brutal, and because there is no road back if the convicted man is later proved innocent ... Finally, I oppose the death penalty because it is grossly destructive of human hopes for a society more amenable to peace and less dependent on violence for the solution of its problems.

Before the Senate, Washington, March 12/
The Washington Post, 3-15:(A)30.

3

Is the health hazard [of marijuana] so great as to endanger society, or is it so minimal that government should refrain from interfering with the individual user? Do the criminal laws impose on the individual and on society a burden which is so great and so unfair that they are far more damaging than the use of marijuana itself could be? Even if we find that marijuana does present serious health hazards, are we justified in using the criminal law to solve a health problem when we do not use it in any similar way to solve the very well-known problems created by the use of such substances as alcohol and nicotine?

At Senate Subcommittee on Alcoholism
and Narcotics hearing, Washington/
The National Observer, 11-30:3.

Clifford Irving
Author   4

[After serving 17 months in prison for writing a fraudulent biography of industrialist Howard Hughes]: Incarceration of men who are not violent and therefore are in jail to be punished is not only kind of barbaric and pointless, but as far as I can see leads to the hardening of the criminal mentality and to further crime. The longer you stay in prison, the more bitter you get. It is my own personal experience and the experience of every man I know.

Interview/
Los Angeles Herald-Examiner, 2-20:(D)8.

Clarence M. Kelley
Director, Federal Bureau of Investigation

1

I have worked with police officers all my life. I have been an officer myself. I know their gripes. I know their joys. I think I know the men and women themselves—as human beings. And I can tell you, honestly and truthfully, you will never meet a finer group of Americans. They work not alone for the salary—if they did, they wouldn't be there. They work not for public acclaim—if so, they wouldn't be there. They work not to be heroes—if so, they would long ago have resigned. They walk your streets, safeguard your homes, keep your traffic going . . . why? Because they believe in the dignity of the law, in the triumph of right over might, and, above all, because they want to do their share in helping protect their communities . . . Today it is not always pleasant to be a police officer. There are many groups and individuals who hate the police, who call the officer vile names. They seek to discredit and impugn our profession. If an officer makes an arrest, he is accused of "brutality." If he maintains order during a demonstration, he is taunted as a "bully." If he enforces the law, he is charged with "harassment." He is called a "pig," and hissed and vilified as he carries out his duties. It takes a man of unique qualities to do his job, honestly and faithfully, amid this barrage of unwarranted abuse and vilification. The excellent record of our officers in meeting these situations is a tribute to their training, skill and patience.

At Outstanding Law Enforcement Officers
Awards Banquet, Birmingham, Alabama,
Feb. 9/Vital Speeches, 4-1:355.

2

[Arguing against the proposed sealing of criminal records after a specified time period] : I am completely opposed to sealing any criminal-justice information against criminal-justice agencies. There is a continuous need for criminal-justice agencies to have unfettered access to prior criminal records for subsequent investigations. The majority of criminal recidivism occurs within a time frame short of the [five-to-seven-year] periods enumerated in some of the bills [aimed at sealing the records] ; *all* criminal recidivism does not. If only 10 murderers or kidnappers repeated their crime outside the statutory time frame, is this not enough to warrant criminal-justice agencies access to offender records which may provide leads in subsequent murder or kidnapping investigations?

The Christian Science Monitor, 4-18:4.

3

Ten years ago, it was not uncommon for police officers generally to be slighted by many as under-educated and poorly trained. Today, these criticisms are infrequent. Now, with higher education standards, sophisticated equipment and vastly improved training efforts, the police are more apt to be criticized for the efficiency of their techniques and programs.

Quote, 7-28:74.

4

The FBI is not a national police and has no aspiration to become a national police. In America there is no place for a national police. I am categorically opposed, in any shape or form, to a national police.

Before Federal Bar Association, Washington,
Sept. 6/The New York Times, 9-7:29.

5

The white-collar criminal characteristically has all the trappings of success and respectability. Not uncommonly, he is a prominent member of the community. People should insist on the same strict enforcement of the law for business and government officials who break the law that they demand for those without status. They ought to be as outraged when bilked by corporate fraud or government corruption as they are when assaulted and robbed by a stranger on the street.

U.S. News & World Report, 12-16:40.

Glen D. King
Director of information services,
International Association of Chiefs of Police

6

The logic which urges an abolition of the death penalty in the interest of human life is

(GLEN D. KING)

more apparent than real. I am convinced that ultimately abolition of capital punishment would result in a much greater loss of human life than its retention.

The Washington Post, 6-16:(F)4.

Edward I. Koch
United States Representative, D–New York　1

[Calling for decriminalization of marijuana possession]: While many thousands are being arrested for possessing marijuana, many millions are not. I think that both Constitutional liberals and Constitutional conservatives will want to rally around this issue—because of the unfairness of it. By an estimate I've seen, it would cost $79 billion a year to put every pot-smoker in jail. And even assuming pot's as vile as its worst critics say, so do you correct that by putting everybody in jail?

Interview/The National Observer, 11-30:3.

John L. McClellan
United States Senator, D–Arkansas　2

[On capital punishment]: Shall the murderer be permitted to live and have another opportunity, or shall we protect society against his dastardly deed? A society that refuses to protect the innocent invites repetition of the dastardly deed.

*Before the Senate, Washington, March 12/
The New York Times, 3-13:21.*

3

[On capital punishment]: What it all boils down to is whether it is ever "just" to impose the death penalty. Can man ever be found to have acted so viciously, so cruelly, so much like an animal as to justify society imposing upon him the ultimate punishment? I firmly believe he can.

*Before the Senate, Washington/
The Washington Post, 6-16:(F)4.*

Patrick V. Murphy
*Former Police Commissioner of
New York City*　4

We have to face the facts. There is too much instability in our cities. As long as we have

unemployment, under-employment, broken homes, alcoholism, drugs and mental-health problems, we are going to have crime.

U.S. News & World Report, 6-10:36.

Ralph Nader
Lawyer; Consumer advocate　5

Newspapers and television highlight bank robberies as major events, yet the white-collar criminal inside the bank, through fraud and embezzlement, took six times more money in fiscal year 1973 than did the holdup men.

*At Senate Subcommittee on Criminal Laws
and Procedures hearing, Washington,
July 19/The New York Times, 7-20:36.*

Aryeh Neier
*Executive director,
American Civil Liberties Union*　6

[Arguing against dissemination of criminal records]: How can we seriously hope to reduce crime if we disseminate records which have the unintended effect of making it impossible for people to stop being criminals? Arrest and conviction records often create social lepers. Dissemination of their past records . . . insures that many of these branded persons will not escape . . . It may take years until they are able to get steady jobs and put down the roots which take them out of the criminal class. The dissemination of records places a series of obstacles in the path of persons who wish to enter society's mainstream and end the half-life of the world of crime.

Los Angeles Herald-Examiner, 4-14:(D)9.

Louis S. Nelson
Warden, San Quentin (Calif.) State Prison　7

I think that all prisons have punishment built into them. We don't normally talk about it, but I think we should face it openly, that sending a man to prison punishes him. We keep using the rhetoric that people are sent here for correction. And this is true; hopefully they'll find some correction. But in the final analysis, the penal code says that a man is punished by being sent to state prison. I would disagree that there is cruelty, that there is barbarism. There is certainly punishment. If that's cruelty, so be it. I think there are humane ways to punish, and I think one of them is to restrict a man's movements. It also serves the dual purpose of protecting the community . . . I would suggest that when the prisoners throw up or cry of brutality, what they're really saying is that the administration has abdicated its responsibility, has lost control, and cruelty is exerted on them by other members of the inmate body. The administration has backed away and allowed the inmates to take charge, and the conditions have been so cruel and intolerable that they've had to revolt.

Interview/
San Francisco Examiner & Chronicle, 9-8:
(California Living)10.

A. L. Palumbo
Director, California State Office of
Criminal Justice Planning
1

Justice is not something a judge metes out to a convicted criminal. It is more than that. Justice is that part of the quality of our way of life which results from the fair and impartial administration of equitable laws. It involves both the rights of the accused and the rights of the victim. And in a larger sense, justice involves the rights of all of us to live and work without fear, to walk freely and safely through the streets of our communities.

Los Angeles Times, 8-5:(2)2.

Henry E. Petersen
Assistant Attorney General,
Criminal Division, Department of
Justice of the United States
2

[Arguing against a number of bills that would limit the scope of government electronic surveillance and wiretapping]: I can be very brief. We oppose the bills. That's it. We maintain that electronic surveillance techniques are, to date, the most effective method to bring criminal sanctions against organized criminals, and are indispensable in developing witnesses with corroborating testimony, and generally in providing a useful tool in the evidence-gathering process.

Before House Subcommittee, Washington,
April 26/The Washington Post, 4-27:(A)2.

Raymond K. Procunier
Director, California Department of
Corrections
3

If there is any way of protecting society without sending a criminal to prison, we should take that course. Long incarceration in big prisons should be reserved for high-risk offenders who cannot be safely controlled in other ways. Now, there are justifications for sending some guys to prison, but simultaneously we should be working on a program to eliminate prisons in their present form. We have to get away from this emphasis on big prisons far away from inmates' homes and friends. We need to regionalize our institutions and have more diversity for different kinds of offenders.

Interview/
U.S. News & World Report, 12-16:46.

4

[Saying he is in favor of capital punishment]: . . . I think that it's more-humane punishment to get the gas chamber than do 45 or 50 years in prison. Further, I think there has to be an ultimate punishment for very extreme behavior. We don't know how else to deal with those people. Let me expand on that: We have now seven different degrees of murder in California, so we're not talking about the death penalty for just any murder. We're talking about the extreme cases, and I don't think you can have a society like ours if law-enforcement people, particularly, are not protected from the predators who attack them. Now, the ultimate punishment in our society has to be judiciously applied, with all kinds of reviews and limits. Everybody who's charged with a capital crime should have the same quality of counsel regardless of his social status. But then we should let the death penalty prevail if there's conviction.

Interview/U.S. News & World Report, 12-16:48.

Ronald Reagan
Governor of California
5

Perhaps the single greatest need is for a change in attitude [toward crime], from the permissiveness of the 1960s to a realistic approach to crime in the 1970s. Unfortunately,

(RONALD REAGAN)

too many people, including those holding public positions of responsibility, persist in viewing crime as a sociological case-study rather than an urgent problem of public safety.

At California Conference on Criminal Justice,
Sacramento, Dec. 4/
Los Angeles Herald-Examiner, 12-5:(A)5.

Milton Rector
President, National Council on
Crime and Delinquency 1

Time and experience have shown that prisons do not and cannot rehabilitate or correct. They deter very little crime, and in the long run they don't protect society. They are ineffectual .... studies have shown the longer the term, the more likely the ex-prisoner is to return to crime ... Prisons themselves are, in fact, one of the causes of crime. They are schools of crime where first-time offenders are thrown together with hardened offenders .... the more one becomes concerned with humanization of prisons, the clearer it becomes that the only way to achieve this is to avoid incarceration altogether, except for the dangerous few.

The Dallas Times Herald, 4-14:(J)1.

William H. Rehnquist
Associate Justice,
Supreme Court of the United States 2

[Disagreeing with those who are against circulation of arrest records by the FBI to other law-enforcement agencies]: [An arrest] is not a private event. I think it would be a rather bold person who would suggest that if one of the suspects in an investigation of a serious crime had a record of several arrests for similar offenses, that sort of information would not be of significant help to the investigating authorities ... To me, the question posed by these situations is not an issue of core privacy since I think as a policy matter it is quite justifiable for the government to collect arrest data. The question is simply whether or not the government ought to spend its funds and use its manpower

to supply this information to inquiring potential employers.

Lecture, University of Kansas Law School/
The New York Times, 9-29:(1)36.

Frank L. Rizzo
Mayor of Philadelphia 3

I'm not sure if the death penalty is a deterrent. But I know one thing—that when they pull that switch, he's not around to commit another crime. I'll tell you this: I will personally pull the switch if they run out of people who want to do it. I'm available.

At Pennsylvania American Legion convention/
Los Angeles Times, 7-19:(1)2.

4

I'm supposed to be a hard-nosed cop. I became a hard-nosed cop because of where I worked. I was a cop 28 years. I worked the toughest areas. I've been there and back. I'm for human rights; a policeman's job is mostly helping people. But when you talk to me about criminals I get hard-nosed, because I've been there, within minutes, and seen the broken bodies. They pick on old gray-haired people to stab and rape. I'm so fed up with the misplaced compassion—and it's getting worse. You kill, you rob, you rape, and you become a hero.

Interview, Philadelphia/
Los Angeles Times, 8-18:(1-A)8.

Donald E. Santarelli
Administrator, Law Enforcement Assistance
Administration of the United States 5

This is a bit philosophical, but, from my view, the causes of crime result from the kind of society that we have become. Crime is the very high price we pay for such progress as urbanization and mobility. We've become a society of highly mobile and, therefore, often anonymous people whose relationship to one another is substantially disrupted—whose relationship with community is substantially disrupted. You have to remember that what really controls antisocial conduct in any culture is societal institutions. The most important of these institutions is the family, then the community, the neighborhood, the church and the school—these are social institutions which best conform to the societal norm. When those institutions don't work very well—as we now find them not working in our society—you can't ask the criminal-justice system to replace all of them by itself. That's what we have tended to do.

Interview, Washington/
U.S. News & World Report, 6-10:39.

William B. Saxbe
Attorney General of the United States *1*

[On gun-control]: I have little confidence in trying to rid the country of guns . . . It is another of our idealistic dreams that fails in practice. Any plumber can make a gun in half a day that is just as effective as the real thing.

Washington/
The Christian Science Monitor, 1-18:7.

2

Somehow, the people in this country have come to think that the courts and the police and the prisons have to solve our criminal problem in this country. This is a mistake that should be set aright . . . It's like trying to say that the schools are responsible for bad behavior of the children. The few police and the few courts in this country can't begin to rebuild a community. The policemen are getting tired of hearing that so-and-so shouldn't be found guilty of mugging because he's poor, he comes from a bad neighborhood, or his daddy didn't take him to see the *Redskins* play football, or something like this. What we have to do somehow is to free the police departments and our prisons from the pressure that it is up to them to make the necessary social changes that solve the crime problem. The courts and the police are not agencies of social change. They are there for one purpose: to catch criminals, prosecute them and put them in jail.

Interview, Washington/
U.S. News & World Report, 2-4:26.

3

. . . I have always favored capital punishment . . . I think capital punishment is a deterrent in the shooting of policemen. I think it's a

deterrent to the heinous crimes of mass murder and terrorism that we're faced with today.

Interview, Washington/
U.S. News & World Report, 2-4:26.

4

[Saying the certainty of punishment is a reliable deterrent to crime]: If the potential criminal knows the odds are against him, he probably won't commit the crime. Most criminals are not insane; most turn to crime as a calculated risk.

At Federal Corrections Institutions convention,
Wisconsin Dells, Wis., May 21/
Los Angeles Times, 5-22:(A)2.

5

[Wiretapping is] a dirty business . . . but sometimes it is a last resort of decent men striving to protect our freedom against activities far, far dirtier.

Before Cleveland City Club, June 28/
Los Angeles Herald-Examiner, 6-30:(A)2.

6

I have at one time or another supported nearly all of the panaceas offered for crime reduction: more policemen, more prosecutors, more judges, more rehabilitation of offenders, and if all else fails, paying them to be good. Yet after years of struggle and billions of dollars, it should be clear to everyone there is no touchstone that can be evoked in crime control. There are no rabbits to be pulled out of the hat; we have to admit now there never were.

Before Major Cities Police Chiefs Committee
of International Association of Chiefs
of Police, Chicago, Aug. 27/
The Washington Post, 8-28:(A)1.

7

If we go on as we are, there is every possibility that crime will inundate us. The nation would then be faced with the prospect of falling apart or devising a national police force in one final effort to restore domestic order . . . As other countries have learned, a police state can control common crime. But that is not our way. And it would be a dreadful mistake to slide inch-by-inch toward that chasm, centralizing the war on crime in the name of effi-

(WILLIAM B. SAXBE)

ciency while meekly accepting a national constabulary.

Before Major Cities Police Chiefs Committee of International Association of Chiefs of Police, Chicago, Aug. 27/ The Atlanta Constitution, 8-28:(A)2.

1

Criminals alone are responsible for crime. [Many offenders commit crimes merely] because they want [to]. A great many feel the chances of apprehension are low—and the risk of going to prison, even if caught, are lower. Some commit crime for gain, others for personal satisfaction, thrill, adventure—or general hell-raising. [For these reasons, it is] beating around the bush to think removing conditions we have come to accept as root causes of crime will end it.

Before Major Cities Police Chiefs Committee of International Association of Chiefs of Police, Chicago, Aug. 27/ The Washington Post, 8-28:(A)7.

2

Too many dangerous convicted offenders are placed back in society in one way or another, and that simply must stop. With so few dangerous offenders being convicted and even fewer being jailed, something has got to be wrong somewhere. Much of the fault, as I see it, must rest with prosecutions and the courts . . . When the bleeding hearts say they [hardened criminals] can be rehabilitated as honest industrious citizens, all I can say is they must have a hole in their head. Prosecutors, court[s] and parole boards must face the fact that some violent offenders cannot be rehabilitated. Dangerous and violent offenders . . . should know that arrest means conviction and conviction means prison.

Before International Association of Chiefs of Police, Washington, Sept. 23/ The New York Times, 9-24:18.

3

[Saying white-collar criminals should be sent to jail]: Price-fixers should go to prison. The man who evades taxes should go to prison. They are not better than the car thief or the burglar or the robber. They are all members of the same fraternity. And it is about time that all of our Federal judges begin realizing that . . . It's one thing for the president of a company to pay a fine out of the corporate treasury. It's another thing for him to pack up his toothbrush and go off to jail.

At conference of industrial leaders, Lake Placid, N.Y., Oct. 4/ The Atlanta Constitution, 10-5:(B)2.

4

The FBI is changing with the times. For years, they saw themselves as the bulwark against Communists or socialists or any kind of infiltration into our government. When it's criminal, that's the way it should be. But when it's not criminal, they should only operate in that area authorized by Congress. They shouldn't have the capability of operating based on their own political philosophy.

Interview, Washington, Dec. 16/ Los Angeles Times, 12-17:(1)7.

Philip G. Tannian
Police Commissioner of Detroit

5

[Supporting proposed Michigan legislation banning handguns]: We as a people cannot afford the terrible toll of death and injury being inflicted through the proliferation and thoughtless use of pistols. We're talking pistol—not gun—control. Pistols, which are readily available throughout the state and easily concealed . . . are weapons designed primarily to kill human beings . . . It may be five to 10 years before this amendment will dramatically cut the homicide rate in Michigan. But for the lives we will save and for the well-being of our children, it will be our greatest contribution to the future of our state and our people.

News conference, Lansing, Mich./ The National Observer, 3-9:4.

Don Weber
Associate Warden, San Quentin (Calif.) State Prison

6

The outside world has moved in on the prisons with all of society's ills and frustrations. Things are no longer as cut and dried as they once were, because everything now depends on what's happening in the streets . . . A con's place in the scheme of things isn't related to his crime as much as it was before, when a "heavy" on the outside was still regarded as a "heavy" on the inside. Now there's something for everyone—more militants, more gangs, more pressure and more trouble. Tempers are shorter and the violence is a lot closer to the surface. The old con bosses of the past couldn't make it in today's prisons, even if they tried.

Los Angeles Times, 2-9:(1)22.

James Q. Wilson
Professor of Government, Harvard University
1

Crime is beyond the control of police. The courts, the prosecutors' offices, the correctional agencies—that's where the big changes have to be made. Until some big gains are made there, I doubt we'll ever know what difference improvement in the police really makes in fighting crime.

U.S. News & World Report, 12-16:43.

Coleman A. Young
Mayor of Detroit
2

I issue a forward warning now to all those (drug) pushers, all ripoff artists, to all muggers: It's time to leave Detroit . . . I don't give a damn if they are black or white, or if they wear Superfly suits or blue uniforms with silver badges—hit the road.

Inaugural address, Detroit/Newsweek, 1-14:20.

Education

Mortimer Adler
Author, Educator

1

If our kind of society and culture is dedicated to the education of a whole people, not just the development of a small class of educated persons, then the notion of the educated person must hold out a goal toward which every human being can strive and which, given facilitating circumstances, he can achieve in some measure. An educated person is a human being who, given the tools of learning, goes on to the fullest possible development of his potential, both mental and moral.

At conference on "The Educated Person in the Contemporary World," Aspen, Colo./ The New York Times, 8-10:16.

Reubin Askew
Governor of Florida; Chairman, Education Commission of the States

2

Taxpayers in state after state are demonstrating their unwillingness to impose added property-tax burden upon themselves to support education. With all its other headaches and responsibilities, education shouldn't have to fight this kind of battle perennially with the people whose support it desperately needs. Our citizens historically have been generous in their outpouring of support for education. Let us regain that support. We cannot assume that the people are going to automatically support education. Education must be ready to prove its case.

Before Education Commission of the States, Miami, June 20/The New York Times, 6-21:15.

Samuel F. Babbitt
President, Kirkland College

3

It used to be that colleges . . . would openly espouse the goal of leadership. My alma mater, for example, was frankly founded, in another century, to produce leaders for church and state. In more recent days we have tended to talk less of leadership and more about the development of individuals; but I think it would be a great injustice if we put those two in opposition to each other in any way. What I propose to you is that the development of one's own potential should include a potential for responsible leadership, a leadership which is informed, trained and, above all, humane.

Before Kirkland College freshmen/ The National Observer, 10-26:15.

John M. Blum
Professor of American History, Yale University

4

During the periods of relative student unrest, from about 1968 to 1970, there was something of a flight from history. Students didn't find it relevant. They were looking for a "now" subject and, at Yale, as in most other colleges, enrollment in history classes fell off. Since 1971, there's been a movement back, however. Students seem less concerned with the merely contemporary. They are more serious about their studies—indeed, sometimes too serious; they don't have enough fun!—and many of them see a great deal of relevancy in history. Instead of viewing it as some obscure subject, they find it enlightens their understanding about people in general, those living today as well as yesterday. So enrollment has risen once again. Not only are history classes larger, but there are more students majoring in history. And the students seem very much to enjoy what they are doing.

Interview, Los Angeles/ Los Angeles Herald-Examiner, 6-2:(G)4.

Daniel J. Boorstin
Historian, National Museum of
History and Technology, Washington
1

One of the problems of educated people is that they talk too much.

At conference on "The Educated Person
in the Contemporary World," Aspen, Colo./
The New York Times, 8-10:16.

William Bouwsma
Professor of History, Harvard University
2

The idea of the educated man is above all the man who is open to new knowledge and able to advance it.

At conference on "The Educated Person
in the Contemporary World," Aspen, Colo./
The New York Times, 8-10:16.

John Brademas
United States Representative, D—Indiana
3

With only a few exceptions, President Nixon has shown no willingness to work together with Congress to strengthen our schools and colleges and improve our system of education . . . . it is Mr. Nixon, through the device of impoundment, the deliberate withholding of school funds Congress lawfully appropriated, who has brought confusion and chaos to thousands of school districts all over America.

Radio address, Washington, March 30/
The Dallas Times Herald, 3-31:(A)29.

Kingman Brewster, Jr.
President, Yale University
4

There is the constant threat that, because we [colleges and universities] receive Federal grants or contracts or fellowships or loans, the Congress will use the spending power to blackmail us into conformity to policies and preferences which they would have no power to impose by Federal regulation or criminal law.

Quote, 1-13:26.

Y. Frank Brown
Chairman, National Commission on the
Reform of Secondary Education
5

The foremost problem in American education is not forced [racial] busing; it is forced

schooling. Too many classrooms are loaded with students who are there because of either parental or societal pressure. High-school students are entitled to an education but should not be forced to acquire one.

The Christian Science Monitor, 1-7:(F)3.

Josiah Bunting III
President, Briarcliff College
6

The mad scramble to go co-ed is finally leveling off, but it still is a serious recruiting problem, getting career-oriented girls into women's schools. The more activist, self-assured young women tend to think their best educational opportunity is in co-educational schools. Our challenge (as women's schools) is to convince them this is not true.

Los Angeles Herald-Examiner, 7-22:(A)9.

Brendan T. Byrne
Governor of New Jersey
7

[Calling for an end to disparities in education between wealthy and poor areas]: To live with an educational system that does not reach and teach as many children as humanly possible, to chart a young child's future on the basis of family wealth or neighborhood affluence, is to impose an unequal burden that mocks the deepest faith of our American system: the faith that ability, not nobility of birth or income, is a test of how well a citizen will achieve in his life.

Inauguration address, Trenton, N.J.,
Jan. 15/The New York Times, 1-16:1.

Kenneth B. Clark
Educator; Director, Metropolitan
Applied Research Center, New York
8

Without apology, I would say I am a traditionalist. I do not see any substitute for the public schools' teaching reading, writing and arithmetic as the base upon which all other forms of education must rest. I don't believe a child can play any constructive role in this society if he is unable to spell or to read or if he does not have an elementary sense of grammatical structure.

Newsweek, 10-21:91.

WHAT THEY SAID IN 1974

Raymond C. Collins
Director of Program Development,
Office of Child Development,
Department of Health, Education
and Welfare of the United States   *1*

I don't think the public schools are beyond help. They are here to stay. But we need to find ways to get them to play a central role in child development. They must take a broader view of how a child learns; must find out what happens in the home, look at health and nutrition and get a general understanding that learning is not just a ritual you go through in the classroom. Kids get turned off when they get to public school. In [HEW's] Head Start [program], children are encouraged to talk, to move around and do things with their hands. [But] when they get to school, they are told to sit in a corner and do what the teacher says. They are rewarded only for how they behave.
Interview/Los Angeles Times, 3-26:(4)1.

Henry Steele Commager
Historian   *2*

If our educational enterprise is in disarray, it is in part because we have asked it to perform a miracle—to teach the young to understand a world they live in and the one they are to live in in the future, when we ourselves show little awareness of our fiduciary obligation to that future. Much of education today is a massive demonstration in hypocrisy, and it is folly to suppose that the young do not know this.
At conference on "The Educated Person
in the Contemporary World," Aspen, Colo./
The New York Times, 8-10:16.

Alan Cranston
United States Senator, D–California   *3*

I believe that bilingual education can be a great force in fostering educational changes in America. It clearly rejects the idea that the prime objective of the school is to wipe out all differences in style, heritage and language background, delivering to society—at the end of 12 years—a nicely packaged, well-rehearsed, automatic reciter of majority maxims. This is the route that schooling in America has traveled

historically . . . and it reflects an anti-minority tradition in American public education that is only now beginning to change.
The Washington Post, 9-22:(F)4.

Lawrence A. Cremin
President, Teachers College,
Columbia University   *4*

Largely because of television, I think we're going through an educational revolution that may be as radical as the original invention of the school. Television now is in 96 per cent of our homes and is being watched on an average of six hours a day, mainly by the very young, the very old and the very poor. People are learning knowledge, values and tastes from television. And youngsters also are influenced by their parents, relatives, churches, museums and libraries, movies, their peers on the street. The teacher must take it from there.
Interview, New York/
The New York Times, 6-23:(4)11.

James P. Dixon, Jr.
President, Antioch College   *5*

Private colleges may well be unable to weather the financial gales unless they subscribe to different purposes, provide educational alternatives, and serve people whom public institutions cannot reach. Failing this, private education may rapidly resemble a vermiform appendix—a vestigial apparatus of enculturation with little real function, heeded only when inflamed.
U.S. News & World Report, 6-3:60.

Peter F. Drucker
Management consultant; Professor of
Social Science and Business Administration,
Claremont (Calif.) College Graduate School   *6*

. . . we are going through a crisis of the schools. You talk to a school administrator: most of them are trying to do a good job, and you would be surprised how many are doing one. But the administrator does not know who his boss is. Is it a school board? Is it the community? Is it the black mothers? Is it the teachers? Secondly, he doesn't know what he is accountable for. So he does the normal thing, which is to try to keep everything a secret, if possible. By contrast, look at the English [British] open classroom. It has one and only one goal: By the end of what, in this country, would be the third grade, every child can read. Writing? All right. Not terribly important. Figuring? All right. Not terribly important. Development of the child? Baloney. Relationship with the parents? No. Parents are never allowed inside an English school. If you want reading and development of the child and development of the community and development of competent parents, you can't do it all. It's impossible.

Interview, Claremont, Calif./
Nation's Business, March:64.

Douglas Edwards
Authority on sales and marketing

1

The [company] recruiters are no longer on [the business-school] campus. They used to flock to the campuses by the hundreds and sometimes by the thousands, but today there is only a handful. Why doesn't the American businessman want today's college student? Simply because he's not being educated to earn a living in the world of business. I believe the accrediting agencies are so overwhelmingly liberal-arts oriented that they have turned business schools into liberal-arts schools.

At seminar sponsored by Sales and Marketing
Executives of Dallas, Jan. 14/
The Dallas Times Herald, 1-15:(D)5.

Harold L. Enarson
President, Ohio State University

2

A university is not just another organization. It is a very special kind of place. It is more like the Metropolitan Opera than the Metropolitan Life Insurance Company. It is more like a church than a factory, more like a research lab than a highway department. The university is an intensely human enterprise. And it is not so much managed as it is led.

Quote, 1-13:41.

Gerald R. Ford
President of the United States

3

I will do everything in my power to bring education and employers together in a new climate of credibility—an atmosphere in which universities turn out scholars and employers turn them on.

At Ohio State University commencement,
Aug. 30/Los Angeles Times, 8-31:(1)1.

4

Why can't the universities of America open their doors to working men and women, not only as students but also as teachers? Practical problem-solvers can contribute much to education, whether or not they hold degrees.

At Ohio State University commencement,
Aug. 30/Chicago Tribune, 8-31:(1)3.

5

... competition in education between private and public is good for the student. There's no reason why there should be a monopoly in education just on the public side. And private education has contributed, over a long period of time, at the primary, secondary and graduate levels, significantly to a better-educated America. And I would hope that we could find some Constitutional way in which to help private schools.

News conference, Washington, Oct. 9/
The New York Times, 10-10:38.

Erich Fromm
Psychoanalyst

6

Education acquaints the young with the best heritage of the human race. But while much of this heritage is expressed in words, it is effective only if these words become reality in the person of the teacher and in the practice and structure of society. Only the idea which has materialized in the flesh can influence man.

Quote, 5-19:464.

Edith Green
United States Representative, D–Oregon

7

As a long-time supporter of Federal financial aid to education, I have come to realize with much pain that many billions of Federal tax dollars have not brought the significant improvement we anticipated. There are even signs that we may be losing ground ... We can no longer afford another new program for each new problem, or another new agency for each old agency that has lost its vitality. We cannot tolerate more

WHAT THEY SAID IN 1974

centralized and Federal control. We cannot afford to enlarge, or even to continue with, a huge administrative apparatus that operates out of public view and beyond public control.

Before the House, Washington/
Human Events, 4-6:5.

Terry Herndon
Executive secretary,
National Education Association 1

I look forward to the day when the schools automatically receive the funds they need, and the Pentagon holds bake-sales to buy tanks.

San Francisco Examiner & Chronicle,
2-10:(This World)2.

John A. Howard
President, Rockford (Ill.) College 2

Among those groups that have defaulted on the obligation to mark the difference between right and wrong, and to uphold that difference vigorously, perhaps the most influential delinquent is the academic community. It is the colleges and universities which in our era gave us the Filthy Speech Movement starting us down the course which led to *Hair* and *Oh! Calcutta* and *The Dirtiest Show in Town*, and other such cultural effluvia which have now become commonplace in our society. It is on the campuses that we first saw brutalization unsuppressed, where arson and massive vandalism and the seizure of buildings inspired such feeble responses that such acts multiplied; and on the campuses that the chapters of the SDS, an organization overtly committed to violence, received the formal blessings of institutional authority. It is probable that college students living in dormitories constitute that group with the highest incidence of the use of marijuana, an illegal drug, of any large group in the country. And now on many campuses, a man and a woman student who are not married may live together with either overt or tacit approval of college officials.

Before Chamber of Commerce, Freeport, Ill.,
Jan. 15/Vital Speeches, 2-15:283.

3

... if the over-all college experience should be characterized by a continuing effort toward a true apprehension of human dignity, the result, I am confident, would be a unity and a vitality and a cumulative satisfaction which has been conspicuously absent in higher education for many years. If a college could, indeed, seriously engage in apprehending human dignity— apprehending not only in the sense of understanding, but also of achieving—if it could do that, then it would not lack for either students or financial support; and what is more, it would be sending out into the adventure of the world confident people of disciplined imagination prepared to grapple with even the most difficult problems of society.

At Rockford College convocation, Sept. 18/
Vital Speeches, 11-1:59.

Robert M. Hutchins
Chairman, Center for the Study of
Democratic Institutions; Former
president, University of Chicago 4

American higher education is unique. In no other nation does the university tangle up academic and athletic programs to the confusion of both. In England, the difference is that winning a boat race doesn't establish the merits of one university over another.

Los Angeles Times, 10-25:(3)10.

Jerome Kagan
Professor of Human Development,
Harvard University 5

Every year, psychologists and educators, administering intervention studies with poor children, demonstrate that sophisticated use of curriculums can facilitate intellectual ability. When educators say the poor are not educable, they mean that it is difficult to close the gap between poor and middle-class with respect to currently accepted levels of mastery.

U.S. News & World Report, 2-18:37.

Kenneth Keniston
Professor of Psychology, Yale University 6

There are few subjects that arouse as much passionate concern on the part of individual citizens as . . . the education of their children, the circumstances under which that education is conducted, whether it's integrated or non-integrated or closed and so on. You can bring out more people on those issues than on almost anything else. And the issues are deeply political in the sense that they involve all of the great tensions of the society: the questions of the relationship between the races, the questions of discipline and permissiveness, the questions of the cultivation of the diversity of individual talents as opposed to the promotion of . . . a smaller number, the questions of cooperation versus individual competition . . .

New York, Feb. 7/
The Washington Post, 2-8:(B)6.

Edward M. Kennedy
United States Senator, D–Massachusetts

1

In five years, the total resources committed by the [Nixon] Administration to the right-to-read program have been less than $40 million. If it were not so tragic, the contrast between the goal of removing illiteracy by 1980 and the level of expenditures of this Administration in pursuit of that goal would be absurd.

U.S. News & World Report, 8-19:37.

Clark Kerr
Former president, University of California

2

So much of higher education today, following a Golden Age of many triumphs, is now mired in an attitude of survivalism, is content to endure rather than to face constructively the new challenges.

San Francisco Examiner & Chronicle,
6-16:(This World)2.

John P. Leary
President, New College, Sausalito, Calif.;
Former president, Gonzaga University

3

I'm convinced that education is off on an enormous jag of premature professionalism—dentists, lawyers, street-cleaners. But the most profound vocation a person can have is to be a human being. Education has forgot what we are supposed to be, and life has become so empty for so many.

The New York Times, 12-1:20.

Philip Lesly
Public-relations counsel

4

We have achieved the mass production of "education." But far from being a cure for our ills, education has proved to be a foment. Education opens the mind not like a cork removed from a bottle but like the entire lid removed from a can. Everything is exposed at the same time and the cover can never be plugged back in. We have been mass-producing dissidents, whose expectations of influence have been built up but whose true role can never fulfill their deluded dreams.

Before Greater Kansas City Chapter,
Public Relations Society of America/
The National Observer, 10-26:15.

Clare Boothe Luce
Former American diplomat and playwright

5

. . . I never went to college. My parents couldn't afford it, and then I married very young. All my life, I have wanted the university experience. But where could a person of 40 or 50 go to college without feeling ridiculous and conspicuous? Education shouldn't be something you can get only in your 20s. I think an old-people's college would be positively jammed. Think how thrilling it would be to get your B.A. at 40 or a Ph.D. at 60!

Interview/U.S. News & World Report, 6-24:55.

Bryce MacKasey
Postmaster General of Canada

6

Education . . . promised to remold man. Education, we said, was the only real counterweight to man's animal nature. But in the '50s educators downgraded the humanities and universities became technical schools. Then, in the '60s, educators rationalized self-indulgence. They tolerated illegal drugs. They let boys and girls sleep together. They recognized student groups committed openly to violence. Finally, even those who condoned this in the name of truth and freedom could see that this wasn't exactly the freedom they had in mind. Man's animal nature is more in evidence than ever.

Before Audit Bureau of Circulation,
Chicago, Nov. 7/Vital Speeches, 12-1:121.

WHAT THEY SAID IN 1974

Harold C. Martin
President, Union College, Schenectady, N.Y. 1

I cannot for the life of me see how, especially in these times, an institution can hope to be good and to remain good unless it protects itself against dominance by a heavily tenured and aging faculty body. If we can learn anything from other institutions, the condition of the Civil Service and the church should have taught us that.

At New York State Board of Regents trustee conference, New York, March 5/ The New York Times, 3-6:21.

William J. McGill
President, Columbia University 2

Private higher education is caught in a cost squeeze that had already forced dangerously high tuitions and is forcing us into unhealthy dependence on public funds. Yet such funds are becoming increasingly crucial for our survival.

At Charter Day Convocation, Lincoln (Ill.) College, Feb. 10/ The New York Times, 2-11:24.

3

Our earlier successes in higher education have bred some curious ideas in the United States. Most middle-class parents believe that their children will be failures unless they complete a four-year college education. So many four-year institutions have been built that corporate and government personnel officers believe it to be necessary to demand a college degree for occupational entry in areas where college training clearly makes no sense. We have thus created the ridiculous situation in which a college degree is deemed necessary to be a policeman or to drive a truck or to operate a telephone switchboard. Legal pressures for equal opportunity in the United States have forced statistical standards of non-discrimination upon employers. Such pressures have generated a rapid deterioration in the quality level of the four-year college degree in many public institutions in the United States. Today's students understand very well that a piece of paper stating educational qualifications is more important for occupa-

tional entry than the educational experience itself.

At Mexican Institute of Culture, Mexico City, April 29/Vital Speeches, 6-1:496.

4

The basic difficulty with proposals that we [universities] engage in ethical instruction is that we are then required to define a preferred ethical system in order to teach it. While it is true that certain basic and timeless ethical concepts dominate the academic life, it is also true that universities must resist even well-intentioned pressures leading us toward moral orthodoxy. Ethical rules are currently devised and administered by the governance bodies of the major professions in the United States. These rules are deliberately kept out of university instructional programs because we do not wish to put universities into a posture of moral advocacy ... Moral advocacy is pure dynamite, as we have learned very painfully in the last decade. Why should we assume that, if we seek to inculcate a preferred ethical system, other moralists will not then use the university for purposes of their own? What principle could be used to bar the university from less-attractive forms of moral advocacy? There is the spectacle of the Free University in West Berlin, where moralism and zealotry have reached a point at which professors are threatened for teaching ideas which seem to violate the currently accepted orthodoxy. Berlin's Free University is no longer free, and consequently it is no longer a university.

At Columbia University commencement/ The National Observer, 6-15:17.

Charles Muscatine
Professor of English, University of California, Berkeley 5

Academic specialization has done a reasonably good job in the junior and senior years, when students are majoring; but nobody is worrying about the first two years. Very many lower-division [freshman and sophomore] students have not only not entered a major but do not even have much notion of what major to prepare for or how to look for one. Despite recent innovations in advising, most students are left free to roam through the great smorgasbord of thousands of courses, with only peer-group gossip and a necessarily superficial orientation and advising system to guide them.

Los Angeles Times, 4-29:(2)1.

Richard M. Nixon
President of the United States

1

. . . parents know that the education of their children can most effectively be carried out in neighborhood schools. They are naturally concerned when the courts, acting on the basis of complicated plans drawn up by far-away officials in Washington, D.C., order children bused out of their neighborhoods . . . A belief in the wisdom of the local communities and the parents of our school-children has been the guiding education philosophy of this Administration since we took office. The Federal government has a role to play in education, but that role must never place Federal employees—your employees—in the role of master social planners.

Radio address to the nation, Camp David, Md., March 23/The New York Times, 3-24:(1)26.

Harris H. Parker
Professor of Religion, Columbia (S.C.) College

2

We [in higher education] have done too much: lectured too often, tested on material "spoon fed," applauded intellectual conformity as if it were a virtue. In short, we have inadvertently encouraged dependence and stifled creativity. The time is ripe for change. Let us covenant among ourselves to provide for *all* students *some* opportunities within every course to determine their own curricula, to choose studies according to their own interests; and let us also design a program for *some* students within which they may determine with appropriate counsel virtually *all* of their own curricula. If our goal is the liberation of the human spirit, then the time is at hand to make a significant shift in educational management, to transfer to the student a larger share of responsibility for her own education. Such change does not mean that the professor will do less than before, play a reduced role in the educational process, but only that he will play a different role. He will do less *for* the student

and more *with* the student. He will function more often as a facilitator of individual inquiry than as a transmitter of information. No teacher, however well-intentioned, renders the student a genuine kindness when he acts as if vicarious learning were a possibility. It is not. It has never been. The fact is simple: We learn only what *we* learn. None can learn in our behalf. Let us beware lest our educational methods encourage the very dependence we seek to erase, and stifle the spark of creativity for which we yearn.

At Columbia College commencement, Aug. 16/Vital Speeches, 9-15:730.

John C. Raines
Assistant Professor of Religion, Temple University

3

The idea has taken hold that part of being middle-class parents means that you are going to send your kids to college. One of the ways you prove you are middle-class and stay middle-class and do right by the kids is send them to college. But, increasingly, people who are middle-class can't finance their kids' college education and are doing it on loans. You can't even get Federally guaranteed loans after your income rises above a certain level.

Interview, Tulpehocken, Pa./ Los Angeles Times, 1-16:(2)7.

John Rassias
Professor of Romance Languages, Dartmouth College

4

Language study should change the student who submits to its discipline. Language study is a route to maturity. Indeed, in language study as in life, if a person is the same today as he was yesterday, it would be an act of mercy to pronounce him dead and to place him in a coffin, rather than in a classroom. Language is a living, kicking, growing, fleeting, evolving reality, and the teacher should spontaneously reflect its vibrant and protean qualities.

Quote, 5-26:485.

Albert Shanker
President, American Federation of Teachers

5

Teachers could be a major force for social progress in this country if they were organized.

Yet they are powerless. They have never been consulted by a [U.S.] President on any major issue. Four days after [Gerald] Ford became President, who did he meet with? It was [AFL-CIO president George] Meany. He represents the largest bloc of organized workers in the country—and if we want a voice, we have to speak in a big one.

Time, 9-16:76.

John R. Silber
President, Boston University   1

The [increased tuition] costs are certainly having the effect of changing school communities to places of the rich who can afford it and the poor who can qualify for aid. We have increased financial aid every time there has been a tuition increase, but middle-income students are having increasing difficulty raising the money, and they can't qualify for aid. We either have to change the criteria for granting aid or deny these students an opportunity to attend college. If we change the criteria, we will also have to have more money, because there just isn't enough now to fund that kind of program.

U.S. News & World Report, 3-18:35.

Barbara A. Sizemore
Superintendent of Schools of the
District of Columbia   2

[On specialized vocational high schools]: ... maybe the general academic high school has had its day. If we really mean what we say about career development—that every career is respectable and that a student has a right to have work-study experience no matter whether he wants to be a lawyer or a plumber—then we've got to think in terms of those directions or else we're really not fulfilling the prophecy of career development. Ultimately we hope to make it so that a student could go part-time in one high school and part-time in another if he or she so desires.

Interview, Washington/
The Washington Post, 7-7:(B)1.

The important thing for me is not what grades my son makes, but what does he know how to *do?* That's what's important to me. I came out of Northwestern University and, listen, I was an honor student at Northwestern University, and one morning I woke up and I realized I didn't know anything! There I was, March 27, 1946, about to get a degree from Northwestern University, cum laude, and I didn't know anything! I didn't know how to make a living! There was no one knocking on my door asking for someone to translate Horace. There was no one asking me to translate ancient Greek. There was no one who was anxious to have somebody who could write poetry. And I didn't know how to do anything else! That was a profound observation for me.

Interview, Washington/
The Washington Post, 7-7:(B)4.

Samuel R. Spencer, Jr.
President, Davidson (N.C.) College   4

[On foreign-study programs]: ... an American college or university can no longer claim honestly to provide an adequate education if it fails to add a strong international dimension to its program. This is not to say that the student who chooses to remain at home cannot be an educated person. It is to say that the institution in which he studies must, in one way or another, create an international consciousness which makes all students aware of the world-wide dimensions of our society and their responsibilities to it. A program of international study, offering opportunities for all who will take advantage of it and leavening the home campus with those who return and with nationals of other countries, is important not only intrinsically but as the visible symbol of institutional interest and commitment. In former days, when the difficulties and expense of foreign travel and study restricted such opportunities to the affluent few, students had to learn of other cultures by other means. But today there is no substitute for first-hand experience, and no excuse for a failure to offer it to the student who wants to learn in depth.

At University of Bonn, West Germany,
June/Vital Speeches, 9-1:678.

Robert E. L. Strider
Chairman, Association of American Colleges 1

It is terribly important for the private [educational] institutions to survive. For them to fail would be not only a monstrous calamity intellectually, but financially as well. Think what it would cost the taxpayers to make up a big share of educating these young men and women . . . The independent colleges offer diversity and pluralism in higher education, and they carry out the educational experiments that later find their way into public institutions.
The Christian Science Monitor, 1-21:(F)3.

James W. Symington
United States Representative, D–Missouri 2

. . . we might need fewer czars for energy, industry, politics or morality if we had more articulate, no-nonsense schoolmasters hammering into the reluctant brain of the American child from the wheat fields to the suburb to the ghetto a sense of history, a knowledge of the classics with emphasis on the durable moral values and the dangers so well demonstrated by their neglect.
Before Sales Association of the Paper Industry/ The National Observer, 4-13:13.

George Wald
Professor of Biology, Harvard University 3

I was full of hope that the stirring-up of the universities [a few years ago] was going to produce the changes that seem to me the only hope for this society. All that came to pieces. We are now in the quiet third year. The struggles have a degree of hopelessness and helplessness I never dreamed would happen.
San Francisco Examiner, 7-12:36.

The Environment

Isaac Asimov
Author
1

Our lifetime may be the last that will be lived out in a technological society. If the world continues to behave as stupidly as it has behaved in the past, we are going to have an increase in population, an increase in violence. We will try to support the population by ripping up earth's resources, producing pollution at a greater and greater rate, ending, perhaps, in a nuclear war. The earth will have its oil burnt up, most of its most easily available coal used up, its metals distributed thinly over the entire world. We simply won't have the material basis to build up another technological civilization. The greater the population, the greater the pressure on technology to produce things. Also, there is a great deal of pressure to produce things that don't directly relate to the quantity of people in the world, but are useless, energy wasting. Socrates is reported to have looked over a bazaar in great wonder and said, "How very many things there are that I do not need." There are a great many things that we don't need.

*Interview, New York/
The Christian Science Monitor, 3-27:(F)1.*

Orin E. Atkins
Chairman, Ashland Oil, Inc.
2

We need to realize [that] both the economic and world political problems growing out of the energy crisis are complex and serious. They will not be solved by half-way measures and attempts to gloss over the facts. We only need to realize that the present economic crisis, with the rapid escalation of oil prices, is probably the most profound economic change which has occurred in the history of the world without resulting in a major war. The impact of higher oil prices is not restricted to the developed nations, for the penalty is much greater on the Third World, or under-developed nations. It is from this source that we face the most serious problem. Suppose you are [Indian Prime Minister Indira] Gandhi: Your borders are less than 1,000 miles from the unprotected sheikdoms on the East Coast of the Arab Peninsula; a number of your nationals are employed in these countries; you have the fourth largest army in the world and you have the atomic bomb at your disposal; your country is in ferment with famine and pestilence brought on by your own mistakes, but politically attributable to high costs for oil and resulting shortage of fertilizer. What would be your course of action? While your answer may seem farfetched today, it may not tomorrow.

*Before Cincinnati chapter,
Ohio Society of Certified Public Accountants,
Oct. 8/The New York Times, 10-20:(3)14.*

Carl E. Bagge
President, National Coal Association
3

The United States need never run out of its prized petroleum products as long as it has abundant coal and the national will to convert the solid fuel into a source of oil not only rich but guaranteed against upheavals in world supply. But to be strong enough to support a synthetic-oil industry later, the coal industry must be fully employed now. It can't make a living as a crisis industry or as stand-by for future needs. The Arab oil embargo spotlighted the nation's need for coal, and it would be a national energy blunder if the United States lapsed so far into euphoria over the lifting of that embargo as to revert to its former neglect of the fuel that represents its best promise of lasting energy independence.

*Before National Petroleum Refiners Association,
Miami, April 1/Vital Speeches, 5-15:466.*

Hans Bethe
Professor of Physics, Cornell University
1

If we follow the advice of these people [who oppose nuclear power, increased strip-mining and stepped-up off-shore oil exploration], we might as well go back into the cave right away. There would be incredible unemployment. Food production would be cut severely. In that direction lies catastrophe.

At City College, New York/
The New York Times, 12-14:58.

Z. David Bonner
President, Gulf Oil Company-U.S.
2

We must stop bickering about whether or not there is an oil shortage. There has been too much finger-pointing and not enough understanding and support. The energy industry desperately needs the active support of the Federal government, not its domination; its cooperation, not its time-consuming questioning and doubt.

Before Senate Permanent Subcommittee
on Investigations, Washington, Jan. 21/
Los Angeles Times, 1-22:(1)18.

Arch N. Booth
President, Chamber of
Commerce of the United States
3

[On the Arab oil embargo]: I think the Arabs have done us a favor in what they have done, because they are forcing us to face up to a crisis, and we people for some reason do better under crisis circumstances, frequently, than we do under normal circumstances. We are doing things now which will make us independent of the Arab nations in a short time, and it is forcing us to do things which will enable us to be in a position where this can never happen to us again, if we conduct ourselves in the right manner.

TV-radio interview/"Meet the Press,"
National Broadcasting Company, 3-10.

Norman E. Borlaug
Director, International Maize and
Wheat Improvement Center, Mexico City
4

There is no reserve of grains of any magnitude in the world today; and to give you a benchmark to go by, annual global consumption of grain is some 1.2 billion metric tons. That's enough to build a highway around the earth's equator 55 feet wide and six feet deep. But unlike macadam, which lasts 30 years, this road has to be rebuilt every year. And every year the world's population increases by about 76 million people. So this requires 28 million to 30 million metric tons of more grain every year.

Interview, Santiago, Chile/
The New York Times, 12-11:13.

Edmund G. Brown, Jr.
Secretary of State of California
5

For nearly 50 years, the oil companies have received massive tax breaks. Now it's time to let them know we are tired of being pushed around ... Less than a month ago, California motorists were forced to wait in long lines to buy gasoline [because of the shortage]. But now that the government has virtually met every oil-industry demand, the lines have suddenly disappeared. All of this makes me very suspicious ... The 65-cent-a-gallon gasoline price is a reality, small independent oil companies have been forced out of business, resumption of oil drilling off the shores of Santa Barbara has been approved and the Alaska pipeline is being readied. Just a year ago, the oil companies were finding their demands in these areas ignored by the American people. And so suddenly—by strange coincidence—we found ourselves in the midst of an energy shortage.

News conference, Sacramento, April 17/
Los Angeles Times, 4-18:(1)3.

Arthur F. Burns
Chairman, Federal Reserve Board
6

[Calling for conservation of gasoline through government action]: These might include a sizable tax on gasoline or on imports of oil or on automobiles according to their weight or horsepower ... We won't be able to drive our cars as much or take as many leisure trips as we are accustomed to. The automobile industry, already depressed, will suffer more. The recreation industry also would be affected more. And home-building, which is already in a decline, would be hurt more. [Nevertheless, unless

(ARTHUR F. BURNS)

stringent energy-cutting measures are taken,] we will be unable to persuade others [around the world] to do their part. Our rhetoric will be ridiculed around the world. [And unless the price of oil goes down,] there will be a massive redistribution of economic and political power among the countries of the world. This of itself carries dangers for our country's future.

Before Congressional Joint Economic Committee, Washington, Nov. 26/ Los Angeles Times, 11-28:(1)1.

Earl L. Butz
Secretary of Agriculture of the United States

1

Concern over our environment is well-founded. However, our people must strike a sensible trade-off in matters concerning the environment. We must help the nation come to its senses on environmental constraints that affect agriculture. Effective poisons and other means of predator control are a well-known environmental issue. People must decide whether they prefer the howl of the coyote to an economically priced sirloin. At a time when meat demand will be straining against supplies— and when all farm costs are increasing—every calf devoured by a coyote represents higher prices ranchers must receive when they sell their calves in order to cover their costs and to earn sufficient profit to keep producing. People must decide whether they prefer the absolute safety of the total ban on DES to the relative safety of DES-fed beef, which is of the same high quality but more abundant and more reasonably priced. People must decide whether they want to seriously curtail the use of antibiotics in feeds—if the action curtails cattlemen's ability to put more abundant, economical and nutritious beef in the retail meat counters. People must decide whether they want to place cost-increasing restrictions on the location and design of waste-disposal systems in cattle-feeding operations. If so, they must expect to pay the added costs which will fall on cattle producers. These are specific decisions the general public must ultimately make.

The general question is really this: At what point, for economic and other reasons, will we finally let objective science take dominance over the emotionalism connected with some of these environmental matters?

Before American National Cattlemen's Association, San Diego/ The National Observer, 2-2:11.

2

I wonder if some of those ill-informed, fuzzy thinking do-gooders who suggest that we eat one less hamburger per week to release more foodstuffs for the world are really serious. If so, they could make the first onslaught on this noble goal by reducing our dog and cat population by 50 per cent, which likewise would suddenly release more grain for the world. We could also make very substantial progress increasing grain supplies by reducing by 50 per cent our horse population—which no longer pulls the plow or the dray. Now, I am not out to limit horse numbers or to cut down on the number of pets. I do not advocate such a thing. On the other hand, if some people are really serious about proposing that we cut back on hamburgers in order to feed the world, then I want to know how they feel about the horses and the dogs and the cats they own.

Before American Society of Animal Science, College Park, Md., July 31/ Los Angeles Herald-Examiner, 7-31:(A)16.

Nicolae Ceausescu
President of Romania

3

One may often hear the pessimistic thesis according to which if the present population growth is maintained, the exhaustion of subsistence resources and a general food crisis will shortly and inevitably be arrived at ... [But] the world still possesses huge unused reserves [and] science will reveal new food resources and increase soil fertility on the entire earth's surface ... Every state has the sovereign right to promote that demographic policy and those measures which it considers most suitable, consonant with its national interests, without any outside interference.

At United Nations World Population Conference, Bucharest, Romania/ The Atlanta Constitution, 8-21:(B)2.

Barry Commoner
*Director, Center of Biology of
Natural Systems,
Washington University, St. Louis*
1

While the nation needs oil, it does not need the oil companies ... The oil crisis is not the running out of a limited natural resource. It is simply another aspect—blown up to a huge, potentially catastrophic scale—of the way oil companies do business for a profit.

*At energy conference, Washington, Feb. 16/
San Francisco Examiner & Chronicle, 2-17:(A)8.*

Donald C. Cook
Chairman, American Electric Power Company
2

... what is going to produce conservation is the high cost of energy. The price will necessarily continue upwards. In the past, energy was cheap and people kept the lights on in every room. Now I think people are properly becoming more frugal. Why? Because when they look at their electric-power bills, they get a shock. They can thank the environmentalists and the fuel merchants for that. The psychology of Americans is such that, without the discipline of price, conservation campaigns can't be expected to do very much. Price, not propaganda, will do a lot.

*Interview, New York/
Nation's Business, September:52.*

William O. Douglas
*Associate Justice, Supreme Court
of the United States*
3

[Saying damage to the environment has been caused partly by apathetic citizens]: How do you cook a frog? Do you put him in boiling water? No, he'd jump right out. Put him in cold water and heat it slowly. He'll like it at first, then will doze off, and soon he's cooked.

*Dallas, Feb. 7/
The Dallas Times Herald, 2-8:(B)1.*

4

Flowers, plants, trees are like one's neighbors. They have names, habits and temperaments. Get to know them; come on speaking terms with them; introduce them as friends to the children. The more one sees and appreciates the beauty of the earth, the less destructive he will be.

*At New York (City) Botanical Garden, May 9/
The New York Times, 5-10:33.*

Rene Dubos
*Environmentalist; Professor Emeritus of
Microbiology, Rockefeller University*
5

Human beings have always lived in an environment they have transformed. People talk about the lovely nature of England, France and Italy. There is not one part of England or France or Italy, or their countrysides, which has not been shaped, molded, created by human beings. People love to go to Vermont, but not to be in the midst of dense woods. We love Vermont because of those beautiful meadows and nice trails—but those are completely made by man. There would be no meadows in Vermont if it were not for man. From the beginning, human beings have transformed the wilderness. Wherever man has lived he has transformed nature. I am completely in favor of transforming nature; but one must do it with thought and knowledge, and not capriciously.

*Interview, New York/
Los Angeles Times, 11-28:(2)7.*

Paul R. Ehrlich
Professor of Biology, Stanford University
6

The population explosion is the most basic problem facing mankind today. It is highly unlikely that we will get through the next two decades without a major disaster resulting in the deaths of hundreds of millions of human beings ... The basic problem is that there is a momentum built into population growth. If, by a miracle, every couple in the world should decide today to limit themselves to just two children, the population would still continue to grow for a considerable time before zero population growth is finally reached. What's more, there is a limited amount of good that can be extracted from the earth. So even if we manage to stop population growth dead in its tracks, but continue an ever-expanding production and rape of the environment, we could still easily destroy the world.

Interview/Chicago Tribune, 9-4:(1)14.

WHAT THEY SAID IN 1974

Gerald R. Ford
President of the United States

1

Everyone can now see the pulverizing impact of energy price increases on every aspect of the world economy . . . All nations have been adversely affected by price increases. When nations use their resources as political weapons against others, the result is human suffering . . . Sovereign nations cannot allow their policies to be dictated or their fate decided by artificial rigging and distortion of world commodity markets. No one can foresee the extent of damage nor the end of the disastrous consequences if nations refuse to share nature's gifts for the benefit of all mankind . . . A global strategy must seek to achieve fuel prices which provide a strong incentive to producers but which do not seriously disrupt the economies of the consumer. We recognize the desires of the producers to earn a fair share or a fair price for their oil as a means of helping to develop their own economies. But exorbitant prices can only distort the world economy, run the risk of a world-wide depression and threaten the breakdown of world order and world safety.

At World Energy Conference, Detroit,
Sept. 23/U.S. News & World Report, 10-7:42.

J. Paul Getty
Industrialist

2

Conservation is very important, and some people think it will take care of itself. It won't. But the modern world is more or less based on oil, isn't it? Without oil, we'd go back one or two generations. I can still remember, about the close of the 19th century, going out for a ride with my father. He was very well-off. He had two horses, a coach and a carriage. But the only oil he needed was a little lubricating oil on the axles. I don't know how many people would be willing to go back to that.

Interview, Woking, England/Time, 2-18:18.

William R. Gould
Executive vice president,
Southern California Edison Company

3

. . . [I] have a few suggestions for critics of nuclear power. Everyone seriously concerned about health and safety, and about the environment, must begin realizing that there are no absolutes in life. Distasteful as it may be, we have to think in terms of costs and benefits, of tradeoffs, of comparative effects. As far as I know, every group of experts that has done a comparative study of realistic energy forms has concluded that nuclear power is the least harmful to the environment and at least as safe as any alternative. Demanding that all effects and risks be kept to zero represents an obstructionalism that has contributed more to our problems than it ever will to our solutions.

At Atomic Industrial Forum conference,
Washington, Oct. 28/
Vital Speeches, 12-15:135.

Mike Gravel
United States Senator, D–Alaska

4

Our energy crisis is the result not of some byzantine conspiracy on the part of private industry, but the consequence of virtually no coherent public policy for the single most important factor in American life: energy. Simply put, we have failed to adequately plan for our needs in this highly cybernated society of the last half of the 20th century.

Quote, 2-3:98.

John Hannah
Deputy Secretary General, United
Nations World Food Conference

5

Nobody can say there aren't going to be a lot of people going to die [of starvation in the world] . . . [However,] I am satisfied the world can feed whatever number of people there are going to be for the balance of this century. It isn't going to be easy, but it can be done . . . We've got to deal with this one without too much regard for national boundaries, or religious differences, or color differences, or the attitudes of people, or even politics. Feeding the hungry people of the world should be an apolitical situation.

Interview, United Nations, New York/
The Christian Science Monitor, 11-4:1,4.

C. Howard Hardesty
Executive vice president,
Continental Oil Company

1

The United States has the strongest economy in the world. In most circles, this nation is the most envied. We owe a good deal of that advantage to the years of cheap and abundant energy provided by the petroleum industry. Just *how* cheap has it been? The United States has only 6 per cent of the world's population, but it consumes 30 per cent of the world's energy. Industry critics rattle off these figures. But they do not mention that for 20 years we've used that 30 per cent of the world's energy for only 12 per cent of the world's cost of energy. This illustrates that the petroleum industry has served the country well. Historically, petroleum products have been the most stable element of our economy. At the same time, the very abundance of low-cost energy masked its importance to our way of life. The minute scarcity arises, how the wolves come out of the woods!

Before Soap and Detergent Association,
Boca Raton, Fla., Jan. 17/
Vital Speeches, 2-15:275.

Wayne L. Hays
United States Representative, D—Ohio

2

[Referring to Administrator William Simon's Federal Energy Office]: All they say is that fuel prices must go up 10 per cent. People are not fooled by this. I mention "Simple Simon" to an audience back home and they stand up and applaud because they know him for the phony and fake that he is. If we're going to impeach anyone around here, it ought to be him.

Before the House, Washington, Feb. 4/
The Washington Post, 2-5:(A)17.

Thor Heyerdahl
Explorer

3

I feel that the [current] Law of the Sea Conference is the most important ever held. But I'm very much concerned, because I have the feeling that the delegates, most of whom seem to be lawyers and politicians, are discussing how to divide and make the best use of an apple which is on the way to rot. And they leave it rotting while they try to find a way to divide it ... People seem to think that the ocean is endless. But it is small and vulnerable. If people can step onto a pile of reeds off Africa and step off onto Barbados a few weeks later, that shows how really small it can be.

Caracas, Venezuela/
The Christian Science Monitor, 7-12:5C.

Ernest F. Hollings
United States Senator, D—South Carolina

4

There was an old saying aboard ship in World War II: "When in danger, when in doubt, run in circles, scream and shout." Such is Washington's reaction to the energy crisis.

Quote, 1-13:26.

Huang Shu-tse
Deputy Minister of Health of the
People's Republic of (Communist) China

5

The superpowers' false alarm of a "population explosion" reminds us of the notorious Malthus, who more than 170 years ago driveled about the impossibility of production's ever catching up with population. Today, the world's population has more than trebled that of Malthus' time, but there has been a much greater increase in the material wealth of society.

At United Nations World Population
Conference, Bucharest, Romania/
The New York Times, 8-26:10.

Frank N. Ikard
President, American Petroleum Institute

6

The [oil-shortage] crisis has been coming for a long time, and many people have been talking about it in industry and in government for, oh, 10 years. The thing that accelerated it, of course, was the [Arab] embargo. But we simply were not developing our resources in this country in a way that was keeping up with our demand. We were not developing the [Alaskan] North Slope, the largest oil field in the Western Hemisphere. We were not developing our marine [off-shore] resources. Our production in Texas and Louisiana and other places was going

(FRANK N. IKARD)

down, and we were administering our import program so that we were discouraging the construction of refining capacity. All these factors could lead but to one final conclusion, and that was a shortfall. It is not contrived. It is very real. And I think people should understand it's going to be around for a long time ... most of the reasons that we are not developing the resources have been government decisions—the failure to build the [Alaskan] pipeline, for instance, has been the deterrent in the development of the North Slope. That was a government decision. The failure to develop the public lands was because there had not been lease-sales to make those lands available. I'm not suggesting this was a conscious decision on the part of government to bring about any shortfall. This is more complicated than just a simple thing of who's at fault. We're all at fault in that we have never had any concern about our energy uses. We've been very extravagant, and when people talked about there being some limitation, no one really listened.

Interview, Washington/
Los Angeles Times, 2-15:(1)30.

Fred C. Ikle
Director, Arms Control and Disarmament
Agency of the United States   *1*

[Warning about possible destruction of the ozone layer in the stratosphere by nuclear war]: We do not know how much ozone depletion would occur from a large number of nuclear explosions—it might be imperceptible, but it also might be almost total. We do not know how long such depletion would last—less than one year or over 10 years. And above all, we do not know what this depletion would do to plants, animals and people. Perhaps it would merely increase the hazard of sunburn. Or perhaps it would destroy critical links of the intricate food chain of plants and animals, and thus shatter the ecological structure that permits man to remain alive on this planet. All we know is that we do not know.

Before Council on Foreign Relations, Chicago,
Sept. 5/The New York Times, 9-6:12.

Henry M. Jackson
United States Senator, D—Washington   *2*

The fact is that the international oil cartel has run up oil prices at will. This plus the dollar drain poses a continuing threat to the American economy that can be removed only by a massive and sustained effort to achieve self-sufficiency in energy ... Creating a self-sufficient energy industry will require enormous investments. But when this program is underway, we're going to have so much business in this country [that] there won't be an idle person who is capable of working who won't have a job.

At St. Patrick's Day dinner, Cranston, R.I.,
March 17/San Francisco Examiner, 3-18:8.

Jesse L. Jackson
President, Operation PUSH (People
United to Save Humanity)   *3*

[On the fuel shortage]: When we consider that 20 companies own 86 per cent of the oil wells and 93 per cent of the pipelines and 75 per cent of the service stations, that is control of production and distribution. In the case of the movies, they [film companies] cannot own [legally] Hollywood movie lots and own theatres; they had to break it up. In the case of the [TV] networks, they can own only five stations or it would be monopoly. But these [oil] companies own the oil wells, the refineries and the service stations and even control the research at government and public expense ... There's more evidence that we're looking at the laws of monopoly than the laws of shortage.

At dinner for Operation PUSH, Chicago/
The Hollywood Reporter, 2-26:10.

Thomas L. Judge
Governor of Montana   *4*

The pressures to mine our coal, pump our oil and build electric generation and gasification plants will increase daily. Carried to its extreme, an unlimited energy-growth policy would simply mean that more agricultural lands will be disturbed and taken out of production, and that our water resources would be irretrievably committed to industrial development. And unless the demand for energy is reduced, we will never catch up. Consequently, there would be no opportunity to expand our agricultural production, and the effects on the nation's and the world's food supply would be devastating... I would be a hypocrite if I did not mention the fact that hundreds of thousands of men, women and little children are starving to death in the worst famine that has ever occurred in the southern hemisphere of this planet. I mention these grim circumstances because the fact remains that we now have the productive capabilities, in our abundance of rich agricultural lands, manpower and technology, to substantially limit this human suffering.

Before Federation of Rocky Mountain States,
East Glacier, Mont., Sept. 4/
The New York Times, 9-5:21.

Henry A. Kissinger
Secretary of State of the
United States

1

... the energy situation poses severe economic and political problems for all nations. Isolated solutions are impossible. Even those countries, like Canada and the United States, capable of solving the energy problem by largely national means, would still suffer because of the impact on them of a world economic crisis. Consumer or producer, affluent or poor, mighty or weak—all have a stake in the prosperity and stability of the international economic system ... this challenge can be met successfully only through concerted international action. Its impact is controllable if we work together; it is unmanageable if we do not.

At Washington Energy Conference, Washington,
Feb. 11/The New York Times, 2-12:20.

Richard Lamm
Governor-elect of Colorado

2

Yes, we've [Colorado] got natural resources and, yes, they're needed by the rest of the country and, yes, Colorado is very definitely a part of the United States. But we do not intend to be the coal bin of the United States. We've looked at West Virginia and we've said that is not the kind of future we want. We're not saying, no, you can't have our coal, our oil. But

we sure as hell are saying that you're going to pay for the [environmental] impact. We're not going to be left with the boomtowns and the immense tax burdens and the wasted landscape, with no money to pay for it. We're saying, to the developers, that the cost of taking a ton of coal or a barrel of oil out of Colorado does not end with the technological costs as in the past. There are social costs as well—schools, sewers, parks, roads. Those are costs for the developer, and the ultimate user, not the Colorado taxpayer alone.

Los Angeles Times, 12-29:(1)14.

Ralph Lapp
Physicist

3

Back of all the charges the anti-nuclear [-power] people make, it isn't anti-nuclear. It's anti-growth. Five years down the road I see the nation in a tight bind on the generation of electric energy. Given a series of black-outs, I believe some people who are now considered heroes for opposing nuclear power may be castigated as villains.

San Francisco Examiner & Chronicle,
11-10:(B)4.

Charles A. Lindbergh
Environmentalist, Aviator

4

I think it is inevitable that we come to government control of natural resources. I see no way to preserve world resources without that control. Obviously, we have to have oil and energy in the future. But how do we balance this with where the lines go and how much is taken?

Interview, Woking, England/Time 2-18:18.

Louis B. Lundborg
Former chairman, Bank of America

5

The current energy crisis provides us with a dress rehearsal, the trial run of a drama that we must some day see enacted on a much larger stage. With this early warning we have the blessing of time to plan an orderly transition into an era that could be catastrophic if we allowed it to overtake us without preparation.

At Western Assembly on the Changing World
of Work, Carmel, Calif., May 31/
San Francisco Examiner, 6-1:1.

WHAT THEY SAID IN 1974

Marvin Mandel
Governor of Maryland

1

... you practice conservation when you have people convinced that there's a problem. It's very difficult to do it when they aren't convinced. And right now they're not convinced that there's a gasoline problem. And they're obviously right about not being convinced because the stations are just loaded with gasoline. It's impossible to talk to one gasoline [station] owner who's having any problem getting gas. In fact, we're getting complaints from station owners about the companies trying to dump gas on them, and forcing them to sell it. And there are price wars going on now in the state of Maryland, in gas. So conservation is not going along that well. In the state agencies, the state departments, sure we can control that. With the public, we can't ...
Interview/The Washington Post, 10-20:(K)3.

Mike Mansfield
United States Senator, D–Montana

2

What Watergate did to public confidence with regard to the nation's politics, the energy crisis has done in the realm of the nation's economy. Grave uncertainties have arisen. It is not merely a question of long lines at the filling stations and slower speeds on the highways. The implications of the shortage are seen to extend far beyond the gas tank into every aspect of our society. Today, the petroleum situation threatens the jobs, the business and even the basic maintenance of the homes of millions of Americans.
Television address, Washington, Feb. 1/
The New York Times, 2-2:11.

William F. May
Chairman, American Can Company

3

For 10 years or more, thoughtful analysts have warned of approaching [energy] shortages. For at least five years, leaders in industry and in ecological sciences have been predicting the very problems that face us today. The government has done nothing, and the total absence of planning is a scandal of appalling dimensions. Mistrust of technology and industry haunts us all. We have the astonishing situa-tion that the current Federal energy agency cannot, as a matter of government policy, use the services of anyone from the energy industries. For an administration to assume that representatives from an entire industry should be so tainted as to be unqualified for government service in the field of their expertise is to reveal, in my opinion, a deep and destructive cynicism. The nation is poorer for it.
Before National Association of Secondary
School Principals, Atlantic City, N.J.,
March 5/Vital Speeches, 4-15:403.

Tom McCall
Governor of Oregon

4

We all have an environment, operating to the laws of nature regardless of what we do to it. But what we do to it may make it unsuitable for habitation by such a complex creature as man ... What we can do is to think and talk about the environments we're living in and try to change what we mutually believe needs changing. But there should be a process available to enable us to reach our decisions—a process, for instance, that will enable us to preclude hucksterism in land sales ... a process that will make us think twice before tearing down a residential neighborhood for business development simply because it's economically feasible ... Think about the decisions made on the basis of expediency, tradition and short-term economic considerations ... Think about whether you need more pavement for private cars or more buses to use the pavement that already exists. Think about the loss of revenue and brainpower that a city suffers when it allows itself to become so unlivable that it forces the loss of land to the buildings that make up suburbia ... I think we're here on this earth in temporary stewardship, and have no right to pass onto future generations a land surface made up of patent pavements, mouldy boots, beer bottles and garbage. We have no right to cover today's river valleys—today's and tomorrow's prime sources of food—with anything except agricultural crops.
At meeting sponsored by University of
California and the Planning and
Conservation League, San Francisco/
The Christian Science Monitor, 7-5:12.

Michael McCloskey
Executive director, Sierra Club

1

[On nuclear power plants] : We are not convinced that anyone knows how safe the emergency core cooling system is and what the risk is of a significant accident. We do not think it is responsible to proliferate radioactive wastes whose safekeeping cannot be guaranteed by those who benefit from their production. And we are profoundly disturbed at the revelations of the dangers of illegal diversion of fissile materials. We believe society should have satisfying answers for these problems before it permits more nuclear plants to be built. Thus, we are calling for a halt in licensing new plants until answers are forthcoming. If the answers can soon be found, the industry has nothing to worry about. It merely needs to learn to speak understandably and convincingly. But if the answers do not exist, and cannot be found in a reasonable time, can we all afford to gamble so much? We are gambling with people's lives, with the well-being of future generations, and with prodigious sums of capital that may affect the viability of our economy.

Before American Nuclear Society,
Portland, Ore./The Christian Science Monitor,
9-23:14.

Ian L. McHarg
Professor of Regional Planning,
University of Pennsylvania

2

Man is an epidemic, multiplying at a super-exponential rate, destroying the environment upon which he depends and threatening his own extinction. He treats the world as a storehouse existing for his delectation. He plunders, rapes, poisons and kills this living system, the biosphere, in ignorance of its workings and its fundamental value.

Los Angeles Times, 12-18:(4)13.

A. J. Meyer, Jr.
Associate director, Center for Middle
Eastern Studies, Harvard University;
Authority on oil

3

The American public, after facing a year's barrage of almost totally undiluted banality on the subject of energy, is now being offered occasional bits of advice based on analysis and good sense. One example is President Ford's suggestion that "Project Independence" be renamed "Project Interdependence"—implying recognition that America will depend heavily on imported crude oil for at least another decade and that we had better keep it flowing. Another example is the growing recognition . . . that not only Arabs raise oil prices but so too do Iranians, Indonesians, Britons, Norwegians, Russians, Venezuelans, and even the Chinese . . . A third example is the spreading recognition that the industrial world's double-digit inflation receives only about two percentage points of its upward thrust from oil-price hikes and that the remaining eight to 10 points is "home made" in various ingenious ways.

Before Near East Foundation, New York/
The Christian Science Monitor, 12-9:16.

Robert T. Monagan
Assistant Secretary for Congressional and
Intergovernmental Affairs, Department of
Transportation of the United States

4

Since the [energy] crunch began, the attitude of the people, the Congress and the Administration has changed. Daylight Savings Time has been fought for 20 years that I can remember, yet it passed in a month recently. A year ago, there would have been howls of protest over lowering the speed limit. Today, motorists are getting used to a 55 MPH limit, and safety experts predict 5,000 lives a year will be saved in the nation as a result.

Los Angeles Herald-Examiner, 2-17:(A)12.

Rogers C. B. Morton
Secretary of the Interior of the United States;
Chairman, Federal Energy Resources Council

5

We have to get the people to understand that the standard of living, and the general well-being of this country and our friends throughout the world who are also consumers, depends on reducing our dependence on these very high-priced [foreign] fuels, which are causing us to transfer wealth out of this country at a rate of $23 billion a year. And the only short-term way we can do this is through the conservation of

(ROGERS C. B. MORTON)

fuel. The question is: Do we do this by controlling and rationing—either by coupon or by inconvenience such as the Arab embargo produced—or do we do this by self-imposed discipline? And do we have to nudge that self-discipline by arbitrarily raising the price through taxes? If the American people will do this, we'll have the least damaging effect on the economy. If the American people decide they don't want to do this, we'll have to come up with some tougher turkey.

Interview, Washington/
Los Angeles Times, 11-10:(1)4.

1

The real [resource] policy question we face is not either conservation or development. The major decision is how do we balance these two strategies. How much conservation can the economy withstand? What should be the pace of resource development? We are well aware that U.S. energy consumption cannot continue to grow at 4 to 5 per cent a year; but it is equally obvious that energy conservation must be blended with a carefully and deliberately planned program of resource development.

At energy-policy hearing sponsored by Energy
Resources Council, Washington, Dec. 9/
Los Angeles Herald-Examiner, 12-9:(A)1.

Ralph Nader
Lawyer; Consumer advocate

2

[Saying nuclear power plants are not safe] : If the public knew what the facts were and if they had to choose between nuclear reactors and candles, they would choose candles.

The New York Times Magazine, 2-10:13.

Gaylord Nelson
United States Senator, D—Wisconsin

3

[The oil shortage demonstrates] unequivocally that mankind can stumble blindly into a resource crisis ... Population growth, greater affluence, technological explosion and a generally increased tempo of human activity have combined, at our moment in history, to burden the world's resources to an extent our fore-

fathers never imagined possible. [The nation has paid] a terrible price in unemployment, restricted mobility, economic retardation, uncertainty, and unplanned change in everything from personal life-styles to urban development [because of the energy crisis]. This happened in energy because there never was a serious attempt to measure the world oil supply or to calculate the implications of a dramatic rise in gasoline and oil-product consumption. Consequently, refinery construction and oil exploration in the U.S. lagged, and serious research to develop substitute sources of non-polluting energy was virtually nonexistent.

Luxemburg, Wis., March 30/
The Dallas Times Herald, 3-31:(A)9.

4

The pollution crisis and the energy crisis are merely different sides to the same coin, and both must be dealt with together. To try to solve an energy crisis while blinding ourselves to environmental problems, or vice versa, as some have been advocating, would be a fool's course. A future of poisoned air, a gutted landscape and dead seas—but abundant energy—would be as insufferable as one with pure air and water, but no heat, light or transportation.

Quote, 4-21:365.

Richard M. Nixon
President of the United States

5

[On the oil shortage] : ... regardless of the success we have in increasing petroleum imports and in stabilizing prices through diplomatic means, we must continue to move forward toward achieving a capacity for self-sufficiency in energy right here at home. America is a rich, a strong and a good country. We must set for ourselves this goal: We must never again be caught in a foreign-made crisis where the United States is dependent on any other country, friendly or unfriendly, for the energy we need to produce our jobs, to heat our homes, to furnish our transportation for wherever we want to go ... The distance between the winter of 1974 and the springtime of energy independence for the United States remains great. We must proceed with confidence in our ability to do the job. Far more importantly, we must act now, as one people, to do the job that must be done ... Where energy is concerned, we, the American people, shall be the sole masters of our fate.

Radio address to the nation, Jan. 19/
The New York Times, 1-20:(1)36.

1

... the whole world has become more prosperous. The whole world demands more energy. And even if there had not been an oil embargo in the Mideast, we would have an energy problem. I said that over a year and a half ago, and I kept repeating it to the Congress. And the thing to do, rather than to blame the big oil companies and say they could do something about it—they could if they had the oil. The thing to do is to develop the resources of this country so that we don't depend on any foreign country for our energy ... How are you going to do it? The way to do it is to increase supplies. We should deregulate natural gas, which is the cleanest fuel, for example, that we have. We should move on the environmental field to relax some of those inhibitions so that we can develop our coal resources and use our coal. We could do that because the United States is blessed with having approximately half the coal in the world, and we're foolish not to develop it, and we can eventually develop a clean fuel out of coal. And third, we should move to develop those energy resources—I refer to shale oil, I refer to Elk Hills and others—which exist in the United States in great abundance. In the long term, of course, we must move forward with the development of nuclear power. It is disgraceful that the United States, that broke the secrets of the atom and was first in that field, has been so far behind in developing nuclear power for peaceful uses, because it is clean fuel and it is safe fuel and we should move forward in that area as well ... The truth is there is an energy shortage. The way to deal with that shortage is not to demagogue about it, but do something about it; and it's time for the Congress to get off its something and do something about it right now.

Before Executive Club, Chicago, March 15/
The New York Times, 3-16:12.

Robert Packwood
United States Senator, R – Oregon

2

Touted by many observers to be the sea monster in this ocean of energy problems are the 8 to 20 major oil companies that dominate the market. The long tentacles which grip the consumer take the name of "vertical integration." From top to bottom, the majors control every aspect of oil. They control exploration, drilling, refining, transportation and retailing of the product. The oil companies own every rung in the ladder, from oil field to fuel tank. And when every rung in the ladder is controlled, the price of using the top rung is easily manipulated.

Quote, 11-10:434.

Charles H. Percy
United States Senator, R – Illinois

3

[On the energy shortage]: I think I could really just summarize the feelings of people by simply saying in summary form: We're in a hell of a mess. The American public doesn't know who or what to believe ... We don't even know how much of a real energy crisis we actually have—whether there are only scattered or regional shortages, or, as some have told me, perhaps we have a wholesale fraud being perpetrated on the American public.

At Senate Permanent Subcommittee
on Investigations hearing, Washington,
January/U.S. News & World Report, 2-4:14.

Russell W. Peterson
Chairman, Federal Council on
Environmental Quality

4

I believe we can markedly reduce the demand curve [for energy] for the next 20 or 30 years, and produce an amount of energy within our own shores and, as a result, stop usurping so much of the world's energy as we have been doing ... I see this as resulting in a marked acceleration in the movement to mass transit, and that in turn would lead to making the central cities more viable, making them a more attractive place to shop, to go for entertainment, to live. It might well play a key role in helping to rejuvenate our central cities.

Interview, Washington/
Los Angeles Times, 2-10:(1)25.

John Portman
Architect; Urban developer
1

My total interest and concern is the central city. That's our greatest need and our greatest opportunity. We have to create a new downtown atmosphere and a new downtown environment... If we build housing first, there's no reason why anyone would want to live in it. That's why the commercial rebuilding must come first. Create the amenities, the environment, and then the housing will follow.
Interview, Atlanta/
The National Observer, 1-12:22.

Allen E. Pritchard, Jr.
Executive vice president,
National League of Cities
2

Urban areas cannot continue to grow by under-utilizing existing facilities and creating new ones. Urban development can no longer consume a disproportionate share of the world's resources. Scarcity diminishes the differences between old cities and new ones. The so-called central-city problems are in fact urban problems. The central-city cycle can be and is being repeated at other places. We are eyeball-to-eyeball with the necessity of changing a way of inefficient urban development born in abundance and no longer supportable in a world where scarcity demands conservation.
At National League of Cities meeting,
Houston/The New York Times, 12-4:21.

John R. Quarles
Deputy Administrator, Environmental
Protection Agency of the United States
3

[Before the House votes on legislation covering strip mining, which is] one of the great and still unresolved environmental issues confronting this country, [the Representatives] will have been cornered by lobbyists and bombarded by statistics. And yet, after all of this, few of them will know what you [who live in strip-mining areas] know or will have seen what you have seen. They will not have seen the miles of ugly scars which encircle the mountains like the coils of an angry snake. They will not have seen the gutted hillsides, raked by the claws of rushing water. They will not have seen the streams choked with sediment. Most of them will never know the acrid stench of a pond or marsh fouled by acid runoff of mine water. Few of them will ever hear of the roar of a power shovel as it chews into a hillside. The nation needs more coal. Much of it will have to be strip-mined. This cannot be avoided. What can be avoided, however, is the senseless destruction which has marked strip mining in the past. No longer will we tolerate those who would make a wasteland out of our mountains. No longer will we tolerate those who would flood our rivers and streams with acid and sediment. No longer will we tolerate those who care only about quick profits, and nothing for the land. The days of the big raid on our nation's resources are over. Controlled development of these resources is the only acceptable course.
At town meeting, DuBois, Pa., July 11/
The New York Times, 7-12:5.

Jennings Randolph
United States Senator, D–West Virginia
4

[On the energy crisis]: I have been warning for years that we had no fuels-and-energy policy. For example, I testified before the Senate Interior Committee in 1961 and said: "Every year that passes in which we become more and more dependent on foreign oil to buttress our national economy and security perhaps is one year nearer disaster... We are gambling with our country's future"... I blame in part the Administrations, both Democratic and Republican. I blame in part the Congress, and both parties there. I blame in part the producers of petroleum. I blame in part, of course, the failure of the American people themselves to come to grips with these problems, because they assumed that we're just going to have an easy time of it. That which we acquire too easily, we tend to value too lightly.
Interview, Washington/
U.S. News & World Report, 1-28:68.

Dixy Lee Ray
Chairman, Atomic Energy Commission
of the United States
5

Everybody's in favor of resolving the energy crisis and everybody is in favor of preserving the environment. But the people in the North-west, where the big coal deposits are, don't want their terrain upset; and the people in the Northeast, who need heating fuel the most, don't want an oil port and refineries on their coast; and some of the [consumerist Ralph] Nader people don't want any nuclear plants at all generating electric power because of some theoretical dangers. I understand these conflicts, but this isn't a perfect world. Somebody—and I mean every one of us—has to make some sacrifices.

Quote, 5-12:438.

1

It's important to emphasize that nuclear power has [safety] problems. But the job [of protection and safety] has been done well. And there has been no serious event that has hurt the public or done any damage. Nuclear power, properly handled, is the safest, cleanest, most versatile . . . it will probably be [in the future] the primary way we generate electricity.

Accepting Man of Science Award of Los Angeles chapter of ARCS Foundation, June 22/ Los Angeles Times, 6-25:(4)2.

Abraham A. Ribicoff
United States Senator, D—Connecticut

2

[On the oil shortage] : The consumer . . . is faced with major disruptions in his life-style—reduced driving, early-morning darkness, school and factory closings, chilly homes . . . At the same time, the oil companies are reaping the greatest profits in their histories . . . They have oil stocks 5 per cent higher than at this time last year. And they enjoy the lowest effective tax rate of all U.S. manufacturing concerns. In other words, while the consumer is suffering, the [oil] industry seems to be receiving a bonanza. How should we . . . explain the situation to the American people?

At Senate Permanent Subcommittee on Investigations, Washington, January/ U.S. News & World Report, 2-4:15.

W. F. Rockwell, Jr.
Chairman, Rockwell International

3

[On the energy shortage] : . . . it is our system which, in response to special-interest groups with legitimate arguments, has brought on this shortage. Let's say you prohibited the use of coal wherever possible because it is a dirtier fuel than petroleum products. Let's say you don't permit the power plants to use the types of coal or oil that are most plentiful. Let's say you pegged the price of natural gas at a level which discouraged exploration and at the same time encouraged excessive use. You imposed smog-control requirements so rigid that they led to devices which in fact contributed to over-use of gasoline. You limited off-shore [oil] drilling for esthetic reasons. You halted development of the largest oil deposit in North America [in Alaska] on ecological grounds. You stopped the construction of nuclear-energy plants because local communities objected to them. The end result would be inevitable: an energy shortage. And this is exactly what's happened. Our system has produced these types of obstacles and this end result. True, each obstacle was raised for a persuasive reason. But the cumulative result has been the most acute energy shortage in American history.

*Before Society of Automotive Engineers, Detroit, Feb. 26/**

John C. Sawhill
Administrator, Federal Energy Administration

4

[On "Project Independence"] : It certainly isn't a government gimmick, [but] I don't think any of us feel that this country can be completely self-sufficient [in energy] —ever. We will always be dependent on foreign sources for some of our petroleum supplies and I think we always should be, because these supplies can be produced more cheaply than domestic supplies. The thing we should avoid is being so dependent on foreign sources that future embargos could seriously affect our economy or . . . our foreign policy.

Chicago/The Christian Science Monitor, 9-13:4.

5

The energy problem is international in scope and every bit as perilous as World Wars I and II. The price and availability of oil will determine whether several million human beings live or starve to death, and whether millions in the

WHAT THEY SAID IN 1974

(JOHN C. SAWHILL)

industrial world will continue to be productive and secure. It is the world-wide question of survival.

At Los Angeles Area Chamber of Commerce Business Outlook Conference/ Los Angeles Herald-Examiner, 11-24:(G)5.

Walter Scheel
Foreign Minister of West Germany

1

[On the shortages of oil and other natural resources around the world]: We are all feeling depressed. Things cannot go on like this. No one with a clear head and feeling heart should still be able to sleep calmly. There is a growing feeling of frustration and inadequacy, of uncertainty and helplessness. The ground on which we stand is shaking. The familiar landmarks have gone. Data we could rely on yesterday are no longer valid today. And who knows what they will be tomorrow?

Before United Nations General Assembly, New York/The New York Times, 4-14:(3)1.

William E. Simon
Administrator, Federal Energy Office

2

I realize that many people still doubt that we have a [gasoline] shortage, but there definitely is one. I have been trying to stress this in numerous testimonies and public appearances throughout this past year. We would have been confronted with shortages even without the Arab nations' [oil] embargo. The embargo heightened everyone's awareness of the problem. If the Arabs lift the embargo in the weeks ahead and if, through our efforts to conserve and distribute equitably the oil that is available, we get through this difficult period, many people will say: "There was no shortage at all. It was contrived by the oil companies to get higher prices. It was contrived by the [Nixon] Administration to get Watergate off page 1." I am aware of this danger. However, our Number 1 job is to educate the American people that there is, in fact, a shortage facing our country and that we must not only do what is necessary to manage it in the short run, but also take the necessary steps now to develop our domestic

resources which hold the answer in the long run. My point is that the energy crisis is the most infinitely solvable problem we face if we take the necessary actions now.

Interview, Washington/ U.S. News & World Report, 1-14:16.

3

[Criticizing those who predicted that the energy shortage would create a disastrous situation]: Contrary to what one reads in the papers, I have patience. Remember, in November and December, the "experts"—I use quotes, some experts!—made predictions of massive unemployment and the rest. Did all these things occur? Brownouts? Unemployment? We opted for comfort at the expense of gasoline. Actually, unemployment went from 4.7 per cent to 5.2 per cent, and, as far as we can determine, the relation of an energy shortage to these figures is less than one-half of 1 per cent . . . I have had a difficult time with Congress and the critics. Nit pickers, cheap-shot critics. Cynics. Cynics are not what made this country great.

Los Angeles Herald-Examiner, 3-25:(A)6.

Charles E. Spahr
Chairman, Standard Oil Company of Ohio; Chairman, American Petroleum Institute

4

[Saying the petroleum industry should face the energy crisis with a united front]: We're in a battle for survival, a national economic battle for survival, that neither we nor our country can afford to lose. As long as we remain fragmented and display to the public and to our opposition our own disunity, policy will be formed by others and we may find ourselves subject to greater restrictions and further governmental interference . . . If the United States is to solve its energy problems in effective and timely fashion, leadership must come from the energy industries. If we fail, the reins of leadership will fall into far-less-capable hands, with potentially disastrous consequences for our country as well as ourselves.

Before Texas Mid-Continent Oil and Gas Association, Houston, Oct. 17/ The Washington Post, 10-19:(A)5.

Maurice F. Strong
Executive Director,
United Nations Environment Program

1

I don't think it's a question of whether man is going to cease to exist, but whether he will lose the qualities that make him human. In polluted waters, what survives? The lowest forms of fish. When soil deteriorates, what grows? Weeds. In the same way, man, too, may degenerate before he becomes extinct. Remember that man's indulgences and appetites don't distinguish him from the animals. It's his moral and intellectual capacity. The golden age of a civilization doesn't consist of eating six meals a day. We're facing a fundamental question: The gods have put into our hands the means of deciding the future. Are we wise enough to handle them? The only attitude to take is enlightened concern—to admit that doomsday is possible, but preventable. My feeling is that, when man faces the ultimate challenge, he responds.

Interview, United Nations, N.Y./
Parade, 2-10:16.

2

A simplistic and illusory notion all too common to the more developed world is that population growth in the less developed countries is the greatest threat to the global environment. The fact is that the main risks of environmental damage on a global scale and the greatest pressures on natural resources come from the population growth and economic activities of the rich countries and the exploding appetites of their inhabitants. A citizen of an advanced industrialized nation consumes in six months the energy and raw materials that have to last the citizen of a developing country his entire lifetime.

At United Nations World Population
Conference, Bucharest, Romania/
The New York Times, 8-26:10.

William P. Tavoulareas
President, Mobil Oil Corporation

3

The oil-exporting countries have shown within the past year that the oil in their countries is going to be used primarily to help them,

not us. Some of the OPEC countries have just in the past month reduced allowable production of crude oil in order to prop up prices. Some of those countries have, or soon will have, all the money in their treasuries that they need or really want for a while. Why, then, should they let greater volumes of their oil be produced just for our benefit—especially if we refuse to help ourselves sufficiently by developing our own resources? Our country can find itself in a situation that is not only ridiculous but also dangerous if we forego developing domestic energy resources on the assumption we can make a large reduction in demand, and suddenly find demand much higher than expected . . . I fervently believe that unless America soon focuses its efforts on increasing its supply of energy—all forms of energy—we and our children could very well be both witness and victim to an economic collapse that leaves our nation in ruins. We must not let that happen.

At National Press Club, Washington,
Sept. 12/Vital Speeches, 10-15:12.

Russell E. Train
Administrator, Environmental Protection
Agency of the United States

4

I don't think there is any basic conflict between environmental laws and energy needs. It is important that we in the environmental field be sensitive to the nation's energy needs. But in return, I insist that our energy leaders also be sensitive to the nation's environmental needs. We should move ahead in tandem, so to speak, in meeting both goals; the Environmental Protection Agency is committed to this approach. An example is in the use of coal. It seems plain to me that, if we are going to be able to use this nation's abundant supplies of coal for the production of energy over the next 15 to 20 years, we must install the necessary technology and make the investments that will make it possible to burn coal without producing emissions that endanger public health. In short, to meet a very real energy need, we're going to have to deal effectively with the environmental problems associated with it.

Interview, Washington/
U.S. News & World Report, 3-11:39.

WHAT THEY SAID IN 1974

(RUSSELL E. TRAIN)

We are starting to see that our energy and environmental ills stem essentially from the same source—from patterns and growth and development that waste our energy resources just as liberally as they lay waste to our natural environment. The energy crisis is part and parcel of our over-all environmental problem—a classic symptom of the strains that occur when an organism begins to exceed the carrying capacity of its habitat.

The New York Times, 3-29:12.

Pierre Elliott Trudeau
Prime Minister of Canada

[On conservation of natural resources]: Time is not limitless; and if we don't change our life-styles, at some point we may have to do without. But I would hope that well before that point is reached we will have had almost a qualitative change in our civilization and we will consider ourselves more as trustees, stewards, of the resources which nature has provided mankind, and that we will transmit this heritage to future generations with more care and less profligacy.

Interview, Ottawa/
Los Angeles Times, 12-5:(1)7.

Morris K. Udall
United States Representative, D—Arizona

[On conservation]: The questions are really much larger than those we have traditionally dealt with. The issue is not whether we will have animal life for the next generation to enjoy, but whether we will have human life; not whether we will pass on isolated plots of wilderness, but whether our descendants will inherit anything like what we know as civilization. Conservation is not a piece of wilderness here, a wildlife refuge there. It is a celebration of life in its totality. It can be found at Yellowstone and in Jacksonville, at the Grand Canyon and in Brooklyn. The more we exploit nature, the more our options are reduced, until we have only one: to fight for survival.

Before National Wildlife Federation, Denver,
March 30/The New York Times, 3-31:(1)47.

The energy crisis is the first in a series of stark realizations that will shock this country in the months and years immediately ahead—one of history's most traumatic transitions, from the last whimpers of an age of abundance to the first painful groans of a new age of scarcity.

Before National Wildlife Federation, Denver,
March 30/The New York Times, 3-31:(1)47.

Stewart L. Udall
Former Secretary of the Interior
of the United States

[On the energy shortage]: We've [the U.S.] been so incredibly successful that we've become arrogant and very self-indulgent. We don't believe—the American people don't believe—you can run out of anything. They think technology waves a wand and the game goes on. So the energy crisis is a very shocking comeuppance; and this is just openers. Within the next decade there are going to be severe world-wide shortages of metals and raw materials. I believe, at the global level, we face a great tragic drama in the next 10 to 20 years.

Interview, Washington/
The Christian Science Monitor, 4-9:5.

Tarzie Vittachi
Director, United Nations Fund for
Population Activities

However successful the family-planning programs of the world are, the fact is that if the children already born each have only two children themselves, just reproduce themselves, in 27 to 35 years the population of the world will double, short of some massive catastrophe. We will have another world on top of this world. How do you accommodate another inevitable world on top of this one? Not just in terms of space—another house on top of this house, another park on top of an existing park—but in terms of food, clothing, medical care, schools, transportation? And this is a problem shared by the rich world and the poor world; the world is too interdependent [for it to be otherwise].

Los Angeles/Los Angeles Times, 10-22:(4)1.

James Abourezk
United States Senator, D—South Dakota

1

I believe very strongly that we must have an intelligence-gathering organization, and I believe the CIA and our defense intelligence agencies do an adequate job in this respect. We have every right to defend ourselves from foreign attack, and that right includes intelligence-gathering to protect our security. But there is no justification in our legal, moral or religious principles for operations of a U.S. agency which result in assassinations, sabotage, political disruptions or other meddling in another country's internal affairs, all in the name of the American people. It amounts to nothing more than an arm of the U.S. government conducting a secret war without either the approval of Congress or the knowledge of the American people.

Before the Senate, Washington, Oct. 2/
The Washington Post, 10-7:(A)22.

Raymond Aron
French political analyst; Member of
the faculty, College of France

2

The main impact [of the Watergate affair] so far has been to increase the strength of [U.S. Secretary of State] Henry Kissinger and weaken the President [Nixon]. In his first term, Nixon was really the boss, and Kissinger was a brilliant operator. But today it's difficult to say whether Nixon is still the boss of foreign policy, because he needs Kissinger. And Kissinger knows it ... He [Kissinger] came to Washington as an unknown, small professor of a big university, without any power base, with only a reputation for writing good books which everybody quoted without having read them. He had to go on with the war in Vietnam. There was every reason why he should have been destroyed. The fact that he not only survived but acquired this extraordinary position is an achievement that every observer of politics

must respect. Of course, he had a certain element of luck. But good luck is one of the ingredients of political genius. His greatest luck was to have Nixon as President—that is, having as President a man as unpopular as Nixon. So when anything went wrong, Nixon was responsible; when anything went right, it was Kissinger's merit.

Interview, Washington/
U.S. News & World Report, 4-29:50,51.

L. A. (Skip) Bafalis
United States Representative, R—Florida

3

[Criticizing the non-payment of debts owed to the U.S. by now-wealthy countries which once received American loans]: There may have been some sense to this program when we taxed ourselves to help those nations torn by war or those whose needs for development were much greater than their financial and technical resources. But that is certainly not the case now. Today, it is our country that needs help. Our economy is lagging, under attack by inflation and recession largely caused by higher [imported] oil prices. We need the money owed us, if only to cut down just a few dollars on each American's tax bill. If all the foreign debts now delinquent were paid, we could balance the Federal budget and beef up the strength of the dollar.

Los Angeles Times, 1-1('75):(1)7.

Lloyd M. Bentsen
United States Senator, D—Texas

4

True detente must address itself to all sources of conflict in a complex and interdependent world. It must not be compartmentalized or limited to certain countries or to specific ideological disagreements. Our national security is at stake. And our national security depends on far more than a lessening of tension with the U.S.S.R. and [Communist] China, as

119

WHAT THEY SAID IN 1974

(LLOYD M. BENTSEN)

important as that might be. It also depends on the strength of the NATO alliance; on our relationships with Japan, with Canada, with our neighbors in Latin America and with other developing countries. Our national security also depends on our response to the potentially dangerous pressures of world-wide inflation; food, energy and raw-material shortages; the population explosion; and havoc in the international monetary system. Finally, we need to reassert our moral leadership and humanitarian concerns in our dealings abroad.

Before Foreign Policy Association of New York,
Sept. 19/Vital Speeches, 10-15:28.

Aristides Calvani
Foreign Minister of Venezuela
1

I know it is often said the delegates talk too much and do too little at international meetings. But I believe that, in order to do something, it is necessary to talk much . . . Thank God there are forums in which we can speak. If not, we would hear only the voices of cannons, not words.

News conference, Mexico City/
Los Angeles Times, 2-21:(1)5.

Chiang Ching-kuo
Premier of the Republic of
(Nationalist) China
2

The democratic countries often consider "detente" a means to avoid war and a road to peace, whereas for the Communists "detente" is a means of pretending to make peace while winning the war . . . To negotiate with the Communists is to make concessions to evil and is tantamount to tying one's hands and throwing oneself into a tiger's mouth.

Before the Yuan (Parliament),
Taipei, September/
Chicago Tribune, 10-9:(4)17.

Frank Church
United States Senator, D–Idaho
3

[On revelations of CIA activity in Chile against the government of the late President Salvador Allende] : I think the fact this has now come to light demonstrates that the covert activities of the CIA are presently under no effective restraint. I would hope that it will be possible to establish, either through a joint committee or by some other means, adequate Congressional surveillance over the activities of the CIA, in order to avoid in the future such unseemly interference with the rights of other peoples. If so, then we will have solved this problem without having to outlaw covert activity outright. I can envision situations in which the national security of the United States, or the survival of the republic, or the avoidance of nuclear war, would have such overriding importance as to justify covert activity. But none of those factors was present in the Chilean case and none of those factors has been present in previous cases which later came to light, wherein the CIA has undertaken to covertly subvert the governments of other countries, contrary to our treaties, contrary to the principles of international law, and contrary to the historic role played by the United States in world affairs.

Before the Senate, Washington, Oct. 2/
The Washington Post, 10-7:(A)22.

Ray S. Cline
Director of studies, Georgetown University
Center for Strategic Studies; Former
Director of Intelligence and Research,
Department of State of the United States
4

Detente is defined by most Americans as peace, stability, international cooperation, tolerance and convergence . . . [The paradox] is that, if detente were really to succeed in our sense of the word, of opening meaningful contacts inside Soviet society, the Soviet internal control system would feel so threatened it would destroy those contacts. Therefore, our concept of detente can continue only so long as it doesn't succeed.

Interview, Washington/
The Washington Post, 7-8:(A)3.

William E. Colby
Director, Central Intelligence Agency
of the United States
5

There have . . . been, and still are, certain situations in the world in which some discreet

[CIA] support can assist America's friends against her adversaries in their contest for control of a foreign nation's political direction. While these instances are few today compared to the 1950s, I believe it only prudent for our nation to be able to act in such situations, and thereby forestall greater difficulties for us in the future ... it is clear that American policy today is different from when it was confronting world-wide Communist subversion in the 1950s or Communist insurgency in the 1960s. Our involvement has been reduced in many areas, in part, I may add, by the fact that many of the Communist efforts during those years were unsuccessful.

At conference on the CIA, Washington, Sept. 13/The Atlanta Constitution, 9-14:(C)7.

1

If we [the CIA] cannot protect our intelligence sources and methods, I fear we may reach a situation in which our adversaries profit from our openness while we are blinded by their secrecy ... In addition, in a world which can destroy itself through misunderstanding or miscalculation, it is important that our leaders have a clear perception of the motives, intentions and strategies of other powers so that they [other powers] can be deterred, negotiated about or countered in the interests of peace or, if necessary, the ultimate security of our country.

At conference on the CIA, Washington, Sept. 13/Los Angeles Times, 9-14:(1)22.

2

The CIA has three major functions: science and technological work, analysis, and the clandestine collection of intelligence. Now, there's been a fourth responsibility, and that is positively influencing a situation through political or paramilitary means. That's the one that goes up and down, depending on national policy. Right now it's way down. The degree of our involvement in covert activities reflects the kind of world we live in. If it's a world where two superpowers are peering over the fence at each other, then it's a matter of concern when a hostile political group is about to take over a country. But if it's a world in which we've worked out a relationship of reasonable restraint, or detente, with the other superpowers, then it won't matter to us who runs one of these countries in a far-flung area. Of course, something very close to us might still be important for political or security reasons. There may still be certain situations where U.S. interests—and I don't mean corporate interests, but fundamental political interests—can be adversely affected. In some of those cases it would be appropriate to take some modest action, such as establishing a relationship with somebody who needs the help. But I stress: It's not now our government's policy to engage in these situations around the world.

Interview/Time, 9-30:18.

Henry Steele Commager
Historian
3

Because of our [the U.S.'] acute fear of Communism, we have come to terms with every non-Communist dictatorship and totalitarian state in the world. This completely turns around the concept of America as the beacon of light for the free people of the world.

At California State University, Long Beach, Dec. 2/Los Angeles Times, 12-3:(1)18.

Valery Giscard d'Estaing
President of France
4

The path of [international] consultation, which is as far removed from confrontation as it is from capitulation, is the only one in keeping with the political, economic and human needs of our time.

At banquet honoring visiting U.S. President Gerald Ford, Fort de France, Martinique, Dec. 14/The Washington Post, 12-16:(A)1.

Thomas F. Eagleton
United States Senator, D—Missouri
5

Our distinguished Secretary of State [Henry Kissinger] is famous for his tilts. He tilts toward the junta in Chile. He tilts toward [President] Thieu in [South] Vietnam. His most famous tilt was his pro-Pakistan tilt. His current tilt, his pro-Turkey tilt, is no wiser than the others.

The Washington Post, 10-6:(A)16.

Gerald R. Ford
Vice President of the United States

1

[Speaking after President Nixon announced his resignation]: It's been my opportunity to watch over a period of nearly 25 years a foreign policy in the last five years that has been most successful in the achievement of peace for all of us here and hopefully the rest of the world. It's been a policy that I think can continue peace in the months and years ahead. Let me say without any hesitation or reservation that the policy that has achieved peace and built the blocks for future peace will be continued, as far as I'm concerned, as President of the United States. We've been fortunate in the last five years to have a very great man in [Secretary of State] Henry Kissinger, who has helped to build the blocks of peace under President Nixon. I think those policies should be continued, and those policies of peace will be continued.

Alexandria, Va., Aug. 8/
The National Observer, 8-17:D.

Gerald R. Ford
President of the United States

2

To the peoples and the governments of all friendly nations—and I hope that could encompass the whole world—I pledge an uninterrupted and sincere search for peace. America will remain strong and united. But its strength will remain dedicated to the safety and sanity of the entire family of man as well as to our own precious freedom.

Inauguration address, Washington,
Aug. 9/The New York Times, 8-10:3.

3

Successful foreign policy is an extension of the hopes of the whole American people for a world of peace and orderly freedom ... Over the past five and a half years, in Congress and as Vice President, I have fully supported the outstanding foreign policy of President Nixon. This I intend to continue. Throughout my public service, starting with wartime naval duty under the command of President Franklin D. Roosevelt, I have upheld all our Presidents when they spoke for my country to the world. I believe the Constitution commands this. I know that in

this crucial area of international policy I can count on your firm support. Let there be no doubt or misunderstanding anywhere. There are no opportunities to exploit, should anyone so desire. There will be no change of course, no relaxation of vigilance, no abandonment of the helm of our ship of state as the watch changes. We stand by our commitments and will live up to our responsibilities, in our formal alliances, in our friendships and in our improving relations with any potential adversaries. On this, Americans are united and strong. Under my term of leadership I hope we will become more united. I am certain we will remain strong.

First address as President before Congress,
Washington, Aug. 12/
The New York Times, 8-13:20.

4

The United States, our allies and our friends must maintain strength and resolve. Potential adversaries watch the state of our readiness and of our strength and our will. I will offer them no temptations. America is not the policeman of the world. But we continue to be the backbone of Free World collective security.

Before Veterans of Foreign Wars, Chicago,
Aug. 19/The Washington Post, 8-20:(A)8.

5

From the time of the founding of the United Nations, America volunteered to help nations in need, frequently as the main benefactor. We were able to do it. We were glad to do it. But as new economic forces alter and reshape today's complex world, no nation can be expected to feed all the world's hungry peoples. Fortunately, however, many nations are increasingly able to help, and I call on them to join with us as truly United Nations in the struggle to produce, to provide more food at low prices for the hungry and, in general, a better life for the needy of this world. America will continue to do more than its share. But there are realistic limits to our capacities. There is no limit, however, to our determination to act in concert with other nations.

Before United Nations General Assembly,
New York, Sept. 18/
Los Angeles Times, 9-19:(1)12.

1

A President has to be able to act. He has to be able to work with allies and with some potential adversaries. And if the Congress is going to limit a President . . . so that he has no flexibility, in my opinion the opportunity for a successful foreign policy is harmed considerably.

News conference, Washington, Oct. 29/
The Atlanta Constitution, 10-30:(A)13.

J. William Fulbright
United States Senator, D–Arkansas

2

Foreign aid has been kept alive over the last several years not on its merits, but primarily through Republican Party loyalty to their President's legislative program.

Before the Senate, Washington/
Los Angeles Times, 2-8:(1)5.

3

The United Nations—despised, neglected and misused—remains nonetheless the greatest potential instrument for dealing with the global problems of our time. When all is said and done—when all the ideologies have been exposited and found wanting, when all the theories of realpolitik have been tested and revealed as dangerous romanticisms—one ancient, still untested, idea persists: the idea that politics can be put to the service of ordinary human needs; the idea that through world law we can free ourselves from the costly and dangerous burden of international conflict; the idea that through cooperation and man's genius we can alleviate poverty and put our technology to humane and rational purposes. It is the age-old dream of beating swords into plowshares, of changing the rules of the old, discredited game by supplanting the anarchy of nations with an effective international organization.

Quote, 5-26:494.

John Glenn
United States Senator-elect, D–Ohio

4

I applaud very much most of what Secretary of State [Henry] Kissinger has done . . . [But] I would like to see this dependent not just on one man. What would happen if Henry Kissinger dropped dead of a heart attack tonight—heaven forbid—not wishing anything like that, but what would happen? Where would our foreign policy be? I want to have us have a broad-based foreign policy, well-thought-out, hopefully with the full support of and with Congress being taken in as an equal partner in some of these decisions; [to] make something that other nations can rely on for an extended period of time so that we are not just running out of a briefcase and depending on one man and his personal relationship with other leaders. I think that is a hazard for the future.

TV-radio interview, Washington/
"Meet the Press,"
National Broadcasting Company, 11-10.

H. R. Gross
United States Representative, R–Iowa

5

Do you realize that, aside from the war costs in Southeast Asia, we have spent $260 billion in foreign aid? I didn't say million, I said *billion!* . . . I would have voted for a minimal amount for Korea and a few selected places, but certainly not $260 billion worth. The best evidence of what it [foreign aid] hasn't done is in the few friends we have around the world today. We've spent $260 billion, and where do we have a solid ally? Look at NATO today; it's a shambles. It's a pretty sad situation, after having dumped $260 billion around the world.

Interview, Washington/
The National Observer, 3-23:11.

Alexander M. Haig, Jr.
Assistant to President of
the United States Richard M. Nixon

6

. . . Americans must understand and realize that America is the hope of the free world—it has been and continues to be—and that it is an obligation that we can't abandon by popular fiat or by legislative fiat. It is destiny, and it is a world-leadership role that history has thrust us into, both as a result of our demographic achievements and accomplishments and resources and the evolution of the post-World War II modern world.

Interview, Washington/
The Christian Science Monitor, 3-13:(F)1.

WHAT THEY SAID IN 1974

W. Averell Harriman
Former United States Ambassador-at-Large
1

Frankly, it bores me very much to hear [President] Nixon say he ended the era of confrontation and started an era of detente. That's an insult to Eisenhower, who deserves much of the credit for the Austrian State Treaty of 1955, and to Kennedy, who brought about the Limited Test Ban Treaty of 1963. Besides, Nixon didn't even begin the present round of detente; [former West German Chancellor] Willy Brandt did, with his Ostpolitik in 1969.

Interview/Time, 7-1:22.

Vance Hartke
United States Senator, D—Indiana
2

Whenever a nation takes money from the U.S. for one purpose—that is, to defend itself— and uses that money as an aggressor nation against another nation, we are going to stop giving them money. That is a rather simple proposition.

Quote, 11-10:434.

Wayne L. Hays
United States Representative, D—Ohio
3

I think the problem [of dissatisfaction over U.S. foreign problems] is that everybody in this country, and I mean everybody, likes instant solutions to problems. The foreign problems facing this country and the world are so complex and so difficult that there are no instant solutions. They are long-term and they are tough and they are hard. I think that is the reason people are unhappy about it.

*TV-radio interview, Washington/
"Meet the Press,"
National Broadcasting Company, 10-13.*

Theodore M. Hesburgh
*President, University of Notre Dame;
Chairman, Overseas Development Council*
4

The food crisis will make the energy crisis look like a picnic . . . this world is going to see an explosion and the cataclysmic revolution we deserve unless aid is provided the poor and hungry nation[s].

The Saturday Evening Post, November:87.

Hubert H. Humphrey
United States Senator, D—Minnesota
5

If foreign policy is a product only of government and not of the people, then it becomes essentially Machiavellian and it doesn't retain a hold on the people.

*Interview/
The New York Times, 1-15:6.*

Henry M. Jackson
United States Senator, D—Washington
6

If we continue to treat our friends as adversaries and our adversaries as friends, we shall find ourselves with a declining number of friends and an increasing number of adversaries. The real test of American statesmanship lies in the consolidation of the Western alliance, in the harmonization of the sometimes divergent interests of us and our allies and in the mobilization of the spirit and resources of the free nations.

March 25/Los Angeles Times, 3-26:(1)14.

James Keogh
Director, United States Information Agency
7

The Voice of America [radio service] is not an international NBC or CBS. Detente has changed what we do in USIA. Our program managers must be sensitive to U.S. policy as enunciated by the President and the Secretary of State. That policy is that we do not interfere in the internal affairs of other countries. We're not in the business of trying to provoke revolutions.

Interview/Time, 12-16:85.

Henry A. Kissinger
Secretary of State of the United States
8

I do not believe that the great departments of the government can be personal fiefdoms of individual men. The Constitutional responsibility for conducting foreign policy resides in the President. The Secretary of State has to be the agent of the President or he represents nothing.

*News conference, San Clemente, Calif.,
Jan. 3/The Washington Post, 1-4:(A)1.*

1

People think that when it's all finished you feel exhilarated. My experience when I'm finished with a negotiation is that I'm usually let down.

The Christian Science Monitor, 1-18:8.

2

The great goal of American policy for the past quarter century has been to try to achieve a more cooperative world, to put permanently behind us the narrowly competitive approach which has traditionally ended in conflict—economic or military or both. We maintain our faith in the validity of this goal.

*At international energy conference,
Washington, Feb. 11/
Vital Speeches, 3-15:323.*

3

Our constant view has been that the necessity for detente does not reflect approbation of the Soviet domestic structure. The necessity of detente is produced by the inadmissability of general nuclear war under present conditions. The accumulation of nuclear arms has to be constrained if mankind is not to destroy itself. This is a question which will be before humanity and before American governments as long as the accumulation of nuclear arms continues. So the United States will pursue a policy to reduce the dangers of war, to increase the possibilities of peace and to limit the danger of nuclear conflict.

*News conference, Washington, Feb. 13/
Los Angeles Times, 2-14:(1)16.*

4

[The U.S.] has changed enormously in the last decade. We have learned that peace cannot be achieved by our efforts alone, and that development is far more than simply an economic problem. Through years of anguish and trial, we have found that the United States cannot remake the world, and that neither peace nor development is achievable unless it engages the effort and commitment of other nations.

*Before Organization of American
States, Atlanta, April 20/
The Dallas Times Herald, 4-21:(A)3.*

5

Weapons of unimaginable destructiveness, global economics and instantaneous communications have thrust nations into a proximity for which they are politically and psychologically unprepared.

*Accepting Golden Jubilee Award
of International House, May/
The New York Times, 6-19:40.*

6

[On his relations with President Nixon in formulating foreign policy]: It almost never reaches the point where he says, "I order you to do this." He'll ask my opinion . . . and I'll give it to him. But finally he makes the decision of what needs to be done.

*Television interview/
"Kissinger: An Action Biography,"
American Broadcasting Company, 6-14.*

7

The President's [Nixon] style in negotiation [with foreign governments] is a very reflective style. That is to say, he does not go in there with 10 specific points to bargain on a specific agreement. He believes, as President, his greatest contribution is to set a general direction to make sure the parties with which we are dealing understand our basic purposes and then to leave it to others to fill in the details of the day-to-day negotiations . . . the President always attempts to make and, in my view does so very effectively, to put across to the leader with whom he is talking what the general purposes are of the United States; he then elicits from them a statement of the direction in which they want to go.

*News conference, Jerusalem,
June 17/The New York Times, 6-18:14.*

8

We must ensure that the heart of American foreign policy, our alliances with the Atlantic community and Japan, can meet the challenges of the next generation . . . America's principal alliances have overcome a period of strain brought about by the inevitable adjustment to new conditions. Maintaining the vitality of our alliances and [giving] even greater impetus to their joint efforts will be one of the principal goals of President Ford's policy.

*Before American Legion, Miami Beach,
Aug. 20/Los Angeles Times, 8-21:(1)6.*

WHAT THEY SAID IN 1974

(HENRY A. KISSINGER)

1

President Nixon's legacy to President Ford is a world safer than the one he found, [but] it is still far short of our hopes. We have eased many crises; we have not yet eliminated their roots. We have begun but not completed the journey from confrontation to cooperation, from coexistence to community. We are determined to complete that journey . . . [The United States] cannot be the world's policeman, [but] we will always use our influence for peace and conciliation.

Before American Legion, Miami Beach,
Aug. 20/The Washington Post, 8-21:(A)2.

2

[On the recent detente with the Soviet Union]: It is too early to judge whether this change should be ascribed to tactical considerations. But in a sense, that is immaterial. For whether the change is temporary and tactical, or lasting and basic, our task is essentially the same: to transform that change into a permanent condition devoted to the purpose of a secure peace and mankind's aspiration for a better life. A tactical change sufficiently prolonged becomes a lasting transformation. Detente is a process, not a permanent achievement.

Before Senate Foreign Relations
Committee, Washington, Sept. 19/
The Washington Post, 9-20:(A)19.

3

In foreign policy, the most difficult issues are those whose necessity you cannot prove when the decisions are made. You act on the basis of an assessment that in the nature of things is a guess, so that public opinion knows, usually, only when it is too late to act, when some catastrophe has become overwhelming. The necessity of the measures one takes to avoid the catastrophe can almost never be proved. For that reason you require a great deal, or at least a certain amount, of confidence in leadership, and that becomes difficult in all societies.

Interview, Washington/
The New York Times, 10-13:(1)34.

4

[On the CIA]: I think an intelligence organization is essential for a great power. I don't think there is much dispute about the part of the intelligence organization that collects information, analyzes it and tries to interpret the world to political leaders. The debate arises where the intelligence organization is operational and attempts to affect political events in other parts of the world. In this case there is a serious problem, because there is a gray area between the exercise of diplomacy and the use of force . . . There is no question that insofar as covert operations are conducted they should be carefully controlled, first of all within the Executive Branch to make certain there is no alternative and that they meet political goals, and secondly, to the degree possible, by Congress. How to do this, I think, requires careful study.

Interview, Washington/
The New York Times, 10-13:(1)35.

5

The old isolationism [in the U.S.] was based on the proposition that we were too good for this world; the new isolationism was based on the proposition that we're not good enough for it. When one looks at the process of growing up, it is largely a process of learning one's limits, that one is not immortal, that one cannot achieve everything; and then to draw from that realization the strength to set great goals nevertheless. Now, I think that as a country we've gone through this. We were immature in the sense that we thought the definition of goals was almost the equivalent of their realization.

Interview, Washington/
The New York Times, 10-13:(1)35.

6

Nations have learned through hard experience that any attempt to secure only their interests leads to confrontation and danger to the interests of all. Today the interests of all nations were never more intertwined.

At United Nations Concert,
Kennedy Center, Washington, Oct. 19/
The Washington Post, 10-21:(B)3.

7

Without the Foreign Service we will not be able to create a consistent foreign policy. We cannot base foreign policy on star performers.

We cannot rely that somebody will come along every few years to manipulate events. What we need is a high average standard of performance that is carried over through the decades. And that cannot be done by any President or by any Secretary of State. That is what I mean by institutionalization of foreign policy.

Before American Foreign Service Association, Washington, Nov. 11/ Los Angeles Herald-Examiner, 11-12:(A)4.

1

[Foreign Service officers, in analyzing future foreign-policy situations, must] do so not on the basis of some sentimental proclivities but on the basis of a hard-headed—if necessary, cold-blooded—analysis of what the various alternatives are that the situation requires... As we go ahead into the future, we will face more and more confusing situations and there will be an overwhelming temptation to let oneself be driven by the emotion of the moment. But the difference between observers and actors is that the actors who are responsible for the conduct of foreign policy do not have the right to let themselves be driven by emotions. They are responsible not only for the best thing that can happen but also for the consequences of failure. They are not conducting foreign policy in order to implement their personal preference, but to carry out the national interest in relation to the global interest.

Before American Foreign Service Association, Washington, Nov. 11/ Los Angeles Times, 11-12:(1)6.

2

Nothing is more dangerous than to claim success in diplomacy. I do not believe in statements of miraculous achievements. Anything that is done is the result of careful preparation and an enormous amount of detail, as well as the result of objective circumstances that exist and cannot be created.

New Delhi, India/ The New York Times, 11-11:2.

3

There is no magic and there are no supermen in foreign policy. The difference between a good and a mediocre foreign policy is the accumulation of nuances. It is meticulousness; it is careful preparation. If a Secretary of State, or anybody concerned with foreign policy, goes out to hit a home run every time he goes up there, he is putting a burden on himself and a strain on the system.

Interview/Newsweek, 12-30:32.

Clare Boothe Luce
Former American diplomat and playwright
4

We live in a jungle of equally sovereign nations, some more equal than others. The climate of the world of sovereign nations is one of hot or cold war, a foul climate and getting fouler by the minute. You cannot clear the air without clearing the international climate. Our problems are not simply American, but problems of every nation: finite natural resources, over-population, pollution, urban disorders, terrorism, violence—we are all experiencing these neurotic symptoms of hate and death.

Interview, Honolulu/Parade, 4-21:10.

Andre Malraux
Author; Former Minister of State for Culture of France
5

[The U.S.] is the first country in history that will have become the most powerful in the world without having sought it—because it is perfectly true that there has never been a will to political conquest in the United States. There were episodes, but that doesn't count. Americans did not enter the great wars with joy in their hearts; they gained little from them politically. They did not seek to gain more. The Treaty of Versailles and the Treaty of Trianon are worth what they are worth, but it is not true that the United States sought the greatest advantage. Thus, they have been master of the world by having wanted to sell what they produced at the best price. That is a completely new fact; it has never happened before. And the consequence is that they have never really had historical designs.

Radio interview, Paris/ The New York Times, 7-27:29.

WHAT THEY SAID IN 1974

Robert S. McNamara
President, International Bank for
Reconstruction and Development

1

We are in an interdependent world. If we ever needed a lesson on that, we got it in the oil crisis. We are getting it in the food crisis; it is the droughts in Africa and Asia that raised the price of bread in the U.S., and our failure and other nations' failure to support a world food-reserve system that would meet these drought conditions. So we are in an interdependent world. Our destiny is linked to the destiny of the developing countries. One-third of our raw materials comes from the developing countries. Fifteen billion dollars of our exports go to the developing countries. We are engaged in political negotiations today to reform the international monetary system. They [the developing countries] are part of it. We have got to have their support if we are going to get a satisfactory conclusion. So, in the narrowest possible way, it is in our interest to help advance their economies and to help ensure political stability in those countries.

TV-radio interview/"Meet the Press,"
National Broadcasting Company, 3-24.

George Meany
President, American Federation of Labor-
Congress of Industrial Organizations

2

I pray every night that [U.S. Secretary of State] Henry Kissinger won't give the Russians the Washington Monument—he's given them every God damn thing else.

Before AFL-CIO Building
and Construction Trades Department,
Washington, April 1/
The New York Times, 4-2:14.

3

Detente is appeasement—nothing else, pure and simple, but appeasement. It's a giveaway in search of profits for our corporations through a combination of American capital and Soviet slave labor.

Before International Ladies Garment
Workers Union, Miami Beach, June 4/
The New York Times, 6-5:15.

Gunnar Myrdal
Swedish economist

4

I think one reason that [foreign] aid is going down in most rich countries is that we are motivating it in a false way. Instead of saying that we should give foreign aid out of compassion, a feeling for the poor, or because other people are hungry and sick, we say it's in "America's strategic interest." This is very bad. The ordinary chap in America, the farmer, the teacher, the clergyman, he doesn't believe you. And he believes you still less after having been defeated in Indochina, and very often seeing that your policies in Latin America have not had good results. No, you should appeal to the true American, the person who is still proud of the American Dream.

Interview/The National Observer, 12-7:26.

Richard M. Nixon
President of the United States

5

It is good that the peace of the world is in our [the U.S.'s] hands. I say that from the standpoint of other nations, because we seek not to insulate them, we seek not any domination over them; we seek only for themselves what we have—the right to independence, to freedom for all of our people.

At Honor America Day rally,
Huntsville, Alabama, Feb. 18/
Los Angeles Times, 2-19:(1)19.

6

With regard to the policy of detente, let us first understand that, whether it is with the Soviet Union or the People's Republic of [Communist] China, neither side—and I have met the top leaders of both—has any illusions about our vast differences as far as philosophy is concerned. Second, the fact that we have negotiations rather confrontation does not in any way imply that we approve of their internal policies, or, for that matter, that they approve of ours.

Before Executive Club, Chicago,
March 15/The New York Times, 3-16:13.

7

. . . it is quite true that the Soviet Union, being a major nation, has great influence within certain bodies within the UN. And I think the only recourse for the United States, rather than getting out of the UN and leaving the whole game to them, is to stay in and attempt to see to it that our influence counterbalances theirs whenever we think theirs is wrong.

Before Executive Club, Chicago,
March 15/The New York Times, 3-16:13.

1

You cannot in today's world have successful diplomacy without secrecy. It is impossible. I used to say that I believe in the Wilsonian doctrine of open covenants openly arrived at. But that was Wilson at his idealistic best and his pragmatic worst. Open covenants, yes; there should be no secret agreements that the country is not totally committed to. But openly arrived at? There would be no convenants. It is impossible. And it is particularly impossible when you are dealing not with your friends but with your adversaries.

Interview, Washington, May 14/
Los Angeles Times, 5-17:(1)7.

2

There are some people here in America who would like to turn inward and away from the world's problems. But like it or not, we are part of a larger world. In a day when atomic weapons are spreading, when famine stalks parts of the earth, and when the tinder that could ignite another massive conflagration exists in many parts of the world, to turn our back on our responsibilities for world leadership would, in the long run, be disastrous not only for us but also for all people in the world who seek peace.

Memorial Day radio address to the nation,
Key Biscayne, Fla., May 27/
The New York Times, 5-28:24.

3

Eloquent ... appeals are now being made for the United States through its foreign policy to transform the internal as well as the international behavior of other countries, and especially that of the Soviet Union. This issue affects not only our relation[s] with the Soviet Union but also our posture toward many nations whose internal systems we totally disagree with, as they do with ours ... Not by our choice but by our capability, our primary con-

cern in foreign policy must be to help influence the international conduct of nations in the world arena. We would not welcome the intervention of other countries in our domestic affairs and we cannot expect them to be cooperative when we seek to intervene directly in theirs. We cannot gear our foreign policy to transformation of other societies. In the nuclear age, our first responsibility must be the prevention of a war that could destroy all society. We must never lose sight of this fundamental truth of modern international life.

At United States Naval Academy
commencement, Annapolis, June 5/
The New York Times, 6-6:16.

Lewis F. Powell, Jr.
Associate Justice, Supreme Court of
the United States

4

Our foreign policy ... is attacked as imperialistic and even as immoral. [But] whatever mistakes have been made over the years—and certainly they are not inconsequential—it can be said with truth that no powerful country, victor in major wars, has sought less for itself or taken less from other nations and people than the United States of America.

At convocation, Washington and Lee
University/The National Observer, 2-9:12.

Peter Ramsbotham
British Ambassador to the United States

5

Diplomacy is the art of extracting advantage from difficult circumstances. The troubles of the past year have shown us that international cooperation is the only way to solve the world's economic and political problems. This cooperation is no longer merely a desirable end; it has now become a vital necessity. No country can hope to solve these problems alone. That is the lesson we learned in 1974. I am confident that it will stand us in good stead in 1975.

Los Angeles Times, 12-29:(4)14.

Dan Rather
News commentator,
Columbia Broadcasting System

6

[Secretary of State] Henry Kissinger, for quite a while now, has been a surrogate Presi-

(DAN RATHER)

dent in foreign affairs. I think one of the keys to whether [President] Ford succeeds or fails as President is whether he'll be able to build any kind of power balance for the foreign-policy decision-making process with Kissinger. Now, have it clearly understood that I think Kissinger is a genius. We were lucky to have him during this period. But even a genius can only play so many chess games simultaneously, and Kissinger has been playing a hell of a lot of chess games lately and it's beginning to show. Our whole system is built on checks and balances and, lately, Kissinger hasn't had any on him at all. What he says goes, whether it's indifferent, silly or brilliant. I admire Kissinger. He's superb at what he does. But nobody ought to have that much power.

Interview, New York/
"W": a Fairchild publication, 12-13:18.

Ronald Reagan
Governor of California 1

I think that detente—the idea of opening up relationships to the point where we can talk to each other—has borne fruit already. As a result of that, we find China, the great Communist colossus . . . is no longer in the Russian orbit, and we find that a President of the United States a few weeks ago was able to pick up a telephone and, with one telephone call, stop the Soviet Union from moving armed forces into the Middle East.

TV-radio interview/"Meet the Press,"
National Broadcasting Company, 1-20.

Zaid al-Rifai
Prime Minister of Jordan 2

In diplomacy, sometimes the appearance of movement is as important as movement itself.
The Washington Post, 11-3:(A)4.

Nelson A. Rockefeller
Vice President-designate of the United States 3

. . . unless we represent our national *interest* abroad as well as our conscience, we will not be serving the American people.

At Congressional hearings on his nomination
for Vice President, Washington/
The New York Times, 12-15:(4)5.

Dean Rusk
Professor of International Law,
University of Georgia; Former
Secretary of State of the United States 4

There's nothing more dangerous than a security treaty you don't mean. If we want to make them a bluff, we'd better get out of them.
The Atlanta Journal and Constitution
Magazine, 8-18:30.

5

Coup d'etats blow up like a summer storm. There were 82 during my term of office, and not one caused by the CIA.
The Atlanta Journal and Constitution
Magazine, 8-18:30.

John A. Scali
United States Ambassador/Permanent
Representative to the United Nations 6

My countrymen have made a great investment in this world organization [the UN] over the years—as host country, as the leading financial contributor and as a conscientious participant in its debates and negotiations and operational programs. Americans have loyally continued these efforts in a spirit of good faith and tolerance, knowing that there would be words spoken which we did not always like and resolutions adopted which we could not always support. As the 29th General Assembly draws to a close, however, many Americans are questioning their belief in the United Nations. They are deeply disturbed. During the 29th General Assembly, resolutions have been passed which uncritically endorse the most far-reaching claims of one side in dangerous international disputes. With this has come a sharply increased tendency in this Assembly to disregard its normal procedures to benefit the side which enjoys the favor of the majority, and to silence, and even exclude, the representatives of member states whose policies the majority condemns . . . We are all aware that true compromise is difficult and time-consuming, while bloc voting is fast and easy. But real progress on contentious issues must be earned. Paper triumphs are, in the end, expensive even for the victors. The cost is borne, first of all, by the

United Nations as an institution, and, in the end, by all of us. Our achievements cannot be measured in paper.

Before United Nations General
Assembly, New York, Dec. 6/
The New York Times, 12-7:15.

Helmut Schmidt
Chancellor of West Germany

1

The difficulty for the Americans is that, on the one hand, they have to act as the most important leaders of opinion and, on the other, they have to avoid appearing as leaders. There are many people in the world who do not like to be led, at least who do not like this to be shown.

Interview, Bonn/Time, 10-7:58.

George P. Shultz
Secretary of the Treasury of
the United States

2

[Saying the U.S. should not reduce foreign aid] : Let's not cut and run. Let's not abandon our principles. Let's not abandon the world. Let's not abandon what we are trying to do. Let's not throw in the towel and say we don't give a damn about anybody else.

Before Congressional Joint Economic
Committee, Washington, Feb. 8/
Los Angeles Times, 2-9:(1)4.

Howard K. Smith
News commentator,
American Broadcasting Company

3

Before [Secretary of State] Henry Kissinger straps on his all-day smile each morning, I am sure he faces the mirror with fear and dread. No public official has ever had such continuing surfeit of success. In an Administration whose members are, charitably put, accident-prone, he alone never missteps. No one ever entered so many foul foreign quarrels and came out every time smelling like gardenias. He is a refugee from the law of averages, a gross violation of Emerson's law of compensation whereby each sweet moment must be paid with a misadventure. He is destiny's scofflaw, and his due bill is astronomical.

ABC News commentary/
The Christian Science Monitor, 1-25:(F)8.

John C. Stennis
United States Senator, D—Mississippi

4

[On the CIA] : . . . I do not approve of such missions as "destabilizing" the Allende government in Chile. That is not the primary mission of the CIA as I see it. And I am sure that [CIA Director] Bill Colby does not favor such missions either. And I tell you this: I am in favor of stopping all of them in the future. And I think he is, too. One thing is to get information, which I regard as the primary function of the Agency. Another thing is to go messing about into the internal affairs of other nations in which you have no business.

Interview/Parade, 10-20:5.

Herman E. Talmadge
United States Senator, D—Georgia

5

In a time when the Federal government is running a $14 billion deficit and domestic inflation is climbing over 15 per cent, it ranks as the height of sheer folly for the Congress to approve a foreign-aid package totaling over $3 billion . . . Public officials simply must realize that placing piles and piles of the taxpayers' hard-earned dollars into the outstretched hands of governments from Afghanistan to Zambia buys no peace in the world and certainly gains America no friends.

Before the Senate, Washington, Sept. 25/
The Atlanta Constitution, 9-26:(C)2.

Henri Troyat
French historian

6

International conferences are the brake marks on the asphalt of history.

San Francisco Examiner & Chronicle,
3-17:(This World)2.

Pierre Elliott Trudeau
Prime Minister of Canada

7

It's obvious that foreign ministers and heads of government now are realizing that discussion of international relations has to be in a large part weighted in terms of the economies, whereas before we talked of power relations in terms of politics and land space and armies. It's obvious now that much of the future of the

(PIERRE ELLIOTT TRUDEAU)

world and of the West, in particular, is being determined by economic considerations. The oil one is the one that looms largest—oil and energy—but to a very important degree the food problem, which has a very heavy human impact, is also [a] matter of economies; and whether the countries have enough to buy and whether they have enough to get the fertilizers and scarce resources attendant to that, mean that resource policies also have a very important aspect in power relationships.

Interview, Ottawa/
Los Angeles Times, 12-5:(1)7.

John Turner
Minister of Finance of Canada   1

I can understand the crisis of confidence in America; disillusionment about foreign aid, the distress of Vietnam and Watergate, the devaluations [of the dollar] have reopened old temptations to turn to isolationism. That must not be carried out. And it won't be . . . the U.S. is still the world's leading nation, the Number 1 economic power and custodian of peace. I am confident that Americans will rekindle their spirit of leadership and reassert their essential moral strength.

Ottawa/Nation's Business, April:58.

Joseph D. Tydings
National co-chairman, Population
Crisis Committee; Former United
States Senator, D—Maryland   2

I don't think any member of Congress would take the same position on committing of resources of the United States on budget proposals before the Senate [last] week [increasing defense expenditures] if he spent two or three weeks in the Sahel and Bangladesh and India and he had some concept of what's happening in the world, and the real threat to the security of the United States if the world catches fire with famine in the '80s or '90s or indeed in the '70s . . . If we ignore the time, if we continue to waste that time that has been bought by the green revolution, the suffering in this world is

going to affect the way we live just as certainly as we sit here. And the vital security of the United States is far more gravely threatened by collapse of governments in India and Pakistan and Bolivia and Ethiopia and Colombia and other spots in the world than it is on whether or not we spend $1 billion on a given weapons system.

Before Senate Select Committee
on Nutrition and Human Needs, Washington/
The Washington Post, 6-22:(A)18.

Kurt Waldheim
Secretary General of the United Nations   3

I know that there are Americans who recall the excessive hopes of 1945 and are disappointed by the achievements of the United Nations. But although it is true that this great and unique human experiment has had its setbacks and failures—and it would be foolish to deny it—I would suggest to you that its achievements have been very considerable. Much of the disillusionment about the world organization that exists in the United States is based upon a misunderstanding of the limits and possibilities of the United Nations. It does not constitute a world government; its strength can only derive from the collective contributions of sovereign independent states. But that strength can be of unique value in facing global problems . . . Conflict anywhere affects us all, sometimes immediately, in others more gradually. Thus, although the United Nations has changed much since 1945, this dominant priority remains: "to save succeeding generations from the scourge of war," in the words of the Charter, and to which I would add the words "anywhere in the world."

At National Press Club, Washington,
Sept. 10/Vital Speeches, 10-1:755,756.

4

[Disputing those who see the majority of Third World countries as having little consequence]: You cannot say any longer today, "Well, they are only small countries with only a few million inhabitants each." They can really decide the fate of the world. Two-thirds of the raw materials of the world are in these developing countries, and they realize this more and more.

Interview, United Nations, New York/
The Christian Science Monitor, 12-27:2.

Louis C. Wyman
United States Representative,
R—New Hampshire
1

It is sheer folly for the United States to continue to acquiesce and be fettered by the actions of an international organization [the UN] whose voting structure is weighted in favor of nations with inconsequential GNP and crassly motivated by unbridled bias and vindictiveness . . . In a world in which the population exceeds three billion, of which the United States has less than 225 million but a substantial portion of the world's wealth and the largest gross national product, it is sheer folly for the U.S. to continue to submit to decisions laid down by a cabal of small nations, rural and undeveloped countries, Communist satellites and blatant dictatorships of one kind and another. If it is to remain to the advantage of the United States to continue as a member of the United Nations, there must be sweeping reform of its voting system to recognize the realities of populations and economic product. Otherwise, the U.S. is going to continue to largely foot the bill, and to have little or no say.

Human Events, 12-21:10.

Government

Henry Aaron
Baseball player, Atlanta "Braves" *1*

Baseball players and Congressmen have something in common. Both of them fall prey to the old adage, "What have you done for me lately?" Each spring, no matter how many home runs or how many hits you had the previous year, you still have to prove to management that you can do the job.

Before the House, Washington,
June 13/Quote, 8-11:122.

Gardner Ackley
Professor of Economics, University of
Michigan; Former Chairman, Council of
Economic Advisers to the President of
the United States (Lyndon B. Johnson) *2*

One reason why I can retain some optimism lies in the many demonstrations that our society—and in particular our institutions of government—can still move surprisingly effectively, when what is proposed by its leaders is clearly right and constructive. Even today's national political leadership was able to move decisively and successfully when it proposed to re-orient our foreign policy toward [Communist] China—something clearly right, even though almost every political expert was convinced that the public was not ready for it. I have recently been amazed by the extent of the public's voluntary compliance with requests, even by today's discredited national leadership, to turn down thermostats and to slow down their driving, and by businesses' apparent willingness and ability to economize on energy, not merely because it is more expensive, but because government tells them that it is in the national interest to do so.

Lecture, College of Business Administration,
University of Texas, Austin, Jan. 30/
Vital Speeches, 5-1:434.

George D. Aiken
United States Senator, R—Vermont *3*

[On revenue-sharing]: The idea was that revenue-sharing would make it possible to cut local taxes, but that is not what has happened. Instead, revenue-sharing funds have been used for things that might not have been attainable otherwise, and in most places taxes have not been cut. My home town—Putney—got $15,000 in revenue-sharing funds in the first quarter of last year. Out of that, $1,000 was voted for care of indigent dogs—and that brought in dogs from surrounding towns. Some people want to use these funds for indoor skating rinks and indoor swimming pools.

Interview, Washington/
Los Angeles Times, 4-15:(2)7.

4

The trend is toward what we used to call socialism. Communities are more and more dependent on the states, and the states are more and more dependent on the Federal government. Government support for education, hospitals and other social purposes has gone up tenfold, I suppose, in the last 10 years. The number of local, state and Federal agencies has increased greatly ... Paradoxically, under a supposedly conservative Republican [Nixon] Administration, the leftward swing has been most rapid in the last five years. The people and the Congress seem to be for it. People are kicking about paying for these programs, but they are demanding to have them.

Interview, Washington/
Los Angeles Times, 4-15:(2)7.

5

We [in Congress] duck too many issues. Somebody said we should take the eagle off the seal and put the duck on instead.

Quote, 6-16:554.

1

The success of a government's administration depends largely upon the qualifications of the party in power. A party may be simply a political organization before election. Yet if it is successful, it becomes the government itself. Therefore, government can be no better than the party in control or about to acquire it. While "government official" is a more dignified-sounding term than "party politician," yet it does not necessarily follow that a person becomes more scrupulous, more efficient, more wise or more tolerant simply because he has been elected or appointed to a position of authority.

Before the Senate, Washington, Dec. 11/
The Washington Post, 12-14:(A)14.

Wendell R. Anderson
Governor of Minnesota

2

There is no school or college that one can go to to qualify you adequately for the Presidency. I think holding elective office is the best background, the best training. I would like to see in [the election of] 1976 frankly somebody on the ticket who is a Governor or has had experience as a Mayor. I think there is too much power in Washington. I think the Governors have the advantage of living in their states, living among their people. I think sometimes the poorest place to find out what is going on in America is to go to Washington, D.C.

TV-radio interview, Seattle/"Meet the Press,"
National Broadcasting Company, 6-2.

Roy L. Ash
Director, Federal Office of
Management and Budget

3

[Saying that since 1968 the big increases in Federal spending have been in income-transfer programs, such as Social Security, and not in direct government expenditures, such as for defense]: The main role of government is no longer governing. The main role of government is now redistributing wealth, taking from some people and giving it to others. [More than half of Federal revenues] now are on their way to somebody else to spend. If we are to reduce the rate of growth of Federal expenditures, we will

have to do it in income transfers, because that's where the money is being spent.

News briefing, Washington, Nov. 8/
The Atlanta Constitution, 11-9:(A)2.

James D. Barber
Chairman, Department of
Political Science, Duke University

4

The active-positive Presidents have been Franklin Roosevelt, Harry Truman, John Kennedy. What they had going for them was a remarkable conjunction of high energy output and enjoyment of what they were doing. They had an ability to roll with the punches. They didn't brood on the defeats and the mistakes. A prime example would be Franklin Roosevelt and his bizarre attempt to pack the Supreme Court in the '30s—a plan he called "the answer to a virgin's prayer." When he propounded that, it ran into terrific opposition and really backfired on him. And when that happened, he simply laughed and said: "Well, we gave it a try. Now let's go on to the next thing." This ability to roll with the punches and to grow in office is terribly important.

Interview/U.S. News & World Report, 9-2:23.

Abraham D. Beame
Mayor of New York

5

Public service in our democracy provides a singular opportunity for men in office to set the moral and ethical standards of our society. Those of us who are entrusted with greater responsibility have a special obligation to elevate those standards, to safeguard the integrity of government by our own actions, by the actions of those whom we appoint, and by the efficiency that we require from all our colleagues in government.

Inaugural address, New York, Jan. 1/
The New York Times, 1-2:33.

Daniel Bell
Professor of Sociology, Harvard University

6

Leaders are not believed. If they propose something, the people are skeptical. How can [President] Nixon, in a situation like the energy crisis, for example, step forward and

(DANIEL BELL)

say, "I ask you to follow me," when this man has skimped at every turn on his income taxes? In terms of credibility, there has been a crisis in the Presidency itself . . .

Interview, Cambridge, Mass./
Los Angeles Times, 3-22:(2)5.

Wallace F. Bennett
United States Senator, R–Utah

1

[The seniority system in Congress] beats any substitute I've heard of. It avoids internal bickering. A lot of firebrands cool off when they get responsibility. I'm reminded of *Horatius at the Bridge*: "Those in back cried, 'Forward.' Those in front cried, 'Back.' "

Interview/U.S. News & World Report, 5-6:25.

Lloyd M. Bentsen
United States Senator, D–Texas

2

The office of the Presidency has deviated considerably from the original intent. It has become more remote, more exalted, more powerful. And it has become more distrusted at home and abroad . . . What is needed most in the White House is a man with perspective. A President should view himself merely as the holder of the nation's top job at a particular point in history, not as a man exalted above other men. It is this perspective that needs to be restored and re-emphasized—by an open President, an accessible President who makes no apology for democracy.

Before Women's National Democratic
Club, Washington, April 8/
The Dallas Times Herald, 4-9:(A)4.

3

A strong President will surround himself with strong and effective advisers. He is, after all, the Chief Executive—not the sole executive. Every member of the Cabinet, every agency head, should be an executive—and a highly competent executive—as well as an adviser to the President, who is then free to fulfill his function as Chief Executive. And right here I would like to say that it is high time to return to the Cabinet system. It has been downgraded

and bypassed for too long. Government is far too complex, and events move far too rapidly, to be managed by a White House clique. The country is dangerously weakened when the Cabinet is supplanted by a team of faceless, anonymous advisers who pay allegiance only to the President. There is no place in a democracy for an elite palace guard composed of men who have never been elected to office, and who have never been formally appointed to office with the Constitutional safeguard of Senate review and confirmation.

At symposium on the Presidency, Reston, Va./
The Dallas Times Herald, 5-12:(B)3.

Alan Bible
United States Senator, D–Nevada

4

My mail reflects that Congress is in disrepute with many, but I don't share [that view] necessarily. I think our record has been a good one. People take out their frustrations on Congress. They hold it responsible for the high cost of living, the gas shortage. As a group, we may be in low esteem. But as individuals, members of Congress seem to come off much better since so many are re-elected time after time.

Interview/U.S. News & World Report, 5-6:25.

Winton M. Blount
Former Postmaster General of
the United States

5

We have the right to expect our President to be a good and an honorable man who does the best he can as he is given the wisdom to do it. But that is all we have the right to expect. It is as much as we could expect of ourselves. Instead, we want a man who has the courage of David, the wisdom of Solomon, the probity of Lincoln, the patience of Job, and the looks of Tyrone Power. We want what never has been, and never will be; and if we persist in demanding this media-manufactured notion of what a President ought to be, we're going to end up with a President whose chief advisers are his make-up man, his tailor and his barber. That is not what the Constitution had in mind. What we need today is not a false image of a President that plays well in the press, and not a king who takes all responsibility for all aspects of our national life and most of our personal life. We need a man capable of meeting his responsibilities within the context of one of three co-equal branches of government; a man who we will permit to decide what he has the right to decide, who we will not permit to decide what the Constitution does not give him the right to decide, and a man who we will permit to be human—capable of both majesty and of mistakes.

> *Before Georgia Highway Contractors*
> *Association, Callaway Gardens, Ga.,*
> *Sept. 21/Vital Speeches, 11-1:64.*

Jack Brooks
United States Representative, D–Texas   *1*

[On TV coverage of Congressional floor debate]: Gavel-to-gavel coverage would be basically dull. You couldn't make people listen. You'd have to chain them and prop their eyeballs up.

> *San Francisco Examiner & Chronicle,*
> *3-3:(This World)2.*

Patrick J. Buchanan
Special Consultant to President of
the United States Richard M. Nixon   *2*

What is needed—and this represents a personal judgment—for restoration of respect for government is for government to begin its own Long March, a strategic retreat from domestic empire. Ultimately: getting out of the business of setting [racial] quotas in public schools, business offices and English and philosophy departments, for that matter; getting out of the business of attempting sweeping re-distribution of income according to the ideology of this or that politician; getting out of the business of controlling wages and prices; getting out of the business of delivering "services," better and less expensively delivered by states and communities and private institutions; getting away from the idea that government in the United States needs one-third or two-fifths of the total income of the American people to fulfill its legitimate responsibilities. If the phrase "bold new program" were temporarily expunged from the vocabulary of politicians, the nation would not greatly suffer. If Big Brother would diminish his boasting and lower his profile considerably, per-

haps he might better win the confidence of the American people.

> *At convocation, Sangamon State University,*
> *Springfield, Ill., Jan. 7/Human Events, 1-19:6.*

McGeorge Bundy
President, Ford Foundation; Former
Special Assistant to the President of
the United States for National Security
Affairs (John F. Kennedy and
Lyndon B. Johnson)   *3*

The Presidency is only a fragment of itself unless it works in open trust with the rest of the Executive Branch, with the Congress and with the people. Even a large-spirited President, as we saw in the late '60s, can be gravely damaged by secretiveness. But in an open Presidency, any fair and honest man has a chance for high success.

> *Interview/Newsweek, 8-19:52.*

Yvonne B. Burke
United States Representative, D–California   *4*

... sometimes there are 200 amendments stacked up for a single bill. Most of them are irrelevant items that should have been taken care of in committee ... When you sit there [in the House] for two or three days and your colleagues have marched only halfway through a bill, it dawns on you that it is a colossal waste of time and money. Saddling a bill with countless amendments is the worst possible way to pass legislation ... Any time you amend anything to death on the House floor, it has not been thoroughly researched. Your staff people haven't looked at it. The amendments are often worded poorly. You just know that someone was sitting around drafting amendments on a note pad. So when people talk about the Supreme Court taking over [judging laws], that's the reason.

> *Interview, Los Angeles/*
> *Los Angeles Times, 2-24:(Home)26.*

James MacGregor Burns
Professor of Political Science,
Williams College   *5*

[On Presidential impeachment]: I've never subscribed to the theory that, if there's an

WHAT THEY SAID IN 1974

(JAMES MAC GREGOR BURNS)

impeachment, men would be shoving each other over bars or fighting in the streets. In fact, it is when nations don't have processes for dealing with problems that people fight in the streets.

Newsweek, 3-25:29.

Jimmy Carter
Governor of Georgia

1

... to a great extent, the attitude of the Governor can shape the expressed attitude of the people of the state. A Governor doesn't have any authority or influence to change the state's makeup or its general political philosophy. But every person has within him a wide range of motivations—fear, doubt, uncertainty, insecurity, hatred and prejudice on the one hand, and hope, self-confidence, compassion, understanding, love on the other. A person in major political office can emphasize those characteristics and express through his personal statements and actions either the lowest common denominator if he wishes to ... or he can strive to express the highest common standards among his people. This has preyed very heavily on my mind, that you can be a leader either in subjugating or in enhancing the best that exists among the people you represent. It's so easy for a person in office simply to seek personal popularity, to avoid any controversy, to make bland statements or to avoid involvement in things that need to be substantively changed.

The Atlanta Journal and Constitution Magazine, 8-11:6.

2

[Since the Constitution leaves to the states all powers not given to the Federal government,] if we have the courage, when a new problem exists, the state governments [should] have first crack at it. If we can take the responsibility, it won't be like in the past, when too often timidity, aversion and distaste caused us to sit back until the Federal government moved in by default. We don't have to wait for the Federal government to act for us to react.

Before Southern Growth Policies Board, Atlanta, Nov. 13/ The Atlanta Constitution, 11-14:(C)2.

Frank Church
United States Senator, D—Idaho

3

[On politicians revealing their personal finances]: Representatives and Senators do differ from other citizens in one important respect: They write the laws that affect business; they write the taxes that corporations as well as individuals must pay. Since members of Congress must regularly vote on legislation which reaches—often in varying ways—every segment of the economy, there is a very legitimate reason for making their private holdings a public matter.

U.S. News & World Report, 3-25:37.

Dick Clark
United States Senator, D—Iowa

4

The biggest problem [with Congress] is one that it's difficult to do anything about: It's the democratic process. When you get 535 members from different parts of the country, you can't ask them to sit there and join hands on everything. That's not democracy. It might be a Supreme Soviet, but it wouldn't be democracy.

The Christian Science Monitor, 3-14:(B)5.

Marlow W. Cook
United States Senator, R—Kentucky

5

[On public criticism of Congress]: Half of our bad ratings are due to our lack of respect for the profession ... Look at the debate we had on the Senate floor the other day on whether Arizona or Texas creates the better chili. What a ridiculous waste of time for a body that has the problems to solve that we do!

Interview/ The Christian Science Monitor, 6-4:(F)1.

Alan Cranston
United States Senator, D—California

6

[Criticizing a comment by Vice President Gerald Ford that, if Democrats sweep the fall elections, the country is in danger of a dictatorship by Congress]: The Vice President knows very well that Congress could not be a dictatorship. Congress has built within it all sorts of checks and balances between the individuals and the committees and the two houses; and the rules and the traditions and the differences make it impossible to be a dictatorship. [What is needed is to] restore the balance of power between Congress and the Executive branch, which is the very basis of our freedoms in this land . . . The people are making clear that they want an effective Congress. They don't want an imperial Presidency. They don't want a dictatorship, and that is the real significance of the [Democratic Party] election victories that we have seen in recent special elections.

At Democratic fund-raising dinner,
San Bernardino, Calif., April 17/
Los Angeles Times, 4-19:(1)23.

Robert J. Dole
United States Senator, R–Kansas
1

[On Senators' salaries] : It has been said that the difficulty with pay raises in the Senate is that one-third of its Senators are millionaires, one-third are statesmen, and the other third are cowards.

Before the Senate, Washington, March 4/
The Washington Post, 3-7:(A)30.

Peter F. Drucker
Management consultant; Professor of
Social Science and Business
Administration, Claremont (Calif.)
College Graduate School
2

I would say the two most dangerous things in the world today are, first, the world-wide inflation; and secondly, the frightening incompetence of government. There is no country today that has a competent government . . . We are probably not at an all-time low in government effectiveness. I think we are not basically weak, insecure or incompetent. We are back to normal, but at a time when we need something much better. We need better than normal.

Interview, Claremont, Calif./
Nation's Business, March:65.

Julie Nixon Eisenhower
Daughter of President of
the United States Richard M. Nixon
3

[On the Presidency] : It's becoming an impossible job. It's just so much for one person

to handle. I look at my father and how hard he works—he tries to keep his finger on the pulse of everything that's happening, and yet it's just a monumental job . . . People go into the Oval Office. They go in and their shoulders are down, really down because they have a problem. They come out and they're okay. They're walking tall or walking faster because they really are leaving their problems with the President. He's the one who's got to make the decisions. I don't know what the answer is. Government is becoming so big—becoming more and more complex.

Interview, Washington/
The Dallas Times Herald, 6-30:(A)22.

Milton S. Eisenhower
President emeritus, Johns Hopkins University
4

The office of the President [of the U.S.] has become impossible. The structure of the Federal government is obsolete. Drastic reform is necessary in the government, in the office of the President and in the manner in which we nominate candidates for President and Vice President . . . Immense changes will have to be made to cope with the size and complexity of the government and the Presidency. The Secretary of Agriculture has a bigger job to do today than the President of the United States had to do in Coolidge's time. When I was growing up in the early 1900s, the total Federal budget was $500 million a year. Today the defense budget is $85 billion. More people work for the Federal government today than lived in the United States when Washington was President.

Interview, Baltimore/
Los Angeles Times, 8-20:(2)7.

Lewis A. Engman
Chairman, Federal Trade Commission
5

. . . the people are uneasy when they don't know how [government] decisions are made which affect their lives; when they don't know why those decisions are made; when they are not even sure who is making them. In a totalitarian state, the solution to this problem—from the government's point of view, at least—is quite straightforward: They identify those who are disaffected and who voice their disaffection,

(LEWIS A. ENGMAN)

and then they either shoot them, lock them up or . . . exile them—depending, I suppose, on logistics or, in some extreme cases, on the pressure of world opinion. In a democracy, the solution is inestimably more difficult because it depends not on good marksmanship but on good judgment.

Before National Press Club,
Washington, Feb. 19/**

John N. Erlenborn
United States Representative, R—Illinois
1

[On Executive privilege]: The problem has been that the only way we could test Executive privilege was to hold the President in contempt of Congress. That is such an awesome weapon, and so abrasive, that the Congress just hasn't done it. What we've done, in effect, is to allow the President to invoke Executive privilege, and, in the process, he defines it.

The Dallas Times Herald, 3-14:(A)9.

Sam J. Ervin, Jr.
United States Senator, D—North Carolina
2

The men and women who made America believed that governments derive their just powers from the consent of the governed. Moreover, they had absorbed the lessons taught by the history of the struggle of the people against arbitrary power for the right to be free from tyranny. Hence, they comprehended some eternal truths respecting men and government. They knew that those who are entrusted with powers of government are susceptible to the disease of tyrants, which George Washington rightly diagnosed in his Farewell Address as "the love of power and proneness to abuse it." For this reason, they realized that the powers of public officers should be defined by laws which they as well as the people are obligated to obey. They also knew the truth subsequently embodied by Daniel Webster in this aphorism: "Whatever government is not a government of laws is a despotism, let it be called what it may." For this reason, they realized that liberty cannot exist except under a government of laws, i.e., a government in which the conduct of the people is controlled by certain, constant and uniform laws rather than by the arbitrary, uncertain and inconstant wills of the men who occupy public offices, and in which the laws accord to the people as much freedom as the commonweal permits.

At National Conference on Church
and State, Orlando, Fla., Feb. 4/
Vital Speeches, 5-15:454.

3

Congress has had a low rating [by the public] throughout history. You have 435 members of the House and 100 Senators representing just about every shade of political opinion imaginable. Congress can hardly speak as one voice, like the President can. A lot of people are unhappy when Congress fails to move on a law they want passed. But a lot of others are equally unhappy when Congress passes a bill they don't want passed. Congress isn't intended to rush through all proposed legislation. In fact, all of this might prove the wisdom of Congress.

Interview/U.S. News & World Report, 5-6:24.

Daniel J. Evans
Governor of Washington
4

It has been the states who have responded most fully to the problems of the day. This has been a response not in terms of empty rhetoric without action or visionary promises without dollars. It has been a response which has required executive and legislative courage, sound fiscal management, plus a willingness to act.

At National Governors Conference, Seattle,
June 3/San Francisco Examiner, 6-3:1.

Roy M. Fisher
Dean, School of Journalism,
University of Missouri, Columbia
5

We have lost faith in government not because we have discovered too many crooks and too much corruption, but because deep in our hearts each one of us knows we have discovered too few and too little.

Quote, 11-10:433.

Gerald R. Ford
Vice President of the United States

1

... those of us who have served here [in Congress] know that this institution adjusts and responds to demands of the times. Sometimes this response is not just in the form or manner the critics demand or envision; but in an over-all way it invariably is consistent with the needs of the day ... At the heart of representative government is the legislature. If it is strong, the republic will be secure.

Before former members of Congress,
Washington, May 21/
The Washington Post, 5-22:(A)4.

2

Truth is the glue that holds government together, and compromise the oil that makes government run.

At Utah State University commencement,
June 8/The Washington Post, 6-9:(A)5.

3

No country as diverse as the United States can be effectively governed with a rigid sameness of categorical standards imposed from Washington.

At Conference of Lieutenant Governors,
Santa Fe, N.M., July 12/
The New York Times, 7-13:10.

Gerald R. Ford
President of the United States

4

As Vice President, I addressed myself to the individual rights of Americans in the area of privacy. There will be no illegal tapings, eavesdropping, buggings or break-ins by my Administration. There will be hot pursuit of tough laws to prevent illegal invasions of privacy in both government and private activities.

First address as President before Congress,
Washington, Aug. 12/
The New York Times, 8-13:20.

5

One of the most important Republican concepts is to reverse the concentration of power in Washington. With revenue-sharing and such important new programs as the Housing and Community Development Act ... we are beginning to see the transfer of power back to the people. You at the state and local level are getting the power to decide where and how your tax dollars are to be spent in more and more areas of human needs.

Recorded message to Michigan State
Republican convention, Aug. 24/
The Washington Post, 8-25:(A)4.

6

[On the current delay in confirmation of Nelson Rockefeller as Vice President]: ... I will propose to the next Congress a re-examination of the 25th Amendment, which has been tested twice in as many years, to see if the provisions of Section 2 [dealing with selecting and confirming a Vice President when the office is vacant] cannot be tightened up either by another Constitutional amendment or by public law. There should be a specific deadline both for the President to nominate and Congress to confirm a Vice President.

Before Sigma Delta Chi, Phoenix,
Nov. 14/The Washington Post, 11-15:(A)7.

7

... I think the general revenue-sharing program has been a good one. It's now provided from the Federal Treasury around $16 billion to state and local units of government ... I think it ought to be extended. I think it's produced a great deal of good at the local level as well as at the state level. Now we're in the process of analyzing any internal changes, but over-all I think the program is good and I want to work with the Mayors and the Governors and the county commissioners to make sure that the Congress extends this sound program.

News conference, Washington, Dec. 2/
The New York Times, 12-3:28.

8

I have some friends, as well as some critics, up on the [Capitol] Hill, who say I should not veto something if I know in advance it is going to be overridden. That is no way to judge from this office whether a piece of legislation is good or bad. They have their obligations; I have mine. And if I predicate my decision on the basis of their responsibility or irresponsibility, I am not carrying out the function of this office. So, I have told every member of the Cabinet that we are not going to decide what we do on

(GERALD R. FORD)

legislation because of critics out there or on the basis of whether they are going to sustain or override the veto.

Interview, Washington/Newsweek, 12-9:37.

Robert F. Froehlke
President, Sentry Corporation;
Former Secretary of the Army
of the United States
1

In business, most of us, at least, know that we're mortal and that we're going to make honest mistakes. That's how you gain experience. We're expected to make mistakes in business, although we're not expected to repeat them. But get ready when you come to Washington [to work in government]. You can't stand up and say: "Yep, that was a boo-boo, an honest error. I learned from it and it's not going to happen again." The press, and properly so, is going to tell everybody about it and imply, at best, stupidity and, at worst, dishonesty. Get ready for it because it hits you right in the pit of the stomach. No one, you'll find, is waiting to tell you what a good job you've done.

Interview/Nation's Business, July:32.

J. William Fulbright
United States Senator, D–Arkansas
2

[Democracy cannot be defended by undemocratic means,] because the values of democracy are in large part the processes of democracy—the way in which we pass laws, the way in which we administer justice, the way in which government deals with individuals.

At University of Arkansas,
Fayetteville, April 13/
The New York Times Magazine, 5-26:35.

3

In a democracy we ought to try to think of our public servants not as objects of adulation or of revilement, but as servants in the literal sense, to be lauded or censured, retained or dispensed with, according to the competence with which they do the job they were hired to do. Bitter disillusionment with our leaders is

the other side of the coin of worshipping them. If we did not expect our leaders to be demigods, we would not be nearly as shocked by their failures and transgressions.

At National Press Club, Washington, Dec. 19/
The Washington Post, 12-26:(A)24.

John W. Gardner
Chairman, Common Cause
4

In government, just about every organization, whatever its intended purpose of service, has a tendency to end up serving the people who run the organization. Every bureaucracy tends, eventually, to serve itself. It has defined purposes, but it becomes a power in its own right.

Interview/San Francisco Examiner, 7-3:31.

Robert N. Giaimo
United States Representative,
D–Connecticut
5

Too many Americans are unwilling to admit even to themselves that a President can be guilty of wrongdoing. They do not want to look at the facts. They consider it unpatriotic or even traitorous to question the acts of a President. They think that by defending the President they are defending the United States.

San Francisco Examiner & Chronicle,
3-24:(This World)2.

Arthur J. Goldberg
Former Associate Justice, Supreme
Court of the United States
6

Mr. Justice Brandeis once observed that, "Our government is the potent, the omnipresent teacher. For good or for ill, it teaches the whole people by its example." Government is not an abstraction; it is people, elected or appointed to serve our body politic. What Justice Brandeis said of government is, therefore, equally applicable to the individuals who run the government—"for good or ill, they teach the whole people by their example." If we have indeed learned the lesson of Watergate, surely it is not too much to expect that public officials do not practice fraud, deception or illegality on the public, the media and the investigatory agencies of government. Instead of exacting too high a standard from public officials, the far greater danger is that we will all too quickly return to business as usual.

Before Senate Rules Committee, Washington, Nov. 14/The New York Times, 11-15:20.

Barry M. Goldwater
United States Senator, R–Arizona
1

In the domestic fields it is becoming more and more almost impossible for a President to offer the kind of leadership that, say, a Franklin Roosevelt or a Harry Truman could, because we keep forgetting that the Congress no longer has any power over the so-called domestic problems. When we create a bureau, we kiss goodbye to Congress' power. So does the President kiss goodbye to the power of the White House. The real power in this government to get something done rests with these innumerable bureaus, with the power that they have that is greater than the Congress' or the President's. So I don't think . . . we will be able to get this government back in line until we get a Congress with enough courage to say to the bureaus, "Look, fellows, you have gone too far and so have we. We are going to start cutting you down until your power is no greater than ours, or is not as great as ours."

*TV-radio interview, Washington/
"Meet the Press,"
National Broadcasting Company, 1-13.*

Julian Goodman
President, National Broadcasting Company
2

[Saying the President should appear periodically at televised question-and-answer sessions with Congress] : I recognize the impracticability of adopting such a proposal during the tensions of today's political climate, and I suggest it be considered for adoption beginning in our bicentennial year, 1976. This is a time-honored practice in Great Britain and other parliamentary democracies, although it is clearly without precedent in this country. I believe it would provide an excellent way to demonstrate graphically to the public the respective, co-equal

rules of the executive and legislative bodies in governing the nation.

*Before Joint Committee on
Congressional Operations, Washington,
March 7/Daily Variety, 3-8:1.*

Katharine Graham
Publisher, "The Washington Post"
3

. . . the government—and especially the President—has come to enjoy awesome powers of communication which can be employed at will . . . a President can command live coverage on all television and radio networks, on virtually any subject, at short notice. He can choose his forum and select the live audience to applaud or ask him questions. His remarks will not only be carried across the airwaves, they will also be reprinted, at least in part, in the daily newspapers of the land. Presidential pronouncements thus enjoy a weight and circulation which no other view or version of the facts is likely to attain. This gives the government enormous power to reveal what it wants when it wants, to give the people only the authorized version of events—and equally important, to conceal that which is unfavorable, untimely or embarrassing. And that power to conceal, to keep information bottled up, is a kind of license to abuse the public trust.

*At Colby College, Waterville, Maine,
March 20/Vital Speeches, 5-15:461.*

Edith Green
United States Representative, D–Oregon
4

Nobody can get a handle on [the Federal bureaucracy]. We pass one program after another without stopping to see whether the last 100 have really worked . . . There are so many programs and promises. Expectations rise and disillusionment sets in when we don't deliver. The reaction is, "My government isn't working."

*Interview/
The Christian Science Monitor, 6-4:(F)1.*

Alan Greenspan
*Chairman-designate, Council of Economic
Advisers to President of the
United States Richard M. Nixon*
5

In the last 10 or 15 years there has been an extraordinary buildup in what I call "fiscal con-

WHAT THEY SAID IN 1974

(ALAN GREENSPAN)

stituencies"; that is, an ever-increasing group of special interests in our society who have on-going commitments from the Federal budget. And, as a consequence of this, over the years what has developed is a rate of increase in Federal expenditures and Federal credit guarantees which is running in excess of the revenue-raising capacity of our tax system ... In fact, I would suspect that it may account for anywhere from 80 to 90 per cent of the inflation in this country and perhaps to a significant extent in the inflation in the rest of the world.

Interview, June/
The Washington Post, 7-28:(H)1.

Martha W. Griffiths
United States Representative, D—Michigan

1

We [in Congress] are a bunch of cowards. We are perpetually jumped on for spending money. Just think of the screams and raving and ranting about the construction of the Rayburn Building so we could have space for more staff. The Executive comes up here and lies, lies, lies, and I don't care whether they are Democrats or Republicans. They won't tell you the truth. And we don't have the staff or the computer capability to counteract the Executive. Some time ago when I decided that the Equal Rights Amendment was going to become a reality, I thought it would be a good idea to check every law, every Attorney General's decisions, every regulation, every court decision to see what we would have to correct. We do not have that computerized, and you can't spend years going through all that. Do you know who has it computerized? The Air Force. Why? Because they can get all the money they want and they don't have to look out for anybody.

The Washington Post, 9-15:(B)4.

H. R. Gross
United States Representative, R—Iowa

2

[On the increasing power of the President]: How in hell did he get all this authority? Because Congress gave it to him, that's how. I say to my colleagues, "Stop your bellyaching and your wailing and groaning about the President usurping all this power. He hasn't usurped it. You gave it to him!" The point is, the President can't spend a goddamn dime, he can't impound a penny—unless we give it to him. Congress ought to get a mirror and look at itself ... Deep in their hearts they know it. But this is the easy way; this makes life more comfortable.

Interview, Washington/
The National Observer, 3-23:11.

Alexander M. Haig, Jr.
Assistant and Chief of Staff to
President of the United States
Richard M. Nixon

3

[On his position as Presidential Chief of Staff]: I don't view myself as an adviser [to the President]; and to the degree that I permit myself to indulge in that personal perception, I think I could be doing a terrible disservice to the President. I view myself as an individual who must insure that all of the best advice that is available within the White House staff, within the Cabinet, in the bureaucracy and outside of government, is available to the President on any particular question that he has to address, and to be sure that a broad cross-section of views are brought to his attention. Now, having said that, if the President asks me a question or asks for my views on a particular issue, I assure you I give it to him. But it's with that conditioning caveat that I preceded that statement ... I'm not going to make any self-serving comments about the importance of my role. I think it's important to the degree I can bring to the President the best views that are available in any field, foreign or domestic.

Interview, Washington/
The Christian Science Monitor, 3-13:(F)1.

4

I think President Nixon is an individual who I find, in many respects, in the mold of many great military leaders I have known. He keeps a degree of formality between himself and his staff. As a general rule, I'm not sure that isn't the most effective leadership mold for a man with the President's responsibilities. Where you break those lines down, it tests human assets which are sometimes fragile in a fast-moving, highly important bureaucratic structure.

*Interview, Washington/
The Christian Science Monitor, 3-13:(F)1.*

Louis Harris
Public-opinion analyst

1

By their own admission, a majority of people are not well informed about what is going on in government or politics at the Federal, state or local levels. Although 89 per cent correctly can identify their own state Governor, no more than 59 per cent can name one U.S. Senator from their state, only 39 per cent can name the other U.S. Senator and a minority of 46 per cent really know who their Congressman is. Substantive knowledge about the details of legislation or foreign policy might be even lower than those levels.

*Before Senate Subcommittee on
Intergovernmental Relations,
Washington/Parade, 1-27:7.*

F. Edward Hebert
United States Representative, D—Louisiana

2

Irresponsibility is so widespread in the Senate that if the Ten Commandments came before it, they would be amended.

Human Events, 2-16:7.

August Heckscher
Former New York City Parks Commissioner

3

There are certain cardinal principles to civic administration: Always put the blame on someone else for anything that goes wrong; and when you're trying to do something, always try to make sure you end up by giving someone else the responsibility for the next step.

Interview/Publishers Weekly, 3-18:8.

Eric Hoffer
Philosopher

4

Don't forget that any common man who becomes President lives in enemy country in Washington.

Time, 8-19:63.

Chet Holifield
United States Representative, D—California

5

You no longer feel that it is an honor to be a member of Congress, because there is so much stigma attached to all elective offices as a result of Watergate and the misdeeds of a few members of Congress. The people lack confidence in us. Everyone is suspected of being a crook.

The Washington Post, 9-15:(B)4.

Marjorie S. Holt
United States Representative, R—Maryland

6

It is time for this Congress to recognize that Federal tax dollars are not inexhaustible ... Some of us have been insisting for years that the Congress must consider the fundamental question of what the people can afford, and balance that consideration against the need or desirability of the many programs before us. But the question of affordability never seems to enter the minds of some members; and the nation continues wallowing toward economic catastrophe.

*Before the House, Washington/
Human Events, 8-10:4.*

Craig Hosmer
United States Representative, R—California

7

[Congress] used to be a place where, in a gentlemanly fashion, people of good-will sought to achieve progress for their country. Today it's a cock pit.

*Interview, Washington, Jan. 21/
Los Angeles Times, 1-22:(1)24.*

Harold E. Hughes
United States Senator, D—Iowa

8

Inside Congress, we seem to be preoccupied with inefficiency. There are too many hearings and too many committees. I'm tired of responding to bells [which indicate when roll calls are being taken], like Pavlov's dog. Why not hold hearings one week, then be in session the next? Why can't we act as a Congress, instead of partisans?

Interview/U.S. News & World Report, 5-6:25.

Hubert H. Humphrey
United States Senator, D—Minnesota

1

The purpose of government is not to be efficient but to do justice. To do the right thing is to do the good thing because, sooner or later, you are judged by what you have done . . .
Interview/The New York Times, 1-15:6.

2

[Calling for TV-radio coverage of House and Senate sessions]: Congress casts a blurred and confusing image for the men on the street, and we are regularly made victim to end-runs and upstaging by the President. We have failed to make ourselves known and understood as an institution with a recognizable and positive identity in the public mind. We have been sluggish in meeting the challenge of the Executive's inherent advantage in competing with us for the public eye and ear.
At Joint Committee on Congressional Operations hearing, Washington/ The Hollywood Reporter, 2-21:1.

Frank N. Ikard
President, American Petroleum Institute; Former United States Representative, D—Texas

3

[On lobbying in Congress]: In the years I was in Congress, I've never seen a lobbyist who could control one vote even . . . There are exceptions, but the moral standards of Congressmen are very high.
Interview, Washington/ Los Angeles Times, 2-1:(1)12.

Henry M. Jackson
United States Senator, D—Washington

4

The most important thing to keep in mind is that in order to have good government you've got to have good people. You can spend all the time in the world setting up an organization; but if you get bad people, they'll wreck it. I try to select people smarter than I am. Some people like sycophants. I want people who are first rate.
Interview, Washington/ Los Angeles Herald-Examiner, 6-9:(A)7.

5

There is a danger that as we [the government] do so many things, the individual can get lost in the nature of things. Programs should be a means to an end, rather than the end. The government's role should be to enhance the opportunity for all our citizens . . . as individuals.
The Saturday Evening Post, Aug.-Sept.:45.

Jacob K. Javits
United States Senator, R—New York

6

When applied to [the] enormous powers of the Presidency, the aphorism that "power corrupts and absolute power corrupts absolutely" is valid today. As the Presidential figure grows in grandeur, the Congressional presence diminishes even in its vision of itself. For too long, we in Congress tended to take our cues from the other end of Pennsylvania Avenue; [and] we waited, if not for instruction, certainly for direction, and the direction was well on the way to becoming dictation . . . The price we have paid is too high: the death and maiming of tens of thousands of our young in Vietnam, the Watergate scandals and the shadow of impeachment, which are expressions of an almost grotesque imbalance of power between Congress and the Presidency.
Before Ripon Society, New York, April 27/ The New York Times, 4-28:(1)27.

7

[On the U.S. Presidency]: It is almost embarrassing to recognize that, in an era in which the U.S. has struggled against brutal totalitarianism, we have lodged, of our own free will, more power in a single individual than does any other system of government that functions today.
Quote, 7-7:2.

Jack Kemp
United States Representative, R—New York

8

In my opinion, the President's [Nixon] budget message has to be the worst-conceived of any on record—at least of any Republican President on record. It embodies the worst of Keynesian economic principles—planned deficits, the use of the government's spending power to compensate for declines in other segments of the economy—all at the taxpayers' expense. It fosters inflation by spending a full $30 billion over this year's budget and by encouraging the Federal Reserve to print ever-increasing amounts of paper money—without increasing what stands behind it—to help pay the bills for which tax revenues are not enough. It is hard, in all candor, to realize that a budget proposal resting on such misguided principles and proposing such outrageous levels of expenditures came from a President whose political party has, historically, been known for the advocacy of fiscal integrity, less taxes and less spending, reducing the size of government and the number of its employees, balanced budgets and paying our own way now—rather than passing on our national debt to our children.

Human Events, 2-16:5.

Henry A. Kissinger
Secretary of State of the United States

1

Any President lives longer in history than in headlines.

News conference, Washington, April 26/
Los Angeles Herald-Examiner, 4-26:(A)2.

2

[On charges that he was a prime mover behind a series of wiretaps of government officials and newsmen several years ago in the wake of government information leaks]: The impression has been created that I was involved in some illegal or shady activity that I am trying to obscure with misleading testimony. The fact of the matter is that the wiretaps in question were legal; they followed established procedures. When they were established, the then Attorney General and the then Director of the Federal Bureau of Investigation assured me that they were reinstituting procedures that were carried out in previous Administrations . . . The history of these wiretaps derived from a series of leaks that occurred in the spring of 1969. As Assistant to the President for National Security Affairs, I had the duty to call the attention of the President to what seemed to me violations of national security. These violations cannot be assessed only by analyzing the intrinsic merit of individual documents, but they must be also analyzed in terms of the confidence other governments can have in a government that seems totally incapable of protecting its secrets. After a series of egregious violations, the President [Nixon] ordered, on the advice of the Attorney General and the Director of the Federal Bureau of Investigation, the institution of a system of national-security wiretaps . . . I did not recommend the program as such, though this does not mean that I disagreed with it. I find wiretapping distasteful; I find leaks distasteful; and therefore a choice had to be made. So, in retrospect, this seems to me what my role has been.

News conference, Salzburg, Austria, June 11/
Los Angeles Times, 6-12:(1)20,26.

3

[Calling for an end to bitter political debate and anti-government feeling in the U.S.]: Governments by their very nature must make difficult choices and judgments when facts are not clear, when trends are uncertain. This is difficult in the best of circumstances. It may grow dangerously erratic in a pervasive climate of distrust and conflict. Debate in a democratic society should find its ultimate limit in a general recognition that we are all engaged in a common enterprise.

Before Alfred E. Smith Memorial Foundation,
New York, Oct. 16/
Los Angeles Times, 10-17:(1)5.

4

. . . it is the absolute duty of [government] leaders to tell the people what they believe is necessary. You can make your life easier by not putting tough choices to the public. But then when the inevitable catastrophe occurs, you have lost not only credibility but legitimacy.

Interview/Newsweek, 12-30:31.

Edward I. Koch
United States Representative, D—New York

5

When I'm asked about Congress, I say it's doing a lousy job. And if I say that, why shouldn't the constituents around the country say it? Look at this crazy Congress. There's an energy shortage, and we couldn't even get a bill to the floor week after week . . . While I have a

(EDWARD I. KOCH)

high personal regard for the leaders of the House on a personal basis, they're not exactly balls of fire. I've never yet been asked by the leadership to vote for some position as a matter of party discipline.

Interview/The New York Times, 3-23:15.

Melvin R. Laird
Former United States Representative,
R—Wisconsin; Former Secretary of Defense 1

There is so much feeling of suspicion and distrust between the Congressional and Executive Branches. One reason that Congress has so low public acceptability is that they fight each other personally inside the system. In my years up there [as a Congressman], we had confrontation of ideas, which is essential to our system; but we tried not to get personal. I've never seen the personal distrust we have now.

Interview/
The Washington Post, 5-5:(Potomac)25.

Clare Boothe Luce
Former American diplomat and playwright 2

Presidents catch hell if the people don't get what they want.

Los Angeles, Jan. 30/
Los Angeles Times, 1-31:(2)6.

Frederic V. Malek
Former Deputy Director, Federal
Office of Management and Budget 3

[In Washington] you need a little charisma. In business you don't need charisma. But in government you've got to inspire people to work toward goals. You can't just tell them like in business. You've got to win them over.

The Washington Post, 8-25:(Potomac)10.

Marvin Mandel
Governor of Maryland 4

I think the biggest challenge in government today is at the state house. Far more than [any other] office, I think the Governor's office today has become the real challenge in government. The big-city problems which were there

many years ago—they're still there with a lot of them—but most of it's moved out to the state house. I think state governments have modernized their operations far more efficiently than the Federal government has. I think there's more being done at the state level than the Federal government level, and I think the real challenge is right in the state house today in government . . .

Interview/The Washington Post, 10-20:(K)1.

John O. Marsh, Jr.
Counsellor to President of the
United States Gerald R. Ford 5

I, for one, don't subscribe to the theory that [the Presidency is] an impossible job. It's a job that is changing because of the demands of our times. But I think it's also a job that is susceptible to both organization and management, and also I think it's susceptible to a great deal of style, meaning the manner in which an individual goes about performing it. Our system is such that the Presidency is a manageable job if you can develop the techniques for it and if the individual has the ability.

Interview, Washington/
U.S. News & World Report, 9-23:33.

Eugene J. McCarthy
Former United States Senator, D—Minnesota 6

I think the office of the Vice Presidency ought to be abolished . . . It clutters up campaigns, it clutters up the Administration, and it generally has had a bad effect on the men who were Vice President.

At National Press Club, Washington, Jan. 16/
The Washington Post, 1-17:(A)7.

Gale W. McGee
United States Senator, D—Wyoming 7

[On Congressional salaries]: We ought to make sure that the office of U.S. Senator or a member of the House of Representatives requires no dependence upon any outside income . . . It is important that we as legislators . . . tell our constituents, "If you want good and responsible government, you are going to have to pay for it." That is the way we brag about our private sector . . . That is how the top executives of General Motors manage to squeeze by on $300,000, $500,000 or $750,000 a year. I do not deplore that they receive that . . . But what, then, is a board of directors worth when they have to administer a $300 billion business? What is it worth when, in all truth, the fate of the world depends on the kinds of decisions that come out of this government?

Before the Senate, Washington, March 4/
The Washington Post, 3-7:(A)30.

Clarence E. Miller
United States Representative, R—Ohio

1

[Criticizing absenteeism among members of Congress]: The place to start in reasserting Congressional responsibilities in the government is by doing the job we are elected and paid to do. And you cannot do that if you are off globetrotting or campaigning. When Congress is in session, the job is here. There could be no better way of promoting public confidence in our abilities and commitment to move America forward than a high level of Congressional attendance and voting participation.

Washington/Quote, 1-20:50.

Walter F. Mondale
United States Senator, D—Minnesota

2

The government has to be strong enough to show power yet diffuse enough to allow liberty.

Before high-school student-government
officers, Washington, Feb. 7/
San Francisco Examiner, 2-8:5.

3

Deceit prospers in secrecy, so what we need to do is open government up. Samuel Johnson said that a good conscience is based on the notion that you might get caught. In our democracy, the whole idea is to keep the pesky press probing all the leaks that are possible, and keep Congressional hearings and governmental processes open so that the people can hear it all and then decide.

Quote, 10-6:320.

4

Our Presidents must be willing to risk their popularity by providing leadership on impor-

tant domestic issues which are open to scrutiny and debate. We need Presidents who can ask questions without being ashamed, develop solutions without being isolated, and provide leadership without being dictatorial. I would like to see a President appear on television some night and say, "Fellow Americans, I really blew it today!" We'd all feel better.

Quote, 10-20:372.

Malcolm C. Moos
President, University of Minnesota

5

Congressional power of the purse has been superceded by Presidential impoundment. The power of investigation has been superceded by the Presidential doctrine of Executive privilege. The war powers have placed the nation's security in hock to Presidential whim; a free reign to the unbounded exercise of Presidential statecraft in its own interest. As a result, we have seen the advent of a Presidency that possesses the power to be arbitrary and even absolute—the characteristics that the great historian of Constitutionalism, Charles H. McIlwain, identified as the immemorial enemies of Constitutionalism. Not even the English kings of the Middle Ages had as much power to be arbitrary and absolute as does the American President today.

At University of Maryland,
Baltimore County, commencement/
The National Observer, 6-29:11.

Richard B. Morris
Professor of History, Columbia University

6

Government is in the hands of the second-rate and the third-rate, and we've got to do something to regenerate that enthusiasm for government on the part of the younger generation and on the part of the first-rate people. No first-rate people want to expose themselves to so many of the rigors and disadvantages of government service, notably the invasion of privacy in their personal lives. I think we have the brains, but I don't think we have the inclination on the part of first-rate minds to get into the government service.

Interview/U.S. News & World Report, 7-8:31.

Daniel P. Moynihan
United States Ambassador to India 1

There is very little success in politics... [The late Secretary of State Henry] Stimson once said that the thing about Washington is that it continues to bring young men full of energy and hope. Energy fails and hope wanes. People get used up in government.
Interview, New Delhi/
The New York Times Magazine, 3-31:17.

Edmund S. Muskie
United States Senator, D—Maine 2

What concerns people most in recent days is that, as exercised by the President, [power] is increasingly unchecked because so often its exercise is secret.
Television panel discussion/TV Guide, 5-11:9.

3

[Saying Federal agencies have over-extended themselves in intelligence-gathering operations]: We have seen alarming evidence that we have created a monster. We have the FBI spying on Congressmen and on domestic political groups. We have had the CIA involved in political she-nanigans spawned by the White House staff. And we have had military agents spying on civilians on behalf of an agency created by Executive order.
At Senate Government Operations
Subcommittee hearing, Washington,
Dec. 9/The Washington Post, 12-10:(A)7.

Richard M. Nixon
President of the United States 4

[On British-style votes of confidence for Presidents whose popularity is down in the polls]: ... I think the Founding Fathers made a very good decision when they rejected that and when they indicated that a President was elected for four years and that he would be removed from office only as defined by the Constitution when found guilty by the Senate of the United States of high crimes including, to be quite specific, the crime of treason, brib-ery or other high crimes and misdemeanors. Now, the reason that they rejected that [votes of confidence] was that they felt that there was a need for stability in the Chief Executive. They did not want the instability that would happen, insofar as the so-called vote of confi-dence always hanging over the President. Now I come to the other point: The reason why I think the Founding Fathers are right—or were right at that point—is that, if a President is always watching the polls to see what he should or should not do, he will be a weak President and not a strong President. Some of the best decisions ever made by Presidents were made when they were not too popular. And I can only say that, as far as I'm concerned, I be-lieve that the American system is a good one. In this time, particularly, it is essential that, when our Presidents are elected by the people, they're in for four years. At the end of four years, the people have then the right to turn them out.
Before Executive Club, Chicago, March 15/
The New York Times, 3-16:12.

Thomas P. O'Neill, Jr.
United States Representative,
D—Massachusetts 5

[On the effect in the House of the electronic voting machine]: A roll call used to take 30 to 45 minutes. In that time, you could move about the floor, talk to wavering members and say, "You'll be with me on this one, won't you, Joe?" Now [with the machines] members come in here, put their cards in the slot and duck out without you even knowing they were here.
The Washington Post, 3-31:(E)5.

Robert Packwood
United States Senator, R—Oregon 6

Nobody can take any legislative body seri-ously that doesn't keep control over its own budget. We [Congress] meet in January, stay till December, add up the bills we've passed and call that a budget. It's the one area where the President is way ahead of Congress.
Interview/
The Christian Science Monitor, 3-14:(B)5.

7

Congress deserves to be censured. We are our own worst enemies... The whole system of

Congress is designed to frustrate, to hamper, to slow things down. It is designed to prevent the leaders from exercising any leadership.

Interview/
Los Angeles Times, 3-17:(1)14,15.

1

All of us [in Congress] spend the better part of our lives running around our state, asking the voters to delegate to us their right to make decisions on their behalf, and then we can't wait to get back to Washington to give it away to the President. We accept the view that to get along we will go along; we won't rock the boat, we won't say or do anything controversial. We avoid voting on imperative issues—keep 'em in committee, table 'em, filibuster 'em. Don't vote on them on their merits, for heaven's sake; don't upset your constituents! If you're non-controversial and unobtrusive, you'll be re-elected many times and then go into that marvel of Congressional operation—the seniority system. And 10 years after you're dead they'll name a dam after you. The answer to America's problems is not to weaken the Presidency, it is to strengthen the Congress.

Quote, 10-6:317.

Charles H. Percy
United States Senator, R—Illinois

2

The Constitutional prohibition against any foreign-born citizen [being eligible for the Presidency] applies not only to talented and valuable individuals such as Secretary of State [Henry] Kissinger, but also to children of American citizens who happen to be out of the country at the time of the child's birth. This exclusion seems unwarranted and unnecessarily deprives America of potential leaders.

"W": a Fairchild publication, 4-5:5.

3

Federal government units that do police, investigative and intelligence work are proliferating. We find ourselves threatened by the specter of a "watchdog" government breeding a nation of snoopers.

Washington, Aug. 4/
Los Angeles Herald-Examiner, 8-5:(A)5.

William Proxmire
United States Senator, D—Wisconsin

4

Too many members of Congress simply don't work at it. There are far too many absences at roll calls, in committee hearings and mark-ups; and the Senate—the so-called greatest deliberative body in the world—hasn't had even a third-class debate in years, and if we had it no one would be on the floor to hear it, except the two or three Senators doing the talking.

Before the Senate, Washington, June 26/
The Washington Post, 6-27:(A)4.

Ronald Reagan
Governor of California

5

Politics ought to be just about as sacred as church. I don't know of anything, other than the church, that is more a temple to the people's rights than a public building and the people who hold office in that building.

Before high-school students, Sacramento,
Jan. 14/San Francisco Examiner, 1-15:8.

6

In the marble halls of government, plans go forward constantly to involve government in every facet of our lives, from material needs to providing for the arts and the nationalizing of health care ... Government programs multiplying like the spores of a fungus have brought an inflation that has robbed our people of their dreams of a good life. Our tax burden approaches one half of what all the toilers in our country earn. And year after year, demagoguery, preached from the podium of politics and even the halls of academia, has created a cynicism and mistrust of all these institutions we refer to as The Establishment.

Before San Francisco Bay Area Council,
June 19/San Francisco Examiner, 6-20:5.

7

[In the 1972 election of Richard Nixon as President,] the voters rejected an invitation to Utopia and reaffirmed the basic values from which our system was built. They voted for fiscal responsibility and individual determination of their own destinies. They repudiated the idea that government should grow bigger and bigger ... that we should embrace more costly

(RONALD REAGAN)

programs to alleviate human misery—programs that somehow never succeed no matter how much money is spent on them. The mandate of 1972 was a matter of the people versus big government.

At Republican fund-raising dinner, Centreville, Md., Aug. 24/ The Washington Post, 8-25:(A)5.

Howard W. Robison
United States Representative, R—New York

1

I am afraid of late what we [in Congress] do best is talk. What we are worst at is finding a consensus for action. I think I keep up with issues pretty well, but I am in constant danger of drowning in paperwork. It would be nice if you could somehow divorce the political side of the job from the legislative side. It is difficult to put the two together, especially when you've got a district as big and as diverse as I've got. If you walk down the main street of your home town on a Monday, they'll say, "What, aren't you in Washington?" If you don't show up back home regularly, they say, "Why don't you come home more often?"

The Washington Post, 9-15:(B)4.

John D. Rockefeller III
Philanthropist

2

Apathy, suspicion and even scorn are the attitudes that many Americans are manifesting toward the affairs of government ... Disinterest in government, a sense of alienation from government, is worse than useless. In a democratic society, it is destructive.

At Rockefeller Public Service Award ceremony, Washington, Dec. 4/ The Washington Post, 12-5:(C)1.

Nelson A. Rockefeller
Vice President-designate of the United States

3

The role of a Vice President totally depends on the President. If the President wants to use him, wonderful. If he doesn't, fine.

News conference, Washington, Aug. 20/Time, 9-2:18.

4

Political authority, the only enduring kind of political power, is not for sale in the American political system. Yes, you can buy some influence; you can bribe and win sordid gains; your wealth can purchase a piece of political power here or there. And we also know that with raw political power without wealth, you can buy some influence; you can bribe and win some sordid gains; and you can acquire some personal wealth here or there. But great political authority in America comes only from the free gift of the people when they vote for you. Wealth only leads to true political power here when it has been transmitted by our Constitutional arrangement into public authority ... It is the unbought voice of the people that here ultimately determines everything. And then when you are in office, true authority in office depends upon a Governor or a President winning the collaboration of the legislative body. Authority in office comes only through public support and the cooperation of all three branches under our separation of powers. And indeed, under our system of Federal decentralization, the system functions effectively only through the willing cooperation of Federal, state and local government. That is what I have in mind when I say that the American Constitutional system is the greatest arrangement ever devised for taming private power and moderating it into public authority.

At Senate Rules Committee hearing on his nomination for Vice President, Washington, Nov. 13/The New York Times, 11-14:40.

Peter W. Rodino, Jr.
United States Representative, D—New Jersey

5

In my judgment, the writers of the Constitution intended that the people should have another recourse against Presidential abuses of power besides the next election. That is why they reposed the awesome power of impeachment in the body closest to the people, the House of Representatives. If they had only criminal offenses in mind, they would have made the punishment fit the crime. They would have provided for criminal penalties. They didn't. They stipulated only removal from office on conviction after impeachment.

Los Angeles Times, 3-24:(1-A)7.

Dean Rusk
Professor of International Law,
University of Georgia;
Former Secretary of State
of the United States
1

There are times when a public official ought to be silent or even when the public would prefer not to know the whole brutal truth.

The Atlanta Journal and Constitution
Magazine, 8-18:30.

Edward B. Rust
President, Chamber of Commerce
of the United States
2

"Big Motherism" is the belief that government should be used to make the world safe for the citizen, right down to the smallest details of his everyday life. Behind this belief is the presumption that decisions made by the government, in behalf of the citizen, will be superior to those made by the citizen in his own behalf, as well as superior to those made by the marketplace. That proposition may be statistically demonstrable in some instances. But government is, after all, an abstraction. *People* must run it. I question whether the people who run it are consistently superior to the average citizen. If they are, we have a two-class society. If they are not, then why should we defer to their judgment? James Madison warned in 1788 that "there are more instances of the abridgment of the freedom of the people by gradual and silent encroachment of those in power than by violent and sudden usurptions."

Before Distilled Spirits Council,
Scottsdale, Ariz., Jan. 8/
Vital Speeches, 2-1:254.

Harrison E. Salisbury
Former assistant managing editor,
"The New York Times"
3

I've always been terribly impressed with the town-meeting concept. I grew up in the Midwest where they don't have town meetings, but for many years I've had a home in Connecticut where the town meeting flourishes, and it's always seemed to me to be the epitome of democracy, a place where everybody in the community gets together and speaks their minds on every possible subject. This is the essence of democracy. We live in an age when people feel dreadfully alienated from their government because it's so big and concentrated in Washington.

Interview, New York/
The Christian Science Monitor, 10-30:10.

John C. Sawhill
Deputy Administrator, Federal Energy Office
4

Without being believed, a government cannot govern, at least not under any system resembling what Americans have come to consider a free democracy. A government does not have the *right* to the confidence, trust and support of the people. It must earn these things. On the contrary, it is the people who have the right to demand and receive trustworthiness from their government. Public officials do not have a right to public credibility and trust, any more than they have a right to hold office without the support of the people. Both public office and public credibility are temporary responsibilities that must be earned to obtain and constantly re-earned to maintain.

Before American Women in Radio
and Television, Feb. 14/
The Washington Post, 2-21:(A)24.

William B. Saxbe
Attorney General of the United States
5

[On wiretapping and other electronic surveillance by government]: The possibility of Big Brother eavesdropping on our thoughts as well as our actions has seeped into our national consciousness in substantial ways. And some of the events related to Watergate have increased public fears on the subject. For the record, let me state that the term "national security" will not be employed by the Department of Justice during my time as Attorney General as some sort of easily obtained hunting license ... The yardstick of fairness must be adhered to doggedly.

Cleveland, June 28/
The Washington Post, 6-30:(A)19.

James R. Schlesinger
Secretary of Defense of the United States
1

There is no alternative to Presidential leadership. The wiser men in Congress recognize that Congressional dominance is no substitute. People must believe in our institutions, including the Presidency. To get belief, the institutions must merit support in each decade or generation.

Interview, Washington/
The Washington Post, 10-6:(Potomac)29.

William W. Scranton
Former Governor of Pennsylvania
2

... the isolation of the Presidency is a fact. It began with F.D.R. during the deep Depression and has gotten progressively worse as the Federal government has become involved in so many endeavors of life ... Why couldn't the Vice President formulate domestic policy? Why shouldn't he take care of regular contacts with the Cabinet, except for the Secretaries of State, Defense and Treasury and the Attorney General? It's almost impossible today for any President ... to escape isolation. If he has to have regular contacts with all of the Cabinet, with the White House staff, with Congressional people, and with leaders in various fields such as labor, business and education, and, quote, 'do the whole foreign thing," unquote, he doesn't have time to be "the people's President" ... I'm very concerned about this whole problem of isolation. It worries me. We must have mechanisms for releasing the President from some of the work so that he can be open and see the people. How will he know what the man in the street thinks if he is so isolated? He may know what [AFL-CIO president] George Meany and [banker] David Rockefeller are thinking, but he'll have a hard time knowing what the average person is thinking.

Interview, Washington, Aug. 20/
Los Angeles Times, 8-21:(1)28.

William E. Simon
Administrator, Federal Energy Office
3

A democracy's validity can be measured by the extent to which a people can know about the affairs of the government. If the government knows or can find out what the people are up to, but the people do not know and cannot find out what the government is up to, then the people don't control their government; *it* controls *them*. How can we regain public confidence if the people hold their government in such low regard that they doubt its word before it speaks? We can get that confidence by being open—not just when we are right and proud of what we have done because we think people will like it, but also when we are wrong, when we have goofed.

At National Press Club, Washington,
Feb. 5/The New York Times, 3-24:(4)17.

William E. Simon
Secretary of the Treasury of the United States
4

The monstrous growth of the Federal budget is a prime example of our troubles. It took 185 years for the budget to reach the $100 billion mark, nine more years to hit $200 billion, and only four more years to reach the $300 billion level. And in only one year of the last fourteen has the government been able to balance its budget books. In the last 10 years alone, Federal deficits have reached a staggering total of $103 billion. Yet even the unified budget, as huge as it is, seriously understates the full impact of the Federal government on the financial markets. What it ignores is the ominous growth in "off-budget financing." A large volume of credit, as you know, is now guaranteed by Federal agencies—to assist public and private housing, urban and rural development, transportation, health, education, small business and other activities. In recent fiscal years, total Federal and Federally assisted borrowings have grown to approximately one-half of all the funds raised through borrowings in the capital markets. It is imperative that we reverse this trend.

Before Economic Club, Chicago, Nov. 6/
Vital Speeches, 12-1:108.

5

When are we going to halt the growth of big government? When are we going to show our concern that one-sixth of the working men and women in this country are now employed by government and more than 30 per cent of our gross national product is consumed by government? When are we going to stop creating new government mechanisms that feed the bureaucracy but strangle free enterprise? It has certainly become apparent to me—and I hope it is evident to you—that we have more government than we need, more government than most people want, and certainly more government than we are willing to pay for.

Before Economic Club, Chicago, Nov. 6/
Vital Speeches, 12-1:108.

John J. Sirica
Chief Judge, United States District
Court for the District of Columbia   *1*

Good government begins on Main Street. The faults of the governments the world over are caused by the indifference and failure of the man in the street to play his proper role and meet his responsibility. We get the kind of government we ask for.

Quote, 6-16:554.

Charles H. Smith, Jr.
Chairman, SIFCO Industries;
Chairman, Chamber of Commerce
of the United States   *2*

One of the serious problems in the United States is that government has been encouraged to enter into more and more elements of individual citizens' lives. In a free society, problems should be solved to the maximum extent possible by non-governmental citizens ... Most things can be done much more efficiently by private groups than by government. Government is the most inefficient method of accomplishing almost anything.

Interview, Cleveland/
Nation's Business, May:49.

Howard K. Smith
News commentator,
American Broadcasting Company   *3*

Congressional committees vote themselves costly junkets at taxpayer expense. Many are helpful. But abuses have been spectacular. Employees and wives are often taken along. Once a

waiter was taken along because he was a friend of a Congressman. One member charged up tickets to nightclubs and an Aegean pleasure cruise. Several charged double the allowed per diem on grounds their plane touched down in two countries in one day. Some years ago a law was passed requiring detailed public disclosure of expenditures on junkets to limit abuses. Well, recently, quietly, almost unnoticed, Congress passed a measure killing the public disclosure requirement. The gates to covert abuse were thrown wide once more. If the essence of Watergate is secret privilege for officials and contempt for the public, it may be in trouble in that hot spotlight on the White House. But it is alive and well in some dark corners on Capitol Hill.

ABC News commentary/
The Christian Science Monitor, 5-31:(F)8.

C. P. Snow
British author   *4*

I think you [Americans] would have been better off if you hadn't invested the Chief Executive power and magic in one person [the President]. It's dangerous for one man to be Chief Executive, chief head of his party and to have the reverence accorded to royalty.

San Francisco Examiner & Chronicle,
12-22:(This World)2.

John C. Stennis
United States Senator, D—Mississippi   *5*

The most important decision a new President has to make concerns his advisers, the men who are going to be closest to him. He's got to be mighty careful about the men he chooses—because a President is so dependent on them, that's why. I remember the late President Kennedy saying, in my presence, that to him the most frightening thing about the Presidency was the small percentage of items that he himself had to make an exclusive judgment on; the very small number of decisions that he could say he had made all by himself. He had to take the word, 90 or 95 per cent of the time, of others. So that would be my first advice to a new President: Be careful of the men you sur-

WHAT THEY SAID IN 1974

(JOHN C. STENNIS)

round yourself with. They will make you look very good or very bad or very in-between.

Interview/Parade, 10-20:5.

Herman E. Talmadge
United States Senator, D–Georgia

1

In my 17 years in the Senate, I've seen decision-making policies shift from Cabinet heads to clerks in the White House. I haven't seen but one Cabinet officer in all that time who ran his own shop, and that was [former Treasury Secretary] John Connally. I think it would be a good idea if we could take that power away from the clerks at the White House and give it back to the appointed officials. That was the idea of the Founding Fathers. These youngsters in the White House don't have the expertise or the competence of people who are appointed to Cabinet posts. Cabinet officers are confirmed by the Senate; these faceless folks in the basement of the White House aren't.

*Interview, Washington/
Los Angeles Times, 3-13:(1)7.*

Meldrim Thomson, Jr.
Governor of New Hampshire

2

[Urging a stronger role for the states, as indicated in the Tenth Amendment to the U.S. Constitution]: Today we hear much ado about the First and Fifth Amendments, the shoehorns of social change, but scarcely a word ever of that great Tenth Amendment, the umbilical cord of Federalism.

*At Conservative Political Action Conference,
Washington/Human Events, 2-9:13.*

Pierre Elliott Trudeau
Prime Minister of Canada

3

I think that governments in complex societies have to be flexible; they have to be accepted by most of the people. But at the same time, they can't run around trying to please everybody, everywhere, all the time, about everything. In that sense they must retain their authority, their ability to act and their integrity . . . Governments must continue to

find ways in which people will continue to want to obey them.

*Interview/
The New York Times Magazine, 11-3:72.*

Al Ullman
United States Representative, D–Oregon

4

[Expressing misgivings about deficit-spending by government]: I don't think I'm less liberal or more conservative than when I came here. I think I'm more conscious of the over-all impact of [Federal spending] programs on the national economy. If the national economy is not strongly based, we destroy all our people-programs through inflation. It's the ultimate liberalism to keep a sound economy going that benefits everyone. A recession or depression is worst of all on the poor, the little people.

The New York Times, 12-15:(4)4.

George C. Wallace
Governor of Alabama

5

[Saying the Federal government is wasting tax dollars on local programs it doesn't understand]: It has come to the point where those who probably have never seen your state have more to do with the lives of the average individual you represent than you or anybody else on the state or local level . . . The average citizen has already found that the answer is not in a big national government. But this local control can be restored in a strong, viable, responsible state government that knows the needs and the wishes of the people it serves and is responsive to them . . . As long as the Federal government continues to absorb such a disproportionate amount of the revenue that can be devoted to governmental purposes, states will remain the slaves of the national government.

*At National Legislative Conference,
Albuquerque, N.M., Aug. 16/
The Washington Post, 8-17:(A)3.*

Earl Warren
Former Chief Justice of the United States

6

It has been urged in some quarters that the Justice Department be taken from the Executive Branch to be placed in an independent agency under the Congress. A similar suggestion has been made concerning the Federal Bureau of Investigation because of the derelictions of a recent Director. But the sponsors of these measures fail to recognize that the conditions they recoil against do not flow from public officials following Constitutional procedures, but, on the contrary, from circumventing them. As a result, they ignore the old truism that we do not tear down good buildings merely because they have been occupied by bad tenants.

Before graduating class, Morehouse College,
Atlanta/Quote, 6-23:584.

Walter Washington
Mayor of Washington, D.C.
1

What's a Mayor for? Anything that falls down, it comes back to what's the Mayor doing about it, including the weather.

The Washington Post, 9-3:(A)14.

Charles E. Wiggins
United States Representative, R–California
2

People's wants are irrational. They want high-quality, high-quantity services at no cost. If we [in Congress] did everything that people wanted in order to make them happy, the doing of it would make them very *un*happy ... The appearance of activity [in Congress] and the passage of legislation may put you temporarily in the sun, but it is the later Congresses which

suffer when the solutions don't work. People should be told that many ... problems are not capable of legislative solution.

Interview/
The Christian Science Monitor, 3-14:(B)5.

Malcolm Wilson
Governor of New York
3

The people have more government than they need, more government than they want, and certainly more government than they can afford.

Television election campaign message/
The Christian Science Monitor, 10-22:5.

Walter B. Wriston
Chairman, First National City Bank,
New York
4

There is a paradox in the fact that those who look to government to remedy every economic grievance in our society also want government to get out of their personal lives and stop telling them how to run their affairs. They cannot have it both ways. They cannot ask more and more government intervention in what ought to be a free market and still insist on more and more freedom for themselves as individuals. No people have ever preserved political liberty for very long in an environment of economic dictatorship. We often learn too late that freedom is indivisible.

Before Economic Club, Detroit, Feb. 25/
Vital Speeches, 4-1:376.

Labor • The Economy

Gardner Ackley
Professor of Economics,
University of Michigan; Former Chairman,
Council of Economic Advisers to the President
of the United States (Lyndon B. Johnson) 1

[Arguing against reduced government spending as a method of fighting inflation]: Slowing down an already slow economy, increasing an already high level of unemployment, creating new excess capacity where there is already more than enough, will have exceedingly little effect in slowing down an inflation already under way. This has been so repeatedly demonstrated—most recently in 1970-71 in the United States—that I am surprised that the idea still survives that further weakening an already weak economy is an effective cure for inflation.
Before Senate Budget Committee, Washington,
Aug. 14/The New York Times, 8-15:22.

2

Almost all of us believe that we are hurt by inflation, whether or not—in some objective sense—we are. So we all seek to find someone to blame—those greedy employers or nasty trade unions; the bankers, landlords, farmers or foreigners; our economic system, the government, society. In my judgment, the most significant real cost of inflation is what it does to morale, to social coherence, to people's attitudes toward each other. Without inflation, we would all feel much better. And our national life would be far healthier.
Quote, 12-22:587.

Roy L. Ash
Director, Federal Office of
Management and Budget 3

A recession is kind of like a bad cold: You don't know when you get it and when it ends; but when you've got it, you know you've got it.
News conference, Washington, Feb. 12/
The New York Times, 2-13:29.

4

For the last 10 to 20 years, we have wrongly concluded that we can consume [far more] than we can produce. Or on the other hand, we can consume what others produce. This is completely counter to basic principles of economics. We must produce in direct ratio to what we consume. If not, we have inflation.
Before Merchants and Manufacturers
Association, Los Angeles/
Los Angeles Herald-Examiner, 7-28:(D)5.

Malcolm Baldrige
Chairman, Scovill Manufacturing Company 5

Unfortunately, there is no way to slow inflation without some attendant pain, which is politically unpopular and so far has been unacceptable to political leaders. Yet the American people have always been willing to sacrifice if they believed the cause was good and, most important, if they perceived everyone to be sacrificing equally.
At conference of business leaders, Pittsburgh/
U.S. News & World Report, 9-30:29.

Lloyd M. Bentsen
United States Senator, D—Texas 6

[President Nixon has said that] "the key to fighting inflation is steadiness." That is why so many of us in Congress have been troubled for the past five years by the drastic fluctuations in the President's economic efforts: the on-again, off-again controls; the sudden freezes and phases; four Treasury Secretaries, four budget managers, six wage and price controllers, five energy chiefs, three chief economic advisers and now another newly created post, an "economic counsellor." . . . Sadly, only four things have really been steady: steadily rising prices; steadily dwindling confidence; steadily cheerful assurances from the Administration—followed by steadily worsening results.

Television address, Washington, July 31/
The Dallas Times Herald, 8-1:(E)9.

Barbara R. Bergmann
Professor of Economics,
University of Maryland
1

All of the natural scientists I have ever heard of generate and record their own data. But economists go down to the library and look up what the Commerce Department and the Bureau of Labor Statistics and the Federal Reserve have chosen to make available. The historian cannot question living men and women because the ones he or she is interested in are dead; the economist voluntarily chooses not to question the living.

Before Eastern Economic Association/
The Washington Post, 12-8:(Potomac)72.

Arch N. Booth
President, Chamber of Commerce
of the United States
2

In his sweeping indictment of government officials and business, [AFL-CIO president] George Meany sullies the meaning of Labor Day. It's time labor leaders learned the economic truism that inflation benefits nobody—least of all business, on whose success workers depend for their jobs.

Aug. 30/Los Angeles Times, 8-31:(3)14.

Alan S. Boyd
President, Illinois Central Gulf Railroad
3

. . . the peril to free enterprise in this country is very great. And in my view, that is bad—bad for the citizens of this country, bad for the economy, and bad for our ultimate efficiency as a functioning society of free men. I said free men—because I see a direct connection between personal freedom and economic freedom. When we see nationalization of basic industry under way in this country, when we see free enterprise burdened hopelessly with political costs . . . we will be well on our way toward a tyranny of the individual—and never mind that it will all be in the name of "the public." Those

who believe—or who behave as though they believe—that politics and economies are unconnected, that freedom is a political problem and that material well-being is an economic problem, are just plain bewildered. The notion that you can adopt the economic framework of a socialist society—in the name of the public's material well-being—and still preserve individual freedom—by a separate apparatus of political machinery—makes the mind boggle.

Before Southern Industrial Development
Council, Louisville, Ky., Oct. 14/
Vital Speeches, 11-15:76.

Peter J. Brennan
Secretary of Labor of the United States
4

[Most labor unions are at the point] where they feel strikes are costly to them as well as to the employer and the general public . . . The average worker today has a little better income, and he's probably able to save a few dollars that he couldn't before. He's paying off a house and car and vacation trip, and sending his children to college . . . He finds now that he's on the other side, thinking like some of the people he was shouting at before. But this, of course, is good. This shows America has been progressing, and the workers have moved into an era that they didn't enjoy before.

U.S. News & World Report, 4-22:91.

5

[On the employment bias against workers over 40 years of age]: . . . age discrimination costs money. It deprives workers of income. It boosts our unemployment rate. And it swells the cost of unemployment compensation. Age discrimination is also expensive for employers. They are cheating themselves out of some of the best talent in America. And they do so because of myths and prejudices that have no basis in fact.

U.S. News & World Report, 6-3:76.

6

More and more we live in a world of scientifically-based industries, resulting in an information explosion and in a society in which knowledge and intellectual processes are more in demand. As a result, new technology can

WHAT THEY SAID IN 1974

(PETER J. BRENNAN)

wipe out established trades and crafts . . . How this affects the employment relationship is illustrated by the recent contract between *The New York Times* and Local 6 of the International Typographical Union. Although an 11-year agreement will smooth the transition, an entire craft has in effect been automated out of existence at *The Times*, as well as at other newspapers. [The real lesson of this post-industrial society] is that we need a program of continuing education and training for executives, engineers, craftsmen and even semi-skilled workers if our economy is to function efficiently and if people are to have meaningful and productive lives.

At Industrial Round Table Conference sponsored by Edison Electric Institute, Chicago, Sept. 23/Chicago Tribune, 9-24:(1)11.

Bill Brock
United States Senator, R—Tennessee
1

[Wage and price] controls have resulted in incredible dislocation in this economy. They have created shortages, unemployment and loss of jobs and property without due process of law, without protection to the individual, the family, the company or anyone else; and I find it difficult to understand how we can go before the people of any state of this country—certainly I cannot in Tennessee—and justify to them a continuation of a policy which has literally clobbered the working people of this country. In the last year they have lost almost 5 per cent of their real income, not as a result of lack of productivity, but because the government of this country imposed restrictions on the production of this country, impeded the processes of the market and made it impossible for them to compete.

Before the Senate, Washington/ Human Events, 5-18:5.

Edmund G. Brown, Jr.
Governor-elect of California
2

[On the Ford Administration's economic policies] : There's a game plan they've got and the game plan is very simple: throw people out

of work; raise the cost of money; cripple the housing industry; in fact, take away all your money. That'll get rid of inflation all right, but it will also get rid of the American economy and the country. I think the way to do it is the way Roosevelt did it, Truman, Kennedy, Johnson, the Democratic tradition of putting people back to work. That's the way to solve the economy.

Before International Guiding Eyes, Los Angeles, Nov. 20/ Los Angeles Times, 11-22:(1)22.

Yvonne B. Burke
United States Representative, D—California
3

The reality today, particularly among low-income, unskilled minority workers, is that the highest possible job is one that is mundane and dead-ended. It just doesn't pay for many people to go through the employment hassle. The challenge is not to provide employment at any cost, but employment that will provide some kind of dignity.

San Francisco Examiner & Chronicle, 8-4:(This World)2.

Arthur F. Burns
Chairman, Federal Reserve Board
4

For our part, we at the Federal Reserve are determined to follow a course of monetary policy that will permit only moderate growth of money and credit. Such a policy should make it possible for the fires of inflation to burn themselves out, while it at the same time provides the financial basis for the resumption of orderly economic growth.

Before House Banking Subcommittee, Washington, April 4/ The New York Times, 4-5:51.

5

Of late, individuals have come to depend less and less on their own initiative and more on government to achieve their economic objectives. The public nowadays expects the government to maintain prosperous economic conditions, to limit such declines in employment as may occasionally occur, to ease the burden of job loss or illness or retirement, to sustain the incomes of farmers, home builders, and so on. These are laudable objectives, and we and other nations have moved a considerable distance toward their realization. Unfortunately, in the process of doing so, governmental budgets have gotten out of control, wages and prices have become less responsive to the discipline of market forces, and inflation has emerged as the most dangerous economic ailment of our time.

At Illinois College commencement, May 26/
U.S. News & World Report, 6-10:21.

1

There are those who believe that the struggle to curb inflation will not succeed and who conclude that it would be better to adjust to inflation rather than to fight it. On this view, contractual payments of all sorts—wages, salaries, social security benefits, interest on bank loans and deposits, and so on—should be written with escalator clauses so as to minimize the distortions and injustices that inflation normally causes. This is a well-meaning proposal, but it is neither sound nor practical. For one thing, there are hundreds of billions of dollars of outstanding contracts—on mortgages, public and private bonds, insurance policies, and the like—that as a practical matter could not be renegotiated. Even with regard to new undertakings, the obstacles to achieving satisfactory escalator arrangements in our free and complex economy, where people differ so much in financial sophistication, seem insuperable. More important still, by making it easier for many people to live with inflation, escalator arrangements would gravely weaken the discipline that is needed to conduct business and government affairs prudently and efficiently. Universal escalation, I am therefore convinced, is an illusory and dangerous quest. The responsible course is to fight inflation with all the energy we can muster and with all the weapons at our command.

At Illinois College commencement, May 26/
Vital Speeches, 7-1:554.

2

Our country is now struggling with a very serious problem of inflation. In the past 12 months, the consumer price level has risen by

11 per cent; wholesale prices have risen even faster. When prices rise with such speed, inflation comes to dominate nearly every aspect of economic life. The inflation that we have been experiencing has already caused injury to millions of people, and its continuance threatens further and more serious damage to the national economy. As a result of the inflation, consumer purchasing power is being eroded. During the past year, the take-home pay of the typical worker declined nearly 5 per cent in real terms. As a result of the inflation, the real value of the savings deposits, pensions and life-insurance policies of the American public has diminished. As a result of the inflation, financial markets are experiencing strains and stresses. Interest rates have moved skyward. Some financial and industrial firms have found it more difficult to roll over their commercial paper or to raise needed funds through other channels. Savings flows to thrift institutions have diminished, and stock prices have plummeted. As a result of the inflation, profits reported by corporations have risen sharply; but much of the reported profit is illusory because it fails to take into account the need to replace inventories, plant and equipment at appreciably higher prices. In short, as a result of the inflation, much of the planning that business firms and households customarily do has been upset and become confused. The state of confidence has deteriorated and the driving force of economic expansion has been blunted.

Before Congressional Joint Economic
Committee, Washington/
The New York Times, 8-16:29.

3

It is sometimes contended that the Federal deficits of recent years have been only a minor source of economic or financial instability, since the amounts are small relative to total borrowing by the private sector. This is a faulty argument. To be sure, the rate of private credit expansion has substantially exceeded the rate of Federal borrowing. But we must never confuse the power or responsibility of private citizens with the power or responsibility of government. Business firms and consumers have no way of acting in concert to prevent an

(ARTHUR F. BURNS)

inflationary expansion of credit, and their private responsibilities may conflict with national objectives. The basic responsibility for economic stabilization lies with the Federal government. Unless our government exercises that function better than it has in the past, there will be little hope for restoration of stability in the general price level.

Before Senate Budget Committee, Washington/
The Wall Street Journal, 10-7:12.

Earl L. Butz
Secretary of Agriculture of the United States
1

[Approving the lifting of price controls] : We should never again interfere with our normal economic system. But you have to teach this to every generation—and in Congress a generation is two years.

Before American Paper Institute, New York,
March 12/The New York Times, 3-13:53.

2

The American consumer has grown accustomed to cheap food. Prices did not increase until the last two years—and, in the last two years, the increase has been steep. But over the last 10 years, food prices have gone up less than prices for clothing, transportation, housing, medical services or appliances. Americans spend less than 16 per cent of their take-home pay on food. That is less than anyplace else in the world and less than ever before in America.

At Japan National Press Club, Tokyo,
April 17/Los Angeles Times, 4-18:(3)15.

3

There can be only one answer to our slipping productivity. It is the new attitude of getting more for doing less. This is taking its toll in reduced output. The new campaign seems to be, "Get mine for me—and the rest be damned!" This is resulting in "less for thee" and the rest as well ... We must recognize as individuals, as professional groups and as labor groups, that if we are to have more, then we must produce more. Nobody else is going to do it for us. Certainly the government can't produce it. Looking to Uncle Sam for bigger pieces of pie obscures

the simple fact that what we need is a bigger pie. Uncle Sam can't make a bigger pie. Only individual productivity can do that.

Before Personnel and Industrial Relations
Association, Los Angeles/
The National Observer, 10-19:25.

Chiao Kuan-hua
Vice Foreign Minister of the People's
Republic of (Communist) China
4

In the final analysis, the present economic difficulties [in the world] are the inevitable outcome of the imperialist system. They are not due to increase in the price of raw materials, still less to any alleged misdeeds on the part of the oil-producing countries.

At United Nations, New York/
The Christian Science Monitor, 10-4:6.

David L. Cole
Lawyer; Chairman, National Commission
for Industrial Peace
5

We must constantly bear in mind that the basic concept of collective bargaining [in labor disputes] in our type of society is that it is a process of trying to arrive at accord with a minimum of economic strife. As such, the parties must be willing to try to agree. Each retains the right to decline to agree. Voluntarism on both sides is the essential characteristic. This is emphasized by the constantly repeated thought that strikes could be avoided by the enactment of compulsory-arbitration laws. Such laws are strongly opposed by both labor and management, with relatively few exceptions. The exceptions are largely in the area of public utilities and government employment. The opposition to compulsory arbitration is for a variety of reasons, mainly that it would be incompatible with our system of free collective bargaining and industrial democracy, and that it ignores the fact that we have always proceeded and must still proceed by the process of agreement. Imposition by law runs counter to the very essence of the proposition that we must look to the parties to reach agreement.

Lecture, New York University/
Vital Speeches, 5-1:440.

John Davis
Member, Council of Economic Advisers
to President of the United States
Richard M. Nixon
1

[Saying the reasons for inflation have been building for years]: It's kind of like a fat person. If you follow his food intake on any one day, you may not understand why he's fat. His weight is a direct function of his eating habits and his metabolism over time. But any one day's contribution to it is infinitesimal.
The National Observer, 8-10:12.

Peter F. Drucker
Management consultant; Professor of
Social Science and Business Administration,
Claremont (Calif.) College Graduate School
2

Inflation is the one economic phenomenon on which we have good records. And every period of inflation has led to a revolt of the middle class. Inflation is a social poison—a corrosive poison—because it destroys the bonds of community and sets group against group.
Interview, Claremont, Calif./
Nation's Business, March:65.

John T. Dunlop
Director, Federal Cost of Living Council
3

The present rates of inflation are unusually high, unprecedented in our country, and probably not likely to last. But we should attend to getting them down; and this struggle to achieve a moderate rate of inflation over a long period of time will be with us the rest of this century. As an economist, I do not think inflation is the unmitigated evil that a lot of people have sometimes said it was. Institutions find ways of adapting to inflation. Many countries have had a heck of a lot worse inflation than we have. So it isn't an unmitigated disaster; nor do I think that, should inflation continue at the rates we have experienced in the past couple of years, the U.S. necessarily will fall into a depression of long duration. But we need to work hard to bring the rate of inflation to more tolerable levels.
Interview, Washington/
U.S. News & World Report, 4-22:23.

Lewis A. Engman
Chairman, Federal Trade Commission
4

An economy as complex as ours is like a gigantic machine with thousands and thousands of moving parts linked together with wheels and gears and belts. You change one part and it is going to affect all the others. This is not to say that you shouldn't change anything, just that you should not do so until you have examined its complexities and thoroughly mapped its consequences. We learned this in trying to solve the energy and environmental problems on a piecemeal basis in an atmosphere of crisis, when we discovered that their solutions related to one another like opposite ends of a seesaw. When our economy is examined in an international context, the complexities become even greater.
Before Economic Club, Detroit, April 29/
Vital Speeches, 6-15:517.

Paul J. Fannin
United States Senator, R—Arizona
5

There is the attitude of a growing number of Congressmen and Senators that free enterprise is an outmoded 19th-century institution, that industry acting alone is incapable of serving the public interest, and that only through massive Federal intervention into the workings of the marketplace can the public interest be served. Many members of Congress do indeed believe that the public interest is served in direct proportion to the extent industry is regulated by the Federal government. An increasing number on Capitol Hill believe that capitalism is inherently evil. They feel that the profit motive only results in the strong exploiting the weak, that the growth necessary to sustain industrial survival will destroy the society itself, that business competition encourages destructive aggression. These foes of capitalism feel that only government is capable of doing good. They argue that, to the extent that government can supplant or control industry in the production of goods and services, justice will be done. I know that many members of Congress believe this, as do even more of their staff members. I know that many, if not most, leaders of the academic community believe this, as do an increasing number of

WHAT THEY SAID IN 1974

(PAUL J. FANNIN)

students who have left the colleges and universities to enter society. I stress these points because I believe that the punitive attacks on the energy industry are merely the beginning of even greater attacks on all industry.

Before Energy Users Task Force, Washington,
May 1/Vital Speeches, 6-15:521.

Paul Findley
United States Representative, R—Illinois

1

[Arguing against forced retirement because of age] : [It is] an outrageous form of discrimination that weakens our society and depresses and debilitates millions of citizens each year. The leaders of American industry are being pushed from their board seats; and the production people, whose skill and hard work have made this country an industrial giant, are being dismissed from the assembly lines. Not because they can't keep up. Not because they are too feeble mentally or physically to attend to their duties. But because they have reached the magical—some say doomed—age of 65.

Before the House, Washington, July 10/
Los Angeles Times, 7-11:(1)29.

Gerald R. Ford
Vice President of the United States

2

We all have our pet whipping boy when it comes to inflation. The real culprit today, as it has been, is excessive demand. Double-digit inflation is a result of double-digit increases in money supply and double-digit budget deficits.

Before Economic Club, New York, May 6/
The New York Times, 5-7:36.

Gerald R. Ford
President of the United States

3

The American wage-earner and the American housewife are a lot better economists than most economists care to admit. They know that a government big enough to give you everything you want is a government big enough to take from you everything you have. If we want to restore confidence in ourselves as working politicians, the first thing we all have to do is learn how to say "no." The first specific request by the Ford Administration is not to Congress but to the voters in the upcoming November elections. It is this: Support your candidates, Congressmen and Senators, Democrats or Republicans, conservative or liberal, who consistently vote for tough decisions to cut the cost of government, restrain Federal spending and bring inflation under control . . . Inflation is our domestic public enemy Number 1. To restore economic confidence, the government in Washington must provide leadership. It does no good to blame the public for spending too much when the government is spending too much.

First address as President before
Congress, Washington, Aug. 12/
The New York Times, 8-13:20.

4

Production must improve if we are to have a less inflationary economy. In the long run, it is the only way we can raise wages without inflationary price increases. It is essential in creating new jobs and increasing real wages. In a growing economy, everyone—labor, management and the consumer—wins when productivity expands.

At Ohio State University commencement,
Aug. 30/Chicago Tribune, 8-31:(1)3.

5

[Addressing economists assembled at a White House conference on fighting inflation] : . . . if we succeed in the job cut out for us, I can promise you there will be statues of each of you in every city park throughout the United States. Economics will never again be called a dismal science; nor will politicians, if we succeed, ever dare again to hide behind the old alibi that the people just don't understand economics. The people understand economics very, very well, and they are sick and tired of having politics played with their pocketbooks.

At White House inflation conference,
Washington, Sept. 5/
The Washington Post, 9-6:(A)6.

6

. . . I know many Americans see Federal [wage/price] controls as the answer. But I believe from past experience controls show us that they never really stopped inflation—not the last time, not even during and immediately after World War II, when, as I recall, prices rose despite severe and enforceable wartime rationing. Now, peacetime controls actually, we know from recent experience, create shortages, hamper production, stifle growth and limit jobs. I do not ask for such powers, however politically tempting, as such a program causes the fixer and the black-marketeer to flourish, while decent citizens face empty shelves and stand in long waiting lines.

Before Congress, Washington, Oct. 8/
The New York Times, 10-9:24.

1

. . . our inflation, our Public Enemy Number 1, will, unless whipped, destroy our country, our homes, our liberty, our property and finally our national pride as surely as any well-armed wartime enemy. I concede there will be no sudden Pearl Harbor to shock us into unity and to sacrifice, but I think we've had enough early warning. The time to intercept is right now. The time to intercept is almost gone.

Before Congress, Washington, Oct. 8/
The New York Times, 10-9:24.

2

Somehow the word has gone out that the best way to defeat inflation and revitalize the economy is to curtail buying. Nothing could be further from the truth, and I strongly oppose that point of view. I believe a free society means precisely that—a free market. And sales are the heartbeat of a free market. Instead of curtailing purchases, I say to consumers: Buy wisely. Shop smarter. [To businessmen:] Sell harder. Sell more aggressively. What we need at this time . . . are more Yankee traders and more super salesmen.

Before National Association of Realtors,
Las Vegas, Nov. 14/
The Washington Post, 11-15:(A)6.

3

Times are nowhere near desperate enough to paraphrase President Franklin D. Roosevelt's great rallying cry that the only thing we have to fear is fear itself. Still, it is a good thing to remember. But I do want to say to my fellow Americans that our greatest danger today is to fall victim to the more exaggerated alarms that are being generated about the underlying health and strength of our economy. We are going to take some lumps and we're going to take some bumps, but with the help of Congress and the American people we are perfectly able to cope with our present and foreseeable economic problems. But action is more helpful than criticism. And every week that the Congress delays [in tackling the economic situation] makes the prospects a little bleaker.

News conference, Washington, Dec. 2/
The New York Times, 12-3:28.

4

Men survive by instinct but make progress by intelligence. Perhaps we could survive by merely following our instincts now—an immediate return to wage and price controls, as some demand; immediate and mandatory gasoline rationing, as others advocate; the enactment of other compulsory programs that treat the symptoms but retard the cure. I have been listening to troubled people long enough, and running for election long enough, to sympathize with those who advocate such fixes. I am also old enough to know they never work. I believe instincts must be overruled by intelligence and politics must yield to principles if we are to make reasonable economic progress that can be sustained. And that is what I intend to do.

Before the Business Council, Washington,
Dec. 11/Los Angeles Times, 12-12:(1)10.

Henry Ford II
Chairman, Ford Motor Company

5

I think it is inevitable that some day we will have a shorter work week, but we are not ready for it in this country yet. It would just cut productivity more and send prices higher. I don't think it is the thing to do now, nor three years from now, nor do I think it feasible six years from now. But if you want a long-term look at the future, I think the work week is going to go down as sure as we are sitting here.

News conference/
The Dallas Times Herald, 8-4:(I)6.

165

WHAT THEY SAID IN 1974

(HENRY FORD II)

[1]

[On fighting inflation]: My first recommendation is that governments should curb their spending and bring the supply of money and resulting demand for goods back into balance with the supply of goods. All nations share the responsibility to keep demand in balance with supply, but the major industrial nations have a special responsibility because they account for the greater part of world demand. Fiscal and monetary restraint must be gradual to avoid a depression but must be persistent to succeed. Inflation will not stop if fiscal and monetary discipline is replaced, as soon as it hurts, by jawboning, price controls or other expedients.

Interview/Newsweek, 9-30:78.

[2]

The time has come for the government to recognize that recession has replaced inflation as the greatest and most immediate domestic problem... Consumers have stopped buying because they are afraid that things will go from bad to much worse. Washington must take steps that will persuade the people that the nation still has control of its fate and is not drifting helplessly into deeper and deeper trouble.

Before National Advertising Bureau,
New York, Dec. 9/
Los Angeles Herald-Examiner, 12-10:(C)7.

Gaylord A. Freeman, Jr.
Chairman, First Chicago Corporation

[3]

Congress has got to stop deferring to the Federal Reserve in taking responsibility for controlling inflation. If Congress will have the courage and fortitude to implement the power they have been given under the new budget law passed this year, that might get us out of this quagmire. Reduction in Federal spending will mean a reduction in aggregate demand for goods and services. When the government has a balanced budget, it doesn't need to enter the money market to borrow, and that would relieve much inflationary pressure.

U.S. News & World Report, 8-19:32.

Milton Friedman
Professor of Economics, University of Chicago

[4]

Up to now, inflation is the taxation we got without legislation.

Interview, Ely, Vt./
The New York Times, 8-4:(1)39.

[5]

We've heard a lot of talk about the costs of stopping inflation, and that's an important question. But it must not overcome the other question: What is the cost of not stopping inflation? The plain fact is that this country, while fundamentally strong, has a serious disease; and that disease is going to take its toll, whether we let it run unchecked or whether we try to check it. The cost, if we let it run unchecked, will be the destruction of our system of society and government. The cure would have to be painful indeed to be worse than that disease. There is one and only one cure and we all know it. We have to slow down total spending. Only the Federal government can do that, and it can do that only by slowing its own spending and by slower monetary growth which will slow private spending... no matter how well we conduct the cure, no matter how many sedatives we impose, we cannot avoid paying a substantial cost. We have to reconcile ourselves to the fact that we will not get out of inflation except by going through a temporary but maybe fairly prolonged period of slow economic growth and higher unemployment.

At White House economic conference,
Washington, Sept. 5/
U.S. News & World Report, 9-16:23.

J. William Fulbright
United States Senator, D—Arkansas

[6]

It appears that no one is yet prepared to take the drastic steps—voluntary and mandatory—to curb inflation. It is almost as if we did not quite believe the evidence before our eyes, or our own words acknowledging that evidence. Is this crisis of democratic capitalism indeed fated and beyond our control? The answer, most emphatically, is that it is not. The cure for inflation is to live within your means, which is something we were not doing before the increase of oil prices.

That comes first—the elimination of the prodigal, outrageous waste of basic resources which has become endemic to the American way of life.

Quote, 12-8:538.

John Kenneth Galbraith
Professor of Economics, Harvard University   *1*

There are two kinds of depressions: the old-fashioned kind like we had in the '30s where people couldn't buy what was available because they didn't have enough money; and the new '70s kind of depression, which the world's greatest economists always maintained could never happen—vast unemployment along with inflation.

*Interview, Cambridge, Mass./
"W": a Fairchild publication, 1-11:14.*

2

The trouble with economists is that they're like generals: They are always fighting the last war. To them, unemployment is the great enemy. They don't seem to realize that inflation is far more serious than unemployment. No Administration can survive on a 10.8 per cent inflation rate, and that's what we've been having in this country... If I were appointed Secretary of the Treasury, I would keep the prime interest rate at 10½ per cent, to discourage expansion. I would increase taxes on those with incomes of $15,000 or more. I'd place a surtax on all such incomes, and I believe that would control 40 per cent of all excessive spending. I am opposed to the reduction of taxes on the lower income brackets right now, but I would ease these taxes just as soon as inflation subsided. I would certainly use wage and price controls on the most highly organized sector of the economy—the nation's 1,000 corporations and the unions they're involved with. I would also ask the Congress for a large sum of money to permit the cities to become the employers of last resort for those who became unemployed; and I would lean toward a system of income-maintenance, probably through the negative income tax.

Parade, 5-26:4.

3

[On economists who write about monetary affairs]: There's a tendency for incantation and

mysticism to take over. It's essentially the same as medicine, psychiatry and the priesthood—it's the natural desire of economists to spread the impression that they have access to knowledge not open to other people. The priest does the same when he bespeaks for himself some kind of special relationship with God... People associated with money not only persuade other people they are in touch with the cosmos, but they persuade themselves. The essential absurdity of man is his inability to see himself in perspective, and money destroys his ability to do that.

*Interview, Newfane, Vt./
The New York Times, 8-4:(1)39.*

4

In this kind of economy there is no alternative to wage and price controls—not across the board, but where the private power exists to fix prices and wages, then the public power to do so must be asserted. Otherwise, we have a spiral which is of such power that it can only be arrested by a volume of unemployment that is socially unacceptable.

*At White House economic conference,
Washington, Sept. 5/
U.S. News & World Report, 9-16:23.*

5

... there must, in regard to particular supplies and shortages, be foresight and planning [by government]. The ancient magic of the market is gone forever. Henceforth, for an increasing range of products, supply will equal demand, and vice versa, only as it is made to do so. Every modern government must have an effective planning mechanism... [My plan] is one that calls for a careful, wide-spectrum management of the economy. I share with my conservative friends no slight sorrow that there is no invisible hand to guide the economy, no automatic mechanism that removes the need for human agency and effort and intervention. But it is by the hope that we might be relieved of such care that we have recently been guided. This is the source, in the most general sense, of our anxieties, of what so many call the present [economic] crisis. It was thoughtless of God so to arrange things that the modern economy

WHAT THEY SAID IN 1974

(JOHN KENNETH GALBRAITH)

requires energy and intelligence if it is to serve. But so it is.

Rome, Nov. 29/
The New York Times, 12-8:(3)16.

J. Paul Getty
Industrialist

1

I think money invested in a company that gives employment to people, and good merchandise at a reasonable price, is better-invested than it would be in charities. I think people want jobs more than they want charity. If I am remembered at all, it will be because I created a lot of jobs for a lot of people.

Interview, Woking, England/Time, 2-18:18.

Nat Goldfinger
Research director, American Federation of Labor-Congress of Industrial Organizations

2

[On the current high rate of inflation]: ... this accelerated rate of inflation started in the second half of 1972, and it was touched off by the huge Russian grain deal, which involved large export sales [by the U.S.] of wheat, other grains and other agricultural products to the Soviet Union. Ironically, this was based upon a U.S. government loan of $750 million at a 6 1/8 per cent interest rate to the Russians for the purchase. And we sold off one-quarter of the 1972 wheat crop in addition to soybeans, hides and skins, and corn and various other agricultural products in large amounts, creating tremendous pressures and anticipations of further pressures. We also created developing shortages of those products here at home, because in the process of those sales, and other large-scale export sales which followed sales to other countries—the Japanese and others—we also created shortages of boxcars, barges and transportation facilities. Now, on top of all that, we had the additional pressures on the price level that came from the excessive speculation in the commodity exchanges, which are essentially unregulated by the United States government. So that we had shortages developing here at home. We sold off our stockpiles and reserves, and we also created for ourselves

shortages of transportation facilities. And then in February, 1973, as if all that wasn't enough, the [Nixon] Administration devalued the dollar in a formal, official devaluation—the second official devaluation in 14 months—which added to the continuing huge export sales, not merely to the Russians but to all other countries. And the sales involved not merely agricultural products, but other kinds of raw materials and crude materials, like copper scrap, steel scrap—even wastepaper and fertilizers. What happened here is that the Administration, in effect, sacrificed the American price level and the standard of living of the American people for a temporary, and it turns out to be just a short-run, improvement in the balance of trade ... This whole process—these export sales and the several periods of wild speculation in the commodity exchanges—built up tremendous pressures on the price level from which we are still suffering, and which are rippling out through the rest of the economy. You get the impact of rising prices of corn and soybeans and wheat, on the prices of beef and hogs and poultry and eggs, and also the sharp rise in the price of cotton eventually turns up in sharp increases in the prices of clothing and other goods. And you go down the line.

Interview/The National Observer, 6-15:6.

Barry M. Goldwater
United States Senator, R—Arizona

3

Economic freedom is inseparable from all the other freedoms and liberties we enjoy. It is, in fact, the essential freedom without which all the rest perish. What good is the right to life if a man does not control the *means* to life? In America, the hope of economic and personal freedom rests in the hands of enlightened citizens and their elected representatives who are convinced by their own experiences that the competitive-enterprise system is the best system available in this imperfect world of ours.

Before American Iron and Steel Institute
board of directors, Washington, Feb. 5/
Human Events, 4-6:19.

4

[Saying President Nixon's fiscal-1975 budget is so large it will further contribute to inflation]: If we refuse to act, the holocaust may not descend upon us this year or next year. But, inevitably, the day will come when the people, distrusting their country's currency, will lose all reason to believe in the integrity of their government, and that most noble of experiments in the freedom of man will be dragged down into the dust. The government of the United States . . . will either disappear or be so distorted as to no longer be recognizable.

Los Angeles Herald-Examiner, 5-8:(A)10.

C. Jackson Grayson, Jr.
Dean, School of Business Administration,
Southern Methodist University;
Former Chairman, Price Commission,
Federal Cost of Living Council

1

Wage and price controls have limited short-term benefits, have now passed their usefulness, become counter-productive in our economic system and, before it is too late, should be discontinued in order to return to the competitive market system . . . Wage and price controls become more dysfunctional and dangerous for the future of our economic system the longer they last . . . I believe that wage and price controls can help attack inflation in the short run by reducing inflationary expectations, intrude on the market power of business and labor and influence the timing of price and wage decisions while waiting for other government policies to take effect. But any favorable impact is short-lived.

Before Senate Banking and Currency Sub-
committee on Productivity and Stabilization,
Washington/The Dallas Times Herald, 2-1:(C)5.

Alan Greenspan
Chairman-designate, Council of Economic
Advisers to President of the
United States Richard M. Nixon

2

I always argued against price controls and wage controls, largely because I submit that they suppress inflationary forces and, by suppressing them, cause them to be pushed out. The simplest way to eliminate inflationary expectations is to allow the prices to rise and those expectations to burn themselves out.

Interview, June/
The Washington Post, 7-28:(H)4.

Alan Greenspan
Chairman, Council of Economic Advisers
to President of the United States
Gerald R. Ford

3

. . . we have to recognize that what is depressing the economic outlook, at least in my judgment, is the underlying inflation psychology. I think if one tracks it through the system it shows up in so many areas; it's so pervasive that it leads you to a conclusion that, if through some means you can defuse this inflation psychology, you're removing a very major depressant on the system. And I think that the policy should in all respects be focused on this particular point. And if we're successful in bringing down the rates of inflation, and it is credible to the American public, I would not be surprised to find a good deal of this gloom, which we now see, dissipate fairly rapidly. And I think this is essentially what we should be focusing on. I certainly don't think that it's easy . . . but unless and until we can do this, I think that we're going to stay with this particular turgid economy.

At White House inflation conference,
Washington, Sept. 5/
The New York Times, 9-6:14.

4

I think that inflation can never be solved on strictly economic grounds. I think that one must confront the problem in a political sense, and in fact that is what is being done; because essentially, as I view it, the basic underlying cause of inflation is a long-term trend in excessive Federal spending. But the Federal spending obviously is created by the political process; and in fact what the President and the Congress are now confronted with at the moment is to try to suppress this expansionary rate, and that essentially is our political process.

TV-radio interview, Washington/
"Meet the Press,"
National Broadcasting Company, 9-29.

H. R. Gross
United States Representative, R–Iowa

5

Do you know that this big, allegedly affluent country of ours has a public and private debt,

(H. R. GROSS)

as of last December 31, of 3 trillion, 200 billion dollars? That's *net,* public and private. That much debt is unmanageable . . . we can't go on piling up debt, paying so much interest. We can't go on—and maintain this form of government. If you can't retire this debt by orderly means, then it will be retired by disorderly means or unusual means . . . by devaluation, revaluation or outright repudiation. You might have a little money in the bank and one fine morning you might wake up and find that each one of your dollars was now worth 50 cents. The other 50 cents would have been confiscated.

Interview, Washington/
The National Observer, 3-23:11.

Gabriel Hauge
Chairman, Manufacturers
Hanover Trust Company, New York
1

Inflation is . . . insidious. It erodes the very fabric of our society. It stimulates a race for pay, profit and power. It sets group against group in a feverish contest for slices of the national pie. It accelerates treadmill consumer spending. It encourages speculation in such things as real estate and commodities as means of making money, and discourages the development of entrepreneurial skills vital to the functioning of our society. Moreover, its soaring cost threatens to socialize many private educational and charitable activities. Inflation is a dangerous disease, not "a bad itch" or an "annoyance," as it was recently characterized by two leading economists. I say to you with all gravity that it is a threat to our society that is real and deeply disturbing.

At Canadian Financial Conference, Toronto,
June 20/Vital Speeches, 8-15:663.

Alfred Hayes
President, Federal Reserve Bank of New York
2

[There is a] profound public disillusionment of the efficacy of official anti-inflationary policies, and widespread fear that inflation will continue unabated for years to come. I hope this nation will refuse to succumb to the siren song of those who would meet this situation by accepting inflation as a way of life and establishing escalator indexing practices for salaries, bonds and other vehicles of income or savings.

Before New Jersey Bankers Association/
The New York Times, 5-28:57.

Walter E. Hoadley
Executive vice president, Bank of America
3

In my judgment, the most pressing problem confronting the American economy—and indeed a great deal of the world—is lack of confidence in the future. This is not to minimize the economy problems, but I'm concerned that there are far too many people in this country who are seeing only more trouble ahead and certainly not judging our basic strengths. Now, unless this is reversed, we can see a worrisome breaking down and weakening of the venturesome spirit in this country which is vital to our future. And if that continues for some period of months or a few years, then obviously there will be erosion in capital expenditures. There will be an aggravation of shortages and a compounding of unemployment, all of which . . . is intolerable. But the doom and gloom, as it's called, is much more profound outside the United States than it is within our own country. And those who have been to Western Europe or to Asia—but particularly to Western Europe in recent days—come back uniformly saying that there is a great lack of confidence. And that, in my judgment, is one of the prevailing concerns which must be an overriding consideration . . .

At White House inflation conference,
Washington, Sept. 5/
The New York Times, 9-6:15.

James D. Hodgson
Former Secretary of Labor
of the United States
4

We know that, until well into this century, employment relationships in the U.S. were largely unregulated by law . . . Today, both the employer and the employed are subject to a wide range of legislated requirements. Some can be characterized as labor legislation. Some not. But all are interrelated. The workplace has become practically a legal world of its own, invaded by a fantastic array of legislated do's and don'ts. The bulk of this legislation has had an objective that may be summed up under one word—protection; four kinds of protection for the worker: protection of persons, of jobs, of income and of rights. It appears that, as a society becomes more mature and an economy more affluent, the protection of its citizens becomes an increasing preoccupation of lawmakers. Statutory protection of citizens in their roles as workers has become part of this pattern—an increasingly large part of it.

*Before Labor Relations Council,
the Wharton School, University of Pennsylvania,
Feb. 19/Vital Speeches, 4-1:373.*

Eric Hoffer
Philosopher

1

We must abandon the idea that jobs should be meaningful. There are simply not enough meaningful jobs in the world for everyone to feel fulfilled. Santayana once said that to demand that your work be meaningful is a human impertinence. In an industrial society, many jobs require doing something that, when you get through with it, you know is pointless. That is why I think people should work no more than six hours a day, five days a week; and after that, one's real life should begin.

*Interview, San Francisco/
San Francisco Examiner & Chronicle,
7-21:(California Living)36.*

Hendrik S. Houthakker
*Former member, Council of Economic Advisers
to the President of the United States
(Richard M. Nixon)*

2

... "stagflation" is intimately related to the weakness of competition ... If competition is sufficiently widespread, the economy as a whole will react to an excess of supply with a fall in the general price level, just as it will respond to an excess of demand by inflation. But if competition is not sufficiently strong, the economy as a whole will behave rather like the automobile industry, where rising prices and declining output go hand in hand ... In

many other markets, lack of competition is a direct result of government intervention rather than inaction ... The list of industries where the government thwarts the beneficial action of market forces, usually at the behest of trade organizations or labor unions, is long indeed and still growing ... Competition is not dead in the American economy, but it is losing ground steadily; and this is one of the principal reasons for our increasing vulnerability to inflation ... We may well be in for a prolonged period of sustained inflation, excessive unemployment and sluggish growth unless we reinvigorate the economy by greater reliance on its mainspring—private competitive enterprise.

*Before Senate Government Operations
Committee, Washington, Nov. 22/
The Washington Post, 11-23:(C)10.*

Hubert H. Humphrey
United States Senator, D–Minnesota

3

Regardless of how you look at it, the American worker suffered [in 1973] both as a wage-earner and as a consumer. Wage rates not only have not kept pace with inflation, but also have undergone a significant setback in terms of purchasing power. Unfortunately, the worst may be yet to come. According to many experts, inflation next year will be even worse than in 1973. A rate of inflation of more than 7 per cent is expected during the first half of 1974 ... Prices on nearly everything we buy have gone up at record rates—food costs rose 19 per cent in the last year, fuel oil and coal prices are up about 20 per cent over last year and are still rising, and housing costs went up by 6 per cent in 1973. Interest rates have soared to new heights, with the prime interest rate at 10 per cent in many banks in December and home loans carrying stiff interest charges of 9 per cent or more. At the same time, industry has reaped a profits bonanza at the expense of the American worker.

The Christian Science Monitor, 1-25:9.

4

For generations economists have claimed that a high rate of inflation could not exist side-by-side in our economy with a drop in economic activity, high levels of unemployment

(HUBERT H. HUMPHREY)

and high interest rates. The Nixon Administration has clearly proved that, with its economic policies, you can have all of this bad news at the same time.

April 21/The New York Times, 4-22:20.

Lee A. Iacocca
President, Ford Motor Company
1

The only way to break inflation is by rolling back costs. We've got to get back to fundamentals. The Federal government is spending $30 billion more than it's taking in, and you can't do that for long. But it has become a way of life. Now, I'm one of those free-enterprisers. I can't deficit-spend. If I don't make a profit—and I don't mean the measly 2.6¢ per dollar of sales we've seen lately—I don't last for long. That's the name of the game.

Interview, Dearborn, Mich./People, 9-23:36.

Henry M. Jackson
United States Senator, D–Washington
2

Full employment would be the greatest social program in our history. This still evades us after all these years of effort... for every able-bodied person to have employment. We have to put first things first. It is at the heart of everything, and is central to all our other problems, such as the need for more health programs and a better environment. I think we must pause and think... what do we really want? Raise a family in a good neighborhood; live in a good home in a good environment; send our children to the best schools possible; have good health care, both preventive and curative; and have leisure time to live in a peaceful world. It will require full employment to create the best possible standard of living for all our people.

The Saturday Evening Post, Aug.-Sept.:45.

Reginald H. Jones
Chairman, General Electric Company
3

We have reason to be concerned whether the corporation as we know it—the characteristic institution of our American enterprise system—

will survive into the next century... The deepest challenge comes from a basic shift in the values that undergird our society. Increasingly, Americans distrust the market system and demand that government step in to assure them of economic benefits. Much of the public has come to feel that controls—in other words, central planning—are not only desirable, but superior.

Before Economic Club, Detroit, Nov. 25/ The New York Times, 11-26:55.

Henry Kaufman
Partner, Salomon Brothers, investments
4

It may... be that we as a people may not be willing to accept harsh government action to deal with the inflational problems because the measures required will deny things to us, hardly a popular political objective. This is why the inflation may lead to... a protracted period in which there are disappointing results and disillusionment. It may well be a rolling period of discipline and disillusionment, moving from one sector to another, forcing both economic and financial expectations lower and ultimately bringing about great efficiency and prudence.

At New School economic forum, New York, Jan. 26/ The New York Times, 1-27:(3)12.

5

When inflation spreads and expectations of hyperinflation appear, governmental countermeasures are unlikely to be even-handed or well-planned. The public anxiety becomes too great and the pressure to do something impetuously is given added impetus not only from the sharply rising prices, but also from strikes, shortages of goods and services, and the increasing skepticism of the people in the governmental process. Consequently, the country becomes ripe for a sharp shift politically, either to the left or to the right.

Before Boston Stock Exchange members/ The New York Times, 7-7:(3)1.

Jack Kemp
United States Representative, R–New York
6

I hear questions daily: "Why shouldn't we extend wage and price controls? After all, don't we need controls now more than ever since prices are still rising? Don't we need more controls to allocate scarce resources and goods in short supply? And even if we are going to end price controls, shouldn't we wait until a more appropriate time?'' Why then do I advocate a refusal to extend these controls? As a nation—and as a Congress entrusted with the exercise of the people's welfare—we are at an historic focal point for major decisions on the role of government in the economy. If we opt for more controls, we invite the potential destruction of the most productive economy in the world—ours. If we opt for restoring freedom to the marketplace, we will not only help to resolve many of our ills, but we will also set the stage for a period of renewed economic expansion and solidity. This period now before us—between now and April 30 [when wage/price control authorization expires]—is when we must make this decision; and I, for one, will be on the side of freedom as I believe I was when I voted against the last extension of the act . . . If we do not learn from the experiences of history . . . and return to a market economy, we are inviting even worse shortages and even higher prices. These may, in the end, produce a severe recession or even a depression. This would stagnate the economy of the entire world, would weaken our position in relation to controlled economies, would result in millions unemployed, and would place additional—and what would have otherwise been unnecessary—burdens upon government to insure the general welfare.

Before the House, Washington, Jan. 28/
Vital Speeches, 2-15:265.

William F. Kerby
Chairman, Dow Jones & Company   *1*

. . . consider these facts: Americans have never had more real income; I am not talking about inflation-eroded dollars but real spending power. We read about unemployment, but did you realize that never in history have more Americans held jobs? Importantly, while we have all experienced and are quite understandably unhappy about high prices, the offset is that never in history has any people been able

to afford such a high standard of living. All this provides an enormously strong, durable and flexible economic base . . . Of all the figures poured out by the statistical mills, none is more widely publicized than that representing the cost of living—an index of consumer prices based on the 1967 price level as 100. The other side of the coin, the size of the American paycheck, gets almost no attention. The cost of living, measured by this cost-of-living index, stood at 66.9 in 1947. By early this year it had climbed to 141.5, a rise of 111 per cent. But now a look at the average American paycheck: In 1947 it stood at, believe it or not, $45.58 a week. By this past February it had soared to $147.10. Now, that's a real leap—up 222 per cent. So we have this interesting comparison: During the post-World War II era we have had weekly earnings rising by almost exactly twice as fast as the cost of living.

At DePauw University commencement, May/
The National Observer, 8-3:11.

2

I have great faith in the good sense of the American people and the resilience of the American economy. So we may fumble, make false starts and do some foolish things. But, in the end, the system works and it will keep on working.

Quote, 11-3:410.

R. Heath Larry
Vice Chairman,
United States Steel Corporation   *3*

There's almost no way the government can involve itself in an effort to control prices and wages—and do it equitably, and do it for very long—without leading to allocation of materials and then to an almost totally controlled economy.

At talks with Steelworkers Union/
The Washington Post, 1-31:(A)3.

Raymond S. Livingstone
Authority on personnel administration
and employment; Former vice president,
TRW, Inc.   *4*

It's a simple fact that many of the jobless don't know how to do much of the work that

(RAYMOND S. LIVINGSTONE)

needs to be done. But many, many others just don't *want* to do work that is waiting to be done. It's too hard, or not interesting enough, or doesn't pay enough, or is hard to get to, or "doesn't lead anywhere," or "isn't in my line," or "the hours are bad." Part of this is that we have inculcated our young people with the idea that it's their right to have a job that is interesting, that has status, that has security, and that they enjoy doing. The term "meaningful work" has been perverted. We haven't told them that there's a lot of work that is just plain hard, tedious and unpleasant—but it's important and has to be done, and it's a means to an end: earning food, clothing and shelter, and then the pleasures that go with it.

Interview/U.S. News & World Report, 11-18:45.

Mike Mansfield
United States Senator, D—Montana

1

I am not an economist and make no pretenses. What is clear to me, however, is that . . . words will no longer satisfy the nation. Inflation is social dynamite; walk through any food market in any suburb and take note of the comments. Recession is social dynamite; walk through areas of high unemployment in any city and ask what lies ahead. The divisions among people, among societies, among nations are on the rise. They will not wait for the "self-adjusting mechanisms" of the economy to self-adjust.

At Presidential conference on inflation,
Washington, Sept. 27/
Los Angeles Times, 9-28:(1)4.

2

I think it's just going to be a matter of time before we come to wage and price controls. With unemployment reaching 6 per cent and going to go above that, with prices still increasing—12.1 per cent from last September to this September—all the elements are there for a recession which, if not corrected, may well plunge us deeper into an economic morass.

TV-radio interview/"Face the Nation,"
Columbia Broadcasting System, 10-27.

Forrest McDonald
Professor of History, Wayne State University

3

What it comes down to is this: Prices are going to increase, taxes are going to increase, waste is going to increase, and unemployment is going to increase. Any effort to prevent the increase in any one of these four areas will produce a corresponding acceleration of the increase in all the others. In sum, the engine grows hotter and hotter.

Interview/
"W": a Fairchild publication, 8-9:7.

George Meany
President, American Federation of Labor-
Congress of Industrial Organizations

4

We've already reached the recession point in my book . . . A recession is when your neighbor is out of work. A depression is when you are out of work.

News conference, Bal Harbour, Fla.,
Feb. 18/ The New York Times, 2-19:13.

5

[Saying Congress should not renew the Nixon Adminstration's wage/price control authority]: We are here to ask the Congress not to give this Administration the legislative authority to further wreck the American economy. Two and one-half years experience under this program are enough. It has failed miserably in its stated aim of curbing inflation. It has been unfair, inequitable and unbalanced. It is a fraud and deception . . . The gimmickry of two freezes and three phases, since August 15, 1971, has helped to create the worst economic mess in over three decades. The controls program has been heavily weighted in favor of big business and the banks, against the worker and consumer. Thirty months of freezes and phases make it perfectly clear that the Nixon Administration will never establish a program of even-handed controls, based on fairness, justice and equal sacrifice.

Before Senate Banking Subcommittee,
Washington, March 6/
The Dallas Times Herald, 3-6:(A)28.

6

The Nixon Administration, by its incredibly stupid policy, placed the American people in the tightening squeeze of an inflationary recession. So what is the logical conclusion as we are confronted by this economic mess, the bankruptcy of the Administration, raging inflation, skyrocketing profits and the highest interest rates since the Civil War? The conclusion is quite simple: Workers and their unions have no other alternative than to seek large wage increases and cost-of-living escalation protection for the sake of their families and living standards.

At carpenters union convention, Chicago/ Chicago Tribune, 8-3:(1)2.

1

Inflation, unemployment—these are people-problems and they call out for humanitarian solutions. Until now, the government has treated the problems as mathematic equations. It is our hope the new President [Ford] will see more than just cold, cruel numbers—that he'll see people, not percentages, and that he will move with compassion.

Labor Day message, Aug. 30/ Los Angeles Times, 8-31:(3)14.

2

Today's inflation is not caused by excessive demand, which is the classic reason for inflation—too many dollars chasing too few goods. Hence we believe that [government] budget cuts, high interest rates and tight money—which might be appropriate weapons against excessive-demand inflation—simply will not work on today's inflation. Indiscriminate budget-cutting could compound recession; higher interest rates could only insure higher prices; tight money only chokes an economy that needs to grow.

At White House economic conference, Washington/Newsweek, 9-23:77.

Walter F. Mondale
United States Senator, D–Minnesota
3

Everyone, from the President on down, should pay their fair share in taxes. The average working American has already seen more than enough of this kind of artful tax-dodging. He is fed up—and rightly so—with a system that forces him to pay more so the rich can pay less.

San Francisco Examiner & Chronicle, 3-10:(This World)2.

Thomas A. Murphy
Chairman-elect, General Motors Corporation
4

In the final analysis, the cure for inflation and our other economic ills lies in the regenerative powers built into our competitive market system, and not in government controls. The time has come to move back, at long last, toward an essentially free economy, and to create the kind of economic climate we all need desperately—a climate conducive to expanded employment, to innovation and risk-taking and to growth.

At Los Angeles Area Chamber of Commerce Business Outlook Conference/ Los Angeles Herald-Examiner, 11-24:(G)5.

Gunnar Myrdal
Swedish economist
5

... there are many effects of inflation that economists are not stressing. One, which I put great emphasis on, is the irritation it creates all around. You get irritation between the house-wife, who goes to the grocery store, and her husband, who has given her the money. Then there's irritation between the housewife and the grocer. You have irritation between employees and employers. And you have irritation—this is the most important thing—between the citizen and his government ... most certainly citizens should blame their government when it doesn't keep a stable currency. And when you have a great instability among governments all over the Western world, I think the basis [for that instability] is their citizens' irritation with inflation, with stagflation.

Interview/The National Observer, 12-7:1.

6

The so-called war against inflation is flowery rhetoric and not reality. [U.S. President] Ford asks the American people to sacrifice them-selves in this war, and the Americans see no incentive to making sacrifices like they did in World War II, for instance. I call it stagflation, and you will not win it if you don't take it as a war. I don't see any clear leadership in either major party against this evil.

At symposium, Palm Coast, Fla./ Los Angeles Times, 12-11:(6)3.

WHAT THEY SAID IN 1974

Richard M. Nixon
President of the United States

1

[The inflationary tide] will go down provided we are responsible in our government spending programs and that the Congress does not go on a wild spending spree. It'll go down, second, because, the energy crisis having been reduced to a problem, we'll have less pressure upwards in that particular area. And it will go down, too, because the prospects insofar as food production appear to be very good at the present time, although this is one that is extremely difficult to project. I would like to tell you that the number will be 4 per cent, 5 per cent, 3 per cent, 8 per cent by the end of the year. I don't know. My economic advisers don't even know, and they used to know everything. So all that I can say is this: We're in this fight with regard to inflation to win it, and we believe that with proper fiscal policies and with increasing production in the energy field, increasing production on the food front, that that is the way to bring down the prices and to take the pressure off of the prices.

Before Executive Club, Chicago, March 15/
The New York Times, 3-16:13.

2

At the end, we will look back and say 1974 was not our best year [economically], as were '72 and '73, but it was a good year. I will say—and I will flatly predict—that '75 will be a very good year. And I say today that '76, the 200th anniversary year for America, will be the best year in America's history, the most prosperous, the most free.

Jackson, Miss., April 25/
The Washington Post, 4-26:(A)4.

3

The requirements for full economic recovery may sound like harsh medicine—budgetary restraint, no tax cut, tight money—but there is no alternative. I wish I could tell you that there is a way out of the present inflation without such measures, but there is not. We cannot spend our way to prosperity. Neither can we achieve prosperity or price stability by putting America back into a straitjacket of controls.

Radio address to the nation, May 25/
The New York Times, 5-26:(1)23.

4

. . . we need in this country the one lobby we don't have: an anti-inflation lobby. This should not be a lobby with plush Washington offices and high-paid officers. This lobby should have an office in every home in America, and every citizen should be an officer of it. When every government official—whether in the Executive Branch, in the Congress or in state and local governments—knows that this lobby will reward anti-inflationary action and punish inflationary action, the fight against inflation will be won.

Before businessmen, Los Angeles, July 25/
The New York Times, 7-26:16.

Arthur M. Okun
Senior fellow, Brookings Institution;
Former Chairman, Council of Economic
Advisers to the President of the
United States (Lyndon B. Johnson)

5

[On the impending end of wage and price controls] : I'd like a continuation of some statutory control or authority that would permit wage or price decisions to be overturned after some due process. Still, I think we'll be out of the controls business for a while. Then, after its bad reputation wears off, we'll be back into it. This has been the history of a lot of European countries. I'm always reminded of the P. T. Barnum story that it's easy to put a lion and a lamb in the same cage as long as you have a large reserve supply of lambs. I think that's the story with the lamb of controls and the lions of business, labor and excessive fiscal and monetary enthusiasm—you need a big supply of lambs.

Interview/The New York Times, 4-28:(3)25.

Don Paarlberg
Director of Agriculture Economics,
Department of Agriculture of the
United States

6

Much as we protest against inflation, we seem to prefer it to a stable price level, with all its related problems . . . We have a love-hate relationship with inflation. We hate inflation, but we love everything that causes it. Farmers hate inflation, but they like high price supports.

Laboring people hate inflation, but they like an increase in the minimum wage. Industrial people hate inflation, but they like to keep out cheap foreign goods. The lending community hates inflation, but likes a plentiful supply of credit ... It is quite possible that the public attitude toward inflation is less adverse than one would think from reading the papers. Whom does inflation help? The borrower, who finds his debts easier to pay; the homeowner, who sees net worth increase; the laboring man who, through his union, is able to keep ahead of the increase in consumer prices; the industrialist, who finds a growing market for his products. Whom does inflation hurt? The widow who must live on her husband's life insurance; the retired people, who must live on fixed incomes; salaried people, whose incomes are administered and are slow to increase; bond holders, who get back less real value than they paid out; low-income working people, who lack the bargaining power needed to keep up with price increases. Altogether, those favored by inflation must be more numerous or more powerful than the others; I can see no other way to explain the behavior of our political economy. As a people, we insist on efforts to retard inflation. We set up a Cost of Living Council and appoint officials to battle inflation. But we don't really want them to win. It is a fundamental principle of sociology that the kind of behavior which develops is the kind that is rewarded. As our elected public officials apparently read the picture, we reward those who oppose inflation with words but cause it with deeds. Since the public apparently wants strong statements in opposition to inflation and actions that induce it, we no doubt shall continue to have both.

*Before Federal Land Bank
of St. Louis stockholders/
The National Observer, 4-13:13.*

W. R. Poage
United States Representative, D—Texas   *1*

Instead of trying to do an honest day's work for an honest day's pay, we have too long tried to get a full day's pay for part of a day's work. If American labor is going to continue this policy, we are going to continue to have inflation regardless of any credit regulations that the government may impose.

*At Food and Agriculture Economic Summit
Conference on Inflation, Chicago, Sept. 12/
Los Angeles Herald-Examiner, 9-13:(A)2.*

2

Labor organizations have done a great deal for our country ... but they have tended, very naturally, to concentrate on programs of direct benefit to their own members—too often without regard to the public's good. I think that we are now suffering from the adoption of a philosophy which I believe was originated by our labor organizations and which has pretty well been accepted by a large part of our population, and that is that every individual should receive the same compensation for the same number of hours on the job regardless of his productivity. I don't believe this. I believe that the compensation of a lawyer, a bricklayer or a farmer should be in proportion to his contribution to society—not in proportion to the number of hours which the clock shows he was on the job. And I think that our departure from that principle has been disastrous to laboring men as well as to the consuming public.

*At Food and Agriculture Economic Summit
Conference on Inflation, Chicago,
Sept. 12/Vital Speeches, 10-1:745.*

George B. Preston
*President, United States League of
Savings Associations*   *3*

We have the housing act of 1968, which promises a decent home for every American family. We have the employment act of 1946, which presses a determination on the part of the Federal government to secure a job for every American able to work. These are landmark declarations of public policy and there are references to them, year-in and year-out, when matters of housing policy and economic policy are discussed in Congress. It seems to me a clear public policy statement on inflation could also become a yardstick against which various social, economic and financial policies of the country may be measured ... I would like to see a major piece of legislation include a declaration

(GEORGE B. PRESTON)

of public policy on inflation that would be broad enough in its scope and strong enough in purpose to hold out hope for those tens of millions of Americans whose real purchasing power has been eroded in recent years.

At California Savings and Loan League management conference, San Diego/ San Francisco Examiner, 2-28:56.

Ronald Reagan
Governor of California   *thats funny-*

1

There is no way that you can condone strikes by public employees. They do not have the same situation that private employees do in private industries. Government cannot go out of business.

News conference, Sacramento, March 12/ Los Angeles Times, 3-13:(1)24.

2

There is no mystery about inflation. Inflation is caused by one thing and one thing alone. It comes when government spends more money than it is taking in.

Aw it spends it on stupid shit like "star Wars"

At Republican fund-raising dinner, Centreville, Md., Aug. 24/ The Washington Post, 8-25:(A)5.

Henry S. Reuss
United States Representative, D—Wisconsin

3

On inflation, I think the time is past when it is desirable to try to maintain a complete apparatus of price/wage control across the entire economy. That's simply too restrictive; and the "on again-off again" conduct last year has made that as impossible as it is undesirable. However, I think we do need to maintain some sort of price-control apparatus, and there I like the idea proposed by Dr. Arthur Burns, Chairman of the Federal Reserve Board, who suggests that there be a more or less permanent price/wage board to examine inflationary increases in those industries that are characterized by huge firms and huge labor unions. Roughly speaking, there we mean automobiles, petroleum, certain heavy chemicals, steel, aluminum—those industries, by [and] large, where just a handful of companies control the majority of production, and where

huge unions are pretty well able to dictate their own wage terms and have those wages passed on in the form of increased prices of the end product. There, Dr. Burns thinks—and I agree— that we need a permanent board to examine existing and proposed price increases, to evolve guidelines, and if it comes down to a crunch, to actually issue mandatory orders.

At Utah State University, Jan. 7/ Vital Speeches, 3-1:296.

4

The causes [of inflation] are complex and multiple. In some areas, such as inventories and industrial supplies, we face an old-fashioned credit-induced demand inflation. In the food and fuel sectors and at various times lumber, scrap and many other commodities, an old-fashioned supply-shortage inflation is going on. We also suffer from an over-extension of our money supply, resulting from the Fed's [Federal Reserve Board's] creation of too much money in the past two or three years. In addition, we suffer from the legacy of a fiscal inflation going back to the guns-and-butter foolishness of us Democrats in the late '60s. That originally gave the inflationary rotor a spin.

Interview/The National Observer, 7-13:6.

John J. Rhodes
United States Representative, R—Arizona

5

[Arguing against a tax cut]: What we have on a global basis is demand-pull inflation. When you have a demand-pull inflation, the best way to cure it is to increase production. You don't cure it by putting more money in the hands of more people to chase fewer goods, which is the classic definition of a demand-pull inflation to begin with. You would merely exacerbate your economic problems if you were to cut taxes at this time. I think most economists agree that, economically speaking, a tax *increase* would make more sense. Politically speaking, that's impossible. It won't happen. But I would certainly hope that a tax cut would be forestalled.

Interview/ U.S. News and World Report, 5-27:30.

Pierre A. Rinfret
Economist
1

If we are going to mount a war on inflation, we should mount a war effort. A war requires war effort. It requires an all-out, dedicated effort to achieve victory. Half measures, partial measures, partial commitment and "business as usual" have never won a war. In my judgment, losing the war on inflation can be as morally and economically damaging as losing a military war. We need to put the American economy on a war footing to beat inflation. By that I mean we have to take stern and drastic measures.

Interview/Newsweek, 9-30:76.

Alice M. Rivlin
Economist; Senior fellow,
Brookings Institution
2

In this country we have had, except for the Great Depression, almost no experience with price decline. Nobody expects prices to decline generally. The best one hopes for now is a leveling off of the inflation or cutting down to 3 per cent or 4 per cent annually. The recent consumer price index shows a rate of 12 per cent or 13 per cent, which is higher than we have ever had except for brief periods after wartime ... The United States has been fairly lucky about inflation, if lucky is not the wrong word. We have not experienced prolonged inflation the way the rest of the world has; and it may be that we will just have to get used to a continuing, somewhat higher level of inflation so that one comes to regard 5 per cent or 6 per cent as normal rather than 3 per cent.

Interview, Washington/
Los Angeles Times, 6-20:(2)7.

Kenneth Rush
Counsellor to President of the United States
Richard M. Nixon for Economic Policy
3

I feel economists are not necessarily the ones who should sit at the policy-making roles in government. I feel economists are absolutely necessary to make studies, to give advice, to play a very major role in the formulation of policy. However, I feel that the broad considerations of economics, of politics, of international relations, of diplomacy, may require that someone other than an economist be at the post of Secretary of the Treasury or head of OMB or Counsellor to the President.

TV-radio interview, Washington/
"Meet the Press,"
National Broadcasting Company, 6-9.

Howard A. Rusk
Director, Institute of Rehabilitation
Medicine, New York University
4

Mandatory retirement policies are causing us to lose our most precious human resource—wisdom. You can be born brilliant, but you cannot be born wise. That only comes with experience, and experience comes with time. Actually, it takes both old and young people to do a job. You need older people for stability and wisdom, and young people for fire.

Interview, New York/
The New York Times, 7-21:(1)10.

Paul A. Samuelson
Chairman, Economics Department,
Massachusetts Institute of Technology
5

The Republican Party has an albatross around its neck, which is Watergate. But in addition, there is another albatross—which would hurt any incumbent—and that is the stagnation of the economy while at the same time we have "double-digit" inflation. That's tough on incumbents. But let me be objective. I'm a Democrat. I criticize the [Nixon] Administration. But it would be wrong to think there exists in Congress a great source of untapped wisdom which knows how to handle the simultaneous problem of stagnation and inflation. No mixed economy—whether it's England with the labor government, or Denmark with a relatively conservative government having turned out labor, or in Sweden, Switzerland or Japan—knows how to have stable prices and high employment. The wonder, you might say, is that things have not been worse.

Interview/
Los Angeles Herald-Examiner, 6-9:(D)6.

Alfred Schaefer
Chairman, Union Bank of Switzerland

1

Americans are too gloomy. America is in better shape than anyone else ... Europeans are going into the American stock markets because America is the last bastion of capitalist thinking and because 90 per cent of production in America goes back into America itself. The Americans can sell what they produce right there in their own market ... [America is] the one nation where capitalism seems safe for the next one or two generations.

Zurich/"W": a Fairchild publication, 1-11:14.

2

If we are realistic, we must conclude that permanent inflation will lead to the downfall of the free-market economy and the social system that goes with it.

U.S. News & World Report, 5-13:29.

William J. Scherle
United States Representative, R–Iowa

3

The guy who hung the first dollar he ever made in a 10-cent frame 30 years ago finds that today the frame is worth a dollar and the dollar is worth 10 cents.

San Francisco Examiner, 5-6:31.

Helmut Schmidt
Chancellor of West Germany

4

[On the world economy] : Inflation is not an inevitable feature of our structure of economy. It is the consequence of a lack of will, of too much permissiveness, of too much opportunism, a lack of decision, a lack of consequence ... Many, many countries have contributed to that process [of inflation] by unsound financing of their public expenditure, by unsound behavior of their banking systems, by letting their banking system step up their volume of credit in a way by no means justified by the increase of production or productivity. One could find the common denominator in saying that many governments and legislatures all over the world have just been too permissive vis-a-vis different pressure groups within their own societies. They tried to satisfy everybody, and in the end they dissatisfied everybody.

*Interview, Bonn/
The Christian Science Monitor, 8-14:1.*

5

There is a danger that, if the United States as a whole goes deflationary, taking into the bargain a high rate of unemployment, this will inevitably spread to the world markets. It will mean less demand from the U.S. on the world market, and it will mean that we can sell less than we sold last year or last month ... You [the U.S.] have to fight inflation, but please don't enter into deflation policy, because you might incur too much unemployment, too much deflation in the world economy. It is for the man in the street a very unclear message and it needs very much, from period to period, from quarter to quarter, feeling in the tips of your fingers.

Interview/The New York Times, 8-25:(1)26.

Charles L. Schultze
*Former Director, Federal Bureau
of the Budget*

6

In the normal inflationary situation, when I pay a higher price for a suit of clothes or a TV set, most of that increase ends up in somebody's paycheck. However undesirable the inflation, it does not normally lead to a reduction in the over-all purchasing power of consumers, since the higher prices are more or less matched by higher money income. But that is not the case today. In 1974, the increase in crude-oil prices alone, as they are passed on to the consumer, will take some $20 billion out of consumer pockets. Part of that money will go abroad to foreign oil-producing countries. Most of the remainder will show up in higher profits for domestic oil companies. Some of those higher profits will be plowed back into the economy through increased expenditures on exploration and development of oil, gas and other fuel reserves. But not all of them—and not right away.

*Before Congressional Committee, Washington/
The New York Times, 5-12:(3)2.*

Hugh Scott
United States Senator, R Pennsylvania

1

I think that one can only candidly say that we are in a recession. I can't quite understand the White House reluctance to actually call this what it is. I think the sooner we admit it's a recession the earlier we have a chance to get out of it, because the existence of the fact presents the necessity for the solutions.

Interview, Philadelphia, Nov. 11/
Los Angeles Times, 11-12:(3)16.

Irving S. Shapiro
Chairman,
E. I. du Pont de Nemours & Company

2

. . . the most difficult problem is inflation. We haven't licked it. All you can hope for is that, once we get through the first pain of the impending [price] decontrol, in which some prices will be forced up, we can get enough stability in the economy to avoid runaway inflation. There will be a higher plateau—you never go back. But, with sensible government policies and some constraints both by labor and management, it doesn't have to mushroom.

Interview, Wilmington, Del./
Los Angeles Times, 3-28:(2)7.

George P. Shultz
Secretary of the Treasury of
the United States

3

I think no one should aspire to manage the economy—the Secretary of the Treasury or whatever. I certainly never had that idea. That is, I think the basic idea about our economy is that it manages itself. And what we should be trying to do in our policies is to get those policies in place that help the economy manage itself. For example, the policy of competition is one that helps the economy manage itself. The policy of promoting supply is one that helps the economy manage the problem of inflation, and so on . . . But that's not the same thing as trying to sort of literally manage the economy from Washington, which I don't think can be done. And I think that, as people try to do it, the results are very undesirable and unsatisfactory.

Interview/The Washington Post, 4-14:(A)21.

George P. Shultz
Former Secretary of the Treasury of
the United States

4

It seems to me that in economics and finance, as we look at the whole range of questions, the thing that we emphasize, naturally, is efficiency. That's what economists are doing. They're trying to maximize things. They're trying to get the optimal solution under all the circumstances, so that the key word in the whole endeavor is efficiency. However, anyone who has spent some time around the political world knows that things are not that simple. The key word there is really equity. So I think that the question we're really dealing with is this: Can we do the things that will give us the efficiency we need in our system, that will give us real growth, that will allow us to exercise the necessary discipline? And can we do all these things in a way that is consistent with the demand of the political process for equity? Can we do them in such a way that, as the fallout occurs and affects different people differently, measures are taken to give a greater sense of equity in the result?

Oct. 29/The New York Times, 12-15:(3)14.

William E. Simon
Secretary of the Treasury of the United States

5

I don't believe that there is necessarily a dramatic trade-off between inflation and unemployment. Indeed, one can make a compelling case that prolonged, excessive inflation creates greater unemployment. It creates many distortions in our economy.

Interview, Washington/
Los Angeles Times, 5-20:(3)13.

6

What we must have is restraint on Federal spending so that the government won't be putting all this pressure on the economy and the money markets, forcing interest rates higher than they should be and keeping the inflation fires burning. This is what has to be reversed. This is fundamental. Then you can deal with shortages and other inflationary problems by acting rather than reacting.

Interview, Washington/
U.S. News & World Report, 6-17:33.

(WILLIAM E. SIMON)

1

Over a long period of time, political decisions have been tilted in the direction of inflation. We have increased government spending faster than we have been willing to pay for it through taxation. We have created too much new money and credit, so that more borrowing has taken place than could be financed out of savings. By those actions, we permitted, encouraged, even forced the demand for goods and services to outrun the productive capacity of our economy. The inevitable result was inflation.

The Christian Science Monitor, 9-18:1.

2

We should think twice about sending liberal spenders, whether Democrats or Republicans, to Washington, because they are the ones who create our problems . . . To go down that path would be an extremely serious mistake, for the bloated Federal budget is one of the prime culprits behind the inflation that is raging in this country.

News conference, Dallas, Oct. 28/
Los Angeles Herald-Examiner, 10-29:(A)6.

3

If I were the President, I'd get rid of Bill Simon about next May, because by that time he will be so bloody that [President] Gerald Ford will get credit for letting him go. I intend to be a pain in the ass. I intend to insist on a budget cut; I intend to insist on a tax increase; I'm going to propose changes in the regulatory agencies at the rate of about one a day. When I get through, nobody's going to like me, and I'll have just one satisfaction: that I've made life easier for the next guy who comes along.

Interview, Washington/
The Washington Post, 11-2:(A)15.

4

Inflation is our Number 1 domestic problem in the United States. Prices are going up faster than at any time in our peacetime history; and if they continue at this pace, they will under-mine the very foundations upon which this nation is built. This is not to say that our problems are of only one dimension. All of you are aware that we are also confronted with a growing sluggishness in our economy. In my judgment, the current economic malaise will eventually be recorded as a recession, but I would urge anyone who calls it a recession to use the term most advisedly. This is not a recession in the classic sense, nor does it call for the classic remedies. Instead, we must recognize that much of the sluggishness in the economy was touched off by inflation. Therefore, the way to cure our economic troubles is to concentrate our attack not on the recessionary aspects of the economy but on the enemy, inflation.

Before Economic Club, Chicago, Nov. 6/
Vital Speeches, 12-1:107.

5

Inflation is like a wild night on the town: The first few drinks have a decidedly pleasant effect, but the hangover is hell.

Before Economic Club, Chicago, Nov. 6/
Vital Speeches, 12-1:109.

Arthur E. Sindlinger
Economic analyst

6

[On what to do about inflation]: What we need is a recession. That is the only solution. We have got to have a recession, and it has got to be deep enough and long enough so that the consumer, in exercising the buyers' strike that is now on, will force prices down. The only way this is going to be solved is for enough people to get hurt. When this happens, the shortages that are causing rising prices will turn into surpluses. Demand will slow down. And my economist friends are whistling in the dark when they say that the consumer does not control the economy. They think the government controls the economy with its fiscal policy. [But] it is the consumer who controls the economy. When he has confidence, he spends. When he does not have confidence, he does not spend. And that is where we are.

Interview, Swarthmore, Pa./
Los Angeles Times, 5-1:(2)7.

Charles H. Smith, Jr.
Chairman, SIFCO Industries; Chairman,
Chamber of Commerce of the United States 1

We learned in this country many decades ago that a monopoly is dangerous to the public good. Yet we have created, in the labor policy of the United States, the biggest monopoly of all—organized labor. Our laws literally legislate a monopoly position for organized labor. Once a union has been certified to represent the employees of a company or a portion of a company, neither the company nor its employees can deal with anybody else. This monopoly power of unions has been augmented by a number of other steps taken by the government—such as welfare, food stamps, and so on, for strikers. These steps have completely destroyed the balance at the bargaining table and threaten to destroy collective bargaining. The threat of a strike used to be the ultimate concern of both parties. The employer knew that if his employees went on strike he would have severe financial losses; and the employees knew that if they went on strike their income stopped. In the last seven or eight years, labor unions have learned to use the government purse, the public purse, to subsidize strikers, so there is no longer the same economic pressure on employees to get a strike settled. Economic pressure to settle a strike is primarily on the company only.

Interview, Cleveland/
Nation's Business, May:48.

2

Despite [the] demonstrated superiority of the free-market system, there are many distinguished leaders from both government and business who warn that future generations of Americans—perhaps even the next generation—will witness the elimination of free enterprise in America—the elimination of capitalism and the substitution of state ownership of the means of production and centrally planned economy ... If our free-market economic system outperforms every variation of government-owned and government-planned economies, we must ask ourselves why it is that so many knowledgeable people are freely predicting the early demise of the free-market system in America.

Those of us who realize that all of our freedoms—freedom of the press, freedom to work at a job of our own choosing, freedom to bargain collectively—yes, even political and religious freedom, are based on the freedom of the marketplace and the private-enterprise system—those of us who realize this must quickly find the reasons for the threat to our free-market economy and rally to its defense ... But the longer we procrastinate ... the more dangerous becomes our position. It is high time that we begin to identify and seek to avoid currents that can carry us downstream at an ever-accelerating pace until we reach a channel from which there is no possibility to return.

At National War College, Washington,
Sept. 9/Vital Speeches, 10-15:25.

3

An increase in productivity can help cure inflation caused by government borrowing; but government borrowing makes an increase in productivity more difficult to attain by disrupting capital markets and impeding the flow of investment funds, and therefore capital formation. We have gotten into this mess by focusing on the desirability of goals while ignoring the availability of means. We have been so busy bickering about the distribution of the golden eggs that no one has given much thought to the nutritional needs of the goose.

Interview, Los Angeles, Sept. 30/
Los Angeles Herald-Examiner, 10-1:(A)5.

Beryl Sprinkel
Senior vice president,
Harris Trust and Savings Bank, Chicago 4

The reason why we're stuck with this sizable inflation rate is that no politician can pay the political cost of keeping inflation under control. The economic solution is simple; it is the political solution that is almost impossible to solve.

San Francisco Examiner, 2-4:54.

Herbert Stein
Chairman, Council of Economic Advisors
to President of the United States
Richard M. Nixon 5

[The key economic issue] is not how we shall get through 1974 ... but how we shall get

(HERBERT STEIN)

through the next generation. The question is whether we shall restore and strengthen the free-market, free-price system which has provided the American people the highest standard of living in history, or whether we are going to be enmeshed in more and more controls, each one designed to remedy the problems created by the last one... Three years ago, people could say that there is a ready remedy in the medicine chest if we would but use it. The remedy was "incomes policy," or in stronger form, "price and wage controls." We have now used the medicine and have learned what others have learned before us: that it gives temporary relief only, followed by many headaches.

Before Congressional Joint Economic Committee, Washington, Feb. 7/ The Washington Post, 2-8:(A)1, 7.

1

... it may be that, while the American people rate the evil of inflation heavily, they are unwilling to pay the price of stopping it; and this is only another way of saying we get the inflation we want and deserve.

At meeting sponsored by American Enterprise Institute/San Francisco Examiner, 5-8:9.

2

Part of economics is that people should understand what they can demand. If people have needless demands, we will have increasing inflation, and that is what's happening around the world today ... We must think in terms of years, not months. We must follow a program of much greater discipline. We need a period in which the economy is not in an exuberant boom, when there is some slack in it.

TV-radio interview/"Face the Nation," Columbia Broadcasting System, 7-7.

Robert Stovall
Vice president and director of investment policy, Reynolds Securities, Inc.
3

We won't have a severe recession or a depression. Remember that the unemployment rate is still under six per cent and nowhere near the 25 to 30 per cent that existed in the 1930s. It's

even lower today than it was during the Eisenhower years, which were considered a period of peace and prosperity. The banking system is completely different from what it was in the 1930s. There was no Federal deposit insurance then, and when banks began to fail, the government was powerless to do anything about it. It's the psychology that is the bad thing today. It's the worst I can recall. It's responsible for turning a lot of events into non-events. There was the ending of the oil embargo, and ending of wage and price controls, the resignation of [President] Nixon, a drop in the prime rate. [But] because of the gloom psychology, these events became non-events. They were shrugged off.

Miami/Chicago Tribune, 10-9:(4)12.

Herman E. Talmadge
United States Senator, D–Georgia
4

We need never to lose sight of the fact that creeping inflation of the variety that has been inflicted upon the United States is only a few steps away from hyper-inflation, or runaway inflation, which has wrecked economies and resulted in dictatorships in Germany, Latin America and other parts of the world. I say it is not only time for the people of the United States, and this government, to become aware of the historical consequences of runaway inflation, it is time we got a little fearful.

Aug. 20/The Atlanta Constitution, 8-21:(A)12.

5

We have near economic chaos and double-digit inflation. Even the most optimistic economists tell us it will take years to unravel the mess ... Watergate no doubt posed a threat to the security of the nation. Inflation constitutes a more serious menace. Watergate no doubt undermined the confidence of the people in government. Runaway inflation can destroy confidence in government, totally and permanently. When people lose all confidence in eroded money, they lose all confidence in the government that issued that money ... When runaway inflation strikes a nation, when its monetary system becomes uncontrollable, its constitution is rendered meaningless and government is reduced to a shambles.

Before Indiana Democratic Editorial Association, French Lick, Ind., Aug. 24/ The Atlanta Journal and Constitution, 8-25:(B)18.

Mayo J. Thompson
Commissioner, Federal Trade Commission

1

Today it is lawful for a single labor union to exercise a complete monopoly over the total supply of labor to even the largest of our greatest industries and to use that power to exact any wage the firms in that industry can successfully "pass on" to the consuming public. Monopoly in the country's labor markets assures that prices will rise . . . year after year, and hence that we will continue to have an inflation problem into all of the foreseeable future. The stronger our unions become—and the more aggressive their numbers and their leaders become—the greater our future inflation problem will tend to be.

Before National Fluid Power Association, Palm Springs, Calif., May 6/ The Washington Post, 5-7:(A)2.

John G. Tower
United States Senator, R—Texas

2

The high rate of inflation and the depressed state of housing cannot be separated. Until and unless inflationary pressures are stymied, the housing sector of the economy will continue the wild "boom or bust" gyrations experienced in recent years. When high mortgage rates are coupled with inflation, a double blow is dealt to the prospective home-buyer. With each one-quarter per cent increase in rates, the terms of the mortgage not only become more financially unattractive but more psychologically unattractive as well.

The Dallas Times Herald, 5-12:(A)26.

Friedrich von Hayek
British economist

3

What I expect is that inflation will drive all the Western countries into a planned economy via price controls. Nobody would dare to stop inflation in an ordinary manner because, as things are at present, to discontinue inflation will inevitably cause extensive unemployment. So, assuming it stops, it will be resumed. People will find they can't live with constantly rising prices and will try to do it by price controls, and that of course is the end of the market system and the end of the free political order. So I think it will be via the fight against inflation that the free market and free institutions will disappear.

Interview/Human Events, 11-16:20.

George C. Wallace
Governor of Alabama

4

[On inflation]: I don't know that there's any solution to a problem that's been brought about through long-term over-spending at the Federal level—foreign aid that was wasted, and our resources wasted on a prolonged no-win war in Vietnam that should have been concluded earlier or should not have been started if you didn't intend to conclude it. As for inflation, I think you ought to cut down on government spending, and then if you had more spending among the broad masses of our people, it would create employment and productivity.

Parade, 6-9:6.

Ben J. Wattenberg
Political analyst

5

[On the current inflation, unemployment and other economic problems] : This is a very serious setback, no doubt about it. But will our economy collapse, as some people are suggesting? Nonsense. The problem will be with us for a couple of years, but nobody is going to starve. Nor are we about to have a '30s-style depression. I find it tremendously amusing to watch well-dressed businessmen complaining about how terrible it's getting over martinis and lunch in a fancy restaurant. As for the blue-collar worker, in 1960 he was living in an urban row house, he could not afford to send his daughter to college and he drove one car. Now he lives in a suburban split-level, sends his daughter to college and owns two cars. He has come to expect this kind of life and does not want to lower his standards. America is not suffering from a revolution of

(BEN J. WATTENBERG)

rising expectations. It is suffering from a revolution of realized expectations.

Interview/People, 10-28:52.

Caspar W. Weinberger
Secretary of Health, Education and
Welfare of the United States
1

The causes of unemployment, and especially of inflation, are no longer influenced as significantly by a [Federal] budget deficit or surplus as they once were. For example, it certainly is not the budget policy of the past three years that has caused a tripling in the price of ferrous scrap and a doubling of wheat and cotton prices. Nor is the unemployment at service stations or automobile assembly plants going to be cured by an increase in aggregate demand. International conditions, private collective-bargaining agreements and scientific discoveries, just to name three, have a far greater influence on our economy today than whether the budget has a deficit of 10 or 20 billion dollars in an economy where the GNP is approaching a trillion and a half.

Lecture/The Washington Post, 6-16:(F)8.

Leonard Woodcock
President,
United Automobile Workers of America
2

... this [Nixon] Administration has thrust the nation into a state of near economic chaos. [It did this] by its ineptness, its outworn conservative policies, its callous disregard of people's problems and its persistent pandering to the powerful interests which paid for its election. The people of this nation have been the victims of isolation and incompetence at best, and deliberate malfeasance and misrepresentation at worst.

At United Automobile Workers
of America convention, Los Angeles,
June 2/Los Angeles Times, 6-3:(1)3.

Walter B. Wriston
Chairman,
First National City Bank, New York
3

If ... you believe in free markets, it is a formidable task to be heard in our town be-

cause *The New York Times* editorials almost daily advance the thesis in one way or another that all of our economic activity should be regulated by the government, except, of course, those corporations which own the press or the media. After three years of price and wage controls and 2,000 years of history which recorded only their failure, one would think that experience would have overwhelmed the editors' theory. Instead, only recently *The Times* called for "a more sensible price-control policy" for what it characterized as an "inflation-racked, monopoly-dominated economy." It seems unable to grasp one of the central lessons of history, which is that you cannot preserve political liberty, which includes a free press, if the economic system is run by a government dictatorship.

The New York Times, 5-16:41.

4

[His suggestion for fighting the current U.S. economic downswing]: The largest employer is private industry. Therefore, you have to do something to get it spending again and you've got to put money in the working man's pocket fast. A cut from 48 per cent to 40 per cent [in corporate tax rates] would see an enormous increase in liquidity, spending and employment. And every 1 per cent cut in unemployment brings $1.8 billion to the U.S. Treasury. We should raise individual tax exemptions from $750 to $1,000. The interesting thing is every time they've cut corporate tax rates, there's been an increase in receipts to the Treasury. It's better to have a piece of something than a piece of nothing.

Interview, New York/
Los Angeles Times, 12-30:(1)4.

Jerry Wurf
President, American Federation of
State, County and Municipal Employees
5

[Criticizing Labor Secretary Peter Brennan's statement that 1973 was a good year for workers]: Frankly, I wonder what Pete is smoking. I think 1973 was one of the most devastating years we've experienced since World War II. We've had high unemployment, unprecedented inflation, an outrageously inequitable wage-control program, and we had the spectacle of an American President [Nixon] chiseling on his income tax. If that's Pete Brennan's idea of progress, God help us.

Jan. 8/The New York Times, 1-9:19.

1

The denial to public employees of the basic protections available to workers in the private sector under Federal law has had a harmful effect on those employees, a harmful effect on the quality of services they produce and a harmful effect on the reasonableness of the labor-relations processes of government in this country. [Public employees] are denied protections at the Federal level on every score: minimum-wage laws, health and safety provisions, and even unemployment compensation . . . Public workers' needs are not very high on the Nixon Administration's priorities list. We rank somewhere between homeless dogs and the Euthanasia League on the President's agenda. Given Mr. Nixon's rock-bottom standing among most Americans, however, that may be a blessing.

At seminar sponsored by Coalition of American Public Employees and American Arbitration Association, Washington, March 25/The New York Times, 3-26:25.

Clayton Yeutter
Assistant Secretary for Marketing and Consumer Services, Department of Agriculture of the United States

2

Perhaps the strongest charge made against free enterprise is that it distributes income unfairly. Here . . . we have to remember our decentralized system works through incentives. Few people work well without incentives. The real key to our prosperity is output—and free enterprise offers a combination of personal incentive and high efficiency that is tough to beat. It produces a bigger, juicier pie so that nearly everyone's slice can be larger. We are better off than we would be under an inefficient system—even if such a system distributed the returns equally. This is not to say the market is perfect. It is not. But it is more efficient and responsive for the people than any of the substitutes thus far devised. I believe prices and free markets do work for the little people, for all the people. I say this not out of concern for big business; I have spent most of my life as a small businessman—a farmer. I do not say it to protect government; I am only a temporary public servant. I say it out of genuine concern for all of us who make up this great country.

Before American Association of Agricultural College Editors, West Lafayette, Ind., July 16/Vital Speeches, 9-1:690.

Law • The Judiciary

Dewey F. Bartlett
United States Senator, R–Oklahoma 1

[Saying all Federal judges should be required to retire at age 70]: It just makes no sense to allow persons executing the authority and responsibility of a Federal judge to continue their duties at a time when they may not be fully capable either physically or mentally.
Before the Senate, Washington/
San Francisco Examiner, 7-23:6.

Warren E. Burger
Chief Justice of the United States 2

I have often suggested that if John Marshall, Thomas Jefferson, Alexander Hamilton and John Adams—all very good lawyers—came back today, it would require only a small amount of briefing for them to go into court and try cases. I limit this to the courtroom, because it is in procedure and method that the law has experienced the least change. The corporate law, tax law, administrative and regulatory law is, of course, a totally new world. Had Rip Van Winkle gone away ... and come back today instead of the short time fixed by Washington Irving, and if he went into the courts, the principal changes he · would have observed would have been the wearing apparel, the increased number of judges, and the air conditioning. Most of the rest would be the same as when he began his legendary exile in the Catskill Mountains.
Before Economic Club, New York/
The Wall Street Journal, 3-15:6.

3

The inequity of failure to provide any increase in pay for Federal judges for almost six years is perhaps felt most extensively in the [Federal] District Courts, where six judges have resigned in the last 13 months to return to private or corporate practice. That was as many

resignations for such reasons in little more than one year as in the previous 34 years. The Federal courts will continue to lose judges and fail to attract many promising young attorneys who must be the mainstays of an effective judicial system; and the nation will suffer for it.
Dec. 28/The New York Times, 12-29:(1)14.

Archibald Cox
Professor of Law, Harvard University 4

[On the legal profession]: We inherit the tradition of seven or eight centuries of continuous concern for the institutions and aspirations ... that make for a free and civilized society. It is not the age of the profession that matters ... what matters most is that, through the centuries, the men of law have been persistently concerned with the resolution of disputes ... in ways that enable society to achieve its goals with a minimum of force and a maximum of reason.
Before law graduates, University of Virginia/
The New York Times, 5-29:37.

5

Law depends upon voluntary compliance, and compliance upon the notion that the law binds all men equally, the judges no less than the judged, the governors no less than the governed, the highest officials equally with the lowliest citizens.
Before law graduates, University of Virginia/
The Washington Post, 6-8:(A)21.

Jack G. Day
Judge, Ohio Court of Appeals; Chairman,
criminal-justice section,
American Bar Association 6

Plea-bargaining can be terrible and terribly immoral—if it is dishonest. If someone of enormous power and money is in trouble and a bargain is made just to save his hide, that is terrible. However, I would defend plea-bargaining when you have a tough and honest defense lawyer and a prosecutor who knows what [charges] he can make ... and they get the deal they can. Most plea-bargaining, in my view, is dead honest.

The Christian Science Monitor, 6-5:3.

Sam J. Ervin, Jr.
United States Senator, D—North Carolina
1

Law merely deters some human beings from offending and punishes other human beings for offending. It does not make men good.

At American Bar Association prayer meeting, Honolulu, Aug. 16/ Chicago Tribune, 8-17:(1)3.

Macklin Fleming
Judge, California State Court of Appeal
2

Procrastination is a sin of lawyers, trial judges, clerks, reporters, appellate judges; in brief, everyone connected with the machinery of criminal law. Procrastination must be recognized for the sin that it is. Once we cease to tolerate procrastination, its use will fall into disfavor and in time acquire the character of unprofessional conduct.

Before Wilshire Bar Association,
Los Angeles, July 23/
Los Angeles Times, 7-24:(2)4.

Gerald R. Ford
Vice President of the United States
3

Even as a lawyer no longer in practice, I am concerned when I see a respected weekly news magazine headline its recent report on America's lawyers with the caption: "A Sick Profession"? The caption is followed by a question mark. That is some consolation for us. But if others are asking the question, all lawyers must be concerned about the state of the profession's health ... Nevertheless, I am not about to apologize for having numerous lawyers in government. Neither am I about to believe that government would be better off without lawyers in positions of public trust and responsibility. I have much more respect than that for law as an intellectual discipline and, I would add, a *moral* discipline. I hold my own legal

education and experience in the highest regard for the help it has been to me in government. Also, I have the highest respect for what the study and practice of law have made of many men I know who have come to serve this nation well—not only as judges and government lawyers but as legislators, executives and administrators. Lawyers of good education and practical competence are generally distinguished for their ability to be resourceful, innovative, orderly and dispassionate in their thinking and in their approach to problems.

Before Georgia Bar Association, Savannah,
June 7/U.S. News & World Report, 6-24:69.

Abe Fortas
Former Associate Justice,
Supreme Court of the United States
4

By and large ... big-city criminal administration is a jungle, a snake pit, an aggregation of horrors. It is the dismal swamp of no-hope for the offenders who make the process necessary. It is livable turf for mean, venal and small-time chiselers whose only qualification is a license to practice law.

San Francisco Examiner & Chronicle,
11-3:(This World)2.

Paul A. Freund
Professor of Law, Harvard University
5

There's a great interest on the part of [law] students in the philosophy and ethics of law, and they see being trained in law as having a great impact on society. In New Deal days, they had the same desire, but they found their outlet in government. Now with government somewhat passive, young lawyers find their outlet in private practice and more especially in local and grass-roots government and politics. In a way, we might be going back to the early days that produced lawyers at the beginning of the American republic. There were no law schools then—law teachers inspired students. They got technical knowledge from Blackstone, along with the philosophy of law; natural law, natural rights—that's what made them great lawyers ... We can't give up specialized training in the highly complex structure of law today, but we do have to return to a feeling of what the whole

(PAUL A. FREUND)

legal system stands for—how it relates to our own conception of the person as a human being.

U.S. News & World Report, 3-25:28.

John W. Gardner
Chairman, Common Cause
1

I am sure when the first code of laws was formulated somebody was asked why in the world he was chipping away on that stone, on something he couldn't change. All laws are an attempt to domesticate the natural ferocity of the species. We can't stop murder, but we can make it tougher to get away with it. We can't stop a banker from stealing the widow's money, but we can make it harder for him to steal it.

Interview/San Francisco Examiner, 7-3:31.

Gerhard A. Gesell
Judge, United States District Court
for the District of Columbia
2

[As a judge,] I obviously try not to let my bias lead me astray. [But] after a long career on the bench, you're a product of everything you've been through. You have to balance this with your obligations as a judge and your view of the law. If you have biases and you can give them a little push while being consistent with the law, you may often do this, either consciously or unconsciously. There isn't any way you can put life out of your mind. You've just got to remember to put the law before your own prejudices.

Interview/Los Angeles Times, 6-13:(1)8.

Howell Heflin
Chief Justice of Alabama
3

[Criticizing the system of electing judges]: It has been said that there is no harm in turning a politician into a judge. He may become a good judge, but the curse of the elective system is that it turns every judge into a politician to some degree.

At American Judicature Society National Conference on Selection and Tenure, Denver, March 21/Vital Speeches, 7-1:556.

Shirley M. Hufstedler
Judge, United States Court of
Appeals for the Ninth Circuit
4

A regular civil trial today, with or without a jury, is beyond the economic reach of all except the rich, the nearly rich or the person seriously injured by a well-insured defendant.

Before American Bar Association, Houston/The New York Times, 2-10:(4)9.

Leon Jaworski
Lawyer; Special government
prosecutor for Watergate
5

Recently, a national magazine carried an article designed to question the status of the legal profession as an influence on society because of some scars it carried. The implication was that the profession may be losing its place of honor in our society. That far too many members of our profession in recent years have failed to live up to the standards of professional responsibility, and failed in even worse respects, is not to be denied. But the immoralities do not begin and end with the legal profession. Not that this should be of any comfort to us, but it is fair to face the total situation as it exists. Of one fact we may be certain: No profession—and least of all the legal profession, whose efforts are based on trust and honor—can long withstand the encroachments of iniquities within its ranks. There is another guilt more widespread—that of too many lawyers viewing with indifference the upholding of the high standards of professional conduct that we insist are ours. And there is yet another—that of too many of our members dismissing with a deaf ear the cries for improvements in the administration of justice, which is our sacred trust.

At commencement, George Washington University National Law Center, Washington, May 26/ The Washington Post, 5-27:(A)6.

6

When dictators and tyrants seek to destroy the freedoms of men, their first target is the legal profession and through it the rule of law.

Before Junior Bar of Texas, San Antonio, July 4/The Dallas Times Herald, 7-5:(A)9.

1

We have experienced in almost all parts of the United States what can only be described as a breakdown in the teaching of the root principles of law in a free society. In saying that, I am not blaming the education system alone. It has in part been a failure of the legal profession and of society itself. We have not paid sufficient attention to what we now realize is a very basic component of preparing our youth for lives of constructive participation in a changing society; we have failed to impress upon the very young how the law functions to protect individual rights—how it provides for orderly, democratic change; what the difference is between dissent and violent protest; why individual rights must be balanced with individual responsibility to the total society.

Before International Platform Association/
The Washington Post, 8-13:(A)18.

2

... while I think our system of justice is the greatest in the world, I have to say also that it has its imperfections. The statement of "equal justice under the law" is a great goal, but actually it's an aphorism, because if we're going to be perfectly honest about it, you have to accept the fact that it's not perfect. You're dealing with human beings and, when you deal with human beings, you find human frailties come in. You also must bear in mind that the law is not an exact science.

Interview, Washington/
The Washington Post, 10-22:(A)15.

Bryce MacKasey
Postmaster General of Canada

3

The law in a free state sets minimal standards of conduct. It assumes that the majority will act responsibly. It assumes that I won't chuck garbage into my neighbor's yard, not because the law forbids it—we'd need an army of policemen—but because I have a moral code and a conscience. If I fail to act responsibly, then the state steps in and makes me; because when everyone is free to do their own thing, no one is free.

Before Audit Bureau of Circulation, Chicago,
Nov. 7/Vital Speeches, 12-1:123.

Margaret Mead
Anthropologist

4

The contempt for law and the contempt for the human consequences of lawbreaking go from the bottom to the top of American society. Watergate is a final expression of contempt for law at the very top. If Americans finally come face to face with this, it may have the same beneficial effect as treating a boil by lancing it at the top.

Quote, 5-12:434.

Earl F. Morris
Lawyer; Former president,
American Bar Association

5

If the bar of this country was concerned with its selfish interests, it would leave antiquated laws on the books and outmoded procedures in our courtrooms. Instead, the lawyers of this country, functioning through their legal organizations at the national, state and local level, seek modernization of our statutes, strive for uniformity of our laws, promulgate standards for civil and criminal justice, and attempt to achieve the improvement of our court procedure and the streamlining of our system of justice. They do not always succeed. But when they fail it is because special interests thwart, political considerations prevail over, or public apathy impedes what the lawyer seeks in the public interest.

At Dickinson School of Law commencement,
Carlisle, Pa., June 1/
U.S. News & World Report, 6-24:69.

Dorothy Wright Nelson
Dean, University of Southern California
Law Center

6

If criminals wanted to grind justice to a halt, they could do it by banding together and all pleading *not* guilty. It's only because we have plea-bargaining that our criminal-justice system is still in motion. That doesn't say much for the quality of justice.

Interview, Los Angeles/
Los Angeles Times, 8-11:(Home)26.

Louis Nizer
Lawyer

1

The day of manipulating a jury is absolutely gone, if there ever was such a day. Cases are won through preparation, dragging the facts into the courtroom. The lawyer excavates the facts, and the more he digs, the more certain he is to win; and then he can pound upon the facts and an emotional appeal—that's the way of persuasion. But to play clever with a jury when you don't have the facts leaves them cold, absolutely cold! They resent it.

Interview/San Francisco Examiner, 5-29:35.

Charles H. Percy
United States Senator, R—Illinois

2

Our system of law is strong enough to deal fairly with the accused in spite of popular opinion and what I call "judicial chic." It ought to give us great comfort for the present and hope for the future that two people like [Angela] Davis [black activist acquitted in a murder trial in 1972] and [John] Mitchell [former U.S. Attorney General acquitted of trying to unfairly influence an SEC investigation]—people whose only similarity would seem to be the contempt with which they are regarded by certain segments of the population—can be dealt justice equally. If our system were weaker and guilt or innocence were meted out at the bar of public approval rather than at the bar of justice, both Davis and Mitchell probably would have been found guilty.

At dinner sponsored by Constitutional Rights Foundation, Beverly Hills, Calif., May 3/Los Angeles Times, 5-4:(1)9.

Ed Reinecke
Former Lieutenant Governor of California

3

The grand-jury system is nothing but a tool of the prosecution. You don't know what is being said about you or who is saying it. Government is getting just as oppressive as it was under George III.

Interview, Placerville, Calif./ San Francisco Examiner & Chronicle, 11-17:(A)27.

William B. Saxbe
Attorney General of the United States

4

[On why he accepted the office of Attorney General]: I'm small town and Ohio enough to think I'm a patriot, which we don't hear much about down here [in Washington]. Also, I think we're in an era of crisis of judicial confidence. People think the "fix" is on, that the system is beyond control. I don't. Most judges and lawyers I know are dedicated people and want to do right. I thought I might be able to hit a lick to get some stability in the Justice Department.

News conference, Washington, Jan. 15/ The Dallas Times Herald, 1-16:(A)27.

5

The thing I want to find out is whether people are willing to live under laws. Everybody says he respects the law, but the people who say they believe in gun laws are the same people who want to tear down the penitentiaries. The other day there were three people with guns at a school—do you think any of the three will wind up in jail? Today I wired all 94 district attorneys that the Justice Department is going to crack down on illegal acts of truckers [protesting the gasoline shortage and gas prices]. We have laws in this country. Already there must be 20 laws broken by some of the truckers. We have civil-rights laws in the country. If a guy parks his truck in your gas station and blocks it, isn't he infringing your civil right to go about your business in peace? . . . There may be a lot that's right in a trucker's cause, and they have every right to strike. What I'm talking about is picking up a hunk of concrete and throwing it.

Interview, Washington, Feb. 5/ The Washington Post, 2-7:(C)3.

6

Each of us with responsibilities to the law must be fair—not a little fair or fair only some of the time, but totally fair and all of the time. In a sense, we all walk a razor's edge—both as individuals and as a society. It is our devotion to decency and fairness—our devotion to law—that keeps us from straying into tyranny. Fairness is most needed when it is in short supply or when a problem assumes such great proportions that we are tempted to resolve it through expediency outside of the law.

Before National Association of Attorneys General, Coeur d'Alene, Idaho, June 24/ The National Observer; 8-10:11.

1

Disrespect for the law by those sworn to uphold it can only encourage a tendency toward lawlessness in others.

Before Major Cities Police Chiefs Committee of International Association of Chiefs of Police, Chicago, Aug. 27/ Chicago Tribune, 8-28:(1)3.

Bernard G. Segal
Lawyer; Former president, American Bar Association

2

[Lauding former President Nixon for his nominees for the Federal judiciary]: You can't take the credit away from him. If you're going to condemn him for the things he did that were wrong, as you must, you should also give him credit for the good things he did. The Federal judiciary is better off for his being President.

Los Angeles Times, 9-18:(1-A)4.

Joe Sims
Special Assistant to the Assistant Attorney General, Antitrust Division, Department of Justice of the United States

3

[Saying that bar associations should allow their member lawyers to advertise their services as a means of promoting competition within the profession]: It may well be that the march of time and the burgeoning needs of our society have made it essential [for the government] to re-evaluate existing constraints on competition in the legal profession and test them against the standards universally applied . . . to the marketplace . . . What is at issue is the right of buyers of professional services to consider all factors, including price, which go into a judgment to choose one among the many who offer the services they need. When the lawyer sells his services, he is engaging in the business of practicing law. The economic principles that apply generally throughout our economy apply to the lawyer as well as to the sellers of other services.

The consumers of legal services are just as entitled to the benefits of competition . . . as are consumers of other services.

Before ethics committee, New York State Bar Association, Rochester, N.Y., Aug. 21/ Los Angeles Times, 8-22:(1)9.

Chesterfield Smith
President, American Bar Association

4

[On the Senate's refusal to authorize salary increases for Federal judges]: As politicians, Senators can now take credit for turning back their own proposed pay increases. Judges, however, are not politicians, and the Senate should not have imposed what it found to be politically expedient for its own members on the principal architects of justice in this country . . . In a real sense, the way in which we treat our judges reflects our attitude toward the functions they perform. By denying them fair treatment, we are casting unwarranted and dangerous doubt on our support of the administration of justice and the rule of law.

Before Federal Bar Association, Washington, March 14/The New York Times, 3-18:19.

Irving Stone
Author

5

The legal profession in America today is in a very bad way. It has been dishonored and is downcast. Perhaps that's why my legal friends are looking back to [Clarence] Darrow with great pride, saying, "This is what law should be about. This is the kind of man we need." When young men come out of law school today, they should be committed, as was he, to social justice. Naturally, they should earn a good living; they've put in years of training. But not all their time should be devoted to working for big corporations. They should spend half their time, as did Darrow, defending clients for no recompense whatsoever. Over half of Darrow's clients never paid him. They weren't able to; they were poor. Yet he realized that you owe half your time to American society and democracy to preserve it. You owe all people equal representation by law, regardless of pay.

At reception in his honor, Los Angeles/ Los Angeles Herald-Examiner, 5-15:(C)2.

Pierre Elliott Trudeau
Prime Minister of Canada

1

The basis of law is not the army or the machine gun. It's the acceptance by the people of the principle that the law should be obeyed. What has worried me in my time, not only about Canadian society but about many others, is that obviously the psychological inclination to obey the law has been eroded. And I'm not making a moral judgment. Perhaps a lot of the laws haven't kept up with the times. Perhaps they should have been changed earlier, and had they been changed they would have been obeyed.

Interview/
The New York Times Magazine, 11-3:72.

John V. Tunney
United States Senator, D—California

2

Lawyers are prominent among the accused and the suspected in [the] Watergate [affair]. They helped to plan it, lent their imaginations to its evolution, gave the honorable trade of plumbing a bad name, covered up, lied under oath, may have tampered with the conduct of prosecutions, lent their talents to the perversion of long-respected limitations on Executive privilege and national security. Nor are those who committed these acts on the fringe of our profession. Most of them were trained and some received distinction in law schools which enjoy national reputations. Many were ornaments of their bar associations. Is it any wonder that this year has seen an accelerating erosion of respect and trust in the lawyer and the legal profession?

At Harvard Law School Forum/
Los Angeles Times, 5-19:(6)6.

Lawrence E. Walsh
President-elect, American Bar Association

3

[On Congress' recent turndown of a pay raise for Federal judges]: This idea of a hierarchy—with the Supreme Court making more than the Appeals Court, and the Appeals Court above the District Court—can be overdone. If $60,000 is right for the Supreme Court, it can't be too wrong for everyone else. Don't we want well-qualified lawyers at every level of the judiciary? I can't think of anything more important, if we want to improve the system of justice in this country, than good judges. We can spend all the money we want for new buildings, for court improvements, for larger staffs; but if we have poor judges, none of the rest matters very much. Killing this raise was just about the most foolhardy thing I've heard of from Congress.

Los Angeles Times, 3-10:(1)19.

Lowell P. Weicker, Jr.
United States Senator, R—Connecticut

4

I'm seriously thinking that the Attorney General of the United States should be elected by the people instead of being appointed by the President. Attorneys General are elected in about 40 states and territories, and I'm inclined to believe the same should hold true in the Federal government. We can live with partisan politics in this country but not with partisan justice. The Attorney General of the U.S. should be held accountable for his actions by the people, and the greatest accountability is achieved through the electoral process.

Interview, Washington/Parade, 7-14:8.

Creighton W. Abrams
General and Chief of Staff,
United States Army

1

Detente may last, but on the other hand it can fade overnight. American strength made detente attainable, and it is hard to see it continuing unless we maintain that strength.

Before House Armed Services Committee,
Washington, Feb. 14/
The Washington Post, 2-15:(A)28.

James R. Allen
Major General, United States Air Force;
Superintendent, U.S. Air Force Academy

2

[Saying he opposes women entering the nation's military academies]: At some time that I can't imagine in the future, when we are challenged in a way that people are landing on our shores and we need our women in foxholes and trenches, with guns in their hands . . . then I will change my views on that.

Colorado Springs, Colo., Aug. 13/
The Washington Post, 8-15:(A)16.

Leonid I. Brezhnev
General Secretary, Communist
Party of the Soviet Union

3

Advocates of the arms race use the argument that, to limit arms and even more to reduce them, involves taking a risk. In practice, it is an immeasurably greater risk to continue the unbridled accumulation of arms.

June 14/The New York Times, 6-24:28.

George S. Brown
General and Chief of Staff,
United States Air Force

4

Our defenses today are good . . . The Air Force, for instance, has very few people in any responsible positions who haven't been in combat. This is a tremendous asset. In the Air

Force's case, we fought the [Vietnam] war with what we had. Now we've got a lot on the drawing boards; we've got a lot in development. We've got one new airplane in production—that's the F-15 fighter. We have the B-1 we're working on, and the A-10 to support ground troops. That's what I mean by modernization.

Interview, Washington/
U.S. News & World Report, 2-25:63.

5

A very dedicated group of citizens recommended the all-volunteer [armed] force. The President and the Congress accepted it. But I think there's a plus in having a citizen Army—at least a meld of professionals and people who are not professionals who are willing to serve their country for a couple of years—and we're not going to have that.

Interview, Washington/
U.S. News & World Report, 2-25:64.

Howard H. Callaway
Secretary of the Army of the United States

6

Historically, nations and armies have made enormous mistakes by trying to evaluate [a potential adversary's] intentions. The old military rule that has been proven true in so many wars is you don't make your plans based on intention; you make your plans based on capabilities . . . When you ask what the Soviet intentions are, I certainly don't know. We take them in good faith and say that their intentions are one of detente, of living together, of negotiation instead of confrontation . . . Intentions, even if you can understand them and know what they are—which is extremely difficult—they can change on five minutes' notice. Capabilities can't change on five minutes' notice. Capabilities require the long lead time of production, the training of troops, the mobilization of economies; all kinds of things enter into capabilities. All of these things take time and

WHAT THEY SAID IN 1974

some of it very substantial time—some of it 10, 15, 20 years in time frame. Basically, we would say that the United States should look at Soviet capability rather than intentions . . . Today they have two million more men in arms than we have—about twice as many as the United States.

Interview/
The Atlanta Constitution, 10-29:(A)8.

Frank Church
United States Senator, D—Idaho

1

[On Defense Secretary James Schlesinger's view that there must be U.S. military balance with the Soviets even if a Soviet superiority is merely "overkill"]: The Secretary's point is that, even though overkill may reduce a possible imbalance of forces to utter meaninglessness, the *delusion* of superiority may nonetheless tempt adversaries to adventure while allies panic and break ranks. Other high-ranking officials dismiss this conception as nonsense, pointing out that no land-based nuclear missile has ever been fired from an operational silo and can hardly, therefore, be regarded as having political value. If we act on Mr. Schlesinger's concept of "perceived equality," it will mean staggering costs and the effective end to meaningful SALT negotiations.

Before the Senate, Washington, Aug. 19/
The Washington Post, 8-19:(A)5.

Albert P. Clark
Lieutenant General,
United States Air Force; Superintendent,
U.S. Air Force Academy

2

[Saying women should not be put in combat roles in the military]: For this nation to open combat roles to our women short of a dire emergency, in my view, offends the dignity of womanhood and ignores the harsh realities of war. Fighting is a man's job and should remain so.

Before House Armed Services Subcommittee,
Washington, June 18/
Los Angeles Times, 6-19:(1)22.

William E. Colby
Director, Central Intelligence
Agency of the United States

3

Today the Soviet attaches can go to almost any newsstand in this country, pick up a copy of a technical aviation or space magazine, and from it learn a vast amount of detail about our weapons systems. Unfortunately, we have to spend hundreds of millions of dollars to get comparable information about the Soviet Union.

San Francisco Examiner & Chronicle,
12-8:(This World)2.

Henry Steele Commager
Historian

4

This fear [of Communism] allowed us to build a fantastic arms-spending race which has seen the United States spend 1,600 billion dollars on armaments since 1945. Instead of spending money on technology, which could help feed the half of the world that is hungry most of the time, world powers have spent 50 per cent of their budgets on armaments since World War II. The recent [U.S.-Soviet] atomic-weapons agreement in Vladivostok sets a very high ceiling on these armaments. We already have enough atomic weapons to destroy the world 100 times—why do we need to be able to destroy it 200 times?

At California State University,
Long Beach, Dec. 2/
Los Angeles Times, 12-3:(1)18.

Michael S. Davison
General, United States Army;
Commander, Seventh Army

5

It seems to me that in today's world the most important strategic consideration is a psychological one. Does the West, by the quality and number of men and weapons in its armed forces, reflect the will and intent to defend its society? Does the size and nature of the American military deployment in Europe convey a message that we, along with the Western Europeans, have the determination to defend our common heritage and interests? Unilateral force reduction would communicate an entirely different message about our will and intent. It is a message we should not want to send.

U.S. News & World Report, 12-30:29.

James H. Doolittle
Lieutenant General,
United States Air Force (Ret.)
1

The military has changed [since World War II] ... But I don't think the men and women in uniform today lack the tenacity and courage that we had during the war. In fact, they have that, plus they are smarter.

Oakland, Calif., April 21/
The Dallas Times Herald, 4-22:(A)2.

Russell E. Dougherty
General, United States Air Force;
Commander, Strategic Air Command
2

Now, and [in] the future, the balance of power is not decidedly ours [the U.S.']. We always could control the last raise in the escalating game; ... we had it in our hip pocket. But now, they've [the Russians] got it in their hip pocket, too.

San Francisco Examiner & Chronicle,
12-1:(This World)2.

Robert E. L. Eaton
National commander, American Legion
3

From the earliest days of the republic, Americans have embraced the fundamental doctrine that the cornerstone of defense is the citizen Army. The first article of the Constitution empowered Congress to "call forth the militia to execute the laws of the Union, suppress insurrection and repel invasions" ... Today, however, it is national policy to build toward an all-volunteer, professional armed force. Without participation by the citizens in selective service, we are moving away from the concept of citizen soldiery. The American Legion supports the personnel of our armed forces. We are convinced that they represent the highest type of individuals who serve our nation. But we are not convinced that the professional armed force is in keeping with the American idea of free government. Nor are we convinced that it is an effective way to fight

our nation's wars. There is a belief—in which I concur—that the principal cause of the Southeast Asia disaster [U.S. involvement in Indochina] was the professional-Army approach. There were draftees in the armed forces, but the Army fighting the war was primarily professional. The reserves were never called into action, and for that reason the nation never realized the full participation of its people.

Before Reserve Officers Association
National Council, Washington, Feb. 22/
Vital Speeches, 4-1:384.

Gerald R. Ford
Vice President of the United States
4

At the moment, I think we are fully prepared to meet any [military] challenge. We don't, however, have the military superiority we once enjoyed—and that worries me. And I am concerned about our military sufficiency in the next five to 10 years. To maintain military adequacy, we cannot affort to neglect adequate procurement as well as adequate research and development.

Interview/Nation's Business, March:58.

Gerald R. Ford
President of the United States
5

A strong defense is the surest way to peace. Strength makes detente attainable. Weakness invites war, as my generation knows from four bitter experiences. Just as America's will for peace is second to none, so will America's strength be second to none. We cannot rely on the forbearance of others to protect this nation. The power and diversity of the armed forces, the resolve of our fellow citizens, the flexibility in our command to navigate international waters that remain troubled—all are essential to our security. I shall continue to insist on civilian control of our superb military establishment. The Constitution plainly requires the President to be the Commander-in-Chief, and I will be.

First address as President before Congress,
Washington, Aug. 12/
The New York Times, 8-13:20.

6

No budget for any [government] department is sacrosanct. And that includes the de-

WHAT THEY SAID IN 1974

(GERALD R. FORD)

fense budget. I insist, however, that sufficient money be made available to the Army, the Navy and the Air Force so that we are strong militarily for the purpose of deterring war or meeting any challenge by any adversary. But if there is any fat in the defense budget, it ought to be cut out by Congress or eliminated by the Secretary of Defense.

News conference, Washington, Aug. 28/
The New York Times, 8-29:20.

1

[On the U.S.-Soviet Vladivostok agreement setting limits on weaponry] : These ceilings are well below the force levels which would otherwise have been expected over the next 10 years, and very substantially below the forces which would result from an all-out arms race over the same period. What we have done is to set firm and equal limits on the strategic forces of each side, thus preventing an arms race with all its terror, instability, war-breeding tension and economic waste . . . This [agreement] does not permit an agreed buildup. It puts a cap on future buildups and it actually reduces a part of the buildup at the present time. It is important, I should say however, in order for us to maintain equality, which is the keystone of this program, to have an adequate amount of military expenditures. But I can say this without hesitation or qualification: If we had not had this agreement, it would have required the United States to substantially increase its military expenditures in the strategic areas. So we put a cap on the arms race; we actually made some reductions below present programs. It's a good agreement. And I think that the American people will buy it because it provides for equality, and it provides for a negotiated reduction in several years ahead.

News conference, Washington, Dec. 2/
The New York Times, 12-3:28.

Robert F. Froehlke
Former Secretary of the Army
of the United States

2

Military strength does not cause wars. But strength matched against weakness does. A pos-

sible exception is the Middle East today, where presumably near-equal strength is being exhibited on both sides. But I assure you there would have been a Middle East war long before October, 1973, if that balance of power had not been maintained. Strength plus weakness causes war, even in a period of detente. Political scientists agree that, at any time, detente without defense is delusion. It is utter delusion for the U.S. to talk with the U.S.S.R. and the People's Republic of [Communist] China while we are slashing our military defenses. Only through talking from strength can detente accomplish what we hope and pray is possible.

Before Town Hall, Los Angeles,
Jan. 22/Vital Speeches, 3-1:298.

J. William Fulbright
United States Senator, D—Arkansas

3

We have, all along, been ahead of them [the Soviets], back to the missile gap of the Kennedy era, when President Kennedy alleged there was a missile gap. There was a missile gap, but it was in reverse. We had about 1,000 weapons and they had about 80, whereas he made the country believe that we had 80 and they had 1,000. It just was not so. But the public believes that we are behind [militarily]. We have had Admiral [Thomas] Moorer and Admiral [Elmo] Zumwalt going about recently— of course, this always happens; this is an annual ritual just before appropriations time—saying we are suddenly inferior, our fleets are inferior, everything is inferior, we are in terrible shape militarily, and therefore we need more money . . . I think the military and its allies have much influence here. In our case, even if the President does not like it, the military can go to Congress and override the President. They do it on their appropriations time and time again, year after year. It has been going on and there is no power that can restrict the military in our political system . . . There is very little counterforce against the power of the military. Look at the votes in the Senate on any effort to reduce in a substantial way anything the military wants. Everybody knows what happens year after year. We have never won a single showdown with the military.

Panel discussion, Washington, Aug. 2/
The New York Times, 8-7:42.

Noel Gayler
Admiral, United States Navy;
Commander-in-Chief,
United States Armed Forces/Pacific 1

I'm not one of those who sees Communists under every bed. We do have a detente with both Russia and [Communist] China, and I welcome it and hope it endures. But the world changes, and we have to deal with uncertainty. You also have to notice the extraordinary and continuing Russian buildup, the way in which force and the threat of force has been used in recent years, and our vulnerability both to attack on us and on other countries who depend on us. The consequences, if an aggressive power were seen to be dominant militarily in the Pacific, would be very unfortunate. Security is not something we can give away to save the money and enjoy something else, because without security there is nothing else. Many an unfortunate nation has learned that too late.

Interview, Washington/
U.S. News & World Report, 3-25:42.

Barry M. Goldwater
United States Senator, R—Arizona 2

I'm very worried about [U.S. defense weakness], because we have obviously entered a period where some of our leaders in Congress feel that we have detente with the Soviet. In fact, we've never been in a worse position to talk about detente than we are today. What happened in the Middle East, where we came up with another confrontation with the Russians, was only the first of a number of these experiences that we're going to go through . . . If you're not first [militarily], you might as well be tenth or twelfth—you won't get hurt too badly down there. As I've said, the Soviets are now superior to us in every category of military equipment. For a while I thought I was wrong, but now I'm more convinced than ever that they are. And with that strength, they're

going to have the ability to convince our allies and our enemies that we are not going to stand up. The only answer to that is to have a President and a State Department who will answer these confrontations, and to have a military capable of going through with whatever is necessary.

Interview, Washington/
U.S. News & World Report, 2-11:41.

3

[Calling for a Constitutional amendment limiting the war powers of the Presidency]: Let's say that the President did want to destroy the world. We haven't taken away the power for him to reach in and punch that red button. If we want to change things—and I wouldn't be opposed to this—let's make punching that red button something that is going to be decided not by one man but maybe by a group of men.

Los Angeles Times, 10-9:(1)2.

Andrew J. Goodpaster
General, United States Army;
Supreme Allied Commander/Europe 4

It is of course our deep and fervent hope that there will never be occasion to use nuclear weapons, or any other weapons . . . But it is perhaps ironic that, in our time, the best way to insure that these weapons are not used is to convince the other side that we have a ready plan for their efficient and coordinated use—effective use of all forces and weapons, including nuclear weapons, if required—for all contingencies.

Before Atlantic Treaty Association,
Ottawa, Canada, Sept. 10/
Vital Speeches, 11-1:50.

Mark O. Hatfield
United States Senator, R—Oregon 5

The Selective Service System is a fine example of bureaucracy that continues to exist and spend the taxpayers' money more by virtue of its own momentum than for any other constructive purpose.

San Francisco Examiner, 3-28:32.

Fred C. Ikle
Director, Arms Control and Disarmament
Agency of the United States
1

Being able to respond in kind to an attack which is less than full-scale does not increase the likelihood of nuclear war. Any use of nuclear weapons would be incredibly dangerous and, in a rational calculation, the risk of national destruction would outweigh any expected gain from initiating nuclear war. On the contrary, the ability to respond in a limited manner against military targets adds a new element to deterrence: It introduces a last chance—should something have gone wrong to avert the utmost catastrophe.

Interview, Washington, Feb. 1/
The Washington Post, 2-2:(A)12.

Herman Kahn
Director, Hudson Institute
2

[On the political benefit of military superiority]: If you have a crisis, both sides [the U.S. and the Soviet Union] say something like this: "Look, nothing at issue is worth the serious risk of nuclear war. It's just crazy for us to continue this terrible crisis. One of us has to be reasonable *and it isn't going to be me."*

Newsweek, 4-22:55.

Henry A. Kissinger
Secretary of State of the United States
3

If we [the U.S. and Soviet Union] have not reached an [nuclear arms curb] agreement well before 1977 [when the present interim agreement expires], then I believe you will see an explosion of technology and an explosion of numbers [of multiple warheads on missiles] at the end of which we will be lucky if we have the present stability. Then it will be impossible to describe what strategic superiority means. And one of the questions which we have to ask ourselves as a country is what in the name of God is strategic superiority? What is the significance of it—politically, militarily, operationally—at these levels of numbers? What do you do with it? Opportunities for nuclear warfare [will then] exist which were unimaginable 15 years ago at the beginning of the nuclear age, and that is what is driving our concern.

News conference, Moscow, July 3/
Los Angeles Times, 7-4:(1)6.

4

[Saying that in an area of rough strategic balance, the threat of all-out nuclear war is less and less credible]: Thus, challenges at the conventional level may become more difficult to prevent . . . our conventional forces must therefore be strong. They keep the nuclear threshhold high by helping to contain, discourage, or altogether prevent, hostilities. They are the essential tool for our diplomacy in times of crisis.

Before American Legion, Miami Beach,
Aug. 20/The Atlanta Constitution,
8-21:(A)7.

5

As I can attest from experience, in time of crisis and at the conference table, America's military might is the foundation of our diplomatic strength. We have made progress toward peace in recent years because we have been flexible, but also because we have been resolute. Let us never forget that conciliation is a virtue only in those who are thought to have a choice. A strong defense is the essential deterrent to aggression.

Before American Legion, Miami Beach,
Aug. 20/The New York Times, 8-21:6.

6

When nuclear arsenals reach levels involving thousands of launchers and over 10,000 warheads, and when the characteristics of the weapons of the two sides [the U.S. and the Soviet Union] are so incommensurable, it becomes difficult to determine what combination of numbers of strategic weapons and performance capabilities would give one side a militarily and politically useful superiority. While a decisive advantage is hard to calculate, the *appearance* of inferiority—whatever its actual significance—can have serious political consequences. With weapons that are unlikely to be used and for which there is no operational experience, the psychological impact can be crucial.

Before Senate Foreign Relations Committee,
Washington/The New York Times, 10-20:(1)2.

Walter Laqueur
*Director, Institute of Contemporary
Affairs, London*

1

There is a tendency in this country [the U.S.] now, particularly among the young, to belittle military power. People say, "Look, all these nuclear bombs won't be used anyway, so what does it matter?" But the Middle East war [in 1973] showed that military strength matters, after all.

*Interview, Washington/
Los Angeles Times, 4-3:(2)7.*

Mike Mansfield
United States Senator, D—Montana

2

The U.S. military presence overseas has been too much, too long. Nevertheless, the Federal government seems to be incapable of a significant reduction of a military presence anywhere abroad, not to speak of a close-out, unless we are "invited" to leave, politely or otherwise.

Quote, 4-21:361.

John L. McClellan
United States Senator, D—Arkansas

3

Traditionally, after each of our major wars, we have followed a naive and reckless policy of quick disarmament. After World War I, World War II and Korea, we put down our arms and indulged the unwarranted assumption and false hope that military preparedness was not essential to our future security and world peace. And once again—this time after Vietnam—the same pressures are being exerted. There are many well-intentioned and patriotic Americans—some of them in Congress—who are convinced that defense spending is wasteful and unnecessary in a period of detente. We must not equate or confuse detente with disarmament. Even with detente we must maintain—pending hopes for effective arms limitation agreements—a military force that provides a sufficient deterrent to ensure peace and our security.

*At Senate Defense Appropriations
Subcommittee hearing, Washington,
March 5/Los Angeles Times, 3-6:(1)12.*

4

Perhaps one of the problems with military spending is that the professional soldiers—the Generals and Admirals who manage programs and projects in the Defense Department—have not had the experience of working in the private marketplace where profits, and not appropriations, determine expenditures. We must get full value for every dollar expended. Our Generals and Admirals must come to realize that we do not intend to appropriate for any purpose unless it is fully justified.

U.S. News & World Report, 10-14:72.

George S. McGovern
United States Senator, D—South Dakota

5

We have a triad system of national deterrents that includes submarines, missiles and our bombers. Already plans are going forward in the Pentagon to build a new bomber to take the place of the one we now have on the theory that that one may be obsolete by 1990. So we have got to start planning for the future. Why is it so hard to get people concerned about the food supply in 1990 or the population pressures in 1990, and yet we don't seem to have any difficulty providing whatever is necessary for a real or imagined threat or threats that might occur 15 or 20 years down the road?

*At Senate Select Committee on Nutrition
and Human Needs hearing, Washington/
The Washington Post, 6-22:(A)18.*

6

With the purveyors and profiteers of militarism, there can be no compromise. We cannot tell the lie that America will be a prosperous and progressive society while we squander our resources on overkill and overruns and for a feast of weapons to nourish dictatorship around the world. Military waste worsens inflation as it worsens the arms race.

*At Democratic Party mini-convention,
Kansas City/The Washington Post,
12-21:(A)15.*

Thomas H. Moorer
*Admiral, United States Navy;
Chairman, Joint Chiefs of Staff*

7

Detente, of course, simply means that we are establishing a situation wherein we can communicate and negotiate before we move into a

(THOMAS H. MOORER)

position of confrontation [with an adversary]; and so I certainly think that this procedure, which permits discussion of problems of mutual interest, is a good one. I would go on to say, however, that it is mandatory, in my opinion, that, in order to make detente work, we must maintain adequate military forces, because you cannot negotiate from weakness; and as [it] has been put before, detente without defense is a delusion.

TV-radio interview/"Meet the Press,"
National Broadcasting Company, 2-17.

1

I think that the war in the Middle East [last year] brought back a recognition of the world-wide interests of the United States and the part that our military forces play in security and in enhancing these interests of the United States. In my view, the Congress was more receptive to our budget requests this year than they were last year. I don't know that the shift in focus to the Middle East accounts for all the change. It may be that they say, "Thank God that we're disengaged from Vietnam."

Interview, Washington/
U.S. News & World Report, 7-8:62.

Ron Nessen
Press Secretary to President of the
United States Gerald R. Ford

2

[Defending the U.S.-Soviet Vladivostok agreement, which puts a ceiling on weapons strength, against criticism by some in the U.S. that the ceiling is too high]: What would have prevented the Russians from continuing to build up at a rapid rate in their nuclear strike force? If they did that, what would have been our two alternatives for action? One, to do nothing, allowing the Russians to gain an ever-larger advantage in missiles. That would have caused some political difficulties in this country as well as strategic problems. Our other alternative would have been to chase them, and you would have been into a new arms race. It's no secret that this is going to cost some money, but think of the difference in cost between building a force of 2,400 [missiles] and build-

ing an unlimited force governed only by the decisions of the other side.

Washington, Dec. 5/
Los Angeles Times, 12-6:(1)6.

Richard M. Nixon
President of the United States

3

... we must not assume that our new [improved] relationship with the Soviet Union allows us to neglect our own military strength. It is because we are strong that such a relationship that we are now developing is possible. In his first annual message to the Congress, George Washington said: "To be prepared for war is one of the most effective means of preserving peace." That statement is true today as it was then. And that is why all of you who are serving in our armed forces today are actually serving in the peace forces for America and the world. We thank you for your service. We are prepared, we in the United States, to reduce our military strength, but only through a process in which that reduction is mutual and one that does not diminish the security of the United States of America. It is to that end that we have been working.

Broadcast address to the nation,
Loring Air Force Base, Limestone, Maine,
July 3/The New York Times, 4-4:4.

William Proxmire
United States Senator, D—Wisconsin

4

I have criticized the Defense Department before and will do so again vigorously. But, in all fairness, they have done well in some respects and deserve credit for it. During a time when the mood of the country seems to be pessimistic and critical of all government bureaucracies, it is reassuring to look back at the enormous problems the Department ... has solved by wise management and sound decision-making.

April 29/The Washington Post, 4-30:(A)2.

5

In any other agency, heads would roll and drastic changes would be made to halt the runaway costs and program failures occurring daily in the Pentagon. One of the most distressing facts is that the quantity cutbacks have usually been made because of the cost overruns. The Pentagon is being forced to buy less while spending more because of its inability to control costs. The result is a double whammy for the taxpayer. He pays higher taxes and receives less defense for the dollars spent.

Before the Senate, Washington,
June 3/Los Angeles Times, 6-3:(1)4.

1

The arms race continues to accelerate despite the obvious conclusions that the numbers of weapons on both sides defy interpretation into the standard context of "who's ahead" ... It appears that we have slipped—from the rational basis for an arms race of keeping ahead or equal to any combination of adversaries—to a strictly psychological arms race where the numbers are meaningless, in a military sense, but all powerful in a bargaining environment.

The National Observer, 9-21:4.

Hyman G. Rickover
Admiral, United States Navy

2

... all weapons of war are expensive. Cheap weapons will not win us a war. And if we cannot win a war, there is no sense in spending money on weapons at all. Rarely in naval history have the leaders looked far enough ahead. They generally build ships that they consider to be adequate for the present. That is why, frequently, naval leadership has been replaced when war broke out. We should be planning now for war that may erupt 15 or more years from now. Therefore, it is time to establish a firm program for making all new major combatant ships for our striking force nuclear-powered. It is a matter of national priority.

Before San Diego Press Club/
Los Angeles Herald-Examiner, 3-31:(A)14.

James R. Schlesinger
Secretary of Defense of the United States

3

I believe that we have already overshot the mark in previous force reductions, and that, to the extent that we can expand the combat structure without adding real costs, we should be authorized to do so ... the military capabil-

ities of those nations in a position to threaten our interests have not declined, they have increased. There is, in fact, no evidence whatsoever that unilateral reductions [on our part] induce reciprocity on their part ... Deterrence must operate across the entire spectrum of possible contingencies. We cannot afford gaps in its coverage that might invite probes and tests.

Before Senate Armed Services Committee,
Washington, Feb. 5/
Los Angeles Times, 2-6:(1)8.

4

I do not subscribe to alarmist statements alleging the current superiority of the Soviet fleet [over U.S. naval strength]. There are circumstances, and there are places in the world, where the U.S. Navy cannot go today with a high confidence of success. But I think that this was built into the cards. We continue to have some edge in naval capability. But we should adjust our naval strength so as to maintain a high-confidence, world-wide balance for the nations of the free world, which are in a sense maritime states.

Before Senate Armed Services Committee,
Washington/The Washington Post, 2-20:(A)2.

5

Now as the Soviet Union reaches nuclear parity with the United States, deterrence will be strongly reinforced if there is a balance of conventional as well as of nuclear forces ... Thus, a strong conventional capability is more than ever necessary—not because we wish to wage conventional war, but because we do not wish to wage any war.

U.S. News & World Report, 4-1:16.

6

If the rate of inflation is 7.5 per cent, it will cost us $6 billion more just to have the same purchasing power as we had last year in the Department of Defense, when the budget was $80 billion. Unless the American public is willing to tolerate a gradual erosion of our defense capabilities, they will have to expect to spend about 6 per cent more on the Department of Defense each and every year just to retain the

WHAT THEY SAID IN 1974

(JAMES R. SCHLESINGER)

same general defense posture as in the previous year.

Interview, Washington/
U.S. News & World Report, 5-13:38.

1

The notion that detente permits us to disarm is a widespread illusion. Nonetheless, it *is* an illusion. It is necessary to maintain a world-wide military balance as the underpinning of detente. Detente rests on an equilibrium of force. If that equilibrium of force is upset, detente and also hopes for improved political relations with the Soviet Union will disappear. We do not base our force structure on the diplomatic atmosphere, which we hope will show improvement. Our force structure must be based upon those external capabilities which we hope to balance. There is a continuing, steady increase in the military capabilities of the Soviet Union, and we must balance that.

Interview, Washington/
U.S. News & World Report, 5-13:38.

2

I don't believe that we are behind the Soviets [in naval strength]. If one is thinking of naval engagements, I think that the United States still has an edge—perhaps a decided edge. The point that worries our naval strategists is this: The free world is dependent upon maritime communications. If the Soviets were able to deny us the use of the seas, that would be a crippling blow. Consequently, one should not think about the naval balance in terms of who is stronger, but in terms of this question: Does the West have sufficient naval capabilities to continue to use the seas rather than being denied the use of the seas?

Interview, Washington/
U.S. News & World Report, 5-13:40.

3

... democracies are suffering from their traditional problem that they need an overt manifest threat in order to bring about the appropriate allocation of resources within the society to maintain a defense establishment

that continues militarily to deter, rather than to rely upon the good-will of potential opponents.

The New York Times Magazine, 8-4:36.

4

We're not putting together a defense establishment which is primarily directed toward protecting the U.S. against an overland attack. The defense establishment of the U.S. is designed to provide world-wide military balance and a vision of the U.S. role. No one else but the U.S. can play that role. There's a tendency now toward the belief that we should go home. We can't go home. There's no one else to pick up that torch if we drop it.

Interview, Washington/
The Washington Post, 10-6:(Potomac)12.

5

There is no conflict between detente and defense. They are inextricably bound up with one another in the maintenance of an equilibrium ... [Russia] has no difficulty in pursuing detente and in simultaneously strengthening its defense efforts ... And next year the Soviets will start what promises to be the most dramatic deployment of offensive forces in the entire history of strategic nuclear arms.

Before Army Association, Washington,
Oct. 16/The Atlanta Constitution,
10-17:(A)14.

6

The American role in maintaining a world-wide military balance is, I fear, better understood in Moscow than it is in this country. It is understood there that failure to maintain a military equilibrium will result in a shift ... adversely against the West with consequent major political adjustments to follow. To understand the requirements of the military balance so necessary to the security of the free world demands intellectual discipline and a rejection of the mindless cliches which all too frequently have characterized our domestic debates on military issues.

The Washington Post, 10-21:(A)2.

7

We [the U.S.] have dropped in terms of military manpower by a million and a half men, and, compared to pre-war, we are down by about 600,000 men. We [the military] have the lowest share of the GNP since before the Korean war. And in terms of public spending, we're at the lowest point since before Pearl Harbor. The Department of Defense of the United States now suffers from a wasting disease and has been so suffering since fiscal year 1968 ... The question is, does the United States wish to maintain a military balance or does it not? If we are to disarm as a nation and accept second-class status as a military power, we should do so consciously, rather than allowing the erosion of purchasing power for the Department of Defense to drive us into that second-class status ... I think that the departure from Vietnam [and] the war in the Middle East eliminated much of the hostilities toward the Department of Defense. Now we're faced with a crueler fate—which is indifference rather than hostility ... People don't care very much.

Television interview/"Morning News,"
Columbia Broadcasting System, 10-22.

John C. Stennis
United States Senator, D—Mississippi
1

Those who are over-zealous or over-concerned or have something to sell have over-sold the [naval] strength of our possible adversaries and have under-sold our own strength. [Such alarmist charges] can be dangerous since they undermine United States naval power in the eyes of our allies, our own seamen and the American people and could encourage the Soviet Navy to react recklessly or belligerently. On a navy-to-navy basis, the Soviet Navy does not match the capability of the United States Navy. The United States Navy should be able to fulfill its missions, both now and in the foreseeable future, except under the most adverse and extreme circumstances, such as being subject to massive land-based air attack without sufficient air defense.

Before the Senate, Washington, Sept. 19/
The New York Times, 9-20:19.

Edward Teller
Physicist
2

The proliferation of nuclear weapons is unavoidable. The Non-Proliferation Treaty has the faults of the Kellogg-Briand Pact, which certainly did nothing to prevent World War II. At the same time, only two countries—the U.S. and the U.S.S.R.—today possess massive nuclear arms. If the limited capabilities of small powers are used purely as a deterrent, they may even have a stabilizing influence in certain parts of the world. I don't want proliferation, but we don't know how to prevent it. And it is totally misleading to use it as a direct measure of global instability.

Interview/People, 8-19:37.

Paul C. Warnke
Former Assistant Secretary for
International Security Affairs,
Department of Defense of the United States
3

Realistically, the United States faces one conceivable threat: the Soviet Union. The problems are, what kind of war would be fought, what does it take to deter a strategic war and what does it take to deter or defeat the Russians in a conventional war? At present levels, we have plenty for both kinds of war—so many nuclear warheads, we'd run out of targets. As for a conventional war, if we don't have enough with all the money spent, someone has blundered.

The New York Times, 3-17:(1)30.

Frederick C. Weyand
General and Vice Chief of Staff,
United States Army
4

[On whether women should be admitted to the military service academies] : The issue is not whether women should become cadets at West Point; the basic question is whether Americans are prepared to commit their daughters to combat. I am not prepared to do that. And I believe that is the sentiment of the majority of Americans.

The Christian Science Monitor, 7-19:5C.

Jerome B. Wiesner
President,
Massachusetts Institute of Technology
5

I think arms control is possible. But I'm not foolish enough to think it's about to happen in

(JEROME B. WIESNER)

the next five years. I think it's worth trying, but I don't know how it's going to come about. I think we could be trying harder, but, on the other hand, I think we have kept the arms race from being worse than it could have been. For instance, we haven't made or bought all the terrible weapons we talked about. At least one thing has come out of the dialog on the subject between the U.S. and the U.S.S.R.: We've both come to understand how nutty the whole thing is.

Interview, New York/
"W": a Fairchild publication, 10-4:7.

Bob Wilson
United States Representative, R—California   1

If we are to learn any lesson from the constantly expanding Soviet naval capability and the oil crisis, it is that we must provide nuclear propulsion in the new warships being built for our first-line striking forces ... It is inconceivable that the Navy should even be considering the design of new ships for our aircraft striking forces which do not have nuclear propulsion.

Los Angeles Herald-Examiner, 7-6:(A)10.

Elmo R. Zumwalt, Jr.
Admiral, United States Navy;
Chief of Naval Operations   2

[On U.S. naval strength as compared with that of the Soviet Union]: We stand now at our point of greatest weakness and in my estimate in our greatest jeopardy ... When I apply the personal assessments of my fleet commanders as to the readiness of the remaining [U.S.] forces to our net assessment, the picture is grim indeed.

Before Senate Armed Services Committee,
Washington, Feb. 19/
The Washington Post, 2-20:(A)2.

3

We are entering an era with the Soviet Union ahead of us, numerically, in the strategic field and having four times the number of ships that we have at sea. We have to ask ourselves what will be the nature of the military-political con-

test in the years ahead. If we do not proceed to maintain the strength that is necessary in the years ahead, it is we who will have to accommodate ourselves to superior Soviet power as they marshal it in support of their vital interests.

Parade, 5-5:39.

4

... I believe it is just very difficult for the man in the street to understand, in an era of apparent peace and tranquility, why one needs military strength. And I think the layman doesn't realize how very long the lead time is in the modern era to recover strength. In each historical cycle, we have won a war, demobilized, become inferior, and tempted prospective adversaries to become aggressive. Fortunately, in the past we have had time to rebuild our strength, trading space and other people's territory for time ... I think it remains to be determined whether this country is going to be able to meet its national-security needs in the years ahead. One can visualize several alternative worlds. One is a world in which we have been successful in maintaining sufficient strength so that detente will continue on terms acceptable to the United States and the free world. A second is a world in which our military strength has become so inferior that the Soviets are tempted to become much more aggressive in their foreign policy. There are two forks in that road: one in which we recognize what is happening and accommodate; the other in which we do not recognize it, fail to accommodate and, through miscalculation, are involved in a losing war ... the lessons of history would teach us that the free world will let its defenses deteriorate until some set of external circumstances creates sufficient concern that we decide to do something about it.

Interview, Washington/
The Washington Post, 6-29:(A)4.

5

[During the last 10 years,] we have seen our once-great fleet cut almost in half and our remaining ships and personnel forced to endure long and continuous deployments as their numbers dwindled while requirements increased. [Those same 10 years has seen the Soviet

Union,] which has no fundamental need to control and use the seas, develop a capability to do so which nearly in every way challenges our own. Our Navy has reached a point where the odds are it can no longer guarantee free use of the ocean lifelines to U.S. and allied forces in the face of a new, powerful and still-growing Soviet fleet.

Upon turning over his command (effective 7/1) as Chief of Naval Operations to Admiral James Holloway, Annapolis, Md., June 29/San Francisco Examiner & Chronicle, 6-30:(A)5.

1

I do agree that inflation is a serious problem. I also think that the insurance policy of adequate defense is a very necessary one; and I think that as we have seen the defense budget fall each year to the smallest fraction of the gross national product since 1950, and each year to the smallest fraction of the Federal budget since 1950, and as we have seen our Navy fall to the smallest number of ships since 1939, that people should be very, very concerned about the ability of the United States to defend its interests.

TV-radio interview, Washington/ "Meet the Press," National Broadcasting Company, 6-30.

2

The Navy is not the only defense we have, but it is the *sine qui non* for the defense of any of our forces overseas or for the reinforcement of our allies. If we are not able to control and use the seas, we simply cannot have armies and air forces operating overseas, since 94 per cent of the millions of tons that it takes to support ourselves and our allies in any kind of an action has to travel on the surface of the seas—even for example, the aviation gasoline necessary to fly the airlift back home.

TV-radio interview, Washington/ "Meet the Press," National Broadcasting Company, 6-30.

Elmo R. Zumwalt, Jr.
Admiral, United States Navy; Former Chief of Naval Operations

3

[On women in the Navy]: We find that the problems are diminutive. They are able to do the work in any rating, and there is no question but that women will be able to serve on all ships effectively when the law in contravention thereof is struck down. I see no limitations on the managerial or leadership capabilities of women, and I see no reason, in principle, why some day a Chief of Naval Operations should not be a woman who has had the opportunity to serve and command at sea and work up through the necessary experiences.

Television interview/ The Dallas Times Herald, 7-7:(B)6.

Politics

George D. Aiken
United States Senator, R—Vermont
1

During most of our existence as a nation, the two-party political system has prevailed. Third-party attempts have been successful only when political evolution has necessitated a general realignment of voters . . . There are many indications that our nation has again reached the point where a realignment of the voters is desirable and possibly even necessary. A large percentage of the voters in opposing parties are in almost full accord with their opponents at the polls. Party allegiance is woefully weak today. The rank and file of both major parties and countless numbers of voters who never belonged to any party are undecided as to their future course. Good administration for the benefit of all the people is what we want. I have no sympathy for Republicans who oppose worthwhile measures for fear the opposition party may get the credit. I have no sympathy for Democratic officials who conduct face-saving campaigns to cover up their failures.

Before the Senate, Washington, Dec. 11/
The Washington Post, 12-14:(A)14.

Joseph L. Alioto
Mayor of San Francisco
2

[On how he makes political appointments]: When I decide to make such a move, I naturally look to qualified friends. If I don't have any qualified friends, I look to qualified neutrals. If I don't have any qualified neutrals that I can find, I look to qualified enemies. Now, it just happens that the circle of my friends is so wide and they are so loaded with talent that I never have to get below that first category.

San Francisco Examiner & Chronicle,
9-8:(This World)2.

John B. Anderson
United States Representative, R—Illinois
3

. . . I think it is very important at this juncture to eliminate the influence of large contributions and special-interest money in election campaigns; and when you do that, then I think you have to find an alternative source of funding. Something like 700,000 people gave contributions to the Democratic [Presidential] candidate of less than $100 in 1972 and some several hundred thousand to the Republican candidate. If we could stimulate gifts in that amount—that is, small contributions—by providing for a Federal matching entitlement fund, we could finance campaigns at the Federal level without appealing to the large contributors or the special interests.

TV-radio interview/"Meet the Press,"
National Broadcasting Company, 3-17.

John M. Ashbrook
United States Representative, R—Ohio
4

[On President Ford's choice of Nelson Rockefeller as Vice President]: The President has correctly stated that excessive government spending is one of the chief problems facing our country, especially in our battle against inflation. It is totally inconsistent, therefore, to choose a man who, throughout his entire political life, has used his energy and prestige to do exactly the opposite—that is, to increase spending by giant steps and increase taxes on the already over-burdened American. I know of no person who can identify less with the problems of the average American than Nelson Rockefeller. No one can less identify with the elderly living on fixed income, the housewife with her budget problems, the small businessman meeting a payroll or the average worker just trying to keep his head above the water, than former [New York] Governor Nelson Rockefeller.

With so many leading Republicans available, it is unfortunate that the President chose a man who has continually been rejected nation-wide by the overwhelming majority of the Republican Party. Nelson Rockefeler now gets indirectly what he never has been able to achieve directly.

Human Events, 8-31:3.

Howard H. Baker, Jr.
United States Senator, R–Tennessee

1

I can assure you that, having been "considered" for that job [the Vice Presidency] in 1968 and having been "considered" for it again in 1974, that I'm the world's leading authority on the proposition that there's the most helpless position in politics that you can be in. I'm not sure that I'll ever be a candidate for anything other than the U.S. Senate again. But if I am, I can promise you that it will not be as a candidate for Vice President.

News conference, Nashville/
Los Angeles Times, 8-28:(1)2.

Lucy Wilson Benson
National president, League of Women Voters

2

No issue is more crucial to the future of democratic self-government in this country than the issue of campaign reform. The anger and distrust felt by millions of Americans is fueled by the gnawing conviction that too many people in politics and government are looking out for special, private interests instead of public ones. This conclusion is perpetuated by an insidious system of campaign financing. It must be cleaned up. The votes of American citizens must count for more than the vices of big-money politics.

San Francisco/
The Christian Science Monitor, 5-20:(F)6.

James L. Buckley
United States Senator, C–New York

3

I believe ... that the public is ready to understand that it is the conservative who truly believes in and trusts the common man. We reject the elitism that is at the heart of so much of liberal policy. Nowhere has this fundamental truth about conservatives been more succinctly stated as when that distinguished columnist, author and yachtsman, my brother Bill [William F. Buckley, Jr.], said some years ago that he would rather be governed by the first thousand names in the Boston telephone book than by the Harvard faculty. We are a scandal to the liberals because we really believe that Americans are intelligent enough to lead their own lives, and that they are competent of responsible self-government at levels less Olympian than the Federal. We do not speak of the "masses" or "minorities" or of any other quantitative misrepresentations so popular in liberal rhetoric. Instead, we focus our attention on the individual. We dare to hold the heretical idea that Americans, irrespective of station or origin, should be treated as citizens and not as ciphers.

Before Conservative Political Action
Conference, Washington, Jan. 26/
Vital Speeches, 2-15:264.

4

[Arguing against public financing of election campaigns]: ... millions of Americans now contribute voluntarily to Federal, state and local political campaigns. These people see their decision to contribute to one campaign or another as a means of political expression. Public financing of Federal general election campaigns would deprive people of an opportunity to participate and to express their strongly held opinions. They would still be contributing, of course, since the Senate [campaign-reform] proposal will cost them hundreds of millions of dollars in tax money. But their participation would be compulsory and would involve the use of their money to support candidates and positions they find morally and politically reprehensible.

Interview/Human Events, 3-30:8.

5

The American political future belongs to that party that will first identify itself fully and frankly with the new mood of the American people, and that mood is conservative ... Republicans need look no further than to the extraordinary mandate of the 1972 election to see how they can consolidate within their ranks a new American majority ... But if this is to be

WHAT THEY SAID IN 1974

(JAMES L. BUCKLEY)

accomplished, Republican leaders must abandon their self-defeating fascination with a theoretical "middle ground" that is forever being redefined by *The New York Times* and *The Washington Post*.

Human Events, 11-23:2.

George Bush
Chairman, Republican National Committee

1

[The Republican Party is strong,] more united than the Democrats, and our programs are much more in keeping with the will of Americans than the tired old centralized "turn it over to the Federal government" answers of the Democrats. When the country looks at what we are for and why it's not being achieved—Democrat inaction in Congress—I am convinced our Party will emerge in good shape in the fall elections.

At dinner honoring Representative Clarence Miller, Lancaster, Ohio, March 30/ The Dallas Times Herald, 3-31:(A)21.

Harry F. Byrd, Jr.
United States Senator, I–Virginia

2

Neither party can count on blind support from the voters, and I think that's not bad. It will force both parties to put up better candidates, be franker with the people, tell them what the parties stand for. Hell, those platforms both parties write—the first thing the nominee does is repudiate it. The tendency of politicians is to say one thing and do another. What this country wants more than anything else is leadership in whom they can have confidence. And they don't care if it comes from the Republican Party, the Democratic Party or an independent.

The Washington Post, 12-23:(A)4.

Robert C. Byrd
United States Senator, D–West Virginia

3

The man who would have been the [Democrats'] chief political target, Richard Nixon, has removed himself from office and from the political arena. Democrats must face the fact that the country—and rightly so—wants the new

Republican President [Ford] to have his chance, and he should have it. Let us not delude ourselves. Gerald Ford is respected and he starts with a built-in advantage of being an incumbent with few if any enemies. Moreover, the naming of Nelson Rockefeller as Vice President is a distinct plus for the Republicans, in my judgment. With a moderately conservative President and a moderately liberal Vice President, it seems to me that the Republicans probably have their 1976 ticket already lined up.

At Democratic rally, Asheville, N.C., Aug. 24/ The Washington Post, 8-25:(A)6.

4

I have always believed—and I still believe—[President] Ford to be a decent guy; but it will take more than that to make the country run. The problems confronting him are going to require initiative and hard choices, and there are already indications that he may lack the decisiveness that is so needed to cope with the nagging and agonizing problems that weigh too heavily upon all of us at this time in our history.

Before Southern Democratic state chairmen, Virginia Beach, Va., Sept. 16/ The Washington Post, 9-17:(A)4.

Liz Carpenter
Democratic National Committeewoman

5

The political fact is that 1974 is going to be a year when we [women] can really score. Big political money is a no-no. Slick campaigns are bad politics. That is one of the constructive fallouts of Watergate. So there are going to be a lot of homemade campaigns in 1974, a lot of campaigns run from the kitchen and the living room. It is a year when imagination can replace cash in politics.

At 1974 Campaign Conference for Democratic Women, Washington/ The Washington Post, 3-31:(A)11.

Jimmy Carter
Governor of Georgia

6

I've never found any conflict in my deep religious convictions with my effort to serve in public office. I don't think there ought to be any different standard of ethics or morality or honesty or compassion or brotherhood in our lives in our own homes, or our lives in our church, or our lives in the Governor's office. This is one of the problems that concerns me about our country. We've been willing in recent years to accept a lower ethical standard in politics than we would in our own personal lives. And I think this ought to be changed.

Interview, Plains, Ga./
The Christian Science Monitor, 12-12:7.

Henry Steele Commager
Historian

1

Practically and symbolically, [former President] Nixon associated conservatism not with conserving the resources and institutions of the nation, but with exploiting them for short-sighted and often private ends; with power—military, economic and personal; with a spurious "honor" which required that we go on for four years fighting a war [in Southeast Asia] that should never have been started in the first place; with inveterate hostility to freedom of speech, of the press, of assembly, and with control of the press and of television; and with private aggrandizement of the natural resources which belong to the whole people; with uncritical approval of corporate practices and malpractices; with the worship of money and wealth in all of its most vulgar manifestations. His "conservatism" and his appeal to what he contemptuously called Middle America meant hostility to the press, to the academy, to the arts . . . to the "liberal establishment" and to the young with all their hopes and idealism. But true conservatism preserves natural resources, human resources, the resources of the law and of the Constitution, intellectual, moral and artistic resources, and the resources of our history, our traditions and our ideals.

Interview/Newsweek, 8-19:56.

Barber B. Conable, Jr.
United States Representative,
R—New York

2

[On the controversy about President Nixon's tax deductions]: I believe in people paying their taxes. And if I feel my position as a member of Congress and the House Ways and Means Committee involves hewing the line on taxes, obviously I believe the President of the United States should, too. Obviously, it is better for him to pay the taxes than to be quibbling about it. But I don't think there'll be a lot of people who will feel immediately that the purging has been complete. People will still be resentful that this whole episode was necessary. It would have been far better for him to pay the taxes due in the first place. What's interesting to me has been the apparent assumption by Mr. Nixon that everything would be all cleared up if he could only get a favorable ruling from the Joint Committee on Internal Revenue Taxation. It is remarkable that he would think people would react with gratitude when the facts show such large-scale tax avoidance. Note, please, I said "avoidance," not "evasion." I just think the President's assumption that the citizenry would react with gratitude if he had been able to prove he was within the law on a very large tax-avoidance scheme is a rather remarkable assumption. It involves some misunderstanding on his part of the symbolic position of the Presidency with respect to confidence in institutions in our country.

Interview/Los Angeles Times, 4-15:(2)7.

Richard J. Daley
Mayor of Chicago

3

The 1972 [Democratic National Convention] was one of the most disgraceful things ever put on television, and I hope to God that it never happens again. They had great plans for winning a convention, but there were no plans for winning the election. No one has a monopoly on righteousness and justice. We all make mistakes. Nobody's perfect . . . But if we operate within the Party, we'll win in 1976. You have my word.

Acceptance address on being elected
chairman of the Democratic Central
Committee of Cook County, Chicago/
The Christian Science Monitor, 4-3:2.

John Z. DeLorean
President,
National Alliance of Businessmen

4

When our forefathers wrote our Constitution and designed our democracy, they did not

WHAT THEY SAID IN 1974

(JOHN Z. DELOREAN)

comprehend the professional politician as we know him today. They planned that all Americans would participate in our democracy—that a concerned citizen would take a year or two or four out of his or her business or vocation and serve in Congress, the Senate, or even as President. In contemporary America, either the professional politicians have usurped this right and privilege or the citizenry, for whatever reason, has abrogated it. Somehow, some way must be found to take our country out of the hands of professional politicians and return it to the people. When an individual's primary measure of success is his ability to be elected and stay in office, he cannot be his own man.

Before Management Alumni Association,
Texas Christian University, April 10/
Vital Speeches, 6-1:499.

Herbert S. Denenberg
Insurance Commissioner of Pennsylvania;
Democratic candidate for the
United States Senate 1

. . . people ask me why do I want to leave this office [Insurance Commissioner] to be a U.S. Senator. They say, "Herb, you've done so much here, why do you want to go to Washington?" Well, isn't that the goddamndest thing? Imagine, thinking you can do more in an obscure office like this than you can in the most powerful legislative body in the world. It's an insult!

The National Observer, 3-23:5.

Jack Dennis
Professor of Political Science,
University of Wisconsin 2

The political party system has undergone a marked erosion of its legitimacy among members of the American mass public in the past 10 to 15 years [and] in several respects . . . has moved to dangerously low levels. Reformers of campaign financing, internal party representatives, rules and procedures and the like—and those who are stimulated by Watergate to do something more generally about the condition of our political parties—should take account of the harsh fact of low public legitimacy of the

institution. A mighty effort will therefore be required to re-establish the parties to the modicum of confidence and commitment they enjoyed even a decade ago. Without such an effort, we may be called upon in the not so distant future to witness the demise of a once prominent institution of American government and politics—[the political party].

Before American Political Science
Association, September/
The Washington Post, 10-9:(A)18.

Thomas F. Eagleton
United States Senator, D—Missouri 3

I have no grudge against [Vice President] Jerry Ford. He is a decent, honest man and honorable gentleman. [But] it is my belief that Gerald Ford, by training and experience, doesn't have the inspirational qualities needed to be President. He likes to use football analogies. Well, in my opinion, he's a blocker and not a quarterback.

Before rural editors and publishers,
Flat River, Mo./
Los Angeles Times, 1-28:(1)7.

4

To achieve the Presidency you have to go through the cruel and inhuman torture of seeking it. You have to have a lust for the office, not just a mild ambition. I don't have it.

People, 8-5:13.

Milton S. Eisenhower
President emeritus, Johns Hopkins University 5

[Former President] Nixon had no guiding philosophy. It is shocking about his taxes and the money spent on private property, to say nothing about Watergate; and now we know he lied to us [about Watergate] for two years. I give him credit for most of his foreign policies and many domestic ones, but I really tear him to pieces on moral leadership.

Interview, Baltimore/
Los Angeles Times, 8-20:(2)7.

Sam J. Ervin, Jr.
United States Senator, D—North Carolina 6

[Agreeing that politicians should disclose their financial and tax situations]: I am right proud of my income-tax returns that have been prepared for me. They are very voluminous. I tell the government about every penny of money I receive and every penny of money I disburse, and why I received it and why I disbursed it. And when they get my income-tax returns, they weigh so much that I am certain the IRS officials say, "Well, this ought to bring enough to liquidate the national debt." But when they examine those returns, they find in every case I have over-paid my taxes, and they have to give me a refund.

Before the Senate, Washington/
The New York Times, 1-24:22.

1

Since politics is the art of science of government, no man is fit to participate in politics or to seek or hold public office unless he has two characteristics. The first is that he must understand and be dedicated to the true purpose of government—which is to promote the good of the people—and entertain the abiding conviction that a public office is a public trust, which must never be abused to secure private advantage. The second is that he must possess that intellectual and moral integrity which is the priceless ingredient in good character.

Before American Bar Association,
Honolulu/The Washington Post, 8-22:(A)20.

2

[Former] President Nixon ran the first time on a conservative platform. He was for fiscal responsibility, and he got strong support among conservative elements on that. Why they didn't discover that he was not a true conservative during the first Administration is something that baffles me, because many of these conservatives stuck with him. But the record shows that Nixon was the most extravagant President in the history of this nation.

Interview/The Washington Post, 12-29:(B)3.

M. Stanton Evans
Chairman, American Conservative Union

3

The Nixon Administration has been a calamitous experience for the American nation, the Republican Party and derivatively for the conservative movement. [While] there is an impression this is a conservative Administration, [its] fundamental record has been to continue and expand the liberal policies of its predecessors—expansion of the money supply, deficit spending, a vast increase in trade with Communist countries . . .

At Young Americans for Freedom meeting,
San Francisco/Los Angeles Times, 7-23:(2)5.

Houston I. Flournoy
State Controller of California;
Republican candidate for Governor

4

Public financing [of political campaigns] in the general elections may, in some cases, be nothing more than a subsidy for those who are already entrenched in politics and not necessarily a way to open up the system. And, indeed, if the subsidy should work to enhance the role of the political party organizations as against the candidates themselves, it may work to close the system. Anyone who looks at the public-financing proposals will find that they are full of room for abuse. They would be an expensive cash subsidy by the taxpayers for politics, and it would be open for much manipulation by those politicians who made up the rules.

Before Chancery Club, Los Angeles,
Feb. 5/Los Angeles Times, 2-6:(1)23.

Gerald R. Ford
Vice President of the United States

5

Our great national [political] parties evolved along the same basic grass-root pattern of widely shared responsibility and local self-determination. The party recruits and trains and nurtures candidates and rewards some with higher office. The party allows for the participation of rank-and-file citizens . . . and forges its party principles from the very broad spectrum of opinions and goals.

At Midwestern Republicans conference,
Chicago, March 30/
The Washington Post, 3-31:(A)10.

6

[On his becoming Vice President as a result of Spiro Agnew's resignation last year] : I happen to be the nation's first instant Vice President. I only

(GERALD R. FORD)

hope that I prove to be as pure, as digestible and as appetizing to consumers who did not have a chance to shop around for other brands of Vice President when I was put on the market.

Before Grocery Manufacturers of America,
White Sulphur Springs, Va./
The New York Times, 6-19:51.

1

[Speaking after President Nixon announced his resignation]: I've been fortunate in my lifetime in public office to have a good many adversaries in the political arena in the Congress, but I don't think I have a single enemy in the Congress. And the net result is that I think tomorrow I [as new President] can start out working with Democrats and with Republicans in the House as well as in the Senate to work on the problems—serious ones—which we have at home. And the spirit of cooperation which I believe will be exhibited with the Congress and the new President, on the problems overseas and the problems at home, will be beneficial not only to 211 million fine Americans, but to the world as a whole. And I pledge to you tonight, as I will pledge tomorrow and in the future, my best efforts in cooperation, leadership and dedication to what's good for America and good for the world.

Alexandria, Va., Aug. 8/
The National Observer, 8-17:D.

Gerald R. Ford
President of the United States

2

[Addressing the American people after being sworn in as President]: I am acutely aware that you have not elected me as your President by your ballots. So I ask you to confirm me as your President with your prayers. And I hope that such prayers will also be the first of many. If you have not chosen me by secret ballot, neither have I gained office by any secret promises. I have not campaigned either for the Presidency or the Vice Presidency. I have not subscribed to any partisan platform. I am indebted to no man and only one woman, my dear wife.

Inauguration address, Washington, Aug. 9/
The New York Times, 8-10:3.

3

... part of my heart will always be here on Capitol Hill. I know well the co-equal role of the Congress in our Constitutional process. I love the House of Representatives. I revere the traditions of the Senate despite my too-short internship there. As President, within the limits of basic principles, my motto toward the Congress is communication, conciliation, compromise and cooperation. This Congress will, I am confident, be my working partner as well as my most constructive critic. I am not asking for conformity. I am dedicated to the two-party system, and you know which party is mine. I do not want a honeymoon with you. I want a good marriage.

First address as President before
Congress, Washington, Aug. 12/
The New York Times, 8-13:20.

4

[On his new Administration]: ... we [will] have an open Administration. I will be as candid and as forthright as I possibly can. I will expect any individuals in my Administration to be exactly the same. There will be no tightly controlled operation of the White House staff. I have a policy of seeking advice from a number of top members of my staff. There will be no one person, not any limited number of individuals, who make decisions. I make the decisions and take the blame for them or whatever benefit might be the case. I said in one of my speeches after the swearing-in [that] there would be no illegal wiretaps, there would be none of the other things that, to a degree, helped to precipitate the Watergate crisis.

News conference, Washington, Aug. 28/
The New York Times, 8-29:20.

5

I have some prejudice to which party I think people ought to belong. But the main problem we have is to make sure that these two political parties [Democratic and Republican] survive, grow and participate in a more meaningful way. This [upcoming November] election has something to do with that. A catastrophic defeat, as some forecasters are predicting, for the Republican Party could have a terribly depressing effect on the Republican Party. It could write

the obituary—I don't think it will happen—[of]
the Republican Party and all for which it
stands.

At Republican fund-raising dinner, Detroit,
Oct. 10/ Los Angeles Times, 10-11:(1)24.

1

[On polls which show Democrats making big
gains in the forthcoming November Congressional elections]: The polls have been wrong in
the past. But let me point out that if the polls
are right—and I don't assume that they are—you
can have what some of the most partisan members of the opposition say [will be] a veto-
proof Congress. Now what does that mean? It
means that you will have a concentration of
power in one of three branches of the Federal
government. In effect, you'll have a legislative
dictatorship. One of the basic strengths of
America in the last 200 years has been balance . . . That finely tuned balance has given us
the great blessings that we have. If you have a
veto-proof Congress, you in effect have one
branch of the government dictating . . . Americans don't like dictatorship. They like a system
of checks and balances.

At Republican fund-raising breakfast,
Kansas City, Oct. 16/
The Washington Post, 10-17:(A)1.

2

[On his campaigning for Republicans when
polls show a Democratic gain in the upcoming
November elections]: I have gotten a lot of
advice in recent weeks that I ought to sit in
Washington, D.C., as President of the United
States, read the polls and get discouraged and
wring my hands. I think that is a lousy approach to responsibilities of the President of
the United States. I know all these experts are
saying these things—that you can't change the
result and if I tried and lost, then my Presidency for the next two years will go down the
drain. I don't believe that. It is a lot better for
me to be out talking to you in Greensboro than
sitting around the Oval Office and wringing my
hands.

At rally, Greensboro, N.C., Oct. 19/
San Francisco Examiner & Chronicle,
10-20:(A)14.

3

[On the controversy over confirmation of
Nelson Rockefeller as Vice President because
of, for example, his cash gifts to various people
over the years]: Nelson Rockefeller has been a
superb Governor of the state of New York. He
served both Democratic and Republican Presidents in the past in the Executive Branch of
government. It is my judgment that he would
be a very good Vice President. And therefore,
these disclosures indicate that he does believe in
helping his friends, and a man of that wealth
certainly, in my judgment, has that right to
give, as long as the law is obeyed, and, as I
understand it, he has. It seems to me that his
qualifications from previous public service fully
qualify him to be Vice President, and therefore
I fully support his nomination.

News conference, Washington, Oct. 29/
The Washington Post, 10-30:(A)10.

J. William Fulbright
United States Senator, D—Arkansas

4

You can't say politics will attract a higher
caliber person now than in the past. That would
imply all past politicians were corrupt. And
they all were not. Young people of all walks
will continue to be attracted to politics. It's a
question of taste. It's a calling, a mysterious art
that attracts people as diverse as the country as
a whole. You can't predict who will be attracted to it any more than you can say who
somebody will marry, or why somebody will
like a Rembrandt better than a Picasso or a
Gauguin.

Interview/
"W": a Fairchild publication, 9-6:12.

John Kenneth Galbraith
Professor of Economics, Harvard University

5

. . . today a politician comes packaged. We
should vote against any politicians using TV
commercials. I have heard some politicians say
they hope to win [their elections] next month
with a last-minute TV blitz. Regardless of their
parties, I hope they are defeated.

At world communications convention,
Acapulco, Mexico, Oct. 26/
Daily Variety, 10-29:39.

WHAT THEY SAID IN 1974

John W. Gardner
Chairman, Common Cause

1

Politics is the only game that begins after the public files out of the stadium.

Quote, 5-26:481.

John J. Gilligan
Governor of Ohio

2

Five years ago I would have considered a request to make public my personal financial records an invasion of my privacy. But in the light of the scandals of government in recent years, climaxed by the continuing revelations growing out of the Watergate break-in, I now feel that the invasion of privacy is warranted if the people of this state and this nation are to regain their faith in their elected and appointed leaders.

Quote, 6-30:602.

Henry Graff
Professor of History, Columbia University

3

We will quickly discover that [President] Gerald Ford's limitations, which seem pretty clear, are not going to seem so horrendous. To be sure, it is a handicap that Ford was not elected to the Presidency. He is unprepared for the office with respect to administrative experience; that certainly is a handicap. But he will triumph because he has not lusted after the office of President. Ford is an honest man. He gets on well with the people. He is an open man, and what our society needs now is openness. Artfulness got Lyndon Johnson in trouble abroad; artfulness got Nixon in trouble at home. Thus the new President may surprise us. The need of the hour and the man may have met.

Interview/Time, 8-19:64.

Katharine Graham
Publisher, "The Washington Post"

4

There is a new sensitivity to [political] wrongdoing abroad in the land, and that is obviously all to the good. [But] there is [also] a new and rather indiscriminate emphasis on disclosure as the index of fitness for public office. And that, I think, is doing harm—harm to the nation in general and to the nation's press in particular ... An emphasis on candor and an absence of wrongdoing, although primary and vital, can distort the process of assessment if it is carried to extremes and distracts the public and the press from other, equally significant questions.

Before Magazine Publishers Association/
The New York Times, 12-2:29.

Richard T. Hanna
United States Representative, D–California

5

[Announcing his forthcoming retirement after 12 years in the House]: I have not been a leader, or a mover or a shaker. I have just been one of those blacksmiths at the forge of democracy.

The Washington Post, 2-13:(A)19.

Julia Butler Hansen
United States Representative, D–Washington

6

[Announcing her imminent retirement after 37 years in public service]: Thirty-seven years is a long time to be pursued by an endless string of people who want everything—from post offices to gasoline. It is also a long time to receive telephone calls, on Christmas Eve or New Year's Eve, from the United Press or Associated Press. Main Street in Cathlamet [Wash.], where I own my home, will never look as good as it will after all my encounters with Washington, D.C.—houses where the plumbing won't work, landlords won't weatherstrip, and charge ungodly rents, particularly to members of Congress ... At the end of the year, when my term expires, I shall return to my home in Cathlamet with my husband to write, garden, do as I please, hang up the telephone or take the damn telephone off the hook; and when people I don't know appear at my door and walk in without knocking, I'll have the great opportunity of telling them it is my private home.

Washington, Feb. 6/
The Washington Post, 2-7:(A)3.

Mark O. Hatfield
United States Senator, R—Oregon

1

[On politics]: Outside of the Metropolitan Opera, I know of no profession that more massages the prima-donna instinct in a person. And the more the ego is massaged, the more it requires.

Interview/
The Christian Science Monitor, 6-4:(F)1.

Wayne L. Hays
United States Representative, D—Ohio

2

... Will Rogers once said, "I belong to no organized political party; I am a Democrat." We have always had difficulty in organizing ourselves, and I suppose that is the reason so many of us are Democrats, because we do not like to be regimented.

TV-radio interview, Washington/
"Meet the Press,"
National Broadcasting Company, 10-13.

Edward Heath
Former Prime Minister of
the United Kingdom

3

[On his conducting the London Symphony Orchestra on its 70th birthday]: I was once told: "If you are prepared to be as unpleasant as most top conductors are, then go into conducting." But as I did not want anything to do with unpleasantness, I went into politics.

San Francisco Examiner, 6-24:26.

Hubert H. Humphrey
United States Senator, D—Minnesota

4

[Saying Democratic Senator Edward Kennedy will be unbeatable in the 1976 Presidential election]: Teddy Kennedy is our Number 1 man. He's head and shoulders above them all. He'll win every primary he enters and he'll beat anyone, including [Republican Vice President] Gerald Ford. I can't explain it. There's a mystique about him. It's just the way things are.

Washington/
"W": a Fairchild publication, 4-19:7.

5

[Political-] campaign financing is a curse. It's the most disgusting, demeaning, disenchanting, debilitating experience of a politician's life. It's stinky, it's lousy. I just can't tell you how much I hate it. I've had to break off in the middle of trying to make a decent, honorable campaign and go up to somebody's parlor or to a room and say, "Gentlemen and ladies, I'm desperate. You've got to help me" ... You've got to get $25,000 contributions, $50,000 contributions in a national campaign. You've got to go on television. You've got a message. Harry S. Truman couldn't even get on the radio in 1948 until somebody raised $70,000 for him ... You've got to have the money—cash on the line—or they won't let you on the radio, they won't let you on the television, they won't put your ad in the newspaper. They want cash on the line. Every campaign I've ever been in I've been short of money.

Interview/The New York Times, 10-13:(4)18.

Henry M. Jackson
United States Senator, D—Washington

6

If we [Democrats] select strong candidates, there isn't an office in this country that isn't up for grabs in terms of the Watergate scandals and other Nixon fluffs. But if we make the mistake of thinking any Democrat can win, and select weak candidates, we will lose. The American people are intelligent. They want positive leadership, not negativism.

Interview/San Francisco Examiner, 3-15:37.

Jenkin Lloyd Jones
Editor and publisher, "The Tulsa Tribune"

7

President Nixon is the only President since George Washington who has no party. Some Republicans are trying to set themselves up for re-election by out-shouting the Democrats for his blood. Most of the rest are holding him at far arm's length and wishing he would vanish. He has no fence-mending to do because he has no fences. He is a wanderer on a vast prairie.

Quote, 3-10:232.

WHAT THEY SAID IN 1974

Clarence M. Kelley
Director, Federal Bureau of Investigation
1

The Communist Party [in the U.S.] is not as prominent as it was, but the Party still is dedicated to changing our form of government, whether by force and violence or by the apathy we exercise with our unawareness of what it stands for and what the Communists will do.

Interview/
San Francisco Examiner & Chronicle, 1-13:(B)3.

Edward M. Kennedy
United States Senator, D—Massachusetts
2

[Calling for public financing of political campaigns]: No one, no candidate or contributor, has a Constitutional right to buy an election. We don't let wealthy private citizens pay the salaries of the President and Senators and Congressmen. Why should we let wealthy private citizens pay the costs of their campaigns?

Before the Senate, Washington, March 26/
The Washington Post, 3-27:(A)3.

3

... I know that seeking the nation's highest office demands a candidate's undivided attention and his deepest personal commitment. If any candidate is unable to make that commitment, he does a disservice to his country and to his party by undertaking the effort. My primary responsibilities are at home. It has become quite apparent that I would be unable to make a full commitment to a campaign for the Presidency. I simply cannot do that to my wife and children and other members of my family. Therefore, in 1976 I will not be a candidate for President or Vice President of the United States. This decision is firm, final and unconditional. There is absolutely no circumstance or event that will alter the decision. I will not accept the nomination. I will not accept a draft. I will oppose any effort to place my name in nomination in any state or at the national convention. And I will oppose any efforts to promote my candidacy in any other way.

Boston, Sept. 23/
The New York Times, 9-24:20.

James J. Kilpatrick
Political columnist
4

I know what I have going for me [when speaking on a college campus], which is that I am a front-office or token conservative on most of the college or university speaking schedules ... I discover, wherever I go, that I'm following on the heels of Dick Gregory and Julian Bond and Harrison Salisbury and Walter Mondale and Gaylord Nelson, and on down the line. Ordinarily, I will be the only conservative in the whole speaking academic year, or often the only one in two years. I have a little something going for me on that: I don't have to be good; I just have to be alive. Then they go to the trustees and say, "What do you mean we've got nothing but radicals and far-out left-wing liberals on our speaking schedule? Look: Kilpatrick. There he is." I'm the raisin in the dough.

The Washington Post, 1-27:(H)11.

Herbert G. Klein
Former Director of Communications for the President of the United States (Richard M. Nixon)
5

They [White House aides H. R. Haldeman, John Ehrlichman and Charles Colson] isolated him [then-President Nixon] from the people, from members of Congress whose counsel was essential to him, and planted in his mind a distrust of his own Cabinet officers. In leading him down the path to disaster, by substituting dishonesty and deceit for truth and openness, they built a wall around him—in the guise of a more efficient staff operation—that shut him off from loyal friends whose contrary views might weaken their influence over him ... Corrupted is not the word I would use, but his sense of values was certainly distorted by these men ... When truth and openness were practiced by members of the Nixon staff, all went well. Yet, at some point that cannot be definitely pinpointed, Mr. Nixon's Administration fell victim to the same credibility gap that had plagued the [Lyndon] Johnson Administration. Deceit began to replace truth. Doors were closed instead of open. Dishonesty came to the Nixon Administration and it was the beginning of the end. It wasn't just Watergate. No single factor or isolated decision was really responsible for the Nixon Administration's change of heart and the turning away from truth and openness.

Interview, Los Angeles/
The New York Times, 8-25:(1)33.

Frank Kowalski
Former United States Representative,
D—Connecticut
1

Politics is funny. Once I called on a delegate when I needed delegates to get on a ballot, and people said he was committed to another man. Well, I found him out milking his cows. I said, "I used to milk cows," and he said, "The hell you say"; so I sat down and showed him. It had been many years in the past, but fortunately cows hadn't changed any, and he was impressed. "I'm your man," he said. A crazy way to get on the ballot, if you ask me.

At Former Members of Congress club reception,
Washington, May 22/
The Washington Post, 5-23:(B)3.

Melvin R. Laird
Former Secretary of Defense of
the United States
2

The real measure of a politician is whether, in certain instances, you vote your conscience or your constituents. You're a more lasting politician when you vote your conscience.

Interview/
The Washington Post, 5-5:(Potomac)25.

John V. Lindsay
Former Mayor of New York
3

[Political] campaigns have been using up too much energy, and, like oil and gas, Americans have to learn to get along with less. Public education is certainly not served by the costly campaigns. In my judgment, a simplification of the process actually will result in more-thoughtful voting. My guess is we'd have better government as a result. Who knows? We might even have better politicians.

Quote, 7-7:1.

Russell B. Long
United States Senator, D—Louisiana
4

[Discussing restoration of public confidence in politicians]: Many years ago, I was asked to participate in a debate where the topic was, "Should ideals be used in politics?" In preparing for that debate, I decided I ought to seek out some sage advice; and so I asked my uncle, Earl, who at that time was Governor of Louisiana. He said, "Son, which side are you taking?" I responded that I was arguing for the use of ideals. He looked me straight in the eye and said, "Hell, yes! Use ideals, and anything else you can get your hands on."

At Louisiana State University, Baton Rouge/
Los Angeles Times, 3-27:(1)2.

Clare Boothe Luce
Former American diplomat and playwright
5

I have always thought [President] Nixon a remarkably competent man. I can think of no political figure today in whose hands I think the republic would be safer. I also think that he will go down in history, despite Watergate, as a great President. I am disappointed, very disappointed, that he put his trust in such a crummy crew of counsellors. But then, Julius Caesar put his in Brutus, with his gang of co-conspirators; and Jesus himself picked Judas. Great men, as a matter of fact, are rather famous for picking unreliable subordinates. Isn't it often the trusted partner who robs the safe?

Interview/
U.S. News & World Report, 6-24:56.

Patrick J. Lucey
Governor of Wisconsin
6

Men elected to solve problems have become problems. Institutions that once breathed with life have become choked in the polluted air of scandal, dishonesty and bureaucratic inertia.

At National Governors Conference, Seattle/
The National Observer, 6-15:5.

Lester G. Maddox
Former Governor of Georgia
7

Four years ago, we elected some new Governors [in the South]—Jimmy Carter here [in

WHAT THEY SAID IN 1974

(LESTER G. MADDOX)

Georgia], and Dale Bumpers in Arkansas, and Reubin Askew in Florida, and John West in South Carolina—and everybody went crazy talking about the "New South." But they were no different than any other politicians who had national aspirations. It's the same old breed of liberals and radicals who have always been willing to sell out the South to their Northern masters for a mess of political pottage. They want the national limelight and they know they can't get it by standing up for private property and individual rights and states rights—the things the people of the South really believe in.

The Washington Post, 9-1:(A)6.

Marvin Mandel
Governor of Maryland
1

[Criticizing the Nixon Administration]: A cynical and arrogant power elite of the highest officials in our government has sold out the citizens of America to a silent partnership with the financial giants of this nation, to the corrupters of our political process, to the beneficiaries of government favors, to an ethic that is rooted in no morality but greed and survival.

At Democratic fund-raising dinner,
Phoenix, June 22/
The Washington Post, 6-23:(A)8.

Frank Mankiewicz
1972 Presidential campaign manager for
Senator George McGovern
2

I think politicians are getting a very bum rap. The most subversive thing [former President] Richard Nixon has done is to convince Americans that all politicians have as few moral convictions as he does. Politicians, as a class, are more honest than businessmen, or anyone else. And the great tragedy is that the public is reacting so badly . . .

Interview/
"W": a Fairchild publication, 11-29:9.

Mike Mansfield
United States Senator, D—Montana
3

[On Gerald Ford's assumption of the Presidency]: Jerry Ford has had a remarkable career

because he has been so unremarkable himself. Now he leaves the House and leaves the Senate and goes to a new home at 1600 Pennsylvania Avenue. He goes there with a clean mind, with a clean heart and with a clean record. I think that we can have a great deal of confidence in this unassuming man from the Midwest who always lets you know where he stands and who always appreciates an opposite point of view and understands it.

Before the Senate, Washington, Aug. 9/
The New York Times, 8-10:2.

4

My ambition originally was to be a Congressman from Montana; and when I got to be Senator that was my *highest* ambition. I have always wanted to be my own man, and a Vice President—or President—is anything *but* his own man. I have never for a moment wanted to be President. I often have wondered why so many other Senators do want it—but I'm glad they do. It has too much responsibility for me.

Interview, Washington/
The Saturday Evening Post, October:89.

Eugene J. McCarthy
Honorary chairman, Committee for a
Constitutional Presidency; Former
United States Senator, D—Minnesota
5

From 1789 to 1972, roughly, we went from [George] Washington to [Richard] Nixon, from John Adams to Spiro Agnew, from Alexander Hamilton to John Connally, from John Jay to John Mitchell. You have to begin to . . . wonder how much of that kind of progress you can stand.

News conference, Chicago/Newsweek, 9-9:22.

Paul N. McCloskey, Jr.
United States Representative, R—California
6

I have puzzled over just exactly what it is that has caused me to have such faith and trust in [Vice President] Gerald Ford's leadership. With some hesitancy, I would like to suggest that it stems largely from my recognition of his absolute—almost painful—honesty.

San Francisco Examiner & Chronicle,
6-2:(This World)2.

George S. McGovern
United States Senator, D—South Dakota
1

[On his loss to President Nixon in the 1972 election]: I think what I've finally accepted is that it really is better to lose honorably than to win dishonorably.
The New York Times, 1-19:50.

2

The people will no longer accept a politics whose only purpose is power. We [the Democratic Party] must offer more than an establishment center, where nothing but the labels ever changes. We must seek a unity of principle as well as party. We cannot be bland in what we say and blind to the evils before us. If we are, we will be united but defeated. We will be in the center, but a dead center.
*At Democratic mini-convention,
Kansas City, Dec. 7/
The Washington Post, 12-8:(A)14.*

George Meany
*President, American Federation of Labor-
Congress of Industrial Organizations*
3

[On the large Democratic Party victory in the just-held national elections]: I don't think the Democratic Party has any mandate. When people get an idea they've got a mandate, somehow or another they don't think straight any more.
*News conference, Washington, Nov. 7/
The Atlanta Constitution, 11-8:(C)3.*

Bernard C. Meyer
*Clinical Professor of Psychiatry,
Mount Sinai School of Medicine, New York*
4

To all appearances, [President] Nixon cannot be himself, because he has no authentic or identifiable self. Psychologically, he seems to fall within the definition of the "as if" person, the individual who, seeking to cover over a hollowness within, decks himself out in the shreds and patches of other personalities and thinks and acts "as if" he were they. It is not only with pieces of [the late President] John Kennedy that he has sought to patch over his porous identity. He has made similar use of the words, the gestures and the behavior of other impressive models, notably [Winston] Churchill and [Charles] de Gaulle. This is the real tragedy of Richard Nixon and of the people he was elected to serve: He cannot communicate who he is; for, like all "as if" persons, he simply does not know.
*Interview/
"W": a Fairchild publication, 5-17:7.*

Clarence Mitchell
*Director, Washington, D.C., bureau, National
Association for the Advancement of
Colored People*
5

I can't see a situation developing in this country where blacks would support a Presidential ticket that included [Alabama] Governor [George] Wallace. I'm very certain that, if the Democrats want to hand the [1976] election to the Republicans, all they've got to do is put Wallace on the ticket as Vice Presidential candidate and you can be sure that blacks could put [in] a Republican Administration.
*Interview, July 14/
The Washington Post, 7-15:(A)2.*

Walter F. Mondale
United States Senator, D—Minnesota
6

[On the resignations of Vice President Spiro Agnew and President Richard Nixon, the assumption of, first, the Vice Presidency and then the Presidency by Gerald Ford, and the nomination for Vice President of Nelson Rockefeller]: We have performed miracles for you in Washington. If you don't believe it, consider this: Who else could have given you two Presidents and three Vice Presidents in two years without even having an election?
*Atlanta/The Atlanta Journal
and Constitution, 10-27:(B)4.*

Richard M. Nixon
President of the United States
7

[Saying political candidates shouldn't wait until they had "a sure thing" in running for office]: Show me a candidate who is not a hungry candidate, show me a candidate who

(RICHARD M. NIXON)

isn't willing to take a risk and risk all, even risk losing, and I will show you a lousy candidate.

Before Young Republicans,
Washington, Feb. 28/
The Washington Post, 3-1:(A)12.

1

[On public financing of political campaigns]: I oppose it for this reason: The public-financing proposals before the Congress for the most part are ones that would have the campaigns financed out of the general Treasury. Now, what this would mean very simply would be that a taxpayer would be taxed to support a candidate or a party to whom he was opposed. That is not right . . . I think that that would in effect be taxation without representation. And so therefore, for that and other reasons, I oppose public financing.

News conference, Washington, March 6/
The New York Times, 3-7:32.

2

I would urge young people to get into politics in America for several reasons. First, if they don't like the way the political system works, the way to do something about it is not to stay out and whine about it, but get in it and change it. Second, because this is a great time to be in politics in America. I realize there are those who would question that, question it because of the problems we confront at home and those we confront abroad. But today, what America does in meeting its own problems at home and what America does or fails to do in providing leadership which, having now won a peace will keep the peace for a generation and longer abroad, what America does is absolutely indispensable. This is a great challenge, and if I were a young person and had the opportunity to get into politics, I'd want to be in there working in politics rather than on the outside. Now, that doesn't mean that everybody should get in and run for office; there isn't room for everybody to run for office. But it does mean that every young person should participate, either by actively being in politics or by supporting the candidate or the party of his choice. And while

he will have his disappointments—he will win some, he will lose some, I'm an expert on both—I can assure you that getting in and participating can be a mountaintop experience, and particularly in America at this time, when what we do in America will determine the future [not only] for 200 million Americans, but the future for 3 billion people on this earth.

Before Executive Club, Chicago, March 15/
The New York Times, 3-16:12.

3

Questions were raised with regard to whether or not I had paid or reported the amount of taxes that I should have. I voluntarily asked the Joint Committee on Taxation of the House and Senate to consider this matter. It has been considering it. And as Chairman [Russell] Long and the ranking minority member of the Senate Finance Committee have indicated, there's been no evidence of fraud on the part of the President. There may be evidence that he may owe more taxes, due primarily, apparently, to the debatable technical point as to whether a gift of three-quarters of a million dollars worth of Presidential papers, which was delivered three months before the deadline, whether the paperwork on it was completed in time to qualify for the deduction. If it was completed in time, as I understand it, I get the deduction. If it was not completed in time, I don't get the deduction; I pay the tax and the government gets to keep the papers. Well, under the circumstances, that's hard for me to realize. But the President, when the IRS is concerned, I assure you, is just another citizen and even more so. And that's perfectly proper.

Before Executive Club, Chicago, March 15/
The New York Times, 3-16:13.

David R. Obey
United States Representative, D–Wisconsin　4

I swear to God that I will never again support anybody for the Presidency who doesn't have a sense of humor. I think that's Richard Nixon's biggest problem.

Los Angeles Times, 6-30:(6)10.

Lawrence F. O'Brien
Former chairman,
Democratic National Committee

1

I've had splendid opportunities [while in politics] for public service, and I've fulfilled a desire to be involved. But I'm depressed. I'm depressed to see, after two decades of constant activity, that the American people feel the way they do. It really makes no difference whether the Democrats or Republicans win now or in 1976 unless something is done about the present wide-spread cynicism to restore confidence in our democratic system. It's the politicians who made the people cynical, with excessive rhetoric and excessive promises.

Interview/The New York Times, 3-10:(1)37.

John O. Pastore
United States Senator, D–Rhode Island

2

Public funds for the public [election] campaigns of public officials make good sense if we want to end political payola. [Watergate is] conclusive proof that the present system of private financing breeds corruption ... Let us not be misled by those who claim that public financing is taxation without representation and a raid on the Federal Treasury. Taxation without representation is precisely what you have when you have corruption.

Radio address, March 15/
Los Angeles Times, 3-16:(1)6.

Charles H. Percy
United States Senator, R–Illinois

3

I am interested—seriously interested—in running for the Presidency [in 1976] ... I will not insult your intelligence by going through the motions of the "non-candidate tango," in which the resistant-yet-persistent politician whirls in and out of state after state, assuring his political supporters of his immense indifference to the idea of running for President. I'll leave that to more accomplished performers.

At Lincoln Day dinner, Chicago, Feb. 8/
San Francisco Examiner, 2-9:4.

Norman Podhoretz
Editor, "Commentary" magazine

4

... the American people have now begun to vote according to the most amazingly complicated patterns. On a single ballot in a given election, an individual might vote for a Democrat running for one national office, a Republican running for another national office, an independent candidate running for a state-wide office, another Republican or Democrat or even a member of one of the smaller local parties running for some city or county office. If there are propositions or referenda on the ballot, he might easily vote the "liberal" position on one—let us say in favor of a bond issue appropriating money for the schools—and then vote the "conservative" position on another—let us say against a motion to legalize marijuana. The point is that the American people are more complex than ever before in their political attitudes and in their political behavior; and this, I think, is a sign of strength and a sign of health.

On Far East tour sponsored by U.S. State
Department's Bureau of Educational and
Cultural Affairs/The National Observer, 3-9:10.

Dan Rather
News commentator,
Columbia Broadcasting System

5

We're not short of people with leadership qualities in this country. Why do we have to think of potential Presidential candidates only as politicians? I think there's some terrific potential Presidential material in people who are running universities, running businesses, running unions, in the arts, and even in journalism. This is a big continental country and leadership is sticking out all over it. Yet, when it comes to picking our leaders, we concentrate on a handful of politicians. Some way, somehow we have to open up the potential of being President to more people.

Interview, New York/
"W": a Fairchild publication, 12-13:19.

Ronald Reagan
Governor of California

6

We've heard a great deal about Republican fat-cats—how the Republicans are the party of

(RONALD REAGAN)

big contributions. I've never been able to understand why a Republican contributor is a fat-cat and a Democratic contributor of the same amount of money is a public-spirited philanthropist.

At Republican fund-raising affair,
Los Angeles, Aug. 4/
Los Angeles Times, 8-5:(1)20.

1

Politics is said to be the second-oldest profession. Sometimes I think it's close to the first.
Los Angeles Times, 10-25:(1)3.

2

I'm going to do my utmost to convince as many people as possible that the Republican Party, on any objective analysis anyone wants to make, is more in tune with the thinking of the majority of the American people than is the other major party or either of the splinter parties that started up . . . I think that the [Republican] Party needs to state to the people once and for all clearly what it represents, what it stands for, and then, having raised that banner, to rally around it and attract those others that like the colors of that banner. I do not believe that for vote-getting purposes you go out and vitiate, water down your true philosophical beliefs in order to persuade someone to vote for you. The Democrats have been doing things like that for years and that's why they have got a weird coalition that can't enjoy itself in one room together.

News conference, Sacramento, Nov. 12/
Los Angeles Times, 11-13:(1)3.

George E. Reedy
Dean, College of Journalism,
Marquette University; Former Press Secretary to
the President of the United States
(Lyndon B. Johnson)

3

[On Gerald Ford's assumption of the Presidency] : . . . I doubt if ever before in history so many people wanted a politician to make it. [In his first speech,] Ford did something that few politicians can do well, and that was to evoke some basic symbols. He called for prayer and he

called for God's help. Most politicians doing that would sound like the choirmaster who had just finished a tumble in the hay with one of the choirgirls. Ford is believable when he says such things. There is in this country today a yearning for simple, natural symbols that people can turn to. That is one of the main reasons why Ford could be so very good.

Interview/Time, 8-19:65.

John J. Rhodes
United States Representative, R–Arizona

4

We [Republicans] intend to take the offensive. We are going into every district to tell the people that the only way they can get Congress off dead center is to change the guard—break up the old crony club. We are going to take the Democratic Party's Congressional record to the people and make their candidates wear it around their necks during the [upcoming election] campaign . . . The Democrats just can't seem to settle their internal squabbling in the public interest long enough to see vital legislation through . . . [The question facing the voters in November] is not which party is best fit to run the Executive Branch—that one is for two years from now. This November, the question is which party is best equipped to run the Congress.

Before National Press Club,
Washington, Feb. 22/
The New York Times, 2-23:13.

Abraham A. Ribicoff
United States Senator, D–Connecticut

5

[Dividing politicians into "wholesalers," whom he admires, and "retailers," whom he disdains] : Wholesalers undertake the big issues, the big picture and the big problems, while retailers devote their lives to all the petty things—door-to-door salesmen who cultivate the political vineyards, backslapping, greeting, doing minor retailing.

The New York Times, 7-30:52.

Nelson A. Rockefeller
Vice President-designate of the United States

6

[On the controversy over monetary gifts and loans he made to people over the years] : I have been dismayed by the embarrassment that has been brought to persons who, without exception, are innocent of the slightest impropriety in accepting the help that I could give them . . . not one of the gifts or loans I have made, not one of the loans I have forgiven during my lifetime, was designed to corrupt or did corrupt either the receiver or the giver. The implication has been made that my financial help to persons associated at one time or another with my Administration as Governor of New York State was given to influence or reward their official conduct. That was not my intent or the fact in a single instance . . . I am not in the banking business. I don't believe that when one makes a loan to a friend, he does so as a commercial transaction. These loans were either interest-free or at nominal rates. There is an unfortunate cynicism abroad in the land. In view of the abuses of trust in high places, it is understandable. But I do not believe the day has yet come in this great country of ours where the decencies of human relationships disqualify one for public office . . . I know that every one of you has helped friends in need. And I don't think there is a man or woman in this country who would not have done the same. The American tradition has been to share—to help one's neighbor in time of trouble, to share one's blessings with friends and family.

At Senate Rules Committee hearing on his nomination for Vice President, Washington, Nov. 13/The New York Times, 11-14:39.

Dean Rusk
Professor of International Law, University of Georgia; Former Secretary of State of the United States

1

At any given point, half of the people want someone else to be President.

The Atlanta Journal and Constitution Magazine, 8-18:30.

Hugh Scott
United States Senator, R—Pennsylvania

2

[Advocating the use of a dollar check-off on personal income-tax returns to help finance political campaigns]: I think it's worth a check-off to every taxpayer to do something to get election reform in this country. The taxpayers themselves should be condemned if they are not willing to put up a buck for honesty.

Quote, 8-11:121.

3

Congress, for 40 of the last 44 years, has been under the control of the Democratic Party, and not a cent of money has been expended by the Federal government that was not first authorized by those Democratic majorities which have forced excessive spending. Now the Congress is even more visibly under the massive control of the Democratic Party—not only in the Federal government, but in most of the states. And I would think that during the next two years the attention of the people may well be directed to the fact that their economic ills stem from lack of fiscal discipline by the majority party . . . I think it may well be one of the major issues of '76. It is now up to the Republicans to inform people of their Party's virtual helplessness in the face of the probable determination of the Democrats to spend money like it's going out of style.

Interview, Philadelphia/ U.S. News & World Report, 11-18:111.

4

[On declarations of non-candidacy for the 1976 Presidential race made by a number of Senators]: I suggest that all our colleagues who are not bitten by the Presidential bug can amass for themselves a certain amount of publicity by announcing consecutively that they are not candidates for the Presidency. I suggest that this be done on Friday, in order to get in the weekend papers. It offers an opportunity for a speech, some philosophical reflections on the state of the Union, and then the Senator's own contribution to the improvement of the state of the Union by his decision not to seek to head it . . . Non-candidacy implies a certain spirit of sacrifice, a certain willingness to abase oneself below the peak or to situate oneself further down the slopes of Everest. So I am in favor of non-candidacy. I think the more non-candidates we have, the better for the country. These are all eminent gentlemen and well qualified. Every

(HUGH SCOTT)

one of them is admirably qualified to be a non-candidate.

Before the Senate, Washington/
The Wall Street Journal, 12-6:10.

Mary Louise Smith
Chairman, Republican National Committee
1

It is time for the Republican Party to come to grips with the shape we're in. Republican registration is down. In too many areas the number of Republican office-holders has declined. Why do polls show that only 23 per cent of the voters call themselves Republicans? Somewhere the Republican Party is doing something wrong. Or else we're not doing enough things right. Either we're being out-organized or out-sold. I suspect it's a little of both.

Accepting the position of chairman,
Washington, Sept. 16/
The New York Times, 9-17:40.

Alan Steelman
United States Representative, R—Texas
2

I think the tax returns [of Senators and Representatives] ought to be made public. I'm going to make mine public this year. It's one way to help restore the confidence of people in their government. We'd be giving up some privacy, but that's a choice we made when we entered public life.

The Dallas Times Herald, 4-10:(A)6.

John C. Stennis
United States Senator, D—Mississippi
3

[President Ford has] barely finished his speeches or his answers to questions before some columnists, commentators and news-papers start cutting him to pieces without any mercy. Every statement and speech he has made is immediately interpreted a dozen different ways. Not only is this confusing to the people, but also it puts the President at a disadvantage. [The public and news media should] give this man a chance. Give him a little time while he seeks and searches for solutions. Be

critical when it is necessary, but not critical just to have something to say or write . . . Normally, a President has anywhere from a year to a year-and-a-half to get ready to serve in that office. In this particular incident, Mr. Ford was virtually thrust into the office overnight. [He] is undergoing pressure and criticisms . . . when he is trying to quickly grasp and solve a great multitude of questions and come forth with policies and remedies.

Television broadcast to his constituents/
The Atlanta Constitution, 9-24:(A)12.

Robert S. Strauss
Chairman, Democratic National Committee
4

[On his job as party chairman] : I'm going to have more and more trouble with the hard-liners on the left and right. I'm going to have to take the 15 per cent at the fringes and keep them in the position of a halfway-mean dog that goes "grr" a lot and that you hope doesn't bite you. If I do that, and I'm fair about it, I'll be the kind of chairman that the majority of the party wants.

Time, 12-16:16.

James W. Symington
United States Representative, D—Missouri
5

We should get over the habit of expecting the worst of politics. We should recognize that the ethics of business and labor invariably be-come the ethics of politics, with or without constraints on campaign gifts and expenses. The remedy isn't to prevent the mix, it is to render the ethics of American private life worthy of emulation in public life.

Before Sales Association of the Paper
Industry/The National Observer, 4-13:13.

Herman E. Talmadge
United States Senator, D—Georgia
6

A lot of people from other parts of the country think a fellow from south of the Mason-Dixon Line is supposed to be a fugitive from a nut camp. That s their off-handed impression. And when they see one with walkin'-about sense, they're impressed.

Interview, Washington/
Los Angeles Times, 3-13:(1)7.

Kakuei Tanaka
Prime Minister of Japan

1

Not only in America, politicians [in all countries] must, to a certain extent, accept restriction on their personal activity and their personal privacy to earn the understanding and support of the people.

*At Foreign Correspondents Club, Tokyo,
Oct. 22/Los Angeles Times, 10-23:(1)5.*

Charles A. Vanik
United States Representative, D–Ohio

2

Money contaminates the political process . . . I will endeavor to campaign [for re-election] without a campaign fund—no contributions to be accepted, no signs, no campaign cards, no advertising, no purchase of time or space in the media. If events of the past year [such as Watergate] are to have any meaning at all, it should be that the American people will never again permit public office to be bought.

Jan. 3/The New York Times, 1-4:30.

Daniel Walker
Governor of Illinois

3

I want to see a Democratic Party that is an open party, a Democratic Party that recognizes the right of [Alabama Governor] George Wallace or anybody else to command whatever support he can and to lay it on the line when he gets there to a convention, in terms of issues. I don't agree with George Wallace on everything, but I will say that he does . . . reflect a viewpoint that is strongly held by a lot of people in this nation, and that viewpoint ought to be reflected in the convention.

*TV-radio interview, Seattle/"Meet the Press,"
National Broadcasting Company, 6-2.*

George C. Wallace
Governor of Alabama

4

[On why the Democratic Party lost the 1972 Presidential election] : It refused to listen to the average citizen of this country and ignored their wishes completely. The people spoke in explicit language that they do not want the so-called New Left. The national Democratic Party will be foolish and doomed to defeat if it ignores

the obvious lesson of 1972. I know, because I went to that [Democratic] convention in 1972 and I was allowed 30 minutes to speak. But it took only 10 minutes to point out that, unless they offered a platform the average American . . . could accept, the Party was going to lose by the biggest margin in history. Average men and women who have been Democrats all their lives do not associate themselves or relate with what they saw at the 1972 National Democratic Convention.

*Before Young Democrats, Albuquerque, N.M.,
Aug. 17/The Washington Post, 8-18:(A)2.*

F. Clifton White
*Political consultant; Chairman,
Public Affairs Analysts, Inc.*

5

For years, the Gallup Poll has been asking people what party they identify with. The number who identify with one of the parties has been declining since 1967. Within the past couple of weeks, it hit a new low. While 42 per cent identified with the Democrats and 24 per cent with the Republicans, 34 per cent did not identify with either. The number of independents was up 8 per cent since 1970 and 14 per cent since 1940. People seem to be turning from our basic institutions these days, and one of the institutions they are turning from are the political parties . . . What's happening in regard to political parties, apparently, is a lack of confidence on the part of the people in their performance and programs and function of selecting competent people for public office. The danger of this is that if you don't have a political party—some kind of organization that is identifiable and can be charged with responsibility—then who's going to select candidates to run for public office? There is no question but what ad hoc groups—responsible or irresponsible—will come along to put up candidates for Governor, Senator and Congressman probably; but who's going to be worrying about candidates for city council, Mayor, supervisor and on down the line to dogcatcher? That is the function of a political party—to provide those candidates. A political party since our beginnings is a legal instrument, regulated by statutes. The value of a political party as an institution is that

(F. CLIFTON WHITE)

it enables the public to hold somebody responsible. Anyone from Common Cause to Ralph Nader can tell you what is wrong; they are public watchdogs—but to whom are they responsible?

Interview, Washington/
Los Angeles Times, 3-11:(2)5.

Frederick Wilhelmsen
Professor of Philosophy, University of Dallas 1

You need a cool image to win in politics. Whether you're right or wrong doesn't matter any more. You will win principally because of the image you project, not by what you say.

At Dallas Women's Club, Jan. 16/
The Dallas Times Herald, 1-17:(C)2.

Betsey Wright
Director, National Women's Education Fund 2

I believe women will clean up politics, not because women are inherently more honest than men but because women have not learned corruption.

U.S. News & World Report, 9-16:30.

Ronald L. Ziegler
Former Press Secretary to the President of
the United States (Richard M. Nixon) 3

I've learned a great deal from the President [Nixon]. Here was a man in the office of the Presidency, making important policy decisions, most recently on Cyprus, on detente, tough decisions, totally overlooked [by the nation]. I have seen him agonize over news stories about his personal finances, property, land deals, the Watergate. He had no idea what people dealing with those matters were talking about. Yet, through it all, he maintained a balance . . . such discipline . . . an ability to cope with his job and to continue . . .

Interview, San Clemente, Calif./
Los Angeles Herald-Examiner, 9-1:(A)9.

THE WATERGATE AFFAIR

Carl Albert
United States Representative, D—Oklahoma   1

[On President Ford's pre-indictment pardon of former President Nixon for any possible Watergate crimes]: I think the President created some problems while trying to solve others. The reaction in Congress has been very adverse. The timing [of the pardon] was very bad ... It leaves a lot of people disturbed that the full story will never come out ... I never wanted to see the former President in jail. I would prefer that he not come to trial. But I think the President [Ford] would have been better off if he had waited at least to the point where the charges [against Nixon] were specified.

The Christian Science Monitor, 9-11:1.

John B. Anderson
United States Representative, R—Illinois   2

[On President Nixon's admission that he withheld from investigators tape transcripts that implicated him in a Watergate cover-up]: Pandemonium erupted on the House floor like it must have been in the pit of the New York Stock Exchange on Black Monday, 1929. The shock waves that went out were almost beyond belief. The results were utterly cataclysmic. Someone asked me if there had been erosion in support for the President. I said, "Don't talk about erosion, talk about total evaporation." The suddenness of the thing was like a Wagnerian climax.

Washington, Aug. 5/
Los Angeles Times, 8-6:(1)13.

3

[On President Ford's pre-indictment pardon of former President Nixon for any possible Watergate crimes]: It certainly demonstrates that President Ford is a man of great compassion, and one cannot help but admire that. Compounded with this admiration, there is a very real feeling of relief that the dismal spectacle of a former President sitting in the criminal dock has been averted.

Sept. 8/Chicago Tribune, 9-9:(1)10.

Lloyd M. Bentsen
United States Senator, D—Texas   4

[On the Watergate investigation process and the recent resignation of President Nixon]: I think it shows the great strength of the American system. Here we had a situation where a President fell from power. And that's the way the Europeans will interpret it. But did you see any tanks rolling in the streets? Did you see any soldiers out there with fixed bayonets? The only soldiers were taking photographs of the Capitol. At the height of the crisis, you saw the tourists going back and forth as though nothing was happening. That demonstrates the strength of this system. If all this had happened in Europe, they'd have swept it under the rug. But that's not the American way. We let it all hang out, and then we let the people judge. And that's the way it ought to be.

Interview/The National Observer, 9-7:3.

Raoul Berger
Professor of Law, Harvard University   5

[Criticizing President Ford's pre-indictment pardon of former President Nixon for any possible Watergate crimes]: It's got to be written in letters of fire that transgressions, even by the highest officer, will not be condoned. This pardon says there are no limits.

Sept. 8/The New York Times, 9-9:25.

229

WHAT THEY SAID IN 1974

Edward W. Brooke
United States Senator, R—Massachusetts

1

[Calling for President Nixon's resignation]: It appears that there will be a substantial Republican vote for impeachment in the House, and I think he will only get 22 votes for sure in the Senate. His place in history is already fixed, and if he resigned now the history books would show he was not impeached but that his impeachment was only recommended by the House [Judiciary] Committee. Why prolong this? We have already heard enough of the evidence; the people have heard enough. The economy is in a mess that won't straighten out until he resigns. He just can't be an effective President.

Los Angeles Herald-Examiner, 8-1:(A)14.

Jack Brooks
United States Representative, D—Texas;
Member, House Judiciary Committee

2

[Criticizing the Nixon Administration for refusing to furnish tapes requested by the House Judiciary Committee]: We've worked with those people [at the White House] for 40 days and 40 nights trying to get some material that they could have sent down here in 10 hours. As I have said all my life, particularly before I was married, fun is fun but you cannot laugh all night.

At House Judiciary Committee hearing,
Washington, April 4/
Los Angeles Times, 4-5:(1)1.

3

This Committee has heard evidence of governmental corruption unequaled in the history of the United States: the cover-up of crimes, obstructing the prosecution of criminals, surreptitious entries, wiretapping for political purposes, suspension of the civil liberties of every American, tax violations and personal enrichment at public expense, bribery and blackmail, flagrant misuse of the FBI, the CIA and the IRS ... Never in our 198 years have we had evidence of such rampant corruption in government.

At House Judiciary Committee hearing,
Washington/U.S. News & World Report, 8-5:58.

Patrick J. Buchanan
Special Consultant to President
of the United States Richard M. Nixon

4

If there is an impeachment of this President [Nixon], an awful lot of things will go down the drain because of what you call "an obstruction of justice" ... This Administration ... has made serious errors and grave mistakes. And apparently in this Watergate matter there was serious wrongdoing. [But President Nixon] is confident he'll see this thing through. As Americans, we ought to see what this impeachment process—what it's going to do to American politics down the road. Would it really be wise to reverse the mandate of 1972, which millions of Americans voted for? [While I admire Vice President Gerald Ford,] I do not think he has the knowledge or range or capacity that the President currently has to conduct American foreign policy. So that's one of the reasons that I feel impeachment would be genuinely harmful to the interests of the United States.

Interview/"Washington Straight Talk,"
Public Broadcasting Service, 3-18.

5

[On President Nixon's use of profanities and obscenities in Watergate-related conversations with his aides as indicated on the just-released transcripts of those conversations]: What has to be recalled is that what is taking place, what is being focused upon here is the most grievous, most tragic and most serious scandal to have erupted in the five and a half years of the Nixon Administration. And what is being focused upon specifically is the one conversation in which that was being related to the President of the United States ... I'm sure when [the late President] John F. Kennedy was told that the Central Intelligence Agency had muffed the Bay of Pigs operation, that the men the Americans had sent in there were being exterminated on the beaches, that Adlai Stevenson's false statements at the UN were being revealed to be false, I'm sure his conversation at that point in time was something the admirers of John F. Kennedy would not like to have recorded. The President was being told in these conversations about serious, damaging things.

*Interview, Washington/
The Christian Science Monitor, 5-10:(F)1.*

James L. Buckley
United States Senator, C–New York 1

Watergate has expanded on a scale that has plunged our country into what historians call a "crisis of the regime." A crisis of the regime is not like a political confrontation or labor dispute or economic recession or any other specific and limited difficulty. A crisis of the regime is a disorder, a trauma, involving every tissue of the nation, conspicuously including its moral and spiritual dimensions. The outward signs of the depth of the crisis are obvious: the unparalleled downfall and departure of virtually the entire staff of the head of government; the formal initiation of impeachment proceedings; the confessions, indictments and trials. I won't repeat the list of what all of us know much too well. Yet, at the very heart of the crisis are things which cannot easily be listed, for they consist of felt truths which do not lend themselves to the confines of charts and graphs and polls and headlines. I speak of the spreading cynicism about those in public life and about the political process itself. I speak of the pervasive and undeniable sense of frustration and impotence that has become the dominant political mood in the nation. I speak of a perception of corruption that has effectively destroyed the President's [Nixon] ability to speak from a position of moral leadership. And I speak of the widespread conviction that Watergate and all that it has brought in its wake has done unique and perhaps irrevocable damage to our entire system of government . . . There is one way and one way only by which the crisis can be resolved and the country pulled out of the Watergate swamp. I propose an extraordinary act of statesmanship and courage—an act at once noble and heartbreaking; at once serving the greater interests of the nation, the institution of the Presidency and the stated goals for which he so successfully campaigned. That act is Richard Nixon's own voluntary resignation as President of the United States . . . I am deeply aware, of course, that in recent weeks Richard Nixon has found several occasions to say that he must defend the office of the President, and that he therefore should not resign because that would weaken the office. But precisely the opposite is the case. In order to preserve the Presidency, Richard Nixon must resign as President. If future Presidents are to carry out their grave responsibilities in the free and unfettered manner President Nixon desires, they must be able to inherit an office that has not been irrevocably weakened by a long, slow, agonizing, inch-by-inch process of attrition. Mr. Nixon also argues that it would be destructive of the office for a President to be hounded out of office because he happens to have a low rating in the polls. In normal circumstances I would agree. But we have in the present case a qualitative difference that hinges not on the *fact* of a low rating but on the *reasons* for that rating.

*Washington, March 19/
Los Angeles Times, 3-20:(2)7.*

Warren E. Burger
Chief Justice of the United States 2

[Saying President Nixon must turn over to Watergate investigators subpoenaed tapes of White House Presidential conversations]: In this case we must weigh the importance of the general privilege of confidentiality of Presidential communications in performance of his responsibilities against the inroads of such a privilege on the fair administration of criminal justice. The interest in preserving confidentiality is weighty indeed and entitled to great respect. However, we cannot conclude that advisers will be moved to temper the candor of their remarks by the infrequent occasions of disclosure because of the possibility that such conversations will be called for in the context of a criminal prosecution. On the other hand, the allowance of the privilege to withhold evidence that is demonstrably relevant in a criminal trial would cut deeply into the guarantee of due process of law and gravely impair the basic function of the courts. A President's acknowledged need for confidentiality in the communications of his office is general in nature,

(WARREN E. BURGER)

whereas the Constitutional need for production of relevant evidence in a criminal proceeding is specific and central to the fair adjudication of a particular criminal case in the administration of justice. Without access to specific facts, a criminal prosecution may be totally frustrated. The President's broad interest in confidentiality of communications will not be vitiated by disclosure of a limited number of conversations preliminarily shown to have some bearing on the pending criminal cases.

Delivering Supreme Court decision,
Washington, July 24/
Los Angeles Times, 7-25:(1)23.

James MacGregor Burns
Professor of Political Science, Williams College
1

We have got to have a much simpler procedure for impeachment and removal from office—a more expeditious way that does not, for example, have to depend on tapes. Obviously, they will not be made any more. We need a system that would operate when only one or two or three charges have been made against the President. The sheer range of misbehavior, the totality of it, simply overwhelmed everybody this time [in the Watergate affair]. What if there had been only one clear-cut impeachable offense? Perhaps what we need is a permanent independent prosecutor, related in some way to or appointed by Congress. Another good step would be increasing the availability of information from the government. When [President] Ford talks about an open Administration I hope he has this in mind. If we are ever to learn from our mistakes, we have got to have information.

Interview/Time, 8-19:66.

George Bush
Chairman, Republican National Committee
2

Resignation [of President Nixon] is a nonanswer. I worry about the instability that resignation without proof of guilt brings to our system. Let the system work—let the [House] Judiciary Committee promptly do its [impeachment-inquiry] work. Let us not inject a whole new concept—namely resignation—into the system.

The New York Times, 3-24:(4)1.

3

I have been critical of some of the White House handling of the Watergate matter, but I retain basic confidence that the President [Nixon] is telling the truth about his lack of involvement in the whole be-damned mess. I have enough confidence in the system to feel that the truth will be clearly established on this point—established by fact, not by opinion nor prejudice ... No man should be convicted on less than factual proof. If I did not have confidence that President Nixon is telling the truth on Watergate, I would not stand here in this posture.

Before Republican National Committee,
Washington, April 26/
Los Angeles Herald-Examiner, 4-26:(A)3.

M. Caldwell Butler
United States Representative,
R—Virginia; Member,
House Judiciary Committee
4

There are frightening implications for the future of our country if we do not impeach the President of the United States [Nixon], because we will by this impeachment proceeding be establishing a standard of conduct for the President of the United States which will for all time be a matter of public record. If we fail to impeach, we have condoned and left unpunished a course of conduct totally inconsistent with the reasonable expectations of the American people; we will have condoned and left unpunished a Presidential course of conduct designed to interfere with and obstruct the very process which he is sworn to uphold; and we will have condoned and left unpunished an abuse of power totally without justification. And we will have said to the American people: "These misdeeds are inconsequential and unimportant."

At House Judiciary Committee hearing,
Washington, July 25/
U.S. News & World Report, 8-5:59.

1

... Watergate is our [Republican's] shame. Those things happened in the Republican Administration while we had a Republican in the White House, and every single person convicted to date has, one way or the other, owed allegiance to the Republican Party. We cannot indulge ourselves the luxury of patronizing or excusing the misconduct of our own people. These things have happened in our house. And it [is] our responsibility to do what we can to clear it up. It is we, not the Democrats, who must demonstrate that we are capable of enforcing the high standards we would set for them.

At House Judiciary Committee hearing,
Washington, July 25/
The New York Times, 7-26:12.

Robert C. Byrd
United States Senator, D—West Virginia

2

I think that the trial of impeachment stands on the highest of Constitutional grounds. I can see no proper invocation of the doctrine of Executive privilege [by which President Nixon might withhold requested evidence from House and Senate impeachment proceedings]. The members of the House—certainly those on the Judiciary Committee [making the impeachment inquiry]—are cleared for national security. We have members of the Foreign Relations Committee, the Armed Services Committee, the Appropriations Committee, who annually listen to matters that deal with national security and the most sensitive and classified of matters, so I don't think that the President could invoke the doctrine of Executive privilege in this kind of situation; because this is the highest inquest of the nation, and it goes to the very core of our Constitutional system of government. I would hope that he would not attempt to invoke that doctrine, and I don't think it would stand up if he did.

TV-radio interview/"Meet the Press,"
National Broadcasting Company, 3-3.

3

I don't envy any member of the House, because there's no way to win on this vote [of impeachment against President Nixon]. Either

way a member goes, he creates for himself an unforgiving segment of his constituency. And if I might be a bit facetious, I think ... the luckiest member of the House on the day on which an impeachment vote occurs would be the fellow who was over at Bethesda Hospital having just undergone a tonsillectomy, a hemorrhoidectomy, and is on his way back to the operating room for the recovery of two kidney stones.

Television interview/
The Wall Street Journal, 3-8:6.

4

Congress did not create Watergate. And Congress is not dragging out Watergate. The President [Nixon] could have done more than anyone else to put Watergate behind us a long time ago, if he had only cooperated with the courts and the special prosecutors in carrying out their responsibilities ... Roadblocks have been thrown up at every turn of the way ... The last 15 months have marked a downward trend in the fortunes of our country. Because of the plethora of scandals involving people in high places in the Administration, and because of the cloud that hangs over the President, our country has been weakened at home and abroad. It has been weakened because the power of the President has been eroded—eroded not from without, but from within. He speaks and the people do not believe him. Only the holder of the office can weaken the Presidency; and the Presidency has been weakened ...

Before National Capital Democratic Club,
Washington, March 27/
Los Angeles Times, 3-28:(1)11.

5

[Arguing against President Nixon resigning]: If a President of the United States should be drummed out of office by intense pressure from the media, members of Congress—indeed by public opinion itself—before articles of impeachment, based on evidence formally presented, have been voted, I fear the impact such an event would have on the Constitutional bedrock of our system ... A significant portion of our citizens would feel that the President has been driven from office by his political enemies. The question of guilt or innocence would never be fully resolved. The country

(ROBERT C. BYRD)

would remain polarized—more so than it is to-day. And confidence in government would remain unrestored.

Before the Senate, Washington, May 13/
U.S. News & World Report, 5-27:17.

Joseph A. Califano, Jr.
Former Special Assistant to the President
of the United States (Lyndon B. Johnson)
for Domestic Affairs   1

Presidents from Washington through Nixon have had different personalities: Some have been outgoing, others introverted; some ideological, others pragmatic; some interested only in broad policy, others concerned with the day-to-day operations of government. But every successful American politician—and Presidents are the most successful—like successful lawyers, businessmen and doctors, makes his own decisions and pays close attention to details . . . Richard Nixon is not misled by bad advice, or unaware of what his closest aides do. Reasonable men may doubt his advance involvement in the DNC Watergate bugging and burglary; [but] they must recognize that he would have been unworthy of his political success if he were not deeply involved in everything that followed the capture of the burglars on June 17, 1972 . . . For what Watergate and its surrounding events involve is Mr. Nixon's place in history, Mr. Nixon's personal reputation, and whether he will be convicted of a crime or impeached, remembered as the man who opened the door to [Communist] China or as the man who headed the most corrupt Administration in the history of the free world. Even White House aides as apparently trusted as [Watergate-implicated former Nixon Assistants] H. R. Haldeman and John Ehrlichman would not be permitted by the President to deal, on their own, in areas as central to Mr. Nixon's personal and political life and reputation as those involved in the present scandals. From my own perspective as a former White House aide, if the press is to be criticized in connection with the reporting of these scandals, it is not, as Messrs. Nixon and [former Vice President Spiro]

Agnew suggest, because it has been careless in printing unverified charges. It is, rather, because of its acceptance, with so little skepticism, of the myth that Mr. Nixon is somehow the uninformed victim of aides and Cabinet officers whose political enthusiasm spilled over into criminality. Yet, this myth defies the reality of Presidential power and the personal, political and historical ambition that accompany the exercise of such power. We do not have to plow through the pages of *Six Crises* to know that Mr. Nixon is most attendant to details that intimately affect his political career.

Before Harvard Law School Association
of the District of Columbia/
The Washington Post, 2-15:(A)30.

Jimmy Carter
Governor of Georgia   2

[On the public's weariness with the subject of Watergate] : It's kind of like having an illegitimate child in the family. You know it's happened. You know who's responsible. But you don't want to talk about it much in public.

Seattle, June 2/
Los Angeles Times, 6-3:(1)9.

Chou En-lai
Premier of the People's Republic
of (Communist) China   3

[On Watergate] : Since it is entirely your [the U.S.'s] own internal affair, we have never published anything about it in our press. It doesn't affect the over-all [U.S.-China] situation. We think it perhaps reflects your political life and social system . . . You have had such things occur in your society and undoubtedly will again. There are many social aspects interwoven into it, and it is better not to discuss this issue. I hope your President [Nixon] will be able to overcome these difficulties.

Interview/The New York Times, 1-16:39.

William S. Cohen
United States Representative,
R—Maine; Member,
House Judiciary Committee   4

[On charges that evidence in the Judiciary Committee's consideration of impeachment of

President Nixon is only circumstantial] : Conspiracies are not born in the sunlight . . . They are hatched in dark recesses, amid whispers and code words. The footprints of guilt must often be traced with the searchlight of probability.

At House Judiciary Committee hearing,
Washington, July 25/
The Washington Post, 7-26:(A)12.

Charles W. Colson
Former Special Counsel to President
of the United States
Richard M. Nixon   1

[On his being convicted for obstructing justice by seeking to discredit Daniel Ellsberg while Ellsberg was under Federal indictment in the "Pentagon Papers" case] : During the time I served in the White House, I rarely questioned a Presidential order. Infrequently did I question the President's judgment. These two things, unquestioning loyalty on the one hand and a feeling of self-sacrifice on the other, caused me to lose sight of some very fundamental precepts. Contrary to my view at the time, one who serves in public office is not doing anyone a favor. He or she is privileged to hold that office in public trust. One's loyalty should go beyond the man he serves to the institutions and people that have reposed that trust in him . . . As to the specific offense charged, the President on numerous occasions urged me to disseminate damaging information about Daniel Ellsberg, including information about Ellsberg's attorney and others with whom Ellsberg had been in close contact. I endeavored to do so— and willingly. I don't mean to shift my responsibility to the President. I believed what I was doing was right. The President, I am convinced, believed he was acting in the national interest. I know I did. Daniel Ellsberg was viewed as a serious threat to the security of the United States in that he had had access to very sensitive information which it was feared he might disclose. The President, [then National Security Affairs advisor] Henry Kissinger, myself and others feared that his action would encourage others to do the same. I saw Ellsberg as a martyr who might rally public support against policies the President believed right for the

country. Many of us thought that his alleged act of stealing documents and having them published was unforgivable—perhaps even bordering on the treasonous. Therefore, whatever we could do, we should do . . . I never once even remotely thought that my conduct might trespass upon the Constitution or anyone's rights under it. I had one rule—to get done that which the President wanted done. And while I thought I was serving him well and·faithfully, I now recognize I was not—at least in the sense that I never really questioned whether what he wanted done was right or proper. He had a right to expect more from me. I had an obligation to do more for him.

At his sentencing in U.S. District Court,
Washington, June 21/
Los Angeles Times, 6-22:(1)12.

2

[On the release by the White House of tape transcripts of Watergate-related conversations between President Nixon and his aides] : . . . to make them all public the way they were made public, to me was one of the poorest exercises of political judgment I've ever seen. I mean, it may have been necessary from the standpoint of showing that he [Nixon] technically wasn't involved in obstruction, as far as the lawyers would argue to the impeachment committee; but in terms of the impact on being able to rally public support, showing a man—any man, you, me, Nixon, de Gaulle—in his inner councils when he's beset with a problem and he's under pressure, is just to me the worst exercise of political judgment I've ever seen, to release them. I mean, it had to have a bad impact. It's just incredible.

Interview, Washington/
The New York Times, 7-7:(1)29.

Henry Steele Commager
Historian   3

. . . there's no reason to suppose that the country fails because it impeaches the President [Nixon]. It may fail more egregiously in not impeaching him. The egregious failure would be to accept this man, and to accept the subversion of the Constitution and the violation of the Bill of Rights as an inevitable concomitant

WHAT THEY SAID IN 1974

(HENRY STEELE COMMAGER)

of the Presidency. I think it's far more important to prove that the Constitution means what it says—that the instrument of impeachment was put there by the Founding Fathers to be used when necessary—and to vindicate that, than it is to avoid the crisis of impeachment.

Television interview, March 26/
The Washington Post, 4-13:(A)16.

John B. Connally, Jr.
Former Secretary of the
Treasury of the United States;
Former Governor of Texas

1

I do think [President] Nixon's ability to lead has diminished [because of Watergate], and his ability to lead with confidence. But many people forget the genesis of Watergate, that it started with a stupid burglary about which the President knew nothing. As for the transcripts and conversations [between the President and his aides, recently released by the White House], I'm sure other Presidents have said other things in the Oval Room of the White House that they didn't intend people to hear, and that includes profanity. We tend to put our people and heroes, including the President, on pedestals; but, as a matter of fact, heroes have feet of clay, too. They often have a greater ruthlessness, greater ambitions, greater weaknesses, greater vanities, or they wouldn't be where they are.

Interview, Milwaukee, May 10/
Los Angeles Times, 5-11:(1)20.

John Conyers, Jr.
United States Representative,
D—Michigan; Member,
House Judiciary Committee

2

[On the Judiciary Committee's consideration of impeachment of President Nixon]: I suppose that we should admit that we sit here not because we want to but because we have to, and we have to because for the first time in the history of this country millions of citizens are genuinely afraid that they may have in office a person who might entertain the notion of taking over the government of this country, a

politician who has more effectively employed the politics of fear and division than any other in our time ... The President took the power of his office and, under the guise of protecting and executing the laws that he swore to uphold, he abused them. In so doing he has jeopardized the strength and integrity of the Constitution and laws of the land and the protections that they ought to afford all of the people. This is why we must exercise this awesome power of impeachment—not to punish Richard Nixon, because the Constitutional remedy is not punitive, but to restore to our government the proper balance of Constitutional power and serve notice on all future Presidents that such abusive conduct will not now nor ever again be tolerated.

At House Judiciary Committee hearing,
Washington, July 25/
The New York Times, 7-26:11.

Norris Cotton
United States Senator, R—New Hampshire

3

It is my visceral feeling that [President Nixon] will be impeached by the House. He was beginning to weather the [Watergate] storm until the [non-allowable income-tax deductions] thing hit. Up where I live, people are not very concerned over Watergate, but they are mad as hell over his taxes.

Interview, Washington, May 2/
Los Angeles Times, 5-3:(1)5.

Archibald Cox
Professor of Law, Harvard University;
Former special government prosecutor
for Watergate

4

[On President Nixon's reluctance to submit subpoenaed material to the House Judiciary Committee in its impeachment inquiry proceedings]: The President's lawyers say that ... his guilt or innocence of wrongdoing must be decided by the process of impeachment beginning in the House Judiciary Committee. Plainly, any such investigation will usually depend upon inquiry into what happened in the Executive Offices, and much of the evidence will be under the President's control. If impeachment is to be a viable method of inquiring into alleged Executive misconduct, the House must have a right to access to whatever evidence it judges necessary. Here the House is the tribunal; no court can judge the question or enforce the subpoena. Withholding from the House evidence it judges necessary to the inquiry is therefore a defiance of the only process the Constitution provides for dealing with substantial charges against a President. If the President refused to supply any evidence in his possession, the defiance of Constitutional processes would be so plain that all would perceive it. The principle is exactly the same when he picks and chooses what he will supply. In my view, the refusal to comply with the Judiciary Committee's subpoenas denies Presidential accountability through a Constitutional process the framers were careful to provide. Failure of the Committee to treat the refusal as a major ground for impeachment would go far to concede that Executive wrongdoing is beyond the reach of any form of law.

At University of Virginia Law School/
The Washington Post, 6-8:(A)21.

1

[On President Ford's pre-indictment pardon of former President Nixon for any possible Watergate crimes] : Confidence in our system of justice depends upon the assurance that the law does in truth apply to all men equally, the highest Executive official as well as the lowliest citizen. I fear that the advance pardon, following the [former Vice President Spiro] Agnew settlement, will seem to too many to carry the lesson that the law does not apply equally to those who achieve our highest offices.

Los Angeles Herald-Examiner, 9-9:(A)2.

Tricia Nixon Cox
Daughter of President of the
United States Richard M. Nixon

2

. . . my father knows he has done nothing wrong. And I think the truth always comes through. You can see it in someone's eyes. You can tell by what a person has done in his lifetime. My father is a completely honest person. He has never lied to anyone, and eventually his honesty will shine through. It really

will, because it has to his family and friends . . . I think the history books will show that Watergate [criticism] was politically motivated. History will show that only a few foolish people made a mistake. This mistake was later used to try to force out of office a President who, by his great achievements, possibly could have reminded those who accused him of wrongdoing that they themselves failed in their own achievements.

Interview/The New York Times, 3-17:(1)29.

Carl T. Curtis
United States Senator, R–Nebraska

3

If a President [Nixon] is forced to resign because he is in disfavor, a disfavor created by a hostile press—not all the press, but there is no doubt about the existence of a hostile press which systematically, day after day and day after day, has filled the minds of the American people, conditioning them for a forced resignation or impeachment and conviction—if we permit that to happen, then it will happen to the next President of the United States . . . Just as surely as they drive this man out of office, there will be fewer men of character, stability and vision who will offer themselves for the Presidency, because they know that, if it happens once, it will happen again. That is not good for our country.

Human Events, 3-30:4.

John W. Dean III
Former Counsel to President of the
United States Richard M. Nixon

4

[At his sentencing in the Watergate affair] : As I stand here at the mercy of the court, the only thing I ask for is your compassion and understanding. I have done wrong, and I realize the wrong that I have done. I was involved in a corruption of government and abuse of high office. To say I am sorry is not enough. I have done everything I can in the last 18 months to right the wrong. Whatever the court judges me, I will continue the same course.

At U.S. District Court, Washington, Aug. 2/
San Francisco Examiner, 8-2:1.

WHAT THEY SAID IN 1974

David W. Dennis
United States Representative,
R–Indiana; Member,
House Judiciary Committee

1

[On the Judiciary Committee's consideration of impeachment of President Nixon] : Any
prosecution is going to divide this country. It
will tear asunder the Republican Party for
many years to come, and this is bad for the
country, which demands for its political health
a strong two-party system. And impeachment is
radical surgery on the tip of a cancer which
needs therapy at the root. I am as shocked as
anyone by the misdeeds of Watergate. Richard
Nixon has much to answer for, and he has even
more to answer for to me as a conservative
Republican than he has to my liberal-leaning
friends on the other side of the aisle. But I join
in no political lynching where hard proof fails,
as to this President or any other President. And
I suggest this: What is needed is moral and
political reform in America. The Nixon Administration is not the first to be guilty of shoddy
practices which, if not established as grounds
for impeachment, are nonetheless inconsistent
with the better spirit of America. Neither the
catharsis of impeachment nor the trauma of
political trial will cure this illness of the spirit.
We're all too likely to pass through this crisis
and then forget reform for another 20 years.
Our business in the Congress is basically legislative and not judicial.
At House Judiciary Committee hearing,
Washington, July 25/
The New York Times, 7-26:11.

John M. Doar
Special Counsel to the
House Judiciary Committee

2

As an individual, I have not the slightest bias
against President Nixon. I would hope that I
would not do him the smallest, slightest injury.
But I am not indifferent, not indifferent to the
matter of Presidential abuse of power by whatever President . . . If in fact President Nixon, or
any President, has had a central part in the
planning and execution of this terrible deed of
subverting the Constitution, then I shall do my
part as best I can to bring him to answer before

the Congress of the United States for his enormous crime in the conduct of his office . . .
Members of the Committee, for me to speak
like this—I can hardly believe I am speaking as I
do or thinking as I do—the awesomeness of this
is so—so tremendous . . . My judgment is that
the facts are overwhelming in this case that the
President of the United States authorized a
broad general plan of illegal electronic surveillance and that the plan was put into operation
by his subordinates . . . But with respect to the
plan, I say that decision came direct from the
President or [was] implemented through his
two closest associates, [H. R.] Haldeman and
[John] Ehrlichman. Following that, I say that
he directed, made the decision, the President
made the decision to cover up this shortly after
the break-in [at Democratic headquarters] on
June 17 [1972], and he's been in charge of the
cover-up from that day forward.
Before House Judiciary Committee,
Washington/Time, 7-29:6.

Robert J. Dole
United States Senator, R–Kansas

3

[On President Ford's pre-indictment pardon
of former President Nixon for any possible
Watergate crimes] : The pardon of Nixon was
premature. Like everyone else, I don't relish the
thought of some former President languishing
in jail. But there was no certainty that he would
have been indicted. The damaging part is the
feeling that people have that this is the same
old ball game. A new player does the same
thing the last one did—he takes care of his
friends. That's what people are saying.
Interview/
The New York Times Magazine, 10-20:101.

Helen Gahagan Douglas
Former United States Representative,
D–California

4

[On President Nixon's actions in the face of
his possible impeachment] : What he's trying to
do now is what he did in the past, and it was
also in the '50 campaign [when she ran against
Nixon for the U.S. Senate in California], to
suggest to the voter that he is the flag, he is the
pure figure, he is the country and, without him,
it's all going to go awry. And this just isn't true.

It wasn't true then and it isn't true now, and it isn't true of any one person. You are what you are and you occupy a given office at a certain time. He is still Richard Milhous Nixon. Now he is the President of the United States, but he hasn't gained stature, a stature that is above the law. He isn't the future of the United States because he is President. The future of the United States will be determined by us, the people—nobody else.

News conference, Los Angeles, May 23/
Los Angeles Times, 5-24:(1)23.

John D. Ehrlichman
Former Assistant to President
of the United States Richard M. Nixon
for Domestic Affairs   1

[On his being found guilty of conspiracy in the break-in at the office of Daniel Ellsberg's psychiatrist] : I am confident, as this process in our legal system unfolds, that justice will be found and done and I will be exonerated and vindicated. I have a clear conscience and I am confident we will see a proper outcome in due course . . . People who are in government are constantly required to balance the interests of the individual against the larger interests of the nation as a whole or government institutions. [For example,] the farmer who is asked to give up his farm so an airbase can be built during a war. There was a balancing of that kind involved in this case.

News conference, Washington, July 31/
Los Angeles Times, 8-1:(1)14.

Joshua Eilberg
United States Representative,
D—Pennsylvania; Member,
House Judiciary Committee   2

[On the Judiciary Committee's consideration of impeachment of President Nixon] : The evidence is clear and overwhelming. Richard Nixon is guilty, beyond any reasonable doubt, of numerous acts of impeachable conduct regardless of any standards we apply . . . What we are faced with is a gross disregard for the Constitution and the very safeguards in it which the framers hoped would prevent the President from becoming a king or a dictator. The evidence presented during our hearings portrays a man who believes he is above the law and who was surrounded by advisers who believed they owe their allegiance to him and not to their country or the Constitution . . . It is my deep belief that, not only is Richard Nixon guilty of bribery, high crimes and misdemeanors, but he must be impeached and convicted by the Senate if we are to remain a free, courageous and independent people.

At House Judiciary Committee hearing,
Washington, July 25/
The New York Times, 7-26:11.

3

We've learned that in Russia you must never hold a serious conversation without turning on the water or radio so the conversation could not be heard by the secret listening devices. It's also an axiom that the telephone is tapped, so in Russia everyone takes long walks in the park so they can communicate. It's become an article of faith that in Russia Big Brother has arrived, that the secret police are always listening. Now we learn that in the late '60s and early '70s and possibly right up to this date secret police have been listening in America. Only now they have special equipment to eliminate the noise of running water or loud radios. In Washington, it's become a sardonic joke to say that the phone is tapped whenever there's a strange noise on the line. We have become a suspicious people, afraid to talk freely, not because what we say might prove that we've committed a crime or endangered the national security, but because our political enemies might use this information against us. The Nixon White House made the secret police a reality in the United States.

At House Judiciary Committee hearing,
Washington, July 29/
The New York Times, 7-30:19.

David Eisenhower
Son-in-law of former President of the
United States Richard M. Nixon   4

[On President Nixon's recent resignation]: Some members of the family thought he ought to go on, to narrow the bill of particulars and essentially to . . . enable historians . . . to decide

WHAT THEY SAID IN 1974

(DAVID EISENHOWER)

if the President should be driven from office for allegedly, or at least proven to the satisfaction of Congress, having acquiesced in the non-prosecution of aides who covered up a little operation into the opposition's [Democratic Party's] political headquarters, which is a practice that was fairly well established in Washington for a long time and that no one took all that seriously. [Fifteen years from now,] it's going to look pretty small, and there will be other grounds on which to judge the [Nixon] Administration... [Those who became entangled in Watergate were] not so much a gang of felons that were out to subvert the Constitution, but by and large people who walked into and indulged in accepted practices within the unwritten rules of executive D.C. which had developed over four years... Maybe it was the personality of Richard Nixon that inspired it. But in either case, I don't think the individuals involved are on a par with Herman Goering, Joseph Goebbels, Rudolph Hess... Look, they [former Nixon Assistants H. R. Haldeman and John Ehrlichman] were efficient, dedicated public servants. You can't escape that... I think, in the context of time, they were not acting as evil men... They weren't henchmen of Stalin... they just weren't. They're paying for it... We're not punishing evil, wicked men... The government is making a point as to the literal extent of Presidential power in Washington. It's a tough time for them individually. It's a tough time for everyone individually. It's very sad.

Interview, Washington/
Chicago Tribune, 9-5:(1)13.

Sam J. Ervin, Jr.
United States Senator, D–North Carolina;
Chairman, Senate Watergate Committee
1

[Saying his Committee will arrive at no conclusions in its Watergate investigation report, and that none were called for]: You know, there are two ways to prove a horse is a horse. One way is to draw a picture of a horse, a very good likeness. The other way is to write under the picture, "This is a horse." We just drew the picture.

News conference, Washington, July 12/
Los Angeles Times, 7-13:(1)10.

2

Unlike the men who were responsible for Teapot Dome, the Presidential aides who perpetrated Watergate were not seduced by the love of money... On the contrary, they were instigated by a lust for political power, which is at least as corrupting as political power itself. They gave their allegiance to the President [Nixon] and his policies. They had stood for a time near to him, and had been entrusted by him with great governmental and political power. They enjoyed exercising such power, and longed for its continuance. They knew that the power then enjoyed would be lost and the policies to which they adhered would be frustrated if the President should be defeated [for re-election in 1972]. As a consequence of these things, they believed the President's re-election to be a most worthy objective, and succumbed to an age-old temptation. They resorted to evil means to promote what they conceived to be a good end.

Before American Bar Association, Honolulu/
The Washington Post, 8-22:(A)20.

3

[On President Ford's pre-indictment pardon of former President Nixon for any possible Watergate crimes]: Ecclesiastes says, "There is a time for everything under heaven," but there is time for a pardon after a trial and conviction and not before.

At party in his honor, Washington, Sept. 17/
The Washington Post, 9-19:(B)3.

Daniel J. Evans
Governor of Washington
4

[Saying President Nixon should not resign]: I think impeachment, while it may be a difficult process, is much more definitive. I believe that, if the end result of impeachment is that the President is removed from office, at least it will be more decisive; more people will accept the end result. I think resignation would leave an immense void and an awful lot of disruption that I don't think is good for the country.

TV-radio interview, Seattle/"Meet the Press," National Broadcasting Company, 6-2.

Walter Flowers
United States Representative, D Alabama; Member, House Judiciary Committee

1

On the one hand, we hear on television about [President Nixon's] full cooperation and the desire for an expeditious [impeachment inquiry], but we see developing the intricate maneuvers of a strategy to limit this [House Judiciary] Committee and confuse the issue. Both the Constitution and historical precedent are clear: The House of Representatives has the solemn responsibility and power of impeachment. And in the exercise of this power and responsibility, the House should not be limited in any way whatsoever in its access to needed material and testimony. There is no requirement, nor should there be, for . . . this Committee to define what constitutes an impeachable offense or set the scope in advance of this or any particular inquiry . . . [President Nixon should not resign, because] to do so would be interpreted by the vast majority of our fellow citizens as an admission of wrongdoing tantamount to a guilty plea in court. So, Mr. President, do not resign. You may be impeached, even convicted; but do not resign. And if you must do battle with Congress, let your sword be cooperation and your shield be the whole truth.

At House Judiciary Committee session, Washington, March 20/ Los Angeles Times, 3-21:(1)6.

2

I wake up nights . . . wondering if this could not be some sordid dream: Impeach the President of the United States, the Chief Executive of our country, our Commander-in-Chief in this cruel and volatile world that we live in in 1974 . . . But unfortunately, this is no bad dream. It is the terrible truth that will be upon us here in this Committee in the next few days. And then there is the other side of the issue that I speak of. What if we failed to impeach? Do we ingrain forever in the very fabric of our Constitution a standard of conduct in our

highest office that in the least is deplorable, and at worst is impeachable? This is, indeed, a terrible choice we have to make.

At House Judiciary Committee hearing, Washington, July 25/ U.S. News & World Report, 8-5:59.

3

The power of the Presidency is a public trust, and the people must be able to believe and rely on their President. Yet there is evidence before us that shows that the President [Nixon] has given solemn public assurances to the people, involving the trust and faith of his office, when those assurances were not true, but were designed to deceive the people and to mislead the agencies of the government who were investigating the charges against Mr. Nixon's men. If the trust of the people in the word of the man to whom they have given their highest honor is betrayed, if the people cannot know that their President is candid and truthful with them, then the very basis of government is undermined.

At House Judiciary Committee hearing, Washington, July 25/ The Washington Post, 8-8:(A)22.

Gerald R. Ford
Vice President of the United States

4

. . . a coalition of groups, like the AFL-CIO, the Americans for Democratic Action and other powerful pressure organizations, is waging a massive propaganda campaign against the President of the United States. And make no mistake about it—it is an all-out attack. Their aim is total victory for themselves and the total defeat, not only of President Nixon, but of the policies for which he stands. If they can crush the President and his philosophy, they are convinced that they can dominate the Congress and, through it, the nation . . . if the relatively small group of activists who are out to impeach the President see that they do not have the strength to do it, they will try to do the next most damaging thing. They will try to stretch out the ordeal to cripple the President by dragging out the preliminaries to impeachment for as long as they can, and to use the whole affair for maximum political advantage. Such a course

WHAT THEY SAID IN 1974

(GERALD R. FORD)

would be bad for the Congress, bad for one Presidency and bad for the nation.

Before American Farm Bureau Federation,
Atlantic City, N.J., Jan. 15/
The Washington Post, 1-17:(A)14.

1

That is what the American people are telling their elected representatives, again and again . . . : Settle Watergate, they say. Write the last chapter; close the book and get on with the vital business of the nation. It is high time we did just that. It is high time we got out of the rut of despair and self-doubt and back onto the high road of progress. Once we do that, America is bound to succeed . . . No one is perfect—no nationality and no Executive. But when you look back on the past years of the Nixon Administration and think of these really magnificent achievements, then Watergate no longer dominates the landscape. Compared with these mountainous achievements, it's a tragic but grotesque sideshow.

Before American Farm Bureau Federation,
Atlantic City, N.J., Jan. 15/
The Washington Post, 1-17:(A)14.

2

I think the best thing to insure that what happened in the Watergate case, in the broader sense, doesn't happen again, is for the President to monitor, to a greater degree, what his top people are doing. I think I understand what happened. If you go back to the spring of 1972, the President [Nixon] was preoccupied with [Communist] China, the detente with the Soviet Union, and he was trying to end the war in Vietnam. I would wager—and give big odds—that the President probably said to [then Attorney General] John Mitchell: "I have all these foreign-policy problems of major consequence; you run the [re-election] campaign." Obviously, the President did not monitor the campaign, the people, the programs, sufficiently. I know that, if the President had known of any of these [Watergate] things going on, he would have categorically cut them off. But he was preoccupied, and unfortunately the people he gave responsibility to were not wise enough,

not ethical enough, to run the campaign properly. But I think, despite the pressing burdens of foreign policy, you just cannot, as a President, let things be under the total responsibility of others without doing some monitoring.

Interview/The Washington Post, 4-14:(B)4.

3

[Criticizing the Watergate role of the 1972 Committee for the Re-election of the President]: I am disgusted with political trickery of the CREEP variety, or any other creeps who are looking for an easy but unethical or illegal road to [election] victory. We must never again permit CREEP or any creepy successor organization to spoil the name of the Grand Old Party.

At California Republican State Convention,
San Jose, April 20/
The New York Times, 4-21:(1)26.

4

[On President Nixon's release of Watergate-related White House tapes]: I cannot imagine any other country in the world where the opposition would seek, and the Chief Executive would allow, the dissemination of his most private and personal conversations with his staff which, to be honest, do not exactly confer sainthood on anyone concerned.

At University of Michigan commencement,
Ann Arbor, May 4/
The New York Times, 5-5:(1)41.

Gerald R. Ford
President of the United States

5

[On his assumption of the Presidency after President Nixon's resignation]: My fellow Americans, our long national nightmare is over. Our Constitution works. Our great republic is a government of laws and not of men. Here, the people rule . . . As we bind up the internal wounds of Watergate, more painful and more poisonous than those of foreign wars, let us restore the golden rule to our political process. And let brotherly love purge our hearts of suspicion and of hate.

Inauguration address, Washington,
Aug. 9/The New York Times, 8-10:3.

1

[Full text of President Ford's statement on pardoning former President Nixon for any possible Watergate crimes]:

Ladies and gentlemen, I have come to a decision which I felt I should tell you, and all my fellow citizens, as soon as I was certain in my own mind and conscience that it is the right thing to do.

I have learned already in this office that only the difficult decisions come to this desk. I must admit that many of them do not look at all the same as the hypothetical questions that I have answered freely and perhaps too fast on previous occasions. My customary policy is to try and get all the facts and to consider the opinions of my countrymen and to take counsel with my most valued friends. But these seldom agree, and in the end the decision is mine.

To procrastinate, to agonize, to wait for a more favorable turn of events that may never come, or more compelling external pressures that may as well be wrong as right, is itself a decision of sorts and a weak and potentially dangerous course for a President to follow.

I have promised to uphold the Constitution, to do what is right as God gives me to see the right, and to do the very best I can for America. I have asked your help and your prayers, not only when I became President, but many times since.

The Constitution is the supreme law of our land and it governs our actions as citizens. Only the laws of God, which govern our consciences, are superior to it. As we are a nation under God, so I am sworn to uphold our laws with the help of God. And I have sought such guidance and searched my own conscience with special diligence to determine the right thing for me to do with respect to my predecessor in this place, Richard Nixon, and his loyal wife and family.

Theirs is an American tragedy in which we all have played a part. It can go on and on and on, or someone must write "The End" to it. I have concluded that only I can do that. And if I can, I must.

There are no historic or legal precedents to which I can turn in this matter, none that precisely fit the circumstances of a private citizen who has resigned the Presidency of the United States. But it is common knowledge that serious allegations and accusations hang like a sword over our former President's head, and threaten his health as he tries to reshape his life, a great part of which was spent in the service of this country and by the mandate of its people.

After years of bitter controversy and divisive national debate, I have been advised and am compelled to conclude that many months and perhaps more years will have to pass before Richard Nixon could hope to obtain a fair trial by jury in any jurisdiction of the United States under governing decisions of the Supreme Court.

I deeply believe in equal justice for all Americans, whatever their station or former station. The law, whether human or divine, is no respecter of persons but the law is a respecter of reality. The facts as I see them are that a former President of the United States, instead of enjoying equal treatment with any other citizen accused of violating the law, would be cruelly and excessively penalized either in preserving the presumption of his innocence or in obtaining a speedy determination of his guilt in order to repay a legal debt to society.

During this long period of delay and potential litigation, ugly passions would again be aroused, our people would again be polarized in their opinions, and the credibility of our free institutions of government would again be challenged at home and abroad. In the end, the courts might well hold that Richard Nixon had been denied due process and the verdict of history would be even more inconclusive with respect to those charges arising out of the period of his Presidency of which I am presently aware.

But it is not the ultimate fate of Richard Nixon that most concerns me—though surely it deeply troubles every decent and compassionate person—but the immediate future of this great country. In this I dare not depend upon my personal sympathy as a long-time friend of the former President nor my professional judgment as a lawyer. And I do not.

As President, my primary concern must always be the greatest good of all the people of the United States, whose servant I am.

WHAT THEY SAID IN 1974

(GERALD R. FORD)

As a man, my first consideration will always be to be true to my own convictions and my own conscience.

My conscience tells me clearly and certainly that I cannot prolong the bad dreams that continue to reopen a chapter that is closed. My conscience tells me that only I, as President, have the constitutional power to firmly shut and seal this book. My conscience says it is my duty, not merely to proclaim domestic tranquility, but to use every means I have to ensure it.

I do believe that the buck stops here and that I cannot rely upon public opinion polls to tell me what is right. I do believe that right makes might, and that if I am wrong 10 angels swearing I was right would make no difference. I do believe with all my heart and mind and spirit that I, not as President, but as a humble servant of God, will receive justice without mercy if I fail to show mercy.

Finally, I feel that Richard Nixon and his loved ones have suffered enough, and will continue to suffer no matter what I do, no matter what we as a great and good nation can do together to make his goal of peace come true.

Now, therefore, I, Gerald R. Ford, President of the United States, pursuant to the pardon power conferred upon me by Article 2, Section 2, of the Constitution, have granted and by these presents do grant a full, free and absolute pardon unto Richard Nixon for all offenses against the United States which he, Richard Nixon, has committed or may have committed or taken part in during the period from January 20, 1969, through August 9, 1974.

In witness whereof, I have hereunto set my hand this eighth day of September in the year of our Lord 1974, and of the independence of the United States of America the 199th.

Broadcast address to the nation,
Washington, Sept. 8/
Los Angeles Times, 9-9:(1)12.

1

[On his pre-indictment pardon of former President Nixon for any possible Watergate crimes] : The purpose was to change our nation- al focus. I wanted to do all I could to shift our attention from the pursuit [of] a fallen President to the pursuit of the urgent needs of a rising nation. Our nation is under the severest of challenges now to employ its full energy and effort in the pursuit of a sound and growing economy at home and a stable and peaceful world around us. We would needlessly be diverted from meeting those challenges if we, as a people, were to remain sharply divided over whether to indict, bring to trial and punish a former President who is already condemned to suffer long and deeply in the shame and disgrace brought upon the office that he held. Surely we are not a revengeful people. We have often demonstrated a readiness to feel compassion and to act out of mercy. As a people, we have a long record of forgiving even those who have been our country's most destructive foes. Yet to forgive is not to forget the lessons of evil in whatever way evil has operated against us. And certainly the pardon granted the former President will not cause us to forget the evils of the Watergate-type offenses or to forget the lessons we have learned that a government which deceives its supporters and treats its opponents as enemies must never, never be tolerated.

Before House Judiciary Subcommittee
on Criminal Justice, Washington, Oct. 17/
The New York Times, 10-18:18.

Fred W. Friendly
Professor of Journalism,
Columbia University; Former president,
Columbia Broadcasting System News

2

[On media coverage of the trial if President Nixon is impeached] : Never before in the short history of mass communications have journalists grappled with a challenge of such magnitude. This is not a trip to the moon; it's not a political convention; not a coronation or a state funeral. It is unlike any event since the birth of radio and television. It is the impeachment of the President of the United States of America. It will be a testing time not only for the President but for the media . . . Journalism, and particularly broadcast journalism, will also be on trial . . . The manner in which it conducts itself and the public verdict on that performance may be, in its way, as historic and decisive as the drama it is reporting from the floor of the Senate. Currently the debate is over whether [TV] cameras and microphones will be permitted . . . The argument is an academic one that may provide good op-ed page material. But at the end of the day the American people will make the decision; they will require a first-person, unabridged view of so historic an event without having it strained and filtered through the eyes and ears of even the most responsible newspapers and broadcast observers. None of us here today can know whether such a trial will take place; but I can assure you that neither history nor the American public will accept surrogate witnesses to so momentous an event.

At Medill School of Journalism,
Northwestern University, June 15/
The Washington Post, 7-2:(A)20.

John Kenneth Galbraith
Professor of Economics, Harvard University
1

[On President Nixon's recent resignation]: While Mr. Nixon's going is good and a definite boost to the republic, we will suffer for it in the days ahead. That is because his departure will bring out all that is loathsome in our literary tradition. There will now be a drawing of morals until healthy stomachs retch. Someone, I promise you, will say that the fault lies deeply within ourselves. Well, the hell it does. It lies with Richard Nixon and the people who voted him into office. The only lesson to be drawn from the Nixon debacle is that the wrong man can be elected in this country after due notice by a landslide. Mr. Nixon has been tediously around and excessively visible for close on to 30 years. Nixon was a premeditated political assault, committed in broad daylight.

Interview/Newsweek, 8-19:52.

Leonard Garment
Counsel to President of the
United States Richard M. Nixon
2

[On charges that President Nixon ordered a campaign to smear or discredit Daniel Ellsberg, who turned over the "Pentagon Papers" for newspaper publication, in 1971]: [The White

House atmosphere in 1971 was] one of very great concern and very great anger at the enormous amount of very sensitive national-security information—namely, the "Pentagon Papers"—that had been leaked as a result of Mr. Ellsberg's unilateral determination that these should be made public. There was concern at that time that, if Mr. Ellsberg became a hero in the eyes of the American public for making this unilateral determination that he was above the law, that this practice would be encouraged and that negotiations of the most delicate character—with the People's Republic of China and with the North Vietnamese—would be seriously imperiled. Our credibility—our negotiating credibility, our ability to maintain secret discussions—would have been seriously impaired. In that setting, I think one can understand the concern on the part of the President and his national-security advisers that Mr. Ellsberg not be considered a hero, that this practice stop.

TV-radio interview/"Face the Nation,"
Columbia Broadcasting System, 6-23.

Gerhard A. Gesell
Judge, United States District Court
for the District of Columbia
3

[On the charges against former Presidential Assistant John Ehrlichman in the break-in at the office of Daniel Ellsberg's psychiatrist]: An individual cannot escape criminal liability simply because he sincerely but incorrectly believes that his acts are justified in the name of patriotism, or national security, or a need to create an unfavorable press image [of Ellsberg], or that his superiors had the authority without a warrant to suspend the Constitutional protections of the Fourth Amendment.

Charging the jury in the case, Washington/
Los Angeles Times, 7-19:(1)18.

Barry M. Goldwater
United States Senator, R—Arizona
4

If it could be shown that the President [Nixon] has lied, that certainly would be grounds [for impeachment]. If it could be shown that he has been directly connected with the Watergate break-in or the "plumbers" bur-

WHAT THEY SAID IN 1974

(BARRY M. GOLDWATER)

glary, that would be grounds. I don't think the President's real-estate transactions are grounds. I don't think his tax problems relate to it. But if there was a showing that he has lied about Watergate, then the demand for impeachment would be universal, and I think that he could be impeached.

Interview, Washington/
U.S. News & World Report, 2-11:38.

Frank Goodman
Visiting professor,
University of Pennsylvania Law School
1

[Saying those convicted in Watergate should get strong sentences]: Precisely because these men in Watergate have been the recipients of so many gifts from society—and precisely because they have been given and have violated a high public trust—they must be held accountable and severely punished for their crimes. Public esteem and status and trust impose high obligations on them and makes them all the more culpable. Their betrayal of their public trust should be an aggravating factor, not a mitigating factor, in their sentencing. To hold otherwise would lead to the rich and powerful paying nothing for their crimes, and the poor and vulnerable paying everything.

Los Angeles Times, 7-21:(1)20.

Billy Graham
Evangelist
2

[Commenting on Watergate after President Nixon's resignation]: As a nation, we have abandoned God and sought to run our own affairs without regard to His law. We are now reaping the bitter fruits of this. We need to turn to God in humble repentance and faith before a worse judgment befalls us. We must not assume our problems are now over. They will only be over when we turn to God and seek His will with all our hearts. I pray that from this whole painful affair may be reborn a new commitment to God and His law in our national life. If this happens, then the tragedy of Watergate might still make a positive contribution.

Interview, New York, Aug. 8/
The New York Times, 8-9:6.

Katharine Graham
Publisher, "The Washington Post"
3

[On her paper's tracking down and exposing Watergate]: . . . I don't feel any different about Watergate than any ordinary citizen would. I feel the same dismay. I don't feel any second thoughts about what we did. That would imply we had a choice. But there was no choice. It was just an unfolding story. And I don't feel maybe it would have been better that the country never knew. That would assume ignorance is better than knowledge.

Interview, Washington/
"W": a Fairchild publication, 8-9:5.

Robert P. Griffin
United States Senator, R—Michigan
4

I think we've arrived at a point where both the national interest and his [President Nixon's] own interest would best be served by resigning. It's not just his enemies who feel that way. Many of his friends, and I count myself one of them, believe now that this would be the most appropriate course. Needless to say, this would be an awesome and very difficult decision for him to reach, but I believe he will see it that way, too.

Washington, Aug. 5/
The Washington Post, 8-6:(A)13.

Andrew Hacker
Professor of Political Science,
Queens College,
City University of New York
5

[On the Watergate experience culminating in President Nixon's resignation and Gerald Ford's assumption of the Presidency]: There will be a large spurt of self-congratulation: how we came out of the crisis, how resilient our system proved itself to be, how Congress rose to the challenge, how the transition was carried out so orderly. We are going to be engaging in a good deal of ego boosting about what fine people we are. At the same time, beneath the surface, there is a bit of Watergate in all of us. Post-war America has been an era of "get where you can as fast as you can." While it is not corruption in the financial sense, it is an excessive personal ambition. Thus I think that the whole Watergate experience has been good in that we are troubled, especially if it means that we will not be cocky and self-confident. Yet there remains the question: Are we willing to think through to the source of our troubles? I am not sure.

Interview/Time, 8-19:67.

Alexander M. Haig, Jr.
Assistant to President of the
United States Richard M. Nixon
1

... I think if the conclusions to be drawn from recent polls are of any substance, attitudes with respect to such as [President Nixon's] impeachment and resignation are running three and four to one against such action—and we see that throughout the country. We recognize that here in Washington, at the center of political activity, there is greater sensitivity to Watergate and Watergate-related matters than we find elsewhere. I don't mean by that that elsewhere there isn't concern also. But I think we see a fairly strong consensus among the majority of the American people that they have elected this President to do a job and that the system suggests that he should do that job regardless of attitudes of those who may or may not agree with the policy—and that the ballot box is the determining factor in making changes based on that kind of situation.

Interview, Washington/
The Christian Science Monitor, 3-13:(F)1.

2

The Watergate climate has been a great discomfiture to me. It has resulted in a diversion of efforts from things all of us would like to accomplish ... historians are going to wonder how in God's name could we be engaging in such a diversion of national effort and energy over such chickenfeed.

Time, 5-27:20.

3

Many public statements have been made that Watergate has not affected government. On the other side are those claiming that Watergate has paralyzed the government. I reject both of these theses. No one who sits where I do today would discount the fact that Watergate has had an impact on the conduct of the nation's business. It has diverted a great deal of time and energy of the President and other key public officials from conducting the tasks to which they should be able to give full time. Having said that, I'm not in the least apologetic over what the Administration has been able to accomplish, despite Watergate. Notwithstanding the difficulties, we've made further progress in bringing government back to the people, in suppressing drug traffic, in bringing back normalcy—the return to sanity, if you will—within our society. This includes the racial area, on the campuses and in our streets. What I'm saying basically is, yes, Watergate has had an impact—but despite this impact, we've been able to move ahead at home and abroad.

Interview/U.S. News & World Report, 6-3:19.

H. R. Haldeman
Former Assistant to President of the
United States Richard M. Nixon
4

[On his being implicated in Watergate]: I know perfectly well that I am considered guilty until I prove myself innocent. And I know that President Nixon is presumed guilty until he proves himself innocent. That ain't right. But realistically, that's the case; that's what we have to deal with. People have not seen to their satisfaction that innocence is abroad here and have perceived, maybe not to their satisfaction but certainly to their deep concern, the possibility that guilt is abroad.

Before Young Presidents Organization,
Acapulco, Mexico, April 3/
Los Angeles Times, 3-4:(1)22.

Philip A. Hart
United States Senator, D—Michigan
5

We have learned to our regret that, with or without sophisticated technology, unprincipled men can find ways to invade our privacy ... When government officials use Army personnel to spy on peaceful political meetings, as the present [Nixon] Administration did, your privacy is threatened. When government officials send burglars to break into the offices of doctors for confidential files, as this Administration did with its "plumbers" squad [in the

WHAT THEY SAID IN 1974

(PHILIP A. HART)

case of Daniel Ellsberg's psychiatrist], your privacy is threatened. [So too] when government officials use the confidential files of the Internal Revenue Service to harass persons on a White House "enemies" list, [and] when government officials eavesdrop on private conversations of political opponents.

Radio address, March 2/
The New York Times, 3-3:(1)40.

1

[On President Ford's pre-indictment pardon of former President Nixon for any possible Watergate crimes]: It is ironic and unfortunate that so shortly after the Supreme Court affirmed that a President is subject to the law of the land, President Ford has placed Richard Nixon beyond the legal process. In that sense, the final sad lesson of Watergate seems to be that the man upon whom we bestowed the Presidency, if he is grieved by the loss of office, shall not even be brought before the bar of justice.

Quote, 10-6:313.

Paul Harvey
News commentator,
American Broadcasting Company 2

I'm not altogether proud of my own profession these days. The media has turned a valid expose [of the Watergate affair] into [a] lynching. When the watchdog hangs on after the police arrive, and hangs on and hangs on and hangs on, then it seems to me that you have a mean dog.

Interview, Washington/
The Washington Post, 6-21:(C)3.

Walter J. Hickel
Former Secretary of the Interior of the
United States; Former Governor of Alaska 3

Watergate is the watershed in 20th-century American politics. America stood naked before the world and said, "We have nothing to hide." In exposing our weaknesses, we showed our strengths.

Interview, Anchorage, Alaska/
Los Angeles Times, 10-6:(1)24.

Lawrence J. Hogan
United States Representative,
R–Maryland; Member,
House Judiciary Committee 4

[Saying he, as a member of the Judiciary Committee, will vote for the impeachment of President Nixon]: The evidence convinces me that my President has lied repeatedly, deceiving public officials and the American people. He has withheld information necessary for our system of justice to work. Instead of cooperating with prosecutors and investigators, as he said publicly, he concealed and covered up evidence, and coached witnesses so that their testimony would show things that really were not true. He tried to use the CIA to impede and thwart the investigation of Watergate by the FBI. He approved the payment of what he knew to be blackmail to buy the silence of an important Watergate witness [E. Howard Hunt, Jr.]. He praised and rewarded those whom he knew had committed perjury. He personally helped to orchestrate a scenario of events, facts and testimony to cover up wrongdoing in the Watergate scandal and to throw investigators and prosecutors off the track. He actively participated in an extended and extensive conspiracy to obstruct justice . . .

News conference, Washington, July 23/
Los Angeles Times, 7-24:(1)33.

Elizabeth Holtzman
United States Representative, D–New York;
Member, House Judiciary Committee 5

[On President Nixon's invoking Executive privilege in refusing to turn over subpoenaed material to the House Judiciary Committee in its impeachment inquiry]: There is no such thing as Executive privilege in an impeachment inquiry. It puts the country in a dangerous position. If you take the position the President isn't accountable to the law, that means he's not accountable to anyone. And that was not the idea of the Founding Fathers.

The Christian Science Monitor, 6-18:3A.

6

[President] Nixon allowed the people's tax money to be used for the enrichment of his personal properties ... He failed to report income and claimed tax deductions totaling almost $1 million. He appointed and kept in office as Cabinet members and close adviser[s] persons whom he knew to be seriously unfit. He repeatedly and knowingly deceived the American people who trusted him and wanted to trust him ... The thousands of pages before this Committee bear witness ... to a systematic arrogation of power, to a thoroughgoing abuse of the President's oath of office, to a pervasive violation of the rule of law. What we have seen is a seamless web of misconduct so serious that it leaves me shaken.

At House Judiciary Committee hearing, Washington/ U.S. News & World Report, 8-5:60.

1

[Criticizing President Ford's pre-indictment pardon of former President Nixon for any possible Watergate crimes]: I am deeply disturbed to find a continuation in the Ford Administration of what we saw under President Nixon—namely, the perversion of the criminal-justice system to shield those in power from accountability under our law.

Sept. 8/The New York Times, 9-9:25.

Emmet John Hughes
Professor of Politics, Rutgers University

2

[On the Watergate investigation, President Nixon's resignation and Gerald Ford's assumption of the Presidency]: We have just watched our balance of Federal powers work with almost wondrous rectitude and effect. We have seen the Judiciary act with impressive art and force. We have observed the Congress perform with patience and poise. It remains only for us now to glimpse again a Presidency not punished but cleansed, not cowed but renewed, and not diminished but inspired.

Interview/Time, 8-19:66.

Henry M. Jackson
United States Senator, D—Washington

3

[On President Ford's pre-indictment pardon of former President Nixon for any possible Watergate crimes]: My immediate reaction was

amazement. I had the impression Ford would await developments in the courts before taking any action. This is a first in this country for a person to receive a pardon before any charges are filed against him ... Now I'm wondering what happens to those who have been convicted and are now serving sentences, and what happens to the [Watergate] trial September 30. The thing that bothers me is how to handle the problem as it affects those individuals who apparently carried out his [Nixon's] orders in the Watergate incident. I think Ford has left many questions open ... I would think most Americans are rather shocked. The issue transcends politics. It goes to the heart of our system of justice and goes beyond Republican and Democratic politics ... I would hate to be a prosecuting attorney trying to get a conviction in a Watergate-related case, when all the defense attorney has to do is ask the jury to do the same thing President Ford did in the case and pardon the defendants.

Atlanta, Sept. 8/ The Atlanta Constitution, 9-9:(C)1.

Leon Jaworski
Lawyer; Special government prosecutor for Watergate

4

Without pointing the finger of guilt at anyone, there already have been enough public admissions of wrongdoing to make what is known as Watergate a dark and tragic episode in the illustrious history of this nation. It is not the first ignominy our nation has had to bear, although its dimensions are of particularly unusual proportion. Let us hope on this day we so proudly observe [Independence Day] that there will never be another such calamitous burden to shoulder in our affairs of government.

Before Junior Bar of Texas, San Antonio, July 4/San Francisco Examiner, 7-5:8.

5

... in his public statements, as we all know, the President [Nixon] has embraced the Constitution as offering him support for his refusal to supply the subpoenaed [Watergate-related White House] tapes. Now, the President may be right in how he reads the Constitution [regarding Executive privilege]. But he may also be

(LEON JAWORSKI)

wrong. And if he is wrong, who is there to tell him so? And if there is no one, then the President, of course, is free to pursue his course of erroneous interpretations. What then becomes of our constitutional form of government? . . . this nation's constitutional form of government is in serious jeopardy if the President, any President, is to say that the Constitution means what he says it does, and that there is no one, not even the Supreme Court, to tell him otherwise.

Before the Supreme Court, Washington, July 8/The Washington Post, 7-9:(A)12.

1

[On President Ford's pre-indictment pardon of former President Nixon for any possible Watergate crimes]: It's a mistake to believe there would have been more evidence for the public if he had been tried. If he had been pardoned after indictment, the public would have had no new information. If he had gone to trial, he could have invoked his Fifth Amendment guarantees against self-incrimination, pleaded *nolo contendere* or even pleaded guilty, and we wouldn't have learned any new details.

Interview/Los Angeles Times, 10-17:(1)25.

Earl Johnson
Professor of Law,
University of Southern California   2

[Disagreeing with those who say that sentences for those convicted in Watergate have been too lenient]: All of these [convicted] men have already been subjected to disgrace and humiliation just by being discovered and prosecuted and convicted. They've been stripped of their power and influence and their status and good name. Some of them may lose their license to practice law. All of them will be stigmatized for life. That is not only sufficient punishment for the individuals involved, it's also more than enough to deter future Presidential advisers and others in similarly high places from doing the same thing.

Los Angeles Times, 7-21:(1)20.

Barbara Jordan
United States Representative, D–Texas;
Member, House Judiciary Committee   3

. . . everybody ought to regret the Watergate and all that word has come to mean. Nobody ought to take comfort in what we are going through in terms of investigations and indictments and trials. One should regret that it happened—then try to find out why. What is it about the American political system which allowed this kind of event to occur? If you find out what it is which allowed it, then maybe we can prevent it in the future. It ought to be an opportunity for a cleansing experience for the political process, and I view it that way. If we don't find out why it happened and how it happened and try to change it—whatever it is— then we leave ourselves open for its reoccurrence in terms of the law, the system, campaign tactics and political rules of operation. And that's what I'm talking about. I'm not talking about "who went to the door and unlocked it or broke in?" I'll let the police reports deal with that. But what I want to know is what is it in the political system that was so soft that this kind of an event could occur?

Interview, Washington/
The Christian Science Monitor, 3-18:6.

4

Beginning shortly after the Watergate break-in and continuing to the present time, the President [Nixon] has engaged in a series of public statements and actions designed to thwart the lawful investigation by government prosecutors. Moreover, the President has made public announcements and assertions bearing on the Watergate case which the evidence will show he knew to be false . . . James Madison said . . . at the Constitutional Convention: "A President is impeachable if he attempts to subvert the Constitution." The Constitution charges the President with the task of taking care that the laws be faithfully executed; and yet the President has counselled his aides to commit perjury, willfully disregarded the secrecy of grand-jury proceedings, concealed surreptitious entry, attempted to compromise a Federal judge while publicly displaying his cooperation with the processes of criminal justice . . . If the impeachment provision in the Constitution of the United States will not reach the offenses charged here, then perhaps that 18th-century Constitution should be abandoned to a 20th-century paper shredder. Has the President committed offenses and planned and directed and acquiesced in a course of conduct which the Constitution will not tolerate? That is the question. We know that. We know the question. We should now forthwith proceed to answer the question. It is reason and not passion which must guide our deliberations, guide our debate, and guide our decision.

At House Judiciary Committee hearing, Washington, July 25/ The Washington Post, 7-27:(A)14.

Edward M. Kennedy
United States Senator, D—Massachusetts
1

[Criticizing President Ford's pre-indictment pardon of former President Nixon for any possible Watergate crimes]: Instead of turning away from Watergate, instead of building on the record of the first weeks in office, instead of setting standards of respect for the office of the President, the premature pardon of the former President has sown new doubts. Do we operate under a system of equal justice where there is one system for the average citizen and another for the high and mighty? It is the wrong time and the wrong place and the wrong person to receive a pre-indictment pardon. And it has led many Americans to believe that it was a culmination of the Watergate cover-up.

Before Brotherhood of Painters and Allied Trades, Los Angeles, Sept. 13/ Los Angeles Times, 9-14:(2)1.

Delbert L. Latta
United States Representative, R—Ohio; Member, House Judiciary Committee
2

No man can foresee the consequences of a President's impeachment and removal by a Congress controlled by an opposition party. Would this mean that future Congresses with heavy political majorities would be more apt to initiate, or threaten to initiate, impeachment proceedings against a President of a different political faith, just to make certain that he adhered to their wishes? Wouldn't the mere thought of impeachment by an opposition Congress cause future Presidents to tailor their acts to the wishes of the Congress, thereby weakening the office of the Presidency? All must agree that today's world demands strength, not weakness, in the office of the President of the United States . . . If the Committee decides to recommend impeachment of the President [Nixon] based on the wrongdoing of others, the evidence is here, and it's clear and convincing. If the Committee decides to recommend impeachment based on direct evidence of Presidential involvement in wrongdoing, the evidence is not here. The case is that simple.

At House Judiciary Committee hearing, Washington/ U.S. News & World Report, 8-5:60.

Clare Boothe Luce
Former American diplomat and playwright
3

Watergate is the great liberal illusion that we can have public virtue without private morality . . . When the moral consensus, based on religion, collapses among the people, it is not surprising that it also collapses at the top.

The Dallas Times Herald, 7-7:(A)25.

4

[On President Ford's pre-indictment pardon of former President Nixon for any possible Watergate crimes]: There is no good time to perform an unpopular action, so the best time is to get it behind you as soon as possible. As Shakespeare said, "If 'tis, 'tis to be done quickly."

Washington/ San Francisco Examiner & Chronicle, 11-3:(Sunday Scene)2.

Jeb Stuart Magruder
1972 deputy director, Committee for the Re-election of the President (Richard M. Nixon)
5

[On his role in Watergate]: I cannot measure the impact on this [Nixon] Administration, or on the nation, of Watergate. Whatever the impact, I am confident that this country will survive its Watergates and its Jeb Magruders . . . .

WHAT THEY SAID IN 1974

(JEB STUART MAGRUDER)

I was ambitious, but I was not without morals or ethics or ideals [when he joined the White House staff in 1969]. There was in me the same blend of ambition and altruism that I saw in many of my peers. Somewhere between my ambitions and my ideals I lost my ethical compass. I found myself on a path that had not been intended for me by my parents or my principles or by my own ethical instincts. It has led me to this courtroom.

*At his sentencing for his part
in Watergate, Washington, May 21/
The New York Times, 5-22:28.*

Mike Mansfield
United States Senator, D—Montana
1

As for the crimes of Watergate—and there were crimes—they cannot be put to rest by Congress. Nor can any words of the President's or from me mitigate them. The disposition of crimes is a function of the Justice Department and the courts. Insofar as I can see, Mr. [Leon] Jaworski, the special [Watergate] prosecutor, is doing his job and so, too, are the courts. There the matter must rest for however long may be necessary. Whether it is months or years, there are no judicial shortcuts. To excise Watergate and what it implies before it becomes fatal to liberty is a fundamental responsibility of this government. The people have a right to an electoral system free of shenanigans, capable of yielding honest, responsible and responsive government, open to all and shaped to meet the needs of all.

*Television address, Washington, Feb. 1/
The New York Times, 2-2:11.*

Tom McCall
Governor of Oregon
2

[Calling for President Nixon's resignation]: A crippled Presidency cannot be allowed to twist in the wind for another three years. Impeachment under present circumstances could well be considered as a denial of due process. Here is a case where the jury is rigged in advance. If this were a court proceeding, not one member of Congress would be allowed to serve.

So if the President is impeached and convicted, his supporters might well say that nothing else could be expected of a bunch of Democrats who are a majority in Congress.

*Before Commonwealth Club,
San Francisco, April 12/
Los Angeles Herald-Examiner, 4-13:(A)2.*

Robert McClory
*United States Representative, R—Illinois;
Member, House Judiciary Committee*
3

I've heard it said by some that they cannot understand how a Republican could vote to impeach a Republican President [Nixon]. Let me hasten to assert that that argument demeans my role here . . . Preserving our Republican Party does not to my mind imply that we must preserve and justify a man in office who would deliberately and arbitrarily defy the legal processes of the Congress, nor can our Party be enhanced if we as Republican members of the United States House of Representatives tolerate the flouting of our laws by a President who is Constitutionally charged with seeing that the laws are faithfully executed as provided in Article 2 . . .

*At House Judiciary Committee hearing,
Washington/Newsweek, 8-5:31.*

John J. McLaughlin
*Deputy Special Assistant to President
of the United States Richard M. Nixon*
4

[On the release by the White House of tape transcripts of President Nixon's Watergate conversations with his aides]: I think that the Presidency has been enfeebled. I think it has been enfeebled by the disclosure of the transcripts of the tapes. It was my view . . . that the President should not have made available to Judge [John] Sirica tapes or transcripts. I share the view of the Constitutional jurist of Yale University, Charles L. Black, Jr., who says that the President has not only the lawful privilege, but indeed the moral obligation to refrain from responding to subpoenas. Mr. Black points out that the Founding Fathers insisted on secrecy, and it was the very first act of their national Constitutional Convention proceedings. He points out that the Supreme Court in its deliberations meets in absolute secrecy. I share the view that the confidentiality of Presidential discussions must be maintained. I also felt that, if he were to make one tape available, how does he then stop?

News briefing/The National Observer, 5-18:13.

Edward Mezvinsky
United States Representative, D—Iowa;
Member, House Judiciary Committee

1

[On the impeachment inquiry against President Nixon being undertaken by the House Judiciary Committee]: I realize this is a decision not just affecting a President, Richard Nixon, or a year, 1974, but it's going to affect the Presidency and the rest of the decade, if not the century. And I know now it has got to be faced. The greatest weakness of institutions is lack of accountability. We're the vehicle—the Committee—to attempt to restore accountability to the system and lay it out to the people, to restore faith. The mere fact that a President has to say, "I am not a crook," is an indication how far we've fallen and why we have to act.

The New York Times Magazine, 4-28:109.

Robert H. Michel
United States Representative, R—Illinois

2

[On President Nixon and his aides implicated in Watergate]: This is not the kind of man I was recommending [when he supported Nixon in the 1972 election campaign]. These are not the men I ever imagined, in my wildest dreams, would be coming to power. I agonize about it all the time. It's been one of the most wrenching experiences in my political life. In 1972 I'd answered charges that the Administration wasn't doing this or that. In summing up, I'd say to people, "You're entitled to your feeling, but one thing's for sure: There's been absolutely no taint of scandal attached to our Administration." And then to find out that what I was saying was very hollow words because I didn't know what was going on. You have a real wrenching feeling inside, an agonizing turmoil type of thing that causes you all kinds of stress and strain. You want to throw in the sponge yourself; but you sleep over it and

get up the next morning and your wife gives you a word of encouragement: "You've got your own field to plow; go out and be the same old Bob."

Interview, Washington/
The New York Times, 5-12:(4)2.

Clarence Mitchell
Director, Washington, D.C.,
bureau, National Association
for the Advancement of Colored People

3

[Saying the NAACP should not take a stand favoring impeachment of President Nixon]: ... no matter how I feel about the President—remember, I was on the White House "enemies" list—I just don't believe you should set a precedent that might rise to haunt us later on ... Some of us have lived through experiences when emotions ran so high that there was no way you could defend a man. [You'd] be cut down and killed for saying that a man deserved a fair trial. When you think of that spirit running on a national scale, it's a very sobering thing.

The Washington Post, 1-21:(A)8.

Walter F. Mondale
United States Senator, D—Minnesota

4

[On President Ford's pre-indictment pardon of former President Nixon for any possible Watergate crimes]: We don't even know what acts by Mr. Nixon the President is pardoning, because all the facts and all the evidence are not yet available. Now, without the help of the legal process, we may never know the full dimensions of Mr. Nixon's complicity in the worst political scandal in American history, even though the pardon itself is further evidence of his direct involvement.

Sept. 8/The New York Times, 9-9:25.

Richard M. Nixon
President of the United States

5

[On attempts to impeach him]: There is a time to be timid. There is a time to be conciliatory. There is a time, even, to fly and there is a time to fight. And I'm going to fight like hell.

Before Republican Congressmen,
Washington, Jan. 22/
The New York Times, 1-27:(4)1.

WHAT THEY SAID IN 1974

(RICHARD M. NIXON)

1

Under no circumstances could I consider resignation. We cannot allow government to be overtaken by a mass assault on the Presidency . . . we cannot have a convulsion in the greatest nation in the world.

Before Republican Congressmen,
Washington, Jan. 22/Time, 2-4:13.

2

There are those who, I think very logically, would raise the question: Well, why not give the members of the [House] Judiciary Committee the right to come in and have all the tapes of every Presidential conversation, a fishing license or a complete right to go in and go through all the Presidential files in order to find out whether or not there is a possibility that some action had been taken which might be and might result in an impeachable offense? The reason why we cannot go that far, the reason why we have gone probably as far as we have and even in going that far have weakened the office of the Presidency, is very simply this: It isn't the question that the President has something to hide. It is the fact that every President—Democrat and Republican, from the founding of this republic—has recognized the necessity of protecting the confidentiality of Presidential conversations with his associates, with those who come to see him—be they Congressmen or Senators or people from various parts of the country to give advice—and if that confidentiality principle is completely destroyed, future Presidents will not have the benefit of the kind of advice that an Executive needs to make the right decision. He will be surrounded by a group of eunuchs insofar as their advice is concerned, always fearful that sometime in the future, if they happen to give an opinion which turned out to be wrong, that then they would be held responsible for it. Wrong, I'm not referring to being illegal, but wrong in terms of whether or not it worked. In order to make the right decision, you have to have opinion expressed very freely, discussed very freely from a completely wide range. And it is that confidentiality that Presidents have

fought for, that Jefferson fought for and other Presidents through the years.

Before Executive Club, Chicago, March 15/
The New York Times, 3-16:12.

3

I'm sure that many people in this audience have read at one time or other, either in news magazines, possibly in a newspaper, certainly heard on television and radio, such charges as this: that the President helped to plan the Watergate thing before and had knowledge [of] it; that the President was informed of the cover-up on September 15 of 1973; that the President was informed that payments were being made on March 13, rather than on March the 21st when I said was the first time those matters were brought to my attention; that the President had authorized the issuance of clemency or a promise of clemency to some of the defendants; and that the President had ordered the burglarizing—again, a very stupid act, apart from the fact that it's wrong and illegal—of Dr. [Daniel] Ellsberg's psychiatrist's office in California. Now, all of those charges have been made. Many Americans—perhaps a majority—believe them. They are all totally false, and the investigation will prove it . . .

Before Executive Club, Chicago, March 15/
The New York Times, 3-16:12.

4

[On the possibility of his resigning]: From the standpoint of statesmanship, for a President of the United States, any President, to resign because of charges made against him which he knew were false, and because he had fallen in the polls, I think would be not statesmanship. It might be good politics, but it would be bad statesmanship. And it would mean that our system of government would be changed for all Presidents and all generations in the future. What I mean by that, very simply, is this: The Constitution provides a method by which a President can be removed from office—impeachment. Impeachment for treason and other high crimes and misdemeanors. Now, if a President is not guilty of those crimes, if only charges have been made which he knows are false, and if simply because as a result of those false charges and as a result of his falling in the polls he decides to resign, it would mean then that every future President would be presiding over a very unstable government in the United States of America. The United States and the free world, the whole world, needs a strong American President—not an American President who every time the polls [go] down says, well, maybe I'd better resign.

Before National Association of Broadcasters, Houston, March 19/ The New York Times, 3-20:28.

1

As people look back to the year[s] of the '70s, Watergate will be written about as being something very difficult to understand, particularly coming in the campaign of an individual who is supposed to be a political pro, which I am. But as often said, I was so busy in the year '72—and this is not said in justification, it is only said by way of truth—I was so busy with my overriding concern to get the [Vietnam] war brought to an end, to do the right things on the domestic side that had to be done, that I frankly didn't pay any attention to the [re-election] campaign. In years past, I have been criticized because I always ran my own campaigns; and sometimes I lost, perhaps because I didn't have anybody else running it for me adequately. In 1972—I don't mean to throw off on those who ran the campaign; they meant well—but I can assure you that, had I been spending the time on the day-to-day operations of this campaign and getting the reports that I always insisted on in my previous campaigns, Watergate would never have happened. [Former Attorney General and Nixon re-election chief] John Mitchell put it pretty well. They asked him [during the Watergate investigation], "Did you tell the President [about what was happening in Watergate during the campaign]?" He said, "No." They said, "Why not?" He said, "Well, because I thought he would blow his stack." Well, he was right; I would have.

Interview, Washington, May 13/ The New York Times, 7-18:20.

2

[My resignation or impeachment] would have a very detrimental effect on our political system for years to come due to the fact that it would weaken the Presidency. It would mean that every President in the future, as he sits in this office, would be afraid to make unpopular decisions; and most of the great decisions that have been made in our history have been unpopular, and have been made by strong men. The moment that a President is looking over his shoulder down to Capitol Hill before he makes a decision, he then will be a weak President and he will always come down on the side of what appears to be the popular move rather than being a strong President coming down on the side of what is right for this country. For that reason, among others, I must fight the impeachment, and I must, of course, as everybody knows, refuse to resign . . . if I do not fight, if I were to run away or walk off the job, and if I do not fight the impeachment as it comes before the House in some form or other, I would leave to my successor—be he Democrat or Republican, not just the next one, but for all time to come—a precedent of a man mortally weakened from this process of destroying a President who was not guilty of a high crime or misdemeanor. If that were to succeed, this office will never then have the strong President that is needed.

Interview, Washington, May 13/ The New York Times, 7-18:20.

3

. . . I am often asked, "How do you really take the burden of the Presidency, particularly when at times it seems to be under very, very grave assault?" Let me say it isn't new for us to be under assault [such as in the current Watergate affair], because since the time I came into office, for five years, we have had problems. There have been people marching around the White House when we were trying to bring the [Vietnam] war to an end, and we have withstood that and we will withstand the problems of the future. People wonder, how does any individual these days, when we have very high-pressure campaigns in the media to take on public figures, how does any individual take it, how does he survive it, how does he keep his composure, his strength and the rest? [I have been able to survive the Watergate onslaught because] I have a strong family and I am very

(RICHARD M. NIXON)

proud of it; I have a lot of good friends who write and call and say, "We're sticking with you." I assure you no man in public life has ever had a more loyal group of friends who stood by in good and tough days . . .

At dinner in his honor, Los Angeles,
July 21/San Francisco Examiner, 7-22:11.

1

[Admitting he withheld from investigators tape transcripts which implicated him in a Watergate cover-up] : On April 29, in announcing my decision to make public the original set of White House transcripts, I stated that "as far as what the President personally knew and did with regard to Watergate and the cover-up is concerned, these materials—together with those already made available—will tell it all." Shortly after that, in May, I made a preliminary review of some of the 64 taped conversations subpoenaed by the special prosecutor. Among the conversations I listened to at that time were two of those of June 23 [1972]. Although I recognized that these presented potential problems, I did not inform my staff or my counsel of it, or those arguing my case, nor did I amend my submission to the [House] Judiciary Committee in order to include and reflect it. At the time, I did not realize the extent of the implications which these conversations might now appear to have. As a result, those arguing my case, as well as those passing judgment on the case, did so with information that was incomplete and, in some respects, erroneous. This was a serious act of omission for which I take full responsibility and which I deeply regret . . . Whatever mistakes I made in the handling of Watergate, the basic truth remains that, when all the facts were brought to my attention, I insisted on a full investigation and prosecution of those guilty. I am firmly convinced that the record, in its entirety, does not justify the extreme step of impeachment and removal of a President. I trust that, as the Constitutional process goes forward, this perspective will prevail.

Aug. 5 *
The National Observer, 8-17:E.

[Full text of President Nixon's resignation address] :

This is the 37th time I have spoken to you from this office in which so many decisions have been made that shape the history of this nation.

Each time I have done so to discuss with you some matters that I believe affected the national interest. And all the decisions I have made in my public life I have always tried to do what was best for the nation.

Throughout the long and difficult period of Watergate, I have felt it was my duty to persevere; to make every possible effort to complete the term of office to which you elected me.

In the past few days, however, it has become evident to me that I no longer have a strong enough political base in the Congress to justify continuing that effort.

As long as there was such a base, I felt strongly that it was necessary to see the constitutional process through to its conclusion; that to do otherwise would be unfaithful to the spirit of that deliberately difficult process, and a dangerously destabilizing precedent for the future.

But with the disappearance of that base, I now believe that the constitutional purpose has been served. And there is no longer a need for the process to be prolonged.

I would have preferred to carry through to the finish whatever the personal agony it would have involved, and my family unanimously urged me to do so.

Interests of the Nation

But the interests of the nation must always come before any personal considerations. From the discussions I have had with Congressional and other leaders I have concluded that because of the Watergate matter I might not have the support of the Congress that I would consider necessary to back the very difficult decisions and carry out the duties of this office in the way the interests of the nation will require.

I have never been a quitter.

To leave office before my term is completed is opposed to every instinct in my body. But as President I must put the interests of America first.

America needs a full-time President and a full-time Congress, particularly at this time with problems we face at home and abroad.

To continue to fight through the months ahead for my personal vindication would almost totally absorb the time and attention of both the President and the Congress in a period when our entire focus should be on the great issues of peace abroad and prosperity without inflation at home.

Therefore, I shall resign the Presidency effective at noon tomorrow.

Vice President Ford will be sworn in as President at that hour in this office.

Confidence in Ford

As I recall the high hopes for America with which we began this second term, I feel a great sadness that I will not be here in this office working on your behalf to achieve those hopes in the next two and a half years.

But in turning over direction of the Government to Vice President Ford I know, as I told the nation when I nominated him for that office 10 months ago, that the leadership of America will be in good hands.

In passing this office to the Vice President I also do so with the profound sense of the weight of responsibility that will fall on his shoulders tomorrow, and therefore of the understanding, the patience, the cooperation he will need from all Americans.

As he assumes that responsibility, he will deserve the help and the support of all of us. As we look to the future, the first essential is to begin healing the wounds of this nation. To put the bitterness and divisions of the recent past behind us and to rediscover those shared ideals that lie at the heart of our strength and unity as a great and as a free people.

By taking this action, I hope that I will have hastened the start of that process of healing which is so desperately needed in America.

I regret deeply any injuries that may have been done in the course of the events that led to this decision. I would say only that if some of my judgments were wrong—and some were wrong—they were made in what I believed at the time to be the best interests of the nation.

To those who have stood with me during these past difficult months, to my family, my friends, the many others who've joined in supporting my cause because they believed it was right, I will be eternally grateful for your support.

And to those who have not felt able to give me your support, let me say I leave with no bitterness toward those who have opposed me, because all of us in the final analysis have been concerned with the good of the country however our judgments might differ.

So let us all now join together in affirming that common commitment and in helping our new President succeed for the benefit of all Americans.

I shall leave this office with regret at not completing my term but with gratitude for the privilege of serving as your President for the past five and a half years.

These years have been a momentous time in the history of our nation and the world. They have been a time of achievement in which we can all be proud—achievements that represent the shared efforts of the Administration, the Congress and the people. But the challenges ahead are equally great.

And they, too, will require the support and the efforts of a Congress and the people, working in cooperation with the new Administration.

We have ended America's longest war. But in the work of securing a lasting peace in the world, the goals ahead are even more far-reaching and more difficult. We must complete a structure of peace, so that it will be said of this generation—our generation of Americans—by the people of all nations, not only that we ended one war but that we prevented future wars.

We have unlocked the doors that for a quarter of a century stood between the United States and the People's Republic of China. We must now insure that the one-quarter of the world's people who live in the People's Republic of China will be and remain, not our enemies, but our friends.

Breakthroughs With Russia

In the Middle East, 100 million people in the Arab countries, many of whom have considered us their enemies for nearly 20 years, now look on us as their friends. We must continue to build on that friendship so that peace can settle

(RICHARD M. NIXON)

at last over the Middle East and so that the cradle of civilization will not become its grave.

Together with the Soviet Union we have made the crucial breakthroughs that have begun the process of limiting nuclear arms. But, we must set as our goal, not just limiting, but reducing and finally destroying these terrible weapons so that they cannot destroy civilization.

And so that the threat of nuclear war will no longer hang over the world and the people, we have opened a new relation with the Soviet Union. We must continue to develop and expand that new relationship so that the two strongest nations of the world will live together in cooperation rather than confrontation.

Around the world—in Asia, in Africa, in Latin America, in the Middle East—there are millions of people who live in terrible poverty, even starvation. We must keep as our goal turning away from production for war and expanding production for peace so that people everywhere on this earth can at last look forward, in their children's time if not in our time, to having the necessities for a decent life.

The Good Life

Here in America we are fortunate that most of our people have not only the blessings of liberty but also the means to live full and good, and by the world's standards, even abundant lives.

We must press on, however, toward a goal not only of more and better jobs but of full opportunity for every man, and of what we are striving so hard right now to achieve—prosperity without inflation.

For more than a quarter of a century in public life, I have shared in the turbulent history of this evening.

I have fought for what I believe in. I have tried, to the best of my ability, to discharge those duties and meet those responsibilities that were entrusted to me.

Sometimes I have succeeded. And sometimes I have failed. But always I have taken heart from what Theodore Roosevelt said about the man in the arena whose face is marred by dust and sweat and blood, who strives valiantly, who errs and comes short again and again because there is not effort without error and short-coming, but who does actually strive to do the deed, who knows the great devotion, who spends himself in a worthy cause, who at the best knows in the end the triumphs of high achievements and with the worst if he fails, at least fails while daring greatly.

I pledge to you tonight that as long as I have a breath of life in my body I shall continue in that spirit. I shall continue to work for the great causes to which I have been dedicated throughout my years as a Congressman, a Senator, Vice President and President, the cause of peace—not just for America but among all nations—prosperity, justice and opportunity for all of our people.

There is one cause above all to which I have been devoted and to which I shall always be devoted for as long as I live.

When I first took the oath of office as President five and a half years ago, I made this sacred commitment: to consecrate my office, my energies and all the wisdom I can summon to the cause of peace among nations.

I've done my very best in all the days since to be true to that pledge.

As a result of these efforts, I am confident that the world is a safer place today, not only for the people of America but for the people of all nations, and that all of our children have a better chance than before of living in peace rather than dying in war.

This, more than anything, is what I hoped to achieve when I sought the Presidency. This, more than anything, is what I hope will be my legacy to you, to our country, as I leave the Presidency.

To have served in this office is to have felt a very personal sense of kinship with each and every American. In leaving it, I do so with this prayer: May God's grace be with you in all the days ahead.

Broadcast address to the nation,
Washington, Aug. 8/
The New York Times, 8-9:2.

Richard M. Nixon
Former President of the United States　　*1*

[Addressing his White House staff on his resignation]: We think sometimes when things happen that don't go the right way . . . We think that when someone dear to us dies, we think that when we lose an election, we think that when we suffer a defeat, that all has ended . . . Not true. It's only a beginning, always. The young must know it. The old must know it. It must always sustain us because the greatness comes not when things go always good for you, but the greatness comes and you're really tested when you take some knocks, some disappointments, when sadness comes, because only if you've been in the deepest valley can you ever know how magnificent it is to be on the highest mountain . . . we leave proud of the people who have stood by us and worked for us and served this country. We want you to be proud of what you've done. We want you to continue to serve in government if that is your wish. Always give your best. Never get discouraged. Never be petty. Always remember others may hate you but those who hate you don't win unless you hate them. And then you destroy yourself. And so we leave with high hopes, in good spirits and with deep humility and with very much gratefulness in our hearts. I can only say to each and every one of you: We come from many faiths; we pray, perhaps, to different gods, but really the same God in a sense. But I'll have to say for each and every one of you, not only will we always remember you, not only will we always be grateful to you, but always you will be in our hearts and you will be in our prayers.

At White House staff gathering,
Washington, Aug. 9/
The New York Times, 8-10:4.

1

[*Full text of his response to President Ford's pardoning him for any possible Watergate crimes*]: I have been informed that President Ford has granted me a full and absolute pardon for any charges which might be brought against me for actions taken during the time I was President of the United States. In accepting this pardon, I hope his compassionate act will contribute to lifting the burden of Watergate from our country. Here in California, my perspective on Watergate is quite different than it was while I was embattled in the midst of the contro-

versy, and while I was still subject to the unrelenting daily demands of the Presidency itself. Looking back on what is still in my mind a complex and confusing maze of events, decisions, pressures and personalities, one thing I can see clearly now is that I was wrong in not acting more decisively and forthrightly in dealing with Watergate, particularly when it reached the stage of judicial proceedings and grew from a political scandal into a national tragedy. No words can describe the depths of my regret and pain at the anguish my mistakes over Watergate have caused the nation and the Presidency—a nation I so deeply love and an institution I so greatly respect. I know many fair-minded people believe that my motivations and actions in the Watergate affair were intentionally self-serving and illegal. I now understand how my own mistakes and misjudgments have contributed to that belief and seemed to support it. This burden is the heaviest one of all to bear. That the way I tried to deal with Watergate was the wrong way is a burden I shall bear for every day of the life that is left to me.

San Clemente, Calif., Sept. 8/
Los Angeles Times, 9-9:(1)13.

Louis Nizer
Lawyer

2

[Saying the fact that Nixon Administration aides implicated in Watergate were lawyers should not reflect badly on the legal profession]: None of these people, with maybe one exception, was a practicing lawyer. They were political figures who happened to have a law degree. What Watergate showed was that some very young men were so awed by being under the auspices of the White House or the Attorney General that they forgot to say "no" when something was wrong. They lost their sense of discrimination. And this is a great tragedy. But it shouldn't be a condemnation of the legal profession.

Interview/San Francisco Examiner, 5-29:35.

Sam Nunn
United States Senator, D—Georgia

3

People tell me they wish I'd worry more about energy and the economy and less about

(SAM NUNN)

Watergate. This is not to say they don't deplore Watergate. But people down here want to keep things in perspective. They want the truth, but they don't want to kill the country. They don't want to wake up six months from now to be told, "Okay, we've got all the truth about Watergate, but now we've got you a depression."

Time, 1-14:12.

Charles H. Percy
United States Senator, R—Illinois   *1*

We [Republicans] must not put ourselves in the position of even seeming to condone or gloss over the misdeeds of Watergate. In no way, shape or form is Watergate what the Republican Party is all about; and we'd better make damn sure the American people understand it, or our Party will be paying for that "third-rate burglary" for decades to come.

At Lincoln Day dinner, Chicago, Feb. 8/
The New York Times, 2-10:(1)29.

2

[On the reluctance of the White House to supply material requested and subpoenaed by Watergate investigators]: I continue to see reluctance, dragging of feet, almost what might be considered the hindrance of justice, and obstruction to justice. On the one hand, the word's being said [by the White House], "Let's get Watergate behind us," and then everything possible is being done to prolong it, rather than get it out on the table—to drag it out. And I feel that we are moving toward a very dangerous position of confrontation if the subpoenas of both the House and the special prosecutor are not fully lived up to. There is a chance now that justice is being impeded. I know, for instance, that the work of the grand juries is being impeded and slowed-up because [special prosecutor Leon] Jaworski in a letter to me this week indicated that much in those same words. The White House seems to be setting up itself as the judge as to what the special prosecutor should have, when Mr. Jaworski has clearly indicated to me that the White House is not privy to the scope of the investigation he is conducting and therefore cannot be the judge

as to what evidence he needs in order to carry out his responsibilities.

TV-radio interview/"Issues and Answers,"
American Broadcasting Company, 4-21.

Otis G. Pike
United States Representative, D—New York   *3*

[On the transcripts of taped conversations between President Nixon and his aides on Watergate, which were recently released by the White House]: The tone is appalling. When you realize any editing that was done was obviously not done to make it sound worse, you just wonder what on earth the unedited things could possibly say that would be worse than what you've got. The image of a bunch of people in the Oval Office sitting around discussing various ways they could appear to be forthcoming ... at the same time doing everything they could *not* to be forthcoming ... When you compare the President's public statements at any given date with private conversations immediately prior, you know the public statements didn't mean what they said.

Interview, May 6/
The Washington Post, 5-7:(A)25.

Ronald Reagan
Governor of California   *4*

[On the moral tone and profanity contained in White House-released tape transcripts of Watergate-related conversations between President Nixon and his aides]: It was just a rude shock. It was a little bit like seeing civilization with its pants down to suddenly see a man, sitting with his most intimate counsellors and associates in a room, obviously talking in ways that none of them would ever talk out in public.

Interview/San Francisco Examiner, 5-31:10.

5

[On President Nixon's admission that he withheld from investigators White House tapes which implicated him in a Watergate cover-up]: Until yesterday, I was not convinced that evidence of an impeachable offense had been presented to the Congress or the people. Now, for the first time, it has been revealed that neither the Congress nor the American people had been told the entire truth about Watergate. In view of the President's statement yesterday, I believe it is absolutely imperative that he go before the Congress immediately and make a full disclosure of all the information he has on this matter, answering any and all questions the members may have. The Constitutional process should then go forward in order to bring about a speedy resolution of this issue. The American people are entitled to this as well as to the whole truth—once and for all.

News conference, Sacramento, Aug. 6/
Los Angeles Times, 8-7:(1)27.

John J. Rhodes
United States Representative, R—Arizona
1

[On President Nixon's admission that he withheld evidence implicating him in a Watergate cover-up]: For me, this is a sad day. I admire Richard Nixon for the great many things he has done for the people of America and the people of the world. I have no doubt whatsoever that the final analysis of history will be that few American Presidents did more for the solid advancement of world peace than Richard Nixon. But the most important aspect of our entire system of government is equal justice under the law—the principle that no person, whether he be rich or poor, black or white, ordinary citizen or President, is above the law. Cover-up of criminal activity and misuse of Federal agencies can neither be condoned nor tolerated. And as long as we adhere as a nation to this principle, our nation will remain great and strong. I have considered the evidence to the best of my ability. When the roll is called in the House of Representatives, I will vote "aye" on impeachment Article I.

News conference, Washington, Aug. 6/
The Washington Post, 8-7:(A)11.

2

[Agreeing with President Ford's pre-indictment pardon of former President Nixon for any possible Watergate crimes]: No man is above the law, but the law is purposely flexible so as to accommodate varying degrees of reality and circumstance. Richard M. Nixon has paid a substantial price for whatever transgressions may

have occurred during his Administration. Anything further would be more overkill than justice, and not be in the national interest.

Sept. 8/The Washington Post, 9-9:(A)1.

Elliot L. Richardson
Former Attorney General of the United States
3

[On the underlying cause of Watergate]: It comes down really to a set of attitudes toward the conduct of the Presidency and the political process—attitudes that this is an adversarial process. The more you look at it in these terms, the more you find it permissible to use tactics that would be used against an enemy. I think this has been a limitation of the Nixon Presidency . . . the tragic flaw of his Presidency.

At breakfast meeting with reporters,
Washington, Jan. 22/
The Washington Post, 1-23:(A)6.

4

[Reflecting on the possible impeachment of President Nixon]: I think an impeachable offense is an action, or a failure to act, which involves the gross abuse of authority or the neglect of responsibility. It may or may not include an offense that is indictable under the U.S. penal code. It seems to me that the framers of the Constitution could not have intended to confine impeachable offenses to those that are specific crimes . . . It would seem clear on the face of it that a President could be guilty of acts that justified his removal because they so flagrantly undercut his official responsibilities and yet not come within the specific language of any crime.

News conference, Sacramento, Calif.,
Feb. 27/Los Angeles Times, 2-28:(1)32.

5

[On former Nixon White House aides' connection with Watergate]: They really didn't know what politics was about. Most of their experience was from being advance-men. They thought that everything was manipulable . . . This kind of calculating approach fails to realize that you can't play a three-cornered billiard shot in a country like this, unless the table is warped and the cues are pitted. When I see someone like that, it impresses me not merely

WHAT THEY SAID IN 1974

(ELLIOT L. RICHARDSON)

as cynical, but as the kind of amateur I used to associate with what we called "drugstore cowboys."

At Federal City Club, Washington, March 5/The Washington Post, 3-7:(B)3.

1

[On White House-released tape transcripts of Watergate-related conversations between President Nixon and his staff]: I was depressed. I was surprised. I was dismayed by the exhibition of a save-our-own-skins attitude which seemed oblivious of the moral elements of the situation or the claims of the judicial process or the national interest itself... I had seen in the President glimpses of a kind of tendency to think of the [political] opposition as the enemy, and had from time to time tried to encourage a broader, more magnanimous outlook in written memoranda and in some contact with him and his staff and in some conversations. But I didn't realize, I always thought it was episodic or aberrant rather than chronic and usual. But I think this is a considerable part of the problem as we see it in the present perspective.

Interview/Washington/ The Christian Science Monitor, 5-30:1.

Nelson A. Rockefeller
Former Governor of New York

2

I deplore Watergate. I feel as badly as anyone in the country about it because I spent my life in politics. And integrity is the essence of effective political action.

Interview, New York, Feb. 11/ The Washington Post, 2-13:(A)2.

3

[On the resignation of President Nixon]: Out of the traumatic events of these past two years has emerged an awareness of the extraordinary strengths and stability of the American people and a renewed awareness of the wisdom of the Founding Fathers and the unique constitutional system they created. They have nobly withstood the unprecedented pressures and strains, and we have emerged with our freedoms intact and the same rule of law—applying with

an even hand from the humblest citizen to the highest office-holder—still the predominating force in American life.

At Republican fund-raising dinner, Bangor, Maine, Aug. 9/ Los Angeles Times, 8-10:(1)8.

Peter W. Rodino, Jr.
United States Representative, D–New Jersey; Chairman, House Judiciary Committee

4

[On the Judiciary Committee's consideration of impeachment of President Nixon]: Let us be clear about this: No official, no concerned citizen, no Representative, no member of this Committee welcomes an impeachment proceeding. No one welcomes the day when there has been such a crisis of concern that he must decide whether "high crimes and misdemeanors," serious abuses of official power or violations of public trust have in fact occurred. Let us also be clear: Our own public trust, our own commitment to the Constitution, is being put to the test. Such tests, historically, have come to the awareness of most people too late—when their rights and freedoms under law were already so far in jeopardy and eroded that it was no longer in the people's power to restore constitutional government by democratic means. Let us go forward. Let us go forward into debate in good will, with honor and decency and with respect for the views of one another. Whatever we now decide, we must have the integrity and the decency, the will and the courage, to decide rightly. Let us leave the Constitution as unimpaired for our children as our predecessors left it to us.

At House Judiciary Committee proceeding, Washington, July 24/ Los Angeles Times, 7-25:(1)24.

Eugene V. Rostow
Professor of Law and Public Affairs, Yale University

5

[Saying a President should be removed from office by impeachment only for criminal offenses]: We now have 200 years of experience since the Founding Fathers. It would be the greatest possible error... for us to move toward a system in which the ultimate authority of the Presidency depended not on a national election but on the majority of the moment in Congress. [Members of the Nixon Administration guilty of crimes in Watergate should be punished, but the] independence of the Presidency ... should never be compromised or diluted. [It is] indispensable to the health and effectiveness of our Constitutional order.

The National Observer, 2-16:14.

1

[On President Nixon's invoking of Executive privilege in refusing to release certain documents in the Watergate case]: Executive privilege exists—I neither deny it or oppose it. You can't run a government without it ... But it has to be adapted to the issue. If the functional problem is impeachment, everything relevant must be given. You can't have a man be the judge of his own case—that's the key issue.

The Christian Science Monitor, 5-7:2.

Anwar el-Sadat
President of Egypt

2

It would be a real tragedy for our area and for the world if he [President Nixon] were impeached, because ... [this] is the first time that we see in the Middle East—which holds vast American interests—a new approach to the solution of our problems. This is the doing of the Nixon Administration, make no mistake about it ... Yes, it would indeed be a terrible tragedy if the American people lost sight of the global picture for the sake of narrow domestic political considerations.

Interview, Borg el Arab, Egypt/
Newsweek, 3-25:44.

James D. St. Clair
Special Counsel to President of the
United States Richard M. Nixon

3

... the President [Nixon] did not delegate to the special [Watergate] prosecutor [Leon Jaworski] the right to tell him whether or not his confidential [taped] communications should be made available as evidence. The right to order the President to give up confidential

communications—that was not delegated. A special prosecutor with the power that [Jaworski] suggests he has is a Constitutional anomaly. We have only three branches [of government], not three-and-a-third or three-and-a-half or four. There is only one Executive Branch. And the Executive power is vested in a President. Now, if for political reasons the President wants to dole out some of those powers, he may do so, and has done in this case. But he cannot vest jurisdiction in a court that otherwise the court would not have. Nor should the [Supreme] Court accept jurisdiction.

Before Supreme Court, Washington,
July 8/The New York Times, 7-9:25.

Charles W. Sandman, Jr.
United States Representative, R—New Jersey;
Member, House Judiciary Committee

4

[Arguing against impeachment of President Nixon]: History tells me that 107 years ago the country was thrown into a fit of hysteria and, in less than three days, President [Andrew] Johnson was impeached during that fit of hysteria. That has gone down in history as one of the darkest moments in the government of this great nation; and I do not propose to be any part of a second blotch on the history of this great nation ... The President should be removed only for the most serious offense ... To do otherwise would place a mechanism in the hands of a majority party that any time they choose they could throw the country into a turmoil and replace the Chief Executive, and that should never happen ... Now, many wrongs have been committed [in Watergate], no question about it; but were those things directed by the President? Is there direct evidence that said he had anything to do with it? Of course there is not.

At House Judiciary Committee
hearing, Washington/
U.S. News & World Report, 8-5:58.

William B. Saxbe
Attorney General of the United States

5

The nature of the evil deeds [of Watergate] that are alleged to the President [Nixon] are

(WILLIAM B. SAXBE)

not of an impeachable nature. They're serious as to the moral turpitude of the people involved, and do reflect on the President. The question is one of great indiscretions in areas which, even then, have not been connected to the President, however. To take this before the American people at a time when they're worried about energy, when they're worried about peace in the world, when they're engrossed in their own affairs in a runaway world—and to neglect the business of government while this [impeachment] show goes on in the main tent—seems to me to be the greatest type of foolishness. If we want to wallow in our own misery for the next couple of years, we have this opportunity. However, I think there are enough statesmen in Congress that will not buy this. I think that, unless more-serious evidence is uncovered in the case, we'll look back at this period 20 years or 50 years from now and say, "What in the world were these people doing—to wreck their country, their economy; to demoralize their people—the greatest nation in the world tearing itself apart?" It seems to me we have to get more-concrete evidence or we're never going to be able to satisfy the solid people of this country that there was great maladministration that would warrant the impeachment of a President.

Interview, Washington/
U.S. News & World Report, 2-4:24.

1

We now live under what I believe historians will conclude is the greatest cloud in our history. Its name is short—Watergate. We have come to accept things in public life and in politics that simply have no place there. The list is a long one: lying to the people, twisting the truth, using public position for private gain, failure to do those things which the oath of office requires ... No one in public life or private life can afford to hunker down until the storm of public distrust passes by, because it isn't going to be that easy. The only good that I can see coming out of Watergate is that it will always be there as a goad to our conscience. In its aftermath, we can set about to fashion new

ways, much better ways, of carrying out matters of public trust.

At Ohio State University Law School
commencement, June 6/
Los Angeles Times, 6-7:(1)11.

2

[Saying prison terms for convicted Watergate defendants have been too lenient]: It is hardly reassuring when one man goes to prison for years for theft while another man involved in a conspiracy to steal our freedoms is in and out of jail in the wink of an eye. The message has got to go out all over the country [that] there will be no more dirty tricks, not by anybody for any reason ... As we have seen in Watergate, men who held positions of great power have defaulted on their oaths of office and to the responsibility they owe to the public. Criminal violations cannot be tolerated on the part of anyone—no matter what position of public trust they may have held, no matter how glib their attempts at justification may be.

Before National Association of Attorneys
General, Coeur D'Alene, Idaho, June 24/
Los Angeles Times, 6-25:(1)1,16.

Richard M. Scammon
Public-opinion analyst

3

[On whether Watergate will have a lasting effect on the Presidency]: If we get into a real national crisis, will people turn less to the President for leadership? Would you have fewer correspondents standing outside the White House reporting on the evening TV news? No, I don't think you would. The Presidency is a reverential institution in the United States. Men can be tarnished, but not the Presidency.

Interview, Washington/
U.S. News & World Report, 11-25:38.

Eric Sevareid
News commentator,
Columbia Broadcasting System

4

[On the transcript of White House Watergate conversations between President Nixon and his aides in 1972 and 1973, just released by the President]: All questions of legal incrimination aside ... these pages constitute a moral indictment without known precedent in the story of American government. There is no talk, in these endless conversations, about the welfare of the American people, their faith in their leaders, the nation's reputation in the world; no awareness of what Jefferson was talking about when he invoked a decent respect to the opinions of mankind. There are minimal references to truth, but innumerable conjectures about the most salable publicity techniques for defending themselves. These are men whose minds are irrevocably fixed in the "we or they" view of life and politics, men holding the supreme power in the land, talking like besieged conspirators, men unforgetting, unforgiving, constantly calculating how they can "get" their opponents and critics. They are not interested in destroying their opponents' arguments but in destroying their opponents personally. Mr. Nixon himself talks of using FBI and other agencies to do this. From these pages rises the rancid odor of hatred.

Television commentary/"Evening News,"
Columbia Broadcasting System, 5-1.

1

I think [President] Nixon and the men around him [during the Watergate occurrence] were totally uneducated men. They were skilled lawyers, great at the nuts and bolts, the mechanics of the law, the pragmatic aspects, but they didn't understand the Constitution. They didn't comprehend that every single paragraph was based upon centuries of human suffering. In some of Nixon's speeches, can you find a sense that he was steeped in history, or the great religions of the world, or in the great philosophers, as men like Adlai Stevenson and John Kennedy were? And that's the education that counts. Even [Harry] Truman, who had no college education at all, had a better grasp of history.

Interview, Washington/
"W": a Fairchild publication, 6-14:11.

Laurence H. Silberman
Deputy Attorney General of the United States *2.*

[On President Ford's pre-indictment pardon of former President Nixon for any possible Watergate crimes]: I believe there was con-

sensus among the American people, the press and Congress that Mr. Nixon should not have been incarcerated, that he should be pardoned at some stage. Once you conclude a pardon is appropriate, I find it difficult to justify going through an indictment, trial and conviction, in terms of a criminal-justice purpose . . . I am satisfied that the action of Congress and the view of the people–after all, the President [Nixon] left office in shame and disgrace– constitute ample deterrence to any future President who would be tempted to engage in illegal acts.

Interview, Washington, Sept. 19/
Los Angeles Times, 9-20:(1)21.

Chesterfield Smith
President, American Bar Association *3*

The President [Nixon] should furnish all information requested by the House Judiciary Committee [in its impeachment inquiry], and I don't feel any evidence is subject to Presidential privilege, Presidential privacy or even national security. By claiming Executive privilege, the President is obstructing justice, whether legally or illegally . . . many Americans are suspicious that the President is concealing and misstating the facts. Until Americans believe him, he can't effectively run the country.

Interview, Miami/
San Francisco Examiner, 3-22:8.

Howard K. Smith
News commentator,
American Broadcasting Company *4*

Vice President [Gerald] Ford . . . was wrong in saying that only extremists keep Watergate suspicions alive. What does it is a repeated, soul-trying procedure: Some new facts are revealed–generally not by anti-Nixon people, often by the White House itself–raising suspicious questions; the White House shuts up too long, then finally responds to the questions too late and too lamely, compounding suspicions. Consider the 18-minute hum, obliterating just that part of the [H. R.] Haldeman-Nixon [taped] conversation dealing with Watergate. The White House knew of the hum two months

(HOWARD K. SMITH)

early. Why did it wait till two months late, the day the tape had to be given to Judge Sirica, to reveal the erasure? Whoever erased the vital segment knew he was doing it. An accidental erasure, the experts said, would hardly have been repeated five or nine times. Why was that person not brought forward to admit and explain [the] error in public as soon as it happened? Why ... when it all came out and we asked for an explanation, did the White House go silent? There will be an explanation. It will be late. It will be lame. It will deepen suspicions.

ABC News commentary/
The Christian Science Monitor, 1-21:(F)8.

1

[On President Nixon's resignation]: Most of us are taking comfort today in the thought that, after all, the system works. I truly hate to be a spoilsport. But I think it is important to point out it doesn't work that well. Other nations, we forget, become unhappy with leaders and change them without a fraction of the torture we put ourselves through. In Britain, [Anthony] Eden in the Suez crisis was removed in days; [Willy] Brandt in [West] Germany recently in a few hours. I don't think we can be self-satisfied with a system that works only after tearing us apart for a year and a half. Moreover, it was not really the system that did it. It was a peculiar, one-time thing: Mr. Nixon taped all his private conversations. Had he not done it, and had they not been revealed, all the same misdeeds would have happened, with no change of government. The system would not have helped ... The cause of Watergate is bad campaign finance practice, too much special-interest loot in politics hunting for mischief to do. It kills needed legislation. It dirties politicians. Half a dozen leading Americans are soiled by it in the news right now. More will be in the future. Punishing Mr. Nixon is not enough. The system needs changing. And Congress is moving with unwilling, leaden feet.

ABC News commentary/
The Christian Science Monitor, 8-20:20.

Frank Stanton
Vice chairman,
Columbia Broadcasting System

2

[As] tragic as the news from Washington has been, it offers reassurance that the Constitutional system of checks and balances—alerted, strengthened and impelled by our free institutions—has worked. Our judiciary, our Senate and our Justice Department, aided and in some cases prompted by our vigorous investigative free press, revealed to the American people ... the internal erosion of the high sense of Executive responsibility on an unparalleled scale in our country. Among these institutions, it is the free press to which our nation owes most, in this crisis, for its persistent inquiries and for the revelations of a strange world of intrigue few Americans believed existed outside of fiction.

At University of Southern California
commencement, Jan. 30/
Los Angeles Times, 1-31:(2)1.

John C. Stennis
United States Senator, D–Mississippi

3

[On President Ford's pre-indictment pardon of former President Nixon for any possible Watergate crimes]: I'm in favor of it. Maybe the timing was premature; but as I see it, from where I sit, I think Nixon has had punishment far exceeding anything that anyone in office has ever had. His punishment will be life-long. To me, a forced resignation from the highest office in the land, *that* is the greatest punishment. At least it is to me. I expect that solitude, his solitude, is worse than death. It would be easier to die, in a way. The problem is to live, live ... I agree with President Ford's action. He had to stop the bleeding some time. And he chose to stop it early in his Administration, when he had his most popular public support.

Interview/Parade, 10-20:5.

Adlai E. Stevenson III
United States Senator, D–Illinois

4

[On President Ford's pre-indictment pardon of former President Nixon for any possible

Watergate crimes]: I regret the President's decision because I cherish our system of equal justice. It is poorly served by a decision which excuses a former President, imprisons his subordinates and reinforces a public impression that, for some, justice is less equal than for others.

Sept. 8/Chicago Tribune, 9-9:(1)10.

Robert S. Strauss
Chairman, Democratic National Committee
1

[On the transcripts of Watergate-related taped conversations between President Nixon and his aides which were just released by the White House, and which some people have interpreted as implicating the President in the Watergate cover-up]: I came up through the ranks in politics in Texas. I think I've seen just about everything. I know not all Democrats are pure. Each of our houses has some unclean spots. I've done things I'm not proud of. But this reading of these tapes has upset me more than anything in my life. I told my wife over the third martini last night [that] I'm embarrassed to have our kids read this and think it's part of the life I'm in. Now, that's an interesting reaction from a guy who's no rose. It's saddening; there's no fun in it [for Democrats]. It's sadder and sicker than I ever imagined. I keep looking for some mention [in the transcripts] of the American people, some concern for the nation.

Interview/The New York Times, 5-4:24.

2

[On President Ford's pre-indictment pardon of former President Nixon for any possible Watergate crimes]: What President Ford has done is a travesty to the judicial process. It unhappily raises the question of a calculated move by President Ford to accomplish, during his [Presidential] honeymoon period, an action that he knows would be considered an absolute outrage during other times.

Sept. 8/Los Angeles Times, 9-9:(1)13.

W. S. (Bill) Stuckey, Jr.
United States Representative, D–Georgia
3

[On President Ford's pre-indictment pardon of former President Nixon for any possible Watergate crimes]: I think he [Ford] did the right thing. I think the man [Nixon] has paid enough and I think he will continue to pay the rest of his life. What more can you do to the guy? He paid the price.

The Atlanta Constitution, 9-9:(A)12.

Ray Thornton
United States Representative, D–Arkansas; Member, House Judiciary Committee
4

[On the Judiciary Committee's consideration of impeachment of President Nixon]: I do not enjoy the duty of sitting in judgment on any other man's fulfillment of his oath of office. But I have an oath of office of my own, to decide this grave matter, not on the basis of political interest, but as a matter of conscience, law and Constitutional principle.

At House Judiciary Committee hearing, Washington/The National Observer, 8-3:4.

Morris K. Udall
United States Representative, D–Arizona
5

Our recent problems have given rise to a corrupting lie that must be answered. That lie is that Watergate is nothing unusual, that they all do it, that all your public leaders are crooks and thieves. This is false, my friends, and it's a slander on the American political system.

May 3/The Washington Post, 5-4:(A)10.

Mike Wallace
News correspondent, Columbia Broadcasting System
6

I don't understand how Richard Nixon can take that pressure–that's what I'd like to talk to him about. Not about the facts and allegations of Watergate–but his person, about his psyche, about pressures. I'm convinced that I certainly couldn't withstand his current pressures. I don't mean I want to do any horseback psychoanalysis–I just want to try to understand what has gone on inside this man's mind and heart and body over these last two unrelenting years. But I'm afraid he is neither willing, nor capable, of articulating that in a public way.

Interview, New York/ The Christian Science Monitor, 8-1:11.

WHAT THEY SAID IN 1974

Lowell P. Weicker, Jr.
United States Senator, R—Connecticut;
Member, Senate Watergate Committee   1

I am deeply concerned that, with Watergate not even concluded, the American people, in their anticipation of some new scandal, or in their preoccupation with the guilt or innocence of individuals, are forgetting matters of over-riding importance that have been made known, are indisputable fact and which could over-whelm a democracy. Specifically, I refer to the fact of those institutions of government that have been smeared and defaced almost beyond recognition by a handful of Constitutional delinquents. What took 200 years to build nearly came down in the quest for four more [years of Nixon Presidency].

Before graduating class,
American University, May 12/
The Washington Post, 5-13:(A)4.

2

Do you know what to me was the most surprising, profound and meaningful revelation of Watergate? It was the incredible abuses committed by our law-enforcement and intelligence community—the FBI, the Justice Department, the Internal Revenue Service, the CIA, the Secret Service, the military. Influenced by the White House, the abuses of these agencies have been unparalleled, at least to my knowledge, in the modern history of this country.

Interview, Washington/Parade, 7-14:4.

Charles E. Wiggins
United States Representative,
R—California; Member,
House Judiciary Committee   3

[On the Judiciary Committee's considera-tion of impeachment of President Nixon]: I cannot express adequately the depth of my feelings that this case must be decided accord-ing to the law and on no other basis. The law, you see, establishes a common matrix for judging human behavior. It eliminates irrelevant subjective concern. Under the law, we cannot be concerned with alleged Presidential impro-prieties, because that is subjective. We really cannot be concerned about the judgments of

the President at any given moment of time unless that falls below the standards imposed by the law. If we were . . . to decide this case on any other basis than the law and the evi-dence applicable thereto, it occurs to me . . . that we would be doing a greater violence to the Constitution than any misconduct alleged to Richard Nixon.

At House Judiciary Committee hearing,
Washington, July 25/
The New York Times, 7-26:11.

4

[Reacting after President Nixon admitted that he withheld from investigators tape tran-scripts that implicated him in a Watergate cover-up]: . . . I believe that this is not the time for the President to meet with his attorneys to plan for his defense in the Senate. It is a time for the President, the Vice President, the Chief Justice and the leaders of the House and Senate to gather in the White House to discuss the orderly transition of power from Richard Nixon to Gerald Ford. Failing such action, with great reluctance and deep personal sorrow, I am prepared to conclude that the magnificent career of public service of Richard Nixon must be terminated involuntarily and shall support those portions of Article 1 of the bill of impeachment adopted by the Judi-ciary Committee which are sustained by the evidence.

Television address, Washington, Aug. 5/
Los Angeles Times, 8-6:(1)16.

A. L. Wirin
Former chief counsel,
American Civil Liberties Union   5

The ACLU wants to discourage violations of the law, especially violations by men of power in high places, but prison sentences [for former Nixon Administration officials convicted in Watergate] won't accomplish that. Prison just isn't the kind of institution that these wily, ambitious, amoral, self-serving President's men will get any benefit from—not for themselves nor for society.

Los Angeles Times, 7-21:(1)1.

Louis C. Wyman
United States Representative,
R–New Hampshire
1

[On President Nixon's admission that he withheld evidence implicating him in a Watergate cover-up]: In the light of his statement yesterday, the best interests of the country would be served by his resignation, and he should meet with the Chief Justice and the Vice President to make the necessary arrangements for an orderly transition of Executive power without delay. I am sorry for the President. He has done much for the good of the world, but it's all over for him now. The admissions he's made—they pull the rug out from under even his staunchest supporters in the House . . .

Interview, Aug. 6/
The Washington Post, 8-7:(A)12.

Ronald L. Ziegler
Press Secretary to President of the
United States Richard M. Nixon
2

[Criticizing press coverage of the Senate Watergate Committee hearings]: The early Watergate reporting was good. But what I'm talking about is the excesses we are moving into on the part of the Watergate Committee and part of the press, where unsupported charges are reported. We [in the Administration] are always put in the position of proving the nega-

tive . . . I can't understand the journalistic code applied by some which fails to examine what the Watergate Committee did, in its hearings, to people. I cannot understand the failure on the part of the major news media to assess the excesses of the Committee and the pre-judgment, conviction and trial of people—no matter what they've done. It's a tragedy in the history of this country—as is Watergate; but I think they are equal tragedies. And if we allow a President [Nixon] to be destroyed as a result of excesses in this system, then we have a real problem in our society.

Interview, San Clemente, Calif./
Newsweek, 1-21:23.

3

[On the House Judiciary Committee's request for White House material in its impeachment inquiry against President Nixon]: Substantial amounts of material have been requested that go far, far, far beyond what the [Watergate] special prosecutor felt was important . . . and what the [Senate Watergate] Committee felt was needed . . . These requests being made are seemingly without limitation on the White House before even a definition of the inquiry is put forward . . . the fact of an impeachment inquiry doesn't give Congress the right to back a truck up and haul off Executive files.

At White House press briefing, Washington,
March 12/Los Angeles Times, 3-13:(1)1.

Social Welfare

Alvin J. Arnett
Director, Federal Office
of Economic Opportunity

1

The agency [OEO] has done very little toward making poor people non-poor. We have been delivering services. We have helped poor people become healthier poor people. But we didn't have the tools to deal economically with poverty.

News conference, Los Angeles, Feb. 25/
Los Angeles Times, 2-26:(2)1.

Lloyd M. Bentsen
United States Senator, D—Texas

2

[On the just-enacted pension-reform bill] : I think it's a landmark piece of legislation ... You've got 30 million Americans who'll know their money's waiting for them when they reach retirement. Now, most private pension plans work fine, but you have a few goats in the crowd, and we had some real horror stories told us on the [Senate Finance] Committee ... people who didn't qualify for a pension till they'd worked for a company 30 years getting fired in the 29th year.

Interview/The National Observer, 9-7:3.

Daniel J. Boorstin
Historian, National Museum of
History and Technology, Washington

3

All definitions [of poverty] are relative. What we define as poverty in the United States would be great wealth in a village in India. There's always going to be a bottom 20 per cent among incomes.

Interview, Los Angeles/
Los Angeles Times, 5-10:(4)12.

Norman E. Borlaug
Director, International Maize and Wheat
Improvement Center, Mexico City

4

It is my fundamental belief that it's the moral right of everyone born into this world to

have the basic ingredients for a decent life—adequate food, basic education, medical care, opportunity for employment, housing and clothing. You can't have peace on an empty belly. And you can't have tranquility with hunger and poverty. You can't apply new technology to improve the standard of living if there is unrest and political instability.

Interview/People, 9-9:57.

James B. Cardwell
Commissioner, Social Security
Administration of the United States

5

The theory of the [Social Security] System, as I've always viewed it, is that it was intended to provide insurance against lost earnings in later life ... the original concept was that it would never provide the full level of benefit insurance or protection that one would need at that stage, but that there would be some augmentation by a second tier—a private pension, personal savings. But there is no longer a strong consensus that that is what is expected of the system ... The pressure from the beneficiaries is to raise benefits as they're struck by the cost of living, and you have to be sympathetic with them ... the poorer you are the more difficult it is. Retired people are obviously feeling that pinch. But this rapid rise in the wage base has created a new pressure in the other direction. It's a pressure that is heard in the voice of the middle-income worker ... [who] feels uncertain whether he's going to continue to be taxed on a higher and higher amount ... and that group, I think, is beginning to grumble.

Interview, Washington/
Los Angeles Herald-Examiner, 6-4:(A)8.

Jimmy Carter
Governor of Georgia

6

I used to think all welfare recipients were absolutely worthless. And I guess some—blacks and whites—are. But put yourself in the position of having three or four children and trying to support them on one dollar a day per person. Try it for a week; then try to buy an LTD [car].

At meeting of Commission on the Future of the South, Helen, Ga., Aug. 17/ The Atlanta Journal and Constitution, 8-18:(A)8.

1

Basically, the present welfare system is a mess. It ought to work to get people off public assistance and into a job so they can earn their own way, live a life of human dignity and pay taxes like the rest of us. It does not. [Instead,] it encourages families to remain dependent on public assistance—even for two or three generations ... many welfare recipients are actually worse off financially if they get a job—because one extra dollar of income may make them ineligible for child day-care, public housing and/or Medicaid care ... Basically, we have got to coordinate the many fragmented programs such as public assistance, food stamps, public housing, school lunches, etc., so that it will never be more profitable for a person to stay home and depend entirely on the government than to go out and get a job.

Aug. 20/The Atlanta Constitution, 8-21:(A)3.

Hiram L. Fong
United States Senator, R—Hawaii

2

There is a need for a new look at retirement practices in this country. We need to reconsider obsession with the numbers game—our pursuit of retirement based solely on artificial chronological rules of age without regard for either actual abilities of older persons to participate in the nation's productive forces or the desire of many for continued involvement in society's mainstream. Deliberations by the real experts on aging—older persons themselves—have been no less emphatic about the need for new approaches to the question of retirement. We need to reinstate the principle that choices should be made by the individual in the light of individual abilities and individual desires ... there are some things that Congress can do. Perhaps most important will be decisions in

Federal programs, such as Social Security, which will offer incentives for continued life-participation by older persons at least equal to current disincentives.

Before the Senate, Washington/ The Washington Post, 4-29:(A)22.

Barry M. Goldwater
United States Senator, R—Arizona

3

The earnings limitation for Social Security benefits should be repealed. I'm speaking of the penalty imposed on individuals who are otherwise eligible for Social Security but who earn more than $2,400 per year. Social Security payments are not gratuities from a benevolent government. They are a repayment of our own earnings, which we have deposited in trust as a regular contribution deducted from our salaries and from our employers on our behalf. This method was designed from the start as a guarantee that benefits would be paid as a matter of right, not of charity.

Quote, 12-1:521.

Louis Harris
Public-opinion analyst

4

It is not hard to predict that we shall see a wave of militance among senior citizens as their numbers rise ... The basic shame ... about the way senior citizens are treated is that people are declared ... useless long before their time. In a society that will be aging dramatically in the next decade, this can be a highly dangerous political fact.

News conference, Detroit/ The Christian Science Monitor, 10-30:2.

Maynard H. Jackson, Jr.
Mayor of Atlanta

5

We must open our eyes if we are to begin to deal with the systematic eradication of poverty and the diminution of crime. There can be no glittering international city as long as grim poverty and dangerous despair tarnish our glow.

San Francisco Examiner, 1-31:32.

Edward M. Kennedy
United States Senator, D—Massachusetts   *1*

[The great obstacle to improving the condition of the cities is] the sense of remoteness that people in the cities feel from their political leaders. One hundred-fifty million Americans—black and white, rich and poor—live in the cities, and it is they who will determine America's future.

> *Before meeting of Martin Luther King Jr.*
> *Center for Social Change, New York,*
> *April 6/The New York Times, 4-7:(1)49.*

James T. Lynn
Secretary of Housing and Urban
Development of the United States   *2*

I would say there's a growing unhappiness in the United States with the way we have helped low-income families. A study by the House of Representatives indicates that what with food stamps, housing construction, job training and so forth, you easily reach a point with some families where, for every dollar they earn, they lose a dollar in benefits. It's a built-in dependency cycle and work-disincentive. Accordingly, it seems to me there is a good deal of receptivity today to explore direct cash assistance where it makes sense. But having been in government five years, I have to say that the result is not determined. I know very well that no program will work perfectly in all cases.

> *Interview/Nation's Business, February:60.*

Robert S. McNamara
President, International Bank for
Reconstruction and Development   *3*

What, after all, really constitutes wealth? And what more fundamental measures of wealth are there than the levels of nutrition, literacy and health? It is in these terms that the average citizen of a developed nation enjoys wealth beyond the wildest dreams of the 1 billion people in the countries with per-capita incomes under $200: His caloric intake is 40 per cent greater; his literacy rate is four times higher; the mortality rate of his children is 90 per cent lower; and his own life expectancy 50 per cent more. Are there any more basic terms in which to compare the wealth of the developed and developing nations?

> *Before World Bank board of governors*
> *and International Monetary Fund,*
> *Washington, Sept. 30/*
> *The Christian Science Monitor, 10-1:8.*

Walter F. Mondale
United States Senator, D—Minnesota   *4*

The more I studied human problems—whether in education or health or housing, minorities, discrimination, you name it—the more I became convinced that the primary focus had to be the family . . . We are talking, for the first time, about setting up a system that would require a family-impact statement to force government to discuss and debate the possible consequences of a given policy on the family. It would be similar to the environmental-impact statement.

> *Interview/The Washington Post, 10-12:(A)20.*

William A. Morrill
Assistant Secretary for Planning and
Evaluation, Department of Health, Education
and Welfare of the United States   *5*

We say that it's okay to help people if you do it with "good things" like housing and food and so on. Somehow, giving money has not been considered a "good thing." I sometimes think that in this system it is the giver and not the recipient who is allowed to feel good. He can say, "Here's a house to live in," or, "Here's a stamp for food." It's like saying, "Here's a Christmas basket." [It is less paternalistic to give cash] because the individual is allowed to choose what he needs most of. Have you ever heard of those awful welfare caseworkers' lists which get down to the point of telling some poor woman how much she needs for stockings? That's government intervention at the most excruciating level. It's demeaning and it's what we're trying to get away from.

> *The Atlanta Journal and Constitution,*
> *11-10:(B)23.*

Frank E. Moss
United States Senator, D—Utah   *6*

The so-called Nixon nursing-home reforms are generally punitive, vindictive, punishing, threatening, oppressive and negative . . . Inspections [have become] bureaucratic rituals, with political influence keeping some inferior homes open. Emphasis is on inspection of physical facilities rather than patient care. Responsibility for nursing-home inspection is fragmented. State inspectors are asked to make Federal Medicare and Medicaid surveys since a different branch of HEW is responsible for each. Lack of communication often results in one agency trying to close the facility while another agency is sending it more patients.

Before American College of Nursing Home Administrators, San Francisco, Nov. 2/ The Atlanta Journal and Constitution, 11-3:(B)3.

Armand Nicholi, Jr.
Psychiatrist,
Harvard University Medical School
1

In many homes child care has shifted from parents to outside agencies. There is no family influence. There are six million pre-schoolers in some form of nursery care today and it is sad to note that only one million of the mothers have to work because of economic necessity. America is also suffering from parents who are at home physically but who are emotionally inaccessible because of business pressures or the television set. A child will resent a parent's participation in even a worthy cause if it makes him or her an absent parent, emotionally or physically.

At meeting of Layman's Leadership Institute, Coronado, Calif./ Los Angeles Herald-Examiner, 11-30:(A)7.

Joseph A. Pechman
Director of economic studies,
Brookings Institution
2

[The Social Security tax] is the most regressive in the Federal revenue system; at current rates, it is extremely burdensome on poor and near-poor workers. The payroll tax is defended by those who think of [the] Social Security system as an insurance system; but everybody knows that payroll taxes do not pay for an individual's retirement benefits, even with accumulated interest. The insurance myth

should no longer be allowed to perpetuate oppressive taxation.

Before Senate Committee, Washington/ Los Angeles Times, 4-7:(9)5.

Ronald Pollack
Director, Food Research and Action Center,
New York
3

Over the past three to four years, our nation's needy have become hungrier and poorer . . . I would be pleased to tell you that we have made substantial progress in the effort to eradicate hunger. However, to do so would be untruthful. For the sad and tragic truth is that, over the past several years, we have moved backwards in our struggle to end hunger, poverty and malnutrition.

Before Senate Select Committee on Nutrition and Human Needs, Washington, June 19/ The New York Times, 6-20:17.

William E. Simon
Secretary of the Treasury of the United States
4

. . . welfare payments have grown 65 per cent in the last three years, and I think we'd better take a pretty close look at that. Are we creating in this country a disincentive to work? Is that what the purpose of welfare is? . . . I think we've overdone it.

Television interview/ Los Angeles Times, 7-24:(2)7.

Steven D. Symms
United States Representative, R–Idaho
5

The welfare state is nothing more than a mechanism by which the government confiscates the wealth of its productive citizens in order to support the non-productive and the incompetent.

Before the House, Washington, Nov. 20/Human Events, 12-21:9.

Caspar W. Weinberger
Secretary of Health, Education and
Welfare of the United States
6

Over-sell begins at the very conception of a government program. The rhetoric of over-promise begins on the banquet circuits, when a

WHAT THEY SAID IN 1974

(CASPAR W. WEINBERGER)

new domestic proposal is first a gleam in the eye of the Congressmen and the special constituencies seeking enactment of the program. But there is always a difference between what is said at the banquet speech and what is actually done to help the aging, the poor or those in need of special help. People are led to expect more than can be delivered by the pre-enactment rhetoric that leads to the selling of a new domestic social program. And those expectations are kept inflated after the law is passed, the money appropriated and the program in operation. Why? One reason is simply that a half-billion dollars a year in taxpayers' money is spent publicizing Federal programs, and the people who run them never spend money to provide the public with information that is uncomplimentary to the programs they operate.

Los Angeles/The Washington Post, 12-27:(A)16.

Joseph L. Alioto
Mayor of San Francisco

1

The automotive industry presents the biggest monopolistic aggregate of power in the history of the world ... There is no doubt that General Motors and other powerful auto-makers have restructured our society to suit their desire for profit. Man's environment has been fouled to create an environment for the automobile. It has been impossible for any means of ground transportation, other than the auto, to find even a niche in American society ... The time has arrived for Congress to begin restructuring monopolies to benefit a nation in need of a pure environment and many modes of transportation. It is time the cities were supplied with the types of buses, subways, electric trolley coaches and streetcar systems denied them by the highway, oil and automobile lobbies.

Before Senate Antitrust and Monopoly Subcommittee, Washington, Feb. 25/ San Francisco Examiner, 2-26:6.

Lloyd M. Bentsen
United States Senator, D–Texas

2

Not since the 1920s, when we became aware of the need for interstate highways and good city streets, has this nation confronted such a compelling need for improved mobility. Transportation has become one of the major issues of the '70s, as more and more of us are forced to ask serious questions about how often we travel, what type of transportation will be available and how we will get to work. Americans deserve balanced transportation as a national priority.

Before National League of Cities, Houston, Dec. 2/The New York Times, 12-3:83.

Alan S. Boyd
President, Illinois Central Gulf Railroad

3

... I think we are on the verge of an era in which there will be much less modal chauvinism

[in transportation] than has been the case. Two things will force this. For one thing, I predict our common carriers will be recognized as an important national resource, and legislation will make the Interstate Commerce Commission re-state the financial needs of the carriers so they can measure up to the capacity requirements of the post-crisis world ahead. For another thing, I predict there will be more business than the common carriers can handle. This will be true because of the end of cheap energy, the end of the proliferation of private carriage, plus the absolute growth in the economy which will force social policies to encourage common-carrier handling of intercity freight. In short, I am bullish on railroads after reflecting on the public policy ramifications of recent events. I am also quite bullish on highway common carriers. They seem well-positioned to benefit from what I perceive to be a new era in our political history—when we turn our efforts toward the pursuit of a more perfect society within the limits we now acknowledge in our resources, our space, our ability to change and our wealth.

Before Highway Research Board, Washington, Jan. 23/Vital Speeches, 4-1:369.

Claude S. Brinegar
Secretary of Transportation of the United States

4

I readily admit that we can do a better job at the Federal level in developing a coordinated statement of national transportation policy, and we are at work on one. But I must offer a word of caution: Please don't expect "policy," by itself, to solve our nation's transportation problems. The move from "policy," no matter how brilliantly conceived, to the details of effective "programs" will always be a rocky and uncertain path. I'm convinced that our country is too big, our mixed public-private economy too complex, and our divisions of responsibility

WHAT THEY SAID IN 1974

between Federal, state and local governments too firmly entrenched and too politicized to permit us, at the Federal level, to be able to lay out the details of the nation's over-all transportation system with any degree of success. What we do want to do, and the goal I have set for myself, is to make sure our various programs are, in fact, consistent with our over-all desired direction of effort—that the sum total of what we do pushes us in the right direction.

Before Aviation/Space Writers Association, Washington, May 13/Vital Speeches, 6-15:527.

James L. Buckley
United States Senator, C–New York

1

[Criticizing Federal regulations requiring new automobiles to have devices which prevent the engine from starting until seat belts are fastened] : I know of no single intervention by government into the lives of its citizens that is more universally resented than the current requirement for 1974-model cars that dictates that we shall not start our engines until we strap ourselves in . . . It is wrong for the Federal government to require an individual to conform with an arbitrary standard of conduct that is unrelated to the public safety. It may well be that any driver who fails to put on a safety harness is an idiot. But freedom implies the freedom to be an idiot so long as one does not endanger others . . . This kind of naked Federal coercion is the wrong approach to auto safety. Unlike the prohibiting of driving under the influence of intoxicating beverages, the implementation of the interlock system has no effect on the lives of those in cars not using the system. The American citizen deserves and demands the right to live his own life, free of the constraints of [those in government] whose lust to interfere in the private lives of others knows no bounds.

The National Observer, 2-9:12.

Edward N. Cole
President, General Motors Corporation

2

One of the institutions of the American auto industry which our critics attack most violently—the annual model change—had a great deal to do with giving mobility to the lower economic classes. You may not have thought of it this way—and of course the annual model change has been modified considerably—but historically it had profound economic and sociological effects on this country . . . The reason is that whenever the owner of a . . . car was enticed into buying a new model—and we don't think much about this—he became, in effect, the "manufacturer" of a used car, at a considerably reduced price. As the used car passes through a chain of subsequent owners, there is an economic wrinkle of very great importance: The largest share of the cost is usually paid by those most able to afford it. The new-car buyer absorbs the greatest depreciation, the second owner the next greatest, and so on down to the last owner—who has found himself quite a reasonable bargain in transportation. It was in this fashion that the individual mobility afforded by ownership of a private automobile was spread further, and lower on the economic scale, in this country than in any other.

The Dallas Times Herald, 6-2:(H)2.

Rene Dubos
Environmentalist; Professor Emeritus of Microbiology, Rockefeller University

3

I believe human beings never abandon the conquests they have made. In the case of the motor car, the conquest we have made is to have freedom of motion. Yet public transportation, as we know, decreases individual freedom of motion very much. It seems to me that once you have gained the sense of freedom that comes from not having to take the train at 7:27 and be carted with 100,000 other persons to one or two points in the city, it will be very difficult to get people to accept that, and for very good reason. So my personal belief is that we will insist on retaining individual transportation which allows each person to retain freedom of motion but which is not as destructive of the environment as the present automobile. Furthermore, American cities are not adaptable to public transportation. Housing is not situated in a way that can be serviced by public transportation.

*Interview, New York/
Los Angeles Times, 11-28:(2)7.*

Lewis A. Engman
Chairman, Federal Trade Commission
1

Under the Federal Aviation Act, the Civil Aeronautics Board controls the entry of new [airline] carriers to the market, controls the distribution of routes and has the power to disapprove or modify an airline's rate-change proposal after hearing complaints from the so-called competition. The result is that in the areas of rates and routes for all intents and purposes there is no competition at all. Competition, where it exists, is concentrated on the one unregulated aspect of airline activity—customer service. That is why the average airline commercial looks like an ad for a combination bawdy house and dinner theatre. This may lead to some pleasing amenities. But it puts the customer in the position of captive buyer. Nobody asks him if he would rather have the money than the movie, or if he would like to brown-bag it from New York to California instead of having the steamship round of beef au jus on the little plastic plate. He is just asked to pay up.

Before Financial Analysts Federation,
Detroit, Oct. 7/
The Washington Post, 10-15:(A)20.

Henry Ford II
Chairman, Ford Motor Company
2

Mass-transit systems are in trouble. BART [the new San Francisco system] hasn't been a great success. It has got a lot of problems. Morgantown [W. Va.] has been a fiasco. There are problems, a lot of problems, even when the systems work. How are you going to pay for the upkeep and losses from an operating standpoint, even after you get them built? There are lots and lots of problems which haven't been totally attacked. And they are not cheap; no matter what system you use, they are not cheap. And you are not going to get people out of their cars in total. There are a lot of systems. You can turn the inner city into a mall and have people park outside and give them public transportation. It doesn't mean, in my opinion, that we are going to sell less vehicles. People are just going to use them differently. No system in the world is going to take people from their

house to their job, or restaurant, or recreation, or whatever, other than the automobile. And as far as transportation of goods and equipment and other things, we've got to have trucks; the railroads are falling apart.

News conference/
The Dallas Times Herald, 8-4:(I)6.

Robert P. Griffin
United States Senator, R—Michigan
3

[On what he calls "government-mandated gimmicks and gadgets" which are more and more being required for automobiles] : Unless we move soon to impose a moratorium in this area, new standards and requirements will raise [the costs of] that [requirement list] to $1,200 in 1977. That is in addition to price increases attributable to inflation. In its rush to turn the automobile into a safe, accident-proof tank—which will not pollute and will play FM music—Congress is creating a nightmare for the average auto worker, who can no longer afford to buy a car and whose job is either in jeopardy or has already been lost.

U.S. News & World Report, 12-9:23.

Vance Hartke
United States Senator, D—Indiana
4

As transportation policy has evolved in the U.S., increasing subsidies have been given to every mode of transport but rail. Aside from the original land grants to the Western roads, there has been little in the way of government subsidies for rail transport in the more recent past; in fact, the railroads need to maintain their own roadbeds and rights of ways and pay taxes on them, which is a striking difference from the treatment of other modes... For example, last year over $28 billion in public funds were spent for transportation purposes; of this amount, approximately 86 per cent was spent for highways, 10 per cent for air transportation, 3.7 per cent for waterways, and less than one-quarter of one per cent for rail transportation.

Quote, 12-22:593.

WHAT THEY SAID IN 1974

Lee A. Iacocca
President, Ford Motor Company

1

[Saying there still is a market for large cars, despite the trend toward small, economy models]: Don't forget, we're a very mobile people. Mobility is part of our freedoms and lives. We've got 42,000 miles of Interstate highway systems without a traffic light, almost. That fact boggles the mind of most people I talk with in Japan and in Europe; they've got little cars on winding roads. Why a big car—standard, family-size car, with trunk space and a comfortable, safe ride? Seventeen to 18 million families have three or more kids, plus mother and dad, that's why. Put them all into a Pinto? Why, they just won't fit. Seventy per cent of the people own only one car, and they tend to the standard or big car for comfort, for room, for the only way the family can move together.

Interview/The Washington Post,
2-10:(Adv. Supp.)3.

2

[On criticism that the U.S. auto industry deliberately delayed introducing small cars so as to be able to continue selling large cars]: Everybody has his own "devil theory" about the auto industry. But I think all the theories are summed up in the one that says car-makers have the uncanny ability to make people act against their own self-interest ... But are we really able to force people to buy what they don't want and need? ... As a company, Ford became successful by providing basic transportation. But failure to understand and keep up with our customers almost ruined us a couple of times. For example, in the '20s we were still trying to sell people what we thought was best for them, after the majority had decided they wanted something more than "any color car, as long as it was black." After World War II, the family sedan that could be used to go for a loaf of bread or take the whole family to Yellowstone was the clear choice of the American car-buyer. That was their choice—they didn't want small cars. Those who are old enough will remember these names: the Playboy, the Henry J, Hudson Jet, Davis, Willys Aero, King, Nash Metropolitan, Woodhill,

Crosley, Nash-Hudson American and the English Ford. These small cars that came into the United States after World War II quietly died because of a lack of customer interest. Maybe they were ahead of their time ... But you show me someone who tries to lead a market too far, and I'll show you a candidate for bankruptcy. It's been widely reported that we took a $250 million bath on the Edsel. We said it was time to sell the public a new medium-priced car. The market didn't agree with our timing. I remember with dread our own pioneering effort to lead the market on safety features in cars. Back in 1956, we offered seat belts, the padded dash, deep-dish steering wheels. Our major competitor talked performance—I believe "sassy" was the word. What happened? We got clobbered in the marketplace. No matter what the poet said, the saddest words in business are these: He was ahead of his time.

At National Press Club, Washington/
Los Angeles Times, 4-1:(2)7.

3

The track record for mass transit looks pretty bad. We haven't technically and economically worked out a feasible system that people want. The new systems like BART [in San Francisco] have flopped. If a small bus line is going under, that doesn't mean that the government should bail it out. That's a bottomless pit. A balanced transportation system is the answer. We've had enough artists' sketches of people going overhead in computerized trains. In the next 10 years, we're not going to see any wholesale mass transit. Those concrete ribbons are just going to keep tearing up our landscape until we can find something better.

Interview, Dearborn, Mich./People, 9-23:38.

William B. Johnson
Chairman, Illinois Central Industries, Inc.

4

In 1973, the Federal, state and local governments invested $29 billion in transportation facilities and services. Of that, about one tenth of one per cent went to the railroad industry. There is simply no way that the industry can meet its capital needs from the private-enterprise markets while its competitors are receiving something like $28.8 billion a year to build highways, waterways, airports, etc. If the Federal government can finance airports, why not terminals for railroads? Or better roadbeds? Not only is government financing needed, but there must be substantial reform of Federal regulatory and taxing policies if we are to avoid nationalization of railroads. We simply have to get with it. The problems of the bankrupt Penn Central are not basically much different from those of other railroads—the Penn Central just had all of the industry's problems, and many railroads have only some of them.

Interview, Chicago/
Nation's Business, November:50.

Charles Kuralt
News correspondent,
Columbia Broadcasting System

1

Came into the Syracuse [N.Y.] airport the other day, picked up my bag at the baggage counter, walked out and caught a cab into town. The Syracuse airport works the way airports ought to work, and that's because Syracuse hasn't built a new airport lately. Old airports work, frankly, and new ones don't. Take Kansas City, for example. Kansas City used to have an old airport, practically in the middle of town. You could get off a plane and be wherever you were going in 10 or 15 minutes. But the airport wasn't big enough or flashy enough, so Kansas City built a new airport on what seems like hundreds of miles out in the Missouri countryside. The planes park right at the terminal, so you don't have long walks. So far, so good. But the baggage is delivered on a laughable slow elevator that keeps whole planeloads of people waiting for up to an hour for their bags. The rental-car desks have been banished to a cornfield farther from the new airport than downtown Kansas City was from the old one; and after you've got your car, you still face that long drive into the city. This is progress? Take Denver. Denver used to have an old airport. Its crowning joy was a big, spacious newsstand in the middle of the lobby where a man could happily pass an hour between planes. Denver has now modernized. There is an empty space where that wonderful newsstand stood. The newsstands are now in-

credibly crowded tiny enclosures which discourage browsing and unstocked with many worth reading anyway. This is progress? . . . I arrived at [New York's La Guardia Airport] in . . . a DC-10. They couldn't get the DC-10 that was already at the gate to start, and so our DC-10 had to wait, since the only mechanized tunnel that can accommodate a DC-10 was occupied. We waited—an hour and 10 minutes . . . That's why it was so nice to come to Syracuse—no mechanized tunnels, no gondolas, or people-movers, or conveyor belts, just a rickety set of stairs to walk down, just an old-fashioned baggage counter, just a taxi at the curb outside, the way airports used to be, before progress.

Radio broadcast/
The National Observer, 3-16:10.

Lewis Mumford
Author

2

. . . Boston can't control its traffic. It is choking on motor cars. The more complex the system becomes, the more open it is to a total breakdown. What is happening here is happening all over the world. It is possible, even, that there will be traffic tie-ups that will last for several days. It actually happened in Hyde Park in London that there was a traffic blockage that lasted half a day. That could occur on a larger scale. What is happening to the great cities of the world is outrageous. In Paris, the glory of the Seine was the embankment. It was one of the early pieces of urban improvement. Now they have thrust through these heavy-duty highways along the river to make more automobiles come into Paris. The great boulevards have been turned into parking lots. You now get a headache dining in the outdoor cafes. Between the noise of the cars and the stench of the fumes, outdoor dining in Paris is no longer the fine experience it was.

Interview, Cambridge, Mass./
Los Angeles Times, 4-8:(2)7.

Richard M. Nixon
President of the United States

3

[Arguing against Federal fund handouts to faltering railroads and the accompanying gov-

(RICHARD M. NIXON)

ernment regulations]: The collapse of the Penn Central Railroad is ample evidence of the wrongheadedness of this approach. While we cannot afford to let our railroads fail, neither can we afford to bail them out every time they do get in trouble. Our economy cannot afford it. Our taxpayers will not tolerate it.

Radio address to the nation, Washington, Feb. 9/The New York Times, 2-10:(1)44.

Charles F. Phillips, Jr.
Professor of Economics,
Washington and Lee University   *1*

Amtrak has indicated it is trying to serve passengers' interests. That's good. In years to come, as gasoline prices rise, highway congestion increases and urban parking spaces dwindle because of pollution-control measures, the car may further lose appeal. Then the trains may be the intercity traveler's best friend.

The National Observer, 1-26:14.

John Pierce
Professor of Engineering,
California Institute of Technology   *2*

. . . I believe the use of public transit has fallen because, like the telegraph and the sedan chair, it uses too much labor in a day in which labor is extremely expensive . . . Subways and conventional rail systems will be built by communities who love dinosaurs and will have them at any cost. Successful mass transit must be automated mass transit; for only through automation can mass transit escape the economic disaster of increasing labor cost.

Lecture/San Francisco Examiner, 7-23:42.

William Proxmire
United States Senator, D–Wisconsin   *3*

[Calling for the abolition of the Interstate Commerce Commission]: Instead of regulating transportation to avoid monopoly and increased prices, the ICC has established monopolies, reduced competition and ordered high and uneconomic rates to cover the costs of inefficient producers. There is now enough natural competition between rail, road, truck and barge transportation that this agency should fold up entirely.

Human Events, 5-4:2.

E. G. Shuster
United States Representative, R–Pennsylvania   *4*

[Arguing against proposed Federal subsidies and expenditures for big-city mass-transit systems]: . . . the taxpayers of small-town rural America should not have their hard-earned dollars spent to help pay transit fares for the people of our big cities. This is especially true since the people of big-city America can save hundreds of dollars each year by using the mass-transit systems available to them rather than using their cars, if they so choose . . . Why should American taxpayers spend their money so city commuters can save theirs?

Human Events, 8-24:4.

Robert D. Stuart, Jr.
President, Quaker Oats Company   *5*

In Britain, and in one country after another throughout the world, when the railroads came upon hard times, were no longer viable private enterprises and could not attract new capital, they were not abandoned. They were nationalized. But nationalization does not solve the problem; it simply shifts the burden. Indeed, the problems and the burden are generally aggravated . . . For those who look to Canada, England and Europe as favorable indications for rail nationalization, I think we should perhaps pay more attention to examples in this country. Amtrak and the Postal Service might indicate the kind of service we could expect. The private U.S. economy is unique in its cost effectiveness. There is a major role for government to play in helping the U.S. railroads. But it should be selectively limited to what is in the public's best interest—which means a strong, competitive railroad system, properly regulated and supported by government, yet not dominated by any special political group or private interests.

Before Traffic Club, Chicago, May 16/Vital Speeches, 7-1:576.

Donald E. Weeden
Chairman, Weeden & Company, investments

1

Wall Street—more than Main Street—knows that the transportation crisis is very real. For private citizens and government officials, the challenge is to control the automobile before it controls us... The emphasis over the next decade will be on governmental incentives for mass transit. The problem for Wall Street is that it is difficult to come up with a domestic company in which to invest because of its future role in mass transit. Investing in General Motors—the leading producer of locomotives and buses—is like investing in a mutual fund for auto stocks... So long as one bus can do the job of 35 Cadillacs, one subway car 50 Oldsmobiles, and one train 1,000 Chevrolets, the pressure on the most public-spirited, well-meaning corporate manager at GM will be overwhelming to push private cars rather than mass transit. Perforce, then, one cannot advise clients to invest in GM even though it also controls the production of diesel buses and diesel locomotives. But if not GM, then what company for the investor sold on the future of mass transportation? That is what I mean when I say the "Street" abhors a monopoly... Dissipate that self-defeating conglomeration of conflicting goals—spin off at least two divisions from GM, buses and locomotives—and Wall Street will more than likely respond with new investment opportunities. And so will the government, with much larger research and development grants.

Before Senate Antitrust Subcommittee,
Washington, March 1/
The Washington Post, 3-3:(A)2.

Malcolm Wilson
Governor of New York

2

[On the possibility of no Federal funds to aid urban mass transit] : That is a prospect that is too devastating even to consider. I've stated this in terms of essentiality. Essentiality does not admit to degrees. A thing is essential or not essential. It is not more or less essential.

At Governors conference, Washington,
March 7/The New York Times, 3-8:40.

Women's Rights

Polly Bergen
Actress 1

My generation was taught that a woman's only role in life is marriage and children. Now I'm facing the fact that marriage may not be the answer. The happily-ever-after syndrome of marriage can be a fantasy, something to hope for, to dream of perhaps, but not to trust your life to. I've learned that a woman can't build her life on a man, or just for men. My present goal is to be happy with me, to accept and fulfill myself. That's my best advice to any woman putting herself together.

Interview, San Francisco/
San Francisco Examiner, 5-29:23.

Lorraine Blair
Financial consultant 2

American women could rule the world if we were half-smart, because we have the money. Eighty-five per cent of every dollar is spent by women; 95 per cent of all advertising is for women. Women control education of children, have the greatest amount of leisure time, inherit most of the money and have the greatest amount of votes. Yet we American women sit here and do nothing. So we're the greatest untapped force in this country.

San Francisco Examiner & Chronicle,
3-24:(This World)2.

Yvonne B. Burke
United States Representative, D—California 3

White women need to rebel until sexism is removed as a barrier for them. It is part of white manhood to keep women down. To the extent that white society changes, ours [black] will change, and we will all live in a system of equality . . . There are those who believe it can't be done—that change can't come. It can. If laws say it's right, it becomes right, and this is the only way women, blacks or any other group reaping injustice in America, will achieve.

U.S. News & World Report, 5-27:42.

Carol Burris
President, Women's Lobby, Inc. 4

I agree with President Ford that today women have to be twice as good as men to get half as far. But it won't stay that way. As it becomes easier to get elected [to political office], we'll have more mediocre women seeking office, just as we now have mediocre men. You won't have to be a Superwoman like [U.S. Representatives] Shirley Chisholm, Bella Abzug, Barbara Jordan. The next generation already thinks our battles are won.

Interview/Chicago Tribune, 10-29:(3)21.

Simone de Beauvoir
French author 5

There are still many women in the United States who want to keep their secondary role; they actually *want* a feminine role. So the leaders, the women who started [the women's rights movement], are disappointed. They believe that their radical, extremist movement has been taken over by women who call themselves "liberal," which basically means that they are very middle-class, want to improve some aspects of women's position, but not to make women effectively equal.

Interview, Paris/
The New York Times Magazine, 6-2:18.

Karen DeCrow
President, National Organization for Women 6

Most of the differences between these two varieties, male and female, have been culturally imposed. Men can be feminists. Sexism can be two ways, too. Anything that is based on putting people into some kind of box or category is sexism, whether male or female. This is the most sex-hung-up culture in the world, female as well as male. We know so little about people, about our own potential. What we're fighting is this male preoccupation with power.

Houston/The National Observer, 6-8:4.

Luis Echeverria (Alvarez)
President of Mexico

1

It is necessary to break the barriers that impede women from achieving their total development within the political, economic and social life, and which obstruct the integral advancement of Mexico . . . It is also necessary that men and women be able to shake off the old mental structures that have caused the current unjustified situation. Women must enjoy absolute equality with men in the exercise of their rights and obligations.

State of the Union address, Mexico City, Sept. 1/Chicago Tribune, 9-2:(1)2.

Betty (Mrs. Gerald R.) Ford
Wife of the President of the United States

2

[Supporting the Equal Rights Amendment]: I believe that every woman has a place in this world; and I believe that whether you are a housewife, a mother or whether you want to go into a business . . . this is your choice and every woman should have their choice. And in that choice I think they should be considered equal, and that's what it's [the Amendment] all about.

Los Angeles Times, 9-9:(1)2.

Gerald R. Ford
President of the United States

3

If our country is to survive and prosper, we need the best efforts of all Americans—men and women—to bring it about. And besides, as a great philosopher once said—I think it was Henry Kissinger—nobody will ever win the Battle of the Sexes. There's just too much fraternizing with the enemy.

U.S. News & World Report, 12-30:15.

Betty Friedan
Founder, National Organization for Women

4

The women's movement is getting to men. It's getting down to middle America. It's not just an extremist sort of thing that will fade out. What was just theoretical discussion among perhaps a minority of women, and treated not too seriously by the media five years ago, is now actually in the lives of a majority of women in the country—and it is one of the hopeful things that is happening in the country.

Interview, New York/ The Christian Science Monitor, 4-1:(F)1.

Burleigh B. Gardner
Chairman, Board of Social Research, Chicago

5

Formerly, the working-class woman accepted with little question the idea that women must be subservient to their husbands and, in the working world, must accept lower pay and fewer opportunities than men. And she firmly reared her daughter to likewise accept this woman's role. Today, the working-class woman is rejecting such limitations. She feels women should have free choice of careers or home-making or of both, and should have equality with men in pay, in choice of jobs and in opportunities—and not be restrained just because they are women. When she hears these demands made in the name of Women's Lib, she heartily concurs. [This represents] one of the most significant changes in attitude we have witnessed in more than a quarter century of probing the attitudes of working-class women.

U.S. News & World Report, 5-27:41.

Francoise Giroud
French Secretary of State for the Condition of Women; Former editor, "L'Express," Paris

6

I am not a feminist. I have no interest in "women" as such. I have good friends among women. I like to work with them. But I don't like the strident, aggressive types. They are out of date. When women were trying to get the vote, then they were very brave. But I can't stand this idea that there is a world plot by men to subjugate women. If it is true and if they have succeeded then women are really stupid. If they think they are victims, well, victims are

WHAT THEY SAID IN 1974

(FRANCOISE GIROUD)

stupid. There is no plot. Women are just at a certain moment in history.

Interview, Washington/
The Washington Post, 10-27:(L)3.

1

You can't fight against men if you want to change the world. It is impossible; they are the masters of the world—so you have to convince them to abdicate.

Interview, New York/
The Christian Science Monitor, 11-8:5.

Helen Hayes
Actress

2

[On Women's Lib]: I don't think I can quarrel with any of the basic things they are trying to do. But I do object to their approach in some instances. I think that feminism sometimes turns into anti-maleism. I don't understand that. Why do so many of them seem to be fighting the loveliest thing that nature ever gave our sex—gentleness and special understanding?

Interview, Los Angeles/
The Christian Science Monitor, 3-19:(F)1.

Matina Horner
President, Radcliffe College

3

There is an increasing awareness that the genuine experiences of equality between men and women depend not only on the opportunities and barriers society has to offer, but also, and perhaps more importantly, on the reactions and beliefs that those men and women involved have about themselves and each other . . . Since people differ from each other as individuals more than men and women do as groups, those who . . . choose to pursue traditional careers or family patterns should be encouraged to do so and to do so with pride— without guilt, discomfort or apology—just as those who seek non-traditional fulfillment and life patterns must also enjoy and exercise their options freely, without fear of retribution and loss of self-esteem.

The Christian Science Monitor, 7-8:14.

Jeane J. Kirkpatrick
Professor of Political Science,
Georgetown University

4

In entering politics women are still defying conventional expectations; they are role-defiants and so should expect to be met with reluctance and disbelief. And they are. One woman legislator . . . talks about a male colleague saying from the floor, "Mrs. So-and-so makes some interesting points and I'm sure we're interested in her opinions. But, for myself, I prefer my women soft, cuddly and sweet-smelling." To which the woman legislator responded that she could understand perfectly; that's just the way she felt about men.

Interview, Washington/People, 11-11:54.

John H. Knowles
President, Rockefeller Foundation

5

By my definition, a home, in contrast to a house, is something that gives shelter from the elements and has someone in residence who cares continually. But all of a sudden, you get women outside the home working to increase the income. The woman may not be home in the morning, may not be home at night. And, furthermore, Women's Lib wants full equality. I agree with them: The option should be there. I don't see for the life of me, though, why anybody should be embarrassed as a woman to be a mother who builds the nest and is continually caring for the home and the people in it. And I think it takes more wit and energy and creativity than anything else women have attempted since time began. That is not to say I don't admire women for careers. They should be in executive ranks, on boards of trustees, in professorships . . . But I would stand up for the values of thoughtful, energetic, creative mothers who care for families and make a home out of a house and provide the best mental, physical and intellectual environment for the development of her children and her husband. I would say the majority of people in this country feel this way and are struggling to maintain the ideal.

Interview, New York/
Los Angeles Times, 2-13:(2)7.

Anita Loos
Author

1

[On Women's Lib]: Today they throw away their bras, which is not at all an attractive gesture. I don't think they gained anything; I can't follow their mentality. I'm mad at them because they tipped off the fact that women are smarter than men, which spoils our relationship. They should have kept it quiet; that's the only way we'll get anywhere. And another thing—they don't amuse me.

Interview, New York/People, 8-5:29.

Jack Nicholson
Actor

2

A certain segment of women say we can't know them, because we're men. Well, they're hurting themselves with their rhetoric and their propaganda. And I'm not talking on a theoretical level; there has been a very real backlash. Men are writing fewer female [film] roles than ever before because they've been made to feel that, if they do write about women, they must give those women a point of view about the [women's rights] movement. And that is very limiting. I'm afraid it will be another five years before this quasi-dance of seduction between the opposing political forces comes to an end. I myself try to duck conversations about sexism. It's all so dehumanizing.

Interview, New York/
The New York Times, 2-10:(2)11.

Adrienne Rich
Poet; Winner, 1974 National Book
Award for poetry

3

I don't think that the women's movement is about women exercising power in the same way that men do. I don't think that the women's movement is about having a woman President of the United States, in a society which would be structured like American society has been structured, and who would be wielding power in the way that [Presidents] Nixon and Johnson wielded power. I think that there's a real philosophical question before the women's movement now whether what we want is to redefine power or do away with power alto-

gether, power relationships. Is power itself meaningful? What would power mean for women? I keep going back to the root of that word which comes from French and from Latin through French. It's *posse,* which means to be able, to be capable of, and it has nothing to do with dominating someone else. It has to do with realizing your own abilities. And I suppose that, for me, a truly feminist society would be a society in which everyone was powerful in that way, in which no one was being told what limits they had to put on themselves because of their role, their sex, their color, their sexual preference, or whatever.

Interview, New York/
The Christian Science Monitor, 5-31:(F)2.

William B. Saxbe
Attorney General of the United States

4

The matter of women's rights is not a frivolous one. No rights are frivolous and neither is any effort to fully achieve them in a responsible fashion.

Before Federal Women's Program, Washington/
Los Angeles Times, 6-6:(1)2.

Phyllis Schlafly
Commentator, "Spectrum,"
Columbia Broadcasting System

5

I don't think the [Women's Lib] movement has been beneficial to women in any way. I think their objectives are radical and do not relate to the true facts about women. The only reason they have gotten where they have is because they appeal to women who know they've been discriminated against. The movement is detrimental to women and is counterproductive and degrading. The greatest put-down is the literature of the movement. They say they want women to be treated just like men, but women don't want to be ... You know, the libbers' movement is predicated on the myth that women are second-class citizens, serfs, chattel. That's ridiculous. We are extremely well-treated. We have it going our way.

Interview, Washington/
The Washington Post, 7-11:(D)1,10.

WHAT THEY SAID IN 1974

(PHYLLIS SCHLAFLY)

1

I don't believe in women's rights. I believe in chivalry.

Quote, 8-4:98.

Mary Louise Smith
Chairman, Republican National Committee

2

I don't think there is any reason to think women are any more honest or fair, or have any more integrity than men. To suggest they do is discrimination in reverse.

News conference/
Chicago Tribune, 10-29:(3)21.

Jayne B. Spain
Vice Chairman, Civil Service Commission
of the United States

3

Women must stand together instead of fighting and scratching like chickens do in a hen house. The housewife downgrades the poor woman who has to work. "Oh, the poor thing," says the housewife. "She's deserting the family who needs her." This, of course, creates guilt. The woman who works, and usually because she has to work, downgrades the housewife. "Oh, the poor thing," says the working woman. "How can she feel fulfilled without any intellectual stimulation?" Then you have the professional woman who downgrades both of the others and wonders aloud how each of them could fail to get a professional education. And then last, but not least, you have the Queen Bee who through her own struggle has made it to the top and likes it in that rarified atmosphere of no women and all those men. She likes it so much that she wouldn't turn a hand to help another woman up the career ladder. It is still too true today that, while men are protective of each other, women will tear each other down to whomever will listen, be it men or women.

Before Junior League, Los Angeles/
Los Angeles Herald-Examiner, 11-8:(B)1.

Barbara Walters
Co-host, "Today" show,
National Broadcasting Company Television

4

It's harder for a woman to reach high positions. You have to give up certain things. You can't have it all. You cannot have the perfect family, the best marriage and a full-fledged career. But I don't believe women should whine because they can't have everything. Whoever said it wasn't supposed to be tough? I think that's one of the problems with young women: They want it all and they forget how tough it can be. Men know how difficult it is. I hear a lot of women say, "I won't take a job if I have to type." Well, yes, it's too bad that you do; but face the world as it is. Stop whining. Get your foot in the door and then if you don't like it, get out. But don't be afraid of hard work.

Interview, New York/
"W": A Fairchild publication, 12-13:21.

Duchess of Windsor

5

. . . to judge by what I see, women are much unhappier as they try to be equal with men. All they succeed in doing is making themselves miserable and discontented with life.

Interview, Paris/People, 8-12:7.

John Wooden
Basketball coach,
University of California, Los Angeles

6

I'm 100 per cent for women's participation [in sports]. But I doubt women are able to participate in contact sports with men—such as football, basketball, wrestling, boxing. And I really don't think they should. The good Lord just didn't build them with sufficient strength. But if you're going to make it perfectly equal— if this is what women really want—then let's have no men's or women's teams, just varsity athletics. You turn out. If you make it, fine; if you don't, you don't participate. I don't think that's really what women want, and I don't think that's the way it should be.

Interview, Los Angeles/
Los Angeles Times, 7-16:(3)5.

PART TWO

International Affairs

Roelof F. Botha
South African Ambassador/Permanent
Representative to the United Nations
                                                    1

We are ourselves an African state. We wish to live in harmony and cooperate with other African states. We complement one another, and we have much to offer one another, much to gain politically, socially and economically from communicating with one another. We should replace sterile confrontation with productive cooperation. We for our part are ready to seek and to explore opportunities for coming to an understanding with Africa.
Before United Nations General Assembly,
New York, Sept. 30/
The New York Times, 10-1:5.

                                                    2

We [South Africa] do have discriminatory practices and we do have discriminatory laws. But that discrimination must not be equated with racialism ... A policy such as ours, which is designed to avoid disaster, to eliminate friction and confrontation between different peoples, to eliminate domination of one group by another and to give to every man his due, can surely not be said to run counter to civilized concepts of human dignities and freedoms ... Why is it, if the position of blacks in South Africa is really so intolerable, that hundreds of thousands of black workers from other countries of Africa voluntarily come to South Africa for employment, many of them entering the country illegally for that purpose?
Before United Nations Security Council,
New York, Oct. 24/
Los Angeles Times, 10-25:(1)5.

                                                    3

We [in South Africa] realize that the development of the black man is essential for security in southern Africa. We realize that it is, therefore—quite apart from any moral aspects— in our own interests to see that this development

takes place at an ever-increasing rate—politically, materially and otherwise.
Interview, United Nations, New York/
The Christian Science Monitor, 11-1:4.

Chou En-lai
Premier of the People's Republic
of (Communist) China
                                                    4

[On the recent coup d'etat in Portugal overthrowing the government of Marcelo Caetano]: The fall of the reactionary Caetano regime in Portugal ... signifies the ignominious failure of Portugal's notorious policy of colonialism [in Africa] and represents a major victory for the persistent and protracted armed struggle of the African people ... We are confident that the great African people, united as one and persevering in struggle, will win complete liberation for the entire African continent.
At banquet honoring the President
of Senegal, Peking, May 6/
The Washington Post, 5-7:(A)12.

Antonio de Spinola
President of Portugal
                                                    5

Our efforts [in Portugal] must be concentrated on re-establishing peace overseas. But the destiny of overseas Portugal must be democratically decided by all those who call these lands their own. They must be allowed full freedom of decision; and in Africa, as here, we must avoid in every way having minority forces, whatever they may be, affect the free development of the democratic process now under way.
At his installation as President, Lisbon,
May 15/The New York Times, 5-16:3.

                                                    6

[Saying Portugal will grant independence to her three African territories]: We are ready from this moment to initiate the transfer of power to the people of the overseas territories

(ANTONIO DE SPINOLA)

considered suitable for this development—namely, Guinea, Angola and Mozambique . . . The moment has come for the President of the republic to reiterate solemnly the right of all people from the overseas Portuguese territories to self-determination, including the immediate recognition of their right to independence . . . This is a historic moment for which the country, the African territories and the world were waiting: peace in Portuguese Africa finally attained in justice and freedom.

Broadcast address to the nation, Lisbon, July 27/The New York Times, 7-28:(1)1,16.

Alec Douglas-Home
Foreign Secretary of the United Kingdom
1

Get it out of your heads that any British government is going to use force in Rhodesia. We're going to use infinite patience to find a peaceful way to [black] majority rule.

News conference, Nairobi, Kenya, Feb. 7/ Los Angeles Times, 2-8:(1)21.

Haile Selassie
Emperor of Ethiopia
2

[Saying he is preparing for a change to democratic government in his country]: We have had a firm conviction since our youth that it is essential for a people and a government to be entwined through a constitutional covenant . . . As it has always been our ardent wish that our beloved people should have a peaceful transition from one era to another and from generation to generation, we have never refrained from effecting the necessary administrative innovations demanded by the changing times.

TV-radio address to the nation, Addis Ababa, March 5/ The New York Times, 3-6:11.

Kenneth Kaunda
President of Zambia
3

For years, inequality and oppression have been accepted as the mode of life [for black Africans] in southern Africa . . . We must move in the direction of more equality among all human beings. The majority must have the right to participate in shaping their own destiny.

San Francisco Examiner & Chronicle, 5-19:(This World)2.

Henry A. Kissinger
Secretary of State of the United States
4

I believe that the embargoing of trade on Rhodesia is not based on its internal policies so much as on the fact that a minority has established a separate state; and it does not, therefore, represent exclusively a judgment on the domestic [racial] policies of the Rhodesian government, but also a question with respect to the legitimacy of the Rhodesian government.

Human Events, 3-30:5.

Connie Mulder
Minister of Information and the Interior of South Africa
5

We [in South Africa] will not be pushed by external or internal pressures in directions that are against our interests. We are going to carry on with our evolutionary policies of separate racial development for all who live here. There will be no panic changes . . . We refuse to share political power over the whites with any other people. There can be no change toward integration.

U.S. News & World Report, 10-7:84.

Hilgard Muller
Foreign Minister of South Africa
6

[On the UN vote to suspend South Africa from the current General Assembly session because of its racial policies]: I think the whole thing is deplorable. It is most irresponsible and immature, not to mention the fact that it is totally illegal. It reminds one of spoilt children.

Nov. 13/The New York Times, 11-14:3.

Ivor Richard
British Ambassador/Permanent Representative to the United Nations
7

I would have thought there was a chance that within the next year or two, within that time scale, the white Rhodesians would decide that it was in their interests to settle with the [black] Africans on reasonable terms. [But] I don't think the white Rhodesians yet have any real idea of the sort of concessions they're going to have to make. I think it's dawning on them, particularly as they see one after another of the white bastions in southern Africa beginning to crumble.

Interview/
The Christian Science Monitor, 10-25:5.

John A. Scali
United States Ambassador/Permanent
Representative to the United Nations

1

[Saying South Africa should not be expelled from the UN because of its racial policies]: My government does not accept the view that the United Nations is powerless. Rather, we strongly believe that it is through both increased bilateral contacts and the strong will of a determined United Nations that a peaceful change will occur in South Africa ... History holds no example of a pariah state that reformed itself in exile. There is no record of good citizenship in the land of Nod, east of Eden, where Cain, the first pariah, was banished.

At United Nations, New York, Oct. 30/
Los Angeles Times, 10-31:(1)19.

Ian Smith
Prime Minister of Rhodesia

2

[Announcing a cease-fire between his government and black nationalist guerrillas and the release by his government of all African political prisoners]: I am taking this step on the firm understanding that everyone concerned will conduct themselves peacefully and within the law. This will, I believe, create the necessary climate for a constitutional conference ... No doubt there will be some among you who feel concerned at the implication of these developments. In the light of events in the past decade, this is understandable. However, let me reassure you all, firstly, that it is the intention of your government to maintain law and order in

Rhodesia; secondly, that we are not prepared to deviate from our standards of civilization.

Broadcast address to the nation, Salisbury,
Dec. 11/The Washington Post, 12-12:(A)22.

Helen Suzman
Member of South African Parliament;
Leader, Progressive Party of South Africa

3

[Criticizing the UN ruling denying South Africa a seat in the General Assembly because of the country's racial policies]: I think it would have been more constructive to have demanded that South Africa spell out the changes envisaged and to set out a timetable for implementing them, and then to take action if South Africa failed to follow through. To take steps which could lead to a withdrawal from the United Nations may well accomplish less in the long run than insuring that South Africa stays in the United Nations, accountable to it and under constant pressure to change.

Lecture, Barnard College, Nov. 19/
The New York Times, 11-20:18.

John Vorster
Prime Minister of South Africa

4

[Saying that, with its eventual independence from Portugal virtually assured, Mozambique will inevitably form a black government]: The fact is there will sooner or later be an indigenous government in Mozambique, which shares a common border with South Africa ... If a government were to be established in Mozambique which wants to use Mozambique as a springboard for attacks against South Africa—and I personally do not think this will happen—then obviously we shall have to defend ourselves ... [But if that government desires economic cooperation with South Africa,] then, irrespective of the color of that government, there will be wholehearted cooperation in the economic sphere despite such political differences as there may be.

Before Parliament, Cape Town, Aug. 30/
The New York Times, 8-31:3.

WHAT THEY SAID IN 1974

(JOHN VORSTER)

1

[Calling for greater cooperation between black- and white-ruled Africa]: I believe the choice lies between peace on the one hand and escalation of conflict on the other. The consequences of an escalation of conflict are easily foreseeable. The price will be high—too high for southern Africa . . . Africa has been good to us [South Africans], and we are prepared to give back to Africa something of what we have so richly received over the years, as far as it is in our power to do.

Before the Senate, Cape Town, Oct. 23/
Los Angeles Times, 10-24:(1)16.

John M. Ashbrook
United States Representative, R–Ohio

1

Recently, the Soviet Union has been urging Cuba to improve relations with the United States. This is understandable, as the Soviets probably hope to have the United States start picking up part of the bill for keeping [Cuban Premier Fidel] Castro in power. Currently, the Soviets give Cuba over $1 million a day to shore up the Castro regime. The Soviets have had to provide Cuba with subsidies and credits. I am sure that the Soviets would not be opposed to the United States granting Cuba some of the same type of American taxpayer-subsidized credits that our government is presently allowing the Soviet Union.

Human Events, 8-17:4.

Joaquin Balaguer
President of the Dominican Republic

2

... there is no danger of internal upheaval here. We have matured as a nation and realize that the well-being of all our people depends on respect for our democratic institutions. We have a great future in our grasp, and we are willing to share it with well-meaning people from anyplace in the world.

Interview, Santo Domingo/
The New York Times, 1-27:(3)69.

David Barrett
Premier of British Columbia, Canada

3

We [in his province] are a democratic-socialist government. To many Americans that means a big Red flag; but actually ours is similar to the British Labor government. We believe in a mixed economy—in a mix of public and private investment ... I'm not anti-American. We have had excellent cooperation with the American companies functioning here. I don't have any particular love for some corporations because I find their practices border on outright

immoral behavior. But it's the company, not the nationality. Also, I feel that most Americans would applaud and support the things we are doing here if they could ignore the "socialist" label. Americans are far more progressive, far more understanding and far more willing to back a government like ours than the deep-core Canadian Tory. If I could talk to Americans about medicare and hospital insurance, about our guaranteed family incomes, our farm programs, they wouldn't give a fig about the "democratic socialist" label. They'd say, "Right on!"—and they'd support what we are doing.

Interview, Victoria, B.C./
U.S. News & World Report, 8-12:60,61.

Mauricio Borgonovo (Pohl)
Foreign Minister of El Salvador

4

[On a vote by OAS members which, although winning a majority, failed to attain the two-thirds majority needed to rescind the blockade and sanctions against Cuba]: Seen in the perspective of time, this is no more than a phase, a step in a journey that will reach a happy end ... We hope that Cuba will comprehend this gesture of friendship from the majority of its American brothers and abstain from acts that might compromise the unification process, of which this conference [and vote] is by no means the beginning nor the end.

Quito, Ecuador/
Los Angeles Times, 11-17:(8)3.

Juan Bosch
Former President of the Dominican Republic

5

I do not hate the U.S., but it is hard to love it. I believe it is true the American people regrets many policies ... but the government still goes on its way. In my own country, here, ideas are very backward. Money from the U.S. comes in very fast now. Ideas come slowly.

Interview, Santo Domingo/
The New York Times, 8-3:23.

Leonid I. Brezhnev
General Secretary,
Communist Party of the Soviet Union

1

We well know, as others probably also know, that Soviet arms in Cuban hands are not weapons to attack anyone nor a means of straining the international situation. They serve the just cause of the defense of revolutionary conquests of the country, the cause of peace and tranquility.

At rally, Havana, Jan. 29/
The New York Times, 1-31:3.

James L. Buckley
United States Senator, C—New York

2

Before we plunge ahead and make concessions to Cuba, we should have a national debate to highlight the issue. We seem to be caught on a drift moving us uncritically toward a relaxation of sanctions against the [Fidel] Castro regime. I have been concerned that practically no one has called attention to serious hemispheric security problems posed by the special relations between the Soviet Union and Cuba.

Interview, Washington, Oct. 1/
The New York Times, 10-2:3.

Fidel Castro
Premier of Cuba

3

There are many examples which demonstrate that we [in Cuba] are not yet prepared to live under Communism. We must be honest about it . . . so that we can recognize and struggle against our faults and defects . . . It is possible to demonstrate that we use a greater work force than used by the capitalists to operate the mills, and with less efficiency than that of the capitalists. The fault is ours, because we have not been capable of developing administrative efficiency so that it can at least be equal to that of the capitalists.

Before Cuban Labor Federation/
Los Angeles Times, 1-14:(1)8.

4

[Criticizing U.S. President Ford for his defense of CIA funding of groups opposed to the late President Salvador Allende in Chile]: The new President of the United States, to the surprise and stupefaction of Latin American public opinion, has declared that such actions were carried out in the best interests of the United States. Thus, the government of the United States proclaims openly the right to intervene by any means, regardless of how illicit, dirty or criminal, in the internal processes of the nations of the hemisphere.

Havana, Sept. 28/Chicago Tribune, 9-30:(1)3.

5

[Former U.S. President] Nixon was personally very much involved with them [Cuban counter-revolutionaries], and we have seen in [current U.S. President] Ford a man who is above this, these relations of friendship. In our opinion, we see Ford with a certain hope in the sense that he may, after all, adopt a different policy toward Cuba.

Television interview, Havana/"CBS Reports:
Castro, Cuba and the U.S.A.,"
Columbia Broadcasting System, 10-22.

6

[Saying the U.S., in pre-Castro days, used to own much of Cuba, while today the Soviet Union, Cuba's principal ally, does not]: In a few words, they [the U.S.] owned the Cuban economy. The Soviets do not own a single mine in Cuba, not a single factory, not a single sugar mill, not one hectare of land, not a single bank, not a single business, not a single utility.

Television interview/"CBS Reports:
Castro, Cuba and the U.S.A.,"
Columbia Broadcasting System, 10-22.

William E. Colby
Director, Central Intelligence
Agency of the United States

7

[On charges of CIA involvement in the overthrow of the government of Salvador Allende in Chile in 1973]: I don't think we've toppled democratic regimes, and I don't think we did so in Chile. First, we didn't bring about the coup, and second, the Allende regime was not democratic. Granted the [current] military regime is not democratic, I don't think a Communist regime is democratic. Our program in Chile was to sustain the democratic forces against the Allende political forces, which were suppressing various democratic elements in a variety of ways—harassing radio stations, harassing some parts of the press and some political groups. We looked forward to the democratic forces coming to power in the elections of 1976.

Interview/Time, 9-30:18.

1

[On U.S. relations with Latin America] : The troubled history of hemispheric relations records many attempts at renewed understanding and announcements of promising eras which never materialized. In fact, the channels of communication between our countries have almost never been closed. What has happened is that they have been inoperative.

At Latin America-U.S. foreign ministers meeting, Mexico City, Feb. 21/ Los Angeles Times, 2-22:(1)20.

Luis Echeverria (Alvarez)
President of Mexico

2

Latin America forms part of the Third World. Its struggles are coincident with and parallel to those being made by other nations against colonialism, modern attempts at subjugation, injustice in international transactions . . . Let us consolidate, in this hemisphere, bonds based on autonomy, equality and justice. And let us exercise the militant solidarity of the peoples of the Third World in our own hemispheric home.

At Latin America-U.S. foreign ministers meeting, Mexico City, Feb. 21/ The New York Times, 2-22:10.

3

[Calling for an end to the OAS embargo of Cuba] : I will travel through South America struggling to stop the unfair blockade. They should not worry about Cuba exporting revolution, because I think they don't want to do it any more.

Mexico City/The Washington Post, 7-8:(A)9.

4

Within our country domestically we are struggling to foster social justice in accordance with all the moral guidelines and with a spirit of cooperation which we believe would benefit all the countries of the world. Internationally we struggle to achieve norms of cooperation, balance, understanding on the part of each nation for all other countries. We in Mexico believe that inflation is only one of the manifestations of lack of balance between the interests of the one and the other, between the rich and the poor, between the people that are just developing and the industrialized countries. We feel we have to reach an equilibrium in order to fight against these problems.

Welcoming U.S. President Ford to Mexico, Nogales, Oct. 21/ The New York Times, 10-22:14.

Daniel J. Flood
United States Representative, D—Pennsylvania

5

As to whether the United States should surrender its sovereignty over the Canal Zone to Panama, there is no doubt as to how our people feel. Following a national TV debate on this question over *The Advocates* program on March 15, 1973, more than 12,000 citizens reported their views, with 86 per cent of them against any surrender at Panama. In recent weeks, my own correspondence from 48 of the United States, and abroad, is almost unanimous in opposition to the projected giveaway. In addition, state legislatures have passed resolutions opposing it and more are in the process of doing so . . . United States policy of exclusive sovereign control over the Canal Zone and Canal is based upon realities, including treaties with Great Britain and Colombia. For the United States to assume the obligation of operating and defending the Canal after surrender of sovereignty over its protective frame of the Canal Zone, would place our country in the position of having grave responsibility without requisite authority, which is unthinkable in the management of a project of such magnitude of importance . . . Most certainly, the Congress will never appropriate huge funds for a Canal project in an area that the United States does not control and that during the last 70 years has had 59 Presidents.

Before National Aviation Club, Washington, April 22/Human Events, 6-22:8,16.

Gerald R. Ford
President of the United States 1

The policy that we have toward Cuba today is determined by the sanctions voted by the Organization of American States, and we abide by those actions that were taken by the members of that organization. Now, if Cuba changes its policy toward us and toward its Latin neighbors, we, of course, would exercise the option, depending on what the changes were, to change our policy. But before we made any change, we would certainly act [in] concert with the other members of the Organization of American States.

News conference, Washington, Aug. 28/
The New York Times, 8-29:20.

2

[On charges that the CIA was involved in "destabilizing" the regime of the late Chilean President Allende which ended in a coup]: Our government, like other governments, does take certain actions in the intelligence field to help implement foreign policy and protect national security. I am informed reliably that Communist nations spend vastly more money than we do for the same kind of purposes. Now, in this particular case, as I understand it and there's no doubt in my mind, our government had no involvement in any way whatsoever in the coup itself. In a period of time, three or four years ago, there was an effort being made by the Allende government to destroy opposition news media, both the writing press as well as the electronic press, and to destroy opposition political parties. And the effort that was made [by the U.S.] in this case was to help and assist the preservation of opposition newspapers and electronic media and to preserve opposition political parties. I think this is in the best interest of the people in Chile, and certainly in our best interest.

News conference, Washington, Sept. 16/
The New York Times, 9-17:22.

Eric M. Gairy
Prime Minister of Grenada 3

I wouldn't kill a moth, spider, snake or lizard. I don't believe in violence. I'm a spiritual man. I am in the mystical world. Few people know how spiritually, mystically inclined I am. They say that man is afraid to unlock the door to himself. I am not one who has to be afraid. My opponents can't beat me. They are based on negativity. I am positivity. When they hate, I love. I send out waves of love to them. I pray for them. They hate me so much they can't eat and they can't sleep. But I laugh, I play tennis, I play cricket, I do yoga exercises, I dance and I am happy inside. Very happy.

Interview/Time, 2-18:51.

Ernesto Geisel
President of Brazil 4

We will insist that they [the developed nations] give us just, if not preferential, treatment [in trade]. They have been shouting at the under-developed world for many years to build up industry, and they cannot now, irresponsibly, block our exports of manufactured goods on allegations of unfair competition.

Before his Cabinet, Brasilia, March 19/
Los Angeles Times, 3-21:(1)21.

5

We will exert sincere efforts for gradual but sure progress toward democracy [in Brazil], broadening honest and mutually respectful dialogue and stimulating greater participation of responsible elites and the people in general.

Before his Cabinet, Brasilia, March 19/
The New York Times, 3-21:2.

Alastair W. Gillespie
Minister of Trade of Canada 6

Americans sensitive to the current Canadian climate must be aware that we are no longer interested in simply supplying rocks, logs and brains to more highly industrialized nations. Canadians want to make greater use of our own economic skills and potential.

San Francisco Examiner & Chronicle,
7-21:(This World)2.

Walter Heitmann
Chilean Ambassador to the United States 7

Everybody criticizes Chile. Why? Because we don't have free elections and courts like the

United States. Is everything in the U.S. a model or a masterpiece to be copied for other countries? We are not afraid of anything; we have nothing to hide. A citizen of any country of the world with which we have relations can go to Chile without a permit. Reporters can go; they can come and see and visit wherever they want ... If that is not freedom and liberty, what else is?

News conference, San Francisco, June 21/
San Francisco Examiner, 6-23:(A)17.

Robert S. Ingersoll
Deputy Secretary of State
of the United States

1

[On a vote by OAS members which failed to attain the two-thirds majority needed to rescind the blockade and sanctions against Cuba]: Our [the U.S.'s] abstention should not be taken as a sign of anything other than the fact that the United States has voted in accordance with its own perception of this question at this time. We respect the views of the majority who have voted for this resolution [to end the sanction/blockade]. We also respect the views of those who entertain such serious reservations with respect to Cuba and who therefore have felt it necessary to vote against.

Quito, Ecuador, Nov. 12/
Los Angeles Times, 11-13:(1)14.

Henry A. Kissinger
Secretary of State of the United States

2

The [Panama] Canal still operates under the terms of a treaty signed in 1903 when the realities of international affairs were still shaped by traditional precepts of power. [Any new treaty] must restore Panama's territorial sovereignty while preserving the interests of the United States and its participation in what is for us an indispensable international waterway.

Panama City, Panama, Feb. 7/
Los Angeles Times, 2-8:(1)10.

3

I know that many of my country's southern neighbors believe they have been the subject of too many surveys and too few policies. The United States is accused of being better at finding slogans for its Latin American policy than at finding answers to the problems that face us all. Some of the criticisms are justified. At times, rhetoric has exceeded performance. But the United States has been torn by many problems; only from afar does it appear as if all choices are equally open to us.

Panama City, Panama, Feb. 7/
The Washington Post, 2-8:(A)20.

4

[Calling for a new community of nations between the U.S., Caribbean and Latin-American countries]: One concern has dominated all others as I have met privately with some of my colleagues in this room. Does the United States really care [about Latin America]? Is this another exercise of high-sounding declarations followed by long periods of neglect? What is new in this dialogue? ... The United States will do its full part to see that our enterprise succeeds. We can make a major contribution; but it would be in nobody's interest if we raised impossible expectations, leaving our peoples frustrated and our community empty. We will promise only what we can deliver. We will make what we can deliver count.

At Western Hemisphere conference,
Mexico City, Feb. 21/
The New York Times, 2-22:10.

5

Since I've become Secretary of State, I've spent a considerable amount of time on Western Hemisphere relationships ... I have found two things: One is that the mere act of dialogue in the Western Hemisphere has had an emotional response; and secondly, I have been struck in my meetings—I've now attended three foreign ministers' meetings in the Western Hemisphere—by the fact that if one reads the records without the mood of the meetings, one would find in them a litany of criticism of the United States. But if one actually was at the meetings, one had the sense that this was a family quarrel; that, in some intangible way, one was talking as a member of the family. So I think that in the Western Hemisphere we have the possibilities of a creative phase, provided the United States can shed its traditional predominance and recognize that the decisions

WHAT THEY SAID IN 1974

that emerge must be genuinely felt by our friends in the Western Hemisphere to be theirs.

Interview, Washington/
The New York Times, 10-13:(1)35.

Ernest W. Lefever
Senior fellow, Brookings Institution   1

[Saying the U.S. should continue economic and military aid to Chile despite criticism of such aid by some U.S. Senators and others who say that Chile's government is repressive]: Since the United States assists other governments to serve U.S. interests and provides aid to the severely repressive Soviet Union through trade and technical exchange, I can see no good political or philosophical reason why the U.S. government cannot provide a modest amount of aid to the anti-Marxist military regime of Chile, just as it has done to the pro-Marxist military regime of neighboring Peru. Further, as far as I can see, Chile is behaving well in the foreign-policy realm. It has restored its international credit. It has no designs on its neighbors. And it is potentially threatened by Peru, which, thanks to Soviet aid, enjoys a four-to-one tank superiority over Chile. I believe Chile deserves American understanding and support.

Interview/Human Events, 12-7:11.

Sol M. Linowitz
Former United States Ambassador to the
Organization of American States   2

[U.S.] President Nixon has been the first President in this century who prided himself on his knowledge of foreign policy and had no policy at all in Latin America.

At Democratic National Committee policy
conference, Washington, June 18/
The New York Times, 6-19:20.

Carlos Lleras (Restrepo)
Former President of Colombia   3

American economic dominance in this part of the world exists as a matter of fact. But the Latin countries have learned, after voting along to keep [Communist] China out of the United

Nations for 20 years, that the U.S. changes its diplomatic position strictly in accordance with its own interests and that there is no need to follow.

Interview/The Washington Post, 11-3:(A)18.

Fernando L. Lopez (Muino)
Cuban Ambassador to Mexico   4

We [Cuba] are not in a holy war with the United States. We would be willing to talk to the United States, given a single and irrevocable condition—that it end the blockade of Cuba.

News conference/
San Francisco Examiner, 4-4:15.

Olof Palme
Prime Minister of Sweden   5

[On Chile's current military government]: Sooner or later, the regime of blood in Chile will vanish in total degradation and humiliation, missed by few, despised by the entire democratic world.

At demonstration against the Chilean
government, Stockholm, Sept. 14/
The New York Times, 9-16:4.

Carlos Andres Perez
President-elect of Venezuela   6

My oil policy will not be anti-United States but by and for Venezuela . . . What I would like to see is the United States being more interested in Venezuela and Latin America than in our raw materials.

Interview, Caracas, March 11/
The New York Times, 3-12:12.

Carlos Andres Perez
President of Venezuela   7

Around us we see millions of men prostrated by wretchedness and ignorance; lives which want to rise up but are wasted . . . An essential plank of my government's action will be the fight against poverty. The Venezuelan state cannot look with indifference on the enrichment of a few with the wealth which belongs to all . . . If we continue to follow the same model of development, our wealth will continue to be concentrated, leaving behind in misery a growing sector of the population.

*Inaugural address, Caracas, March 12/
The Christian Science Monitor, 4-1:5B.*

1

We must take up the defense of Latin-American rights, trampled by the economic totalitarianism of the developed countries . . . Venezuela now has the opportunity to offer Latin America, with the backing of oil, efficient cooperation to carry out the common struggle for independent development, decent prices for other raw materials and a just and balanced participation in world trade.

*Inaugural address, Caracas, March 12/
The New York Times, 3-13:4.*

2

. . . democracy is in crisis in Latin America. [There] are very few countries whose governments are the result of popular elections. If these countries, Venezuela among them, do not prove now that democracy is a system with sufficient force to generate an order of social justice, then democracy will suffer the same fate here that it has suffered in other parts of Latin America. This circumstance should be taken into account by nations like the U.S. But we see that it is the other way around—that for having democratic governments perhaps we are considered weaker, for we are treated with less respect.

Interview, Caracas/Time, 12-16:48.

Isabel Peron
President of Argentina

3

[On her campaign to improve her country's economy]: We will not use complicated systems which, in the long run, break down. Instead, we will base our joint action, by the people and the government, on a saying of [the late President] General [Juan] Peron: Only the people will save the people.

Los Angeles Herald-Examiner, 8-18(F)5.

Augusto Pinochet (Ugarte)
President of the governing junta of Chile

4

Everywhere I go, I find popular support for the junta. The economic situation of our coun-

try is serious. But all the people say: "We know we are hungry. But we must tell you something, General: We're happy, because we have freedom. And that is worth all these sacrifices" . . . I am referring to individual freedom, where a man may think as he wants, [not] group-type freedom, which the Marxists took advantage of.

*News conference, Brasilia, Brazil, March 16/
The Washington Post, 3-17:(A)16.*

5

[Saying there are no plans to return Chile to civilian rule in the near future]: Let's imagine that our government took power, cleaned things up, held free elections and sent the military back to the barracks. What would happen later? The same tendencies that led the armed forces and the Federal police to take over the government would be back in three years. We have totally discarded this position.

*News conference, Brasilia, Brazil, March 16/
The Washington Post, 3-17:(A)16.*

6

When we [the military junta ruling Chile] accomplish our objectives, we will call clean elections and will turn over power to whoever wins the majority. But, in the meantime, these objectives have to be accomplished and they have no time limit. I said this the first day and I say it now . . . I have never said, and neither has anyone else, that this is a transition government. I have said that a transition government would mean a return of the delinquents who would act as they did before.

*News conference, Santiago, Sept. 4/
Los Angeles Times, 9-5:(1)23.*

Guillermo Rodriguez (Lara)
President of Ecuador

7

An end of the blockade against Cuba [by members of the OAS would mean] re-establishment of the full dimension of communications among the peoples of the continent, a diminishing of tensions and a halt to violence. The future of the Americas is at stake. [Full cooperation among Hemispheric countries is incompatible] with all forms of isolation or resistance in respecting the free decision of every state to

(GUILLERMO RODRIGUEZ [LARA])

have the form of government it considers most convenient.

Before Western Hemisphere foreign ministers, Quito, Ecuador, Nov. 8/ Los Angeles Herald-Examiner, 11-9:(A)4.

James R. Schlesinger
Secretary of Defense of the United States 1

[Defending U.S. arms sales to Latin America]: It is and has been fruitless for the United States to dictate to the governments of such sovereign nations the extent to which they should satisfy what they have determined to be their military requirements. By refusing to help them achieve modest modernization programs, we do not spur economic development or an alternative distribution of resources; we simply encourage them to make their military purchases elsewhere. This is inconsistent with a foreign policy which seeks strong regional associations with the nations of the Western Hemisphere.

Congressional testimony/ The Christian Science Monitor, 8-21:(B)3.

Mateo Marques Sere
Uruguayan Ambassador to the Organization of American States 2

Now ... that the specific proposal has been made [in the OAS] to lift the sanctions on the government of Cuba, the government of my country, after careful consideration, has decided that it should oppose this measure ... [T]he position of Uruguay ... is very simple: It is based on the fact that to permit the lifting of the sanctions would be equal to saying, on the part of Uruguay, that Cuba has not intervened recently in my country, or that its intervention has not been serious, or to considering that there has been a new categorically clear event that ensures that Cuba will not continue its intervention. In the view of my government, none of these hypotheses is true, and to have maintained otherwise would have been to fool ourselves, the Uruguayan people, and the American governments.

Before Organization of American States Permanent Council, Oct. 22/ Human Events, 11-9:4.

Juan Antonio Tack
Foreign Minister of Panama 3

The problem for Panama does not end with a simple negotiation of a juridic [Panama Canal] treaty [with the U.S.]. Instead, we have a very fundamental objective—of perfecting the national independence of Panama. We believe that, as long as we accept a colonial enclave like the Canal Zone in the heart of our country, we shall never be truly independent.

News conference/ Los Angeles Times, 2-17:(8)2.

Charles Thone
United States Representative, R–Nebraska 4

[Saying the U.S. should reassert its sovereignty over the Panama Canal]: Giving away the Panama Canal would make as much sense as giving Alaska back to the Soviet Union or Nebraska and the rest of the Louisiana Territory back to France.

Human Events, 5-11:2.

Strom Thurmond
United States Senator, R–South Carolina 5

[Arguing against the return of the U.S. Canal Zone territory to Panama]: [The Canal Zone was] obtained [by the U.S.] both through treaty and purchase of all the lands in fee simple. It is the most expensive territorial acquisition of the United States ... We own it. We bought it. It's ours. The President of the United States has no authority to dispose of this property except by an act of Congress. The State Department has no authority to dispose of this property except through an act of Congress.

Human Events, 4-13:4.

Pierre Elliott Trudeau
Prime Minister of Canada 6

[On the Prime Minister's limits of power]: A ship of state is a big thing to turn around and give another direction. And it isn't just the bureaucracy. It is the whole strictures of a society which is as large as ours, with such different regions where consensus is difficult to obtain. So, a society isn't a plastic thing that you mold after the particular image of the day. I think the important thing is that over a period of time, even if you are only acting at the margin, as it were, you can choose your priorities and objectives that give a different direction to society. But it's not the Prime Minister alone. It's the Prime Minister, and the Cabinet, and the Parliament, and the party, and everything else. It's a heavy apparatus. But, if you choose certain priorities, they will be achieved, perhaps longer than in the time span you had planned for.

Interview/
The New York Times Magazine, 11-3:53.

1

[On his country's influence with the U.S. resulting from U.S. energy shortfalls and Canadian oil and gas resources] : In a very short run we do have some leverage. But it would be ridiculous to think that you can use that kind of leverage over any long period of time with a neighbor which is obviously so much bigger and stronger and heavier than we are. I think it would be a very unwise government which would say, "We've got the U.S. in a bind because they need our energy." They [the U.S.] could have us in a bind over so many other things. The U.S. understands that, and we

understand that, and because of that, relations have been quite good.

Interview/
The New York Times Magazine, 11-3:62.

2

Our first priority is the defense of Canadian sovereignty. Our second is defense of the North American continent. The United States does not have to fear any changes in these priorities. Military cooperation with the United States always will rank very high with us.

Interview/
U.S. News & World Report, 12-16:28.

Leonard Woodcock
President, United Automobile
Workers of America

3

If U.S.-model cars are going to Cuba [through American auto manufacturers' foreign subsidiaries] anyway, isn't it about time for our government to amend the embargo so that Cuba can buy motor vehicles produced in this country? With more than 100,000 auto workers on indefinite layoffs, such trade opportunities should not be ignored. [The U.S. government has] approved massive trade with the powerful Soviet Union and sees no threat to national security in it. Surely, then, trade with its small satellite in the Western Hemisphere holds no danger for us.

March 15/The Washington Post, 3-16:(D)7.

Asia and the Pacific

Lance Barnard
Minister of Defense of Australia   1

You [the U.S.] must expect that we shall wish our [military and defense] relations with you to be consistent with our status as an independent nation. There is no other basis for our relationship. You yourselves will not be behaving in any other way. We are no longer able to behave as a junior partner dependent on the strategic and military policies of more-powerful friends.

New York, Jan. 4/
The Washington Post, 1-5:(A)14.

Zulfikar Ali Bhutto
Prime Minister of Pakistan   2

[Announcing his country's recognition of Bangladesh]: It is not a happy decision for me. I do not say I want this decision or am happy with it or that I'm not speaking out of sadness. But there is no other way. In Lahore today we have our friends, our [Arab] brothers, our well-wishers. They would never give us wrong advice. There are some among them who have not recognized Bangladesh because of us. I have sought their opinion and they all said the same thing—that you must take this step. It is in the interest of Pakistan . . .

Lahore, Pakistan, Feb. 22/
The Washington Post, 2-23:(A)14.

3

I might . . . be prepared to call the Prime Minister of India [Indira Gandhi] my sister. I might even be prepared to call her my elder sister. But my people, the people of Pakistan, will never call India their big brother.

Los Angeles Times, 6-4:(1)17.

4

[On India's recent detonation of an atomic device]: If India builds the bomb, we [Paki-

stan] will eat leaves and grass, even go hungry, but we will have to get one of our own.

Los Angeles Times, 6-4:(1)17.

5

[India's making Sikkim an associate state last week is] simply the latest demonstration of their [India's] psychosis—a craze to dominate, to spread their wings. We stand vindicated in our analysis. Half of our country is gone; half of Kashmir is gone. They marched into Goa and took that. They have gone nuclear. And now they have swallowed up Sikkim.

Interview, Rawalpindi, Sept. 10/
The Washington Post, 9-11:(A)13.

6

[Saying the U.S. should relax its ban on arms shipments to his country]: There is no question of encouraging an arms race [between Pakistan and India]. The disparity is so preponderant that it is not accurate to describe it as a race. There is this vast disparity in military position between Pakistan and India. Why should Pakistan be singled out for an embargo? India is receiving assistance from all over the world, including the Soviet Union. She's got her own ordnance factories, her own capacity. It's only an embargo on Pakistan. It baffles us why Pakistan should be singled out.

Interview, Rawalpindi, Oct. 9/
The New York Times, 10-14:10.

Birendra (Bir Bikram Shah Deva)
King of Nepal   7

[Saying he has no intention of liberalizing his rule over Nepal]: It's not that I'm against the norms of democracy. But there are different ways of achieving these norms. You can walk up the stairs or you can run. If you run, you fall . . . Since the beginning of recorded history in Nepal, we have known no other form of government other than that of monarchy.

And the experience that history conditions in the shaping of men's minds is not something that can be brushed aside . . .

Interview, Katmandu/
The Washington Post, 11-24:(B)3.

Chiang Ching-kuo
Premier of the Republic
of (Nationalist) China

1

The current turbulence [in Communist China] is a result of increased contacts with the outside world and the consequent exposure of the weakness of the regime. The struggle is an attempt to eradicate the after-effects of such contacts. The Communists are doing everything possible to suppress the people. I am confident the people will rise up and overthrow the Communists.

Interview, Taipei/Time, 3-11:52.

2

To negotiate [with Communist China] is to commit suicide; to compromise with them is to decease . . . For the Communists, detente is a means of pretending to make peace while winning the war.

Before Yuan (Parliament), Taipei, Sept. 17/
Los Angeles Times, 9-18:(1)5.

Chou En-lai
Premier of the People's Republic
of (Communist) China

3

At present, the Chinese people, tempered in the great proletarian Cultural Revolution and fighting with high spirit and militancy, have, under the leadership of the Party's Central Committee headed by our great leader, Chairman Mao, launched a surging nation-wide campaign to criticize [former Defense Minister] Lin Piao and Confucius. Lin Piao and Confucius were both reactionaries who tried to turn back the wheel of history. [The present campaign] is of far-reaching historic importance in strengthening and expanding the great achievements of the great proletarian Cultural Revolution, consolidating the dictatorship of the proletariat and preventing a capitalist restoration . . . Social-imperialism and foreign die-hards hostile to the Chinese people are . . . viciously attack-

ing this campaign. This shows that we are doing the right thing.

At dinner honoring Zambian President
Kenneth Kaunda, Peking, Feb. 24/
The New York Times, 2-25:4.

4

The Chinese people consistently support the just struggles of all oppressed nations and oppressed peoples. This is our international duty. We hold, at the same time, that the social system of a country can be chosen and decided only by its own people and cannot be imposed by other countries. Countries with different social systems can develop state relations on the basis of the five principles of mutual respect for sovereignty and territorial integrity, mutual non-aggression, non-interference in each other's internal affairs, equality and mutual benefit and peaceful coexistence.

At banquet honoring Malaysian Prime
Minister Tun Abdul Razak, Peking/
The Washington Post, 6-23:(A)14.

Henry Steele Commager
Historian

5

[On former U.S. President Nixon's accomplishments in improving U.S. relations with Communist China]: To hang medals on Nixon for China is like pinning medals on someone who sets your house on fire for 20 years and finally puts it out.

At Hill Preparatory School, Pottstown, Pa./
Los Angeles Times, 11-6:(1)2.

Eric P. W. de Costa
Director, Indian Institute of Public Opinion

6

[Saying a majority of the Indian people want India to have atomic weapons]: It appears clearly enough that public opinion does not reflect the government's determination to confine atomic power to peaceful uses. There will be pressure to create nuclear weapons to be used defensively, and the moral force of the Ghandian age has been eroded so greatly that the government cannot rely on its small residue . . . it is for the Indian people to recognize that their terrible ambivalence will engender

(ERIC P. W. DE COSTA)

less credibility abroad on India's assurance of her ultimate peaceful ends.

New Delhi, July 29/
Los Angeles Times, 7-29:(1)5.

Gerald R. Ford
President of the United States 1

To the People's Republic of [Communist] China, whose legendary hospitality I enjoyed, I pledge continuity in our commitment to the principles of the Shanghai communique. The new relationship built on those principles has demonstrated that it serves serious and objective mutual interests and has become an enduring feature of the world scene.

First address as President before
Congress, Washington, Aug. 12/
The New York Times, 8-13:20.

Takeo Fukuda
Former Minister of Finance of Japan 2

[On his resigning as Finance Minister because of his Liberal Democratic Party's poor showing in the recent election]: Never in my worst dreams did I expect that sort of outcome. It was a complete defeat. The result must be interpreted as a cold, severe criticism of the Liberal Democratic Party's image. If this situation is allowed to continue, there is a possibility the Liberal Democratic Party will disintegrate. That, in turn, means the disintegration of Japan.

Tokyo, July 16/
Los Angeles Times, 7-17:(1)7.

Indira Gandhi
Prime Minister of India 3

[On the feeling of many Indians abroad that there is no place for them in India]: ... I would say there is *some* truth in it. You see, life here can't possibly be easy. So if they go abroad, they have a much easier time. They earn more. They have better opportunities to go higher up, and so on. We are still at perhaps the equivalent of the pioneering stage in the U.S. At that time, everybody had to work very

hard in order just to survive. This is, to some extent, the situation here, especially for the average person. But I think that life is much more exciting here than anywhere else, because you still are at the building stage, and you still can have the feeling that you are molding the future. So it depends how you look at life. I mean, if you want it easy, then obviously there isn't that ease here. But if you are looking for challenges, there is no shortage of them.

Interview, New Delhi/
The Christian Science Monitor, 1-7:(F)1.

4

[On foreign criticism of India's detonation of an atomic device]: Is it the contention that it is all right for the rich to use nuclear energy for destruction but not right for a poor country to find out whether it can be used for construction? We have been taunted that a poor nation cannot afford this luxury of nuclear tests. This same argument was advanced when we established our steel mills and machine-building plants. They were necessary for development; for it is only through acquiring higher technology that we can overcome backwardness and poverty.

At function marking the anniversary
of the founding of the Organization
of African Unity/
The Christian Science Monitor, 5-30:3C.

5

[On India's recent detonation of an atomic device]: There is a difference between a nuclear country and a nuclear-*weapons* country. We are not a nuclear-weapons country; we don't have any bombs. We don't intend to use this knowledge or this power for any other than peaceful purposes. Our neighbors need have no fear. We view the explosion as an extension of our work of research and keeping abreast of developments in science and technology; we have not viewed it in the light of strengthening or creating fear or prestige or pride.

Interview/Newsweek, 6-3:37.

6

In the U.S., you tend to see [relations with India] in terms of aid and assistance. We have needed help and credits, and we do need them now. But why should this color a relationship of one country with another? A basic friendship is an understanding of what the other country is trying to do ... My impression is that it's the Americans who are browned-off about giving aid. First, they stopped everything after the Bangladesh war. Then they said they would resume in a very limited manner what had already been in the pipeline ... As a matter of fact, we give some aid to the U.S. in the form of a brain drain; America manages to take some of our best scientists.

Interview/Newsweek, 6-3:37.

1

Our problems are special. We have a far greater population than any other country. We are trying to solve our problems in an open, democratic society. No system is perfect; but in a country of India's vast diversity, there is one system, the democratic system, that listens to the voice of the people.

Madras, India, Sept. 9/
The New York Times, 9-11:6.

Noel Gayler
Admiral, United States Navy;
Commander-in-Chief, U.S. Armed Forces/
Pacific

2

I happen to be one of those who believe that the Pacific is the area of the future. It's the area where the rate of change is greatest. It's a very large area of the world, and it contains two-thirds of the human race. It is the area where the potential for conflict is certainly as sharp as anywhere, because the gap between the rich and the poor is increasing, both within countries and between countries. And it's an area where the military might of Russia impinges very badly. The Russians have twice formally offered to organize the area under their tent. They haven't gotten very much political support. But it's quite clear that, if Russia were seen to be the dominant military power out there, the political situation would change a great deal.

Interview, Washington/
U.S. News & World Report, 3-25:43.

Jiro Inagawa
Japanese Ambassador to Lebanon

3

Japanese-Arab relations are now going into a new phase, as a result of the influence of Arab oil and the dependence of the world economy on it. Since Japan is an economic power and an industrialized country, it is natural for us to cultivate very good relations with the Arab world—particularly the oil-producing countries.

Interview/Los Angeles Times, 5-5:(6)1.

Walter H. Judd
Former United States Representative,
R–Minnesota; Former medical
missionary in China

4

[On Nationalist China]: Some thought those island refugees couldn't survive their obstacles, but they did so well that we [the U.S.] stopped our aid to them nine years ago. Except for the United States, Taiwan now has the greatest percentage of children in its schools; when everyone else is having to tighten controls, they don't need to; and above all, they speak of renaissance, not revolution, for they realize that they, not Mao [Tse-tung], represent the store-house for their magnificent heritage.

Before American Bureau for Medical Aid
to (Free) China, Los Angeles/
Los Angeles Herald-Examiner, 10-8:(B)2.

T. N. Kaul
Indian Ambassador to the United States

5

[On foreign criticism of India's recent detonation of an atomic device]: Our priorities in India are different from those of the more developed countries. We have been hit hard by the hike in oil prices and the increasing costs of food, fertilizer, industrial raw materials and transfer of technology. Our needs and requirements are more urgent. We see great potential in nuclear technology, not only for producing power which we already do, but also for cheaper and quicker exploitation of underground coal, gas and minerals. We spend only about one per cent of our total outlay in the public sector on nuclear research as against five per cent on health and family planning, six per cent on education and social welfare, 16 per

WHAT THEY SAID IN 1974

(T. N. KAUL)

cent on irrigation and power, 20 per cent on transport and communications, 20 per cent on agriculture and 24 per cent on mines and metals. The nuclear explosion and nuclear technology open up vistas of more power, more tube wells, more agricultural pumps, more fertilizer, better seeds, better utilization of our installed capacity in industry and greater employment to thousands of unemployed engineers and others. Our nuclear experiment cost us less than $400,000—in rupees and not in foreign exchange—as against billions spent by others. There is no limit to research and development of science and technology, and maybe our scientists can show a better way of using nuclear technology for peaceful purposes than the nuclear-weapon powers have done, whose main aim has, so far, been to use it for weaponry. Let us learn from each other and place the benefits of our technology, research and development at the disposal of all mankind, especially the developing countries which need it most.

At National Press Club, Washington, June 17/
The Washington Post, 6-21:(A)22.

Kim Dong Jo
Foreign Minister of South Korea 1

[Saying there are no political prisoners in his country and that the U.S. should not cut military aid because of recent prosecutions of dissenters]: What is the motive of cutting? Do they want to give a hard time to the [South] Korean government by which ... Korea would become softer and insecure, with an unstable government? I don't think the U.S. government would do that ... As a friend, as an ally, why don't you [the U.S.] understand [South] Korea is under threat from North Korea? It is not only a threat externally but also internally. Do you think [North Korean Premier] Kim Il Sung is only sticking to military action against South Korea? He is also expecting revolution and instability and confusion, an uprising of the people [in South Korea].

Interview, Seoul, Aug. 14/
Los Angeles Times, 8-15:(1)14.

Kim Il Sung
Premier of North Korea 2

Today, the Korean question ... boils down to the question of reunification or division; whether one Korea or two Koreas. The entire Korean people unanimously aspire to the reunification of their country. But the great powers want the division of our country. To divide and rule is an old method of imperialism. The U.S. imperialists and the Japanese militarists seek the permanent division of Korea, the former to reduce South Korea to their permanent colonial military base and the latter to take hold of South Korea as their permanent commodity market ... Those who love the country and the nation should not tolerate the machinations of the U.S. and Japanese reactionaries to convert South Korea into a permanent colony, but compel the U.S. troops out of South Korea, forestall the infiltration of the Japanese militarists and actively turn out to build a sovereign, reunified and independent Korea. What is the use of holding the North-South dialogue if our nation is to live divided? The North-South dialogue must be conducted for the purpose of achieving the reunification.

At rally, Pyongyang, North Korea/
International Herald Tribune, 10-9:9.

Kim Jong Pil
Premier of South Korea 3

When we have only $500-a-year per capita income, we can enjoy only that much democracy.

Interview/The New York Times, 8-5:6.

Henry A. Kissinger
Secretary of State of the United States 4

Any attempt [by the U.S.] to play off the Soviet Union and Communist China against each other would have a high risk that, at least for tactical reasons, they would combine against us. The rivalry and tensions between the Soviet Union and Communist China were not created by the United States. In fact, we didn't believe in their reality for much too long a time. They cannot be exploited by the United States. They can only be noted by the United States. The correct policy for the United States is to take account of what exists and to conduct a policy of meticulous honesty with both of them, so that neither believes we are trying to use one against the other. In the course of events, it may happen that one may feel that it is gaining benefit against the other as a result of dealing with us, but that cannot be our aim or purpose. We have meticulously avoided forms of cooperation with the Soviet Union that could be construed as directed against China. We have never signed agreements whose chief purpose could be seen as directed against China. And conversely, we have never participated with China in declarations that could be seen as aimed at the Soviet Union. We have developed our bilateral relationships with both, and left them to sort out their relationships with each other. In fact, we have rarely talked to either of them about the other.

Interview, Washington/
The New York Times, 10-13:(1)35.

Walter Laqueur
Director, Institute of Contemporary
Affairs, London
1

[Communist] China, in Russian thinking, is the Number One problem—not America. The Russians recognize America as a status-quo power; America wants to leave things alone. But whereas the Chinese may be weak today, economically and militarily, they have the unbounded self-confidence of people knowing time works for them. Their population is 700 million. They are making slow progress. They are in a strong position as far as the Communist parties in Asia are concerned. I think the Russians have given up hope of permanent reconciliation with China. But it is with hope that they see that the Chinese leadership is nearer 80 than 70. Soon a new generation will come up, with which there may be at least a normalization of relations or, alternatively, there will be a struggle for power in China. As in the days of the warlords, the Chinese may fight each other, or there may be another cultural revolution. Thus, China, at least for a number of years, would no longer be an active power in world politics.

Interview, Washington/
Los Angeles Times, 4-3:(2)7.

Salvador P. Lopez
President, University of the Philippines
2

The present martial-law regime [in the Philippines] is itself an example of the adaptive capacity of the Filipino. Thousands of people have been arrested, detained and then released. There appears to be no deliberate policy of physical torture, and no political prisoner has been executed. The military is firmly under civilian control, and there is a noticeable absence of uniformed authority in the streets or public places. If President [Ferdinand] Marcos is a dictator, he is too mild to be an effective one. I suspect that he is a crypto-democrat—an authoritarian who cannot quite get over his democratic upbringing. Incredulous foreign observers have dubbed it "martial law-Philippine style." It is, indeed, peculiarly Philippine in that, contrary to the American practice, martial rule co-exists with and is subject to civilian authority. Martial law in the Philippines may have certain affinities with the dictatorships of ancient Rome, but little if any with those of recent or contemporary history ... It is, however, too early to say whether President Marcos is ready to lead the nation on the long road back to a democratic polity. Since he has repeatedly stated that martial law is a "temporary constitutional expedient" and that he is running a race with time, there is at least reason to hope that the Philippines might avoid the disastrous consequences which in other countries have come in the wake of the imposition and subsequent overthrow of authoritarian regimes. On the other hand, there are signs, also, of a growing restiveness among the people arising in part from the adoption of policies crucially affecting the country's future without prior public discussion and consultation, and partly from the worsening economic situation which is seriously eroding one of the regime's principal claims to public support.

Honolulu, Oct. 30/Vital Speeches, 12-15:157.

Ferdinand E. Marcos
President of the Philippines
3

Our goal is to guarantee every Filipino a decent minimum of food, clothing and shelter; and opportunity for every citizen to have

WHAT THEY SAID IN 1974

(FERDINAND E. MARCOS)

something socially useful to do; and for everyone to share in our nation's progress.
San Francisco Examiner, 6-11:31.

1

[Criticizing wealthy Filipinos who used their wealth to corrupt and control political power]: It is that combination of wealth and political power which has brought about this objectionable type of rich men. These are the oligarchs that we sought to dethrone. They symbolize the old society. They prevented the small man from equal opportunity and even from exercising freedom of the ballot. We will ultimately return to complete individual freedom and civil rights. When we do, these rich men and oligarchs will not have the control over political power that the old oligarchs had. So they will not be able to build their enclaves, their kingdoms, their private armies.
Interview, Manila, June 13/
The New York Times, 6-17:7.

2

[On whether, because of the current martial law, democracy is dead in the Philippines]: No, of course not. Even the proclamation of martial law and the setting up of a corresponding crisis government is a part of democracy and in accordance with our Constitution. When democracy is threatened, it exercises certain powers to protect itself. Either a constitution or a law usually provides for what is known as "crisis government," with a history going all the way back to the Roman republic. The Romans provided for a dictatorship in the event of a crisis. Some call it dictatorship; others call it "crisis government" or refer to it as military necessity; I call it authoritarianism. If the republic is endangered, then the commander-in-chief provision in our Constitution is invoked temporarily, for the period of the crisis. This is true of our country. However, in our particular case, I ordered that it be decided by the people. That is why we submitted it to the people in January, 1973—asking them what we should do—and again in the referendum of July, 1973. The people decided we should adopt a new Constitution and continue the exercise of the powers

of a crisis government. Therefore, I have my own marching orders to exercise these powers.
Interview, Manila/
U.S. News & World Report, 8-5:37.

3

[On whether the Philippines is no longer so anti-Communist as it once was]: We believe in peaceful coexistence. The cold war divided the world into watertight compartments—those sympathetic to Communism and those who identified with the free world. Bipolarization has now not only become unfashionable, but there is a new flexibility in the policies of those supporting the conflicting ideologies, Communism and democracy. We feel it unhealthy for a country to deal only with part of the world when it poses as a modern and progressive country. We have, therefore, modified and changed our orientation. We cannot close our eyes to the 800 million people of mainland [Communist] China nor the 200 million people of Russia.
Interview, Manila/
U.S. News & World Report, 8-5:38.

Takeo Miki
Prime Minister of Japan

4

As I look at the grave [political and economic] situation today, I recall that our forefathers successfully overcame the great difficulties of the Meiji Restoration and the defeat of World War II. Our forefathers surmounted their trials because they made self-sacrificing endeavors with courage, wisdom and perseverance. We have the responsibility to uphold the great achievements of our predecessors.
Televised address to the nation before
the Diet (Parliament), Tokyo, Dec. 14/
The New York Times, 12-15:(1)8.

5

We must shift gears from our high growth rate to a more stabilized growth. Total demand must be successfully curtailed. The Japanese economy, which was so abnormal in terms of the rest of the world, will now return to normal. Our life-style will have to be reoriented from quantitative to a more qualitative style . . . This, however, does not mean that a [wage- and price-control] policy—in the strict sense of the word—will be adopted. Since inflation is a world-wide phenomenon, it cannot be successfully tackled without international cooperation . . . We will refrain from promoting our exports in such a way as to disrupt international order. We do not want to be looked upon by the rest of the world with suspicion.

Interview/Newsweek, 12-16:38.

1

[On his country's relations with the U.S.]: I'm afraid thus far undue attention was paid to military aspects. Henceforth, I'd rather underline economic cooperation. It is essential that food and energy problems be resolved; U.S.-Japan cooperation in this area is indispensable. In regard to nuclear matters, though Japan may have the capability of developing nuclear weapons, the overwhelming majority of Japanese remain totally opposed to either our possession or manufacture of such weapons. Thus we must continue to depend on the nuclear deterrence of the United States.

Interview/Newsweek, 12-16:38.

Daniel P. Moynihan
United States Ambassador to India

2

[On U.S.-Indian relations]: Whether we've reached a dead end or started a new relationship, I just don't know. What I do know is that I think I've learned a fair amount about a country that will be much more important to us in five or 10 years. Perhaps few people are paying attention to India now, but they should be. India is the biggest democracy in the world, and the United States is the second largest. Our mutual concern and interest that each other's institutions should prosper and prevail and endure is fundamental. This is not simply rhetoric. It's a hard-headed assessment of mutual self-interest. There are not many practicing democracies today. There is little pleasure, and less prospect, in being the last of a disappearing species. In every important sense, we need each other.

Interview, New Delhi/
The New York Times Magazine, 3-31:17.

3

[Disputing those who say or suggest that the U.S. supplies arms to South Asian countries]: I am enough of a professor of government to know that some things sink in pretty slowly, but what in the hell do we have to do? We are the only country in the world which does *not* sell arms to South Asia that has any arms to sell. We are the only ones . . . Can anyone here name a country that produces arms for sale that does not sell them to Pakistan, India, Bangladesh, Ceylon, excepting the United States? We are the only one. And we've had the policy in effect since 1965 . . . and yet continually we are asked whether we are going to stop arms to South Asia. We adopted this policy with the expectation that it would be met with approval in the region to which it has applied, and approval at least involves some measure of acknowledgment . . . If a policy designed to win a measure of approval wins none, then it clearly is a failed policy. I don't think this is a failed policy, but I hope it does not become one.

News conference, New Delhi, Dec. 15/
Los Angeles Times, 12-16:(1)1,8.

4

[Saying the U.S. pays too little attention to India]: This [India] is a democracy—a huge Asian democracy—and there aren't many around. Half of the people on earth who live in a society with civil liberties live in India. If that disappeared, you would know it. I can understand the [U.S.] fascination with [Communist] China, but I don't understand the corresponding [U.S.] disinterest here . . . I have been here two years and only one Congressman has come here and four Senators—one stayed 16 hours and took his wife to the Taj Mahal and the other was on his way to Bangladesh and had to change planes. Obviously, most people don't think it's interesting or important here, and that's wrong. They also don't think that they'll be welcome here, and that's wrong. They're all trying to get visas to China. It's not wrong to get visas to China, but they should see India, too. We've spent 25 years talking about democracies, and the only places we seem to be interested in are dictatorships. A dictatorship will assure you a friendly press and enthusiastic

(DANIEL P. MOYNIHAN)

crowds at the airport, and India can't do that because it's free. India is the largest nation committed to a free democratic society, and we should simply not forget that.

Interview, New Delhi/
The New York Times, 12-15:(1)1,4.

Palden Thondup Namgyal
Chogyal (King) of Sikkim

1

What choice has Sikkim but to live under the protection of India? The only choice is [Communist] China, but any practical-minded person will know that is not in the interest of Sikkim. All that I said and wanted was that India be the big brother and Sikkim the little brother. You [India] give us love and support, which we will reciprocate. Under your protection we will become strong, economically viable, which will be a good thing for you. After all, we also want a place under the sun.

Interview, Gangtok, Sikkim, April 18/
The New York Times, 4-23:4.

W. R. Poage
United States Representative, D–Texas

2

[On India's detonation of a nuclear device earlier this year]: They spent a lot of money on that bomb that should have been spent on something productive instead of something provocative. India has received more food from us than any other nation, and I'd rather give it to a country that isn't using every possible forum to condemn us before the rest of the world.

U.S. News & World Report, 12-16:21.

Mujibur Rahman
Prime Minister of Bangladesh

3

[On the achievements of his government since taking power after the 1971 war of independence against Pakistan, and the problems the country still faces]: My factories are working, my jute mills, my industries, my cultivators are working. I am a member of the World Bank; I am a member of the IMF; I am in the Asian Development Bank; I am in the Islamic Bank; I am in the Commonwealth; I hope to become a member of the UN . . . We have suffered from a terrible cyclone in 1971. Then the Pakistani murderer killed 3 million of my people, destroyed my houses and my factories, insulted my women. Then we have a drought and then floods. Then the war in the Middle East and oil prices went up. Now this flood. We are only 32 months old, but some people expect us to perform like a long-established country. The Pakistanis diverted all our assets. We started our government with less than zero, with liabilities. I had to rehabilitate 10 million refugees. The efficiency you expect we cannot give. We need time.

Interview, Dacca, Aug. 27/
The Washington Post, 8-29:(A)25.

Jagjivan Ram
Minister of Defense of India

4

[On foreign criticism of India's detonation of an atomic device]: Why should there be this kind of reaction? We are doing this for peaceful purposes and not for military uses. The armed forces know this is not for their use. It is only for peaceful uses, for mining, for oil prospecting, for finding underground water. It is for scientific and technical knowledge.

Interview, New Delhi, May 22/
Los Angeles Herald-Examiner, 5-23:(A)6.

Carlos P. Romulo
Foreign Secretary of the Philippines

5

Everyone knows that in the Korean war and the Vietnam war Japan was the one Asian power that reaped financial and economic benefits from both wars . . . Asians are looking with anticipation to the steps that Japan will take to help in the reconstruction and rehabilitation of Asia, and to continue with its non-military policy and the fight against imperialism. Imperialism is of two kinds: the military kind and the economic kind. Japan should beware of both. Economic imperialism is more dangerous than military imperialism.

San Francisco Examiner & Chronicle,
1-13:(This World)12.

John A. Scali
United States Ambassador/Permanent
Representative to the United Nations
1

[Disputing claims by exiled former Cambodian Chief of State Norodom Sihanouk and his supporters that he controls over 80 per cent of Cambodia's territory and population]: The fact is that despite the best efforts of a foreign-inspired and assisted insurgency, and of the North Vietnamese Army, the Khmer [Cambodian] government has never ceased to maintain control over the vast majority of Cambodia's people and over the territory in which they live. The truth is that Prince Sihanouk does not return to lead his people because he has no safe haven in Cambodia.

Before United Nations General Assembly,
New York, Nov. 27/
Los Angeles Times, 11-28:(1)5.

Karan Singh
Minister of Health and Family
Planning of India
2

The population of India has increased by 100,000 since you began this meeting. Population explosion is the basic evil behind all our problems, and yet the Prime Minister [Indira Gandhi] never speaks about birth control in her speeches, nor does it find a place in her policy resolutions.

At All-India Congress Committee meeting,
New Delhi, July 21/
The New York Times, 7-22:3.

Kakuei Tanaka
Prime Minister of Japan
3

As a homogeneous people, the 100,000,000 citizens of Japan within their island country have no ethnic conflicts, no religious or language disputes. Thus, we have been able to concentrate our efforts solely on rehabilitation and construction. In this respect, we may be regarded as extremely fortunate among the nations of the world. At the same time, it is because of this peculiarity that we have yet a great deal to learn and criticize ourselves for in the areas of international cooperation and dealings with other peoples. The exclusive, narrow-minded manner of pursuing national interests, which may have been overlooked and justified to some extent in the process of rehabilitation in the midst of the ruins immediately after our defeat in war, is not only no longer internationally valid but also a possible source of misfortune. Today, we must listen with an open mind to just criticisms of us, rectify what ought to be rectified, and try to maintain and augment an exchange and relationship of mutual benefit based on a long-term perspective. Only when we judge not with our own yardstick, become good neighbors to the other Asian nations and share both pain and pleasure with them, can we contribute to the establishment of an everlasting peace in Asia.

Before the Diet (Parliament), Tokyo,
Jan. 21/Vital Speeches, 2-15:270.

4

[On what has caused anti-Japanese outbursts during his current trip through Southeast Asia]; That's really a very difficult question. When you have a disease, you have to have a proper diagnosis before you can prescribe the medicine. You are asking me to diagnose the causes. Let me venture to say that one possible cause is that the growth of our economic exchanges has been very speedy. Apart from the economic problems, there is a language barrier and differences in social customs. Also, our Japanese businessmen are not infallible and are not all divine creatures.

News conference, Malaysia/
The New York Times, 2-21:3.

5

Nuclear weapons absolutely must not be used. Japan, as the only nation among 140-some countries of the world to have suffered atomic attacks, makes that appeal to all mankind. Thus, Japan has made it clear it will not use or possess nuclear weapons. Since we have no such weapon, it is only natural that we depend upon the nuclear umbrella of the United States.

At Foreign Correspondents Club, Tokyo,
Oct. 22/Los Angeles Times, 10-23:(1)5.

6

It is a readily accepted notion that the United States of America has often tended to

(KAKUEI TANAKA)

look toward Europe, the major ethnic as well as cultural source of its people. At the same time, the United States has built up a position of enormous influence from which it can decisively affect the political and economic situations in all parts of the world. It is therefore necessary for the United States to work toward peace in its Pacific as well as Atlantic dimensions in order to maintain effectively peace in the world. I feel that America's contribution toward world prosperity can be truly fruitful only when it is motivated by its constructive hope to develop its friendship with countries across the Pacific, as well as by its feeling of close affinity with countries across the Atlantic.

At luncheon for visiting U.S. President Ford, Tokyo, Nov. 19/ Los Angeles Times, 11-19:(1)6.

Teng Hsiao-ping
Vice Premier of the People's Republic of (Communist) China 1

China is not a superpower, nor will she ever seek to be one. What is a superpower? A superpower is an imperialist country which everywhere subjects other countries to its aggression, interference, control, subversion or plunder, and strives for world hegemony ... If one day China should change her color and turn into a superpower, the people of the world should identify her as social-imperialism, expose it, oppose it and work together with the Chinese people to overthrow it.

At United Nations/ The Washington Post, 4-26:(A)30.

Fumihiko Togo
Vice Foreign Minister of Japan 2

Since the end of World War II, for more than two decades, the Foreign Ministry, and Japan as a whole, have been adopting the attitude that we must avoid becoming wrapped up in any political or military problems of the outside world. Even more than the Foreign Ministry, Japan in its entirety has adopted this attitude. We were able to succeed in developing economically such a policy and, for that era, such an attitude was probably appropriate. But when we look at the future, there is doubt how much further we can advance with such a policy. We are now being questioned quite sincerely by foreign nations not about what military responsibility Japan will take but about what political responsibility it will assume. Even in the field of economic aid, Japan must clarify its political position to be able to perform any meaningful task.

Before Japan National Press Club, Tokyo, May 24/Los Angeles Times, 5-25:(1)17.

Pierre Elliott Trudeau
Prime Minister of Canada 3

[On India's recent detonation of an atomic device]: I'm very disappointed that they have joined the nuclear-bomb club. I'm very disappointed that they spent all this money to explode a nuclear bomb when their people are starving.

Before high-school students, May 24/ The Dallas Times Herald, 5-26:(A)2.

Jerome B. Wiesner
President, Massachusetts Institute of Technology 4

I have just been in the People's Republic of [Communist] China, where 25 years ago there was a lot of hunger. It was the kind of situation in which most people would have thrown up their hands and said it is impossible to do anything about such a society. China is not affluent, yet they have made impressive progress and have managed their agriculture, distribution and social system so that they have now eliminated starvation and the worst kind of poverty you see in most other developing countries.

Interview, Cambridge, Mass./ Los Angeles Times, 12-12:(2)7.

INDOCHINA

Daniel Bell
Professor of Sociology, Harvard University
1

The war was a misjudgment. Maybe it was in the [U.S.] national interest to maintain a degree of balance in Southeast Asia; but the means were highly disproportionate to the ends. It was an incredible failure not to have maintained proportionality of ends and means.

Interview, Cambridge, Mass./
Los Angeles Times, 3-22:(2)5.

Leo E. Benade
Lieutenant General, United States Army;
Deputy Assistant Secretary of Defense
for Personnel Policy
2

[Opposing amnesty for U.S. Vietnam draft-dodgers and deserters]: The alternatives were clear at the time a choice was made, and an individual should be required to face the consequences of the choice he made ... [Other men had to take their places and] were just as reluctant to participate in a war. But they served their country. Some suffered temporarily. Some suffered permanently. Some died. [Amnesty would] dangerously impair any future draft, undermine military justice and hurt military morale and discipline. In a future conflict, service members would certainly be less hesitant to desert if they felt that they could do so with reasonable confidence that, once the conflict was over, they would be granted immunity.

Before House Judiciary Subcommittee,
Washington, March 13/
The Dallas Times Herald, 3-13:(A)10.

James L. Buckley
United States Senator, C—New York
3

[On amnesty for U.S. Vietnam draft-dodgers and deserters]: There is no greater injustice than to demean the sacrifice of those [who]

gave their lives in past wars by restoring to the full privileges of citizenship, without individual review, those who deliberately chose to shirk their clear responsibilities under the law ... Our legal system has always been capable of providing leniency to the accused when it is appropriate. We can rely on our legal process to reliably distinguish between the genuine conscientious objection to all warfare and those others who sought to provide safety for themselves only by increasing the danger to which fellow citizens were exposed.

Quote, 12-22:579.

Tran Quoc Buu
President, Confederation of (South)
Vietnamese Trade Unions
4

The popular movements [demonstrating against President Thieu's Administration] have reappeared at a time when the nation is becoming more and more upset by an inefficient and corrupt leadership. In order to achieve national reconciliation, the government must first of all try to restore the faith of the people by a thorough review of national policies, by cleaning the leadership from the central to the local level and by vigorously eradicating corruption and social injustices. Peace is the key to unlock all of the present national impasses. Only peace can help put an end to a policy carried out in the name of national security to limit or delay the real implementation of democracy.

At the Confederation's 25th anniversary
meeting, Saigon, Oct. 29/
The New York Times, 10-30:10.

Charunphan Issarangkun na Ayuthaya
Foreign Minister of Thailand
5

We are certain that there is ... ample room for improvement in our relations with the

(CHARUNPHAN ISSARANGKUN
NA AYUTHAYA)

Soviet Union. Being a great country and world power, the Soviet Union can perhaps be expected to foster mutual relations and imbue them with warmth, trust and friendship to the benefit of the people of the two countries. As regards the conflict in Indochina in particular, we believe that the Soviet Union is in a strong position to contribute to the restoration of peace and harmony to the long-suffering people living there, and thereby contribute positively to the stability of the entire region.

At Foreign Correspondents Club of Thailand, Bangkok, Jan. 16/The New York Times, 1-17:3.

William P. Clements, Jr.
Deputy Secretary of Defense of the United States 1

[Asking for $424 million in additional U.S. aid for South Vietnam]: We have invested heavily in lives and treasure in Southeast Asia. The results could be tragic if we should fail to give this modest additional support, which is but a fraction—a sorely needed fraction—of our prior efforts.

The New York Times, 4-18:2.

Alan Cranston
United States Senator, D–California 2

[Arguing against increased U.S. aid for South Vietnam]: We have finally stopped wasting lives in Vietnam. We must now stop wasting American dollars there, too.

The New York Times, 4-18:2.

Robert F. Drinan
United States Representative, D–Massachusetts 3

. . . only history will discover why the greatest deception and possibly the most impeachable offense of [U.S. President] Richard Nixon may not become [an impeachment] charge against him. I speak of the concealment of the clandestine war in Cambodia [in 1969-70]. I do not here reach the claimed merits of the bombings. I speak only of its concealment . . . I remember well my absolute consternation on July 16, 1973, when the Cambodian bombings were revealed for the first time. I learned on that day that President Nixon had misled me and misled the entire nation when he had said three years prior to that time on April 30, 1970, that: "For the past five years, we have provided no military assistance whatever and no economic assistance to Cambodia." The calculated cover-up of Cambodia, like the cover-up of Watergate, unraveled by accident. We heard of it in the Congress and in the country because a foreign correspondent happened to report on his discovery in Cambodia of the thousands of craters made by American B-52s. There was, in my judgment, no justification for maintaining secrecy about that war. [Cambodian] Prince Sihanouk knew; the Cambodians knew; the North Vietnamese knew; everyone knew except the people of America, and this information was withheld from them until it happened to come out.

At House Judiciary Committee hearing, Washington, July 25/ The New York Times, 7-26:13.

Gerald R. Ford
President of the United States 4

[On U.S. Vietnam draft-dodgers and deserters]: These young Americans should have a second chance to contribute their fair share to the rebuilding of peace among ourselves and with all nations. So I am throwing the weight of my Presidency into the scales of justice on the side of leniency. I foresee their earned re-entry [to the U.S.] into a new atmosphere of hope, hard work and mutual trust . . . I will act promptly, fairly and very firmly, in the same spirit that guided Abraham Lincoln and Harry Truman: as I reject amnesty, so I reject revenge. I ask all Americans who ever asked for goodness and mercy in their lives, who ever sought forgiveness for their trespasses, to join in rehabilitating all the casualties of the tragic conflict of the past.

Before Veterans of Foreign Wars, Chicago, Aug. 19/Los Angeles Times, 8-20:(1)1,12.

5

[On his conditional-clemency program for U.S. Vietnam draft-dodgers and deserters]: The program provides for administrative disposition of cases involving draft evaders and military deserters not yet convicted or punished. In such cases, 24 months of alternate service will be required which may be reduced for mitigating circumstances. The program also deals with cases of those already convicted by a civilian or military court. For the latter purpose, I am establishing a Clemency Review Board of nine distinguished Americans whose duty it will be to assist me in assuring that the government's forgiveness is extended to applicable cases of prior conviction as equitably and as impartially as is humanly possible. The primary purpose of this program is the reconciliation of all our people and the restoration of the essential unity of Americans within which honest differences of opinion do not descend to angry discord and mutual problems are not polarized by excessive passion. My sincere hope is that this is a constructive step toward a calmer and cooler appreciation of our individual rights and responsibilities and our common purpose as a nation, whose future is always more important than its past.

Sept. 16/The Washington Post, 9-17:(A)8.

1

It has been said that [the] forgotten men of the Vietnam conflict are those [Americans] who served. They're the silent heroes of their generation. Too often, those who failed in their duty [U.S. Vietnam draft-dodgers and deserters] have monopolized the headlines and distorted the image of their generation... They [the veterans] served in spite of the most difficult psychological pressures. They served at a time when many of their peers and their elders were denouncing service to one's country as immoral. They served while some avoided service. They served without the full moral support that this nation has usually given its fighting forces.

At Veterans Day ceremony,
Arlington National Cemetery, Va., Oct. 28/
Chicago Tribune, 10-29:(1)1,11.

J. William Fulbright
United States Senator, D–Arkansas

2

As we all know, the U.S. forces were withdrawn [from Vietnam] on schedule and the North Vietnamese returned nearly 600 American military and civilian prisoners. Since then, unfortunately, the North Vietnamese and their allies in the South have refused to cooperate with our efforts to account for some 1,300 Americans still missing, to explain the more than 50 discrepancies in their earlier accounting, or to permit the recovery of the remains of any of our known dead from North Vietnam. [The] message which Hanoi is seeking to convey [would require] agreeing to discuss Hanoi's concerns about the over-all implementation of the cease-fire agreement... The pitfalls in such an approach are obvious; but in the apparent absence of military or other political leverage on the North Vietnamese, it is a possibility which should be considered, [although] Hanoi should recognize... the inhumanity of this attitude...

The Washington Post, 1-27:(A)4.

Noel Gayler
Admiral, United States Navy;
Commander-in-Chief, Armed Forces/Pacific

3

I don't think that North Vietnam has given up or is about to give up its drive to put all of Vietnam under its control. They play both political and military forces and rely heavily upon assassination and terrorism. They've murdered over 100 South Vietnamese hamlet and village chiefs since the cease-fire a year ago. Despite these political assassinations, they haven't had the political success that we know they expected to have. But they have not stopped. They are trying to improve their position with the people and the control of land in South Vietnam.

Interview, Washington/
U.S. News & World Report, 3-25:42.

Vo Nguyen Giap
Minister of Defense of North Vietnam

4

Now that the U.S. is beset with difficulties—its military, economic and political weakening, its many other troubles at home and abroad—the prospects of the revolution in South Vietnam are very good. [The U.S.' only purpose for continuing military aid to the South is] to carry out the Nixon Doctrine minus [former

WHAT THEY SAID IN 1974

(VO NGUYEN GIAP)

U.S. President] Nixon in order to maintain the puppet regime without the U.S. presence, thus making South Vietnam a separate state in the U.S. camp, to the perpetual partition of Vietnam. There is every possibility for the national, democratic revolution of South Vietnam, despite the hard journey ahead, to achieve complete victory.

Before National Assembly, Hanoi, Dec. 23/
Los Angeles Times, 12-26:(1)4.

Barry M. Goldwater
United States Senator, R—Arizona

1

[Criticizing President Ford's "conditional amnesty" proposal for U.S. Vietnam draft-dodgers and deserters]: I think the man who will not serve alongside his fellow man in war is not deserving of being called an American citizen. I think the man who would rather run away from his responsibilities to his country and take refuge in some foreign land is not to be considered an American citizen. [The President's action] is like throwing mud in the faces of millions of men who have served this country. I think it is a travesty on justice. I think it is going to be an insult to every man who has ever worn the uniform of his country, and is going to be a challenge to every traitor living in our midst.

Human Events, 9-28:4.

Hubert H. Humphrey
United States Senator, D—Minnesota

2

[On the U.S. experience in the Vietnam war]: Like many things in our national life, we miscalculated. We overestimated our ability to control events, which is one of the great dangers of a great power. Power tends to be a substitute for judgment and wisdom. I can't help but feel that in those postwar [World War II] years the tremendous power of America and its development—economic—that we really saw ourselves in almost God-like proportions. And the President of the United States obviously found himself affected by that.

Interview/The New York Times, 4-15:26.

3

I refuse to sit back and help perpetuate the delusion that massive American military aid somehow will end the fighting [in Indochina]. I sat at [the late U.S. President] Lyndon Johnson's side during his years of agony over Vietnam. I supported his policies because I believed they would bring peace to that country and allow its people to determine their own political destiny. But President Johnson's policies did not bring peace to Vietnam. The policies of [former U.S. President] Richard Nixon brought about the withdrawal of American troops four long years after he took the oath of office. But the fighting still continues and our nation is spending billions of dollars in Southeast Asia as yet another President [Gerald Ford] urges the American people to stand firm and support policies which mean only more fighting and destruction in Indochina. This is not a course which I support. This is not the course the Senate should support as the elected representatives of the people . . . Let us seek the path of negotiation once again. Let us stop this official self-delusion which says, "just a little more, and victory will be certain." Let us turn our attention to obtaining political settlements in Indochina so that we can end the expenditure of billions of dollars in Vietnam and Cambodia while widespread starvation and poverty rage throughout the developing world. Common sense, if nothing else, should tell us that our policies need to be rethought and options re-evaluated after years of fruitless war.

Before the Senate, Washington, Oct. 1/
The Washington Post, 10-4:(A)22.

Robert W. Kastenmeier
United States Representative, D—Wisconsin

4

[Supporting amnesty for U.S. Vietnam draft-dodgers and deserters]: I find it ironic that one year ago the Nixon Administration was recommending foreign assistance to the North Vietnamese. If we're ready to forgive our enemies, it might be time to consider forgiving our own sons.

The National Observer, 3-23:4.

Edward M. Kennedy
United States Senator, D—Massachusetts 1

We [the U.S.] are still involved in Indochina, even if indirectly, for America continues to provide the weapons of war—to the tune of some $2 billion for fiscal year 1974, and a supplemental request for more is anticipated soon. We also help finance the economies of the governments in the area. If that were not sufficient involvement, we now hear our national leadership warn of direct American military retaliation, and the Pentagon saber-rattles about bombing North Vietnam. Each side competes with the other in violating the Paris [peace] agreements.

Jan. 26/The Washington Post, 1-27:(A)4.

Henry A. Kissinger
Secretary of State of the United States 2

[On recent cuts in aid to South Vietnam voted by the U.S. Congress]: We must strengthen the ability of the peoples of Indochina to determine their own destiny. After a decade of war, and the loss of 50,000 American lives, some hesitate to give to South Vietnam—for whom the war has not yet ended—the help it so desperately needs to maintain itself as an independent nation. It would be tragic, it would break faith with all those Americans who have fought and died there, if we now fail to make the relatively modest effort that the Administration has proposed to the Congress to enable South Vietnam to survive.

Before American Legion, Miami Beach,
Aug. 20/The New York Times, 8-21:6.

Melvin R. Laird
Former Secretary of Defense
of the United States 3

. . . if they [South Vietnam] don't have the will or the desire to protect their own in-country security, we should not do anything else. We have given them the tools. We continue to give them the military supplies and equipment that are needed and necessary for them to do the job. And I would not recommend to the Congress, and I'm sure the Congress would re-

ject, the idea of reinserting Americans—whether it be on the ground or in the air—in Southeast Asia. We should not get in a position where we assure that all of the various groups in Southeast Asia will not raise arms against one another, because that fighting in Laos has gone on for many years, in Cambodia, in North and South Vietnam it has gone on for many years; and I don't believe that the United States of America can ever insure that there will be no more fighting in that area. I think we can insure the non-involvement of America; and I think the Vietnamization program was the vehicle by which we gave the South Vietnamese the capability to protect their own in-country security.

Television interview/
"Panorama," WTTG, Washington, 1-15.

Delbert L. Latta
United States Representative, R—Ohio 4

[Defending, against Congressional criticism, U.S. President Nixon's bombing of Cambodia several years ago]: . . . when [President] Nixon took office he had a very serious problem. We had over 500,000 American troops in South Vietnam. The casualties were heavy; we had hit-and-run activities by the enemy [who returned to] sanctuaries that were not being hit. Action had to be taken to save American lives . . . we didn't have very much dissent from the Cambodian government. In fact, they indicated that publicly they couldn't say anything but they were giving us passive consent. I think it's important that we continue to have in this country co-equal branches of government, that we don't reduce that office of President to chore boy, that we let him remain as Commander-in-Chief. It seems as though we forget that responsibility given to him under the Constitution. And a Commander-in-Chief sometimes has to take actions to protect the lives of his troops. And here we had a Commander-in-Chief taking decisive action.

At House Judiciary Committee hearing,
Washington, July 30/
The New York Times, 7-31:15.

Robert L. Leggett
United States Representative, D—California

1

[On U.S. aid for South Vietnam]: Nothing we can do there is going to affect the final outcome; we can only delay it, and break our own bank in the process. If we help them do it, they can keep this war going for 100 years, by which time *we'll* be ready to be on the receiving end of somebody's foreign-aid program.

The Christian Science Monitor, 4-24:5C.

Lon Nol
President of Cambodia

2

[On the cut-off last year of the U.S. combat role in support of Cambodia]: The American Air Force planes were flying in our skies until August 15 of last year. On that day, August 15, 1973, many observers predicted the early fall of our republic. As everybody can see today, we are still here, and we have succeeded in repelling all enemy efforts to impose his will on our people.

On anniversary of U.S. cut-off, Phnom Penh, Aug. 15/The Washington Post, 8-16:(A)20.

Long Boret
Prime Minister of Cambodia

3

International opinion seems not to react to the suffering of the Khmer [Cambodian] people. When American airmen were bombing Hanoi [North Vietnam] in December of 1972, the whole world condemned the action. But when the other side [the Communists] kills our innocent women and children, there is no reaction. We do not understand this.

Interview, Phnom Penh, Feb. 15/ The New York Times, 2-16:2.

Graham A. Martin
United States Ambassador to South Vietnam

4

[Saying the U.S. should not reduce or cut off its aid to South Vietnam]: [If South Vietnam were to become Communist,] after it was very clear that we did everything reasonably we could have done, that's one thing. But to walk away from it just at this moment in time would be something else again ... The United States would pay an enormous cost, a cost in a turning inward in a new kind of isolationism which would provide enormous dangers for the people of the United States and for the people of the world. My concern with Vietnam is not so much with the Vietnamese. My concern is what happens to us [Americans] as a people, the whole intricate power balance in the world, as the world perceives us and perceives our will to do what we said we'd do.

Interview, Saigon/ The Washington Post, 3-15:(A)25.

5

The important questions remain: How do we [the U.S.] end our involvement [in Vietnam]? How quickly can this be accomplished? My personal belief is that we should end it very quickly, and I believe this can be done. How we end it is of crucial importance. I have said our objective should be to end it leaving a [South] Vietnam economically viable, militarily capable of defending itself with its own manpower and free to choose its own government and its own leaders. I believe this can be done within the next three years. I believe that the effect on our power relationships elsewhere in the world of being able to walk away from such a Vietnam with the evidence of American commitments fully discharged may well determine whether our grandchildren will live in a peaceful world or one where senseless violence will be the daily norm. Only those who are incapable of understanding the intricate interplay of the balance of forces now loose in the world, or those who refuse to think about it, will contend that the preceding sentence is other than a dispassionate statement of a simple fact.

Interview, Saigon/ U.S. News & World Report, 4-29:74.

Thomas H. Moorer
Admiral, United States Navy (Ret.); Former Chairman, Joint Chiefs of Staff

6

[On U.S. bombing of North Vietnamese sanctuaries in Cambodia several years ago]: Yes, we should have bombed them. We should have bombed them sooner and harder. The whole point of a war is to get it over with as soon as possible, and that was one way of doing it.

News conference, San Francisco, July 31/ Los Angeles Herald-Examiner, 8-1:(A)4.

Aryeh Neier
Executive director,
American Civil Liberties Union

1

[Criticizing President Ford's conditional amnesty plan for U.S. Vietnam draft-dodgers and deserters, saying the plan assumes those men are guilty to begin with]: Thousands of them were wrongfully denied conscientious-objector status in disregard of standards established by the Supreme Court. Others were wrongfully denied deferments or physical exemptions. Many induction orders were based on declarations of delinquency, which is also illegal. Some men are in hiding for no reason because the Justice Department never brought an indictment down on them. Tens of thousands of these men are guilty of nothing, and they should have the right to exonerate themselves. Yet there apparently will be no review of anyone's file in Mr. Ford's amnesty.

News conference, New York, Sept. 30/
The New York Times, 10-1:12.

Le Thanh Nghi
Vice Premier of North Vietnam

2

In 1974 and 1975, the North's task consists of rapidly completing and healing the wounds of war; making strenuous efforts to restore and develop the economy and develop culture; continuing to build the material-technical bases of socialism; consolidating socialist production relations; comprehensively consolidating the socialist system; stabilizing the economic situation and the people's living conditions; consolidating national defense and making strenuous efforts to fulfill our duties to the heroic South.

Before National Assembly, Hanoi/
Los Angeles Times, 2-17:(1)1.

Richard M. Nixon
President of the United States

3

We have . . . succeeded in ending our military involvement in Vietnam in a manner which gave meaning to the heavy sacrifices we had made and which greatly enhanced the preservation of freedom and stability in Southeast Asia. One result is that today the 20 million people of South Vietnam are free to govern themselves and they are able to defend themselves. An even more important result is that we have proved again that America's word is America's bond.

At United States Naval Academy
commencement, Annapolis, June 5/
The New York Times, 6-6:16.

Norodom Sihanouk
Exiled former Chief of State of Cambodia

4

The Khmer Reds [Cambodian Communists] are very clever. They know that, without Sihanouk, they are regarded by many just as rebels against [Cambodian President] Lon Nol. But with Sihanouk, they have legitimacy. They have a monarchy. We have a very Red monarchy. But I am glad of it . . . They may not like the monarchy, but they respect it; and they respect our ancestors in a way that the Phnom Penh—please excuse me—running dogs of the Americans do not. Whether or not the Cambodian monarchy continues after my death will be up to the Khmer Reds, but whatever their decision they are a thousand times better than the Blues, or whatever you want to call the Phnom Penh gang . . . The Khmer Reds insist, and they are 100 per cent right, on the complete liquidation of the puppet government before making peace. In a military sense, we are much stronger than our friends of the Pathet Lao [Communists] in Laos and the national liberation forces of Vietnam. Why should we agree to the ridiculously unworkable conditions in which those countries find themselves? It is like putting a tiger and a dog in the same cage. Things will be settled only when one animal eats the other. And that is how it will be in Cambodia. We are the tiger, and Lon Nol and his people are the running dogs.

Interview, Bucharest, Romania, Aug. 24/
The New York Times, 8-25:(1)13.

Nguyen Xuan Phong
South Vietnamese negotiator at Paris
talks with the Viet Cong

5

[On the year-old Vietnam peace agreement]: Call it anything you want to describe a non-achievement. There has been no stop to the fighting in South Vietnam, with more than

WHAT THEY SAID IN 1974

(NGUYEN XUAN PHONG)

60,000 killed and some 120,000 wounded . . .
The Communists have not abandoned all hope
of seizing power in the South by the force of
arms. The big offensive we have been waiting
for did not come. But bitter fighting goes on
unabated.

Interview, Paris, March 18/
San Francisco Examiner, 3-19:12.

William B. Saxbe
Attorney General of the United States   *1*

[Saying that U.S. Vietnam draft-dodgers and
deserters should make an act of contrition as
condition for their return to the U.S. and in
lieu of prison terms] : . . . [but] they don't
want to make this act of contrition. They don't
want to have to come back and say "we were
wrong." As a result, I don't think we are going
to see a great many of them coming back under
any amnesty programs even though the President [Ford] is determined to . . . open the door
to them. They are not going to be welcomed
back as heroes, and this is very disappointing to
them.

Television interview/"Today" show,
National Broadcasting Company, 8-29.

William J. Scherle
United States Representative, R–Iowa   *2*

[On U.S. Vietnam draft-dodgers and de-
serters] : I have sympathy and compassion, but
I've got to reserve that for the 1,200 missing
POWs and MIAs. My first consideration is for
them. Once this is attained, we can think about
those who deserted and dodged the draft and
fled to a foreign country.

The Christian Science Monitor, 8-21:6.

James R. Schlesinger
Secretary of Defense of the United States   *3*

[Congressional cuts in U.S. military aid for
South Vietnam have] put an ally on the military equivalent of starvation rations. We informed them that we would provide them with
the tools and munitions—and would expect
them to do the job. Since that time, the South

Vietnamese have done the job, our assistance to
Saigon has declined and outside aid to Hanoi
has increased. A small nation, beholden to us,
still struggles to survive, but we have neither the
temerity to sever its lifeline nor the resolution
to pay the relatively small but necessary price
to assure its continued existence.

Washington, Sept. 24/
Los Angeles Times, 9-26:(1)10.

Chesterfield Smith
President, American Bar Association   *4*

[Advocating amnesty for U.S. Vietnam draft
evaders and deserters] : A citizen of a free country should not be forced to fight in a war that
neither he nor his elected representatives chose
to initiate or declare.

Before American Bar Association, Honolulu/
The Washington Post, 8-13:(A)4.

Nguyen Van Thieu
President of South Vietnam   *5*

In the last few months, I have busted and
taken away medals from 40 or 50 [military]
officers for involvement in smuggling. I have
also busted and taken away medals from several
battalion and company commanders for being
cowardly in the face of the enemy. These people have been prosecuted by the military court
and may be given death sentences. If thousands,
tens of thousands of commanders, leaders, must
be sacrificed in order to save one million people
in the armed forces, so that the one million
people will save the remaining 19½ million people of South Vietnam, I will be ready to do it
without hesitating.

At Armed Forces Day celebration, Saigon,
June 19/The Washington Post, 6-20:(A)11.

6

We don't have our allies here any more. This
permits North Vietnam, which now is not being
bombed, to build in peace, while we have to
struggle alone against aggression. [South Vietnam must remain strong and] I think the
American people and their elected representatives understand that. But they are not living up
to their promises . . . This year, aid will be
reduced to even a lower level than last year. It

is not only that we do not have an excess of funds from which to draw, we have been cut back below our lowest expectations.

Television address, Saigon, Oct. 1/
Los Angeles Times, 10-2:(1)25.

Nguyen Duy Trinh
Foreign Minister of North Vietnam

1

[On current Communist priorities in Vietnam]: The safeguarding of peace—making it stable and durable; the dressing of the wounds of war and the building of socialism in the North; the completion of the national and democratic tasks in the South; and movement toward peaceful reunification of the motherland.

Interview/The New York Times, 1-24:2.

Lowell P. Weicker, Jr.
United States Senator, R—Connecticut

2

Last year, in February, I was invited to the White House for a "Peace with Honor" reception. I learned that invitations were extended, not to the whole Congress in celebration of getting us out of Vietnam, but only to those of us who had supported the President's [Nixon] position. Since the reception was designated "Peace with Honor," the implication was clear: Those who had disagreed either did not want peace or they were dishonorable men and women. Apparently it never occurred to the White House that the people who doubted the correctness of our role in Vietnam were just as patriotic and helpful in getting us out of the quagmire as were the President and his supporters. Just thinking about that got me so mad I refused the invitation, and I haven't been asked back since.

Interview, Washington/Parade, 7-14:5.

William C. Westmoreland
General (Ret.) and former Chief of
Staff, United States Army; Former
Commander, U.S. forces in Vietnam

3

[Reflecting on U.S. participation in the war]: The amount of civilian control was truly

unprecedented as a result of experiences like the Bay of Pigs and because of the fear of the [Communist] Chinese. It was the first war fought in the eye of the television camera. It was, *per se,* a long war, and the American political system, with its elections every two years, makes for impatience. No wonder it was the first war in which the Commander was called back to make speeches explaining what it was all about.

Interview, Charleston, S.C./
The New York Times, 1-13:50.

4

[Amnesty for U.S. Vietnam draft-dodgers and deserters would be] unfair to those young men who served loyally and honorably and gave their lives. National policies set the course in Vietnam, not the military. Despite the fact this was an unpopular war, this was the national policy. I do not believe in the right of an individual to contravene and take the matter into his own hands.

News conference, Los Angeles, March 13/
Los Angeles Times, 3-14:(2)5.

Charles Wilson
United States Representative, D—Texas

5

I will strongly oppose the granting of American economic aid to North Vietnam as long as Hanoi continues to withhold information concerning our dead and missing servicemen. Hanoi's chances of getting aid have been shaky at best, and I believe Congress will oppose that kind of relationship with North Vietnam while our dead pilots and soldiers are, in effect, being used to blackmail us. My impression is that they are linking the release of information to concessions they want us to make. We know they know what happened to some of our missing men. They have even hinted they have the information and want some concessions for it. Nothing is to be gained by punishing the families of the missing men by withholding information about whether they are dead or not.

Interview, Geneva/
Los Angeles Herald-Examiner, 3-13:(A)5.

Europe

Giovanni Agnelli
Chairman, FIAT Company (Italy)   1

The economic situation [in Italy] is very grave, but even more dangerous are the ills which undermine the economic, political and social system and the environment in which we operate. When there is a choice between hunger and liberty, it is liberty that is in danger. Both these prospects are on the horizon in Italy today.

May 30/
Los Angeles Herald-Examiner, 6-12:(A)10.

Vladimir S. Alkhimov
Deputy Minister of Foreign Trade
of the Soviet Union   2

[On complaints in the U.S. that that country's sale of wheat to the Soviet Union in 1972 was at too low a price]: We bought the wheat at market prices in 1972. They may have been low, but look at Alaska, which we sold you [the U.S.] for $7 million back in 1867. That was cheap, too, but you don't hear us complaining.

San Francisco Examiner & Chronicle,
10-13:(This World)9.

Anthony Ambatielos
Member, politburo,
Communist Party of Greece   3

[On the just-announced legalization of the Communist Party in Greece]: The common people in the street, the leftists, the progressive people—I've seen them crying for joy. They feel Greece has entered into a new period, that the lion will lie down with the lamb and live peacefully. But to tell you the truth, being a scientific Communist and knowing the laws that prevail in society, I'm not so overcome by the change. Legalization is a great thing, but it's just another phase in the long revolutionary history of the Party.

Interview, Athens/
The New York Times, 9-27:14.

Kingsley Amis
British author   4

[On Britain's forthcoming October national election]: It may seem perverse or ungrateful not to vote in what will probably be our last democratic election, but I just can't bring myself to. [The Labor Party] is so dishonest, the Tories are so wet, and the Liberals are funny without being vulgar. And in any case, it has already been decided who governs the country: the trade unions.

Newsweek, 10-21:46.

Raymond Aron
French political analyst; Member of
the faculty, College of France   5

. . . the fact is that people in Europe do see the number of American troops [stationed in Europe] as a symbol of the degree of American commitment. Now, you might say that's crazy. But people who are not crazy—like [West German] Chancellor [Willy] Brandt—believe that the withdrawal of American troops would increase the disparity between NATO and Warsaw Pact conventional strength. They fear that this would increase the moral pessimism of the people on the Western side and give the impression to the Russian side that the American commitment had been reduced. My own view is that you [the U.S.] should begin a campaign to explain that one American division more or less does not really change the picture. But you have to convince the people of Western Europe of that—and also the Russians, which might be more difficult.

Interview, Washington/
U.S. News & World Report, 4-29:50.

George W. Ball
*Former Under Secretary of State
of the United States*

1

Neither [U.S. President] Nixon nor [Secretary of State] Kissinger has been fundamentally sympathetic to the idea of a united Europe. Both are Gaullists. The thrust of Kissinger's foreign policy has been away from alliances toward maneuver, toward manipulation.

*Interview, Brussels/
The New York Times, 3-24:(1)13.*

Anthony Barber
*Chancellor of the Exchequer
of the United Kingdom*

2

[Arguing against the impending coal-miners' strike]: The issue at stake is whether our affairs are to be governed by the rule of reason, the rule of Parliament and the rule of democracy. The vast majority of people in Britain detest the alternative, which ultimately can only be chaos and a totalitarian or Communist regime.

*Before House of Commons, London, Feb. 6/
Los Angeles Times, 2-7:(1)5.*

Anthony Wedgwood Benn
Secretary for Industry of the United Kingdom

3

[On Britain's plan to nationalize the ship-building industry]: The government believes that necessary changes will not come about while the industry is in fragmented private ownership and that public ownership of the major companies . . . offers the only effective prospect of achieving the objective of enabling British ship-building and ship repair not merely to survive but to prosper in the highly competitive markets of the world.

*Before Parliament, London, July 31/
The New York Times, 8-1:34.*

Willy Brandt
Former Chancellor of West Germany

4

For us, there is no substitute for a good relationship with America. That is, there is no alliance we can conceive of without America. For us, the United States is irreplaceable as an alliance partner.

San Francisco Examiner, 5-8:36.

Leonid I. Brezhnev
*General Secretary, Communist Party
of the Soviet Union*

5

I've had a bumper crop of Americans visiting me, and I want more.

Quote, 2-10:122.

6

Those circles in the United States and allied countries that oppose relaxation of international tensions try to whip up the arms race and are trying now to put responsibility for this race on the Soviet Union. This is a clear distortion of reality. Perhaps it is not always necessary to recall the past, but in this case I consider it perfectly appropriate. It is generally known that the arms race, the competition to produce the most dangerous weapons of mass destruction, was imposed on us. It was not we who began to create atomic bombs, submarines armed with strategic rockets, multiple warheads and many others.

*Election campaign address, Moscow,
June 14/The New York Times, 6-15:3.*

7

The relaxation of tension in Soviet-American relations, as in international relations generally, comes up against rather active resistance. There is no need for me to dwell on this subject since our American guests know better and in more detail than we about those who oppose international detente, who favor whipping up the arms race and returning to the methods and mores of the cold war. I just want to express my firm conviction that the policy of such individuals—whether they themselves know it or not—has nothing in common with the interests of the peoples. It is a policy that attests most likely to the unwillingness or inability of its proponents to take a sober look at the realities of the present-day world. We are confident, however, that the peoples will support those who seek to assure their peaceful future and a tranquil life for millions of people, not those who sow enmity and distrust. That is why we believe that the good results it has proved possible to achieve in Soviet-

WHAT THEY SAID IN 1974

(LEONID I. BREZHNEV)

American relations during the last two years shall not be erased...

At dinner honoring visiting U.S.
President Nixon, Moscow, June 27/
The New York Times, 6-28:2.

1

... we received with satisfaction the statement by [U.S.] President Ford about his personal intention and that of his Administration to continue the course for further development of relations between our countries in the same direction. On our part, we told the President that we are for maintaining contacts for [consolidating] good neighborly relations between our countries. We feel that at present there are quite good prerequisites for continuing the new concrete acts of cooperation in various fields, in the interests of the peoples of both countries and of universal peace... The recent change of leadership in the U.S.A. attracted close attention in the world. We in the U.S.S.R., of course, do not interfere in the internal affairs of the United States, but we are far from indifferent as regards the state and development of Soviet-U.S. relations, to which we attach great significance for quite understandable reasons.

At dinner honoring Hungarian leader
Janos Kadar, Moscow, Sept. 25/
The New York Times, 9-26:2.

2

[Criticizing those in the U.S. who would condition improved U.S.-Soviet trade on the Soviets' easing of restrictions on Jewish emigration]: Attempts to condition the development of trade and economic ties by putting demands on the Soviet Union in questions totally unconnected with the trade and economics field, and lying utterly within the domestic competence of states, are utterly irrelevant and unacceptable... It is high time there should be a clear understanding that such attempts at interference in internal affairs do nothing but harm, including harm to trade and economic relations between our countries... [Soviet leaders] continue to be optimistic and still think that the prospects of business relations between our countries will be determined by real economic

and political interests of the two states, and not by egoistic calculations of certain individuals and narrow political groups whose mentality has not yet been freed from the outdated legacy of the cold war. Economic relations between our two countries are, I should say, in the period of early spring, when the sun shines brighter but there is not enough warmth and the temperature varies greatly. But we believe that, even as in nature, summer will inevitably come in these relations. What is important is for this process not to be delayed too much.

Before American industrialists,
Moscow, Oct. 15/
Los Angeles Times, 10-16:(1)1,11.

Erling Brondum
Minister of Defense of Denmark

3

[On his country's welfare state]: There is a reaction against the too-fast development of the welfare state. There is a lot of bureaucracy. We have so developed the tax system that it's no longer worth working. A truck driver told me the other day there is about $1.50 a day difference whether he works or not. He doesn't want to work eight hours for $1.50 a day.

Interview/The New York Times, 3-22:3.

Zbigniew Brzezinski
Director, Research Institute on
Communist Affairs, Columbia University

4

... the Soviet Union, in many ways, much less than the United States, does not have a global perspective. It has a rather narrow vision of its interests. There is much less of a willingness to respond to the new global problems that impose themselves on us. The longer-range threat is not Soviet domination, because I don't think the Soviets are strong enough to impose it on anyone—but world chaos to which the Soviets would be able to make a very major contribution.

Panel discussion, Washington, Aug. 2/
The New York Times, 8-7:33.

5

The Soviet view of detente—explicitly and openly articulated by Soviet leaders—is that of a limited and expedient arrangement, which in no way terminates the ideological conflict even as it yields tangible economic benefits. On the contrary, it has been emphasized over and over again that "peaceful coexistence" is a form of class struggle and that ideological conflict, far from abating, is to intensify during detente ... it is clearly in the U.S. interest, and that of peace in general, deliberately to seek a more comprehensive and therefore a more enduring U.S.-Soviet detente which is not artificially compartmentalized to economics alone and which is not offset by officially sustained ideological antagonism. Such a more comprehensive detente—which should be our explicit goal— would involve a broader social, cultural and political accommodation, the shaping of more extensive social links, the expansion of political collaboration especially in regard to the many new global problems, the adoption not only of the principle but also of the practice of true reciprocity in our relations, and a rejection of the harmful and antiquated concept of an intensifying ideological and class struggle being part of the detente relationship.

Before Senate Foreign Relations Subcommittee on Multinational Corporations, Washington/ The Washington Post, 8-4:(C)4.

1

Nationalism is a real danger in both societies [the U.S. and U.S.S.R.]. In our country, when problems abroad seem to grow too complex, we'll draw back from them. And in the Soviet Union, as the ideology wanes, there may be much more emphasis on nationalism, Great Russian nationalism, which is at an earlier stage of development than American nationalism. It's more like Teddy Roosevelt nationalism— manifest destiny and all of that. And that could be dangerous, not only to global stability, but also to detente.

Interview/Los Angeles Times, 12-29:(6)4.

James Callaghan
Foreign Secretary of the United Kingdom

2

We [Britain] repudiate the view that Europe will emerge only out of a process of struggle against America. We do not agree that a Europe which excludes the fullest and most intimate cooperation with the United States is a desirable or attainable objective.

Before House of Commons, London, March 19/ The Christian Science Monitor, 3-21:1.

Constantine Caramanlis
Premier of Greece

3

[On his assumption of the Premiership] : I have come to contribute to the best of my ability to the restoration of normal conditions and democracy. In the lives of nations there are crises which can be turned into a starting point for national regeneration and a better future. I am optimistic about the future.

Athens, July 24/Time, 8-5:30.

4

[On Turkey's invasion of Cyprus]: I denounce the Turkish behavior to the entire civilized world. On her side, Greece will take all suitable measures to face an attack which is not only directed against the independent state of Cyprus, but also shakes the institutions and the prevailing order of the whole world.

Aug. 14/The New York Times, 8-15:14.

5

The majority of the people, the real Greeks, have shown a unique, a quite extraordinary maturity. It's thanks to them and this newfound maturity that I have managed, painlessly and without bloodshed, to open the road to democracy within three months. It is going to be necessary to sustain the momentum over the next four years in order to lay the real foundations for a healthy and responsible democracy. Do you realize that the coming elections are the first this country has had in 10 years? If I secure a sufficient majority, I will be able to succeed in giving Greece that democracy.

Interview, Athens/Time, 10-28:29.

Clifford P. Case
United States Senator, R—New Jersey

6

We [the U.S.] are defending Western Europe not because we are defending democracy there, but because we are defending ourselves.

The Washington Post, 3-17:(A)12.

Prince Charles
Prince of Wales
1

[On British parliamentary democracy]: This, I do believe, is the only system mankind has so far evolved which comes nearest to ensuring stable government; and I also believe that the institution of monarchy—to which, rightly or wrongly, I belong and which I represent to the best of my ability—is one of the strongest factors in the continuance of stable government. Stability can only be maintained when the body you wish to remain stable has one constituent element that displays continuity—and which can also adapt itself to a changing environment . . . All too often, I find, one hears the cry that our system of parliamentary democracy is on the verge of collapse, that it has outlived its usefulness, that the politicians are all the same and spend their time squabbling over issues that bear no relation to the major questions of the day. However, it is rare to hear of anyone who has been able to suggest a sensible or realistic alternative—geared to the peculiar characteristics and mores of those with our type of heritage. No—the truth of course is that "the system" is, on the whole, basically sound. Obviously, it can always do with adaptions, additions, subtractions and reforms; but, generally speaking, the entire apparatus of parliamentary government, as we know it, has developed gradually from primitive origins and has been constructed on sound experience and expertise.
On 150th anniversary of founding of Parliament in the Australian state of New South Wales, Sydney/The New York Times, 11-19:43.

Glafkos Clerides
Acting President of Cyprus
2

[On his just-announced assumption of the Presidency]: . . . during my Presidency I will uphold with absolute respect all the democratic principles and will safeguard fully the human rights for the entire Cypriot people, irrespective of race, community or political affiliation. I assure the entire Cypriot people—and particularly the Turkish elements—that my intention is to pursue the closest cooperation with them so as to create in Cyprus conditions of prosperity for all of us. Let us leave for the future any criticism of the past and the present. What matters most now is the salvation and the good of our country . . .
Broadcast address, July 23/ The Washington Post, 7-24:(A)15.

3

[Arguing against a proposal to form a federation in Cyprus between two separate and apart Greek and Turkish Cypriot communities]: In my opinion this will not serve the cause of peace and peaceful coexistence in Cyprus. It is by having common institutions, by working together as Cypriots that it will be possible to create that spirit of cooperation that will eventually lead Cyprus into peace, tranquility and progress.
News conference, Geneva, Aug. 9/ Los Angeles Times, 8-10:(1)3.

4

[On Turkey's invasion of Cyprus and its continued ultimatums]: Under such conditions, I am not prepared to negotiate [with Turkey] at Geneva or in Cyprus or anywhere else in this world—or in the next world.
News conference, Nicosia, Aug. 19/ Los Angeles Times, 8-20:(1)8.

5

[Calling for a Greek-Turkish federation on Cyprus]: I see no prospect of the Turks accepting any settlement that does not include federation and some geographical basis for it. I am sorry to disappoint you, but we must not make the same mistakes as before—confuse what we want with what is possible.
Addressing Greek Cypriots/ Los Angeles Times, 11-8:(1)2.

Ray S. Cline
Director of studies, Georgetown University Center for Strategic Studies; Former Director of Intelligence and Research, Department of State of the United States
6

[In Europe there is] fear that a new Soviet-American relationship will lead to a diminution of the U.S. commitment to NATO, that there will be a withdrawal of U.S. forces and a lessening of economic cooperation, and hence increasing pressure on them to enter into long-term understandings with the Soviet Union which, in time, would neutralize them politically and strategically and, even sooner, provide opportunities for united-front governments, getting Communist parties into power through the "parliamentary road to socialism."

Interview, Washington/
The Washington Post, 7-8:(A)3.

William E. Colby
Director, Central Intelligence Agency of
the United States

1

There are three main reasons for Soviet interest in promoting detente with the United States. First, they obviously want to prevent the kind of horrendous confrontation that is possible in this age of superweapons. The result of a nuclear exchange between us would be just so incredible now that they realize that something has to be done to avoid it. Secondly, they insist that they be recognized as one of the world's two superpowers and get the status that their strength implies. They might also benefit from a relaxation of the Western solidarity that characterized the 1950s and 1960s. Thirdly, they would like to accelerate their development in economic and technical terms, because as they look at the enormous power of the West— America particularly, but also the other countries—they see it moving at a tremendous rate. They hope to benefit by a greater degree of exchange, and borrowing from that movement. Generally, the Soviet concern over their internal discipline is very high. This is partly a result of detente. They are nervous about what detente can do in terms of getting new thoughts and new political drives going within the Soviet Union. And they just don't want that to happen.

Interview, Washington/
U.S. News & World Report, 12-2:30.

Liam Cosgrave
Prime Minister of the Republic of Ireland

2

The factual position of Northern Ireland is that it is within the United Kingdom, and my government accepts this as a fact. I now, therefore, solemnly reaffirm that the factual position of Northern Ireland within the United Kingdom cannot be changed except by a decision of a majority of the people of Northern Ireland.

Before Parliament, Dublin, March 13/
The Christian Science Monitor, 3-14:1.

3

[On the situation in Northern Ireland] : All of us who live today in the island of Ireland have inherited an immensely difficult and complex problem which has brought suffering and death to innocent men and women in each generation. It is a problem which no previous generation in our history—whatever else it may have achieved—was able to resolve. The way is open to us who live in Ireland at this particular time to begin to resolve it. The House [Parliament] can be assured that this work, pursued in recent years, will be carried forward by my government with energy and resolution.

Before Parliament, Dublin, March 13/
The New York Times, 3-14:5.

Earl of Cromer
British Ambassador to the United States

4

[On the current strained relations between the U.S. and the nine European Community nations] : I hope that you [the U.S.] will not allow such frustration to become the key to your policies toward Europe. It would be ironic indeed if, after a generation of support for European unity, the United States were to lose heart at the crucial moment. I don't believe European unity is any less an American interest now than it was 20 years ago . . .

Farewell retirement address/
The New York Times, 1-17:38.

Francisco da Costa Gomes
President of Portugal

5

The previous government [before the coup last April] was an extreme right-wing dictatorship. Thus the present government will have to maintain its rudder on a leftward course. That is imperative. If we have only one year to rid ourselves of a half-century of extreme reaction, what climate do you think we should create to guarantee victory for any democratic party?

Interview, Lisbon/Time, 10-28:33.

WHAT THEY SAID IN 1974

Rauf Denktash
*Vice President of Cyprus; Leader,
Turkish Cypriot community*   1

[On exiled Cypriot President Makarios' imminent return to Cyprus]: I hope he is having second thoughts about coming and may decide . . . not to come at all. I feel very gloomy. I know the man. I know of what substance he is made. I know how he thinks about Turkish rights. I find it a misfortune for Cyprus that a man who has caused Cyprus so much trouble, hardship and bloodshed through his leadership will now come back at a very crucial time.

*Interview, Nicosia, Dec. 5/
The New York Times, 12-6:4.*

Joop den Uyl
Premier of the Netherlands   2

[On the resignation of West German Chancellor Willy Brandt as a result of the discovery of a Communist spy on his staff]: His resignation, like his political conduct, marks his total integrity. But without him, Europe is impoverished.

May 7/San Francisco Examiner, 5-7:15.

Antonio de Spinola
President of Portugal   3

It is time for every Portuguese to conclude by himself that any form of anarchy ends fatally and opens the door to new dictatorships, to regimes like the one overthrown April 25 . . . I alert all Portuguese that the democratic ideas of liberty that inspired the Movement of the Armed Forces [in the April takeover] is being criminally undermined by counter-revolutionary forces. These forces are situated in diverse sectors of the nation and have as their objective destruction, anarchy, economic chaos and unemployment . . . If sometimes they [the armed forces] are obliged to respond to violence with force, they will do so without hesitation, now reinforced with the legitimate authority acting in defense of the authentic liberty of the Portuguese people.

*Oporto, Portugal, May 29/
The Washington Post, 5-30:(A)15.*

4

[Announcing his resignation]: [The country's well-being is being compromised] by an economic crisis to which we are fast heading, by unemployment, by uncontrolled inflation, by business recession, by the retraction of investments and by the ineffectiveness of the central powers. [In this general climate of anarchy, in which everyone dictates his own law,] crisis and chaos are inevitable in flagrant contradiction to the aims of the [current armed forces] movement . . . Under these conditions, and in the face of the total impossibility in the present climate of constructing an authentic democracy in the service of the peace and progress of the country, I resign my office as President of the republic.

*Broadcast address to the nation, Lisbon,
Sept. 30/The New York Times, 10-1:11.*

Stane Dolanc
Secretary, Communist Party of Yugoslavia   5

. . . Yugoslavia is not a kingdom. We need no heir to the throne. We are a country which self-manages itself, and our society is one which makes every provision to express the will of the people through the self-management system. We know that many people abroad are wondering what will happen to Yugoslavia after [President Josip Broz] Tito; and I will be frank. Tito's greatness is not only in his personality and genius, which in themselves would be incomplete without the materialization of his ideas in society. He is the symbol of self-management and non-alignment, which are permanent features of our society . . . Our statutes already specify the means by which elections are carried out, and we have no intention of preparing ourselves for any special situation, because there is no need for it.

*News conference, Belgrade, May 24/
The New York Times, 5-25:4.*

Bulent Ecevit
Premier of Turkey   6

We believe in real democracy, that expression of one's opinion should not be forbidden. There is no sound criterion which can differentiate between political opinions that are harmful or beneficial for the nation. The nation should decide what is good and what is not good for itself. If this element of democracy does not exist, it is like an empty building.

Interview, Ankara/
The New York Times, 5-5:(1)2.

1

[On his country's invasion of Cyprus where there was a recent coup]: We are not going to Cyprus only to bring peace to Turks. We are going there to bring peace also to the Greeks. I sincerely believe our decision will be a great service to all humanity and to world peace. We were forced to take this decision after trying all political and diplomatic paths. I hope no fire will be opened on our forces and a bloody conflict [thus] avoided. We are going to Cyprus not to make war but to restore peace.

News conference, Ankara, July 20/
San Francisco Examiner, 7-20:4.

2

[On current antagonism between his country and Greece]: We cannot be allies and yet arm against each other. It is illogical, paradoxical. We should either cease our collaboration within the framework of the [NATO] alliance or fully cooperate. [Turkey] certainly would prefer the second alternative. It is a paradox that we have very good and friendly relations with all our neighbors with one exception, our NATO ally, Greece.

Ankara, July 31/Los Angeles Times, 8-1:(1)20.

3

[On his country's invasion of Cyprus]: Our main concern is the large Turkish community [on Cyprus]. It is our moral responsibility to help when needed. The Greeks had been violating Cyprus agreements for a decade by illegally shipping in troops and military equipment. In the crises of 1964 and 1967, when Turkish Cypriots were being massacred, we wanted to go in and help, but our allies put obstacles in our way. Thus we hesitated. This time we knew we could not delay. If we did, then everything would have been lost for all Cypriots. The independent state of Cyprus would have ended, and de facto enosis [union with Greece] would have occurred [as a result

of the coup on Cyprus ousting Archbishop Makarios]. It was our duty [to intervene]. So we took the initiative. We limited our objectives to providing security and to restoring the constitutional status of Cyprus. We have now reached a position where we can ensure that any new solution to the Cyprus question does not conflict with the interests of Turkey or with the interests of the Turkish community on the island. For example, it is a fact that the Turks on Cyprus can no longer live under Greek rule. This fact should be made part of the new constitutional solution for Cyprus. Separate government for Greeks and Turks on the island is essential after all that has happened.

Interview, Ankara/Time, 8-12:29.

4

[If Greece refuses to resume negotiations with Turkey on the political aspect of the situation in Cyprus, Turkey] shall not be able to help interpreting it as an unexpressed Greek plan to annex part of the island. As weeks pass, administrations on both sides in Cyprus will have to take shape; they will take roots, and their autonomy may increase as time passes to the degree that, after a certain point, it might become incompatible with a Federal state. The partition of the island would create a lot of implications and complications we don't want. It is a very small island, but the whole world has been concerned with what is going to happen on Cyprus. It seems to be one of the vital knots of balance in the world and of detente.

Interview, Ankara, Aug. 22/
The New York Times, 8-23:2.

Elizabeth II
Queen of England

5

[On the economic and other problems her country is facing]: The trouble with gloom is that it feeds upon itself, and depression causes more depression. There are indeed real dangers and there are real fears, and we will never overcome them if we turn against each other with angry accusations. We may hold different points of view, but it is in times of stress and difficulty that we most need to remember that

(ELIZABETH II)

we have much more in common than there is dividing us . . .

Televised Christmas message, London,
Dec. 25/Los Angeles Times, 12-26:(1)19.

Gerald R. Ford
Vice President of the United States
1

I have always supported, from the outset, the NATO Alliance. I always thought that the joint efforts with Western Europe were of great importance. At the same time, I recognize that we cannot expect as many nations as are included in the Alliance all to play to precisely the same tune, year after year; different governments come and go, different countries have problems that are unique one year and require, in another year, a different direction as far as economic policy is concerned. Therefore, although I get a little disappointed with some of the countries going off on tangents, I would still strongly support the continuation of NATO and the Alliance with the hope that I would understand individual problems on a day-to-day basis.

Interview/The Washington Post, 4-14:(B)4.

Gerald R. Ford
President of the United States
2

To the Soviet Union, I pledge continuity in our commitment to the course [of detente] of the past three years. To our two peoples, and to all mankind, we owe a continued effort to live and, where possible, to work together in peace; for, in a thermo-nuclear age, there can be no alternative to a positive and peaceful relationship between our nations.

First address as President before
Congress, Washington, Aug. 12/
The New York Times, 8-13:20.

Joseph Fromm
Senior European editor,
"U.S. News & World Report"
3

I think that all across Europe you'll find most people believe it is important for the U.S.

and Russia to reach some accommodation, if for nothing more than to lower tensions and reduce risks of war. But there is also a feeling that [U.S.] President Nixon and [U.S. Secretary of State] Henry Kissinger have oversold detente. They have shown too few reservations, too little skepticism, in their dealings with Moscow. Officials in Europe were shaken by the sight of [Soviet Communist Party Secretary Leonid] Brezhnev and Nixon sort of embracing on television. West Europeans still consider the Russians as adversaries, and they don't like the idea of Mr. Nixon playing games with the Soviet leader. Also, West Europeans are worried that the U.S. will become so preoccupied with developing its relationship with the Soviet Union that some agreements may be made which compromise European interests, perhaps even their security.

Panel discussion, London/
U.S. News & World Report, 2-4:65.

J. William Fulbright
United States Senator, D–Arkansas
4

[On U.S. dealings with the Soviet Union]: I never like to put it as trusting people. It is a matter of recognizing and adjusting the interests of the two countries. Where their interests are in variance with ours, I don't think you can trust them or other governments. The only possibility of making progress is to discover, if possible, areas of mutual interest on which they can agree . . . where we attempt to make them abide by our ideas of morality or ideology and so on, there is no mutual interest there and you can't trust them to do something in reformation of their own society that they don't want to do.

Panel discussion, Washington, Aug. 2/
The New York Times, 8-7:33.

Edward Gierek
First Secretary, Communist Party of Poland
5

Once or twice a week I visit regions of my country, not to be given flowers—though I like flowers—but to listen. Sometimes this is quite troublesome, but it is correct and necessary. And I'll tell you more—it is contagious. It breaks the tradition of those who love to sit behind their desks.

At National Press Club, Washington/ The New York Times, 10-10:10.

1

One can be a good Catholic, like most Poles, and be an active participant in the construction of a socialist society at the same time—as most Poles are. We have never considered the church a challenge to the Polish Communist Party or our system, and in fact that church has never tried to endanger the system or the Party. We, on our part, have never tried to endanger the church. In both our practice today and our endeavors for the future, we will not attempt to minimize the role of the church in Poland. It is a basic assumption of our government that the church is a substantial force in this nation [that] can participate in keeping moral values and virtues that are common to all people irrespective of their faith.

Interview, Warsaw/Time, 10-14:60.

Valery Giscard d'Estaing
Minister of Finance of France; Candidate for President

2

[If he is elected President]: I am ready to discuss issues with Communists any time; I recently received their delegation on a discussion of inflation. But there is danger in having Communists at the helm in key ministries for seven years.

Television debate, Paris, May 10/ The New York Times, 5-11:3.

3

I heartily want to continue the historical friendship which links us with the American people, and I will not leave the present security system [NATO] before holding firmly on to another. We owe the U.S. much gratitude—but not submission.

U.S. News & World Report, 5-20:33.

4

[The late] President Pompidou modernized France's economic life, and I want to modernize its political and cultural life. For me, France represents what is best in the world. It is a difficult and complicated nation; but on intel-lectual and human levels, it is the best. My idea is to have an exemplary political life, very democratic and very modern. If this idea does not shock you, I see, roughly speaking, two types of political organizations in the world as models: first, the [Communist] Chinese type, however you may judge it, for nations with large populations and under-developed countries; and second, the French society, which would be the type for middle-size, advanced industrial countries with considerable political and cultural maturity. In a few years, with a bit of effort, we can achieve a way of life and a political climate that will be among the most advanced. Perhaps not the most advanced, but the most modern. That is the best reconciliation between traditionalism and an advanced society.

Interview/Time, 6-3:20.

Valery Giscard d'Estaing
President-elect of France

5

[Addressing the French people on his election to the Presidency, which he barely won over his rival]: You want changes—politically, economically and socially. You won't be disappointed . . . Of course, one could have imagined a larger margin. But what matters is decision and responsibility. You have made the decision. I will exercise the responsibility.

Television address to the nation, May 19/The New York Times, 5-20:1.

Valery Giscard d'Estaing
President of France

6

[Saying the French people want change from his newly elected government]: It is I who will lead this change. But I will not lead it alone. While I intend fully to assume the task of President and to assume the responsibilities which this attitude implies, the action to be undertaken will associate the initiative of the government with the control and the rights of Parliament. I will not direct it alone, because I listen and because I can still hear the immense clamor of the French people. We will undertake this change with them and from them in all their number and diversity; and we will direct it

(VALERY GISCARD D'ESTAING)

in particular with the youth carrying joy and the future like torches.

At his installation as President, Paris, May 27/Los Angeles Times, 5-28:(1)4.

1

At the time of the change-over [of Presidents in the U.S. earlier this month], the outgoing President [Nixon] and the new President [Ford] made speeches on the situation at home and abroad, and in neither of these two speeches was the word Europe mentioned . . . From these events [in the U.S. and the Greek-Turk conflict over Cyprus] I draw two conclusions. The first is that Europe must rely on itself alone to organize itself. The second is that the modern world will really be the modern world only when the international map ceases to be torn where Europe should be.

Television address to the nation, Paris, Aug. 27/ The Washington Post, 8-28:(A)18.

2

It was easy to brand me as a conservative when I was Minister of Finance. One expects a Finance Minister to be conservative. But since I became President I do not hear much criticism of my conservatism. People are more inclined to say that I carry change too far. I am a traditionalist who likes change.

News conference/ Los Angeles Times, 9-5:(1)4.

3

My idea [for France] is to create, to organize a model, or potential model, of a liberal advanced society. We have models of socialist advanced societies, like Sweden, or in some ways Germany. But we have not had in Europe, until now, a real model for a liberal advanced society . . . France is a traditionalist country, one that hangs on to its past and traditions while leading a rather active intellectual life. There is an apparent contradiction between intellectual life and the sentiment for traditions. But from time to time one must try to reconcile those, and I would like to use the

intellectual capacity of France to invent, to organize a genuinely liberal advanced society. Why do I say liberal? It could be socialist. But the French nature, instinct and behavior are profoundly based upon individual freedom, and the feeling of security acquired through individual ownership. Sometimes it borders on anarchy, as you know.

Interview, Paris/Time, 10-7:56.

4

Europe is at the present time threatened with a declining population. As you know, for the past 10 years all European countries—and they are not alone in this—have been experiencing a rapid slowdown in their demographic growth. Europe has been additionally impoverished because resources from the industrial countries have been transferred to countries that possess energy and raw materials. Thus there is a danger that in the next few years Europe might drop behind, so to speak, while at the same time other countries will move up. In a way, this is a revenge on Europe for the 19th century. And it is this that prompts us to pursue with patience—and patience is needed—the organization of European union; for perhaps one day we will have to organize together a Europe in need . . .

News conference, Paris, Oct. 24/ The Washington Post, 11-5:(A)18.

Andrew J. Goodpaster
General, United States Army; Supreme Allied Commander/Europe

5

For almost a quarter of a century now, it has been the North Atlantic Treaty Organization, above all else, that has preserved the peace and safeguarded the freedom and prosperity of Western Europe and North America. Since the end of World War II, almost 29 years have passed without war in Europe. For comparison, 29 years after the end of the First World War, Europe had undergone the six years of death and destruction of World War II. This is in fact the first time in many centuries that Europe has had so long a period of peace. We cannot remind ourselves too often that, since the Allied military command was activated by

General [Dwight] Eisenhower in Paris in April, 1951, not one square foot of Allied territory has fallen under Soviet domination. Not one NATO nation has found itself forced to yield to military or political pressures from the East. And ancient enmities that bred two devastating world wars have given way to consultation, cooperation and collective security. I would be the first to agree that we cannot attribute this historic achievement solely to NATO's military strength. We cannot replay history to determine for sure what would have happened without NATO. Nevertheless, the 29 years of peace, progress and prosperity in Europe contrast sharply with the wars and threats of war which have plagued Southeast Asia, South Asia and the Middle East during this period.

Before Central Florida Section,
American Institute of Aeronautics
and Astronautics, Orlando, Feb. 25/
Vital Speeches, 4-15:390.

Andrei A. Gromyko
Foreign Minister of the Soviet Union   *1*

[On his country's recent expulsion of dissident author Alexander Solzhenitsyn]: Solzhenitsyn is now outside the borders of the Soviet Union, outside our country. This poisoned brew is not necessary for the Soviet Union.

Paris, Feb. 18/
Los Angeles Herald-Examiner, 2-19:(A)8.

Turan Gunes
Foreign Minister of Turkey   *2*

[Saying federation is the only realistic solution for the problems of Cyprus]: There is no such thing as the Cypriot nation or the Cypriot people. There are two completely different communities [Greek Cypriots and Turkish Cypriots]. A federation is the only system whereby they can live separately, yet collaborate in the development and prosperity of the island. It is the only system which can guarantee the continued sovereign independence of the island.

Interview, Geneva/
Los Angeles Times, 8-1:(1)18.

3

It's not the Cypriots who decide the fate of Cyprus. It's the Turks and the Greeks, and all the rest is blah-blah. [Deposed Greek Cypriot President] Makarios . . . always blocked any plan for the advancement of the Turkish Cypriot community. The Turks were kept in their place as second-rate citizens. If a Turkish Cypriot wanted to travel abroad, he had a hard time getting a passport from the Makarios Administration, unless he wanted to emigrate to Australia. Then they were delighted to give him a passport and pay for his fare—one way. Turkish Cypriot farmers received less for their produce than Greek Cypriots. There are hundreds of other examples of discrimination. The only solution is to give Turkish Cypriots a fair share of the island . . . Look, we want to live in peace and friendship with Greece. We won't chase Greek Cypriots out of the new Turkish zones [formed as a result of Turkey's invasion of the island], and we hope that Turks can continue to live in the Greek-Cypriot zones. In its new federative form, Cyprus can remain independent. We don't want double enosis [union of Cyprus with Greece and Turkey]. But enosis with Greece is out as well.

Interview, Geneva/Time, 8-26:38.

Jermen Gvishiani
Deputy Chairman, State Committee for
Science and Technology of the Soviet Union   *4*

We [the U.S.S.R. and the U.S.] have two different systems and different orientations. Still, we have much in common. First of all, we are human beings. We live on a planet that is becoming smaller and smaller. Its resources are becoming more scarce. We understand that we cannot live in isolation. We have to ask ourselves whether we should allow these differences in ideology to jeopardize our very existence. There are no other alternatives but for us to live in peace. We have to avoid competition in military power, realizing how dangerous it is and realizing that the world is becoming more and more complicated. At the same time, this doesn't mean that coexistence excludes differences in ideology.

Interview, Washington/
U.S. News & World Report, 10-28:58.

WHAT THEY SAID IN 1974

Robert A. Haeger
West German correspondent,
"U.S. News & World Report"

1

Frankly, the [Atlantic] Alliance seems to be in worse shape now than at any time in 25 years. And one of the reasons is that Europe is unable to act in any unified sense. [West German Chancellor] Willy Brandt keeps making anguished speeches about how West Europe "ought to be treated as a unity." In fact, Western Europe is not a unity, so nobody is going to treat it as such.

Panel discussion, London/
U.S. News & World Report, 2-4:64.

W. Averell Harriman
Former United States Ambassador
to the Soviet Union

2

The Russians don't like to play games . . . they have no "brinkmanship" policy, and they believe they can gain more by international stability than instability.

Interview, Paris/
Los Angeles Herald-Examiner, 6-9:(A)11.

James Haughton
President, British Association
of Chief Police Officers

3

Anarchy was never associated with the British character, but I now see this as a distinct possibility. An ever-increasing population in an already over-crowded island with rapidly dwindling resources, aggravated by greed, violence and corruption, provides little optimism for the survival of our present way of life. We are in a Nero Rome situation with too many fiddlers while the country is being burned and blasted to death.

At conference of police chiefs,
Eastbourne, England, June 19/
Los Angeles Herald-Examiner, 6-20:(A)10.

Denis Healey
Chancellor of the Exchequer
of the United Kingdom

4

[On Britain's economic crisis]: The picture is a somber one. It is the gravest situation Britain has faced since the last war . . . In one way or another, my budget calls on the majority of the British people to make some sacrifice for the survival of their way of life. Unless we can halt the accelerating inflationary trends in our economy, the political and social strains may be too violent for the democratic fabric of our institutions to withstand.

Before Parliament, London, March 26/
Los Angeles Times, 3-27:(1)6.

Edward Heath
Prime Minister of the United Kingdom

5

. . . there is still much disillusion among the people of Britain about the value to this country of Community [Common Market] membership. You know us well. We are a pragmatic people. It is no use telling us something is going to be good for us—we like to see a bit of proof before we believe it. Furthermore, this first year has coincided with an enormous rise in world food prices; and as these have filtered through to the consumer, the Community has wrongly been given the blame for them. When the rewards of membership are seen, as I certainly believe they will be, the disillusion among ordinary people will dwindle, as it did during the early years of the original Community of six. At the outset of any major new enterprise, expectations are high. My own remains so, despite a year in which I admit there were many frustrations. The Community is still in the building stage, and we have got the foundations right.

Interview, London/
The New York Times, 1-8:10.

6

We [Britain] aren't in a state of continual crisis. I know anybody reading the American press will think this was the case because this is all that has been reported for the past few weeks. They have shown no interest in Britain for months and years, ever since the war. Now all they do is describe Britain as being in a state of decay and one of perpetual crisis, which does not bear any relationship to the facts.

Interview, London/
The New York Times, 1-8:10.

1

[Calling for a general election to serve as a referendum on an imminent coal miners strike]: The election gives you, the people, the chance to say to the miners and to everyone else who wields similar power: "Times are hard; we are all in the same boat; and if you sink it now, we will all drown" ... There are some people involved in the mining dispute who have made it clear that what they want is to bring down the elected government—not just this government, but any government. They have made it clear they want to bring down the whole democratic way of life. The majority of you are fed to death with them and the disruption they cause. We have had enough. For heaven's sake, let's get on with it.

Broadcast address to the nation, London, Feb. 7/Los Angeles Times, 2-8:(1)7.

Anthony Howard
Editor, "The New Statesman," London

2

Unlike other parts of Europe, where prosperity has helped to blur social barriers, the classes in Britain keep very much to their own. You would never find a working-class man dining in the same West End restaurant used by his boss, even if he could afford it. But what has changed is that working people in this country will no longer ... shore up a way of life for those who are better able to protect themselves against the ravages of inflation with their perks, their expense accounts and the other benefits that property-owning middle and upper classes enjoy in this country.

Newsweek, 10-21:47.

Fred C. Ikle
Director, Arms Control and Disarmament Agency of the United States

3

We find in the Soviets considerable emphasis on fighting and even winning a nuclear war, rather than on deterrence ... disturbing references to rapid launching and pre-emption which could lead to the destruction of both countries [the U.S. and U.S.S.R.] through an accident. To the extent that they [the Soviets] have been investing in this land-based force,

they have been moving in the wrong direction from the view of strategic stability.

Interview, Washington, Feb. 1/ The Washington Post, 2-2:(A)12.

Hasan Esat Isik
Minister of Defense of Turkey

4

[On the U.S. House of Representatives vote to cut off military aid to Turkey until substantial progress is made toward a military settlement in Cyprus, which Turkey recently invaded]: It is true that America can cut its military aid, but it is not good practice in international relations to tell a country, "If you don't do this, then I will do that." We are not accustomed to this sort of treatment. We are ready to do everything with the United States that is in our mutual interest, and to help a friend. But if they threaten us, this has always brought about in Turkey the opposite result of what was sought.

Television interview, Ankara, Sept. 25/ The New York Times, 9-26:6.

Henry M. Jackson
United States Senator, D—Washington

5

[On U.S.-Soviet relations]: The [U.S. Nixon] Administration has posed a false choice between avoiding nuclear war and keeping faith with traditional values of human decency and individual liberty. It is false and misleading to suggest that the pursuit of peace requires official indifference to the fate of those brave men and women who are struggling to resist tyranny [in the Soviet Union]. It is high time for the Administration to indicate that the pace of the developing detente, and the inevitable accommodation on our part that this will require, must be conditioned on reciprocal accommodation by the Soviet Union.

Feb. 15/The New York Times, 2-16:4.

Michel Jobert
Foreign Minister of France

6

As far as I am concerned, I don't think Europe's future is black to the extent that there is a will to make a European Europe. If, on the other hand, some want to receive advice and

(MICHEL JOBERT)

sometimes directives from the other side of the Atlantic, it's a different Europe they want to make.

The New York Times, 2-15:14.

1

[U.S. Secretary of State Henry] Kissinger's attitude toward Europe seems to me, in the first place, to be artificial, and in the final analysis, excessive. Dr. Kissinger does not have the feel of Europe. The Europeans are hagglers, distrustful and crafty. Some are soldiers; others are jurists. Still others are merchants. All indulge in intellectual speculation or just plain speculation. You can exert pressure on such and such a group, but what you obtain against their will is no victory.

Interview/The Washington Post, 3-13:(A)17.

2

[On U.S.-European relations]: I hope that no one in Europe or the United States boxes himself into an excessive reasoning which could be prejudicial to everyone . . . [The NATO Alliance has] two pillars: the United States and Europe. I think it's better to be two-legged than one-legged; and I plead for European bipeds.

At Gaullist Party parliamentarian meeting, Nogent-sur-Marne, France, March 17/ Los Angeles Times, 3-18:(1)7.

Means Johnston, Jr.
Admiral, United States Navy; Commander-in-Chief, Allied Forces/Southern Europe
3

My primary responsibility is defense of the borders of the NATO countries in this command should NATO ever be drawn into war. Those countries are Italy, Greece and Turkey . . . In the event NATO were ever drawn into a sustained conflict, the southern region, as all of Europe, would rely very heavily on the shipment of supplies across the Atlantic. Hence, Portugal would play a key role, just west of Gibraltar, in helping to protect convoys en route to the southern region and providing bases for assistance in prosecuting the anti-submarine warfare campaign. The Azores are extremely important to us as far as any future anti-submarine warfare may be concerned.

Interview, Naples/ Los Angeles Herald-Examiner, 8-7:(A)6.

Edward M. Kennedy
United States Senator, D—Massachusetts
4

In time, of course, there will be some reduction in U.S. forces based here [in Europe]. It will happen as a result of allied agreement and allied effort, along with East-West negotiations, or it will happen as a result of our failure to act and to act together. It is for us to choose, but an orderly and agreed reduction of U.S. forces during the next few years does not have to mean any lessening of U.S. concern either for Europe's defense or for its future. At the same time, we can and must revitalize our relations, both in politics and economics. And if we do so, then a change in our defense relations can be part of the natural evolution of the Atlantic Alliance, and be in the interests of all.

Bonn, West Germany, April 8/ The Washington Post, 4-9:(A)16.

5

Today, without announcement, the Soviet government is building new missiles and testing still others. What does this mean? Does it mean preparations for the next round of arms competition? Or does it merely represent the momentum of research, pursued without intention to deploy? In the United States we would be greatly aided in assessing Soviet developments that do not threaten us if we could hear clear and public statements of your [Soviets'] intentions.

At U.S.A. Institute, Moscow, April 19/ The New York Times, 4-20:4.

6

[On his recent talks with Soviet Communist Party leader Leonid Brezhnev]: I found him a warm individual, highly intelligent, highly aware, a sense of humor, completely at ease, very informal . . . Here was a man who believes that important progress has been made with [U.S. Secretary of State Henry] Kissinger and [U.S.] President Nixon in the area of reduction of tensions, particularly in the area of strategic arms, and [he] wants that continued . . . And I have every intention of supporting those efforts of Mr. Kissinger and President Nixon to see that those efforts are continued.

Television interview, Washington/
"Washington Straight Talk,"
WETA-TV, Washington, 5-6.

Henry A. Kissinger
Secretary of State of the United States

1

I do not oppose the objective of those who wish to use trade policy to affect the evolution of Soviet society; it does seem to me, however, that they have chosen the wrong vehicle and the wrong context. We cannot accept the principle that our entire foreign policy—or even an essential component of that policy such as a normalization of our trade relations—should be made dependent on the transformation of the Soviet domestic structure. I say this with some anguish, since both as an historian and as one whose own origins make him particularly conscious of the plight of minority groups, I would prefer that we could do otherwise. Let us remember that we seek detente with the Soviet Union for one overwhelming reason: Both countries have the capability to destroy each other—and most of the rest of the world in the process. Thus, both of us have an overriding obligation to do all in our power to prevent such a catastrophe.

Before Senate Finance Committee, Washington,
March 7/The New York Times, 3-8:6.

2

I would say that the biggest problem American foreign policy confronts right now is not to regulate competition with its enemies—we have a generation of experience with that, and with ups and downs we are going to handle it—but how to bring our friends to a realization that there are greater common interests than simply self-assertiveness, and that the seeming victory they are striving for is going to prove hollow in an atmosphere of constant strife and endless competition . . . The United States has no objection whatever to an independent European policy. It does have an objection when independence takes the form of basic hostility to the United States. It does have an objection when, in a crisis which can only be dealt with cooperatively, the Europeans deliberately adopt a competitive posture . . . We [the U.S.] are going to win that competition if it takes place, because we have infinitely more resources.

Before Congressional wives, Washington,
March 11/Los Angeles Times, 3-13:(1)20.

3

[On whether the current trouble in Cyprus—coup, successive changes of government, Turkish and Greek fighting—had caught the U.S. by surprise]: If I answer this question I get into major difficulties, because if I say it took us by complete surprise, you will say, "Intelligence failure." And if I say it didn't take us by complete surprise, you will say other things.

News conference, Washington, July 22/
The National Observer, 8-3:7.

4

The tormented island of Cyprus is [an] area where peace requires a spirit of compromise, accommodation and justice. The United States is convinced that the sovereignty, political independence and territorial integrity of Cyprus must be maintained. It will be up to the parties to decide on the form of government they believe best suited to the particular conditions of Cyprus. They must reach accommodation on the areas to be administered by the Greek and Turkish Cypriot communities as well as on the conditions under which refugees can return to their homes and reside in safety . . . The United States is prepared to play an even more active role than in the past in helping the parties find a solution to the centuries-old problem of Cyprus. We will do all we can, but it is those most directly concerned whose effort is most crucial.

Before United Nations General Assembly,
New York, Sept. 23/
The New York Times, 9-24:12.

5

. . . in early 1973 I thought the time was opportune to move toward a serious dialogue with Europe; and I thought it was all the more essential because I did not want success to

WHAT THEY SAID IN 1974

(HENRY A. KISSINGER)

become identified in the public consciousness only with relations with adversaries; and I felt that the old Atlantic relationship would over a period of time become so much taken for granted and so much the province of an older generation that the next generation would consider it as something not relevant to itself.

Interview, Washington/
The New York Times, 10-13:(1)34.

1

The problem of Italy . . . [is] that you have there a residual vote that has never been reduced by prosperity and goes to the Communists. This shows that there is a significant percentage of the population that does not consider itself part of the system. If you take the authoritarian parties in Italy on the left and the right, you have only about 60 per cent of the spectrum to work with for a democratic policy. When that is split you have an inherent weakness; and it will be split, because that's the nature of the democratic process.

Interview, Washington/
The New York Times, 10-13:(1)34.

2

When I came to Washington, the Soviet Union was considered a permanent adversary. Today we can already say that the possibilities of war between our two countries have been reduced to negligible proportions and the tensions which were so characteristic of earlier periods have largely been stemmed. Now our objective is to give this condition a permanent and irreversible basis.

At luncheon, Moscow, Oct. 24/
The Washington Post, 10-25:(A)24.

3

[Saying the U.S. should not press too hard for easing of Soviet emigration policies as a condition in a U.S.-Soviet trade agreement]: We had . . . been told repeatedly that the Soviet Union considered the issue of emigration a matter of its own domestic legislation and practices not subject to international negotiations. With this as a background, I must state

flatly that if I were to assert here that a formal agreement on emigration from the U.S.S.R. exists between our governments, that statement would immediately be repudiated by the Soviet government . . . I am convinced that additional public commentary, or continued claims that this or that protagonist has won, can only jeopardize the results we all seek. We should not delude ourselves that the commercial measures to be authorized by the trade bill will lead a powerful state like the Soviet Union to be indifferent to constant and demonstrative efforts to picture it as yielding in the face of external pressures; nor can we expect extended debates of domestic Soviet practices by responsible U.S. public figures and officials to remain indefinitely without reaction. We should keep in mind that the ultimate victims of such claims will be those whom all of us are trying to help.

Before Senate Finance Committee, Washington,
Dec. 5/The New York Times, 12-19:18.

4

[On criticism in the U.S. of American military aid to Turkey in light of Turkey's involvement in the Cyprus crisis]: Military aid to Turkey is not given as a favor to Turkey; it is not given to influence a particular negotiation. It is given for the security of the West, for the common interest of all the Western countries in the defense of the Mediterranean.

Brussels, Dec. 11/
The Washington Post, 12-12:(A)30.

Alexei N. Kosygin
Premier of the Soviet Union

5

The general economic situation in the capitalist countries exhibits a downward trend. Crisis tendencies are to be seen in . . . practically the whole capitalist world—the United States, Japan and the West European countries. The crisis has gripped not only the economy but the politics, culture and ideology of bourgeois society. [In the Soviet Union, however,] we have not just increased by far the economic potential of our state but have entered a qualitatively new stage of economic development which is characterized by a high level of technical progress.

*On 50th anniversary of Khirgiz Soviet
Republic, Frunze, U.S.S.R., Nov. 2/
The Atlanta Journal and Constitution,
11-3:(B)2.*

Bruno Kreisky
Chancellor of Austria

1

There is no doubt that we are based on Western democracy and belong to the Western world. Yet the Russians like to hold international conferences in Vienna. They know that Austria's neutrality and unqualified independence under international law mean more than any paper agreements. No one can guarantee what kind of government there will be in France, or Britain, or the United States, or the Soviet Union, or any other country; but neutrality is neutrality—a small country has to respect international law.

*Interview, Vienna/
The Christian Science Monitor, 4-17:2.*

Melvin R. Laird
*Former Secretary of Defense
of the United States*

2

The U.S.S.R. is going ahead full steam with about 12 per cent of their gross national product allocated to their military base. And we [the U.S.] gave 6 per cent. True, their GNP is half [of] ours, but that really shows how determined they are. On top of that, they spend more for modernization than we do. Our defense program is about 55 per cent for manpower and their total expenditure is about 26 per cent for manpower. The rest goes into modernization of forces and new weapons and equipment. They are continuing to do that, and in five or six years they will have a much more modern force. And they have the time . . . So far as the Soviets are concerned, they have made no moves to reduce their national-security and defense efforts. They have done just the opposite. The [U.S.-Soviet] agreements signed up to date have made no effort to reduce the Soviet Union's power. I think that has to be understood when we look for progress from detente.

Interview/Human Events, 7-20:4.

Walter Laqueur
*Director, Institute of Contemporary
Affairs, London*

3

Your idea in America that Europe had become strong and united is not true. On the contrary, it is becoming weaker and more disunited. I say that in sorrow. [U.S. Secretary of State Henry] Kissinger was angry, but that is wrong. The belief that he and [U.S.] President Nixon seemed to have that Europe is ganging up on the United States is a mistake. If Europe did gang up, I would be happy. Europe can't gang up against anyone. In history, from time to time, you have an hour of truth. The recent Middle East war and the resulting oil embargo was such an hour for Europe, revealing its weaknesses, disunity and lack of leadership. Americans have this kind of Marxist assumption that, once you have a strong economy, you are strong. Europe and Japan developed big industries and prosperous trade. So you concluded that, once they had a big GNP, they are a big power; but it just isn't so. It overlooks the military side.

*Interview, Washington/
Los Angeles Times, 4-3:(2)7.*

Georg Leber
Minister of Defense of West Germany

4

Although the [West German] Army takes into consideration military, political and other factors of a potential enemy, the soldiers are not taught to hate the enemy. We teach the soldier that he has never lived in such prosperity, freedom and security as now. We don't need an enemy image. This policy does not result from psychological considerations, but from political ones—that we are *for* something, not *against* something.

*News conference/
The Christian Science Monitor, 1-23:5.*

Joseph Luns
*Secretary General, North Atlantic
Treaty Organization*

5

As allied countries seek to overcome balance-of-payment difficulties brought about by rising prices, pressures to reduce defense

(JOSEPH LUNS)

budgets will inevitably increase. Much will therefore depend on the resolve of governments, backed by public opinion, to allocate enough resources for defense; on the readiness of the European allies to shoulder their fair part; on the ability of the United States and Canada to resist pressures to withdraw U.S. and Canadian forces from Europe; and, ultimately, on the maintenance of a strategy of flexible response [combining] credible conventional defense and the nuclear deterrent.

At NATO 25th anniversary ceremony,
Brussels, April 4/
The Dallas Times Herald, 4-4:(A)3.

Donald Maitland
Chief British delegate to the United Nations 1

What the members of the European community are doing today is not as well understood on this [American] side of the Atlantic as it should be. The construction of Western Europe is, first and foremost, an act of reconciliation, an ending of the civil war which has wracked and ravaged the continent since the collapse of the Roman Empire and disturbed the peace of the world far too often. Our second aim is to restore to our continent the influence in world affairs of which our disunity has deprived us ... Those on this side of the Atlantic who rebuke us for our failure to produce an instantaneous united response to every major event might recall how many years it took the 13 original states to reconcile their conflicting interests and devise a coherent American policy.

Before the Pilgrims, New York, Jan. 23/
The New York Times, 1-24:14.

Makarios III
Exiled President of Cyprus 2

[On the take-over of the Cypriot government by Glafkos Clerides, who in turn took over from Nikos Sampson who took control after a coup which exiled Makarios]: [Clerides] took over the function of acting as President during such time as I may be absent from Cyprus and until my return ... His assumption of such duties is in accordance with the Cyprus Constitution and therefore a step toward return to the Constitutional order as provided in the recent resolution of the [UN] Security Council ... The restoration of democracy in Greece gives me great satisfaction even if it was achieved with the sacrifice of the lives of so many Greeks of Cyprus.

News conference, New York, July 23/
The Washington Post, 7-24:(A)18.

3

I understand that Turkey will insist on a geographical federation [of Greek and Turkish sectors on Cyprus], and I will never accept a federation on a geographical basis because it would lead eventually to a partition of the island and to a double enosis [incorporation of Cyprus into Greece and Turkey]. In other words, it would mean the end of Cyprus as an independent state. What I'm prepared to discuss is a federation, yes, but not a geographical one, a communal one. For instance, there are areas with three or four or more Turkish villages, and these could be grouped and administered by a Turkish administration. It's one thing to have areas administered by Turkish Cypriots, others administered by Greek Cypriots, and it's another thing to have mass movements of the population. A geographical federation would move more than 200,000 people from one area to another area, and that would be inhuman, to say the least. How can you say to 200,000 people, "Leave your house, your land, and go somewhere else, because we want to form a geographical federation?"

Interview, New York/
The Washington Post, 11-17:(C)1.

Makarios III
President of Cyprus 4

[On his return to Cyprus following a five-month exile]: This is not the time to set out my views as to how the [Greek-Turkish Cypriot] problem should be solved. I only say that we shall not accept any solution involving transfer of populations and amounting to partition of Cyprus. It is possible to find a way for the self-government of the two communities, and it is possible to find a way to safeguard the rights of the Greeks and the Turks of Cyprus and their peaceful coexistence and cooperation to their mutual benefit and for their common welfare.

Addressing crowd on his return, Nicosia, Dec. 7/The Washington Post, 12-8:(A)25.

1

[On his return to Cyprus following a five-month exile]: I do not wish to rake up old wounds that I want to see heal. And for this reason it is not my intention to persecute my enemies and opponents or to bring to justice those involved in political offenses or those who took part in the coup against me [last July]. I forgive them all for their sins and grant them amnesty in the hope that the desired concord and unity among our people will come out.

Addressing crowd on his return, Nicosia, Dec. 7/The New York Times, 12-8:3.

George Mavros
Foreign Minister of Greece

2

[On Turkey's invasion of Cyprus]: Can anyone be blind enough not to see that partition is Turkey's objective. Turkey is aiming for the establishment, in the second half of the 20th century, of a Turkish protectorate over the Republic of Cyprus. In short, a satellite state.

*Athens, Aug. 14/
Los Angeles Times, 8-15:(1)6.*

3

The fact · that Greece has pulled out of NATO does not signify that we are a non-aligned power, nor that we have changed the orientation of our policies. We want to have good relations with all our neighbors, even the Soviet bloc. But Greece remains European. That is a fact. We belong to Europe and we are for European integration.

*News conference, Paris, Sept. 6/
The New York Times, 9-7:3.*

4

[On his country's withdrawal from the military branch of NATO]: Our decision is not a bluff. The Alliance proved to be unable to prevent a military conflict between two member countries [Greece and Turkey's conflict over Cyprus this year]. What use is it? Everybody in Greece wonders how this Alliance can protect us from outside aggression if it cannot prevent aggression from within. We know very well what Greek withdrawal means to the status of the Western world. It is ridiculous to think that Turkey can fill the gap. Without Greece, the entire Western strategy— the entire defense structure—will crumble. Can you imagine what would happen if Greece fell [to the Communists]? Italy and Turkey would fall in the same afternoon, and the lives of 300 million Europeans would be at stake. But we Greeks cannot bear alone the responsibility for the security of the Western world at a time when we are so bluntly attacked by a member of the Atlantic Alliance—and the other members of this Alliance are simply looking on. Greece had no other alternative but to withdraw from the military branch of the NATO Alliance.

Interview/Time, 9-9:34.

Francois Mitterrand
*Leader, Socialist Party of France;
Candidate for President*

5

France belongs to the Western world, to the Atlantic world. It is a member of the Atlantic Alliance, and the problem for the French people is to know if it would be good to leave this security system. I would say yes, on condition that there was another system . . . As for myself, for the present, we are in the Atlantic Alliance, and we are staying there.

*News conference, Paris, April 12/
The New York Times, 4-13:9.*

Thomas H. Moorer
*Admiral, United States Navy; Chairman,
Joint Chiefs of Staff*

6

[On whether the U.S. should withdraw its military forces from Europe]: . . . I'm fully aware of all of the arguments: that the war has now been over nearly 30 years, and now that Western Europe has 300-plus million people,

(THOMAS H. MOORER)

why can't they take care of themselves, and so on. Of course, the forces we have in Europe are over there to protect the interests of the United States in the over-all context. And I think that, until we can work out some progressive agreements, such as mutual and balanced force reductions [between East and West], that the presence of our forces in Europe provides a stability that is worth what we put into it. If the forces are withdrawn—assuming we don't demobilize them—we would not save any money of any consequence. As a matter of fact, if we still maintained our commitments to NATO, the withdrawal of the forces would generate a requirement for sea and airlift to get them back, which would cost a considerable amount of money. So, primarily in the interest of deterrence and political stability, the forces in Europe are necessary. It would be a major mistake at this point in history to make a unilateral withdrawal. After all, there's been no war there for nearly 30 years, which is a rather long time for Europe not to have a war. So the record speaks for itself.

Interview, Washington/
U.S. News & World Report, 7-8:60.

Richard M. Nixon
President of the United States

1

As far as our relations with the Soviet are concerned, we shall continue. We shall continue to negotiate, recognizing that they don't like our system or approve of it, and I don't like their system or approve of it. [Soviet Communist Party Secretary] Brezhnev knows that, and I know it, and we have discussed it quite bluntly and directly. However, it is essential that both nations, being the superpowers that we are, continue to make progress toward limiting arms, toward avoiding confrontations which might explode into war ... and also continuing those negotiations for reduction of forces in Europe and reduction of arms, or certainly the limitation of arms, and the various other initiatives that we are undertaking with the Soviet. In a nutshell, this is what we have to consider: Do we want to go back to a period when the United States and the Soviet Union—the two great superpowers—stood in confrontation against each other—and risk a runaway nuclear arms race and also crisis in Berlin, in the Mideast, even, again, in Southeast Asia or other places of the world—or do we want to continue on a path in which we recognize our differences but try to recognize also the fact that we must either live together or we will all die together.

News conference, Feb. 25/
The New York Times, 2-26:22.

2

There are those who say [that], because of the way the Russians treat their minorities, we should break off our relations with them, we should not trade with them, we should deny them credits, and then maybe they will change. Well, first, they aren't going to change if we do that. It will have exactly the opposite effect. But the second point is, if we go back to the old policy of confrontation, not negotiating to limit nuclear arms and other arms ... not negotiate with the hope of resolving differences at the conference table rather than on the battlefield, then what you have to do is to face the necessity for the United States to enter an arms race; and instead of an $8 billion increase in the arms budget, you'd have $100 billion increase in the arms budget; and eventually you confront what would be a massive crisis between the Soviet Union and the United States in the Mideast, in Europe, possibly even in the Mediterranean as well as in the Caribbean area, where our interests are in conflict ... it's far better to have the voice of the President of the United States heard from within the Kremlin than on the outside, because those walls are mighty thick, I can tell you. So, therefore, let's continue to talk to them so we won't have to fight them.

At Executive Club, Chicago, March 15/
The New York Times, 3-16:13.

3

... the Europeans cannot have it both ways. They cannot have the United States participation and cooperation on the security front and then proceed to have confrontation and even hostility on the economic and political fronts ... The United States has been very generous to its allies and friends and to its former enemies. We will continue to be as generous as we can. But whether it's in the field of trade or whether it's in any other field, it is essential that we get what I would say is a fair break for our producers, just as we try to give a fair break to *their* producers ... I have had great difficulty in getting the Congress to continue to support American forces in Europe at the level that we need to keep them there. In the event that Congress gets the idea that we are going to be faced with economic confrontation and hostility from the [Common Market] Nine, you will find it almost impossible to get Congressional support for continued American presence at present levels on the security front. Now, we do not want this to happen; and that is why I have urged my friends in Europe—our friends in Europe—to consider this proposition. It doesn't mean that we are not going to have competition, but it does mean that we are not going to be faced with a situation where the nine countries of Europe gang up against the United States—the United States which is their guarantee for their security. That we cannot have.

Before Executive Club, Chicago, March 15/
The New York Times, 3-16:13.

Olof Palme
Prime Minister of Sweden

1

[On problems of the welfare state in his country, Norway, Denmark, etc.]: The crisis is deeper than the welfare state and possibly more dangerous. It is the hangover of the industrial society. We have all doubled production in the last 20 years. The benefits are material, and we are more free and more secure. Company directors, politicians, trade-union officials all rode on that wave. Now they see there's a price to be paid: inflation, structural changes in the economy. People shift here and there. The gaps between the groups are increasing. People begin worrying what's going to happen to them. There is a sense of fear. There are wars, alienation, multinational companies, things beyond people's immediate influence, redundancy. This has created instability. I'm rather worried

looking around Europe. The stock of democracy is in decline.

Interview/The New York Times, 3-22:3.

2

[On West German Prime Minister Willy Brandt's resignation as a result of an East German spy being found on his staff]: The East German state has committed a shocking breach of faith. In its Stalinistic zeal, it has not been understood that detente must be built on honesty and trust ... His departure as Federal Chancellor is a grave loss for the continuing struggle for peace and detente in Europe and the whole world.

May 7/The Washington Post, 5-8:(A)29.

William Proxmire
United States Senator, D—Wisconsin

3

[On CIA estimates that, percentage-wise, the Soviets are spending less on military equipment and weapons but more on military research]: The figures suggest that, rather than building up the momentum to forge ahead of the United States, the Soviet Union is still trying to catch up with us, and they are having a hard time doing that. If the Russians are planning to mount a massive effort to gain superiority in the area of strategic weapons, they will either have to cut back their other defense programs or completely reverse the long-term trend of their over-all military spending. There is no evidence they are following either course.

The New York Times, 7-22:2.

Peter Ramsbotham
British Ambassador-designate to the United States

4

[On strains in British-American relations since Britain joined the Common Market]: I see no merit in mutual recrimination, irritation or frustration. On both sides of the Atlantic we shall need to exercise the virtues of patience and trust and show a readiness to give each other the benefit of the doubt.

Before Pilgrims Society, London/
The New York Times, 2-8:36.

WHAT THEY SAID IN 1974

Harry Reasoner
News commentator,
American Broadcasting Company

1

Russia is still motivated by Marxism, a religion that promises them the future if they will lie, cheat, threaten, subvert and occasionally fight to get it. That national religion is the single biggest threat to world peace in this half-century. The nice thing about Marxism is, it is dead wrong. In free countries where it has enjoyed brief vogues, the free exchange of opinion has eroded it to ineffectiveness. It can only be sustained in places where thought is tightly controlled.

ABC News commentary/
The Christian Science Monitor, 3-8:(F)8.

Merlyn Rees
British Secretary of State
for Northern Ireland

2

It is all well to say that, politically, we [Britain] have to get out [of Northern Ireland] and let the people there settle it [the Catholic-Protestant conflict] themselves. But when you ask people who call for the pullout about the security situation, they have no answer. The point is that if we withdraw, then there would be serious trouble not confined to Northern Ireland—it could well spread to the Irish Republic and even to cities in England and Scotland.

Interview, London/
The Atlanta Constitution, 11-11:(A)13.

David Rockefeller
Chairman,
Chase Manhattan Bank, New York

3

One of the difficulties in the world today is that the Atlantic nations, which were united after World War II by concern over Soviet aggression, now, because of detente, see that danger abating. Their unity has been weakened because they lack an external force to draw them together. In my judgment, the energy crisis could be a new binding force to reunite them. And if that happens, a threatening problem could be turned into a benefit for all nations.

Interview, Washington/
U.S. News & World Report, 8-12:42.

Eugene V. Rostow
Professor of Law and Public Affairs,
Yale University; Former Under Secretary
of State of the United States

4

The crisis in Atlantic relations revealed by the October [1973] war in the Middle East was more serious than the other crises in the history of the Atlantic Alliance, because the struggle in the Middle East manifests a major and continuing Soviet threat to the security of Europe which the Allies did not face together.

San Francisco Examiner, 3-27:34.

Andrei D. Sakharov
Soviet physicist

5

We all welcome the [U.S.-Soviet] negotiations that are now being held aimed at preventing a thermonuclear world war, as well as the armaments race, and to promote negotiations aimed to increase . . . detente. But at the same time, there continue to be [in the Soviet Union] arrests, interrogations and searches of dissidents, religious persecutions, harassment of honest writers, obstacles placed in the way of free emigration, and discrimination against national minorities. In an irrefutable way, this shows that the external detente is tragically not accompanied by an internal and human detente.

Telephone message accepting the U.S.
Social Democrats' Norman Thomas
Freedom Award, Feb. 1/
Los Angeles Herald-Examiner, 2-19:(A)12.

Nikos Sampson
President of Cyprus

6

[On the coup which just installed him to office] : In the name of God and the people and in the name of the armed forces, I have taken over the Presidency of Cyprus . . . [There will be free elections] as soon as the necessary conditions are created, and in any case within a year, so that the Greek Cypriot people may be given the right to express their will and choose the government of their liking and by free vote and not by acclamation.

Radio address to the nation, July 15/
Los Angeles Times, 7-16:(1)8.

1

There is no difference between me and former President Makarios on this issue [independence for Cyprus]. The difference is that he established a personal regime and violated human rights and did not care that it was leading the country to civil war.

News conference, Nicosia, July 18/
The Christian Science Monitor, 7-19:2.

Nikos Sampson
Former President of Cyprus

2

[On his relinquishing the Presidency to Glafkos Clerides]: Mr. Clerides' experience as a negotiator calls for his presence in the Presidency. My conscience is clear as to my having done my duty . . . at a particularly critical moment.

Radio address, July 23/
The Washington Post, 7-24:(A)15.

James R. Schlesinger
Secretary of Defense of the United States

3

We are not dealing with NATO because of nostalgia. We are committed to the Alliance because of present and prospective advantages for the United States and for the free world. As long as the most critical region in the world continues to be Western Europe, I think the United States may well bear the low costs of maintaining its forces in Europe. The Europeans are offsetting right now the balance-of-payments effects of our forces being stationed in Germany. In addition, in budget terms it costs no more to station them in Germany than it does in the United States. Relocating those troops strikes me as providing no great additional advantages. The maintenance of a free Europe is essential to the United States, and I think our forces should remain there as long as they are necessary.

Interview, Washington/
U.S. News & World Report, 5-13:44.

Helmut Schmidt
Minister of Finance of West Germany

4

If Europe wants to have a decisive word to say in international politics in between the U.S.

and the U.S.S.R., the superpowers, and the emerging power center, [Communist] China, it must come to terms on common policies. The offer to cooperate and to reach equitable compromises in dealings with the outside world will be more convincing if it reflects a similar behavior in dealings within the Community. Among members of the European Community there is certainly no argument about the fact that there is no other alternative to Europe. But this conviction is of not much use unless we stop asking what Europe can do for us and instead ask what we can do for Europe.

At Institute for International Affairs,
London, Jan. 29/Vital Speeches, 3-15:330.

Helmut Schmidt
Chancellor of West Germany

5

We want our friends and neighbors, our alliance and treaty partners in the world, to know that the positions of our foreign and security policy remain unchanged. We shall continue our policy of safeguarding peace and we shall guard and strengthen our country's security. We shall actively contribute toward maintaining the balance of power which is requisite to peace . . . The Atlantic Alliance remains both the elementary basis of our security and the political framework required for our efforts to promote international detente. We shall continue to work for the political strengthening of the Alliance, and by means of our armed forces render our contribution to collective security as agreed within the Alliance.

Before Bundestag, Bonn, May 17/
Vital Speeches, 7-1:548.

6

I truly am an advocate of close cooperation between the European countries and the United States and Canada; but secondly, I am also a deeply convinced advocate of progress in the field of European integration; and thirdly, I am a convinced advocate of detente with the Soviet Union.

Interview, Bonn/
San Francisco Examiner & Chronicle,
7-21:(A)10.

345

WHAT THEY SAID IN 1974

(HELMUT SCHMIDT)

1

The Federation of Europe is a very, very difficult thing to bring about. You don't only have six or seven languages ... The tax problems, for instance, in Italy and in Germany, have been developed within three, four, five generations. They are absolutely different from each other. The credit system. The economic structure of southern Italy still is much more equal to Anatolia than to Europe. All your institutions differ from each other many, many times more than the institutions of California and, let us say, Cambridge, Massachusetts. So it takes a long, long time. And, in the meantime, you are always responsible to your national Parliament and to your national voters, who are very careful that you avoid any sacrifices today out of their pockets or at their expense. It might have been possible to make greater progress with such a super-human leader like [the late French President Charles] de Gaulle appeared to most Europeans. But he isn't any longer here. You might gain something by the personal friendship between [current French President] Valery Giscard d'Estaing and me for the time, as long as these people can act independently. But this just isn't enough. You don't have this great moving personnel, this great moving idea. And you don't have this menace at the horizon which we had in the '50s, when you had this pressure from the Soviet Union.

Interview/The New York Times, 8-25:(1)26.

2

... the social framework in this country doesn't offer the Communists any opportunity for agitation. This is a society in which trade unions, with a very cautious but at the same time energetic policy, have achieved great gains in social justice and social security over the past 25 years. Nobody in Germany really feels the Communists could do any better. We have, for instance, within those 25 years, managed to achieve an average real income that is fourth in the world—behind only the United States, Switzerland and Sweden. Who could have fore-

seen this 20, or even 10, years ago? Under such conditions, there is really no room for Communist agitation or propaganda.

Interview, Bonn/
U.S. News & World Report, 12-9:34.

Mario Soares
Leader, Socialist Party of Portugal

3

So long as the other side maintains the Warsaw Pact, there is no question but that I believe in cooperation with the West and in the collective-security alliance which NATO represents ... The Communist goal of a dictatorship of the proletariat ... is not for us socialists. Yet we are ready to collaborate with the Communists in the period of transition to a democracy [since the recent coup installing a new military junta in Portugal]. As you know, there can be no democracy without all parties—even the Communists—playing a part.

Interview, Lisbon/
The Washington Post, 5-8:(A)36.

Alexander I. Solzhenitsyn
Exiled Soviet author

4

[On his recent expulsion from the Soviet Union]: Actually, a person in many ways is similar to a plant. When he is pulled out of a place and thrown far away, it disturbs hundreds of tiny roots and nerve centers. All the days and each minute, you become aware of inadequacies, of abnormalities. You become aware of yourself, not being yourself. But I do not think that it is hopeless. Even old trees, even they are transplanted and they take root in a new place ... I am an optimist from birth and I do not consider my exile as final. I have the feeling that, in a few years, I will return to Russia. How it will happen, how changed will be the conditions, I cannot foretell. But no one and nothing can predict the future. Wonders never cease to occur in our lives. The last years of my life in Russia, I was already robbed of my country. The pressure and surveillance by the KGB, the opposition of authorities in all instances didn't give me access to either the scenes of my novels or to eyewitnesses. Nevertheless, as I already said, and I repeat now: I know myself that my right to Russian earth is no less than the right of those who took upon themselves the audacity to physically throw me out.

Interview, Zurich, Switzerland, Feb. 18/
Los Angeles Times, 2-19:(1)5.

1

The Soviet Union lives under the rule of serfdom. I have said [this] so many times, but people seem to take it for an artistic metaphor. Free citizens are not at all free. They are free neither to choose their employment, nor to fight for a fair wage for it, and even in their day-by-day lives they are obliged to conform to the whims of the petty local party bosses. Those who anger the bosses can be oppressed without recourse to any process of law. Soviet people cannot choose where to live in their own country. How much more intolerable is this oppression than lack of freedom to emigrate, which has caused so much justified protest all over the world.

Telephone message to British Broadcasting
Corp., April 5/Los Angeles Herald-Examiner,
4-6:(A)4.

Franz-Josef Strauss
Former Minister of Defense and
Minister of Finance of West Germany

2

The Europeans had an almost hostile attitude toward the Americans during the Middle East crisis [late last year]. Then they—primarily the French—tried to solve the energy crisis on their own. All this has brought relations between the United States and Europe to the point at which we are standing today—on the ruins of the Atlantic Alliance.

Interview/Los Angeles Times, 3-18:(1)7.

3

I have a fundamental belief in the future of the U.S. I believe America is indispensable for the world in its present situation and its future. If I were not capable of believing that, I would migrate to another planet—because Europeans will only be able to solve their problems if they get assistance from a closely allied, sound,

strong America. My political background has not necessarily been "pro-Atlantic." I have been a European, sometimes erroneously labeled a "Gaullist." But I have never advocated, nor agreed with, a European future without, or against, the United States. When the Middle East flared up last autumn, it was the U.S., shaken as it was by the Watergate scandal, which immediately took things into hand and squelched the conflict. Europeans did nothing. I believe the future of the world is dependent on the U.S., and we should build on this. Otherwise, we can write about our future, as Dante wrote in *The Inferno:* "All hope abandon, ye who enter here." The more Europeans fail as true partners of the Americans, the more the Americans are forced to coordinate their worldwide policies with the Soviets.

Interview/Nation's Business, April:61.

Mikhail Suslov
Secretary, Central Committee, Communist
Party of the Soviet Union

4

Our foreign-policy initiatives aim to make the relaxation of international tensions irreversible. We want the positive trends in Soviet relations with France, the United States, West Germany and other capitalist states and the new favorable climate that is emerging in Europe to develop and spread further.

On 50th anniversary of Uzbek Soviet
Republic, Tashkent, U.S.S.R., Oct. 22/
The Atlanta Constitution, 10-23:(A)13.

Jeremy Thorpe
Leader, British Liberal Party

5

Liberals are unashamedly committed to breaking the two-party [Conservative-Labor] system in which the party of management alternates with the party of trade unionism, each committed to the reversal of their predecessor's policies. Both interest groups represent vital elements in our society. Neither should ever be allowed to dominate the thinking of the government of the day.

News conference, London, Sept. 17/
Los Angeles Times, 9-18:(1)9.

Kurt Waldheim
Secretary General of the United Nations

1

[On the current conflict in Cyprus]: To this moment, heavy fighting in Cyprus continues. This situation, which clearly represents a threat to international peace and security, calls in question the very essence of the UN Charter and the *raison d'etre* of our organization. I believe it is vital that this [Security] Council, which has the primary responsibility for the maintenance of international peace and security, should give the most immediate and searching attention to the implications of this situation both for the immediate problem of Cyprus and for the future effectiveness of the United Nations.

Before United Nations Security Council,
New York, Aug. 15/
Los Angeles Times, 8-16:(1)22.

2

There is unhappily a tendency—and this is particularly true in the Cyprus situation over the past 10 years—for the parties to a dispute, and other concerned parties, to relax their efforts to reach a political settlement when a United Nations peace-keeping operation is functioning effectively. For the past 10 years in Cyprus, all the instrumentalities for a peaceful solution were there except for the political will and sense of urgency. The result of the absence of that will and that sense of urgency has been a tragedy for the people of Cyprus and has created acute and grave new tensions.

At National Press Club, Washington,
Sept. 10/The New York Times, 9-11:11.

Alfred Wentworth
Senior vice president, Chase Manhattan Bank

3

Detente may be unraveling in the United States—I don't know. But it's not unraveling on this side [in the Soviet Union]. In fact, there's a greater impetus to speed up trade [with the U.S.], to accelerate . . . The Soviets are not going to grant full freedom of emigration [in return for U.S. trade]; nor will they grant freedom of the press. But if [U.S. Secretary of State Henry] Kissinger's requests were any-

where near reasonable, I think he may have got them. The Russians will do everything they can to ease trade. Their desire to trade with the West is a deep conviction, not a surface thing . . . We're talking in terms of billions of dollars and the most fantastic projects. American businessmen who come here are surprised at the size of the deals. "How about 20 tractors?" they ask. And the Russians reply: "How about 200?" Everything is Bolshoi-big in this country.

Moscow/Los Angeles Times, 4-12:(3)16,17.

William Whitelaw
Member, British Parliament; Former
British Secretary of State
for Northern Ireland

4

A separate Northern Ireland would have the effect of increasing pressure for Scottish and Welsh separatism, and the unity of the United Kingdom itself would be in jeopardy.

London/Los Angeles Times, 11-8:(1)22.

Harold Wilson
Leader, British Labor Party; Former
Prime Minister of the United Kingdom

5

We [the Labor Party] stand for something far different than the Tories: a society in which ordinary people can flower and flourish [unhindered by] a school tie [or] the accent they speak. This lot [the Heath government] doesn't know anything about miners or other ordinary people.

Campaigning for the forthcoming February
national election, Huyton, England/
The Christian Science Monitor, 2-28:4.

Harold Wilson
Prime Minister of the United Kingdom

6

[On the continued violence in Northern Ireland]: What I want to make clear today is the utter determination of Her Majesty's government that violence will not succeed. [The men of violence are not going to] bomb their way to the conference table—nor must they be allowed to bomb Northern Ireland into the abyss.

News conference, Belfast, April 18/
Los Angeles Times, 4-19:(1)4.

1

[On the troubles in Northern Ireland, such as the current strikes by militant Protestants]: Northern Ireland faces the gravest crisis in her history. It is a crisis equally for all of us who live on this [London] side of the water. We will not negotiate on Constitutional or political matters in Northern Ireland with anyone who chooses to operate outside the established Constitutional framework, with non-elected thugs and bullies who are systematically breaking the law and intimidating their fellow citizens.

Television address, London, May 25/
San Francisco Examiner & Chronicle,
6-2:(This World)10.

2

[On the collapse of Northern Ireland's coalition Catholic-Protestant government]: This is the gravest crisis seen in Northern Ireland since World War II. It is trying the patience of the people of Britain very much, not only because troops are being murdered, but also because of the vast sums of money pouring into Northern Ireland to get jobs for the people ... We have been glad to do this, but not on the basis that they are themselves imperiling the jobs we are helping to create.

London/U.S. News & World Report, 6-10:68.

3

The coming [October] general election is not just a decision about political power, about personalities or about the ins and outs and party machines. It is a decision, perhaps a once-for-all decision, which will settle whether an undue degree of power is to adhere to the big battalions, the rich and powerful, or whether power is to be exercised under democratic government.

Before Trades Union Congress,
Brighton, England, Sept. 5/
Los Angeles Times, 9-6:(1)4.

4

We [in Britain] cannot look forward over the next two years or more to any general increase in living standard. But when it is tough going, we believe that that means we have to devote more—and not less—of all we produce and enjoy to those who are hardest hit and least able to help themselves—the elderly, the sick and the disabled ... We cannot afford the "big battalion" philosophy, with power groups, whoever they may be, trying to seize more than their share of what is available.

Television broadcast, London/
The Atlanta Journal and Constitution,
10-20:(A)22.

Elmo R. Zumwalt, Jr.
Admiral, United States Navy;
Chief of Naval Operations

5

It is now evident that the historically land-oriented Soviet Union has embraced naval power as a major element of their foreign policy. The balance ... has shifted during the past five years, and now we are at a very critical point. The Soviets have a capability to deter or thwart U.S. movements in certain sea areas and may well be building a capability of their own for intervention overseas.

Before Senate Armed Services Committee,
Washington, Feb. 19/
Los Angeles Times, 2-20:(1)18.

The Middle East

Yigal Allon
Foreign Minister of Israel

1

I do not see any contradiction between the improved status of the United States [with the Arab countries] in the Middle East and the continuation of friendly relations between Washington and Jerusalem. In my opinion, [Egyptian] President [Anwar] Sadat and [Saudi Arabian] King Faisal have reached the conclusion that their national interests compel them to move closer to the U.S., even if it means that Egypt is compelled to break further away from the Soviet Union. They have learned that the Soviet infiltration policy is based on a continued conflict between them [the Arabs] and Israel, while the American influence is based more on a settlement. The capability of the U.S. to help the Arab states is greater than that of the Soviets.

Israeli television interview, June 14/
The Washington Post, 6-15:(A)18.

2

If we seek prospects of a political settlement [with the Arabs], we shall not find a more faithful ally than the United States nor a personality more able and friendly than [U.S. Secretary of State] Dr. [Henry] Kissinger. And, by the same token, if we are fated to have another war, we shall not find at our side better and firmer friends than them.

Before the Knesset (Parliament), Jerusalem,
Aug. 28/The New York Times, 8-29:11.

Ali Amin
Editor, "Al Ahram," Cairo

3

Can Israel and its Arab neighbors live side by side in peace? Of course. The Israelis are beginning to realize that the Arabs, who have resisted, fought and conquered Turkish imperialism, British imperialism and French imperialism, can never tolerate any form of Zionist imperialism. If the Israelis bury any thought of a "Greater Israel," if they treat the Arabs in Israel on a par with their Jewish citizens and not as second-class people, if they behave as good neighbors do all over the world, then I am sure they will enjoy lasting peace and share in the future prosperity of our area.

Interview, Cairo/Newsweek, 2-25:50.

4

The Arabs now have undreamed-of billions of dollars and a tremendous supply of manpower. Soon we will have new pools of technical know-how that will make the Middle East a unique part of the world. And if we are happy and free and unsuspicious, as I think we will be, we will want the whole world to partake of this new age. We will have everything we need to make our deserts bloom and turn our mud huts into decent houses. Ignorance breeds prejudice. And the ignorance will rapidly vanish, too. The Middle East is where East and West are finally going to come together. Perhaps I am a dreamer, but I also see a United States of the Middle East. Israel would not be included in such a grouping in the foreseeable future. But once a Palestinian state is set up, it will obviously have to live in peace with its neighboring Jewish state. After that, there are many hopeful options. The time has come for all of us to develop a more generous vision of the future—and to act boldly and decisively.

Interview, Cairo/Newsweek, 2-25:50.

5

The Soviet Union has lost 80 per cent of its prestige in this area. They want desperately to hold onto the other 20 per cent, but they will lose this, too, if they are not careful . . . The trouble with the Russians is that they don't ever learn from their mistakes. They tried pressure tactics on the Yugoslavs, the Poles, the Czechs, the Romanians and with [Communist]

China. They failed with all of them. With us Egyptians they tried pressure, too. They were always trying to tell us how to use the arms they sold us. If we had done as they wished, our own soldiers would have become like a regiment of the Russian Army.

Interview, Cairo/
The Christian Science Monitor, 5-8:3C.

Jamshid Amouzegar
Finance Minister of Iran

1

[On higher export prices being charged for oil by the producing countries in the Middle East]: How come when the price of exported wheat from industrialized nations increased threefold in a year, or when the price of their exported oil seeds, cement, sugar and petrochemical products are increased ninefold, the nations who import these commodities are not allowed to criticize? But when we reasonably increase our oil price, we are criticized. If the industrialized countries are to determine the price of our exported oil, in turn we regard ourselves as entitled to determine the price of their exported commodities.

Teheran/The Washington Post, 1-22:(A)10.

Yasir Arafat
Chairman, Palestine Liberation Organization

2

Commando raids [against Israel] are one of the political means we use ... Our basic aim is the survival of our people, their right to go home and the formation of a modern democratic state. Every sensible person in the world concedes today that a racist state is an obsolete concept—whether it's South Africa, Rhodesia or Israel. How do you think we feel when we see that any Jew from any part of the world has the right to settle in Israel and we are prevented from going back to our homes? ... If the Israelis are serious about a real peace in this part of the world, [then] a democratic state in which Jews, Christians and Moslems would coexist—as they do in Lebanon—is clearly the best and most idealistic solution. And for that, we have to carry the fight inside Israel.

Interview, Beirut/Newsweek, 7-22:55.

3

It pains me to see a very big country like the United States standing against the legitimate rights of a young people and a young country like Palestine, which is fighting for its freedom and liberty, while at the same time all the peoples of the world stand behind our struggle. Our people have never done any harm to the American people. But the United States offers napalm and all the up-to-date, most modern weapons, such as the *Phantom* jets, to our enemy [Israel] who kill our people and their children in the refugee camps. And who pays for these weapons and killings, too? It is the American taxpayer. Does the American taxpayer know he is paying taxes to kill another innocent people?

Interview, Beirut/
The New York Times, 11-10:(4)4.

4

It's not a question of discussions between us and the Israelis. The question between us and the Israelis is do we [Palestinians] exist or don't we? Do we have a right on our land or don't we? Any Israeli who accepts and believes in the basic premises and objectives on which the PLO stands is welcome and is a partner with whom we can negotiate ... Personally, we are not the enemies of the Jews ... What we want to dismantle is the aggressive, the expansionist attempts and attitudes of the Jewish state.

TV-radio interview/"Issues and Answers,"
American Broadcasting Company, 11-10.

5

Violence is a method used by every oppressed people. However, terrorism is something that goes against our [the PLO's] humanistic principles. We, as people who fight and struggle, cannot possibly adopt terrorism, particularly against civilians ... We had no other way but to use armed struggle, exactly as used in the United States during the time of George Washington. [But as for terrorist attacks on Israelis at the Munich Olympics and at Maalot, Israel,] there are some splinter, small groups that at times out of desperation commit some of these acts.

TV-radio interview/"Issues and Answers,"
American Broadcasting Company, 11-10.

WHAT THEY SAID IN 1974

(YASIR ARAFAT)

1

Palestine is the cement that holds the Arab world together, or it is the explosive that blows it apart.

*At Arab summit conference,
Rabat, Morocco/Time, 11-11:27.*

2

Personally, we [Palestinians] are not the enemies of the Jews. Don't forget, this part of the world is the place for the religions, the important religions, one of which is Judaism. Don't forget, we and the Jews are Semites. Over the years our hearts were open, and our homes too, to the Jews, and we lived together on our land without discrimination and with love and peace.

*Television interview/
The New York Times, 11-13:16.*

3

... if the immigration of Jews to Palestine had had as its objective the goal of enabling them to live side by side with us, enjoying the same rights and assuming the same duties, we would have opened our doors to them as far as our homeland's capacity for absorption permitted ... But that the goal of this immigration should be to usurp our homeland, disperse our people and turn us into second-class citizens— this is what no one can conceivably demand that we acquiesce in or submit to. Therefore, since its inception, our revolution was not motivated by racial or religious factors. Its target was never the Jew as a person, but racist Zionism and undisguised aggression. In this sense, ours is also a revolution for the Jew as a human being as well. We are struggling so that Jews, Christians and Moslems may live in equality, enjoying the same rights and assuming the same duties, free from racial or religious discrimination.

*Before United Nations General Assembly,
New York, Nov. 13/
The New York Times, 11-14:22.*

4

This war [against Israel] has just started. We are just beginning to get ready for what will be a long, long war, a war that will run for generations ... You asked: How long can we go on? The question was phrased wrong. What you should have asked is: How long can the Israelis go on? We shall never stop until we can go back home and Israel is destroyed ... The goal of our struggle is the end of Israel, and there can be no compromises or mediation ... We don't want peace; we want victory. Peace for us means Israel's destruction and nothing else ... We ... have the right to return to our homes without conditions or compromises ...

Interview/Los Angeles Times, 11-18:(2)7.

Hafez al-Assad
President of Syria

5

For Israel to continue, with the support she receives, to play the role of the privileged party who is able to decide the area and extent of withdrawal [from occupied Arab land], and to decide whether the people of Palestine have rights and the extent of those rights—all this is proof that Israel is not desirous of peace and believes that its interest lies in continued expansion and aggression.

*At Islamic summit conference, Lahore,
Pakistan, Feb. 22/Los Angeles Times, 2-23:(1)3.*

6

The Arab people cannot keep silent while Israeli occupation of their lands continues. Since the October [1973] war, this area cannot return to the previous condition of no peace, no war. What is now happening is war. It is at present confined to the Syrian front. It depends on Israel whether it is escalated and whether Israel is prepared to relinquish the Arab territories she seized in 1967 and to restore the rights of the Palestinian Arab people. If Israel is not ready to do this, the war will inevitably escalate ... Wars are not our hobby. But our interpretation of United Nations Resolution 242 means Israeli withdrawal from all territory occupied in 1967 and since, plus recognition of all Palestinian Arab rights. That alone will comprise a just peace.

*Interview, Damascus/
The New York Times, 5-2:10.*

1

Israel now faces the same problem I had. My doctor told me I had to give up smoking—or face a dangerous health hazard. Continued occupation [of Arab territory] has become injurious to Israel's health. When they occupied our land, we were faced with two alternatives— either to find some political and diplomatic way to get them to withdraw, or fight to get our land back. Six years of talking led to nothing, so [in October of last year] we opted for war. It was the only choice after exhausting all other avenues prior to October 6. Like when I gave up smoking, Israel will have withdrawal symptoms. But they'll get over it. As you know, all we want is a just peace. It's not much to ask. And when the prerequisites for this peace have been realized, there will be no need for special measures, such as demilitarized zones. These zones mean nothing in the age of rockets and missiles and long-range artillery. We can hit their settlements and their cities, so a narrow demilitarized stretch on Golan won't make a particle of difference to Israel's security.

Interview, Damascus/Newsweek, 6-10:34.

Abdel Rahman al-Atiqi
Minister of Finance and Oil of Kuwait

2

[On higher prices charged for oil exports by producing nations]: Everyone knows that the dollar was devalued and that the United States had balance-of-payments deficits before oil prices were raised ... We reject propaganda that tries to cover the political and economic failures, whether in the U.S. or Europe, [that cause world inflation] ... Europe and the United States have determined the "place" for the developing nations, and the Arabs in particular, and they want us to stay there forever. What causes the whole bad propaganda is not because we [the oil-producing countries] are destroying the economy of the world but because we are trying to move a little bit forward from the place that Highest Grade Human Beings have determined we should stay.

Interview, Kuwait, Oct. 14/
The Washington Post, 10-15:(A)1,14.

Abdullah Azmeh
Deputy Minister of Economy of Syria

3

[On the cost of the Arab-Israeli conflict]: We need peace and capital. Just think: If we had used the money spent for military items since 1948 to develop our economy—think where we would be now.

Damascus/
San Francisco Examiner & Chronicle,
3-24:(Sunday Punch)1.

Lloyd M. Bentsen
United States Senator, D—Texas

4

[On the U.S. decision to send nuclear reactors to Egypt]: It is ludicrous for the U.S. to be sending nuclear reactors for electrical generators to an area of the world that cannot properly clothe, house or feed millions of its people. Rather than "atoms for peace," we should help with agriculture research for improved crops. We should be providing the necessary technology and materials for fertilizer production and for the desalinization of water supplies.

Quote, 8-18:146.

Zulfikar Ali Bhutto
Prime Minister of Pakistan

5

The root cause of the conflict [with Israel in the Middle East] is not an innate animosity between the Moslem and the Jew or even between the Arab and the Jew. To Jews as Jews we can only be friendly. To Jews as Zionists, intoxicated with their militarism and reeking with technological arrogance, we refuse to be hospitable. The pogroms inflicted on them during the centuries and the holocaust to which they were subjected under Nazism fill some of the darkest pages of human history. But redemption should have come from the Western world and not have been exacted, as it was, from the Palestinian people.

Before Islamic heads of state,
Lahore, Pakistan, Feb. 22/
The New York Times, 2-23:12.

Eugene A. Birnbaum
Vice president for international monetary affairs, Chase Manhattan Bank, New York   1

I believe that there can be little hope of getting a constructive solution to the oil [price] problem by browbeating the Arabs. To countries that consume the imported oil, it is understandable that the massive increase of its price looks like "artificial rigging . . . which sovereign nations could not be expected to tolerate," as [U.S.] President Ford put it. But to the oil-producing countries, the price increase represents a long-delayed act of international equity and social justice. From their standpoint, the rules of the game have long been rigged against them. Therefore, the oil price increase is seen as a redress of the balance of both inflation and power.

At Wall Street forum, New York/
The New York Times, 10-27:(3)14.

Houari Boumedienne
President of Algeria   2

[On high oil export prices being charged by Arab countries]: The prices of many materials [from industrialized Western countries] . . . have increased in recent years—before [Arab] oil prices increased. The price of sugar went up; the price of wheat went up. Knowledge and modern technology, which industrialized countries alone have, also doubled. There are substantial examples. At the same time when, for example, the price of iron ore remained fixed, the price of tractors was doubled because companies wished to double their profits due to the monopolist [system]. The cost of a factory went up by more than 50 per cent in the last two years. These prices were imposed [on the Arabs and developing countries] unilaterally without taking the interests of others into consideration. They [the oil consumers] do not talk about all this. They talk about the phenomenon and ignore its deep roots. The industrialized world has not yet learned how to face the problem of inflation, for which it is responsible in the first place; yet *we* have suffered its consequences. They are shouting because of inflation, although it existed before October, 1973 [the beginning of the new Arab oil

policies]. All this because they want to get rid of their responsibilities by placing the responsibility for the real problem on what they call the artificial raising of oil prices. The question is evoked here by the fact that talk on oil is always on the Arab countries as though they were the only ones who produce oil and raise its price. This attitude does not encourage a positive and fruitful dialogue . . . It is unreasonable that some regard the lowering of the temperature of the heating in their homes by two degrees [to save fuel] to be a great disaster when many who live on mountains in the Third World do not know the meaning of the word heating. It is not logical that a fruitful dialogue can be held between those who cannot sleep because they cannot use their cars on weekends and those who use animals for their movement and whose main interest is to survive. In other words, we can say that the industrialized world has been living for many years beyond its real means and refuses to accept this fact. If it accepted this it would understand that what really needs to be changed is the unjust economic system which it created, and this is inescapable. Thus, through frank dialogue we can reach equilibrium in the interest of all and solutions that take into consideration the interests of all sides.

Radio broadcast, Algiers/
Los Angeles Times, 12-27:(2)7.

Leonid I. Brezhnev
General Secretary,
Communist Party of the Soviet Union   3

[The explosive Mideast situation] cannot be different until the main causes of tension are removed, until [Israeli] occupation of Arab lands is ended, until the consequences of the Israeli aggression are liquidated and reliable guarantees for security of all the countries of the area are ensured. All this should be realized by everyone. The danger lies in the fact that, against the background of a certain decrease of tensions, the aggressor and his patrons may try again to avoid a radical, all-encompassing solution of the problem.

At dinner honoring Syrian President
Hafez al-Assad, Moscow, April 11/
Los Angeles Times, 4-12:(1)11.

George S. Brown
General, United States Air Force;
Chairman, Joint Chiefs of Staff

1

[On U.S. support for Israel and the resultant use of oil by the Arabs as a weapon]: . . . you can conjure up a situation where there is another oil embargo and people in this country [the U.S.] are not only inconvenienced and uncomfortable, but suffer and they get tough-minded enough to set down the Jewish influence in this country and break that lobby. It's [the Jewish lobby] so strong you wouldn't believe now. We have the Israelis coming to us for equipment. We say we can't possibly get the Congress to support a program like that. They say, "Don't worry about the Congress. We'll take care of the Congress." Now, this is somebody from another country, but they can do it. They [U.S. Jews] own, you know, the banks in this country, the newspapers; you just look at where the Jewish money is in this country.

At Duke University, Oct. 10/
Los Angeles Times, 11-13:(1)10.

2

[On the controversy over allegedly anti-Jewish statements he made recently at Duke University]: . . . my improper comments could be read to suggest that the American Jewish community and Israel are somehow the same. Americans of Jewish background have an understandable interest in the future of Israel—parallel to similar sentiments among other Americans, all of whom at one time or another trace their descent to other lands. I do in fact appreciate the great support and the deep interest in the nature of our security problems and our defenses that the American Jewish community has steadily demonstrated; and I want to re-emphasize that my unfounded, all-too-casual remarks on that particular occasion are wholly unrepresentative of my continuing respect and appreciation for the role played by Jewish citizens . . .

Nov. 13*/The New York Times, 11-14:26.

Chiao Kuan-hua
Vice Foreign Minister of the People's
Republic of (Communist) China

3

In this Middle East war, the Arab countries used oil [export embargoes and price hikes] as a weapon to deal a heavy blow at Zionism and hegemonism. This was an historic pioneering action. Its impact far exceeds the scope of the Arab people's anti-imperialist struggle. It has offered up a new dimension for the Third World's struggle in defense of national resources against imperialist plunder and exploitation.

Before United Nations General Assembly,
New York, Oct. 2/Chicago Tribune, 10-3:(1)6.

Donald C. Cook
Chairman, American Electric Power Company

4

[On Arab oil-producing countries' price increases for their oil exports]: . . . they go beyond what Americans regard as appropriate business practices. We have strong antitrust laws in the United States and, at least for the most part, they are enforced. On the other hand, the Arabs are not subject to such restraints. They have put together a vicious seller's cartel. If any in our country tried it, they would all go to jail. The Arabs are capitalizing on a tight energy situation, which they greatly accentuated. They are asking prices for their products that most reasonable people would agree are extortionate . . . In America it is not regarded as either good economics or good manners to price-gouge. Americans and Middle Easterners have different points of view on what is a legitimate margin of profit.

Interview, New York/
Nation's Business, September:52.

Moshe Dayan
Minister of Defense of Israel

5

I think we can survive without U.S. support in manpower. We never asked you [the U.S.] to fight for us or send soldiers over there [the Middle East], but I do think we have a problem. We are three million people there surrounded by many Arabs, a lot of money, a lot of influence now, and with the Russians now with them; so I think we must have somebody to help us, too—to sell us arms, to help us technically and politically; we do hope that this is the United States of America. But not to fight for us—just to help us, having the arms, having the money, having the political aid.

TV-radio interview/"Meet the Press,"
National Broadcasting Company, 3-31.

WHAT THEY SAID IN 1974

(MOSHE DAYAN)

1

[On the recent Arab guerrilla raid which killed 18 Israelis, and Israel's retaliation raid into Lebanon]: The relationship between Lebanon and Israel must be based on normal relations between two countries where each government is responsible for what is taking place inside its territory. We have no doubt that the government of Lebanon knows that the three murderers who killed the Israelis in Qiryat Shemona came from the headquarters of the [Achmed] Jabril group in Beirut. The government of Lebanon knows where to find him and his group of murderers, and it is their job to do it ... If we cannot live in peace on our side of the border, then eventually the entire southern part of Lebanon won't be able to live in peace.

News conference, Tel Aviv, April 13/
The New York Times, 4-14:(1)1,3.

Moshe Dayan
Former Minister of Defense of Israel

2

If Egypt is not willing to make a separate settlement [with Israel], then not even the most tempting proposals will do any good unless we include settlement with Syria on the Golan Heights ... If, and as long as, we [Israel] are sitting on the Golan Heights, then the dangling sword of war exists above our heads. It is not only an open wound that cannot heal, the Golan Heights is the key to the problem of war.

Israeli television interview, Dec. 20/
Los Angeles Times, 12-21:(1)20.

Simcha Dinitz
Israeli Ambassador to the United States

3

All depends on the strength of Israel—not only her strength in the number of tanks and men, but on the kind of society we build. We will always be in the minority, but our strength must be in a stable society that can produce a nation which can fight against all odds.

Before B'nai B'rith Women, Dallas, March 28/
The Dallas Times Herald, 3-29:(C)3.

Abba Eban
Foreign Minister of Israel

4

[On U.S. Secretary of State Henry Kissinger's role in Arab-Israeli relations]: I think that Secretary Kissinger's role refutes the view that history is the product of impersonal forces and objective conditions in which the personal human factor doesn't matter. I think it does matter. I believe that the association of American prestige with Secretary Kissinger's skills have been crucial in creating a new climate. After all, the position after the October [1973] war is not the same as b   . Instead of deadlock, there is movement; instead of rhetoric, there is also negotiation. And for this I think the United States and its Secretary of State have a large amount of credit.

The New York Times, 3-25:19.

Abba Eban
Former Foreign Minister of Israel

5

While Israeli opinion has been moving forward on the issue of territorial compromise, Arab governments have been moving backward on the issue of peace. If the Arabs will give us a great measure of peace, they can recover a great measure of lost territory. The way out of deadlock lies through reciprocal concession.

At fund-raising dinner, New York,
Oct. 11/The New York Times, 10-12:6.

6

The United Nations, in its present composition and mood, would refuse to support the Ten Commandments because they came out of Israel.

San Francisco Examiner & Chronicle,
11-10:(This World)2.

Faisal (ibn Abdel Aziz)
King of Saudi Arabia

7

The injustice and aggression which were wrought upon the Arabs of Palestine are unprecedented in history; for not even the darkest ages had a whole population of a country been driven out of their homes to be replaced by aliens [the Israelis]. The Arab nation has appealed to the conscience of the world for more than a quarter of a century to regain their lost rights and to undo the injustice which was committed. But those appeals were in vain and they had no alternative but to resort to arms in the defense of their rights, their land and their sacred shrines.

At banquet in honor of U.S. President Nixon, Jidda, Saudi Arabia, June 14/ The Washington Post, 6-15:(A)1.

1

[Addressing U.S. President Nixon on his efforts to improve U.S. relations with the Arab countries]: What is very important is that our friends in the United States of America be themselves wise enough to stand behind you, to rally around you, Mr. President, in your noble effort—almost unprecedented in the history of mankind—the effort aimed at securing peace and justice in the world. Anybody who stands against you, Mr. President, in the United States of America and outside the United States of America, or stands against us, your friends in this part of the world, obviously has one aim in mind, namely causing splintering of the world, the wrong polarization of the world, the bringing about of mischief that would not be conducive to tranquility and peace.

Jidda, Saudi Arabia, June 15/ The New York Times, 6-16:(1)26.

2

We believe that there will never be a real and lasting peace in the [Middle East] area unless Jerusalem is liberated and returned to Arab sovereignty, unless liberation of all the [Israeli-] occupied Arab territories is achieved, and unless Arab peoples of Palestine regain their rights to return to their homes and be given the right of self-determination.

Jidda, Saudi Arabia/ The Christian Science Monitor, 6-17:2.

Gerald R. Ford
President of the United States

3

To the nations of the Middle East, I pledge continuity in our vigorous efforts to advance the process which has brought hopes of peace

to that region after 25 long years as a hotbed of war. We shall carry out our promise to promote continuing negotiation among all parties for a complete, just and lasting settlement [of the Arab-Israeli dispute].

First address as President before Congress, Washington, Aug. 12/ The New York Times, 8-13:20.

4

The United States has been proud of its association with the state of Israel. We will continue to stand with Israel. We are committed to Israel's survival and security.

Washington, Sept. 10/ The New York Times, 9-11:17.

J. William Fulbright
United States Senator, D—Arkansas

5

Israel, I am convinced, can and should survive as a peaceful, prosperous society—but within the essential borders of 1967, as called for by the [UN] Security Council's Resolution 242 of November, 1967. That resolution calls as well for a settlement "guaranteeing the territorial inviolability and political independence of every state in the area . . ." This provision, as I have suggested in the past, can be implemented by great-power guarantees contracted through the UN Security Council and, in addition, by an explicit, binding American treaty guarantee of Israel. That much we owe them, but no more. We do not owe them our support of their continued occupation of Arab lands, including Old Jerusalem and the Palestinian West Bank. The Palestinian people have as much right to a homeland as do the Jewish people. We Americans—who have always professed adherence to the principle of self-determination—should be the first to appreciate that . . . So completely have the majority of our office-holders fallen under Israeli domination that they not only deny the legitimacy of Palestinian national feeling; but such otherwise fair-minded individuals as the two candidates for Senator from New York [Jacob Javits and Ramsey Clark] engage in heated debate as to which one more passionately opposes a Palestinian state. We have nearly allowed our detente

WHAT THEY SAID IN 1974

with the Soviet Union to go on the rocks in order to obtain an agreement on large-scale Jewish emigration—a matter of limited relevance to the basic issue of human rights in the Soviet Union, and of no relevance at all to the vital interests of the United States.

At Westminster College, Fulton, Mo.,
Nov. 2/The National Observer, 11-16:17.

Ashraf Ghorbal
Egyptian Ambassador to the United States

1

[On recent events that could lead to peace in the Middle East]: There is no place now for delaying tactics. Either the Israeli leaders must come to grips with the full dimensions and implications of the new situation in the Middle East, or they throw the Middle East and the world into a turmoil. The U.S. must make abundantly clear to Israeli hawks that the U.S. is not ready to play again their game.

Before Commonwealth Club,
San Francisco, March 15/
Los Angeles Herald-Examiner, 3-16:(A)4.

Andrei A. Gromyko
Foreign Minister of the Soviet Union

2

There are some who try to present the Soviet Union's [Middle East] position as one-sided and only serving the interests of the Arab states [against Israel]. Yes, we do support, and we will support, the legitimate demands of the Arabs. But it would be wrong to see only this particular aspect in our position. When we insist that territories acquired by force should not become a prize for the aggressor, the purport of our demand goes beyond the limits of the Middle East. It reflects intolerance of aggression in general. What this involves, therefore, is a major international principle, and the question of consistency in policy. Furthermore, the Soviet Union stands in favor of Israel existing and developing as an independent sovereign state. We have said so many times and we reaffirm it once again. Real, not illusory, progress toward a Middle East settlement will create prerequisites for the development of rela-

tions between the Soviet Union and all the states of the Middle East, including Israel.

Before United Nations General Assembly,
New York, Sept. 24/
Vital Speeches, 11-1:36.

Alexander M. Haig, Jr.
Assistant to President of
the United States Richard M. Nixon

3

The successes we have achieved in the past few months [such as the easing in the Arab-Israeli conflict] have not been the result of fancy stepping by [U.S. Secretary of State] Henry Kissinger through the Middle East, although that was an integral and crucial part. Rather, the successes have been the result of decisions made in 1969 and 1970 at a time when the U.S. and Israel were totally isolated from the Arab world, backed by the Soviet Union. Except for the decisions made by [U.S.] President Nixon, we would never have achieved the accomplishments we have to date.

At Lincoln dinner, Lower Merion, Pa.,
Feb. 12/San Francisco Examiner, 2-13:14.

Mohammed Hassanein Heikal
Former editor, "Al Ahram," Cairo

4

[On U.S. President Nixon's recent visit to Egypt]: I think he made a mistake coming here and talking so much about economic factors, promising us $250 million. So what? A week ago, Abu Dhabi, one of the smaller [Persian] Gulf oil producers, gave us $1.2 billion, not as a loan but as a gift. The Saudis a little earlier gave us another $200 million. We got $150 million from Kuwait and $80 million from Algeria. Money is not the problem in the Arab world.

Interview/Christian Science Monitor, 6-25:4.

Hussein I
King of Jordan

5

We are confident peace will come [in the Middle East]; and when it does come, we are confident that the contribution of the United States will be a major one. We are proud of the cooperation that has existed between us over the years, and we always remember the sympathy, understanding, support and warmth we found through many a crisis and difficult time.

Toast at dinner in his honor,
Washington, March 12/
The Washington Post, 3-14:(C)3.

1

... a younger generation has come to power in Israel [since Prime Minister Golda Meir's government stepped down]. At the beginning, they will probably have to speak out from both sides of their mouths to avoid offending others. A clean break with the bankrupt policies of the past is perhaps too much to ask. But we hope they have the capability to see Israel in a different light. There is movement—and it's hopeful. With foresight and courage, it can lead to a just and durable peace . . . It's up to them. Either they can continue on the same path and become another Rhodesia—[in that case,] they would eventually be destroyed; it would only be a matter of time; dangers to world peace and stability would also be very real—or they can return the occupied [Arab] territories and end hostility.

Interview, Aqaba, Jordan/
Newsweek, 6-17:44.

Henry M. Jackson
United States Senator, D—Washington

2

... a more vulnerable Israel would mean a more vulnerable peace and ultimately a more vulnerable American position in the Middle East. The search for stability is inseparable from the search for Israeli security.

At Hadassah convention, Atlanta,
Sept. 8/The New York Times, 9-9:7.

Abdel Haiim Khaddam
Foreign Minister of Syria

3

Israel must understand once and for all that it must recognize the obligation to withdraw from all the Arab territories it occupies—not only Syrian territory, but all Arab territory without exception. Furthermore—and this is very important for the Arabs—Israel must recognize [the] legitimate national rights of the Palestinian people. Both these conditions must

be fulfilled before there can be any agreement on the separation of forces between Syria and Israel.

News conference, Tunis, Tunisia,
March 28/The New York Times, 3-29:3.

Henry A. Kissinger
Secretary of State of the United States

4

No people has suffered more for the past generation than the people of Israel. No people has more cause to wish for peace than the people of Israel. This country has never known what other countries take for granted: a period of acceptance by other countries and a period of peace.

San Francisco Examiner, 2-4:32.

5

In the past year we have witnessed both the fourth Arab-Israeli war in a generation and the hopeful beginnings of a political process toward a lasting and just peace. One side seeks the recovery of territory and justice for a displaced people. The other side seeks security and recognition by its neighbors of its legitimacy as a nation. In the end, the common goal of peace surely is broad enough to embrace all these aspirations.

Before United Nations General Assembly,
New York, Sept. 23/
The New York Times, 9-24:12.

6

Unlike food prices, the high cost of oil is not the result of economic factors, of an actual shortage of capacity or of the free play of supply and demand. Rather, it is caused by deliberate decisions to restrict production and maintain an artificial price level. We recognize that the [producing countries] should have a fair share; [but] the fact remains that present prices even threaten the economic well-being of producers. Ultimately they depend upon the vitality of the world economy for the security of their markets and their investments. And it cannot be in the interest of any nation to magnify the despair of the least developed who are uniquely vulnerable to exorbitant prices and who have no recourse but to pay. What has

WHAT THEY SAID IN 1974

(HENRY A. KISSINGER)

gone up by political decision can be reduced by political decision.

Before United Nations General Assembly, New York, Sept. 23/ The New York Times, 9-24:12.

1

I think the survival of Israel is essential. The United States—and finally in the last analysis Europe—will not negotiate over the survival of Israel. This would be an act of such extraordinary cynicism that the world would be morally mortgaged if it ever happened. But it won't happen.

Interview/Newsweek, 12-30:31.

Clare Boothe Luce
Former American diplomat and playwright

2

[On the Arab oil embargo]: The Arabs will eventually, I am sure, face up to the fact that nations who cannot survive without their oil will go to war for it.

News conference, Los Angeles, Jan. 30/Los Angeles Times, 1-31:(2)1.

James A. McClure
United States Senator, R—Idaho

3

[On U.S. backing of Israel in the Arab-Israeli confrontation]: Eventually, material assistance would not be enough and the United States would be called upon to contribute manpower as well. We should have learned by now from our involvement in Vietnam that this won't work ... We must say to our friends in the American Jewish community that we admire and respect what has been accomplished in Israel. They have accepted the risks of war. Now it is not unreasonable for us to ask them to accept the risks of peace.

At U.S.-Arab Chamber of Commerce meeting, New York, March 22/ Los Angeles Times, 3-23:(1)4.

Golda Meir
Prime Minister of Israel

4

We are striving for a peace settlement between ourselves and Jordan which would be based on the existence of two independent states—Israel, with united Jerusalem as its capital, and an Arab state to the east of Israel. In the neighboring Arab state, the identity of the Palestinian and Jordanian Arabs could find expression in peace and good neighborly relations within Israel. Israel rejects establishment of an additional separate Arab state west of the Jordan [River].

Before the Knesset (Parliament), Jerusalem, March 10/The Dallas Times Herald, 3-11:(A)3.

5

[On Egypt's announcement that it would divert war funds toward internal development]: When the head of an Arab state starts worrying about his own people, then there is hope. When an Arab leader starts comparing the cost of killing one Israeli to the cost of saving one infant born into poverty in his own country, then we are beginning to talk the same language.

At convention of American and Canadian rabbis, March 15/ The Washington Post, 3-16:(A)14.

6

[On the Arab terrorist attack at an Israeli school in which many schoolchildren were killed]: I can't promise that they [the terrorists] will let us live in peace. But I want to and can promise that the government—any government of Israel—will do everything in its power in order to cut off the hands that want to harm a child, a grown-up, a settlement, a town or a village. And for all of us there is only one thing left: to guard in the most careful manner our strength and our spirit ... I want to hope that the international community will finally recognize who they are who stand at the head of so-called liberation movements, to what they send their men and to what they educate their people.

Television address to the nation, Jerusalem, May 15/The New York Times, 5-16:18.

7

[On U.S. Secretary of State Henry Kissinger's successful negotiation of a Golan Heights troop disengagement between Israel and Syria]: He's fantastic, fantastic. Better than any others, he learned the land—every hill, every road, every street in Quneitra. Nobody in the Cabinet knows so much . . . There is no doubt that this is a great event, an event that spells great efforts, soul-searching and searching for possibilities that maybe some time ago appeared impossible. It brought home to mothers and wives and children, Syrian and Israeli, that they could sleep without the nightmare of killing and war . . . On behalf of the people of Israel and the boys still on the front, I want to express our great appreciation, admiration and wonder at how you [Kissinger] did it.

At party honoring Kissinger, Jerusalem,
May 29/Los Angeles Times, 5-30:(1)6.

Golda Meir
Former Prime Minister of Israel
1

[On calls for Israel to give up occupied Arab land and go back to the borders of pre-war 1967]: It has become boring and almost idiotic, but I ask this question over and over again. In '67, on the 5th of June, Sinai was in Egyptian hands, the West Bank was Jordanian and the Golan Heights was Syrian. In that case, why was there a war? There seems to be only one logical explanation: that the Arabs saw this as the proper period to destroy us. So now we're asked to restore exactly the same situation, which the Arabs in '67 thought was a good starting point to destroy us. If a person's house is broken into once, twice, three times, he can either move out and go somewhere else or else he puts iron bars on the windows and puts up fencing. Maybe it doesn't look nice, but you can't expect him to take it off because of that. Even half-intelligent people learn from experience.

Interview, Ramat Aviv, Israel/
The New York Times, 12-2:14.

Hisham Nazer
Minister of Planning of Saudi Arabia
2

Oil is a depletable resource, and it is the only resource we have at this time. We must plan very carefully and wisely, because when the oil runs out—and with it the dollars—I don't think many people will say "hello."

Newsweek, 1-28:58.

Richard M. Nixon
President of the United States
3

[Announcing a just-reached agreement for disengagement of Israeli and Egyptian forces along the Suez Canal]: This, I would say, is the first significant step toward a permanent peace in the Mideast. I do not understate, by making the statement that I have just made, the difficulties that lie ahead in settling the differences that must be settled before a permanent peace is reached, not only here but between the other countries involved. But this is a very significant step reached directly as a result of negotiations between the two parties and therefore has, it seems to me, a great deal of meaning to all of us here in this country and around the world who recognize the importance of having peace in this [Mideast] part of the world . . . Our [the U.S.'s] role has been one of being of assistance to both parties, to bring them together, to help them narrow differences, working toward a thorough and just settlement for all parties concerned, where every nation in that area will be able to live in peace and also to be secure insofar as its defense is concerned.

TV-radio address to the nation,
Washington, Jan. 17/
The New York Times, 1-18:2.

4

. . . the Mideast has had four wars in a generation. That's just four too many in an area that's very poor and one that needs peace and needs it desperately. And at the present time, the influence of the United States in the Mideast—the fact that we have restored relations with Egypt, that we're moving in all of the areas of the Mideast toward creating a permanent peace—is going to be one of the major legacies of this Administration, I would hope.

Before Executive Club, Chicago,
March 15/The New York Times, 3-16:13.

5

I realize that many of those who support Israel and its independence—as I have since that state came into existence—wonder about the policy of the United States which is now one

WHAT THEY SAID IN 1974

(RICHARD M. NIXON)

designed not only to be a friend of Israel but to be a friend of Israel's [Arab] neighbors. And I would only suggest that, in terms of the future of Israel, it is much better to have the United States a friend of Israel's neighbors, and thereby able to influence and perhaps restrain their policies, rather than an enemy or with no communication. And so therefore our policy is designed to accomplish these things: One, we will continue to support the independence and the integrity of the state of Israel. Two, we will continue to try to seek not only renewed relations with Egypt but with other countries with which those relations have been broken . . . growing out of the June, 1967, war. But let me make one thing very clear: Being a friend of one of Israel's neighbors does not make us an enemy of Israel.

Before National Association of Broadcasters,
Houston, March 19/
The New York Times, 3-20:28.

1

The October [Arab-Israeli] war of last year, while tragic, also presented a unique opportunity. Because for the first time it was clear to us and clear to the moderate leaders of the Arab world that a positive American role was indispensable to achieving a permanent settlement in the Middle East. And it was for this reason that I sent Secretary of State [Henry] Kissinger to the Middle East to offer our good offices in the process of negotiation. The results, which reflect more than anything else the vision and statesmanship of the leaders of both sides, have been encouraging: An agreement to separate military forces has been implemented on the Egyptian-Israeli front, and now a similar accord is being negotiated between Israel and Syria. For the first time in a generation, we are witnessing the beginning of a dialogue between the Arab states and Israel. Now, the road to a just and lasting and permanent peace in the Mideast is still long and difficult and lies before us. But what seemed to be an insurmountable roadblock on that road has now been removed, and we are determined to

stay on course until we have reached our goal of a permanent peace in that area.

At United States Naval Academy
commencement, Annapolis, June 5/
The New York Times, 6-6:16.

2

[On the peace negotiations and cease-fire recently agreed upon in the Arab-Israeli conflict]: The historians later will perhaps see all of these great events in perspective, but one fact stands out today: that without the wisdom, without the visions, without the courage, without the statesmanship of President [Anwar] Sadat of Egypt, we would not have made the progress toward peace that we have made, and the world owes him a great debt for what he has done.

Cairo, June 12/
The New York Times, 6-13:10.

Mohammad Reza Pahlavi
Shah of Iran

3

In 10 years' time, we [the Persian Gulf oil-producing nations] are going to have a tremendous purchasing power. We will have the same per-capita income as in Germany today . . . We are going to be a member of your [industrialized nations] club. It is a question of readjusting the relation between the industrial world and the oil-producing countries. We have said that the era of cheap oil is finished. We must add that the era of exploitations is finished.

Interview/The Washington Post, 1-31:(A)19.

4

I can forgive people who make attempts on my life, but I cannot forgive people attempting to put an end to the sovereignty of my country . . . What is happening in my country is that Communism is prohibited because they are people who have sworn no allegiance to our flag and allegiance to some other country. In addition to being outlawed because they are Communists, they are terrorists. They throw bombs.

News conference, Canberra, Australia,
Sept. 26/The New York Times, 9-30:6.

5

. . . if we [oil-producing nations] cannot link the price of oil [exports] with the price of [world] inflation, there will not be any pressure or incentive for the industrial world to check their inflation. If they do not check their inflation, we can defend ourselves with the pricing of our oil. But who is going to suffer? The poor countries, or the developing countries. They will suffer on both fronts. So to keep our whole world together in one piece we will have to have a very comprehensive talk between the developed industrial countries of the world and we, producers of energy, in the immediate future.

News conference, Teheran, Nov. 2/
Los Angeles Times, 11-11:(1)17.

1

We are not going to go nuclear. But discipline we will have, and knowledge we will have. We are working like mad training our people and enhancing their military knowledge. We are buying the best. If we make our forces mobile, then I think that, with what we are planning now, in five years' time we will be among the top non-atomic armies of the world. Every day I find additional reasons to continue this policy because of the impotence of the United Nations. First of all, there is that UN veto. We also know that as long as detente persists between the U.S. and the Soviet Union, wherever they agree—as on the Middle East cease-fire—they only agree that their two countries will not go to war.

Interview, Teheran/Time, 11-4:34.

Shimon Peres
Minister of Transport of Israel

2

[On criticism by other countries that Israel is too militarist]: Survival is more important than image. It is better to remain alive with a critical image than disappear with a wonderful halo. The European nations, where people criticize us, were rescued by American troops and are protected by the American military umbrella now. We prefer that our labor force work harder and protect ourselves. It's nice to be under the American military umbrella—and preach to others not to be militarists.

The New York Times, 2-2:3.

Shimon Peres
Minister of Information of Israel

3

[On the Arab-Israeli conflict]: We keep our ears open for the song of the bird [of peace] — and keep our powder dry. There's no other alternative. It is not a plain, one-dimensional situation but very complex. We don't lose sight of the guns or the olive branch. The olives are still young.

Interview, Tel Aviv, March 29/
The New York Times, 3-30:10.

Shimon Peres
Minister of Defense of Israel

4

The Palestinians are represented in three ways: by the Jordanians, by the Palestinians on the West Bank and Gaza, and by the Palestine Liberation Organization. We refuse to talk to the PLO because they are not necessarily representative of the Palestinian people. They are a small group of armed terrorists who impose themselves on the rest of the population. There is an African saying that, if you put a stone in a basket of eggs, you had better worry. We consider the PLO a stone in a basket of eggs. They are basically against a compromise by the Palestinians. They see a Palestinian state as the first step in a long road to overthrow Israel.

Interview, Washington/Time, 7-8:20.

5

The ones planning the war [against Israel] are, in my opinion, the Syrians. The terrorist organizations are dreaming of war. Less enthusiastic about it all are the Egyptians ... As for Syria, as long as she remains unable to pronounce the word "peace" without severe stomach cramps, we must remain on the alert on that front. Here, we must stand fast and fortified, prepared and determined, and not mince words.

Interview, Sept. 7/
The Atlanta Journal and Constitution,
9-8:(A)24.

Muammar el-Qaddafi
Chief of State of Libya

6

There has been enough chatter about Arab unity by men who run away when the time comes to translate it into reality. Those who try

WHAT THEY SAID IN 1974

(MUAMMAR EL-QADDAFI)

to escape from Arab unity are running away from the truth and from the progress which, in the end, will catch up with them in their own countries.

Feb. 10/Los Angeles Times, 2-11:(1)11.

1

Those who speak of a rift between our two countries [Libya and Egypt] are wrong and are plowing in the sea. What happened in the [recent Arab-Israeli] war has strengthened my belief that Egypt is the fortress of the Arab struggle. This is not just praise but an historical truth.

Before Parliament, Cairo, Feb. 19/
The Washington Post, 2-20:(A)13.

Yitzhak Rabin
Prime Minister of Israel

2

Egypt is the principal country in the Arab world. Without her not a single war has been launched against Israel; without her not a single war against Israel has ever ended. I also believe that no significant conflict of interests exists between the Egyptian people and ourselves. A vast desert separates us . . . There is no conflict between the solution of Egypt's problems and the continued existence of Israel . . . after a certain period of time we shall have to look for a way together with Egypt to take a further step toward peace. And by this I mean not only an understanding but also a search for ways of giving this understanding practical expression.

Television interview, June 7/
The Christian Science Monitor, 6-11:8.

3

It's Lebanon's responsibility as a sovereign state to prevent the use of its territory as a base for terrorist activities against Israeli civilians. Recent atrocities showed the terrorists murder indiscriminately whomever they find, mainly women and children. We are determined to do everything possible to stop this. We are now trying our best to seal the Lebanon-Israeli border—electrified fences, mine fields, electronic devices and so forth. But it seems that defense measures alone will not be enough. Therefore, as long as Lebanon doesn't assume

its responsibility to prevent infiltration across our border—as some other Arab states have done—we will feel free to hit the terrorist headquarters, concentrations and stores, wherever and whenever we so decide.

Interview/Newsweek, 7-8:37.

4

The creation [of a Palestinian state between Israel and Jordan] will not solve what is considered to be the Palestinian problem. It will serve as a country that will bring about more tension and will serve as a time-bomb against both countries—Israel and Jordan.

The Christian Science Monitor, 7-19:2.

5

We face today a continuous influx of Soviet arms to the Arab countries. They are of high quality and are delivered in great quantities. You can find now the most sophisticated Russian jet fighters such as the MIG-23, tanks, ground-to-air missiles and ground-to-ground missiles in the Arab arsenals, which are bulging with arms of aggression. Israel has to maintain a balance of arms in order to prevent another aggression like the Yom Kippur war [of 1973] . . . In order to maintain a balance of arms, Israel must turn to the United States. We have all reason to believe that the U.S. government understands the situation. The Administration of President Nixon has until now proved this understanding by helping Israel get the weapons it needs to survive, and we hope that this American policy will be continued.

Interview, Tel Aviv/
San Francisco Examiner, 7-20:4.

6

When it comes to Jerusalem, I believe one has to distinguish between the political issue and the religious issue. I know that many people don't know that for the last 150 years the majority of the population in Jerusalem was Jewish. I believe this majority has been increased today. It is a living city that should be part of Israel, the capital of Israel. But at the same time we realize that Jerusalem is holy not only to the Jews, but also to the Christians and the Moslems; and I believe that arrangements can be made to make sure of free access to the holy places of the other two religions and certain controls of the places of each religion by those who would be delegated to do so ... [But] no doubt the sovereignty [over the city] should be in Israel.

TV-radio interview, New York/
"Meet the Press,"
National Broadcasting Company, 9-15.

1

We don't believe in [security] guarantees. I believe that no one in this world believes any more in international guarantees. You see what happened [during the recent Turkish invasion] in Cyprus. There were United Nations forces there; they did not prevent anything. Our experience in the last 26 years proved to be that we can rely only on ourselves when it comes to our defense. Therefore, we don't ask guarantees because we don't believe in guarantees. We want, therefore, to have secured—to be more specific, defensible—boundaries. They cannot be the pre-'67 war. Therefore, we are ready to compromise, but by no means to return to the lines that existed before the [1967] Six Day War.

TV-radio interview, New York/
"Meet the Press,"
National Broadcasting Company, 9-15.

2

The menace to Israel stems from Arab belligerency supported by Russian backing—political, military and, to a lesser degree, economic. If this menace didn't exist, Israel would be in the same position as other free-world countries, each of which would, of course, be affected if the gigantic U.S. economy were to dip. But our case is special because of the menace I described. Thus, if the present Middle East situation continues and the U.S. also suffers a real depression—which I will hope will not be the case—that would produce a major threat to Israel. Frankly, nevertheless, I am more optimistic about United States prospects and capabilities than many Americans.

Interview/The New York Times, 10-16:43.

3

I would phrase my question to [Egyptian President Anwar Sadat] this way: "If you really want peace, why do you just say so for propaganda purposes on American television? Why do you not rather take a real concrete step? Let us sit together, in the presence of others, with the purpose of the meeting and the dialogue being a peace between Egypt and Israel. If you, President Sadat, are ready for that, I am ready—at any place and at any time."

At businessmen's luncheon, Tel Aviv,
Dec. 20/The New York Times, 12-21:45.

Anwar el-Sadat
President of Egypt

4

We shall not sleep for a moment in obtaining the objectives we have pledged before God and our people. Our pledge is to continue bearing arms until all Arab territory is liberated from [Israeli] aggression and occupation. Our pledge is not to bargain over the rights of the people of Palestine.

Before Parliament, Cairo, Feb. 19/
The Washington Post, 2-20:(A)13.

5

The United States has always been aligned with Israel and has provided Israel with from the loaf of bread to the *Phantom* [fighter plane]. When the United States changes its policy toward justice—not to be on our side, but toward justice—and I think they are changing, I think then everything will be easier.

News conference, Lahore, Pakistan,
Feb. 24/The New York Times, 2-25:7.

6

If you compare what happened in [the Arab-Israeli wars of] June, 1967, and in October, 1973, you cannot escape the conclusion that there has been a fundamental change in U.S. policy ... In 1967, the U.S. prevented the UN Security Council, for the first time in its history, from ordering withdrawal along with the cease-fire. The U.S. twisted arms, threatened and did its level best to inflame further what already was the most dangerous situation in the world. Not so in 1973. Though the U.S. heavily supplied Israel with the most sophisticated weapons and military equipment, it very quickly understood the implications of the October 6 war. This was the turning point which led the U.S. to take a new look at the

(ANWAR EL-SADAT)

Middle East and to embark, as a result of that, on a policy of working toward peace based on justice for the region. My talks with [U.S. Secretary of State Henry] Kissinger convinced me that he rejects the simplistic notion of some of your [U.S.] strategists who see—or saw—Israel as the American gendarme in this part of the world.

Interview, Borg el Arab, Egypt/
Newsweek, 3-25:44.

1

. . . let me state as categorically as possible that I vehemently reject the way of thinking that says that, in fulfilling complete [Israeli] withdrawal [from Arab lands occupied in 1967], there will be a risk for Israel. I can assure you there won't be. To say that there is a risk is a reflection of the June, 1967, mentality. If the Israelis continue to think that withdrawal entails a risk, then we shall be back in the vicious circle . . . What I think is this: There must be new thinking in Israel as a result of [the 1973 war of] October 6, as there is new thinking in the Arab world. The end of the state of belligerency is the achievement we should all think of—and work toward. Let us concentrate on our pending problems—the ways and means and the international guarantees necessary to insure a permanent and honorable peace.

Interview, Borg el Arab, Egypt/
Newsweek, 3-25:45.

2

[Criticizing Arab leaders who have criticized him for his cooperation with the U.S.]: [The United States has changed its attitude in the Middle East] from recklessness to an understanding of the gravity of the situation and . . . to serious participation in the search for a settlement. There are political adolescents who do not see the changes that have taken place on the Arab and international levels. When [U.S. Secretary of State Henry] Kissinger goes to Moscow and Peking, that [say these adolescents] is fine, but when he comes to Cairo, Damascus or Algiers, then that is treason. Kissinger's mediation in Vietnam? That is a

victory for Vietnam and is not directed against the Soviet Union; but Kissinger's mediation in the Middle East and his talks with us is an act directed against the Soviet Union. The opening of a branch of the [U.S.] Chase Manhattan Bank in Moscow is a good thing, but the opening of an office for it in Cairo is a danger for us. The use of American, German and Japanese capital for building factories in Russia and extracting natural gas in Siberia is acceptable; but its use to reconstruct the cities of the Suez Canal and for rehabilitation in the Western Desert is not acceptable. This is political adolescence symptomatic of sickness and lack of self-confidence. Those who are trying to restrict our efforts by making irresponsible noises will not succeed.

May Day address, Helwan, Egypt,
May 1/The Washington Post, 5-2:(A)30.

3

I am ready for a peace agreement with Israel. The matter is complicated, however. For one thing, we must satisfy the legitimate rights of the Palestinians, which is the core of the problem. On this point, I agree completely with the United Nations resolutions calling for self-determination and also for some repatriation. Then there is the future of Jerusalem. As a matter of principle, no Muslims will agree to let the Arab sector of Jerusalem remain under the sovereignty of Israel. As far as I am concerned, internationalization of the city would be acceptable—if it includes the entire city, not just the Arab part.

Interview/The Reader's Digest, June:118.

4

The role of the United States under the leadership of President Nixon is vital to promote peace and tranquility in the [Middle East] area. It is a great challenge, but I am convinced that, with good-will and determination, statesmen of the stature of President Nixon are apt to meet it.

Cairo, June 12/
The New York Times, 6-13:1.

5

[Americans should remember that] you have friends in this area. As a superpower responsible for peace, and specifically in this area, I want you to look objectively at the whole problem. I am not asking you to be on my side against Israel at all, but I am asking you to be objective. Just as you have friends in Israel, you have friends in the Arab world also—and your main interests in the area are with the Arabs.

Interview, Cairo/
The Christian Science Monitor, 10-25:6.

Omar Saqqaf
Foreign Minister of Saudi Arabia

1

[Saying his government will work with other oil-producing countries to bring down the price of oil exports]: Saudi Arabia is following a policy on oil which bespeaks a sense of responsibility toward the welfare of the world community. As part of the world, we want to build the world and not destroy it. And we hope that other members of the world community come to appreciate the gravity of this responsibility and the importance thereof. Oil is not everything but it is a great thing . . . We sincerely hope and it is our prayer that all of the oil-producing countries will come around to following the policy of Saudi Arabia.

Oct. 13/Los Angeles Times, 10-14:(1)1.

John A. Scali
United States Ambassador/Permanent
Representative to the United Nations

2

Last year's outbreak of war in the Middle East demonstrated for the fourth time in a quarter-century that military force cannot resolve the issues which divide Arab and Israeli. It must be clear by now that more violence cannot bring peace. It will only intensify hatreds, complicate differences and add to the sum of human misery. The sole alternative to the sterile pursuit of change through violence is negotiation. This path is less dramatic, but in the end it is far more likely to produce acceptable change . . . War has ravaged the Middle East four times in 26 years because people did not believe that constructive dialogue between the parties was possible. A fifth war would

threaten the security of every country and produce no permanent gains for any.

Before United Nations General Assembly,
New York, Nov. 21/
The New York Times, 11-22:15.

James R. Schlesinger
Secretary of Defense of the United States

3

[On whether the U.S. might forcibly take control of Arab nations which embargo oil exports]: I think that that is a risk. It is plain, I think, that one should not tempt fate by pushing the concept of national sovereignty [in this case, Arab sovereignty over their oil] too far. But the United States is dedicated, and has remained dedicated, to the independence of free states. And that includes the states in the Middle East. We should recognize that the independent powers of sovereign states should not be used in such a way as to cripple the larger mass of the Arab world. That is running too high a risk, and it is a source of danger, I think, not only from our standpoint, but from the standpoint of the oil-producing nations.

Interview/
The Christian Science Monitor, 1-11:2.

4

I believe that polarization in the Middle East would diminish if the United States and Egypt should resume more-normal relationships. To the extent that it is perceived that Israel and her Arab neighbors are being supported by competing suppliers, I think this inflames tensions in that region. To the extent that both of them might draw upon the U.S. as a source of supply, I think that might help to alleviate tension. It is not likely to affect the arms balance. Countries in that area can get their weapons from a variety of sources. If we were to assume an increased role in supporting both sides—as we are doing in supporting Egyptian efforts to clear the Suez Canal—this would provide the United States with influence which hopefully could be used to achieve something close to a permanent settlement in the Middle East.

Interview, Washington/
U.S. News & World Report, 5-13:43.

WHAT THEY SAID IN 1974

Ariel Sharon
General, Israeli Army; Member of
the Knesset (Israeli Parliament)

1

[Criticizing the Israeli-Egyptian agreement whereby Israeli forces would pull back from the Suez Canal]: The Egyptians have won something they never dreamed they could get in their lives ... We have lost our strongest trump cards against another Egyptian attack. All the declarations we have made all these years about no withdrawal till a declared end to hostilities, or a general peace settlement, or a demilitarization of the Sinai, have collapsed ... If war breaks out again, we will not be able to return the situation to what it is now, not unless we intend to attack the Russians, and I don't propose to do that.

News conference, Tel Aviv, Jan. 20/
Los Angeles Times, 1-21:(1)7.

2

In 25 years, Israel has managed to become an international force from just a small, isolated place somewhere in the Middle East. The Zionist dream has become such a reality that we don't even bother to discuss it any more. In our history there were always Jews living here. Sometimes there were hundreds of thousands, sometimes just tens of thousands, but always there were Jews—a non-stop Jewish population. I regard Israel as the spearhead of the Jewish nation. The main body is abroad, but the spearhead is here.

Interview, Tel Aviv/
The National Observer, 2-2:1.

3

Who says that everything we [Israel] do is good? Six years ago, after the 1967 war, I went to the Prime Minister [the late Levi Eshkol] and told him the right thing to do is solve the Palestinian-refugee problem. We could have done many, many things differently; I personally believe we have not treated the Arabs who live here in the way they should be treated. After 25 years there is no reason why we shouldn't have Israeli Arabs working in our missions abroad, and having posts in the government here. Many things we did were wrong.

Interview, Tel Aviv/
The National Observer, 2-2:14.

Howard K. Smith
News commentator,
American Broadcasting Company

4

The Arabs ... have assigned the militant Palestine Liberation Organization control of lands neighboring Israel. That increases the danger of conflict. With that in mind, King Hassan of Morocco warned the West not to interfere, for Arab control of oil would bring us to our knees. We need to free ourselves from that pressure, that limitation on [U.S. Secretary of State Henry] Kissinger's power to negotiate peace, and to tell the Arabs so. Very tough [oil] conservation measures [in the West] would say it most clearly. Also, computations of Western wealth that will have to be shifted to the oil countries to pay their new high prices are now clear. By 1985 our side shall have surrendered to them a total of $1,200 billion— an unheard of draining of the West and swelling of their [oil-exporting countries'] coffers. It can bring chaos to world currency and bankruptcy to industrial nations.

ABC News commentary/
The Christian Science Monitor, 11-8:12.

Yosef Tekoah
Israeli Ambassador/Permanent
Representative to the United Nations

5

[Criticizing the UN's decision to invite PLO leader Yasir Arafat to participate in its debate on Palestine]: On October 14 the General Assembly opted for the PLO, it opted for terrorism, it opted for savagery ... The United Nations, whose duty it is to combat terrorism and barbarity, may agree to consort with them. Israel will not. The murderers of athletes in the Olympic Games of Munich, the butchers of children in Maalot, the assassins of diplomats in Khartoum do not belong in the international community. They have no place in international diplomatic efforts. Israel shall see to it that they have no place in them. Israel will pursue the PLO murderers until justice is meted out to them. It will continue to take action against their organization and against their bases until a definitive end is put to their atrocities. The blood of Jewish children will not be shed with impunity . . . No resolution of the General Assembly can mask the murderous nature of the PLO. No resolution can wash the hands of Yasir Arafat and his henchmen clean of the blood of their innocent victims. No resolution can confer respect on a band of cutthroats. No resolution can establish the authority of an organization which has no authority, which does not represent anyone except the few thousand agents of death it employs, which has no foothold in any part of the territories it seeks to dominate. The PLO will remain what it is and where it is—outside the law and outside of Palestine.

Before United Nations General Assembly,
New York, Nov. 13/
The New York Times, 11-14:24.

Khalifa bin Hamad al-Thani
Emir of Qatar

1

We are striving . . . at the present time for a united Arab policy. We are trying to concentrate our powers and our strength on a single goal: to win back Arab [Israeli-] occupied territories and realize the rights of the Palestinians . . . I would like to emphasize, however, that we are striving for a peaceful solution . . . Instead of asking us whether we have become presumptuous because of this [oil] power, you should ask why the world has shut its eyes to the fact that, for a quarter of a century, we have been trying to draw the world's attention to the injustices shown toward the Palestinians . . . However, we want no revenge. On the contrary, we have again shown our goodwill by canceling our [oil-export] reduction of five per cent to the European Community, with the exception of Holland. Does this not prove that we are not extortioners, that we do not want to see the world on its knees before us? . . . I would like to make this very clear to the world: The actions of the oil-producing countries are exclusively motivated by our national interest, as Arabs, in the rights and

freedom of the Palestinians . . . Those who occupy Palestine are foreign elements, not Arabs but European Jews. Is it not natural that we should react to this danger? Israel is only a transitory phenomenon in the long history of the Arab world . . . An Arab nation existed until we were divided up into autonomous countries. The root of this Arab unity has not withered. It exists—in our history, our language and our culture, and now in our struggle for the rights of Palestinians.

Interview/The New York Times, 1-27:(3)38.

Ahmed Zaki al-Yamani
Minister of Petroleum of Saudi Arabia

2

[On his country's relations with Japan]: We have a very unique possibility to establish extremely strong ties . . . the same way you need us, we need you. In the future, what we want for our oil is not the amount of money that we get; it is the technology and industrialization of Saudi Arabia more than anything else. If there is any nation in the whole world who can satisfy our demand . . . it is Japan . . . Therefore, Japan is nation Number 1, who is in a position to have a continuous supply of crude oil from Saudi Arabia on a long-term basis much more than any other nation on earth.

News conference, Tokyo, Jan. 27/
Los Angeles Times, 1-28:(1)10.

3

[Warning against greed in setting oil-export prices]: The oil exporting countries shall not entertain any suggestions that aim to impose upon them a trusteeship for determining the prices of their oil . . . Individual self-interest must not be permitted to persuade us to ignore the issues, for the danger which threatens us is no less than a world-wide recession . . . The international community cannot go through a world-wide depression without risking devastating war.

At United Nations, New York, April 16/
Los Angeles Times, 4-17:(1)6.

War and Peace

Leonid I. Brezhnev
*General Secretary, Communist Party
of the Soviet Union*
1

We now have the first generation of Soviet people who did not live during the war period. We want our children to be able to say, "War, what's that?"

Quote, 10-27:386.

Chou En-lai
*Premier of the People's Republic
of (Communist) China*
2

The revolutionary people do not at all believe in so-called lasting peace or a generation of peace. So long as imperialism exists, revolution and war are inevitable.

*At banquet for Cambodian Communist
leader Khieu Samphan, Peking, April 1/
The Christian Science Monitor, 4-3:1.*

William E. Colby
*Director, Central Intelligence
Agency of the United States*
3

America has gotten into several wars in this century, started by people who thought we either would not or could not stand up to them. Kaiser Wilhelm thought we would not join World War I. Adolf Hitler was quite certain that we would stay out of World War II. Josef Stalin thought we would not fight in Korea. And Ho Chi Minh certainly felt we could not stop his effort to take over South Vietnam. Where people realized we not only could but would fight—for example, in the Berlin crisis, the Cuban missile crisis—we have had no war.

Interview/Parade, 7-21:5.

Archibald Cox
Professor of Law, Harvard University
4

In the U.S. and most of Europe, three of the four forces of the apocalypse have retreated: ignorance, disease and poverty—all except war; and war is now, as always, within human control and only the result of human perversity.

*Before graduating class of Stanford University/
San Francisco Examiner, 7-19:35.*

J. William Fulbright
United States Senator, D—Arkansas
5

When the two great nuclear powers [the U.S. and Soviet Union] signed the ABM treaty, they in effect said we have no defense against nuclear power. This is the first step toward the acceptance of coexistence. If that rules out the use of nuclear power, then the struggle to prove which concept of society is a valid one will be confined to negotiations, diplomatic and economic means. The nature of international relations has been transformed by the power of complete destruction. But the cold-warriors refuse to recognize that. They still look upon warfare, the threat of warfare, the great huge stockpiles, as definite tools and weapons in international relations. I don't think they are.

The New York Times Magazine, 11-24:93.

Arthur J. Goldberg
*Former United States Ambassador/
Permanent Representative to the
United Nations*
6

[Supporting a "right to peace through law" resolution by the U.S. House and Senate]: The resolution may seem to some to be Utopian, and indeed all agree that this will not be achieved today—or even tomorrow. But achievement of world peace through law may, in the long run, be the highest realism. We hear it said that what nations really respect is not law but political power. My own reading of the facts leads me to a very different conclusion. Power not ruled by law is a menace; but law unserved by power is a delusion. Law is thus the higher of the two principles; but it cannot operate by itself. Our hopes for world peace depend on our ability to extend to the international sphere a dual concept of law, both creative and coercive.

Before House Foreign Affairs Committee,
Washington, March 13/
The Washington Post, 3-14:(A)2.

Barry M. Goldwater
United States Senator, R—Arizona
1

...if we [the U.S.] continue to remain Number 2 [militarily] and eventually Number 3—when Red China passes us, and that's not too far off—then we will no longer be the leader of the world. Now, the world has to have a leader. So there will be a war to decide who's going to be that leader, and the war will be between Red China and Russia. We'll be right back in it on the side of Russia, and it will be called World War III. That's my worry—that we're getting sucked slowly once again into a world situation that's going to result in war. Twice in my lifetime we've gotten sucked into major world wars, because we would not remain strong or even want to be strong or even want to use strength that we had.

Interview, Washington/
U.S. News & World Report, 2-11:42.

Mark O. Hatfield
United States Senator, R—Oregon
2

We are beset with the psychology of war, we are overladen with the means of war, we are addicted with the ways of war, and we are enslaved by a belief in war.

Quote, 6-9:529.

Fred C. Ikle
Director, Arms Control and Disarmament
Agency of the United States
3

Even scientists have become unable to express the full range of physical effects of nuclear warfare... The damage of nuclear explosions to the fabric of nature and the sphere of living things cascades from one effect to another in ways too complex for our scientists to predict... We have imposed on our-

selves an inner secrecy [about the dangers of nuclear war]. We have lost comprehension—in emotive and human terms—of the reality of nuclear weapons.

Before Council on Foreign Relations, Chicago/
San Francisco Examiner & Chronicle,
9-15:(This World)9.

Lewis Mumford
Author
4

Civilization is going downhill. Very definitely. The two world wars brought on violence never before practiced. Whole populations have been exterminated. We civilized nations used the most barbarous means to wage wars and then undermined the recovery of defeated people by destroying their food supplies. We do what the Assyrians did when they went to war. They conquered, destroyed, slaughtered by hand, then salted the land so no more food could be grown. That is exactly what we have done in the Vietnam war. There was wholesale slaughter in Europe and Japan on an order never reached before... And we have closed our eyes to it; that is what is so dangerous. The point is that our technology, which we always hoped would be the means to make men more happy and prosperous and give them full possession of the earth, is in danger of doing just the opposite.

Interview, Cambridge, Mass./
Los Angeles Times, 4-8:(2)7.

Richard M. Nixon
President of the United States
5

In today's world, without America and its strength and its will and its respect and its determination, peace and freedom will not survive. What a great challenge for a great people.

At Lincoln Day ceremonies,
Washington, Feb. 12/
Los Angeles Herald-Examiner, 2-13:(A)8.

6

Lasting peace can be achieved only through lasting awareness, lasting preparedness and lasting strength, both physical and moral. As America and other nations have learned only

WHAT THEY SAID IN 1974

(RICHARD M. NIXON)

too well through experience, weakness invites aggression, and aggression triggers war.

Memorial Day radio address to the nation,
Key Biscayne, Fla., May 27/
The New York Times, 5-28:24.

1

If a structure of peace is to endure, it must reflect the contributions and reconcile the aspirations of nations. It must be cemented by the shared goals of coexistence and the shared practice of accommodation. It must liberate every nation to realize its destiny free from the threat of war, and it must promote social justice and human dignity. The structure of peace of which I speak will make possible an era of cooperation in which all nations will apply their separate talents and resources to the solution of problems that beset all mankind— the problems of energy and famine, disease, suffering—problems as old as human history itself.

At United States Naval Academy
commencement, Annapolis, June 5/
The New York Times, 6-6:16.

2

Waging peace is in fact more difficult than waging war because it's more complex. The goal sometimes one loses sight of as he becomes involved in the tactics that are necessary to achieve that goal. But while waging peace is more difficult than waging war . . . the rewards are infinitely greater.

Washington, June 19/
The New York Times, 6-20:10.

3

Traditionally, when peace has been maintained it has been maintained primarily because of the fears of war. Negotiators have been spurred in their efforts either by the desire to end the war or by the fear that their failure would begin a war. The peace we seek now to build is a permanent peace, and nothing permanent can be built on fear alone.

Broadcast address to the Soviet people,
Moscow, July 2/
The New York Times, 7-3:2.

Paul VI
Pope

4

We all know peace is an extremely important theme. It is not superfluous or ornamental in the life of peoples; it is substantial. It deals with life itself, more even than the physical safety of populations, of their honor, of their name, of their history. Peace must guarantee the life of nations. It is an urgent theme. It weighs on our destinies. It presses on our human and civil conscience. Indeed, it knocks on the doors of our own interests. [The] daily and domestic interests which today disturb ordinary daily family life—such as inflation, the shortage of consumer goods, the bans on driving—are indeed nothing in the face of this theme [of peace] and which indeed has tremendous urgency.

New Year's Day sermon, Rome, Jan. 1/
Los Angeles Times, 1-2:(1)16.

Helmut Schmidt
Chancellor of West Germany

5

We are living in an era of detente. And it's really detente. It is a much less dangerous world than it was at the time of the Cuban missile crisis and the Berlin crisis. We have had enough of it. The menace has gone; at least it has shrunk.

Interview/The New York Times, 8-25:(1)26.

Herman R. Staudt
Under Secretary of the Army
of the United States

6

I don't think one can study our [the U.S.'s] history and not perceive that wars and warfare are less and less a battle for material wealth or land or property than they used to be. After all, in World War II the winner got to rebuild the loser at the winner's expense. In North Vietnam, the [U.S.] offer to assist with rebuilding was an incentive to bring peace. In the Mid-East, we're offering both sides help if they will only be more cooperative. So certainly the American motive for participation in war is not one of coveting something which someone else has, which we then—as an extension of our foreign policy—use our military force to obtain. It's quite the opposite—quite the opposite.

Well, if war is less and less a battle for real estate or riches, looking at it from our peculiar American point of view, then what is it all about? Let me suggest that, as the emphasis on the [real-estate] point of view has been declining, warfare has increasingly become a battle for men's minds, their souls—their spirit. That is really the battlefield.

At Chaplain's Conference, July 16/
Vital Speeches, 10-1:761.

Stuart Symington
United States Senator, D—Missouri
1

One miscalculation, one sudden terrorist activity, one paranoid leader, could set the spark to a world-wide nuclear holocaust. There are now six members of the nuclear club—six scorpions in the bottle instead of the original two, as once described by a great nuclear scientist; and as each month passes it becomes more probable that soon there may well be 20 scorpions in the same bottle. At that point, what a few of those scorpions decide could make little difference.

At United Nations, New York, Oct. 21/
Los Angeles Times, 10-22:(1)9.

Edward Teller
Physicist
2

The danger [of nuclear war] is greater than it was a decade ago. Peace depends on power in the hands of those who want peace. I'm sure the United States wants peace. I'm also certain that the Russian people want peace; but unfortunately they have very little influence on their government. The fact is that the Soviet Union is now stronger than we [the U.S.] are.

Interview/People, 8-19:37.

Teng Hsiao-ping
Vice Premier of the People's
Republic of (Communist) China
3

The two superpowers, the United States and the Soviet Union, are vainly seeking world hegemony. Each in its own way attempts to bring the developing countries of Asia, Africa and Latin America under its control and, at the same time, to bully the developed countries that are not their match in strength. The two

superpowers are the biggest international exploiters and oppressors of today. They are the source of a new world war. They both possess large numbers of nuclear weapons. They carry on a keenly contested arms race, station massive forces abroad and set up military bases everywhere, threatening the independence and security of all nations. They both keep subjecting other countries to their control, subversion, interference or aggression. They both exploit other countries economically, plundering their wealth and grabbing their resources. In bullying others, the superpower which flaunts the label of socialism [the Soviet Union] is especially vicious. It has dispatched its unarmed forces to occupy its "ally" Czechoslovakia, and instigated the war to dismember Pakistan. It does not honor its words and is perfidious; it is self-seeking and unscrupulous. Since the two superpowers are contending for world hegemony, the contradiction between them is irreconcilable; one either overpowers the other or is overpowered.

Before United Nations General Assembly,
New York, April 10/
The New York Times, 4-12:12.

Kurt Waldheim
Secretary General of the United Nations
4

The big powers know very well that a new world-wide confrontation would be detrimental to all of them. This gives me the impression that we won't have world-wide confrontation in the next years or the near future. This will reflect positively on the world situation and on the future of the great majority of small and medium-sized countries.

Before World Press Institute journalists,
New York/Los Angeles Herald-Examiner,
10-18:(A)4.

Gough Whitlam
Prime Minister of Australia
5

There is no war, nuclear or conventional, by which the so-called winner, assuming there was one, could conceivably win back by war the resources used and destroyed in waging it.

Before United Nations General Assembly,
New York, Sept. 30/
The New York Times, 10-1:6.

PART THREE

General

Ansel Adams
Photographer

1

Every photograph I make is a departure from reality. People see the Tetons and complain to me that they're not the same as they are in my pictures... There are no forms in nature. Nature is a vast, chaotic collection of shapes. You as an artist create configurations out of chaos. You make a formal statement where there was none to begin with. All art is a combination of an external event and an internal event. "I perceive something that excites me, that gives me an emotional or spiritual reaction," Alfred Stieglitz used to say. I make a photograph to give you the equivalent of what I felt. Equivalent is still the best word.

Interview/
"W": a Fairchild publication, 12-13:7.

Amyas Ames
Chairman, Lincoln Center for the
Performing Arts, New York

2

We have a double standard in this country [the U.S.]. If the price of our concrete highways doubles, we put up the extra money. If the cost of art institutions doubles, as does everything else, we take no action appropriate to the crisis... We have an artistic trust held in common by all, and we are failing in that trust. We are letting beauty atrophy.

Before House subcommittee, Washington/
Nation's Business, August:16.

Warren Beatty
Actor

3

Anyone who says an artist should stay out of politics is a *fool*. I'm talking about an artist who is able to say what truth is. The real artist—the person who is able to perceive and clarify the truth—if that person is activated, then that artist is what [Soviet author Alexander] Solzhenitsyn says he is: an alternative government. And you know, he's right.

Interview, Beverly Hills, Calif./
The New York Times, 3-17:(2)40.

Leonid I. Brezhnev
General Secretary, Communist Party
of the Soviet Union

4

Over their long history, Soviet literature and arts have known many attempts to sidetrack them from life, to tear away from our ideals. Even now, those in the West have not abandoned such aspirations. Individual renegades and people astray in our country as well tried to echo our class and ideological enemies. But all their endeavors proved futile. Ours is an utterly unfit soil for the growth of such weeds.

Before Young Communist League,
Moscow, April 23/
Los Angeles Herald-Examiner, 4-23:(A)11.

Chaim Gross
Sculptor

5

Art gives me great happiness, and when I'm not working I'm miserable. I tell my students, "Don't wait till the muse wakes you up at night and says do this and that. Make a point of working all the time."

Interview, New York, March 17/
The New York Times, 3-18:24.

Peggy Guggenheim
Art patron

6

... I don't go to the galleries much because they are very boring... It is a low period for art. Terrible... It's the era of the cheap objects. The galleries in New York are responsible... because they want to make a lot of money... Today's artists get more and more degenerate. I hope they don't leave behind these awful things they make nowadays.

Interview/
"W": a Fairchild publication, 11-15:7.

WHAT THEY SAID IN 1974

Nancy Hanks
*Chairman, National Endowment for the
Arts of the United States* 1

The most exciting thing I've seen, because of the potential, is that people are no longer separating in their minds the fine arts and the other arts. Now all the arts—including folk arts and handicrafts, orchestras and dance, street theatre and festivals and all such activities—are viewed as part of a whole, and not something belonging to just a few. In the past, a lot of people thought of the arts as just the concert stage, the theatre, and pictures hanging on the museum wall—almost all of it Western European. Now there is a recognition that the art of jazz, for example, is just as great as other arts, and all part of a continuum of artistic activity that is partly American and partly from other countries. We were very wrong in separating these fields before.
Interview/U.S. News & World Report, 10-7:60.

John Hightower
President, Associated Councils of the Arts 2

Many people consider art a luxury, and therefore it is the first to go in a crunch. But in a time of joylessness, the arts are one feature that helps to make life bearable.
The New York Times, 1-20:(2)23.

Celeste Holm
Actress 3

There is something terribly wrong with culture in this [U.S.] society. We think of it as something women drag their husbands to when they don't enjoy it. If husbands prefer to go bowling, that is their culture and that is what they should do. The arts should be a pleasure.
*Moscow, Idaho/
Los Angeles Herald-Examiner, 10-18:(C)5.*

Thomas P. F. Hoving
*Director, Metropolitan Museum of Art,
New York* 4

We have worked very hard to broaden our over-all constituency of the museum and the exhibits. And after we did this, we found ourselves working just as hard to get out and tell everyone what we have. You must make the public comfortable in the museum. We transferred the gloomy main hall into a light, airy place and now have volunteers to greet the people. You also have to "hype"-up the exhibits to bring in a little excitement. An interesting note here is that, since the onset of the energy crisis, our attendance has risen some 20 per cent. People are being forced to discover what is available to them in the way of cultural activity in the city ... Ours is a great museum, but it is also a very important cultural center. We have concerts, lectures and far more than just galleries of art. We have an obligation to the public to provide pure recreation and popular instruction. It really should be fun to come to the museum.
Dallas/The Dallas Times Herald, 2-6:(E)7.

5

A great work of art has to have a very significant spiritual impact. I don't mean religious impact but spiritual. It moves you, changes you, when you see it. You have to go back, and every time you do go back you gain something. It points out some of your failings or pettinesses... I feel that works of art change because of the eyes of people observing them. Like plants, they bloom or they don't. They become greater through appreciation, and I'm not sure that they don't change subtly themselves. It's very hard to explain ... it's a whole process of discovery.
*Interview/
The Christian Science Monitor, 12-19:11.*

Garson Kanin
Author, Playwright 6

On the matter of public taste, I'm the wrong guy to ask. I'm not sure I know what taste is; but I think it is a continual struggle involving life and art; and out of the struggle, somehow, we all improve one another and civilize one another. We [in the arts] like to feel we have something to do with shaping, with opening up. But we have to recognize that the public is smarter than we are. As individuals, one by one, perhaps no. But when that thousand-headed monster sits out there in the auditorium or sits reading your book of fiction, suddenly that mass audience is what the late Moss Hart called "an idiot genius."

At Best-Sellers Panel discussion,
Los Angeles/Los Angeles Times, 4-3:(4)8.

Richard Kiley
Actor   1

I can't stand to work in an atmosphere of strife. Everything gets turned off; what creativity I have is immediately stifled by any yelling . . . I simply walk out of those situations. Because I have a feeling that art or real creativity is not a negative thing; it's not a kind of fungus that grows in that atmosphere; it's not a mushroom. It's more like a rose, I suppose—something that needs a healthy kind of creative atmosphere . . .

Interview, London/
The Christian Science Monitor, 1-22:(F)1.

Sidney Lumet
Motion picture director   2

. . . if somebody asked me if I would let my own children go into the arts, I'd say, "As a child [actor], I was exposed to Maxwell Anderson, Kurt Weill and Sidney Kingsley. Believe me, worse things can happen to a child." So what if you don't get to see kids your own age—all that means is you don't learn to pick your nose and scratch your butt the way they do. But to be taken by somebody you respect to see Chagall—first the paintings and then the *man*—which is what Philip Loeb did for me when we worked together in *My Heart's in the Highlands* . . . well, is that such a bad thing?

Interview, New York/
The New York Times, 1-20:(2)11.

Paul Mocsanyi
Director, Art Center, New School
for Social Research, New York   3

Art should be concerned with the human condition. I try to choose exhibitions that show the nobility of man or attack his failings . . . I am convinced that Western civilization can only survive if it goes back to the traditional moral values that made it great and made its art great. As Machiavelli said, if the army is in disarray, the only thing to do is assemble around the flag . . . Art is only great when it is in service of something higher than itself—whether it be religious, political or humanistic ideals—and it disintegrates when it becomes preoccupied with itself and its technical problems.

New York/
The Christian Science Monitor, 5-16:(F)8.

Igor Moiseyev
Director, Moiseyev Dance Company,
Moscow   4

Each art is an image of the world. Each composer depicts it through sounds, artists through paints, writers use words, and a choreographer uses the expressive means of the human body.

Interview, New York/
The Christian Science Monitor, 6-27:(F)6.

5

Civilization is the greatest enemy of folk art. Civilization tends toward uniformity. Every little village once created its own local costume, with its own special cut, design, coloring and embroidery. Nowadays, you go in the villages and everyone is wearing suits, all the same. Instead of altering our costume, to accommodate climatic conditions, we switch on the heat or the air-conditioning. That's how folk crafts disappear. It's the same with folk music and folk dance. They are slowly dissolving like sugar in the tea of civilization; and the more water we add, the less sugar we have.

Interview, Washington/
The Washington Post, 8-4:(L)3.

6

[On dancers and other artists who defect from the Soviet Union for careers in other lands]: I can't understand them, frankly. I cannot understand how an artist can leave his native land for personal motive or gain. If one doesn't agree with something back home, then one should fight to fulfill one's needs, fight for what is lacking. I can't believe in order to create you have to go somewhere else. If you leave your artistic roots for a foreign land, you may

(IGOR MOISEYEV)

gain riches, property, villas, but it will rarely enhance one's artistic talents. The artist who quests after wealth acquires it only at the expense of his interior wealth. This is my view.

Interview, Washington/
The Washington Post, 8-4:(L)3.

Eugene Ormandy
Musical director, Philadelphia Orchestra 1

In music, I very definitely think we [the U.S.] are the capital of the world. In dance, perhaps so, because we have some great dancers. I'm not sure we are at the top in painting. In the past, of course, most of the great painters came from Spain, Holland, Italy, France and Germany. I don't know if we have reached their quality yet. We are trying to do in 200 years what they have done in 500 years. In drama, I think we are also ahead. We have some great dramatists—as many as Europe. Yes, I think we are coming along very beautifully in the arts.

Interview/U.S. News & World Report, 6-3:57.

Claiborne Pell
United States Senator, D—Rhode Island 2

A civilized society is judged by the values it places on cultural advancement. How will history eventually judge us as a nation in these terms? Will some group of historians in the future say that somehow the United States faltered—that it became paramount in industry, pre-eminent in science, expert in the design of weaponry, a genius in mass communication, but that it neglected, or paid too little attention to, the diverse art forms which signal like beacons the imperishable achievements of the human mind and spirit?

Quote, 4-14:340.

Nikolai V. Podgorny
President of the Soviet Union 3

At a time when the ideological struggle between socialism and capitalism is becoming even sharper, our art is called upon to constantly raise its ideological arsenal [and] its irreconcilability to manifestations of alien views . . . The slightest departure from our principles is inadmissible in any kind of art. True art, which includes the theatre, ends whenever its exalted spiritual, cultural and moral principles are replaced by lack of ideological content, philistinism, shallowness . . .

Los Angeles Times, 11-15:(1)14.

John D. Rockefeller III
Philanthropist 4

To me, when I say "culture," I think more than art. To me, the cultural field is really everything that isn't political or economic. So it's a very broad front. Art is obviously a key element in the culture picture. Art is tangible. Art is real. Art has tremendous appeal. And I would hope that, with greater emphasis on the art factor in the total cultural picture, it would give [culture] the prominence that I feel is important if we're going to develop really a basic appreciation and respect and understanding between ourselves and any other country. To me, progress in relationships depends on respect and understanding and appreciation. This is true in any relationship, international as well as individual. And I really believe that the art factor coming into this picture can greatly enhance that respect and appreciation and therefore forward the general relationship between . . . countries.

News conference announcing his giving
of an art collection to the Asia Society,
New York/The Washington Post, 2-8:(B)9.

Robert W. Sarnoff
Chairman, RCA Corporation 5

[Advocating greater public support for the arts] : It is well enough to speak of art for art's sake. But in the real world, no enterprise can respond indefinitely to a growing demand when it cannot even cover its current costs. We have no right to expect a free ride at the expense of those who satisfy our yearnings for the best in music, drama, dance or the visual arts.

At dedication of College of Fine
and Communication Arts,
Loyola Marymount University, Los Angeles/
The Wall Street Journal, 11-18:16.

Beverly Sills
Opera singer

1

Although we [the U.S.] may be remembered as the country that put men on the moon, art is the signature of civilization.

Quote, 8-25:170.

Norton Simon
Industrialist

2

... what is art but a man's creativity put down on canvas? When you look at the work of a serious artist, you know that here is a man groping through life to paint in his own peculiar manner. Cezanne, for example, worked day after day within the same framework, struggling to reach a mirage at the end of the road. The mirage changed constantly, so he never finished a canvas but kept starting new ones. Look at his work and you see it all there—the struggling, the mirage, the new attempts. Great art is never finished, because the artist is trying always to modify it, to create more, to create differently. What's important is *how* the artist communicates, and what he leaves behind as an abstraction of his work.

Interview, Los Angeles/
Los Angeles Times, 12-15:(Home)60.

Alexander I. Solzhenitsyn
Exiled Soviet author

3

We all know that an artist's work cannot be contained within the wretched dimension of politics. For this dimension cannot hold the whole of our life, and we must not restrain our social consciousness within its bounds.

Accepting Nobel Prize for literature,
Stockholm, Dec. 10/
The Christian Science Monitor, 12-11:6.

Joshua Taylor
Director, National Collection of
Fine Arts, Washington

4

We're very concerned with *how* you see pictures. We don't believe in just taking a room and hanging pictures around the walls. We like to hang pictures so you ... discover individual paintings and don't just see batches of things. Museums can be frightfully boring, not because the paintings aren't fine but because they're always presented in the same way. We've tried to keep the art in what I call bite-size portions ... and to make sure that, as you move through, there's variety and changing atmosphere in terms of color, light and the kinds of things you're looking at ... Naturally, we're concerned with quality all the way through. On the other hand, I hope you noticed a great many paintings in the galleries by people you had never heard of. That's not by chance, because our theory is you hang a painting because it's an interesting painting, not because it's by somebody who's well known. After all, the history of American art has been pretty well schematized, and to suppose that the scheme is the history is a major fallacy. So we're very concerned with flavors that are not the common ones, and quite deliberately included these. We like people to discover new things, not simply find confirmation.

Interview, Washington/
The Christian Science Monitor, 5-3:(F)1.

Fashion

Bill Blass
Fashion designer
1

"Investment clothes" are here again. These are fashions made to look right for a long time, just as your fine rugs and chairs and tables are meant to last, not forever maybe, but certainly not just for a season. Who wants to put money into clothes that have to be chopped off or let down every few months, any more than who wants to redecorate a room every spring? Extravagances like that just aren't chic any more.

Interview, New York/
San Francisco Examiner, 6-14:23.

Donald Brooks
Fashion designer
2

Expensive ready-to-wear will be worn by fewer and fewer women. On the other hand, more and more women who can afford expensive clothes will be requesting clothes specifically designed for them, be it ready-to-wear or custom. Prices must go down for mass America and in turn will go up for specialized America.

Interview/
"W": a Fairchild publication, 8-23:9.

Andre Courreges
Fashion designer
3

It is grotesque that women in 1974 should be dressed in clothes borrowed from the '30s. The whole world—its way of life, its psychology, its attitude and its environment—has changed. Even the shape of women has changed. We have had a major war, depressions, social unrest, men in space since then. This is the nuclear age. In the '30s there was no long-distance air travel, everything was more leisurely—it took eight days to cross the Atlantic. Clothes that were suitable then are obviously out of place in the modern world.

The Washington Post, 3-31:(L)2.

Hubert de Givenchy
Fashion designer
4

Fashion today is so capricious. No designer should be influenced by a wave. Each designer should think about the body of a woman. Each woman should develop her own taste, should wear what is best for her. I am not a designer to change proportions, to change the look each season. This is not good for women. I believe you must have fidelity to your clothes. The most important thing for a designer is to be honest with his customer.

Los Angeles/Los Angeles Times, 9-16:(4)11.

Lydia de Roma
Fashion designer
5

All my dresses and skirts are still hand-buttonholed, hand-hemmed, hand-embroidered and hand-appliqued. In the American world of mass production, your manufacturers used to laugh at such "archaic" old-world practices. Your business was geared to a consumer economy, a throw-away economy. Waste helped to make it work—not just for you but, through your generosity, for the entire world. Americans have always wanted to have a good time, and thank God they've always wanted other people to have a good time—to share their wealth. Now I sense that more and more Americans want to have not just a good time, but a lasting good time.

Interview, Los Angeles/
Los Angeles Times, 2-13:(4)3.

James Galanos
Fashion designer
6

Taste is difficult to define and rare to find. I am weary of all the messiness around. When you do see something of beauty, someone with style and a certain class, you become very excited. It can be a young girl in blue-jeans. If they are handsome and she has a good figure and a certain know-how and way of putting the blouse, chains, scarves together, it doesn't have to be a Galanos. One thing you cannot buy is taste. That is something you have to have or develop. For some it seems to be inbred. For others it's a searching and wanting to learn and gained by observing the best, following reliable fashion sources rather than the things in the press. Finally, your eye has to adjust if you have any intelligence in a person. This is the way I trained myself.

Interview, Los Angeles/
Los Angeles Herald-Examiner, 12-16:(B)1.

Rudi Gernreich
Fashion designer

1

The designer of tomorrow will be more of an engineer and less of an artist. People no longer want to wear someone else's statement or to call that kind of attention to themselves. It is part of a sociological phenomenon. We want both liberated clothes and we want to avoid clothes that provoke hostility in public... What we will wear in the future will be a kind of uniform in public.

San Francisco/
San Francisco Examiner, 5-13:21.

2

A lot of things are going to have to happen in fashion. New technology will have to apply. This is the one industry not growing in step with other areas. If someone, for instance, comes up with a better icemaker, everybody tries to create a better one. In clothing we're going back. I really don't like nostalgia at all. And then you have to remember there are still people sitting at sewing machines and we are still using thread instead of heat fusion or sound fusion.

Interview, Dallas, June 17/
The Dallas Times Herald, 6-18:(C)1.

3

... I think people in the daytime are going to want to "disappear" in public—not make any specific statement about their individuality on the street. That would tend toward a sort of uniform look, so that you're not attracting

attention to yourself. As a counter-reaction to that, people will want to express their individuality in their private environment, in clothes for their home, and in a selected environment which is going to be more imaginative. The awareness of your own surroundings, your own privacy, is going to express your sense of individuality. That's why people become so much more conscious of home products and what they surround themselves with. I don't think they will want to expose themselves in public, not to invite hostility.

Interview, Atlanta/
The Atlanta Journal and Constitution,
9-29:(G)9.

Robert L. Green
Fashion director, "Playboy" magazine

4

The more we feel victims of the work syndrome and the anonymity of it, the more there is a desire to shed the clothes we work in ... Clothes tell other people about you; and if you're still wearing the suit you wore to the office by nightfall, your head is probably still at the office.

Washington/The Washington Post, 3-10:(H)5.

Kasper
Fashion designer

5

This is not the moment to make a strong fashion statement. There has to be some gentleness, some sensitivity in life, and fashion can provide it. All we designers have to do is make women feel good in their clothes. That's the only way to end once and for all this whole thing about designers making clothes just so women will have to throw them out one season later.

Interview, Los Angeles/
Los Angeles Times, 2-15:(4)1.

Ralph Lauren
Fashion designer

6

Nobody is impressed with elaborate clothes any more. A man doesn't automatically have class because he wears custom-made suits. A girl who is solid doesn't want to be known as a

(RALPH LAUREN)

fashion-lady . . . If we go out in the evening, we go to a movie and have a cheeseburger after. We don't go to big restaurants—God forbid I should have to wear a shirt and tie. I just want to be comfortable and relaxed, and so does my wife.

The New York Times, 3-31:(1)56.

Edith Raymond Locke
Editor-in-chief, "Mademoiselle" magazine

1

Fashion "dictators"? Of course there aren't any today. But it's just a change in semantics. Of course, women still follow the ideas of creative designers, only today we say a certain style is "recommended," or that one may choose from several of the new looks in skirts. The days of "Everybody into pink this spring" are gone forever.

San Francisco, March 7/
San Francisco Examiner, 3-8:26.

Stanley Marcus
Chairman, Neiman-Marcus stores

2

Fashion is part of life and life is going on whether the economy is booming or receding. Undoubtedly it [the economy] will affect the ways people spend their money. In all probability it will put greater emphasis on quality than has been put on it in the past. A person, in thinking of a purchase, will say, "Is this the best I can get or does it have just a 'look'?"

The Atlanta Constitution, 9-24:(B)3.

3

. . . I think women have improved, fashion-wise, over the last 25 to 30 years. The main thing is that they have learned to eliminate instead of supplement decoration. That's today's women. They're simpler in their use of accessories—no longer tend to load themselves up with all the jewelry, those matching earrings, bracelets, necklaces and so forth. As in all art forms, so it is in fashion. That which looks simple and effortless makes for greatness.

Interview, Beverly Hills, Calif./
Los Angeles Herald-Examiner, 10-25:(D)1.

Bob Miller
President, Concept VII, fashions

4

Right now, women are looking for escape clothes. They must act out their dreams. They're inundated with reality—no gas, the high cost of living. There is no escape in the movies—they're all so realistic—so there must be in fashion.

Los Angeles/Los Angeles Times, 1-8:(4)1.

Yves Saint Laurent
Fashion designer

5

I'm for the principle of elegance, and I'm very influenced by the 1930s. I'm influenced by the spirit and the extreme elegance of the '30s. I'd like to make this same elegance and refinement part of the future of fashion.

Paris/"W": a Fairchild publication, 1-11:13.

6

For a woman to look marvelous, she should first *think* she is marvelous. She should wear pink, preferably with red lipstick, and try to seem as much like a flower as possible—in soft dresses with sensuous forms.

Interview/"W": a Fairchild publication, 2-8:2.

7

Fashion is less intense these days. It has less importance. And I don't think its importance will come back. What will be more and more important is to be able to create, through a style, clothing that won't go out of style, which can blend in with things of past seasons, giving women a wardrobe like a man's wardrobe.

Interview/"W": a Fairchild publication, 6-28:7.

8

Haute couture is obviously the highest point of perfection in the trade, but it is evident that the future doesn't belong to haute couture. It is one of the last trades where everything is done by hand. It ought to be saved, if only for that reason, but I don't know if it can go on existing. It's not even certain that the basic materials will be there. Prices are going up and up. Soon there might not be any silk or wool, or even cotton. Everything is being replaced by synthetics.

Interview, Paris/People, 9-9:44.

George Stavropolous
Fashion designer

1

My clothes speak for themselves . . . They are expensive, but money has nothing to do with elegance. I think there are still women who appreciate elegance. They also appreciate the beauty of a flower; and that costs little. But it is the beauty that I want in my clothes.

Interview, Beverly Hills, Calif./
Los Angeles Times, 9-23:(4)7.

Diana Vreeland
Former editor-in-chief, "Vogue" magazine;
Former fashion editor,
"Harper's Bazaar" magazine

2

Fashion is affected by economic and social times. We [in the U.S.] have no social times now; we are making our own as we go along. It's a hell of a time; we're economically crippled and frightened. Attractiveness goes hand-in-hand with pleasure. Unless people hang on to their *joie de vivre*, we won't have fashion.

Interview, New York/
The New York Times, 12-31:8.

Norman Wechsler
President, Saks Fifth Avenue

3

There will always be a place for expensive ready-to-wear in an affluent American economy —providing, of course, there continues to be an affluent American economy.

Interview/"W": a Fairchild publication, 6-14:2.

John Weitz
Fashion designer

4

Grown-up women have given up making asses of themselves with their fashions. It's the men who are making really furious asses of themselves today. They have those $60 hairdos that look like Arnel or polyester or one of those synthetics, all silver-grey plastic with messy razor jobs. And those high heels some men are walking around in look like debs enroute to their first party.

San Francisco Examiner & Chronicle, 4-7:(B)2.

385

Journalism

Elie Abel
Dean, Graduate School of Journalism,
Columbia University
1

One of the first lessons I learned was that, when the government, any government, suddenly offers to dump information on a reporter, share what it knows with a reporter, that is the time for the reporter to become just a little skeptical.

At Press-Enterprise Lecture,
University of California, Riverside,
March 4/San Francisco Examiner, 3-5:32.

2

A degree of tension between President and press is, in my judgment, inescapable and, for all the bitterness it sometimes engenders, a wholesome thing.

At Press-Enterprise Lecture,
University of California, Riverside,
March 4/San Francisco Examiner, 3-5:32.

Harry S. Ashmore
Journalist; Senior fellow, Center for
the Study of Democratic Institutions
3

For almost a century, leading newspapers and magazines have been major commercial enterprises as well as quasi-public institutions, and this has been the situation of the broadcasters from their beginning. Having long ago abandoned any systematic criticism of each other's performance—except for the largely theatrical critique of TV programming by newspapers—they generally unite in condemnation of any outside agency that dares to subject them to the kind of criticism they apply to every other enterprise colored with the public interest.

Los Angeles Times, 5-17:(4)23.

Roscoe C. Born
Vice editor, "The National Observer"
4

I have come to the belief that there lurks in the character of nearly every journalist a fundamental flaw. I now believe that this flaw is probably there in even the most honorable and decent journalists, even though some have managed to overcome it in the same way that decent and honorable men and women have learned, over the years, to suppress or mask some of their baser instincts. I suspect this flaw I am trying to describe is an inborn desire to "get" somebody, anybody; to publish a startling story that will result in an indictment, will get somebody fired, will get some public official ousted from office or defeated for re-election. A reporter who takes the hide off somebody in print reaps immense rewards and satisfactions. His colleagues praise him. His editors praise him. His non-journalist friends suddenly are aware that he has done something remarkable, and they tell him about it. He may even win one of journalism's most famous awards. For it is a fact, known to journalists everywhere, that if one hopes to win a big award for reporting, one must be able to show that his stories got results: someone indicted, someone fired, someone ousted, someone sued. That is the path to journalistic glory . . . This instinct cannot be banned by legislation. It will not disappear by changing the criteria by which great journalistic feats are judged and prizes awarded—although that might help. I think journalists must learn to be more self-critical; we must learn a bit of humility; we must stop telling ourselves incessantly how damned noble we are in everything we do. The conscience of the journalist must be pricked. He must stop and think and remember that the right to gather and print information about people and institutions is an awesome power. And somehow we must come to realize that the abuse of our power can no more be tolerated than the abuse of the awesome power of the Presidency and the government.

Before Railroad Public Relations Association,
Colorado Springs, Colo./
The National Observer, 8-3:10.

Patrick J. Buchanan
*Special Consultant to President
of the United States Richard M. Nixon*
1

[Broadcast-network news correspondents] have claimed a very special right—the right of immediate and first rebuttal to all Presidential addresses to the American people, on all issues of controversy and moment before the nation. When one considers that few if any network correspondents have ever carried the burden of public office ... that most of them have advanced to their current stations less as a consequence of their conspicuous intelligence, wisdom, knowledge and experience than as a result of their verbal agility, stamina, youth and physical appearance, this is indeed a sweeping assertion of political power.

Los Angeles Times, 5-14:(4)12.

2

Why can't the [broadcast] networks run their news operations the way the wire services do? Instead of sending out boxed half-hour shows every night, why can't they send out something like two hours of material—covering a broad spectrum—from which each local station's news editor could then select? With wire services, you have more than 1,600 newspaper editors across the country deciding how to play a story. Once you have that variety of decisions, you also have a viable marketplace of ideas which nobody can criticize.

Los Angeles Times, 5-17:(4)23.

Erwin D. Canham
*Editor emeritus,
"The Christian Science Monitor"*
3

While television may have the advantage of speedy transmission of events, newspapers can and should provide better background coverage and news analysis. Newspapers enable the reader to absorb detailed information at his own pace.

*At Communication in the Americas conference,
Stanford University, June 19/
San Francisco Examiner, 6-20:46.*

John Chancellor
*News commentator,
National Broadcasting Company*
4

[On the death of veteran news commentator Chet Huntley]: I have always believed that his success was based to a great extent on the fact that television ... displays character. The inner man is finally perceived by the viewers. And by the millions, they perceived Huntley to be honest, hard-working, honorable, courageous, warm, patriotic and decent.

March 20/Los Angeles Times, 3-21:(1)5.

Marquis Childs
Political columnist
5

[On U.S. Presidential press conferences]: The question I raise is this: Do the media have a right to interrogate the Chief Executive? Is the confrontation an inherent right or is it the privilege of the man who occupies the office to use it [the press conference] to his own ends, to diminish it or perhaps to let it fall entirely into disuse? In my opinion, it is a fundamental right. Under the American system of divided powers, there is no question period during which the Executive can be called on for an accounting. Limited as it is, the press conference is the only medium of exchange between the public and the President, whose powers have been so greatly enhanced. This becomes all the more important as the claims of Executive privilege and national security have narrowed the response of the Executive to Congress.

*At Frank R. Kent Symposium,
Johns Hopkins University/
The Washington Post, 4-27:(A)22.*

Ken W. Clawson
*Director of Communications for President
of the United States Richard M. Nixon*
6

[On Nixon Administration criticism of the press]: I separate out TV from the print media when it comes to criticism. Newspapers are privately owned, but we all have a piece of TV's ass, and we're entitled to do something—although I'm not sure exactly what—if it offends us.

Interview/Los Angeles Times, 5-14:(4)12.

Charles W. Colson
*Former Special Counsel to President
of the United States Richard M. Nixon*   1

[On the Nixon Administration's attitude toward the press when he was Special Counsel]: Anybody in the White House staff ... who got good press had to automatically be suspect because, *a fortiori,* you must have been cultivating the press; and to cultivate the press meant you had to give them something, and the whole attitude was don't give them a damn thing.

*Interview, Washington/
The New York Times, 7-7:(1)29.*

John B. Connally, Jr.
*Former Secretary of the Treasury of the
United States; Former Governor of Texas*   2

We live in a time when the mass media has become a pervasive influence on all our lives; when instant communication has exposed and magnified every failing of our society; and even when manipulation of the news to accomplish a desired end has become an art for any number of self-serving practitioners.

*San Francisco Examiner & Chronicle,
7-14:(This World)2.*

Helen K. Copley
Chairman, Copley Newspapers   3

In its purest form, freedom of the press exists when the printing press is neither subservient nor responsive to the will of the state. Only when it achieves that condition can it guard the people's interest against excesses by those to whom power has been entrusted. And that is the real problem which we face around the world today. In scores of places there is a steady erosion of the wall that separates the state from a free and honest press. We see totalitarian governments in many places simply knocking aside traditional protections and moving to make the press say what they want it to say, or just preventing the press from saying anything. The problem is growing and holds the gravest of warnings for every one of us. Because it could happen here [in the U.S.]. We already have seen a few warning signals. There have

been bills introduced in Congress aimed at limiting the press in political criticism. There have been recent rumblings that antitrust laws might be used to stifle the news media. There have been repeated proposals that the judiciary power be used to coerce and punish uncooperative news media. Reporters actually have been prevented by judges from reporting upon open court hearings. While we enjoy a tremendously strong position in our country, there still is a clearly visible trend. It is not a good one, and we in journalism had best acknowledge the reality, and do something about it.

*Before San Francisco Press Club, Sept. 27/
San Francisco Examiner & Chronicle, 10-6:(B)3.*

Archibald Cox
Professor of Law, Harvard University   4

The media certainly [are] turning gradually to a more active role in shaping the course of events through their news columns and commentaries as well as on their editorial pages. It isn't true of smaller papers around the country, but I think it's true of *The Washington Post, The New York Times, Newsweek,* and a number of big papers, and I rather think it seems to be true of some of the [broadcast] network presentations. It does seem to me that the selection of items emphasized often reflects the sort of notion that the press is the fourth branch of government and it should play a major role in government. I'm not sure that I want it that way when there are only three networks; to me, that's an awful lot of power to give to whoever runs the three networks.

*At St. Paul's School, Concord, N.H./
The National Observer, 3-2:11.*

Thaddeus J. Dulski
United States Representative, D–New York   5

Since the passage of the Postal Reorganization Act in 1970, postal rates have been increased by the U.S. Postal Service at an alarming rate. The detrimental effects of these increases on all classes of mail, and especially on magazines and newspapers, is well known ... It is in the best interest of this nation that the printed news media remain vital and viable ... It is inconceivable to me ... that a "break-even" policy for the Postal Service is appropriate. This policy necessarily results in exorbitant rates, which will drive many excellent publications, economically marginal, to go out of business. No matter how you analyze it, freedom of the press, recognized by our Founding Fathers as the foundation of the republic, is directly endangered by high postal rates.

Los Angeles Herald-Examiner, 5-30:(A)13.

Marshall Field
Publisher, "Chicago Daily News" and
"The Chicago Sun-Times"

1

Today we are constantly hearing, "Never believe what you read in the paper" or "All news broadcasts are biased." The sad fact is ... there is a certain amount of truth to some of these charges. Personally, this disturbs and concerns me. To encourage more responsible reporting, I think an individual who feels he has been wrongly or unfairly treated in a story in press, radio or TV should be able to sue not just the media that printed—or broadcast—the story, but also the individual who wrote or reported the story, even if there is no malice.

Before communications and advertising
executives, Chicago, June 20/
The Dallas Times Herald, 6-21:(A)21.

Gerald R. Ford
Vice President of the United States

2

[Saying he reads the sports page of the newspaper the first thing every morning]: I read it before the front page because at least on the sports page you have a 50-50 chance of being right.

Los Angeles Times, 2-20:(3)2.

3

[Freedom of the press is] a product of the American Revolution. There is not a member [of Congress] here who has not felt the criticism of the media. There are times when this criticism has not been just. But, not withstanding, neither is there anyone here who does not recognize that one of the safeguards of individual liberty is a free press.

Before former members of Congress,
Washington, May 21/
The Washington Post, 5-22:(A)4.

4

[Newspaper political cartoons] are much more widely scanned than ponderous editorials ... A cartoon says, in effect, that this complex situation is really simple. An editorial says this situation which seems so simple is really very complicated and proceeds with the ramifications.

Before Association of American
Editorial Cartoonists, Boston,
June 1/The New York Times, 6-2:(1)59.

Gerald R. Ford
President of the United States

5

I differ with those who categorize the journalist as a different kind of American. I prefer to consider everyone on his or her merits and to treat each one of them as I would hope to be treated if our jobs were reversed ... As President, I am trying to continue the same free and pleasant relationship with the press that I enjoyed as Vice President and throughout 25 years in the Congress. I do not believe that I am doing things differently than before, except that the press seems a lot more interested now in what I have to say.

Anderson, S.C., Oct. 19/
The Atlanta Journal and Constitution,
10-20:(D)21.

Fred W. Friendly
Professor of Journalism,
Columbia University; Former president,
Columbia Broadcasting System News

6

I don't know which alarms me more—prosecutors and jurists flooding the courts with subpoenaed reporters and contempt citations or newsmen and publishers crying "First Amendment" every time they are challenged ... When challenged for publishing harmful grand-jury leaks, the press decries censorship. Claims of First Amendment interference are used as the handy smokescreen ... If the Chairman of the FCC in 1973 made that speech describing TV as a "vast wasteland," as [then FCC Chairman] Newton Minow did in 1962, he would probably be crucified. There is no excuse for the epi-

(FRED W. FRIENDLY)

demic of wounds which journalists seem to invite, however unwittingly, in reaction to the disease that [President] Nixon cultured and [Vice President] Agnew carried.

Before Federal Communications Bar Association, Washington, Jan. 10/ Variety, 1-16:50.

1

To the extent that journalists fail, democracy falters. A lazy press and a responsible government have about as much chance to co-exist as a totalitarian government and a free press.

The Washington Post, 7-2:(A)20.

J. William Fulbright
United States Senator, D—Arkansas

2

The media has become the fourth branch of government in every respect except for their immunity from checks and balances. This is as it should be. [But because the press] cannot and should not be restrained from outside, you have a special responsibility to restrain yourselves... What I do deplore, and with all possible emphasis, is the shift of the attack [by the news media] from policies to personalities; from matters of tangible consequence to the nation as a whole to matters of personal morality of uncertain relevance to the national interest. A bombastic accusation, a groundless prediction, or best of all a leak, will usually gain a Senator his heart's content of publicity. A reasoned discourse more often than not is usually destined for intonement in the *Congressional Record.* [Since Watergate,] the media has acquired an undue preoccupation with the apprehension of wrongdoers; a fascination with the singer to the neglect of the song.

At National Press Club, Washington, Dec. 19/ The Christian Science Monitor, 12-24:5.

Barry M. Goldwater
United States Senator, R—Arizona

3

[Criticizing *The Washington Post* for printing secret FBI documents recently leaked to

it] : It's very obvious to me that any information that the government has can be obtained by *The Washington Post* or any other newspaper that wants to pay the price. This is plain, outright treason, and I won't stand for it ... I'm worried about the fact that *The Washington Post* can print a facsimile of a top-secret paper stolen from the FBI, and nobody does anything about it. I think the Attorney General should haul *The Washington Post* in and demand an explanation of how they got it, what they paid for it, who gave it or sold it to them, and go through the FBI and find the same thing.

To reporters, Washington, June 12/ The Washington Post, 6-13:(A)18.

Katharine Graham
Publisher, "The Washington Post"

4

It's a basic press difficulty that the object of the story never perceives the story in the same way the reporter sees it. Obviously, I have my Walter Mitty dreams. We all have. We're 25 and brilliant and beautiful and articulate and we do everything well and if you report anything else I'll think you're unfair... [When a friend] calls and says, "This is an outrage," you have to say you'll look into it. If the comment is fair, it may be the end of your lovely relationship.

Interview/Los Angeles Times, 1-27:(4)9.

5

I don't have any new view of the press. It's a very old view—that the First Amendment gets strengthened by exercise ... The press role is still the same—to bring information to people— and only that. Our only power is to inform.

Interview, Washington/ "W": a Fairchild publication, 8-9:5.

Paul Harvey
News commentator, American Broadcasting Company

6

I still write everything myself. I feel when you express an opinion it must be in your own words ... I do worry sometimes if the well will run dry. But at least we have 200 million Americans doing crazy things at night so that we have something to write about in the morning.

Interview, Chicago/
Chicago Tribune, 9-11:(1)1.

F. Edward Hebert
United States Representative,
D—Louisiana; Former city editor,
"New Orleans States"

1

[Addressing news reporters]: I'm not a school boy when it comes to journalism. I know what you're all about. I came straight from the city desk to Congress, you know. I know all the tricks—where all the bodies are buried. I know how reporters can distort the news. I know that a reporter's so-called "reliable sources" are usually his own feelings. To subject Americans to this [harsh treatment of President Nixon] is torture. It's horrible, absolutely horrible.

News conference, Los Angeles, May 16/
Los Angeles Times, 5-17:(1)13.

Clare Boothe Luce
Former American diplomat and playwright

2

Our press has become so neurotic that we pick up each day's paper with dread . . . The newspapers give us a daily false view of life. Anyone looking about him can see that the American world is not a place of unalleviated crime, riots, misery and pollution. We might well think [from our newspapers] America is living in a perpetual hell. The only sane parts of the papers are the women's pages, showing that someone still cares for children, enjoys a family, a garden, or watching a souffle rise in the oven . . .

Interview, Honolulu/Parade, 4-21:10.

3

The press, which yells and screams about the size of the profits being made by the oil companies and other businesses, has shown no inclination to cut down their profits. Yet, as a business, the media is making among the highest profits in the whole country.

Washington/
San Francisco Examiner & Chronicle,
11-3:(Sunday Scene)2.

Bill Monroe
Washington editor, "Today" show,
National Broadcasting Company Television

4

The Fairness Doctrine is nothing but government editing under a sunshine label . . . Under [it] you have news executives who have no choice, as they make their journalistic decisions, but to consult their fears and their lawyers.

At panel discussion sponsored
by (MORE) magazine, New York/
The Christian Science Monitor, 5-30:(F)8.

5

The American press has undergone a technological change. News is now distributed, not just by print, but by electronics. The Fairness Doctrine represents an effort [by government] to take advantage of that change, to take advantage of the necessity of channel allocation, to deprive the electronic part of the press of genuine First Amendment rights. We have slipped into this government-knows-best kind of regulation quietly over a period of 50 years without anybody paying much attention to it. It was already in effect before anyone realized that the infant media of radio and television were destined to become news media as important as print itself . . . Under the Fairness Doctrine, we see ascending an entirely new concept of *fair press,* government certified, at the expense of the old idea of *free press,* with its independent editors. Democracy requires risks, taking a chance on people. We take a risk with voters, a risk that *most of the time* they'll make the right choices. We take a risk with jurors. We take a risk when we depend on independent newsmen and editors not accountable to government. I say it's as good a risk now as it was 200 years ago.

At panel discussion sponsored
by (MORE) magazine, New York/
The Christian Science Monitor, 6-4:(F)10.

Edmund S. Muskie
United States Senator, D—Maine

6

The dialogue—in which the press is the essential intermediary—between the people and their

(EDMUND S. MUSKIE)

leaders is being interrupted and distorted. To restore it will take a change of manners, not laws, on both sides. The change will have to begin with a new acceptance by officials of the necessity of submitting their public conduct to continual scrutiny and a new willingness by journalists to conduct that scrutiny with an eye to information as much as sensation.

Quote, 5-5:422.

Ron Nessen
Press Secretary to President of the United States Gerald R. Ford   *1*

... I will never knowingly lie to the White House press corps. I will never knowingly mislead the White House press corps, and I think if I ever do, you would be justified in questioning my continued usefulness in this job. My concept of the job is that a Press Secretary does not always have to agree with the decisions of the President. I think a Press Secretary's job is to report to you [the press] the actions of the President, why he has taken the actions, how he has arrived at the action. I don't think that the Press Secretary and the press are natural antagonists ... but I think we have the same aim, which is to get as much news as possible about what goes on in this place [the White House] to the American people.

News conference, Washington,
Sept. 20/Parade, 12-8:6.

Richard M. Nixon
President of the United States   *2*

[Referring to Alice Roosevelt Longworth's 90th birthday]: If she had spent all of her time reading *The Washington Post, The Washington Star-News,* she would have been dead by now. [She stays young by not worrying about] the miserable political things that all of us unfortunately think about in Washington; by thinking about all those great issues that will affect the future of the world, which *The Post* unfortunately seldom writes about in a responsible way.

Washington/Los Angeles Times, 2-13:(1)2.

3

Sometimes there is a tendency in the reporting of news—and I do not say this critically, it is simply a fact of life—that bad news is news and good news is not news.

At Honor America Day rally, Huntsville,
Ala., Feb. 18/Los Angeles Times,
2-19:(1)19.

4

I know in the press room that my policies are generally disapproved of, and there are some [newsmen], putting it in the vernacular, who hate my guts with a passion. But I don't hate them, none of them ... They are consumed by this issue [Watergate] and I can see—not all, but I can see in the eyes of them, not only their hatred, but their frustration; and as a matter of fact, I really feel sorry for them in a way because they should recognize that, to the extent they allow their own hatreds to consume them, they will lose the rationality which is the mark of a civilized man.

Interview, Washington, May 13/
Los Angeles Times, 7-29:(1)3.

William S. Paley
Chairman, CBS, Inc.   *5*

Government should simply as a matter of asserted national policy ... repudiate the Fairness Doctrine and specifically immunize news and public-affairs broadcasting from any form of governmental oversight or supervision whatsoever ... The very fact that the Fairness Doctrine confers on a government agency the power to sit in judgment over news broadcasts makes it a tempting device for use by any Administration in power to influence the content of broadcast journalism.

At dedication of Newhouse Communications
Center II, Syracuse (N.Y.) University, May 31/
Los Angeles Herald-Examiner, 6-2:(A)2.

William Proxmire
United States Senator, D—Wisconsin   *6*

Throughout all of human history, events not only tended to creep up on people, but the reporting of those events lacked the standards of accuracy, objectivity, balance and comprehensiveness that virtually every reporter in every city room and television and radio station is held [to] today. What I am saying is that, for the first time in this nation's history, we have a professional and more competent press.

Before the Senate, Washington/
Los Angeles Times, 5-8:(1)8.

Dan Rather
News correspondent,
Columbia Broadcasting System

1

They [the Nixon Administration] talk about a television bias against [President] Nixon, but from the very beginning they brought in a load of bias against the press. They've always had an attack-group philosophy—they get together to determine an individual reporter's vulnerability and how to take advantage of it. The mystery to me has always been why they're not smart enough to see that this philosophy·is counterproductive to everything they're' trying to accomplish.

Interview/Los Angeles Times, 5-15:(4)19.

2

Press relations [with the Nixon Administration] have never been worse in any past Administration. You can't find one oldtimer on the press corps, even one who goes back for years, who can remember the kind of acrimony that existed with Nixon—even though some of it was our fault.

"W": a Fairchild publication, 8-23:6.

Harry Reasoner
News commentator,
American Broadcasting Company

3

[Criticizing *Time* and *Newsweek* magazines for their coverage of the Watergate affair]: Week after week, their lead stories on the subject have been more in the style of pejorative pamphleteering than objective journalism; and since they are highly visible and normally highly respected organs of our craft, they embarrass and discredit us all ... [There are in this week's *Newsweek*] more than 30 instances of phrases that any editor should automatically

strike out—and I assume they have editors ... No one questions the right of magazine editors and columnists to have opinions and put them into editorials and columns. But the sordid story of Watergate writes its own editorial—and for most citizens, without the patronizing help of journalists who would deeply and rightly resent any similar attempt to spoon-feed them their conclusions.

Commentary/"Evening News," American
Broadcasting Company Television, 3-12.

George E. Reedy
Dean, College of Journalism,
Marquette University; Former Press
Secretary to the President of the
United States (Lyndon B. Johnson)

4

Every President has fought with the press, except William Henry Harrison, and he died after a month in office ... [The] problem is the press presents a picture of the world and events which is much closer to reality than any politician can.

News conference/Los Angeles Times, 3-28:(1)2.

5

The Press Secretary should mirror the President because that's his only reason for existing. He has no other function, authority or mandate. A Press Secretary hasn't been elected to anything and no one gives a damn what he thinks. They only care what the President thinks ... He's [the President] a monarch, a sort of king, and if he wants to say something stupid, a Press Secretary should say something stupid. If he [the President] wants to lie, it's the responsibility of a Press Secretary to lie.

Los Angeles Times, 10-4:(1)23.

Elliot L. Richardson
Former Attorney General of the United States

6

So far as the press is concerned ... we have no recourse but to trust you. The problem of how you can most effectively earn, maintain, reinforce and deserve that trust is, of course, a tough problem ... One thing, in any event, is clear: that there cannot be, there should not be, any external authority capable of reviewing the

WHAT THEY SAID IN 1974

degree of responsibility with which you exercise your own obligations to the truth . . .

Before American Society of Newspaper Editors/The Washington Post, 6-6:(A)22.

A. M. Rosenthal
Managing editor, "The New York Times" 1

American journalists have not found all the answers yet and have not even asked all the questions. We never achieve total satisfaction, and we get tired and grumpy. But we are sustained always by the realization that tomorrow there is another question to be asked, another answer to be dissected, another paper to put out, and that we can try yet again. I suppose that, if anything, that's our rose garden.

At City College of New York commencement, June 6/The New York Times, 6-7:20.

Dean Rusk
Professor of International Law, University of Georgia; Former Secretary of State of the United States 2

The press has a duty to get the news. There are times when public officials have a duty to keep their mouths shut. This creates a built-in tension between press and officials, which in my view is wholesome and must never be eliminated either by law or some sort of treaty between the press and public officials.

The Atlanta Journal and Constitution Magazine, 8-18:30.

3

The press demands complete candor from a public official on every subject except one—namely, what he thinks about the press. I think it's fair to say the press can dish it out, but doesn't like to take it.

The Atlanta Journal and Constitution Magazine, 8-18:30.

4

Let's get rid of this genial myth of the Fourth Estate . . . You [in the press] speak *to* the American people, not *for* them . . . That this should be so would seem to be elementary, because the American people have nothing to say about who are to be publishers and editors and reporters and columnists. We cannot admit in our constitutional system room for something called a "Fourth Estate," which has no democratic base.

Before American Society of Newspaper Editors/The Wall Street Journal, 9-25:14.

Jeffrey St. John
Political commentator 5

. . . organs of the media—be they liberal or conservative—maintain a split-level mentality over the "market of goods" and the "market of ideas." The media, with some exceptions, believes that the marketplace of ideas should enjoy freedom, yet it pursues a policy of advocating government control over the market of goods, i.e., business. Nevertheless, it is vigorous business enterprise that makes the market of ideas possible. It is my considered view that unless the mass media cures itself of this affliction of refusing to see that the market of ideas and the market of goods must have freedom from government controls, both markets will eventually perish and be replaced by the all-powerful authoritarian state. It is this fragmentation of freedom that poses the greatest danger, not just to the press, but to the entire American culture.

At Robert A. Taft Institute of Government seminar, Pepperdine University, July 11/ Vital Speeches, 8-15:661.

Richard S. Salant
President, Columbia Broadcasting System News 6

[On criticism about imbalance in news coverage]: What I have to worry most about is whether some of the younger, more timid reporters on my staff don't say, "What's the use of making waves—I'll just skip this sentence." I keep on telling them that they mustn't give in to that pressure. The whole thing does create a certain state of mind, however; and I have to admit that when I see a story with a couple of very strong lines in it . . . I say to myself, "Oh, my God, this is going to bring in lots of complaints; wouldn't it be nice if it hadn't happened." But I never let my feelings go any further than that.

Los Angeles Times, 5-16:(4)30.

Harrison Salisbury
Host, "Behind the Lines," Public Broadcasting Service; Former assistant managing editor, "The New York Times"

1

TV has demonstrated in the last couple of years that it's superlative in covering Washington; and this is, I think, something that nobody ever realized before. There's no question that the coverage of the Ervin Committee hearings [on Watergate] —not just having the cameras on those fellows, but all the commentary and explanations that went with it—was excellent. Even more so with the House Judiciary Committee hearings [on Watergate]. I think most people who witnessed those Judiciary proceedings on television are bound to conclude that far from cheapening the government process—as many commentators had predicted—the truth is that if you could get television into Congress it would probably revivify Congress.

Interview, New York/TV Guide, 11-30:16.

Eric Sevareid
News commentator, Columbia Broadcasting System

2

I've been in this business 40 years. I remember the real yellow press—the bad tabloids, the radio screamers like Walter Winchell who used to tout his favorite stocks on the air. That would never be allowed to happen today. The press is much better educated, much more responsible. Bias is not the basic internal enemy of the press, as the White House charges. It is haste. And in broadcasting, it is not only haste that is our enemy, but a compression of material.

Interview, Washington/ "W": a Fairchild publication, 6-14:11.

Frank Sinatra
Singer, Actor

3

Reporters are parasites . . . They're the hookers of the press. I wouldn't drink their water, let alone speak to them.

Melbourne, Australia/ Los Angeles Times, 7-10:(1)2.

Frank Stanton
Vice chairman, CBS, Inc.

4

[Calling for TV stations to present editorials]: To be a force [in the community] you [stations] must speak out boldly on controversial issues arising out of national and international, as well as local, events. To avoid controversy on major issues is sometimes to avoid disfavor—but also to avoid distinction.

Before National Broadcast Editorial Association, Washington, June 26/ The Washington Post, 6-27:(B)2.

Potter Stewart
Associate Justice, Supreme Court of the United States

5

It is quite possible to conceive of the survival of our republic without an autonomous press. For openness and honesty in government, for an adequate flow of information between the people and their representatives, for a sufficient check on autocracy and despotism, the traditional competition between the three branches of government, supplemented by vigorous political activity, might be enough. The press could be relegated to the status of a public utility. The guarantee of free speech would presumably put some limitation on the regulation to which the press could be subjected. But if there were no guarantee of free press, government could convert the communications media into a neutral "marketplace of ideas." Newspapers and television networks could then be required to promote contemporary government policy or current notions of social justice. Such a constitution is possible; it might work reasonably well. But it is not the Constitution the Founders wrote. It is not the Constitution that has carried us through nearly two centuries of national life. Perhaps our liberties might survive without an independent established press. But the Founders doubted it, and, in the year 1974, I think we can all be thankful for their doubts.

At Yale University Law School Sesquicentennial Convocation, Nov. 2/ The Washington Post, 11-11:(A)20.

Arthur Ochs Sulzberger
Publisher, "The New York Times"

1

[On being publisher of *The New York Times*]: You have to have highly competent people around you who aren't fearful of talking up. God knows, my editors aren't fearful and my business managers aren't fearful. You just can't live in isolation. You know, if I ran down to the city room with a front-page editorial and said, "Stop the presses," they'd put me in a white suit and have me taken away.

Interview, New York/
"W": a Fairchild publication, 1-25:11.

Jerald F. terHorst
Press Secretary to President of the
United States Gerald R. Ford

2

[On his relationship with the press]: I think it's essential for the country that the process continues as an adversary role. I think it would be just as bad if we had a cozy relationship as if we had a total breakdown in communications, which many of us in the press corps seemed to think existed at the [Nixon] White House at least the last year. So I think the absence of an adversary relationship would be very bad. However, I don't think it has to be a hostile relationship. There's no reason why we shouldn't be adversaries in the same way that Republicans and Democrats are adversaries, but still able to walk arm-in-arm out of the chamber after they've voted against each other; or lawyers [who] can maintain a friendly relationship after having fought each other in a court case. I think the adversary relationship ought to be on issues, not on a personality basis. Because once you slide off the issue ... and get into personality clashes, neither the press can serve its role well, nor, I don't think, the spokesman for the President can.

Interview, Washington/
The Christian Science Monitor, 8-19:3.

Clay T. Whitehead
Director, Federal Office of
Telecommunications Policy

3

[On Nixon Administration criticism of the press]: If you ask me the question the way the networks might phrase it, are they being any more favorable to Nixon, I'd have to say no. But this Administration has never worried about that; we're more concerned with over-all balance on all stories. In this regard, I think the situation has improved. And it has improved because we raised the subject. If we didn't do it, who would?

Interview/Los Angeles Times, 5-14:(4)12.

Richard E. Wiley
Chairman,
Federal Communications Commission

4

On the question of fairness in television news coverage, we [the FCC] have and will continue to intervene. But when it comes to objectivity, unless we find some solid extrinsic evidence—memos, edited film to show rigging, etc.—we simply can't step in. This policy predates the present Administration. Although we feel strongly that objectivity is part of the responsibility of a licensed station, there's nothing the FCC can do to make them include it in news broadcasts.

Los Angeles Times, 5-16:(4)29.

5

[On the TV Fairness Doctrine]: I think any kind of governmental intrusion into the journalistic process is not desirable. The Fairness Doctrine ... is premised on scarcity [of channel space] and the concept that TV licensees must act as public trustees. I look on it as a sort of necessary evil. On the other hand, I think that, in its dual obligation on broadcasters to devote a reasonable amount of time to discussion of controversial issues and to give an opportunity for contrasting views, it represents nothing more than the essence of good journalism. What I'm saying is that, if we don't have *unwarranted* governmental intrusion, if we don't second-guess every licensee's judgment, and only intervene where the case is clearly arbitrary and unreasonable, I think the Fairness Doctrine is a viable concept.

Interview, Washington/TV Guide, 7-27:29.

Robert D. Wood
*President, Columbia Broadcasting
System Television*

1

[On public criticism of news reporting] : The sensitive times are contributory. Nobody likes the news today. The news is upsetting . . . It's hard for many people to swallow. It does something to the psyche. It's the old story of blaming the messenger for bad news.

*Before CBS-TV affiliates, Los Angeles,
May 14/Daily Variety, 5-15:14.*

Ronald L. Ziegler
*Press Secretary to President of
the United States Richard M. Nixon*

2

I have not lost faith in the nation's press. I have become disappointed in certain segments of the Washington press—for its excesses, for its pre-judgments about people, and some of the professional conduct as exhibited in the briefings. People are preoccupied with the answers to the questions, and I think they should look to the questions asked as well. It takes courage for the press to break out of the herd instinct. More of the press should back up and assess itself.

*Interview,
San Clemente, Calif./
Newsweek,
1-21:23.*

Literature

Isaac Asimov
Author

1

I enjoy the mechanics of writing. Almost everybody that I know [who writes] would like to hold a finished book in his hands. But almost nobody that I know of likes the *process* of writing. But I do. I enjoy the act of typing. I enjoy the process of turning thoughts into words.

Interview, New York/
The Christian Science Monitor, 3-27:(F)1.

2

We say that television has replaced the book, that the reason few people read books nowadays is because everyone is watching TV. Nonsense! In the days before TV, everybody watched radio. In the days before radio, everyone went out to look at ball games. In the days before sports, people sat and looked at nothing.

Quote, 7-14:26.

Louis Auchincloss
Author, Lawyer

3

I enjoy [reading] William Styron, Norman Mailer, Jean Stafford and Mary McCarthy. Yet most of my reading is in the past. I like to take an author whose work is complete and go right through it. Most recently I have read Anatole France—some 30 volumes. I enjoy the sense of saturation in another writer. He need not be great. The sense of comprehension that comes with an inclusive reading can be its own reward.

Interview, New York/
Publishers Weekly, 2-18:12.

Daniel J. Boorstin
Historian, National Museum of History
and Technology, Washington

4

[On his recently being awarded a Pulitzer Prize in history for a book he wrote]: Of course, if you're a writer you want people to read your books. A prize also encourages you to go back to your typewriter. And it's nice to be put in the company of many who have won a Pulitzer. But it's best not to take these things too seriously. There's always the danger that the author and others may think the book is better than it is.

Interview, Los Angeles/
Los Angeles Times, 5-10:(4)13.

Jorge Luis Borges
Author

5

I'm not a writer at all. I'm a bogus writer. One day soon I will be discovered. They will find me to be an imposter—just like the characters in some of my stories. Personally, I don't like my stories, but one writes what one can. If I could write like Conrad or Emerson . . . But to write like Borges—it is not so much.

Interview, Buenos Aires/
Los Angeles Times, 6-30:(1)2.

Ray Bradbury
Author

6

. . . science fiction makes metaphors of ideas, turns ideas into toys. It's the most incredible field to be in . . . philosophy, architecture, ecology, political science, urban planning, transportation, literature, poetry, theology . . . it includes everything. Even if you're self-educated, as am I, by the time you're 35 you have a total education!

Los Angeles Herald-Examiner, 3-10:(F)4.

Matthew J. Bruccoli
Professor of English,
University of South Carolina

7

Perhaps the greatest flaw critics make is judging a book in terms of its material . . . You can imagine Herman Melville coming to his publisher with his new manuscript. They ask him what it's about, and he says, "It's about a one-legged captain who's had his leg bitten off by a whale, and his search for the whale." It wouldn't have sounded that promising. When [F. Scott] Fitzgerald wrote *[The Great] Gatsby,* he was told you couldn't write seriously about a bootlegger. If a man cares intensely enough about tiddledy winks, his book about tiddledy winks will be a great novel.

Interview/
"W": a Fairchild publication, 2-8:9.

Agatha Christie
Author

1

...if you really want to write, you must first of all decide the kind of style you want to write in, and then read books that have that style. That will really give you your own information and you will know what you want to do. Then you will have to put up with a lot of publishers returning books that you have written or magazines returning stories; and that, of course, is very depressing because you feel that you will never progress. But you have got to go through that period, probably. Everything in life is partly hard work and partly luck. And luck is really the important thing. There are lot[s] of lucky things: You may win a large sum on a premium bond, or you may find that some publisher likes your book. When those things happen to you, it is very encouraging and you go ahead with a feeling that there is a chance for you and that you can go on.

Interview/Los Angeles Times,
12-15:(Calendar)65.

Archibald Cox
Professor of Law, Harvard University

2

Contemporary literature and the arts tell of man the absurd, the pervert, the dropout, but rarely man the hero, or even the tragic—for the tragic requires a degree of nobility, and few current authors see nobility in man.

Before graduating class of Stanford
University/San Francisco Examiner, 7-19:35.

Joan Crawford
Actress

3

Books—be they rare, first or early editions, current best-sellers or reference volumes—are a way of life for me. I take as much pleasure thumbing through a dictionary as I do the works of an essayist, dramatist, librettist or composer. Books can be like old and trusted friends. They are there when you want or need them, and they offer knowledge as well as comfort, peace as well as pleasure, and affection as well as companionship.

Interview/The Dallas Times Herald, 7-5:(F)3.

Len Deighton
Author

4

Just as cowboys are good for movies, spies are good for books. Part of the reason for this is that in this century we have for all sorts of reasons—some of them political—become interested in the phenomenon of people saying one thing and meaning another.

San Francisco Examiner, 6-11:30.

John Fowles
Author

5

I love it when a story is still alive. Then it's still changeable, still fluid, and you can take it anywhere, do anything with it. Once it's printed, it's set and frozen, like a bronze cast of a sculpture. You can't shape it any more. My whole interest is in the act of writing itself. Being published is a kind of death.

Interview, New York/
Publishers Weekly, 11-25:6.

6

In theatre or cinema you are presented with an image. It's a passive experience. Reading is an active experience. You have to create your own image. That's one reason why fiction cannot die.

Interview, New York/
The New York Times, 11-27:24.

Ernest K. Gann
Author

7

I don't like any of my books. You start out [writing] and you know it's going to be the

(ERNEST K. GANN)

greatest masterpiece ever written—better than Hemingway or Steinbeck or any of those guys ... Two-thirds and I wish I'd never started it; but I tell myself, "I'll try to rescue it." When it's finished I say, "Let's tear it up" ... It's pure frustration. I've never written a book I'm anywhere near satisfied with.

Interview, San Francisco/
San Francisco Examiner, 3-3:(A)4.

Raymond C. Hagel
Chairman and president,
Macmillan, Inc., publishers
1

Publishers often tend to do what their competitors do because of their own insecurity. One's associates are likely to point to another house and say, "Well, look what they are doing," as if the other fellow's opinion represents a safe-conduct pass for us. A fair number of our more successful books, and I dare say those of other publishers also, are books that previously were turned down by a lot of people. You have to have the courage to rely on your own judgment. It doesn't make a particle of difference whether the manuscript before you is a first novel or a last novel. What counts is whether you think your house can bring it in as a successful book, whether you want the author and whether you think he will stay with you.

Interview, New York/
Publishers Weekly, 7-22:37.

Joseph Heller
Author
2

I don't think I could write a full, straight narrative book. I couldn't make it interesting. I can't describe things well and dislike the logical progression found in traditional novels. I started out as a kid copying Hemingway, John O'Hara and anybody else I read in the magazines. With *Catch-22* I finally derived my own style, and a lot of reviewers said it wasn't a novel. But I have to lead with my strengths. I tend to rely on my imagination, sense of the bizarre, and the comic ... I don't think litera-

ture is a reproduction of life. I think it has to distort reality.

Interview/Chicago Tribune, 9-30:(3)14.

3

I think when a book is finished, and the editors like it, and it's been handed in, an author goes through a period of nervous craziness. Some writers invest in Canadian Uranium stocks, others change agents or wives or commit suicide. Some writers hear "voices." It's not a good time in which to trust one's own judgment.

Interview/
The New York Times Book Review, 10-6:30.

Eric Hoffer
Author, Philosopher
4

For me, writing is a physical necessity. I have to write in order to feel well. I think it is that way for many people. D. H. Lawrence said that you shed your illnesses—your neurosis—while writing. That explains why there are so many volumes and volumes in the libraries: People write one book, and then they keep on writing because they discover that they feel better while doing it.

Interview, San Francisco/
San Francisco Examiner & Chronicle,
7-21:(California Living)38.

Eugene Ionesco
Author, Playwright
5

I've never had the impression that I was doing something important or profound. But since others say that my work is important and have written so many books on me, either they must be right or mad.

At Teheran University, Iran/
The New York Times, 10-22:37.

Louis L'Amour
Author
6

Readers want to be entertained, and they are curious about how other people solved their problems. A good Western does both. Readers, unfortunately, have been short-changed because most modern novelists are so hung-up on Freud, on ideology, on sex and on violence that they can't tell a good story. It's no wonder people are charmed by a fast-moving action-packed Western. I strive for a simple storyline and relatively uncomplicated characters. And though I wasn't influenced by Zane Grey, I respect his ability to tell a good, accurate Western story. My own writing is sparse. And I don't look down on my readers. I try to pretend I'm a guy sitting around a campfire telling a story.

Interview, Los Angeles/
Los Angeles Times, 5-19:(Calendar)22.

Cornel Lengyel
Poet

1

The poet tries to translate the buzzing confusion that surrounds him from birth to death. He strives to interpret his particular pains and pleasures, to appease his private fears and hungers, to give form and meaning to the more permanent and perplexing facts of life.

Interview, Georgetown, Calif./
Los Angeles Times, 2-13:(4)4.

Anita Loos
Author

2

I write for money. Writing is the only racket I know. If I were Shakespeare, I wouldn't use that word; but I think the great majority of authors shouldn't be dignified too much, including myself. Not that I don't work at writing. I will say I write and re-write about 20 times, but it is not a struggle. I look on it more as a crossword puzzle. It is the thing I enjoy most in life; but I don't look at it as literature, just crossword puzzles.

Interview, New York/People, 8-5:26.

Norman Mailer
Author

3

I always start a book for money. If you've been married five times, you have to . . . There are a lot of writers making money. Why is it only news when I do?

People, 3-11:22.

Andre Malraux
Author; Former Minister of State
for Culture of France

4

Of the great novelists of my generation, who is [still writing fiction]? Hemingway did not finish his last novel. Gide did not write a real novel in the last 10 years of his life. Sartre abandoned the novel. So have I. Why? I do not really know. Perhaps because the novel calls for a strong narrative power. Narration today has been replaced by the image. The publicized and televised violence of every-day existence, hijacking and all sorts of minor events that used to be a mystery for the novelists in the past have helped to kill the narrative novel. I mean a certain kind of novel with which we are all familiar—going from Balzac to Tolstoy. This sort of narrative novel had already received a blow with the publication of *Madame Bovary.* Do you know what Alexandre Dumas' reaction was when he read *Bovary?* He told his son, "If this is what literature has become, we've had it!" And right he was. Just compare *Bovary* with *The Three Musketeers.*

Interview, Verrieres-le-Buisson,
France/Time, 4-8:34.

James A. Michener
Author

5

. . . there is a special satisfaction in [writing] books; a tremendous satisfaction in seeing it done, knowing it'll be around for the next several years and that you've done it and there it is: a permanent record of your thoughts and experiences as of that date.

Interview, Greeley, Colo./
Los Angeles Times, 8-28:(1)28.

6

I have always felt talent is common. There is much more of it around than we suspect. But disciplined talent, organized talent, apparently is pretty rare. It's a valuable commodity. I think that anybody could write a book; anybody can write as well as I write, but very few do.

Interview, Greeley, Colo./
Los Angeles Times, 8-28:(1)28.

WHAT THEY SAID IN 1974

(JAMES A. MICHENER)

1

If there's a young person around who really wants to write, and he or she does not feel to begin with that they can write a hell of a lot better than me or John O'Hara or Pearl Buck or Saul Bellow, then he's not really needed. Without that arrogance you don't have much to work on.

Interview, Pipersville, Pa./People, 9-30:57.

Henry Miller
Author

2

It's true that art never changes anything. Every writer, when he begins, thinks he'll devastate the world. But you can't cure injustice. You can't eradicate evil. When he's working, the artist thinks he's a god. But by the time the publishers, the public and the critics get through with him, he's lucky to feel that he's alive. He's nobody . . .

At Actors and Directors Lab, Los Angeles, July 20/Los Angeles Times, 7-24:(4)11.

Anais Nin
Author

3

[Why she writes]: To create a world of my own . . . a climate, a country, an atmosphere in which I could breathe, reign and recreate myself.

At Authors and Celebrities Forum, Los Angeles/ Los Angeles Herald-Examiner, 4-11:(A)17.

Lance Rentzel
Football player, Los Angeles "Rams"

4

[On the books he has written]: An athlete gets a measure of personal reinforcement every day. When you run a pass pattern and get open, you know you've accomplished something even if nobody throws you the ball. You always have something tangible to tell you that you're doing well. When you're writing, you have nothing until you're finished. That was very hard for me to adjust to. It's the loneliest job in the world.

Los Angeles Times, 6-17:(3)1.

Adrienne Rich
Poet; Winner, 1974 National Book Award for poetry

5

I think women's poetry is becoming very tribal. Instead of sitting alone in your garret scribbling love verses which nobody will ever read, I think a lot of women's poetry is becoming very oral. It's not written just to be read on a page but to be read aloud. At the end of her career, [Sylvia] Plath said that she had this compulsion to read her poems aloud that she'd never had before. She was always wanting to read them to people, and I think that, in a sense, that's been happening to a lot of us. I know it's been happening to me. Without consciously trying for a more oral style, it's been evolving out of necessity and out of my concerns, and I think that's been happening to a lot of women. There's a tremendous desire to communicate and a feeling that there are people you can communicate with . . . I think a lot of women feel that in poetry they're finding roots into the unconscious, and a voice, and it's very important to them.

Interview, New York/ The Christian Science Monitor, 5-31:(F)2.

Francoise Sagan
Author

6

There are moments when you feel trapped, ill at ease. A year later, the same feeling can turn out to be the theme of a book. To write a book you have to be tormented by something.

Interview, Paris/ "W": a Fairchild publication, 5-17:2.

J. D. Salinger
Author

7

[On not, by his own choice, having had anything published since 1962]: There is a marvelous peace in not publishing. It's peaceful . . . publishing is a terrible invasion of my privacy. I like to write. I love to write. But I write just for myself and my own pleasure.

Telephone interview, Cornish, N.H./ The New York Times, 11-3:(1)1.

May Sarton
Author, Poet

1

[On the somewhat late recognition she is now receiving]: For many years I felt I was under a gravestone. I wanted to push it up and shout, "Here I am." It is very hard to really *know* your work is good, but I have always had some proof of it in the very strong, moving letters I have received from my readers. This kind of support is very important to a writer who does not make money. You cannot live on no recognition. You must have some.
Interview/Publishers Weekly, 6-24:16.

Jean-Louis Servan-Schreiber
Author, Journalist

2

The book is today almost certainly the best vehicle for the communication of important ideas. Nothing else is nearly as effective if you have a message. Whatever is printed in a book automatically commands more respect and attention than anything in newspapers and magazines. An article, a speech, a TV appearance produces no echo, no fallout. But an author of a book can be sure that the right people will read what he has to say. Reviewers, often experts in the same field, will discuss his ideas. Perhaps he will be interviewed, and therefore can expand on them further for a wider audience. As a result, a book's message is very widely dispersed, and in that sense it is the most modern and efficient of media.
Interview, New York/Publishers Weekly, 9-2:6.

G. Roysce Smith
Executive director,
American Booksellers Association

3

Of the 10 novels you find on a best-seller list today, the last five aren't selling well enough to have been on a best-seller list five years ago. Today a best-seller in non-fiction sells twice as much as a novel. For example, *Everything You Always Wanted To Know About Sex* just about doubled compared with the sales of *Love Story*. Today people want help and most non-fiction is designed for that type of survival tactic. How-to-do books, crafts books, *The Whole Earth Catalog, The Joy of Sex, I'm OK, You're OK*—these are the kinds of things people want today. Fiction has had a lot of the wind blown out of its sails by things that have happened. The other day, [Watergate-implicated former aide to President Nixon] Jeb Stuart Magruder was autographing his book here and he got more attention than a movie star would have.
At American Booksellers Association
convention, Washington/
The Washington Post, 6-6:(B)10.

Mickey Spillane
Author

4

A "writer" is someone who always sells. An "author" is one who writes a book that makes a big splash, and then never comes up with another one. James Jones, for instance, hasn't really had a major hit since *From Here to Eternity.*
Interview, Los Angeles/
Los Angeles Herald-Examiner, 1-14:(B)3.

Sol Stein
Author; President, Stein & Day, publishers

5

The performing arts are not part of our culture in terms of passing them on from generation to generation. The only way is through hardbound permanent books. There were 10,000 books in my father's library; I got my early education according to my ability to climb. People don't have libraries now; they have bric-a-brac. And it worries me.
Interview, San Francisco/
San Francisco Examiner, 4-18:24.

Gloria Steinem
Author; Editor, "Ms." magazine

6

When a woman actually writes a book and takes the manuscript in to a publishing house, it is regarded as a "woman's book." They will say things to you like, "Well, we've already done 2 women's novels this year," just as they would say, "We've done a black novel this year."
Quote, 3-10:218.

403

Irving Stone
Author

1

There are only two kinds [of writers]: the natural and the unnatural. If a person takes up writing because it looks easy, simple, a surefire route to fame and fortune, that person is unnatural, and the writing process is slow and painful. But if he has great stories to tell or important values to communicate, that person is a natural, and the writing process flows easily. That's the way it is for me.

Interview, Beverly Hills, Calif./
Los Angeles Times, 5-12:(Home)18.

Studs Terkel
Author

2

I think there's a declining interest in fiction because the life we lead today is fiction. It's so surreal. If *Catch 22* came out today, it would be a documentary, not a satire.

At American Booksellers Association
convention, Washington/
The Washington Post, 6-6:(B)10.

Gore Vidal
Author

3

The novel is dead, because it's impossible to create characters as one-dimensional as today's reader.

Interview, Beverly Hills, Calif./
The Dallas Times Herald, 1-22:(C)1.

4

When I started, novelists were at the center of the culture. Now we're on the periphery; we're where the poets used to be. Now it's the film director or the trendy politician or the talking head on television—these are the hot people. And guys like [Norman] Mailer, [Truman] Capote and myself have never given up the dream of being central to our culture, so we have become performers. Truman became a novelist in order to climb into the society into which I was born and have been trying to escape ever since. My real contempt for Truman is that he could take that world seriously. But I'm more tolerant as I get older, and there is a marvelous line in Henry James in which he said that a career as a social climber is as legitimate a career as any other.

Interview/Newsweek, 11-18:97E.

Irving Wallace
Author

5

When I was very young, I created a mythical person in my mind who kept saying, "Where are the pages?" For me, there are two unhappy states: One is writing and the other is *not* writing. I work harder today than when I really needed money. I have so many stories to tell. I'm full of things I want to write . . . When I write "The End," I have a sharp sense of loss— because I've *lived* with the characters. I really hate to let go. And I wonder what happens to them afterwards.

Interview, Los Angeles/
Los Angeles Times, 2-17:(Home)27.

6

I'm simply driven to writing like an addict; but it wasn't always that way. I used to believe, in my youth, that writing was something you did when a flash of inspiration hit you—you only worked when you felt like it. And of course, I never felt like working that much. Then I went through a period of reading biographies of great writers, and it turned out that all of them—from Tolstoy to Flaubert—just glued themselves to the desk. I was first forced to write a certain number of pages each day in the Army, which was the beginning of discipline. But when I started writing my own books, I had to create a mythical taskmaster for whom I labored. I developed intricate systems of bookkeeping, numbers of pages, charts and other paraphernalia to force myself to write. Once I get into a book, however, I'm off and can't be stopped.

Interview, Los Angeles/
Los Angeles Times, 3-31:(Calendar)65.

Frederick Wilhelmsen
Professor of Philosophy, University of Dallas

7

This nation [the U.S.] is unique in that it is grounded in books and the written word. If you learn to read young and reading becomes your dominant way of communication, you're going to develop into a certain kind of person. The person who reads a great deal projects into the future—he dreams a dream, he visualizes the distant future, he uses his imagination.

At Dallas Women's Club, Jan. 16/
The Dallas Times Herald, 1-17:(C)2.

Tennessee Williams
Playwright

1

Writers are the most disagreeable, unpleasant people in the world.

Television interview, New Orleans/
"The Dick Cavett Show,"
American Broadcasting Company, 8-22.

Medicine and Health

James Armstrong
Bishop, Dakotas area,
United Methodist Church
1

[On the Roman Catholic Church's stand against abortion]: With all due respect, should a male-dominated religious hierarchy determine the moral posture and legal status of the opposite sex when the woman in question is caught up in a dilemma no man can fully understand? ... A church that proclaims celibacy to reflect the highest levels of excellence and that takes the dimmest possible view of scientific methods of birth control is not in a logical position to impose its view on abortion on the remainder of the citizenry.

Before Senate Judiciary Subcommittee,
Washington, 3-8:(A)2.

Christiaan Barnard
Surgeon; Heart-transplant specialist
2

[On his transplanting a second heart in a patient while retaining the first]: You know, I've never claimed to be original in what I do because there are very few things in this world today that are original. But the funny thing about it is that when you do something, they [other doctors] always have a lot of criticism about what you do. Someone once told me that it is much better to light one candle of knowledge than to sit around all day complaining about the darkness of ignorance. I've lit one candle. Maybe it's going to be blown out. But at least I've tried to put some light in this darkness of ignorance.

Interview/The New York Times, 11-29:24.

John R. Bartels, Jr.
Administrator, Drug Enforcement
Administration of the United States
3

Anyone who says heroin is not as debilitating as alcohol has been living in an ivory tower. If I'm an alcoholic I can still hold a job. Sure, it brings heartbreak and tragedy. But the one thing I don't do as an alcoholic is steal $40 to $50 a day to support the habit.

The National Observer, 7-20:3.

Harry A. Blackmun
Associate Justice, Supreme Court of
the United States
4

[On last year's Supreme Court ruling legalizing abortions]: The thing that interests me about the decision is the personal abuse heaped upon me. I've never seen such an outpouring of hate mail, a lot of it form mail. It chills me to think that someone can sit down and say, "Forty of us must write letters." And it's a new experience for me to go places ... and be picketed and called Pontius Pilate, Herod and the Butcher of Dachau and accused of being personally responsible for 500,000 deaths in the past year.

News conference, St. Paul, Minn.,
Feb. 4/The Washington Post, 2-6:(A)11.

Balfour Brickner
Rabbi; Director, New York Federation of
Reformed Synagogues, Union of American
Hebrew Congregations
5

[Approving of abortion]: [Women should be free] from the whims of biological roulette, and free of the ideologies and theologies which insist that, in a world already groaning to death with over-population, with hate and poverty, that there is still some noble merit or purpose to indiscriminate reproduction.

Before Senate Judiciary Subcommittee on
Constitutional Amendments, Washington,
March 7/The New York Times, 3-8:11.

Morris E. Chafetz
Director, National Institute on Alcohol Abuse and Alcoholism, Department of Health, Education and Welfare of the United States
1

By every measurement, alcohol is the major drug problem this country faces. We Americans as a society have never learned how to use alcohol. But you can teach your children how not to abuse it; you can teach them there are ways to develop responsible drinking behavior . . . It means not tolerating drunkenness. If you and I go out drinking and I get drunk, you may laugh or humor me or something like that; but our society would not put pressure on me as having behaved in a very negative way. Yet we know that those societies that use alcohol and do not permit or accept getting drunk have fewer alcohol problems. I'm speaking of Italy, Israel, China, Spain, Greece and Japan before World War II when the Japanese took on the American drinking mode.

Interview, Rockville, Md./
Los Angeles Times, 1-24:(2)7.

2

[On how much a person has to drink to be an alcoholic]: I don't care about the amount. If you come to interview me and have to pop in two shots, you've got an alcohol problem. If I have to pop a couple of shots to get up to the podium, I've got an alcohol problem. I don't have to knock off a fifth and be lying in the gutter. That's crazy. Same thing with malignancy. If you've got a tumor, it doesn't have to spread all over your body before it's a problem.

Interview/People, 12-23:24.

John Cardinal Cody
Roman Catholic Archbishop of Chicago
3

[Arguing against abortion]: Unless America is prepared to protect unborn human lives, it cannot with confidence guarantee the protection of any human life.

Before Senate Judiciary Subcommittee on
Constitutional Amendments, Washington,
March 7/San Francisco Examiner, 3-8:12.

Alistair Cooke
Chief United States correspondent,
"The Guardian" (England)
4

The thing that horrifies me most about [TV] commercials is the medical brainwashing that the family gets on television. It seems to me that it easily outweighs any lessons in chemistry or biology that the child picks up in school. When my own children were very small, I used to say, "I'll show you a book which tells you that that is not the way the stomach works at all—that you don't just take a tablet that goes 'pssssst,' and then feel great." We [the U.S.] as a nation pride ourselves on being medically very literate. We love medical jargon: We prefer "lesions" to "swellings," and "clavicles" to "shoulder blades," and so on. Yet I truly believe that the body of our knowledge about medicine is fed to us from a very early age by commercials—and it's idiotic medicine. Mostly, it's either harmful or useless.

Interview, Washington/
U.S. News & World Report, 4-15:49.

Terence Cardinal Cooke
Roman Catholic Archbishop of New York
5

[Supporting a proposed Constitutional amendment against abortion]: No person has the right to say that the innocent life of another human being may be taken at a particular point in time. Last year's Supreme Court decision [in favor of] abortion was, in effect, an attack on human life. [The proposed amendment] would clearly establish that the unborn child is a person in the eyes of the law. It would insure that the child would no longer be victimized by a so-called right of privacy which in fact permits abortion as a matter of convenience.

At Family Life Celebration, New York,
Jan. 13/San Francisco Examiner, 6-14:8.

John A. D. Cooper
President,
Association of American Medical Colleges
6

There is a lot of public criticism of the medical profession [in the U.S.]. Certainly, in some geographical areas there is a doctor shortage. Twenty to 40 million people don't have

WHAT THEY SAID IN 1974

(JOHN A. D. COOPER)

adequate care; 131 U.S. counties are without a physician. But we do have 180 physicians per 100,000 people in this country—more than Canada, Great Britain and Sweden.

Interview, Washington/
"W": a Fairchild publication, 1-11:15.

Darrell C. Crain
Physician; Former president,
Medical Society of the District of Columbia 1

... it [is] time to address the larger problem of when life might be terminated in those people who no longer live in a productive manner. I [am] thinking of the large number of aged and infirm persons in nursing homes who are a burden to themselves and to their families and to society as a whole and who are being kept alive without any particular purpose. This is an extremely broad subject with many complications. I would include in it such cases as hopeless cancer, stroke, post-accident paralyses, advanced senility, that sort of thing ... There are immediate thoughts against it. Those opposed said, "Who are we to play God?" My point is that people play God all the time. For example, judges play God when they pass sentences. Having a commission such as I suggest [to make euthanasia decisions in specific cases] would be the humanitarian thing to do. That's the argument in favor of it.

Interview, Nov. 1/
The Washington Post, 11-2:(B)4.

Robert L. DuPont
Director, Federal Special Action Office for
Drug Abuse Prevention 2

[Saying heroin is often used casually]: It's very much like people who drink. We're taught that having a drink is a pleasant experience. This attacks the concept held by so many people that any person taking heroin must have a desperate problem. Many do it for recreation, just like having a drink. It's not an attempt necessarily to solve a deep psychological problem.

The Washington Post, 2-5:(C)5.

3

... I have become convinced that our attitude toward the problem of marijuana use is both fragmented and largely counterproductive. We do not want our young people to use marijuana, yet they are using it in record numbers and telling us as they do so that it is probably safer medically than our pills and alcohol. We fear that the use of marijuana will lead to deeper involvement with other drugs, yet fail to perceive that the use of any drug—alcohol and pills included—can create a climate in which more drug use is tolerated and thus lead to the same end.

Before Senate Subcommittee on Alcoholism
and Narcotics, Washington, Nov. 19/
The Christian Science Monitor, 11-20:6.

4

A year ago we had talked about turning the corner [on drug abuse]. But now ... I don't think realistically we can talk about ending the problem. The idea was that we were going to wage a war on drug abuse and that if we just put in enough troops and enough armament, we would have a victory and there would no longer be a problem. The better analogy now would be to weeding a garden ... it's a constant problem and we have to keep at it all the time.

News conference, San Francisco,
Dec. 12/Los Angeles Times, 12-13:(1)18.

James O. Eastland
United States Senator, D–Mississippi 5

If the cannabis [marijuana] epidemic continues to spread at the rate of the post-Berkeley period [since 1965], we may find ourselves saddled with a large population of semi-zombies—of young people acutely afflicted by the amotivational syndrome. The spread of the epidemic has been facilitated by the fact that most of our media and most of the academicians who have been articulate on the subject have been disposed to look upon marijuana as a relatively innocuous drug.

San Francisco Examiner & Chronicle,
10-6:(This World)2.

Gerald R. Ford
Vice President of the United States

1

[A U.S. national health-insurance system should include a continuance of] our present system which allows a patient to choose his own physician. I doubt that any other approach would be acceptable to the great majority of Americans seeking health care or to those that deliver the health care. The integrity of the patient-doctor relationship must be maintained. It is essential that any plan be based on our present delivery system of private health care. To let a vast new Federal bureaucracy take over our health-care system would be a burden which would be unbearable in cost. And to many, unbearable in principle.

At dedication of Annenberg Building of Mount Sinai Medical Center, New York, May 26/The New York Times, 5-27:15.

Ephraim Friedman
Dean, Boston University Medical School

2

Enactment [in the U.S.] of a comprehensive program of national health insurance is only a matter of time. This will increase the demand for more and better training of physicians. Society, for better or worse, right or wrong, wants more doctors and more-complete health care.

Interview/The New York Times, 6-2:(1)51.

Paul Harvey
News commentator,
American Broadcasting Company

3

In an [era] of sterile, clinical, computerized medicine, you wish that all doctors might have the bedside manner of the TV doctors. But a real-life Marcus Welby—for all his empathy, for all his immense compassion and genuine concern for alleviating human suffering and extending human life—might not be accepted in any of today's medical schools where the sole criterion for admission is academic excellence.

Quote, 8-25:180.

Robert Heath
Chairman, department of psychiatry,
Tulane University

4

[Saying marijuana is not safe to use]: The active ingredient in marijuana impairs the brain circuitry. We seem to be playing with dangerous, dangerous stuff ... Alcohol is a simple drug with a temporary effect. Marijuana is complex with a persisting effect ... I personally don't give a damn if people drink whiskey or smoke pot, but the facts should be out. Marijuana damages the brain.

People, 12-9:12,13.

Charles B. Huggins
Professor of Surgery, University of Chicago

5

[Saying he does not believe the viral theory of cancer]: Not only am I not buying it, I am denying it. Oh, there may be a few types of cancers involving viruses; but to attribute all cancers to a virus is to ignore a variety of other causes. Focusing on the virus fills a logical need of man—logical but wrong—to find a single, simple enemy to shoot at. It will make everybody happy. But nature cannot be forced.

At seminar sponsored by American Cancer Society, St. Augustine, Fla./ The Washington Post, 5-26:(K)5.

Clifford H. Keene
President, Kaiser Foundation Hospitals and
Kaiser Foundation Health Plan

6

[On his organization's health-maintenance, group health-care system]: The reason our plans work is because we hire the best managers and take full advantage of central planning and purchasing, quick assessment of needs, and skilled administration. Our major aim is to do a good job and reflect well on the Kaiser name. Health care is a big business that needs to be run with that in mind ... Doctors are basically arrogant people who make their own decisions and don't take advice easily. That's why they cannot organize things well. That's where we come in.

Interview, Oakland, Calif./ San Francisco Examiner, 1-22:3.

John H. Knowles
President, Rockefeller Foundation; Former
director, Massachusetts General Hospital

7

I believe that in the macrocosm of world health there is a striking similarity among physi-

WHAT THEY SAID IN 1974

(JOHN H. KNOWLES)

cians and medical educators, regardless of their countries' level of development, what with their emphasis on acute, curative medicine, their de-emphasis on or neglect of public-health programs designed to detect and prevent disease, and their unwillingness or inability to see health in the larger context of population size and density, and of the total environment—locally, nationally and internationally. Perhaps we should all settle for this, but I for one am unwilling to do so; for quite aside from the crucial functions of acute, curative medicine, I know of no other group which has as much power in its hands to improve the quality of life—no other group whose professed calling has a more humanitarian and philanthropic base—no other group of similar high intellectual capacity.

At Hunter College-Bellevue School of Nursing, New York/The National Observer, 4-27:18.

1

They [the American Medical Association] are very powerful and have almost consistently lobbied against things that were needed by the people—the public-health program and Medicare, which they fought for 30 years. They lobbied against the group-practice mechanism hammer-and-tongs. Every major piece of legislation or social change in this country which has benefited the people has been steadfastly fought by the AMA. I think they are a relatively humorless bunch of merchants and that's it. But they are the far right keeping the far left honest; and so I think they do perform a function, because their counterpart, the far left, is equally doctrinaire and ideologically frozen.

Interview, New York/People, 5-6:26.

John Cardinal Krol
Roman Catholic Archbishop of Philadelphia

2

[Arguing against abortion]: Every week, since the Supreme Court's decision of January 22, 1973 [legalizing abortion], there have been as many deaths from abortion as there were deaths at Nagasaki as a result of the atomic bomb . . . The right to life is not an invention of the Catholic Church or any other church. It

is a basic human right which must undergird any civilized society.

Before Senate Judiciary Subcommittee on Constitutional Amendments, Washington, March 7/The New York Times, 3-8:11.

3

[Arguing against abortion]: If unborn infants in the protective wombs of their mothers are not innocent and defenseless human beings, then—in God's name—what are they? And if unborn infants are human beings, then no human court has the authority to define away their rights and no conscientious person has the right to remain silent or satisfied while the tragedy of the wanton destruction of innocent, unborn human life continues. We cannot, we dare not and we will not remain silent. In determining our priority for social action, there would seem to be no task more urgent, no need more immediate and, in fact, no work more meritorious than that of guaranteeing to infants for generations yet to come the sacred God-given right to life.

Before National Conference of Catholic Bishops, New York, Nov. 18/ The New York Times, 11-19:15.

Jean Mayer
Professor of Nutrition, Harvard University

4

No one should be able to graduate from high school or university without a solid course in human health. The absence of adequate health education is deplorable when it is realized that nobody tells people how to prevent heart disease but the government is willing to spend [through a projected national health-insurance program] thousands of dollars after you get sick.

Los Angeles, April 15/ Los Angeles Times 4-16:(2)1.

5

The glamor in medicine is with acute treatment. Doctors find it much more exciting to revive a patient after a coronary than to help him prevent it in the first place.

Quote, 10-6:313.

Karl Z. Morgan
Health physicist,
Georgia Institute of Technology

1

I believe members of the medical professions in these countries [Europe] are much better informed [than those in the U.S.] about the risks of exposure to ionizing radiation [in X rays] and have given more attention to avoiding unnecessary patient exposure. The average doctor or dentist in the United States knows absolutely nothing of the effects of ionizing radiation in man and yet he insists he has the absolute right to deliver any form of radiation he wants.

Before American Cancer Society seminar for
science writers, St. Augustine, Fla., March 29/
The Washington Post, 3-31:(E)1.

Robert Moser
Physician; Editor, "The Journal of
the American Medical Association"

2

I cherish the opportunity to speak to the patient; and the first five minutes with him is the most precious interval in the entire interview. I do not want to read from a computer printout as I address my patient. I want eyeball-to-eyeball contact. I want to listen to the inflection of voice. I want to study body language, facial expression, color, sweat, thought sequence and the other hidden or open messages that pass between two human beings when they talk to each other. If this is done by some other person or by some blasted machine, the initial energy of the interview is siphoned off.

Before American Medical Association,
Chicago/San Francisco Examiner, 7-4:18.

Richard M. Nixon
President of the United States

3

[Saying a health-insurance program run solely by the Federal government would reduce medical-care quality]: If medical care is free but poor, that's not right, and it is not the American way of doing things. When I go to a hospital or a doctor, I want the doctor working for the individual and not for the government.

At dedication of Cedars of Lebanon Hospital,
Miami, Feb. 14/Los Angeles Times, 2-15:(1)5.

Paul VI
Pope

4

. . . the precious right to life—that most important of all human rights—must be affirmed anew, together with the condemnation of that massive aberration which is the destruction of innocent human life, at whatever stage it may be, through the heinous crimes of abortion or euthanasia.

Before United Nations Committee on
Apartheid, Vatican City, May 22/
The Washington Post, 5-23:(C)6.

Ronald Reagan
Governor of California

5

I know when an American goes abroad he has to get punctured about 15 times to guarantee his health while he's there. But I understand that when people come to America from other countries they don't have to get punctured. We must be doing something right. Here is one country in the world that, if you have to be sick, this is the place to be sick, not someplace else. Have we ever checked up . . . to see how unsuccessful government medicine has been in the rest of the world?

At National Governors Conference, Seattle,
June 3/Los Angeles Times, 6-4:(1)16.

Abraham A. Ribicoff
United States Senator, D—Connecticut;
Former Secretary of Health, Education
and Welfare of the United States

6

The implementation of the Medicare program was a monument to what dedicated civil servants can do. However, implementation of that program stretched our administrative capacity close to the limit, creating . . . a host of difficulties, some of which have still not been resolved successfully . . . A fully Federalized health-insurance program would, of course, pose enormous administrative burdens well beyond the Medicare program. Imposing a giant new Federal health program would only disillusion many by promising more than it can deliver. We simply do not have the administrative capacity to administer and pay claims for over 200 million Americans, deal with 7,000

WHAT THEY SAID IN 1974

(ABRAHAM A. RIBICOFF)

hospitals, over 320,000 doctors and countless other segments of the health industry. Nor does our health-care system have the capacity to deliver all the increased demand for services which fully Federalized national health-insurance would induce.

Before House Ways and Means Committee,
Washington/Human Events, 6-1:1.

Russell B. Roth
Former president,
American Medical Association

1

[On proposed national health-insurance programs] : Time was when our profession was accused of being against everything, and those times have changed. We are now attempting to be constructive, and if national health insurance is indeed the way to go, we think it is important that our profession enunciate the principles which should apply. The question that I had in mind . . . is a matter of priorities. Inflation is the Number 1 problem before our country today. Any one of these [insurance] plans would be to some degree inflationary. That is a decision for Congress to make, as to what the priorities are. The public rated health care 15th among 16 issues of importance. First was inflation.

TV-radio interview, Washington/
"Meet the Press,"
National Broadcasting Company, 8-11.

Nathan W. Shock
Gerontologist

2

I don't think there's going to be a sudden breakthrough that's going to double or triple the life span, simply because in order to do that you'll have to engage in "genetic engineering." Obviously, there's a genetic pattern that determines the average age of men and animals. But so far, nobody has been able to find a specific gene or chromosome that codes for life span. To alter the genetic code, you've got to have an identifiable locus to work with. That's a long way off, in my opinion.

Baltimore/The National Observer, 1-19:17.

Samuel Silverman
Associate Professor of Psychiatry,
Harvard University Medical School

3

[Saying there are psychological causes for many illnesses] : It wasn't chance that [former U.S. President] Richard Nixon's phlebitis flared up after his resignation . . . If as many people learn to recognize the psychological clues as have become familiar with the physical indicators of body illness, we will be well on the way to more effective prevention of untold personal suffering and economic loss . . . After interviewing hundreds of patients in over 25 years of clinical experience, I have concluded that calling only certain illnesses psychosomatic is misleading. I have found that emotional factors precede the onset and influence the course of all sickness, whether it be cancer, arthritis, pneumonia, tension, headache or whatever. My research has included a study of physically well people who subsequently became ill. It revealed that in addition to the highly publicized physical indicators, there are specific psychological clues which forecast the likelihood of illness.

Interview, New York/
The Washington Post, 10-27:(L)4.

Malcolm C. Todd
President, American Medical Association

4

We of the AMA believe that health care should be regarded not as a private advantage but as a public right. We are on record in asserting that every American should have access to adequate medical service . . . regardless of who he is or what he can afford. We support national health insurance as the logical means of financing such access. Again, our position is on record—emphatically so! For we have our own NHI plan, called Medicredit . . . and we are working hard to get it enacted into law . . . However, national health insurance—for all that is said and thought of it—is not addressed to complexities. It is not addressed to bad social and economic conditions of which bad health is more a result than a cause. It is not directed at the basic despair that breeds self-neglect and self-destruction. NHI—for all that is said and thought of it—is essentially just a financing mechanism.

Before American Public Health Association, New Orleans, Oct. 23/Vital Speeches, 12-1:124.

Ruth Tibbits Tooze
President, National Women's
Christian Temperance Union
                                                    1

In every crisis, Americans have turned to drink. Liquor dealers admit that, since the energy crisis began, the consumption of alcoholic beverages has greatly increased. The need for conserving gasoline may even enhance their "take," since people will remain home and drink more ... It's a little early to get actual figures, but we know—how well we know—that it happens ... The only place for a cocktail is after the rooster.

Time, 1-28:12.

Caspar W. Weinberger
Secretary of Health, Education and
Welfare of the United States
                                                    2

Medicare was very faultily designed ... in my opinion, because it did not have anything like an effective cost-control system. In effect, it provided for reimbursement of every medical supplier at any amount which the supplier billed. That is not very effective cost control. And when you guarantee at the same time the repayment of all of those bills by government underwriting, you have absolutely built-in inflation. That is what we cannot and should not do with any health-insurance bill, because otherwise you will so erode the benefits that no one will benefit.

TV-radio interview, Washington/
"Meet the Press,"
National Broadcasting Company, 8-11.

Sidney Wolfe
Director, consumerist Ralph Nader's
Health Research Group, Washington
                                                    3

A well-trained actor could probably prescribe drugs as rationally as the thousands of American doctors whose prescribing practices reflect drug-company indoctrination in lieu of scientific evaluation. It is now known that billions of wasted dollars, hundreds of thousands of unnecessary hospitalizations and thousands of lives needlessly lost are the price society pays for the promotional excesses of the drug industry.

Before Senate Subcommittee on Health, Washington/San Francisco Examiner & Chronicle, 3-10:(This World)9.

The Performing Arts

MOTION PICTURES

Robert Aldrich
Director
1

The star system is back, absolutely and strongly. Five years ago, it looked like the counter-culture was the movie audience; and if a movie worked well, that audience didn't require stars. [Peter] Bogdanovich's *Last Picture Show,* a wonderful film, seemed to confirm that. It's still true that a movie will work without stars, but you better believe that the odds against you are astronomical.

Interview/Los Angeles Times,
8-25:(Calendar)37.

Woody Allen
Actor, Director, Writer
2

People always ask me why there are no comedies any more. There are none because they are hard to do. I like to make them. I certainly don't make them that easily. I struggle and sweat for over a year, and sometimes I don't make it. I may just get enough laughs to get by.

Interview, New York/
Los Angeles Times, 1-12:(2)10.

Alan Arkin
Actor
3

I am a movie junkie. I love the form and I love making films. That's what I want to do. But it's a mass medium. To pretend you're a pure artist in a social art-form is madness. You must bend, you have to, or else you have to get out of the business or go to Stratford and do *Hamlet* for the rest of your life.

Interview/
Los Angeles Herald-Examiner, 11-26:(B)4.

Samuel Z. Arkoff
Chairman, American International Pictures
4

[Saying films his company makes may never win Academy Awards, but they are popular with audiences]: I'm not concerned with art. No movie is art. A hundred years from now nobody is going to look back on today's movies and call them art. A movie is like a pair of shoes: They're wasted unless somebody gets some use out of them.

Interview, Los Angeles/
Los Angeles Times, 2-20:(3)10.

5

Producers and directors with a big hit think of themselves as geniuses. They take on the trappings of royalty. In Hollywood, 90 per cent of the people consider themselves geniuses. In actuality, 10 per cent are brightly creative, and the other 90 per cent do a competent, workmanlike job.

Interview/
The New York Times Magazine, 8-4:34.

Fred Astaire
Actor, Dancer
6

I have no feeling about the past. I'm not a nostalgia buff. And I'm not crazy about discussing the things I did in those [past musical] movies. I came from the stage. When a play had run its course, it was over and forgotten. I made one movie after another the same way. There was no way to guess they would all come back in bunches on a television tube. I'm happy they were successful and people enjoyed those musicals. However, I don't watch them on television because I'm not interested in what I did in the past.

Interview, Los Angeles/
The Dallas Times Herald, 7-15:(B)5.

1

I love [show] business. I don't need it. I may never do another picture. I always say, "This is my last picture," though I've been saying that for 20 years. It's not easy to work hard, and that's what I've done all my life. Besides, there isn't that much material for someone at my exalted age. But it's great—everybody wants to help you up the curb. I usually end up helping them.

Interview, Beverly Hills, Calif./
"W": a Fairchild publication, 10-4:10.

Lucille Ball
Actress

2

There are too many lines around the wrong movie houses these days. *Last Tango in Paris,* for instance. I don't know why Marlon Brando would lower himself to do a film like that. I think there are a lot of dirty old men out there making a fast buck—and confusing young people. Too many of the themes of current movies place difficult loads on the shoulders of young people. The kids are beginning to think that the degrading way of life portrayed on screen must be the norm and that maybe there is something wrong with them if they don't conform. People deserve more than that. They deserve to see something they can enjoy, come out of the theatre happy instead of upset by so much kinky violence and sex.

Interview, New York/
The Christian Science Monitor, 3-12:(F)1.

Anne Bancroft
Actress

3

Acting—it's this early need, made of dozens of ingredients, the strongest of which is, you've got to say something to people and they *must* pay attention, listen to *you* say it . . .

Interview, Los Angeles/TV Guide, 11-23:17.

Warren Beatty
Actor

4

I really don't look upon myself as an actor. An actor acts. I do think of myself as a *some-time* actor. I don't like to evaluate my experiences only in relation to the profession of

movie acting. When you have a big success like *Bonnie and Clyde,* there is a tendency for people to want you to repeat it, to make more and more money. I don't see anything to be gained from that. If you take the movies too seriously—success too seriously—if you think it's important to turn out a bunch of hits, well . . . that's kind of a boring way to live.

Interview, Beverly Hills, Calif./
The New York Times, 3-17:(2)15.

5

Being the producer and star [of a film] is almost impossible. A good actor has to be child-like and maintain a feeling of make-believe. He has to learn to put himself out of control and respect that state. A good film-maker needs to be in complete control. So in doing both you pay a price.

Interview, Los Angeles/
Los Angeles Times, 5-31:(4)15.

Candice Bergen
Actress

6

There is something warm and comfortable about being a movie person. I know the values are all wrong. I know I should be thinking about the horrors taking place in the rest of the world. And I do—sincerely. But it is a nice feeling to call and get a good table in a packed restaurant or be given a seat on a plane even when it's badly over-booked.

The Dallas Times Herald, 7-14:(F)1.

Ingrid Bergman
Actress

7

People still think that actresses lie around on sofas and eat chocolates, pick up a fur coat and come down for a couple of hours to say a few lines. I would say a young girl wanting to be an actress should only think of acting if she was first talented and dedicated. Because it isn't easy. It's hard work. You have to have health, strength and a passion for it. Those who are not strong enough can't take it.

Interview, London/
"W": a Fairchild publication, 5-3:11.

415

Bernardo Bertolucci
Director

1

A film is a collective work. I am no boss, no dictator—just a collaborator. That man over there [a technical-crew member] is a contributor, too. If he bungles his job, what can I do? A satisfactory film is a miracle of synchronized effort, of teamwork. There is always an element of confusion in movie-making which acts as a stimulating challenge. Out of chaos rises the phoenix—well, at least quite often.

Interview, Parma, Italy/
The New York Times, 8-26:39.

Peter Bogdanovich
Director

2

One does a film basically for himself. I make it because it's something I want to see. If I want to see a film which no one has yet made, and I want to see it very much, I must make it myself.

Rome/San Francisco Examiner & Chronicle,
4-21:(Datebook)18.

John Boorman
Writer, Director, Producer

3

The act of watching a film is somewhat close to dreaming . . . There's a traffic between a film and the unconscious, which is very interesting. [TV, on the other hand,] gets a very low level of response; the picture you're looking at is so small in relation to the rest of your vision . . . Any kind of serious endeavor is totally destroyed by those endless commercials, especially here in America . . . The difference between this and going into a darkened theatre with a big screen is unbelievable.

Interview, New York/
The Christian Science Monitor, 3-8:(F)1.

Mel Brooks
Director, Screenwriter

4

I know comedy. It's my job and I'm a good craftsman. I'm a laugh-maker, and there aren't many of us around. There certainly aren't many of us making movies any more. Woody [Allen], Elaine May, me. Few, few, few. Too few. And the laughs have to be there. If they're not, nothing else helps and nothing else matters.

Los Angeles/Los Angeles Times,
12-29:(Calendar)30.

Richard Burton
Actor

5

[On giving autographs]: I don't mind it. It's part of the job. I've noticed that some American actors don't feel that way; they turn the autograph-seekers away, sometimes rudely. That seems to me symptomatic of the differences between English and American actors. Acting is a profession in England; we view it that way. But many American actors somehow feel that acting isn't manly, it's something for sissies. So they compensate by being gruff and rude.

Interview, Oroville, Calif./
The Dallas Times Herald, 3-24:(F)7.

James Caan
Actor

6

I'm an actor, and as long as I can feel that way about it, I'll be happy in what I'm doing. What I mean is—not long ago I was offered a "starring" role at so much money, plus a percentage, that I couldn't believe the figures. But the story was a dog. The producer kept telling me, "It's a great James Caan role—right up your street." That did it. I think, rather I hope, there's no such thing as a "James Caan role." I want to play human beings. The football player in *Brian's Song* was nothing like the gangster's son in *The Godfather*. And both were far removed from the timid, intimidated sailor in *Cinderella Liberty*. He, in turn, is miles away from the smart aleck with the Narcissus complex I play in *The Gambler*. Coming up is little Billy Rose, the show producer in *Funny Lady*. These are "people" roles—not "James Caan roles . . ."

Interview, Beverly Hills, Calif./
Los Angeles Herald-Examiner, 2-10:(F)4.

James Cagney
Actor

7

[On sex in today's films]: We used to have a saying in vaudeville: "He would take his pants

down to get a laugh." That meant the guy was so deficient in comedy he had to resort to such means. I have the same feeling about any gal who has to take her clothes off to get attention.
Interview, Beverly Hills, Calif./
San Francisco Examiner, 3-9:9.

1

[On the suggestion that he is a living legend]: If the others choose to think so, that's fine. But I can't accept any of this hullabaloo; I really can't. Acting was a job to be done, and I liked doing it. Apparently, whatever equipment I had seemed to lend itself to the job, and it worked; and inasmuch as it worked and the pay was good, why not? I had no idea of performing high art. The axiom for me has been this very self-evident truth: that you're only as good as the other fellow thinks you are because he buys the tickets. You leave that all to him. You don't sit in judgment on your own work. You hope it's right; and if it isn't, too bad. This has become a big thing among the youth in the business, this so-called "creativity." We were workers, we were professional workers, that's all we were. We'd go from one job to another, go where the job was, do it, and go away. We had no idea of the so-called artistic urge—at least I never felt any and neither did any of the fellows that I knew.
Interview, Beverly Hills, Calif./
The Washington Post, 3-15:(B)11.

2

[On his being called a superstar]: I hate the word "superstar." Silly word. Who hung it on the [film] business? I have never been able to think in those terms. They are over-statements. You don't hear them speak of Shakespeare as a superpoet or Michelangelo as a superpainter. They only apply the word to this mundane market.
Interview/
The Christian Science Monitor, 3-21:(F)6.

Charles Champlin
Film critic, "Los Angeles Times"

3

A lot of people who have been turned off by movies because of the candor, language, behavior, images and so on ought to look more care-

fully because, underlying some of the candor in both movies and literature, the value system looks upon examination to be not much different than the traditional value structures.
At Best-Sellers Panel discussion,
Los Angeles/Los Angeles Times, 4-3:(4)9.

Francis Ford Coppola
Director

4

[On the pressure of costs in making films]: You know what it's like to be a director? It's like running in front of a locomotive. If you stop, if you trip, if you make a mistake, you get killed. How can you be creative with that thing behind you? Every day I know it's $8,000 an hour. It forces me into decisions I know will work. I can't afford to take a chance.
Newsweek, 11-25:74.

Valentina Cortese
Actress

5

For me, the greatest richness for an actor, rather than to go up, up, up, up and own villas and yachts, is that moment when he's there on the set or on stage, and he gives something—a message of love or of life—to his own public, and he does it with *truth.*
Interview, New York/
The New York Times, 2-17:(2)22.

George Cukor
Director

6

What bothers me about the movies today is the narrowing-down of subjects. The thing that built this industry was its willingness to express the whole range of human experience. There's an awful lot of life besides crooked cops. And I don't see many funny pictures any more, do you?
Interview, Los Angeles/
Los Angeles Times, 3-31:(TV Times)2.

Bette Davis
Actress

7

I think stars from my era believed we should look like stars in public. I'm not a fashion person—I'm a dungaree person in private. But stars today all look like bums and tell every-

(BETTE DAVIS)

thing. The public gets disappointed. There should be an air of mystery. Exactly. That sense of mystery. You know, we're really not the kids next door. It doesn't mean the Silent Era with orchids and ermine like [Joan] Crawford and [Norma] Shearer. But I believe we are entitled to have a right to three-quarters of our private lives.

Interview, New York/
"W": a Fairchild publication, 10-4:5.

I. A. L. Diamond
Screenwriter

1

My feeling about the motion-picture industry is that it's not that important. Nobody takes it that seriously. There has been so much artistic presumption in the last few years. Over the history of film-making, out of a lot of journeyman work, came some artistic achievements. Now we're told something is an artistic achievement even before we see it. These days no one seems to consider "What's the best way to tell the story?" That's really the most important thing.

Interview, Beverly Hills, Calif./
Los Angeles Times, 12-15:(Calendar)56.

Kirk Douglas
Actor

2

[On the motion-picture ratings system]: There should be only one kind of rating—parental guidance. That puts the responsibility where it belongs—inside the family. I don't think I have the right to impose my standards on my neighbor, nor does he have the right to impose his on me. I might be too strict for him, he might be too permissive for me. It becomes a question of the individual point of view. The underlying problem of whether a film is acceptable for kids is, in my view, a matter that should be left up to their parents.

Interview, Beverly Hills, Calif./
Los Angeles Times, 5-26:(Home)35.

3

In making movies, the spotlight is never really comfortable, especially when there's criticism to be handed out. A director is somewhat removed from the line of fire. He can blame his troubles on the script or on the producer. But an actor has no place to hide. The critic is *looking* at the actor, and if he doesn't like the performance, the actor takes the punishment.

Interview, Beverly Hills, Calif./
Los Angeles Times, 5-26:(Home)35.

Melvyn Douglas
Actor

4

I think there's much more freedom today for the creative people in films than there was—chiefly writers and actors, and probably even directors. Directors, especially the successful ones, always carried a clout. But writers and actors very often, no matter how important they were, were much more at the behest of the money men, of the administrative crowd, than I think they are today . . . I notice when I go out every now and then to do something, that, compared to the earlier days, there's a kind of respect for integrity that did not always exist then . . . because actors and writers and producers have insisted upon it. They've broken away from just being cattle that were employed and sold.

Interview, Los Angeles/
Los Angeles Herald-Examiner,
4-7:(California Living)4.

5

You remember the good ones, not the junk [that was made in the "golden age" of movies]. But the good ones were rare. In spite of all the trash we produce [today], all of the hardcore porn and the softcore porn, films are much more interesting than they were in my day. That's the trouble [for actors]. Films today—and I mean either movies or television, it's all the same—deal in subjects that interest me, in ideas that are interesting. And they provide the sort of parts that seduce you. An actor can resist anything but a good part. Wave the right part under his nose, and his most carefully-considered plans go to hell.

Interview, Los Angeles/
Los Angeles Times, 4-8:(4)18.

Clint Eastwood
Actor

1

[On his experiences directing films]: Directing opens you up as an actor. You are putting together all the components. I like knowing that. As a director, you have problems with cameramen, problems with the actors—all kinds of problems to resolve. I guess it's a wonder any film ever turns out to be good considering how many elements are involved in putting a film together, how many problems inevitably develop. The writer pulls his idea out of the air; the director's job is to interpret that idea on film.

Interview, Dallas/
The Dallas Times Herald, 5-12:(D)1.

Robert Evans
Executive vice president in charge of
world-wide production, Paramount
Pictures Corporation

2

The habit of going to "the movies" is over. But the desire to see *a* movie is bigger than ever. I would rather put more money into fewer films than less on a lot of them. If you're making just another picture, forget it; you can't even get your advertising costs back. But if you have one or two big captivating entertainments a year, it's oil-rush time.

Newsweek, 11-25:72.

3

[On why there are so few good roles for women in films today]: A hero has many props he can work with. He can be athletic, a gangster, he can have his business or perform physical feats. A woman only has her mystery, part of which is her femininity. To me, a woman is far more complex than a man, but these qualities don't come off on screen. Most women's things are in their relationship to men; but when a woman tries to compete with a man, it doesn't make her any more attractive to him. Despite Women's Lib, I don't think people want to see a woman in a man's world. She loses her femininity. The two men in *The Sting* have something more visual and romantic, something more exciting, than two women would.

The New York Times, 12-15:(2)19.

Federico Fellini
Director

4

I make all of my films in the studios, because the only true way of showing things as they are is to reconstruct them. One must reinvent everything.

Interview, Rome/
San Franciso Examiner & Chronicle,
2-17:(Datebook)17.

5

Making a picture is like making a high jump into a swimming pool. You have to breathe. You have to know you go into the water—not onto the stone. But when you jump, you have to abandon yourself.

Interview, New York/
The New York Times, 10-1:34.

6

To realize that what you say [in film] is liked by people—it's good, nourishing, stimulating. But the critics that are bad—against—I am very weak; I think that maybe they are right, so I don't care to know. For a creative person to be criticized can be very dangerous. A creative person needs an atmosphere of approval. Like a fighter. Even a strong fighter, if the atmosphere around him is against, he feels weaker. You need to be drunk, you need to be exalted, to believe in what you are doing.

Interview, New York/
The Washington Post, 10-6:(E)1.

Bryan Forbes
Director

7

[On directing women in films]: One has to approach a woman with a velvet fist in a velvet glove, whereas you might approach a gentleman with an iron fist in a velvet glove. You have to make more allowances for the fact that when you're directing women you have to kind of—well, everybody has to take more care of them. Oh, not because they are frail creatures, because they're not. I mean, they are very determined and very capable in every direction. But I think that women care more how they look than men do on the screen. Makeup is more important. Photography of women is more critical than it is for men. These things have to

(BRYAN FORBES)

be taken into account when you're scheduling and budgeting a picture ... And if you upset a woman, you're liable to have her spoil her makeup. I treat women more gently than I do men. You can say things to an actor that you wouldn't dream of saying to an actress, just out of consideration. Now, that probably is something the Women Libbers won't like. But the fact is that if you had an all-male cast, you wouldn't perhaps watch your language quite so much.

Los Angeles Herald-Examiner, 12-28:(B)8.

William Friedkin
Director

1

I believe to the end ... that the major reasons to make a film are to move people emotionally, to move them either to laughter, tears, or to fear. Now, there are other reasons to make movies—like to educate them, like documentaries, to reveal some social factor, and I've done that and I would do it again ... But if you're working for the Warner brothers or the Metro brothers or the Paramount brothers or whoever—all these guys who are putting up a lot of bread here and hope to get their investment back—and you're working for them and you're working for an audience, which has got to stand in line with $3, $3.50 on weekends, whatever—I don't know anybody who ever said, "Go see this picture because it's got a wonderful philosophy discourse in it." Or, "Go see this picture because it's really interesting." People want to see movies because they want to be moved viscerally. I do.

Interview/The National Observer, 8-10:11.

Will Geer
Actor

2

I believe actors, by and large, are becoming very tired of not being able to explode once in a while, even if they go off like a rocket and fizzle out. We have been in an era for a long time when the director is everything. The actor is told every move he must make, and it has got so you can hardly move. So as a result, you

have a lot of really extraordinary and interesting acting that is being thwarted. The big movements that are part of the dance and swirl of things are entirely lost and the actor isn't allowed to have much freedom. It is always very easy to tone an actor down, but it is exceedingly hard to build him up.

Interview, Los Angeles/
Los Angeles Times, 7-2:(4)11.

Joan Hackett
Actress

3

It used to be so easy to be a movie star. The "daddies" at the various studios took care of their children, protected them from harm, sheltered them from reality. Now an actress has to take care of herself. It's impossible to be a star and not be real smart. If you're not smart you won't last long. I have to find my own scripts, locate somebody willing to finance the project, choose a director, agent my agent ... I don't mind taking care of myself. But God, if I'm so busy wheeling and dealing, when am I ever going to have time or energy to act again?

Interview, Beverly Hills, Calif./
Los Angeles Herald-Examiner, 3-3:(E)1.

Richard Harris
Actor

4

... I take acting very seriously ... I prepare every part thoroughly, developing it like a mosaic—grading the texture of the role, colors against colors. All too often, some producer doesn't like something about it and pulls a piece out of the picture which destroys the balance. I'll have wasted my time—months and months of it—for practically nothing. People like Steve McQueen, Clint Eastwood, Robert Redford and Paul Newman—they can get away with it. They are more performers than actors. They start at point "A" and finish at point "A"! That's their scale of acting. You can pull out enormous chunks of their performance and it doesn't change a bit.

Interview, London/
San Francisco Examiner & Chronicle,
4-21:(Datebook)10.

Anthony Harvey
Director

1

I think that everything one makes in films, or wants to make, should have some feeling of hope. We're going through a very desperate and despairing age, and I think there are enough films that deal with the horrifying aspects of life.

Interview, Caprarola, Italy/
The Christian Science Monitor, 1-10:(F)6.

Rita Hayworth
Actress

2

They do a lot of pornography pictures now. I wouldn't work on those . . . I haven't seen the picture [*Last Tango in Paris*], but from what people tell me it's disgusting. If you don't do that, you can't get work. I wouldn't be in a picture that had three four-letter words. I don't get a job because there's nothing for me to do here.

Los Angeles Times, 3-3:(Calendar)13.

Joseph Heller
Author

3

There's still nothing to compete with the novel as a vehicle for ideas. Movies can be very interesting, but they're not a thought experience, like novels are. When I go to the movies, I often try to go to the very bad ones, so I won't get my expectations up.

Interview/
"W": a Fairchild publication, 9-20:13.

Alfred Hitchcock
Director

4

A good film is when the price of the dinner, the theatre admission and the babysitter were worth it.

Los Angeles/Chicago Tribune, 8-15:(3)23.

5

Tell your story. Tell it with great potency. Tell it visually. Be as simple as you can. That is my summation of film-making . . . The essential thing is to make the audience participate. My films are designed to create emotion in the audience; it's what makes suspense.

Interview/Los Angeles Herald-Examiner,
9-29:(California Living)29.

Dustin Hoffman
Actor

6

. . . when a writer gets an idea, the whole idea is right in front of you, all there, and then you walk 10 feet to the typewriter and 50 per cent of the idea has already gone somewhere; and then you hit the keys and, when it comes out, you wind up with 20 per cent of what was there less than a minute ago. So, on a movie, you [the actor] start out with a character in a screenplay. You start out with a masterpiece, you think, and then you get into it and hope it'll be just a good film, and halfway through it you hope it won't be a bad film, and three-quarters of the way through it you just hope you'll get a film done.

Interview, New York/
The Washington Post, 11-17:(G)3.

Hal Holbrook
Actor

7

Acting is a selfish life—and terribly unfair to one's family. Actors shouldn't own property. We shouldn't even make much money, because it tempts one to attempt to establish roots—and that's impossible to do.

Interview, Los Angeles/
The Atlanta Constitution, 8-16:(B)18.

8

I used to think the highest point for an actor was to play a character so well that nobody knew it was you. Then I grew older and worked more as an actor; I realized that it is impossible to be somebody else. Then I began to realize that, until you can bring your own self into a role, you don't really fill it. The next thing you're faced with is who are you, what are you. It takes a lifetime to figure that out. Acting to me is a process of discovering who I am and where I'm weak or strong. It's amazing how much I discovered about myself. Then I began to trust myself.

Interview/
The Christian Science Monitor, 9-5:11.

WHAT THEY SAID IN 1974

Celeste Holm
Actress
1

Acting is controlled schizophrenia. That sounds neurotic, but isn't. You are playing someone else while being yourself.

Quote, 12-1:506.

Thomas P. F. Hoving
Director, Metropolitan Museum of Art, New York
2

... film doesn't click unless it has explicit language, explicit sex and perhaps some form of violence. My feeling is that this juggernaut of sex is a mark of decline. They try to explain that this is a great freedom, a getting away from taboos; but I am not convinced by that, because in the vast percentages of cases it takes this raw commercial tinge.

Interview, New York/
Los Angeles Times, 5-14:(2)7.

John Huston
Director
3

The only interesting thing [in movies] is magic. What you try to become is a bringer of magic. For magic and truth are closely allied, and movies are sheer magic. When they are misused, it's a debasement of magic. But when they work, it is glorious.

Interview, Los Angeles/
Los Angeles Times, 8-4:(Calendar)26.

Norman Jewison
Director
4

... films are a form of escapism. They're about our dreams and our fantasies. They're about our illusions and what we want life to be. They can also have a tremendous impact upon us because they show us how life can be if we're not careful.

Interview, Munich/
Los Angeles Times, 9-29:(Calendar)26.

Stanley Kramer
Director, Producer
5

When I was growing up in films, there were a lot of stars: Garbo, Hayes, Crawford and Bette Davis. And you had to find roles for those stars ... Today the film is the director's medium. They put an emphasis on the material as against stars. This may be more suited for the reality in which we live, but I think we'll miss eventually all the romance that was the film. I cannot envision not missing Cagney and Bogart and Tracy and Vivien Leigh and Garbo. They were larger than life, and they took us to another land, and that was very entertaining.

The New York Times, 2-12:42.

Burt Lancaster
Actor
6

I've been bored with acting for years. I never had that usual kind of actor's mentality anyway. But everything has changed in the cinema as well. Like cynicism in the world now, it's so enormous, with so much lack of faith in the leaders and in everything. The dreams have changed for the world. It has become a very harsh kind of place, and there's no room for the kind of movies we used to make. It's all reflected in the world of art. I don't think the days will ever come back when the hero will be able to ride off into the sunset the way he used to. It will have to be a whole lot better world before people can sit back and believe the fairy tale again.

Interview, London/
San Francisco Examiner & Chronicle,
2-10:(Datebook)12.

Elsa Lanchester
Actress
7

Most actors, bound up in their enormous egos, are given to believing that they can follow just this one craft; that it is beneath their dignity to learn how to sew, or type, or sell something. That's why so many wind up broke. What is so anointed about acting? An actor leaves nothing of himself to posterity. He arrives, he charms, he succeeds—hopefully. But unlike a painter with his canvasses, a musician with his poems or melodies, a writer with his books, when the actor dies—poof! There remains nothing, except maybe a rerun or two on the late, late show.

Interview, Los Angeles/
Los Angeles Herald-Examiner, 7-7:(E)1.

Henri Langlois
Director, Cinemateque Francaise, Paris
1

Cinema today is made for few people. In the past it was made for all people. Cinema has lost its power over the masses. I don't know why. People say it's because of television. It's not true. People say it's because of the automobile. It's not true. If you discover why it is, you save the future of the cinema. Maybe it's because the pioneers disappear. There are too many successors and not enough pioneers. The new generation of pioneers has not yet arrived.

Interview, Los Angeles/
Los Angeles Times, 4-16:(4)11.

Sam Levene
Actor
2

. . . the theatre is a very precarious business. It's not worth it, at least not for me, anyway. If I knew some 40 years ago what I know now, I certainly wouldn't have gone into it. I could have done something better with my life. I would like to have been a doctor. I think then I would have contributed something. I don't think an actor contributes that much. Maybe if I were a writer. I don't think an actor is creative. I think it's an interpretive art. And it doesn't mean anything. At least it doesn't mean anything to me. But I didn't know that then. I only know it now.

Interview, Los Angeles/
The Atlanta Constitution, 8-17:(T)18.

Joseph E. Levine
President, Avco Embassy Pictures Corporation
3

I remember years ago we used to go to the movies one night a week. Sometimes we didn't know where we were going or what we were going to see. People went to "the movies." Now they go to see a *particular* movie. It's sold to them; it appeals to them—in many instances you don't know why. A picture that is successful can go up to the sky; there's no limit to the amount of business it can do. There is no in-between. Fifteen years ago, if you made a film that wasn't a hit, you could recoup—if it was a modestly budgeted picture—by playing it as a double feature. That is no longer possible. A picture the public decides is bad now doesn't do business. You've got to hang it up. It doesn't do anything.

Los Angeles Herald-Examiner,
3-24:(California Living)26.

Anita Loos
Author
4

The old movies still have vitality because, as long as we were free to kick up our heels, the spirit in which they were made got into the films. Then people started to think and they got to be bores. Messages came in and dealt the movies a terrible blow. They're still suffering from that even though the messages have disappeared. Porno has taken their place. Between the two, porno is much better.

Interview/
"W": a Fairchild publication, 9-20:18.

Sidney Lumet
Director
5

It's funny, but when I look at the directors whose work I like, the careers I most admire are the careers of quantity . . . All I want to do is get better, and quantity can help me to solve my problems. I'm thrilled by the idea that I'm not even sure how many films I've done. If I don't have a script I adore, I do one I like. If I don't have one I like, I do one that has an actor I like or that presents some technical challenge. I did *That Kind of Woman* because I was enchanted with Sophia Loren. I did one movie simply because I wanted to see what it would be like to do a dramatic story in color; before that, I snobbishly thought you could only tell a *serious* story in black and white. I want to learn as much as I possibly can.

Interview, New York/
The New York Times, 1-20:(2)11.

Louis Malle
Director
6

For me, film is a fantastic means of investigation. You see the world much better through a camera. The act of filming obliges you to see the world differently and to interpret it . . . It's

WHAT THEY SAID IN 1974

(LOUIS MALLE)

reality plus me, a way to know yourself and therefore to know the world.

Interview, Paris/
The New York Times, 3-10:(1)3.

Abby Mann
Screenwriter 1

All that matters here [in the Hollywood film industry] is [commercial] success; achievement doesn't mean a damn thing. You can do a marvelous movie and it doesn't matter unless it's successful. I'll never forget after *Ship of Fools* came out—and I'm not saying it's a paragon, but we had won eight nominations—I walked into the commissary at Columbia, and people hardly said hello to me because the picture wasn't doing any business. I don't think it was so bad when I first came here 13 years ago. But it's become a very small business—only a few agencies, and a few pictures being made, so everybody lives in terror. Everybody feels unworthy, and most of them *are* unworthy. Most of them are dull as blazes. I think this is the dullest town, the dullest group of people. I'd rather be talking with some bigoted sheriff, because at least he's alive; at least he's part of the world. People are so cut off here. They're a bunch of boors.

Interview, Los Angeles/
Los Angeles Times, 12-1:(Calendar)39.

Roddy McDowall
Actor 2

[On acting]: Any professional endeavor is predicated on hard work and progress, or growth. This is a workaday business. It is tiring, mentally and physically. By 3 p.m. there's no oxygen left on the set, and by 4 p.m. you have cotton wool in your brain. There can be no illusions. Acting is creative. Acting is hard. I'm impatient with the rest of the nonsense actors speak of when they talk about their craft. It's all claptrap.

Interview, Beverly Hills, Calif./
San Francisco Examiner & Chronicle,
11-10:(Datebook)21.

Burgess Meredith
Actor 3

I hear actors say, "I accept only big parts in important pictures." Nonsense. Every picture is important. They all contain creativity and—sweat. Some turn out better. But the effort cannot be lessened, at least on my part.

Interview, Beverly Hills, Calif./
Los Angeles Herald-Examiner, 8-25:(D)4.

David Merrick
Motion picture and stage producer 4

The biggest difference between the movies and the theatre is that in the theatre you raise the money and give the backers tickets to opening night, and that's that. But in Hollywood, you live with the moguls forever. On the positive side, the camera gives you a much greater range in picking story material. Of course, in the theatre, you can take it to Philadelphia or Boston and fix it; but here, you just have one shot—and you'd better be right.

Interview, Los Angeles/
The Christian Science Monitor, 4-4:(F)5.

Ray Milland
Actor 5

[Saying he is retiring from acting]: I've won the "Oscar," starred with 80 different leading ladies and have lived well. But I want to go back to being comfortable with myself. I don't want to go on making an ass of myself in public, which is what acting is.

San Francisco Examiner, 2-9:33.

Ricardo Montalban
Actor 6

You continue to be a child in this business. In most other careers there are certain limitations imposed by the outside world. If you are an accountant or lawyer or doctor, you cannot keep dreaming in your work. But acting is like *living* in a dream. You become *part* of the story you tell. As an actor, I can continue dreaming for the rest of my life.

Interview, Los Angeles/
Los Angeles Times, 3-31:(Home)39.

Ronald Neame
Director

1

I was always taught that a director was somebody who helped the stars give their best. But the tendency these days is for directors to play the star roles themselves—right down to parading around with a viewfinder round their necks, even when they're not shooting. I can't do that. I can't give that kind of performance. When I see the way some of them behave, it irritates me enormously.

Interview, London/
San Francisco Examiner & Chronicle,
10-20:(Datebook)16.

Gregory Peck
Actor

2

I don't believe audiences are particularly moved by fellows who merely transform themselves with makeup and heavy accents. That's strictly mimicry and it belongs in amateur theatricals. The art of acting is to communicate an *experience* to the audience. That experience is filtered through the personality of the actor, whether it's Steve McQueen or Robert Redford. The outer transformation is incidental.

Interview, Los Angeles/
Los Angeles Times, 7-21:(Home)33.

Sam Peckinpah
Director

3

[On why he always makes violent films]: I'm not hired to do Tennessee Williams or William Saroyan movies. I'm hired to do violence. I don't like it, but I've learned to live with it. Also, I recognize violence in my own nature. And I have five children. If I don't make movies, they don't eat.

Interview, New York/
The Atlanta Journal and Constitution,
8-24:(T)4.

S. J. Perelman
Author, Playwright

4

I noticed something a long time ago, when I worked for the Marx Brothers... We would watch the audiences emerge from previews of their pictures helpless with laughter, tears streaking down their faces. A minute later their faces would freeze and they would say, "Wasn't that silly?" But they'd go to a Garbo picture or a "serious" play, come out with tears in their eyes and feel ennobled. People feel comedy is somehow beneath their dignity. They feel humor is trivial.

Interview/
"W": a Fairchild publication, 11-15:7.

Christopher Plummer
Actor

5

I think it's terribly important for actors to do films—simply because when you're making a movie you see the world and you live a little, and you learn about life a little more, and you bring that back with you. If you're intelligent at all, you make use of a film and see the country and work with foreign people. It not only influences your work, it influences your life. That's how you find out what the world is like. When temperament meets temperament, that's when people get to know each other.

Interview, London/
San Francisco Examiner & Chronicle,
11-3:(Datebook)16.

Nikolai V. Podgorny
President of the Soviet Union

6

[On the content of Soviet motion pictures]: We are emphatically against all that causes harm to the working man; against the denigration of the personality; against savoring filth and meanness; against the distortion of the truth of life and history. We are equally resolutely against political indifference and the sentiments and tastes alien to us. We openly criticize, and shall continue to criticize, hack-work films which do not present a real picture of life and which we regrettably still see on our screen. Apparently, it is necessary to show greater exactingness in respect to all film workers, to control all the stages of film production and to make greater demands of those who give the green light to new films... Cinema was and remains one of the major battlefields of the ideological struggle raging in the world today. The Soviet cinematographers' duty is to constantly fulfill their revolutionary, humanistic mission—to create a

425

WHAT THEY SAID IN 1974

vivid image of the Communist truth, to expose the true face of imperialism and its lackeys.

At ceremony marking 50th anniversary of Mosfilm, Moscow/Variety, 3-13:34.

Robert Radnitz
Producer

1

... I have never set out to make a children's picture per se. Merely because a film is based on young people's literature or has a child as protagonist does not automatically qualify it as a kiddie show. Children resent being patronized by sentimental drivel that masks and disguises the reality they know only too well in this electronic era.

San Francisco, March 21/ San Francisco Examiner, 3-22:30.

2

I frankly don't really care particularly what kids see in the area of sex [in films]. If they're too young, they're going to be bored; if they understand what's going on, then they understand what's going on in their own lives, anyhow. But what I am enormously concerned about is gratuitous violence, and I think there are too many films that have been rated "G" or "PG" that are filled with gratuitous violence. I'm concerned about it because I think we [in the U.S.] are becoming rapidly a nation that is virtually inured to violence. I don't say, obviously, that movies are exclusively to blame for that, but we do have a responsibility in that area and I don't think we are fulfilling it. Having said all that, I would probably be the first guy on the battlements to fight for people doing any kind of film that they want to do.

Interview, Washington/ The Washington Post, 4-17:(D)1.

Robert Redford
Actor

3

The actor doesn't have any control over the film that results from maybe months of shooting. The director and the producer have their say. All right. But [so] do the censors, the sales people, the studio heads, the bankers—so many people have a say in what finally shows up in the theatres. What's all that got to do with the art of movie-making? Maybe the scene I most enjoyed doing doesn't wind up on the screen. Your work is chopped up and manipulated so much that sometimes you can barely recognize it. Of course, sometimes your performance is better for cutting and editing ...

Interview, New York/ The Washington Post, 12-3:(B)6.

Paul Roth
President, National Association of Theatre Owners

4

[Addressing film-makers]: Don't confuse shock and embarrassment with entertainment. Communicate, yes. But please, gratuitous sex, violence and vulgar language are not substitutes for good stories, good acting and good production. Audiences are looking for escape from their day-to-day problems. They don't want to escape by having to cover their eyes or plug their ears.

At Show-A-Rama convention, Kansas City, March 12/Variety, 3-20:26.

Albert Ruddy
Producer

5

[On the lack of major roles for women in films]: Writers look for intriguing people. They intuitively think of men because men function on a more important level than women. It may not be right, but it's the reality. It's a joke when I see housewives saying, "I want to run GM." *You* try to get a big male star to accept a good script where the action belongs to the chick.

Newsweek, 3-4:51.

Rosalind Russell
Actress

6

Sex for sex's sake on the screen seems childish to me, but it's violence that really bothers me. I think it's degrading. It breeds something cancerous in our young people. We have a great responsibility to the future in what we're communicating. It's terrifying to hear a young person—or anyone—say, "Well, that movie wasn't as good as the last one; they only lopped off six heads." Yet we always seem to muddle through. I think the picture business may be moving into another plateau. Perhaps there will be a return to quality. Quality is important in everything, and it pays, pays and pays.

Interview, Beverly Hills, Calif./
Los Angeles Times, 3-31:(Calendar)25.

Telly Savalas
Actor

1

The concentration of an actor is something I question—particularly since I don't have it myself. We're getting into spontaneity and instinct, which I think are more important than concentration in acting.

Interview, Los Angeles/
The Washington Post, 8-18:(K)6.

Maximilian Schell
Actor, Director

2

I think that the art of movie-making is basically the art of expressing a picture in motion. You need a story, of course; but sometimes you can say more with cuts than with a lot of words. Hitchcock used to talk about this, but I think Pudovkin was the first to describe it. You take the expressionless image of a man's face, cut to a table heavily laden with food, and then back to that expressionless face—and he looks hungry. Do the same thing cutting from the face to lovers in an embrace and back to that same face—and now he will look jealous. So much storytelling in a movie can be done in this way—and done better.

Interview, New York/
The National Observer, 3-30:18.

John Schlesinger
Director

3

I hope the films I make aren't just depressing. I hope they communicate some kind of understanding to people. That's what interests me. When I go to the cinema, I want a human experience of some sort, which is why I like Truffaut's work so tremendously. Sometimes romantic, but human. And Fellini's work: Beneath all the fantasy, there's an enormous

human being with all the excesses. I like, when I go to the cinema, to see something of the person who made it there. Very often, you see nothing.

Interview, Beverly Hills, Calif./
Los Angeles Times, 7-14:(Calendar)19.

George C. Scott
Actor

4

Acting is a very difficult life, very damaging psychologically . . . the earlier you make it, the less chance you have to be a human being. I don't think it's a wholesome profession for anybody, certainly not for young people.

Interview, Los Angeles/
The New York Times, 7-28:(2)14.

5

For reasons baffling to everyone, actors worry endlessly about whether they are any good. It does not help when a director like Otto Preminger jumps up and down screaming, "You have no talent." An actor worries about that from the beginning of his career until he draws his last breath. It's worse than death or taxes. It's a fear that's with an actor all the time. It never stops. Go to the greatest actors in the world and they will say, "I'm not quite sure that I really have any talent." Laurence Olivier suffers the torments of the damned because *he's* not yet sure.

Interview, Beverly Hills, Calif./
Los Angeles Times, 11-24:(Home)68.

Sid Sheinberg
President, MCA, Inc.

6

I'm not at all sure what the most important thing is in a film, but I'd guess finding something valuable and unique in a property is most important. That, of course, can be lots of things: a story, a star, special effects. I [as head of Universal Pictures' parent company] look for something within the project that will hopefully make it an event. I try to avoid the mundane and the ordinary. We're constantly looking for elements or ingredients that make a project special. The difficulty is in implementing the objective.

Interview, Los Angeles/Los Angeles Times,
5-26:(Calendar)24.

James Stewart
Actor

1

I lament the passing of the big studio. I'm sorry they're gone. I think it's a disadvantage to young actors. It wasn't a question of going to acting school. We got training for acting by acting all the time. We had a little part in a big picture or a big part in a little picture. It was vocational training for the craft of acting. There was more chance of training. They got hold of you, made you belong. They gave you a home. They had special means of publicity for you and gym for you to work out. I'm sorry young actors now don't have the chance I did. The way it is now, it's everybody for himself.

Interview, Los Angeles/
Los Angeles Herald-Examiner, 3-5:(A)14.

Gloria Swanson
Actress

2

I've been offered so many roles in these pornographic films! Where are you going to show them? On 42nd Street and Broadway? They've had it all. But where's the romance? I want romance. There's no poetry now. Nobody serenades you. And if they should decide to serenade you, the music is so loud it would only break your eardrums.

Interview, Los Angeles/
Los Angeles Herald-Examiner,
2-24:(TV Weekly)6.

3

The violence, the cruelty, the despair of American movies in recent years makes me mentally and emotionally sick.

Paris/Los Angeles Times, 3-28:(1)2.

4

Why do women have to look dug-up and drunk if they play older parts? A woman should be able to play any age if she can create the illusion. In Hollywood, any woman over 40 is thought to have lost her sex appeal. The curious part of it is men seem to be virile enough to take elephants and throw them over their left shoulder in film. This is false. This is not honest. Stories have been geared to heroes.

Now, maybe as we go along, more good roles will be written for women.

Interview, New York/
"W": a Fairchild publication, 10-4:4.

Rod Taylor
Actor

5

Not in 10 years has the American film been as supreme as it is now in England, France, Italy and everyplace else. The pictures that are currently packing theatres in the U.S.A. are going equally strong abroad. The foreign film industry is practically in ashes. Production is almost at a standstill in Italy even though subsidized by the government. That's because the government is economically at a standstill and suffers from crippling strikes. But beyond the national crises, the European movie-makers got too artsy-crafty, pornographic, sexy, slutty for their own good. Now they have fallen on their prats. Their native audiences are passing them up for American product. Viva good old entertainment!

Interview, Beverly Hills, Calif./
Los Angeles Herald-Examiner, 9-8:(E)2.

John Wayne
Actor

6

A star has to have his own personality. He projects himself into the action, because the audience comes to see *him.* You may say all my parts are the same, but that's just what I want you to think. I want people to say, "Hey, let's go see Duke at the pictures." I'm one of them. I try to do things the people can identify with . . . It isn't a man of many faces that stays on top. You get lost on the screen if your personality doesn't show through.

Interview, London/
San Francisco Examiner & Chronicle,
12-15:(Datebook)18.

Paul Francis Webster
Composer, Lyricist

7

. . . there is a special character to songs written for films. A successful song captures a certain flavor of the film that contains it, but the song is also constructed to have an independent life. The reason is that if the song mirrors the film too closely, people who haven't seen the picture won't understand what the song is all about. Also, while he wants the movie to succeed, a [song] writer very selfishly hopes his song will endure. I was sorry to see *Captain Carey, U.S.A.* disappear swiftly from the movie screens, but I was happy that a song I wrote for it, "Mona Lisa," lived long afterward.

Interview, Los Angeles/
Los Angeles Times, 11-3:(Home)30.

Billy Wilder
Producer, Director, Writer

1

It's enormously difficult to make a good picture anytime. And it's miraculous any more to make a successful picture, which is not necessarily the same thing. But the gamble is so rewarding when you do hit, that people are willing to take the gamble. At the same time, once you start calculating, you're in trouble. You have to make pictures you believe in and have a feeling for. You can't make a phony DeMille-type picture, because it will look and play phony. DeMille believed in what he was doing, as unlikely as that seemed now and then, and it showed on the screen.

Interview, Los Angeles/
Los Angeles Times, 7-14:(Calendar)78.

Robert Wise
Director

2

... whatever the possibilities [of a potential movie], you [the film-maker] have to be turned on. If all you can say is that a project has good commercial prospects, you're on your way out from the start. You can't do a film mechanically. We've all done things that didn't work. But you don't know that at the beginning. The major, crucial decision we all make is that very first one—"Yes, I'd like to make that

into a movie." There are a million decisions which follow, but that's the big one.

Interview, Los Angeles/
Los Angeles Times, 9-29:(Calendar)27.

Joanne Woodward
Actress

3

Not that anyone in Hollywood really cares what I think, but awards now rarely mean what they say they mean. The "Oscar" has become a political gesture or a business gesture. They say an "Oscar" adds $5 million to a film's gross, and I believe it. But that's not what the "Oscar" is for. It didn't used to be that way. I remember winning, and I remember loving it. I just wish there was an award around that you could believe in again.

Interview, New York/
Los Angeles Times, 1-13:(Calendar)25.

Frank Yablans
President, Paramount Pictures Corporation

4

The business of a motion-picture company is to manufacture, finance and *promote* motion pictures. It's to build audience awareness and to stimulate a want-to-see syndrome among those people who are going to put down their money at the box office. We're in competition for the leisure dollar, and our greatest competition is not television: it's golfing, tennis, country clubs, automobiles, mobile homes—all the things that consume off-work time and dollars.

Interview, New York/
The Dallas Times Herald, 7-31:(G)7.

5

I don't know a more cutthroat business than this one. It's partly so because we're dealing with all the instabilities inherent in a creative process. And it's also because we're playing in an enormously high-rolling crap game.

Newsweek, 11-25:71.

MUSIC

Peter Herman Adler
Conductor, Metropolitan Opera, New York

1

In the old times, a conductor was creative. When Beethoven conducted, he didn't care at all about technical perfection. Actually, any creative conductor cared infinitely less about it. You'll never read in the 10 volumes which Wagner wrote any complaints about the players being together. What was interesting was the spirit, the attention, the tempos. Only in modern times, because we live in an age of technical perfection, do we care about this. How many rehearsals did Beethoven have for his "Ninth Symphony"? Three. Can you imagine what kind of performance that was? Ghastly! Still it made a tremendous impression because the audience heard the essence. Today the orchestral technique is such that you're like an elevator man. Anybody can get up, give a downbeat, and technically they'll play together. That is why so many untalented conductors can flourish. If they have enough *chutzpa*, they give a kind of beat and the orchestra plays.

The New York Times Magazine, 9-29:52.

Elly Ameling
Lieder singer

2

The possibilities of communicating with an audience here [in the U.S.], be it in a big city or a small college, are so easy. I find that you [Americans] as a people react to music naturally with your whole being—brains and heart. In Europe, you have the idea that they come to do justice to their critical sense toward or against a singer. Their brains are always at work, but where is the readiness to receive music?

Interview, New York/
The New York Times, 2-10:(2)16.

Chet Atkins
Guitarist

3

I kind of hate to see country music get all mixed up with other musics. I hate to see country music lose its identity, which it gradually is doing. All musics are losing their identities; they're all coming together. It's been happening ever since Elvis Presley. Back before Elvis, you had country music and it seldom, if ever, crossed over into pop. And you had rhythm-and-blues and it never crossed over . . . It depends on the writers, the creativity of our musicians. If they come up with great material, then country music will grow and grow. A music dies when it becomes a parody of itself. It's happened to some extent in rock music. It can happen to country music. It all depends on the creative people.

Interview, Nashville/
San Francisco Examiner, 8-2:28.

Charles Aznavour
Singer, Composer

4

I am not a [song] writer in the strictest literary sense of the word. But I am a writer in the sense that my songs are the truth and come from my own experience. That is the only thing that gives legitimacy to the title of writer.

Interview/
Los Angeles Herald Examiner, 11-17:(E)2.

Tony Bennett
Singer

5

When I was a teen-ager, I liked all kinds of music. I think today's teen-agers are the same, when they're given the chance. Take a bunch of kids at a rock 'n' roll concert, and when it's over put them all on a bus and take them to hear Segovia at Carnegie Hall. I guarantee you they'll like it. Take them to a club where Count Basie is playing. The Count has got to reach them! . . . It proves that teen-agers and adults alike, whatever their special favorites—the Rolling Stones or Pearl Bailey—will always respond to other good performers, too. I'm not trying to point to myself, because wherever I turn in an under-par performance I know it before anyone. I also know it when I've done a performance I don't have to be ashamed of. The point is, a good performance—by Segovia, Count Basie, Sinatra, Bailey or the Rolling Stones—gets through to anyone. Any age, any sex, any background. There's no mystery in music. If it's good it will sell.

Interview/The Dallas Times Herald, 7-22:(C)3.

Maria Callas
Opera singer

1

[On her being 50 and having been away from public singing for eight years]: Nobody can sing as well as the old days. You are not as you were. You don't have the strength of an athlete who's young, who has less experience and great possibilities. The same it is with us [singers]. But the line of the music, the whole feeling, the atmosphere [is still there]. You are born an artist or you are not born an artist. Even if the voice is less of a firework . . . the artist is still there.

News conference, New York, Feb. 7/
The Washington Post, 2-8:(B)9.

Schuyler Chapin
General manager,
Metropolitan Opera, New York

2

[On the Met]: I'm stuck with this quixotic, unreal, impossible and glorious mistress. When the lights go down and the curtain goes up, so do the hackles on the back of my neck.

Newsweek, 10-7:76.

Joan Crawford
Actress

3

Music is oft times the staff of life for lovers, famous or obscure. It's a bond between them, a hands-across-the-sea tie that is as binding and as secret as thought itself. Lovers, separated by

miles, continents or traditions, can be happy by having "their song" follow them wherever they may go, separately or together. Past and present composers must be recognized as creative cupids whether or not they knowingly have written words and music to soothe the so-called savage beast. With today's music to love, read, sleep, work and play by . . . the sounds of music are everywhere. Whether it's hot rock, cool jazz, a melodious torch song or a toe-tapping polka tune, there will always be a song lovers, young and old, can make their very own.

Interview/The Dallas Times Herald, 7-5:(F)3.

James DePreist
Associate conductor,
National Symphony Orchestra, Washington

4

I can't stand conductors who think they're doing the whole job, who fail to acknowledge the pivotal role of the orchestra. The vision, thrust and goals are mine, but in achieving this you have to have everybody pulling together. It's marvelous when you can be human and flexible and it's seen as openness, not weakness.

Interview/The Washington Post,
7-21:(Potomac)18.

Neil Diamond
Singer, Composer

5

Writing takes precedence with me. It always has. It's a direct reflection of myself. The music is an expression of what I see. If I feel something strongly, I can represent it in music. If it affects me, it will affect other people. I try never to approach these songs intellectually. If they come out naturally, then they have their own reason for being. And if they're done well, they have a greater reason for being. I let them pour out. It's more a feeling than a message.

Interview, Los Angeles/
Los Angeles Herald-Examiner,
9-1:(California Living)8.

Rafael Druian
Concertmaster,
New York Philharmonic Orchestra

6

I hope I'm not romantic in my remembrance of the past, but one would be hard put today to

WHAT THEY SAID IN 1974

(RAFAEL DRUIAN)

name conductors of the stature of 30 years ago—men like Reiner, Klemperer, Beecham, Furtwaengler. When you don't have them, you don't have the kind of music they performed. Now they're all gone—Koussevitzky, Toscanini, Szell . . . not only in music but in other fields, too. Years ago one used to work hard and develop a talent. Nowadays the idea is first to become famous and then become good. Conductors [today] aren't aware of the sociology of the orchestra and what makes it tick. They don't make use of concertmasters, with the result that some of us don't do much more than play the soft passages.

Interview, New York/
The National Observer, 6-22:18.

Art Garfunkel
Singer
1

It's a long time since I'd rush out to buy an album, already salivating, eager to bring it home, knowing I was going to like it . . . [Music today is] very serious big business, and it really excites the greed glands, you know; and that's very anti-musical. Pop culture seems a little vacant to me, a missing substance. But in the golden age of the Beatles it was really worth taking seriously—you could put it next to Bach or Beethoven.

Interview, New York/
Los Angeles Times, 2-9:(2)6.

William H. Hadley
Finance director,
Metropolitan Opera, New York
2

Tickets have never paid the price in opera. Right now, adding up all our costs, about two-thirds of the sum total of a performance is paid for by ticket sales—which means that we'd have to charge about 50 per cent more to make up the difference, and that would chase away the audience. Historically, there's always been some kind of subsidy to make up the difference. In Europe, where opera really got started, the governments feel that it's their thing, and they support it. Our [U.S.] government has never really sponsored any sort of entertainment,

except Watergate. What's been the subsidy in this country has been the contributions of people who wanted opera.

Interview, New York/
The New York Times, 1-27:(2)15.

Earl "Fatha" Hines
Jazz pianist
3

Jazz, too, has become a big money thing, and in some ways it has suffered for it. But jazz is still reaching out. It is America's best ambassador. The Europeans have always dug it. The Russians can't get enough of it. They adore it in Japan. In South America, especially in Brazil where they've got such great music of their own, they go mad for jazz. You see, it makes people smile. They feel the music, and that's happiness.

Interview, Nice, France/
The Christian Science Monitor, 8-29:12.

Vladimir Horowitz
Pianist
4

The pianist must have brain, heart, feeling, emotion and command of his instrument, which is technique. The brain is a control, like a policeman. But the brain is not a guide. If there is too much brain, that is not good. If there is too much feeling and not enough technique, that is not good either. The artist must have a goal when he plays: not to stun the audience, but to move them, to touch their hearts.

Interview, Washington, May 31/
The Washington Post, 6-3:(B)6.

Elton John
Singer, Pianist
5

I can't understand those people who say they don't like doing concerts. It's the greatest thing in the world to stand on a stage and see people in the front rows smiling and know they came to see you. The stage, in reality, is the closest you can ever get to most of the fans. I mean, they can't come any closer than that. They may say hello backstage or in a hotel or something; but that's not even as close as seeing a show and being affected by the music. That's why I get so upset if I play badly. Not only for

432

me, but because I know I've disappointed the audience. There's nothing worse than knowing everybody went home thinking, "Oh boy, that sure was a drag." That's what you struggle against every night.

Interview, Dallas/
Los Angeles Times, 10-1:(4)9.

Henry A. Kissinger
Secretary of State of the United States
1

It is amazing that what seems so simple and inevitable in music—concord, harmony and cooperation—seems so difficult in international politics. If we can produce something as complex and beautiful and satisfying as music, there is hope that we can conserve peace.

At United Nations Concert, Kennedy Center,
Washington, Oct. 19/
The Washington Post, 10-21:(B)3.

Michel Legrand
Composer
2

[Music] can be good or it can be bad in any form. An accordian player in Paris in the streets can be beautiful and fantastic, and I could love it very, very much, I could cry for it. And I'm hearing some pretentious symphonic works that are . . . nothing. If it's good, it's good. And I don't believe in dimensions—why a song should be one pebble and why a symphony should be a mountain. Not at all. Not at all . . . Music is music everywhere it is, if it is for one instrument, a string quartet, or a symphonic orchestra, or a movie, or a song, or even a dance.

Interview, New York/
The Christian Science Monitor, 9-26:11.

Stanley Marcus
Chairman, Neiman-Marcus stores
3

[On the lack of financial support for the Dallas Symphony Orchestra]: I suspect that many of our community and corporate leaders are committed to basically three things: making money, supporting the State Fair of Texas and the Dallas *Cowboys* [football team]. This is not said in any way as an indictment but as a commentary of what interests them. From a corporate point of view, the symphony has always

received somewhat begrudging support in times past to keep it alive. Most symphonies are fast becoming dinosaurs because of their cost of operation; and eventually the only way to save symphonic music is through massive Federal funding to match community grants and community support. I am very discouraged about the state of regard in which symphonic music is held in Dallas.

Los Angeles Times, 4-8:(1)21.

Zubin Mehta
Musical director, Los Angeles
Philharmonic Orchestra
4

When a musician is busy playing notes, he is not really thinking of where the music is *going*. When you put a number of musicians together, the problem is multiplied. An orchestra by itself cannot make music *logical* for the listener. The conductor's job is to rehearse, organize and put it all together logically.

Interview, Los Angeles/
Los Angeles Times, 2-10:(Home)36.

Gian Carlo Menotti
Composer
5

. . . when I read a critic on *The [New York] Times* calling the music of *The Consul* merely serviceable, I can only feel discouraged, and can only ask myself why it is that so many critics continually repeat the same old boring cliches about me. I am, of course, aware that most music critics are unimaginative and undiscerning people—that they are people who read each other's reviews and keep repeating themselves endlessly. But what is really discouraging is that the younger critics do not have the courage to express a different opinion. They all follow the opinions of their chief critics—their bosses—and don't dare to strike out on their own. I mean, after 25 years of uninterrupted triumphs of *The Consul* all over the world, it is most unimaginative of a so-called younger critic to mimic the sentiments of his so-called superior. In fact, it is downright cowardly!

Interview, New York/
The New York Times, 4-14:(2)1.

433

Robert Merrill
Opera singer

1

When you really get down to it, a singer is his own true critic. I have to please myself. Even when the audience applauds enthusiastically, if I'm not satisfied with what I've given, I don't even feel like acknowledging the applause with the customary bow. I have to satisfy either my own high standards or those of someone very close who really understands.

Interview, Los Angeles/
Los Angeles Herald-Examiner, 8-25:(D)6.

Mitch Miller
Conductor

2

I've always thought music had to be a part of people's lives, and that's one reason I have enjoyed, so much, the last few years—which have been mostly devoted to conducting symphony orchestras that play music understandable to the average guy. I believe in people participating—singing, clapping, enjoying themselves. When a soloist whips out a brilliant effort during a concerto, I think people ought to applaud. In ballet and opera, supposedly far more sophisticated art forms than symphonic music, the audience applauds a good performance on the spot; they even interrupt the performance. I think symphony audiences should do the same thing . . . Music ought to be a part of everyday life, for everyone. No fancy clothes, no cultural snobbism.

Interview, Oakland, Calif./
San Francisco Examiner, 2-9:11.

Birgit Nilsson
Opera singer

3

Most Italian singers approach opera as if it is much too easy, as if they were born to sing; and they don't last . . . Most Italian singers have poor techniques. They develop a chest voice and three or four registers, but soon the holes appear. If a violinist were to play a "scrunch," everyone would object, but not when singers do that with their voices. The Italian bel canto is dying out. It is not only to sing Wagner that we must concentrate on our techniques. One should be able to go back and sing an *Aida* and

to know you have your voice under control. You have to work finer, like clockwork.

Interview, San Francisco/
San Francisco Examiner & Chronicle,
10-13:(This World)24.

Buck Owens
Country-music singer

4

[On his forthcoming performance in New York]: New York, with Broadway and all, got to thinking they were too sophisticated for country music. The people were afraid to get manure on their boots, afraid country music might smell up the place . . . I think the mood is changing, though. Maybe it's because we're getting away from that nasal twang, but country music is becoming more acceptable, and it seems to me that the 1950-type rock sounds a lot like country music—the modern kind. There is a lot of that kind of rock, which is real popular now, in country music, and vice versa. It's a cross-over. That all helps.

Interview, Bakersfield, Calif./
The New York Times, 1-11:18.

S. J. Perelman
Author, Playwright

5

Broadway has been reduced in quality and importance. The theatres—and the theatre sections of newspapers—have been taken over by rock stars and blue movies . . . Whenever there is a successful revival, I find myself hoping for a return of the polite *incisive* comedy. No one, for example, could write about women like George Kelly. But the day of such creations is gone.

Interview, New York/
The New York Times, 11-3:(2)5.

Tony Randall
Actor

6

Popular music is in a state of extreme boredom. Nothing is happening in it. The reason seems to be that music, as we know it today, is dominated by the record business and the record business is dominated by children. Something took place in our culture that had never occurred before: Small children now have lots of money. The record business is meeting the standards of small children. It has become incredibly lucrative and, at the same time, ridiculously retrograde.

Interview/Los Angeles Herald-Examiner, 6-23:(TV Weekly)5.

Buddy Rich
Drummer

1

I love this business. It's been good to me. I've made six and a half million dollars. I've been totally broke. I've been rich again. And broke again. Because I love what I'm doing, money is secondary. The first thing is to try to keep the beautiful alive. And music is a very total, beautiful thing. With music, you can lift people out of their every-day, dull life. Good music makes you forget all that terror of the outside.

Interview, New York/ The New York Times, 6-2:(2)22.

Julius Rudel
General director and conductor, New York City Opera

2

Conducting is a question of communicating by whatever mysterious means. And they *are* mysterious, there's no question about it. There are some things you cannot explain—like why the same orchestra will sound different for different people. An orchestra sometimes reacts as a body to or against something, sometimes for God knows what reason. Maybe you can begin to explain it, but it isn't enough. There's still a large residue that really cannot be defined, and that's the essence of the thing.

The New York Times Magazine, 9-29:52.

Bobby Short
Singer, Pianist

3

[On his using mostly traditional music in his act]: Don't get me wrong. I'm not Mr. Nostalgia. If I sing an old song, it had better be a damn good old song or I don't sing it. There aren't many good songwriters around these days—*that's* the dying art. [Rock music] said what it had to say long ago. Now it just makes

kids into millionaires. I couldn't care less about it—there, it was time I said that.

Interview, Washington/ The Washington Post, 3-31:(F)10.

Beverly Sills
Opera singer

4

[On temperamental opera singers]: Temperament to me means that quality a singer has that holds your eyes riveted to him from the moment he steps out on the stage. I don't see great flaming temperamental exhibitions in the opera houses I sing in, and I sing all around the world. I don't have the energy to waste in being temperamental, and I don't think anybody else has, either.

Interview, Washington/ The Washington Post, 7-2:(B)2.

Georg Solti
Musical director, Chicago Symphony Orchestra

5

There are two ways to conduct badly. One is by the man who has no ideas at all. He just beats the air and tries to cope with his life. He is hopeless. The other man is a more unfortunate—an average—case. He has ideas, but he can never put them across for reasons of technique and communication. The difference between a mediocre conductor and a very good one lies in the ability to recognize whether what he gets is what he wants or not. The really great conductor has ideas that are better than the rest of the group *and* he is able to put them across.

The New York Times Magazine, 9-29:32.

William Steinberg
Musical director, Pittsburgh Symphony Orchestra

6

[On conducting]: Who gave me the right and power to hold Mozart and Beethoven's fate in my hands? Someone who did not know what he was doing, or someone who knew exactly what he was doing. Anyway, I soon became aware of my—pardon the expression—job. Therefore, I always refer to conducting as a calling—not a job or profession. Who called me?

WHAT THEY SAID IN 1974

(WILLIAM STEINBERG)

I don't know. But it was discovered that I was pre-destined to lead men, and this is the reason why I actually became a conductor. It's the most important part of conducting.

The New York Times Magazine, 9-29:32.

Robert Stolz
Composer, Conductor
1

The moment I pick up the baton I forget how old I am [94]. As soon as I hear the music I go into a trance and the years slip away. I think that is the main reason for the success of my records—one thinks one is listening to a 20-year-old conductor.

Interview, Vienna/
Los Angeles Times, 12-11:(4)26.

Jule Styne
Composer
2

Look at the harm these all-rock radio stations have been doing. Hours and hours of that noise, noise, noise. Don't people see the relationship to dope-addiction and the general disintegration all around us? It's a clear result of that hammering, hammering, hammering. I'm not against rock, per se. I'm against the constant din of it. What I am for is mixing it all up—rock, country music, classical, ballet—mix them all up. If you don't hear the other music, how do you know what's good? You need all kinds of music to really hear, to discriminate.

Interview, Washington/
The Washington Post, 8-25:(L)5.

Michael Tilson Thomas
Orchestra conductor
3

[On conducting]: I don't want to be Big Papa—"Ach, now my children, I vill tell you how you must play the music." I don't want to say, "Listen, you idiots, pay attention!" either. I don't want to be either of those people. I want to be someone who is considered to be a help by the players. This is a spiritual question that is important. I know that eventually this way of working will triumph—when the process of rehearsing becomes more and more a way of

understanding a piece, not just fulfilling the specifications that the "foreman" is laying down. Young musicians of my generation, or younger, are certainly not about to put up with the nonsense that has gone on in regard to the relationship between conductor and orchestra.

The New York Times Magazine, 9-29:34.

Virgil Thomson
Composer
4

... a music critic has only got to ask himself, "Did I say what I mean, and am I willing to mean what I said?" In the last analysis, liking or disliking a piece of music has nothing to do with the critic's responsibility. But if he can find out what the music's about, and tell his readers—well now, that's a good idea.

News conference, San Francisco, July 31/
San Francisco Examiner, 8-1:24.

Peter Ustinov
Actor, Director, Writer
5

Opera is a great medium, because you can't be subtle. You have to resign yourself to the fact no one hears a word—and be happy no one does. Operas in translation are ridiculous... Another thing I love about opera is there is a kind of "improvise" tradition. You know someone is going to catch a cold before the third performance and someone will be flown in from Thessalonika as a replacement and go on without a rehearsal—and no one in the audience will even notice.

Interview/
"W": a Fairchild publication, 2-8:9.

Sarah Vaughan
Singer
6

I've been singing the same way since the first note left my mouth, and it's always been jazz. Jazz may go through some style changes, but it's always been here and it always will be. Of course, the sound may change, because the material may dictate a lush background or a three-piece combo. Even the rock groups are adding to their following by incorporating jazz into their acts. Young people are even discovering me. They tell me they play their jazz records in secret; because jazz was their parents' music, and it proves they were right all along.

Interview/
Los Angeles Herald-Examiner, 5-4:(B)8.

Herbert von Karajan
Orchestra conductor

1

[On critical notices of his work] : I do it as I do it; he who likes it, likes it. It's not good to read reviews at all. If you believed in one man, you must ask why another says the contrary. Where is the truth? The truth is nowhere.

Interview, New York, Nov. 9/
The New York Times, 11-12:44.

Harry Warren
Composer

2

[Criticizing much of today's music] : . . . the trend to make songs socially significant, to abandon the old moon-in-June tradition. Maybe I'm old-fashioned, maybe I've lived too long, but the kids today—they put a lot of words together, and most of the time they don't even rhyme; then they add some music, and they call it a song. I don't know. For instance, a guy says, "I woke up this morning, and I wasn't feeling good. I went into the kitchen and drank some orange juice." What the hell kind of song is that?

Interview, Beverly Hills, Calif./
Parade, 5-26:9.

Paul Francis Webster
Composer, Lyricist

3

If you're a novelist or a playwright or doing a screenplay, you can wait years for a reaction. But while a song is still hot in your hands, it can be introduced on the air. Suddenly your words are shooting all over like skyrockets and you hear people singing your words back to you, with deep feeling. That can be quite a moving experience.

Interview, Los Angeles/
Los Angeles Times, 11-3:(Home)30.

Franco Zeffirelli
Director

4

I have done 42 opera productions, but no Wagner. You have to love what you do, and Wagner is so arrogant, so presumptuous, so boring.

Interview/
"W": a Fairchild publication, 2-8:9.

THE STAGE

Alan Arkin
Actor

1

I can't stand being on stage. I was in two long runs on Broadway and they almost drove me crazy. It was just horrible. The excitement for me has always been in creating a character. The audience was always a hurdle to get over. And repeating a performance for any great length of time was something I never liked. Then, on Broadway, they put your name above the title of the play, and up until then I always thought I was other people when I was on stage. Really, I was kind of crazy, I suppose, but I really believed I was someone else when I got on stage. But the minute they put my name above the title, I felt like the audience was coming there in part to see *me*.

Interview/
Los Angeles Herald-Examiner, 11-26:(B)4.

Elizabeth Ashley
Actress

2

I've spent my life sashaying my fanny on and off the stage and I usually take my money for simple endurance. You get a script and you say, "How the hell am I gonna wrap my mouth around this garbage?" The tragedy is that nobody is writing relevant journalistic theatre. By that I mean plays and films that deal with the way we live now.

San Francisco Examiner & Chronicle,
9-29:(Datebook)15.

Alan Ayckbourn
Playwright

3

The longer television continues, the greater the future theatre will have. That is, providing theatre continues to stress its assets, the main one being that it can offer live performances—a spontaneous bond between actor and audience

which none of the mechanical media can offer. To this end, I am all for the final breakdown of the conventional proscenium-arch theatre and a return to the more natural open stage. More and more theatre people are beginning to realize that this is essential to our survival. By this I am not necessarily advocating that actor-browbeating-and-assaulting-the-audience type of theatre, which is usually embarrassing and sometimes little short of alarming. I mean merely that it is necessary to bring the actor into close enough contact with his audience that he can properly sense them and they him. Theatre is, and always will be, a celebration of the art of acting. We playwrights are there to assist and to shape the event. We're invaluable.

Interview/The New York Times, 10-20:(2)7.

William Ball
General director, American
Conservatory Theatre, San Francisco

4

We haven't got too many wise men today who are popular. We have too many people who are spreading garbage around. If just once in our lives the first thing we heard in the morning was these words from *Cyrano*, "I love you beyond life, beyond breath, beyond any human reach," there is nothing we couldn't accomplish all day. That's what the theatre does for us . . . touches our lives in a way that makes life more possible.

At luncheon honoring him,
Beverly Hills, Calif., April 19/
Los Angeles Herald-Examiner, 4-23:(B)5.

5

[On the repertory nature of ACT]: An actor should be kept busy to the maximum. The company starts out at 10 in the morning and ends at 11:30 at night. Most of them don't have very much spare time. They teach, they study, they perform. An artist is a person who is "proliferating." A painter works all the time at his art; so does a pianist. In the theatre, the custom has been to spend a great hunk of time trying to get a job, then a lot of time trying to keep it, then a long time in a single role. These are all the signs of a non-productive, non-creative person. It is going fallow by repetition. I once knew a woman who had been in *Life with Father* for 11 years. I doubt very much if, at the end of that time, she should have called herself an actress any more.

Interview, San Francisco/
The New York Times, 7-7:(2)5.

Kermit Bloomgarden
Producer

1

If one believes in the quality of the work he's doing, it stands a 35 to 40 per cent chance of being successful. If one produces a work because he thinks he's going to make money on it, it stands a 5 per cent chance. On the one hand, you're backing your own judgment; on the other, you're deciding what the public wants.

Interview/
"W": a Fairchild publication, 3-8:2.

2

[On the large number of British-originated shows on Broadway]: It's much easier to see a finished product and bring it in than it is to originate one here [in New York]. There are not that many originals around here that I want to do. Each one of us [Broadway producers] who is doing a British play here found one we liked—it's not just that we all decided to do English plays this year. We're fortunate to have the Royal Shakespeare and the National Theatre to draw from. British subsidized theatre is giving us an opportunity to see plays, better plays than are being done in the British commercial theatre.

Interview, New York/
The New York Times, 12-5:56.

Ernest Borgnine
Actor

3

Perhaps the best answer [to improving the state of the theatre] would be the establish-ment of state-sponsored theatrical companies. Ideally, each state would allocate funds to a stock company that would represent the particular state. Actors, actresses, playwrights, composers and lyricists would be accepted into the company and develop a year-round program of theatre ... Those joining the company would be obligated to participate for three years, at the end of which time they could "graduate" into film or television or work for the commercial theatre. The most significant aspect of this far-ranging plan would be the development of new talent from all over the country. There could arise a national competition where the most praised productions and new works could be offered in a repertory competition, at a national theatre. To me, a plan like this, if it were to be effected, would stimulate interest in the theatre all across the country. Individuals who are chauvinistic about their state would take an interest in the arts if only because it would enhance the reputation of their state. More people would go to theatre and see new talents; they would also experience the reality behind a live performance.

Interview, New York/
The Dallas Times Herald, 7-14:(F)11.

Peter Brook
Director

4

What makes theatre legitimate is whether it reflects a search for something real. Today, our theatres are often narrow, parochial, class-bound, closed in style or closed in content to the richness and contradictions of human experience. Each theatre tradition, from the musical comedy to the Noh, covers only a tiny corner of the canvas. There is where the international experience lies; for actors of different cultures working together can sometimes crack open the cliches that their cultures have become. Buried behind the mannerisms of cultures lurk true cultures, and they in turn each express a different part of the human atlas. The complete truth is global. The theatre is the place where this great jigsaw can be played.

San Francisco Examiner & Chronicle,
3-17:(Datebook)9.

Yul Brynner
Actor

1

I get very intimidated by audiences. I have stage fright until I'm on. Waiting in the dressing-room until the curtain goes up is always a problem for me. I have never grown accustomed to that. I suffer hell, really; in fact, I hope hell is not that bad.

Interview, New York/
The Washington Post, 11-9:(B)2.

Abe Burrows
Playwright

2

I'm always talking to drama students who have a contempt for happy endings. Well, there are different kinds of "happy." Look at the end of *Hamlet*: Everybody's dead; the whole stage is littered with bodies. Then, suddenly, Horatio bends over and says, "Good night, sweet prince, and flights of angels sing thee to thy rest!" And Fortinbras says let four captains bear Hamlet's body out, and suddenly you feel better. You go out of the theatre on an upbeat note. I think you should be able to say "The End." I'm tired of taking people to the theatre and having them say, "Is it over?" My role as a playwright is to make an audience go out feeling complete. You may have saddened them, but you owe them a satisfactory exit—you know, catharsis, or whatever you call it . . . You notice how on TV they end with the credits because there's no end to the story? Well, millions of us grew up on "happily ever after" and, true or not, *that's* an ending.

Interview, Washington/
The Washington Post, 2-2:(B)5.

Carol Channing
Actress

3

New York always is the worst opening [for a show], not a representative audience at all. There's always a hundred-odd down-front seats for the press; and then the backers, who've already seen the show somewhere and know all the jokes, always want to come and see how the opening-nighters are receiving their investment. That means that opening night audiences are

sneaking looks at everybody else and ignoring the show.

The Washington Post, 2-3:(E)3.

Alexander H. Cohen
Producer

4

The appeal of the stage is universal. The union of actor and audience can strike a spark of human recognition that pierces all barriers, including language.

The Christian Science Monitor, 4-4:(F)6.

Hume Cronyn
Actor

5

Acting is monastic. It sure as hell isn't a rich, full, social experience. The opposite of that is to be unemployed, and that's a real unhappiness.

Interview, New York/
The New York Times, 3-13:39.

Charles Dillingham
General manager, American
Conservatory Theatre, San Francisco

6

When I was a theatre-management student at Yale, everybody tried to proselyte us on repertory. I couldn't figure out why. It seemed better to do one play at a time. It is certainly more economical. But I've finally realized that repertory is the only way you can build a company with real quality. The people get to know each other personally and professionally. They're not going to let each other down. There's no one-upmanship among them.

Interview, San Francisco/
The New York Times, 7-7:(2)5.

Anthony Dowell
Dancer, Royal Ballet, London

7

What does bother me an awful lot about being a dancer is the constant tension of performing. I get frightfully nervous. It's at those lonely moments when you're on your own—waiting to go on. It's that feeling that you can't relieve your nerves. I always slightly resent the people out in the audience, because they're not at all as nervous as I am. Their stomachs are not doing dreadful things. You see, dancers can't take calming pills or drink to quiet down. With us it's a continual battle, coping with nerves.

Interview, New York/
The New York Times, 5-19:(2)14.

1

I'm afraid I like the old-fashioned story bit. I like to identify with someone when I go to the theatre. I feel cheated if I see an abstract ballet with no sets and no costumes. I don't get a kick out of it, really. It's so much easier to dance, too, if you have a character, if you are someone—you are able to hide and use something instead of just being exposed as a classical machine.

Interview, New York/
The Christian Science Monitor, 5-23:(F)6.

Martha Graham
Dancer

2

The experience of knowing the body, not just as something lovely to look at, but as a wonder to experience, is the reason dancers are like shells. Shells are a tiny bit of life, an instant of life, that demands a place. And it begins to weave its own house and it makes its own body. A dancer takes about 10 years to be made—10 years of constant daily work for the body to be so steady and strong that you are not afraid of it any longer. But this is only the beginning.

Interview/
Los Angeles Herald-Examiner, 1-12:(B)9.

3

As a dancer, you are not dancing for the 3,000; you are dancing for the one—for the one to whom that night your dancing will be a revelation.

At "An Evening With Martha Graham,"
University of California, Los Angeles,
Oct. 29/Los Angeles Times, 10-31:(4)11.

Helen Hayes
Actress

4

The trouble with too many actors is that they regard themselves as Artists, upper case. In my long career I've only come across three or four artists. Larry Olivier and the Lunts come immediately to mind. I shouldn't make lists

because I'm sure there are several others. But the rest of us are merely performers who have tried to perfect our craft within those limitations. I'm still working on perfecting my craft.

Interview, San Francisco/
San Francisco Examiner, 6-21:27.

Lillian Hellman
Playwright

5

The theatre has gone downhill, in part because it has deserved to go downhill. In the last 10 years, perhaps since World War II, movies have been truly better than the theatre, and we might as well face it.

Before Smithsonian Associates, Washington,
Nov. 11/The Washington Post, 11-13:(B)2.

John Houseman
Producer, Director

6

There's so much going on in theatre around the country. The universities are the heart of it. No, I don't mean that all the drama students are going to be great professionals, not a bit of it. But think what great audiences they are becoming! They're being exposed to things of the mind, the spirit. There are all those splendid theatre buildings around the country, and not just in the big towns, either. They're in middle-towns, places that have a much higher intelligence quota than is popularly supposed.

Interview, Washington/
The Washington Post, 11-17:(G)10.

Thomas P. F. Hoving
Director, Metropolitan Museum of Art,
New York

7

Not too many years ago, 36 Broadway theatres were flourishing. With the works of such playwrights as Tennessee Williams, Arthur Miller and others, you had a never-ending procession of things that were the highest quality—even experimental things. Now that is not so true. Theatre people get out their pocket calculators and say, "Let [producer Joseph] Papp do it; let somebody else do it." To solve the problem of inflation, they renovated theatres, put in vastly more seats. This caused public discomfort, and they were in a vicious circle, with

WHAT THEY SAID IN 1974

(THOMAS P. F. HOVING)

the whole environment becoming a money thing. That generated off-Broadway and off-off-Broadway, where one would think the slack would be picked up; but it hasn't, curiously enough. I guess the big stage is still very important.

Interview, New York/
Los Angeles Times, 5-14:(2)7.

Trevor Howard
Actor 1

In playing for any medium, including stage, you've got to project the truth. It sounds terribly pompous to say, but all you have to do is be real.

Interview, New York/
Los Angeles Herald-Examiner, 1-19:(B)9.

Gene Kelly
Actor, Dancer 2

Dancing is the only art form in which the artist decreases in skills as he grows older. Just as a dancer is becoming knowledgeable about his work, his tools grow weaker, just like an athlete. Painters, writers and musicians mature as they get older, polishing their skill. Dancers are more like boxers. A writer may improve with age, but it is a simple fact that a dancer cannot do at 40 what he could do at 20.

The Dallas Times Herald, 6-25:(B)4.

Deborah Kerr
Actress 3

People talk about different schools of acting. I see acting as much more within the individual . . . What I do is look for the "me" in the character I'm playing and then build from that. It's easier in the theatre because you can change nuances from performance to performance.

Interview, Klosters, Switzerland/
"W": a Fairchild publication, 10-4:10.

Angela Lansbury
Actress 4

Where are the great new works, the great new roles, the great new musicals? Survival is

the name of the game; and if I've survived and developed a career with some longevity, it's because I've never been willing to sit around and wait. If something I can create from scratch doesn't come along, I'll do something that's already been done. I've played some despicable dames in my checkered career . . . but I've always searched for the honest, underlying human element behind the words and actions of the characters. As a woman, I look for the fascinating facets and truths behind people that can make the worst bitch in the world a palatable human being.

San Francisco Examiner & Chronicle,
9-29:(Datebook)15.

Sam Levene
Actor 5

In those [early] days, there were so many theatres that I never had trouble getting a job. The pay wasn't terrific, but I was always working and that was the most important thing. After all, an actor without a stage is a bum. If you are a painter or a writer, you can paint or write even if nobody buys. But acting must have an outlet. The outlet is the stage—any stage.

Interview/Los Angeles Times,
1-20:(Calendar)30.

Shirley MacLaine
Actress 6

[On her new one-woman musical stage revue]: You want to know why it takes guts to do all this? Because you can't hide behind your character. Nobody can yell "cut" and let you do it again. You're totally exposed up there—naked to the world. You live or die. The stage is the hardest place because it makes you expose so much of yourself. It proves the talent you really have.

Interview, Los Angeles/
San Francisco Examiner & Chronicle,
10-20:(Datebook)9.

Marcel Marceau
Mime 7

In films, the art is to create illusions through reality; whereas in the theatre, the object is to create reality through illusions: We make visible the invisible.

*Interview, Boston/
San Francisco Examiner & Chronicle,
4-28:(Datebook)16.*

Walter Matthau
Actor

1

... I think the New York theatre is primarily a showcase for other, more rewarding, financial institutions. I mean, people do Broadway plays more or less to get seen so they can get into movies or a TV series. Someone like Jason Robards is an exception—he's an excellent actor and he loves the stage. But I don't give a damn.

*Interview, New York/
The New York Times, 4-21:(2)11.*

David Merrick
Producer

2

Broadway is in a terrible state. The material is bad. You can't get people to write or direct or act. [But] I was in California 3½ years ago, and it was funereal. Now there is a very happy buzz and excitement in films. It's a normal cycle. The wheel will turn, and theatre will be back in favor again.

*Interview, Chicago/
The Washington Post, 4-14:(G)4.*

3

[On the large number of British-originated shows on Broadway]: I haven't been able to find any good American plays ... Virtually everything, but a few, comes from the British subsidized theatre. You should have a subsidized theatre here [in the U.S.]. But even the Royal Shakespeare and the National Theatre [of Britain] are in such desperate straits that they are making some choices of plays on the basis of what might go here [in New York]. They have had to be commerical-minded, with their costs up and subsidies down. As for the future of Broadway, if there are a lot of hits on Shaftesbury Avenue [in London] this season, it will be all right on Broadway next season. But there's not much there now.

*Interview, New York/
The New York Times, 12-5:56.*

Arthur Miller
Playwright

4

The production of a new play, I have often thought, is like another chance in life, a chance to emerge cleansed of one's imperfections. Here, as when one was very young, it seems possible again to attain even greatness, or happiness, or some otherwise unattainable joy.

*San Francisco Examiner & Chronicle,
2-3:(Datebook)17.*

5

For myself, the theatre is above all else an instrument of passion.

*At "Evening With Arthur Miller"
symposium, San Francisco/
Los Angeles Times, 2-6:(4)13.*

Igor Moiseyev
Director, Moiseyev Dance Company, Moscow

6

I believe that dance, like any kind of art, is an expression of human feelings, ideas and emotions. It reveals, in plastic form, the human being and the character of the whole nation it depicts. This is its strength.

*Interview, New York/
The Christian Science Monitor, 6-27:(F)6.*

Rudolf Nureyev
Ballet dancer

7

It's not easy, not an easy metier, to dance. It is really very hard and very inadvisable; you have to love it more than yourself in order to do it.

*Interview, San Francisco/
San Francisco Examiner & Chronicle,
4-7:(Datebook)11.*

8

Before every performance I am nervous and frightened. Putting on my make-up, for example, is a way of becoming acquainted with the inevitable fact that I will *have* to go out and dance. I feel like cattle before slaughter. There is no escape. Really, what it boils down to is that we are paid for our fear.

*Interview, New York/
The New York Times, 5-5:(2)15.*

Joseph Papp
Producer   1

[On his Public Theatre in New York]: People think of me as the major thrust of this theatre, but I follow the lead—of writers first, and of directors and actors... I provide the power, context and the audience. My taste and judgment comes in at all times, but I have no grand design... The ingredients that make the cake are not mine. I am the leavening force. At some point, I become an ingredient, but never the basic ingredient... It's not a one-man theatre. I'm helpless without playwrights and actors. I'm a sponge—ready to absorb.

The New York Times, 3-4:38.

Robert Preston
Actor   2

You know what a long run [in the theatre] means to me? Sheer heaven. Yes, I know that some actors can't stand doing the same role night after night... To me, repeating a performance is like telling a joke. If a man tells a joke to a different audience every time, he will always get laughs and find it rewarding; only his wife is bored by hearing the same joke over and over. Well, when you're doing a long-run show, you have a different audience every night and you always get a new reaction. So it never gets boring.

Interview, Los Angeles/
San Francisco Examiner, 7-30:20.

Harold Prince
Producer   3

[In the theatre,] you can't begin with an idea: You've got to begin with people—and within the first three minutes; later than that, you're lost... theatre is about people, characters; and unless the audience is quickly given its characters, you're not going to hold them. Take the beginning of *Fiddler on the Roof.* That's what proved it to me—Tevya and *all* the villagers setting themselves in the audience's mind with "Tradition." That song immediately gives you the characters, their background, their present situation. In *A Little Night Music*, after Stephen Sondheim's evocative overture, you meet the characters in "Night Waltz," and the idea of the story is held off until the characters, in a sense, introduce themselves in song.

Interview, New York/
The Washington Post, 3-17:(E)1.

4

I think Broadway is still the important place... But we can't get anything done in New York until the economy of the theatre is locked into the people, until solutions are found for people worrying about the price of mayonnaise at the supermarket. I'm glad I'm not faced with raising money this year for a musical. It's a hard year ahead, and I'm taking some time off.

Interview/
San Francisco Examiner & Chronicle,
9-29:(Datebook)11.

Anthony Quayle
British actor   5

[On his being involved in a traveling repertory company that performs on U.S. college campuses]: ... I am interested in the preservation of good theatre, and in the preservation of some of the greatest plays that have ever been written, which are now too expensive to put on. I also think, without being overly pompous, that it is important to enlighten people in the widest sense of the word, whether it's through good journalism, good writing or good plays. If we don't look out we're going to have an entirely materialistic society, with no idea of literature, language, history or the past, and therefore of the present. The theatre is one of the most potent means of opening peoples' minds. What happens to it in the U.S. is of tremendous importance to the world.

Interview, Greensboro, N.C./Variety, 12-4:63.

Ralph Richardson
Actor   6

The theatre is a magnifier. Everything is still; the audience, the proscenium, everything is frozen but the actor. I can do things at a much lower key, and the attention is concentrated. But on the screen you've got that great big face, and yet the effect is diminished.

Interview, Washington, June 28/
The Washington Post, 7-1:(C)4.

Jerome Robbins
Choreographer

1

I think ballets are the closest to the life experience. I don't mean life-like. But every second that we're living is past us before we know it. Irretrievable. And there's something about the transient quality in ballet—a fixed period of time that's going by and that can only exist at that moment. It's possibly the most exciting and perhaps the most terrifying experience for the spectator, without his knowing it. The world which it creates has its own manners, its own logic and its own relationships.

Interview, New York/Los Angeles Times,
8-11:(Calendar)58.

Erich Segal
Author, Playwright

2

[Saying that, when he writes a play, he likes to stir up an audience's emotions]: I believe that when you have 'em down and they're weeping, you should keep 'em down and drain 'em. Then pick 'em up with a blotter and put 'em in their cars at the end of the evening. I'm a great believer in emotion, even at the risk of sentimentality. I don't like "cool."

Interview, New York/
The Washington Post, 11-9:(B)2.

Peter Shaffer
Playwright

3

The stage is dependent on its audience. A serious play, a play that's not just superficial or prosaic light comedy, must in some area be about conjuring the gods. And like the initiates in any religion, the priest is not the only one who has to be trained. The congregation must be prepared, too. When you experience something bigger than life, something that casts shadows longer than ourselves, you have to be prepared. A lot of people misunderstand the concept of serious theatre. They think a serious play has a specific message. But if a play has a message that can be abstracted to a simple formula, it's not very good.

Interview, New York/
"W": a Fairchild publication, 9-20:10.

Antoinette Sibley
Dancer, Royal Ballet, London

4

[Ballet] is an art without speaking, so that everybody can understand it; everybody can get joy and relief—even if for an hour. Everybody has problems now; I mean, really everybody. I would say that anything that can get somebody an hour, or two, away from those problems has to be something marvelous. I went through the stage about five years ago when I thought: "What really is one doing with one's life? Is one being selfish doing it [dancing] because it is the one thing that means a lot to you, when the world is in such a mess? Shouldn't one be a nurse, or a this, or a that?" And then I realized that in actual fact—because I know this myself—if one goes to a theatre, or an opera, and is taken away from one's problems, one can then come back to them, see them clearer and get a tremendous amount of happiness.

Interview, New York/
The Christian Science Monitor, 5-23:(F)6.

Paul Sills
Director

5

The popular theatre must go back to the *story*. It's the spoken word that keeps the theatre alive.

San Francisco Examiner & Chronicle,
4-7:(Datebook)9.

Donald Sinden
British actor

6

There is always change [in the theatre]. Since 1955, there have been enormous injections into theatre by [John] Osborne, [Harold] Pinter, [Arnold] Wesker and others. They changed the course of acting. But with one or two exceptions, these plays were not "box office." Theatre, here [in the U.S.] more than in England, depends upon the public paying. The only way is to find a play that the public wants to see. Then there were the newer plays. One had to go through it. You had to have copulation on the stage to see how dull it was, except for the participants; but you have to go through with it, with the permissive society. Still, the lines in *Romeo and Juliet* achieve such heights; and it is better, more alluring, to see a

WHAT THEY SAID IN 1974

(DONALD SINDEN)

woman dressed rather than undressed. Life is depressing enough, isn't it? One should be taken out of one's self in the theatre. I don't want to see the death of the other kind of theatre, but we should give the public an alternative. If they would rather see a kitchen-sink play, then God bless them.

Interview, New York/
The New York Times, 12-23:34.

Hugh Southern
President, Theatre Development Fund,
New York 1

There is more theatre production than at any time in our history. I'm not referring to quality or attendance. It was estimated about two years ago that 600 plays were being presented in New York during one year. Now it's probably 800. This is a tremendous period of ferment . . . As for Broadway, I don't think it is the measure of our theatre, though it is still an important institution. There will probably be more one-man or, more precisely, one-woman shows on Broadway. This is a return to the kind of mix Broadway used to have, when it included not just theatre, but burlesque and vaudeville. I consider this mix an excellent one. A lot of people who came to see Bette Midler's one-woman show had never been in a theatre before. These shows can only have a healthy effect.

Interview, New York/
"W": a Fairchild publication, 1-11:16.

Michael W. Straight
Deputy Chairman, National Endowment
for the Arts of the United States 2

Traditionally, a symphony orchestra is looked on as something of renown for a city.

Theatre is not looked on quite that way. It's just not traditionally true; it doesn't have that ceremonial role. [For example, Washington's Arena Stage] can't have a white-tie ball; it is not considered symbolic of the national commitment to culture and fine arts. It's unfortunate, but people still look on theatre as a "low" art form; it is still struggling to place itself on a par of respectability with things like opera companies and symphony orchestras.

The Washington Post, 11-10:(F)4.

Jule Styne
Composer 3

You've got to bring the theatre to the people, to where they want to go. Dinner theatres are the coming thing. And the price is right: parking, good surroundings, dinner, theatre and dancing—an 11-in-one stop at one price. That's what the public is looking for . . . What these dinner theatres will lead to is a new surge of musical plays. That period of four-year runs is over with. In future, there will be more decentralization, and the major cities will have new works all at the same time.

Interview, Washington/
The Washington Post, 8-25:(L)5.

Peter Ustinov
Actor, Director, Writer 4

I've had no ego bruises because I've become absolutely convinced that theatre, like the movies, is a collaborative art. Even if you quarrel, more good is likely to come from that than not being able to cut your teeth on any hard object.

Interview, New York/
The Atlanta Journal and Constitution,
11-10:(F)7.

TELEVISION / RADIO

Steve Allen
Entertainer, Humorist

1

... there is only one comedy show left [on TV], and that is Carol Burnett's. Why the decline? It goes back to my theory about the number of comedians in the world. Out of three billion people in the world, there may be 300 comedians, probably closer to 200. I don't mean actors who can do cute comedy like Cary Grant, James Garner or James Stewart; I mean comedians. Most of them have had their go at television and then move on to the status of guest stars. I don't think we will ever [again] see the kind of television comedy that reached its peak with Sid Caesar and his fantastic group of comics and writers.

Interview, Los Angeles/
The Atlanta Constitution, 10-30:(B)11.

David L. Bazelon
Chief Judge, United States Court of
Appeals for the District of Columbia Circuit

2

The broadcast media know, or should know, when their programming is simply and only mass-appeal pablum, designed to titillate a sufficiently large majority to enable the broadcasters to sell the most advertising. They know when they are presenting only one side of a major public issue, when they are shading the facts to present their own point of view and when they are ignoring the concerns of the industry. They know the impact of their programs on children. They know about the marketing of human emotions and of the prurient interest of violence and sex. They know when they subvert the professionalism of their own news teams in order to reach the demographic audiences which will attract advertisers. They know that wide exposure of subjects ranging from the names of rape victims to the private grief of a mother on the death of her son constitute unconscionable invasions of privacy. And they know when they are over-commercializing their programming to amortize the inflated cost of the broadcast license. In sum, I think they know the times they may have prostituted the tremendous potential of television as a human communications tool. They know this, and they know what should be done about it. The programming executives and their advertiser clients must stop their single-minded purpose to achieve higher ratings, more advertising and greater profits, and stop to consider what greater purposes television should serve. And they must do it soon if we are to preserve our First Amendment values for telecommunications... The broadcast media surely must strenuously resist all government attempts to interfere with their wide legitimate discretion. [But] they must also have the strength to admit their shortcomings, their abuse of the immense power of television for the private profit of a few, to the serious detriment of the nation at large.

Before Federal Communications Bar
Association, Washington, Nov. 15/
The New York Times, 11-16:50.

Johnny Carson
Television talk-show host

3

The substance of humor has changed because of what you can say now. You have a greater latitude. Five or 10 years ago, you couldn't say "pregnant." Even in the movies. You had to say the girl was "in a family way" or "with child." Now you can come out and say almost anything. You can talk about drugs. You can do jokes about pot. The kind of material I do is reflected in my awareness of the audience. There's no longer that mythical little

(JOHNNY CARSON)

old naive lady from Dubuque, Iowa, watching the tube. [Today] she sees everything that's on television. She knows what's going on politically. Her tastes become more eclectic. So you can be quite outspoken now, as long as you don't get vicious or espouse a particular cause.

Interview, Los Angeles/TV Guide, 7-13:26.

Alistair Cooke
Chief United States correspondent,
"The Guardian" (England)   1

The most striking thing to me is that television has produced a generation of children who have a declining grasp of the English language, but also have a visual sophistication that was denied to their parents. They learn so much about the world that appeals immediately to their emotions, but I'm not sure it involves their intelligence, their judgment . . . Things can come at you on television in a flash—in three seconds—which would take a fine teacher an hour or so to interpret.

Interview, Washington/
U.S. News & World Report, 4-15:47.

2

The thing that alarms me is that you can pick up bad habits quicker from television than anything else. I notice children really picking up the butchery of the English language from television, and especially from advertising prose. "Genteelisms" are absolutely riddling the language. I mean, people don't ever moisten their lips any more; they "moisturize." It doesn't rain in Chicago; we now have "precipitation activity in the Chicago area." Between Madison Avenue and the Pentagon, nobody's ever going to be able to read the first chapter of Genesis. "Let there be light" will have absolutely no meaning. I heard a Defense Department official the other evening, and what he wanted to say was that we've got to be able to attack where we choose. But he didn't say that; he said he was going to "preserve our targeting options." I hear children talking about "dentifrice." They don't know what toothpaste is.

Interview, Washington/
U.S. News & World Report, 4-15:52.

Joseph Cotton
Actor   3

[On working in TV]: There is no room for experimentation or correction. One prepares himself the best he can, and then it's damn lucky if the show turns out well. The procedure for TV is slipshod, best likened to a group of musicians who are given a score and told to work separately and then report in the morning and work together professionally. In TV there's the additional difficulty of falling into the director's concept of the teleplay. One can only hope for the best when a project is done so rapidly and tailored for the mass audience that will buy products advertised.

Interview, Los Angeles/
Los Angeles Herald-Examiner, 8-14:(B)8.

James E. Duffy
President, American Broadcasting
Company Television Network   4

[On children's programming]: During those specific hours when our chief concern must be the welfare of our children, we are far too concerned with out-rating the competition . . . No matter how brilliant we may be in other areas of our programming day, if we are not superior here—when our children are held captive, so to speak—then we are crippled in our superiority everywhere.

Philadelphia/
San Francisco Examiner & Chronicle,
3-17:(Sunday Scene)14.

Leslie Fiedler
Professor of English,
State University of New York, Buffalo   5

[On TV soap operas]: If you sit before those programs, you get out of your head the condescension that says nobody watches those things except the clichéd tired housewives doing their laundry. I tell you—freaky and hippy kids watch those daytime serials, men and women watch those things, old and young people watch them. And what you get by watching those things is a moment of release, a moment of illumination and refreshment, a moment of escape—escape from the bounds of ordinary routine and ordinary consciousness.

At symposium sponsored by ITT Community Development Corp., Palm Coast, Fla./ The National Observer, 11-30:6.

Thomas P. F. Hoving
Director, Metropolitan Museum of Art, New York

1

A lot of people shriek about TV, but I have a feeling that TV is greater than the great Hollywood epoch. We remember the great old movies, but below them the support level was not so great—the movies that carried the business. The sludge that was given to us when we were growing up was more linear even than TV. The effect of TV has been extraordinarily important in education. People without formal education have gained a great deal of knowledge watching TV. When you get a fine series, it has a laser effect. Not just PBS—there have been spectacular things the [commercial] networks have put on; not all *I Love Lucy* reruns . . . Then you have this curious phenomenon of things that could only be on TV and that are excellent. *Upstairs, Downstairs* is really a purely TV series. You couldn't have it any other way. *War and Peace* was a TV series that was the equivalent of the 19th-century novel.

Interview, New York/ Los Angeles Times, 5-14:(2)7.

Robert T. Howard
President, National Broadcasting Company Television

2

We [commercial television] present what the American public indicates a desire for, what they actually watch and what they keep watching until they tune out, giving us our cue to move on to something else. There is a fine non-commercial television service in this country called Public Broadcasting. But it is misnamed. Because it is non-commercial, it does not have to attract the mass audiences advertisers are interested in. It is basically a selective service. It selects a certain taste of interest and programs to accommodate it. I don't think we [commercial TV] could have

registered 11 straight years of increasingly higher television viewing levels if we were not delivering the kinds of programs the general public wants and watches.

Before Georgia Association of Broadcasters, Jekyll Island, Ga./ The Hollywood Reporter, 6-19:8.

Ross Hunter
Producer

3

[On his upcoming entry into television production]: . . . I've never done TV before, except talk shows. But they want me to bring to television some of the same kind of romantic things I've done in movies, to bring back some of the beauty and joy and excitement that is what entertainment is all about. I'm sick of all the filth and pornography in films. I think the time is ready for us to bring back the hero and heroine and some of the glamor in film-making.

Los Angeles/Chicago Tribune, 8-30:(1)14.

John Huston
Motion picture director

4

I think differently about television than most. It has become the father in the house, and it speaks with a rare eloquence—unlike the real father who comes in from laying his bricks and treats the children with the loathing they inspire. It's the most hopeful aspect of the American scene. The integration of American life is achieved on television in a way I did not think possible.

Interview, Los Angeles/ Los Angeles Times, 8-4:(Calendar)26.

Fay Kanin
Writer; Vice president, Writers Guild of America

5

Television comes into the living room and takes off its shoes and loosens its belt and opens a can of beer. Sometimes it yawns and falls asleep. When it doesn't, it has the ability to reach into the people's minds and hearts and change their lives—as movies, for all their excitement, never can.

The Atlanta Constitution, 8-27:(B)8.

Elia Kazan
Author, Director 1

[On TV program content]: Get your hero up a tree in act one; throw rocks at him in act two; and get him down alive somehow in act three. I don't mean that all TV shows are that way, but the manufactured stuff has to be that way. And that pleases everybody because you're able to have a villain that everybody loves to hate.

Interview, New York/TV Guide, 12-7:14.

John H. Knowles
President, Rockefeller Foundation 2

[One] thing that is hurting family life is everybody's being glued to that God-forsaken TV. It has done away with discord and discussion of ideas and has caused less coherence and cohesiveness in the family.

Interview, New York/
Los Angeles Times, 2-13:(2)7.

Glen A. Larson
Writer, Producer 3

If in fact TV influences some people into violent acts—and I can't accept that—there is also a possibility that there is a deterrent effect if TV is as powerful as everyone maintains it is. TV is the great pacifier. It probably prevents more crime than anything else, because people are watching TV; and statistics of the New York police show that, when they are watching in Harlem, the crime rate is down. TV is the only place where you see crimes solved—and no one gets away with it. In the press and on the TV news, that's not so. It's possible that TV can, in marginal cases, help keep crime down. Police shows help to offset the stigma which exists in some places against the police. We are on their side . . . Why not see what good we have done? Why not have a study to determine *that*, instead of confining them to possible harm which is alleged? Nobody has ever gone into that phase of it. I believe TV has a deterrent effect on crime.

Interview, Los Angeles/Daily Variety, 2-25:9.

Norman Lear
Writer, Producer 4

I don't think there is any danger in over-estimating the intelligence of TV audiences—the real danger lies in underestimating it . . . I think it is arrogant of some television people to say that we [his shows] overestimate the intelligence of audiences. I have sat with hundreds of network executives and most of them have no more intelligence than the average American. They are usually no brighter than the less-educated fellow I met in, say, Winterset, Iowa, working in a carwash who, by virtue of native shrewdness and basic intelligence, is often able to fit more of life properly into his skull and come up with more of the proper answers than most TV executives!

Interview, New York/
The Christian Science Monitor, 7-25:13.

5

The essence of what I bring to all of this [his programs] has been, from the beginning, my feeling that a problem can't go too far into drama without coexisting with comedy. You know the old expression, "I laughed until I cried"—that may express it all. Working comedy and drama together has always been my special love. It's always been apparent to me that people laugh hardest when they care the most.

Interview, Los Angeles/
The National Observer, 8-24:22.

Piet Meyer
Chairman, South African
Broadcasting Corporation 6

[The television camera has] its own inherent preferences and prejudices, which, if not controlled, lead to one-sided, distorted, provocative and even false images.

The Christian Science Monitor, 8-26:3B.

Igor Moiseyev
Director, Moiseyev Dance Company, Moscow 7

TV? I try to watch it as rarely as possible. TV is not a means of art but only information about art. Yes, it is seen by millions of people, but the next day they say, oh, well, I've seen it, and then they don't go out to the theatre. I'm grateful when it informs me what took place— floods, fires, political events—but when it comes to the arts, I prefer to go to the theatre.

Interview, Washington/
The Washington Post, 8-4:(L)3.

Garry Moore
Television personality

1

When TV started, people were excited over anything they saw on the set . . . good or bad. Pioneers always get a position in history they may or may not deserve. It's like John Glenn. Everybody knows he was the first American in space. But they can't name the first three Americans who landed on the moon. We TV pioneers are the John Glenns. But we didn't make it to the moon.

Interview/Los Angeles Times, 8-9:(4)9.

Frank E. Moss
United States Senator, D—Utah

2

[Addressing broadcasters]: When you justly express fear of government encroachment of the freedom of the broadcasters to resist government-sponsored propaganda in any form of programming, I'm with you and the American public is with you. But when you allow yourselves . . . a rather exaggerated sense of deference to your advertisers for the simple human wish to avoid controversy, or to shield the American public from a hard look at the realities of our problems and institutions, then *you* have become the censors, and you are violating our First-Amendment rights—the right of access . . . We need the kinds of information which will enable us to perform our responsibilities, to perform our judgments and to perform our duties as informed citizens of a democracy. Whether you call it freedom of expression, consumerism, fairness, freedom of access or corporate responsibility, it amounts to the same thing. You have an enormous responsibility. It is clearly in the best interests of our society that you perform that responsibility without calling down upon your own knees the

leaden and stifling hand of government, or the growing cynicism of the American public.

Before National Association of Television
Program Executives, Los Angeles,
Feb. 18/Daily Variety, 2-19:1,19.

Everett C. Parker
Director, office of communications,
United Church of Christ

3

The FCC is more protective of the broadcasting industry than any mother was ever protective of any child in the history of mankind.

At panel discussion sponsored
by MORE magazine, New York/
The Christian Science Monitor, 5-30:(F)8.

4

Broadcasting [in the U.S.] as we have chosen to make it is a private business and I favor that. The investment is low. The return is astronomical, [but] the broadcasting industry is not willing to give up one-half of one per cent of its profits for the benefit of the country. They are not pleasing the majority of their audience. They are occupying the audience. And the audience is occupied because it can't get anything better.

Television interview/"Prime-Time TV:
the Decision Makers,"
American Broadcasting Company, 9-2.

Tony Randall
Actor

5

I don't think there has been any progress in television; no, none whatsoever. Artistically, it only has interest in what's commercial. What television is keyed to is what the advertiser feels will sell products . . . Television was in its element when it accompanied man to the moon. If there's an impeachment [of the President], TV would be the right medium. Football, again, is television doing what it ought to do—it's television at its best. Otherwise, there isn't much to it.

Interview/Los Angeles Herald-Examiner,
6-23:(TV Weekly)5.

Elton H. Rule
President, American Broadcasting Companies [1]

[On criticism of commercial broadcasting]: I would like to suggest that those who would attack us—by seeking to over-regulate us or otherwise to keep us from performing the kind of service in the public interest for which we are respected by the American people—be as open as we are. I would like to see those who would determine what our role should be, grant that with as massive and heterogeneous an audience as ours, all of our people have to be served. We always welcome constructive, progressive recommendations that will make broadcasting even more excellent as an informational, entertainment and cultural medium. But we are not interested in devoting ourselves to matters that would have the effect of deterring us from our true public responsibilities. [Broadcasters too often] over-react whenever we respond to specific regulatory matters or to frequent public criticisms which usually are based on infrequent viewing, with little or no acknowledgment of our major accomplishments and contributions to society. This often creates a void in which we—for no good reason—suddenly find ourselves on the defensive.

Before California Broadcasters Association, Palm Springs, Jan. 22/Daily Variety, 1-23:1.

Robert W. Sarnoff
Chairman, RCA Corporation [2]

I have always believed it's in the public interest for broadcasters not to have to apply for license-renewal every three years. The real broadcaster can perform a better service if he knows he has a longer period and isn't subject every few years to a challenge by somebody who's just making promises of what he will do. You're going to get a bad egg here or there in any line of activity, but on balance I think broadcasters have done an extraordinary job. There are a lot of people still in broadcasting today, by the way, who are pioneers, who were willing to take risks. Sure they are making good money, a high rate of return on their investment. But why shouldn't they? That's the name of the game in our country and in our economy. The risks and expenses in broadcasting are enormous. All you have to do is look at the many unanticipated things that the networks and stations had to cover in the past year. It was fantastic.

Interview, New York/ Nation's Business, March:51.

John Saxon
Actor [3]

A lot of television writing amounts to the clever wrapping up of a theme. Any theme. It offers all the right equations, sums them up neatly and shuts them off. There's no question of an allusion to something not yet understood. That has been the difficulty. Television people have been afraid of offending somebody. They're afraid of having a reaction that finds someone asking, "What the hell was that about?" They've wanted something that could be summarized neatly in a log rundown: "Tarzan goes into the jungle, wins treasure."

Los Angeles Herald-Examiner, 1-23:(D)7.

Herbert S. Schlosser
President, National Broadcasting Company [4]

[On criticism that TV is behind the times in its programming]: Television has been bringing up the rear in certain areas, to be sure. We're never going to be up with movies, books or the stage in permissiveness, for instance—nor do I think we should be. However, there are many things we do that the other fields can't or won't do. Forms of entertainment such as *Laugh-In*, or series like *All in the Family* and *Sanford and Son*, don't exist in other media. Also, television has a financial freedom which puts it ahead of other media. Films have to think seriously about getting their investment back; Broadway is even more risky. But if television wants to make a show like *The Execution of Private Slovick* or *The Autobiography of Miss Jane Pittman*, it just goes ahead. And if there should be a slight falling off in ratings, it isn't so drastic. Everything television does is immediately and vastly visible; that's why people tend to run it down. You don't have to pick and choose through a rack of paperback books or go out to a movie—it's all there in front of you. Any medium that is so visible to so many people tends to be denigrated. Don't forget—Hollywood movies only really began to be spoken of as an art form when the size of the audience shrank. I hope that never happens to us.

Interview, Los Angeles/
Los Angeles Times, 4-9:(4)18.

1

The strength of television comes from the 185 million people, in all walks of life, who, every week, are its voluntary viewers. Over the last 25 years, the American public has made television its primary medium of entertainment and its most trusted source of news and information. The average American home gives television well over six hours of its time each day. No other popular medium approaches its impact or has come anywhere near its record of growth . . . Television is many different things to different people. It comes before them variously as a source of fun and laughter; as a bearer of good news and bad; and as teacher and salesman. It is a theatre for drama, and an arena for the greatest sports events. It is a political tool and a civics course. It is an art form. It is a profitable business.

Before Association of National
Advertisers, Hot Springs, Va.,
Oct. 29/Vital Speeches, 12-1:119.

John A. Schneider
President, Columbia Broadcasting
System/Broadcast Group

2

Free commercial television is serving and satisfying the American public. That's my visceral feeling. Our critics have their visceral feelings, but mine is supported by fact, research and the largest viewing audience in the history of television.

Before CBS-TV affiliates, Los Angeles,
May 14/The Hollywood Reporter, 5-15:1.

Walter A. Schwartz
President, American Broadcasting
Company Television

3

[Saying TV today is much better than in the so-called "golden age of television" in the 1950s] : Television has become the showplace—for the vast majority of our people almost the only place—where they can witness the very finest in film and drama . . . [In the '50s,] poor and lukewarm reviews far outnumbered favorable notices . . . In the '50s, the medium was almost overwhelmed by what was mediocre at best and scandalous at worst . . . There have never been such great opportunities nor such a receptiveness within the medium and among our audiences for taking on the most challenging themes [than there are today].

Before Hollywood Radio and Television
Society, Beverly Hills, Calif.,
Feb. 12/The Hollywood Reporter, 2-13:1,9.

William Self
President, 20th Century-Fox Television

4

[Saying TV programming hasn't really changed creatively in the past 15 years]: I suspect we can't get out of the rut. When a network schedules a new show, hopefully it will sell; the network wants a show which will fit in with its programming for a particular night; it doesn't want the FCC to say it's too violent, sexy or adult; it wants a good counter-program; it doesn't want a show which might jeopardize the shows around it. [By the time all these considerations go into decision-making,] it's pretty hard to be innovative, and you're doomed to mediocrity.

Interview, Los Angeles/
Daily Variety, 11-4:9.

Lee Strasberg
Artistic director, Actors Studio

5

Anybody who becomes a star has earned it. You don't become a star in any medium accidentally. It means there is *something* there. In television, however, a lot of people become stars because they satisfy the requirements of the television medium. They would not necessarily satisfy the requirements of other mediums. I see many people on TV and I say, "Gee, this person is good." But what happens—especially if they get into series—is that they simply repeat the same tricks, play the thing as it comes along—easily, smoothly and with the

WHAT THEY SAID IN 1974

(LEE STRASBERG)

illusion of naturalness. They're not doing what they're capable of doing.

Interview, New York/TV Guide, 12-7:16.

1

Television drama can be even better than theatre drama because you can get *the* one performance you want. Television, like movies, has one great capability that theatre doesn't have: You can freeze excellence. That's why creating plays for television requires a greater responsibility. These are the documents upon which the history of our culture will be written.

Interview, New York/TV Guide, 12-7:18.

Gore Vidal
Author

2

It's Andy Warhol's genius to have said that people will always look at something rather than nothing. And that's the secret of television: Nothing has to be going on. It's better than looking at four walls.

*Interview, Beverly Hills, Calif./
The Dallas Times Herald, 1-22:(C)1.*

Lawrence R. White
*Vice president in charge of programming,
National Broadcasting Company Television*

3

[On the cancellation of programs with low ratings]: An audience of 15 million people seems large, but it isn't when you have the potential of reaching 80 per cent of the whole population of the United States. There are 70 million homes. For the most part, we have to reach the broad general public, as close to these 70 million homes as possible. Some shows are worth doing because they have significance, even though the audience may be more limited. But these are more likely to be specials rather than regular programs. We are running a business, and we have to keep that very much in mind.

*Interview, New York/
San Francisco Examiner & Chronicle,
3-24:(Datebook)25.*

Frederick Wilhelmsen
Professor of Philosophy, University of Dallas

4

... the book no longer dominates us. Television does. Images are now imaged for us; they are prefabricated, and it happens without us knowing it. If you discount the hours we sleep, many of us spend one-fourth of our lives watching television, and it is amazing how it affects us. We are medium massaged ... Television has divided us into special tribes or interest groups. The members of the tribes don't have to live together to identify with each other, because television brings them together wherever they are. Television was responsible for organizing the black and Chicano movements and women's liberation. It permits people who think alike to be together. And this new tribal system is shattering our nation. We are now a bleeding country, shattered, and this makes it difficult to govern.

*At Dallas Women's Club, Jan. 16/
The Dallas Times Herald, 1-17:(C)2.*

Robert D. Wood
*President,
Columbia Broadcasting System Television*

5

I think one of the most democratic institutions in this country is the television industry ... Our programs are being voted upon 365 days and nights every single year ... I think that the system that we have today gets closest to reaching what the American public wants from television. For me to substitute my judgment as to what they should look at as opposed to all kinds of input that we now get ... I much prefer what we're doing now.

*Television interview/"Prime-Time TV:
the Decision Makers,"
American Broadcasting Company, 9-2.*

Vladimir K. Zworykin
Inventor of the television tube

6

When broadcasting began to develop, I hoped TV would be used for educational purposes, especially so that different cultures could learn to understand each other. Instead, most of the time when I turn on the TV—bang, bang, bang.

Los Angeles/The New York Times, 7-31:39.

Judith Anderson
Actress

1

As for myself, I sit up here in Montecito [Calif.] and I say, "Oh, nobody wants me, nobody wants me." I have my garden and dogs and parties... I'm completely content until I think, "Oh, Lord, the clock is ticking and I haven't much longer and I'm not wanted."

Interview, Montecito, Calif./
Los Angeles Herald-Examiner, 8-18:(D)1.

Arthur Ashe
Tennis player

2

Tennis is an outlet for me. I can be volatile on the tennis court... without hurting anybody. If I didn't play tennis, I probably would have to see a psychiatrist.

Interview, Washington/
The Washington Post, 8-16:(D)6.

Elizabeth Ashley
Actress

3

A man I was married to once said to me, "Everything you do I could hire done better." And I thought to myself, oh my God. Is *that* what it's about? Loving, in marriage, becomes for a woman doing for free what he can hire done better. Well, I don't care for that, myself. I found marriage to be mutilating, barbaric, inhumane. People get married for social reasons, for convenience, for emotional safety. It wasn't for me.

Interview, New York/
The New York Times, 9-22:(2)3.

Isaac Asimov
Author

4

[On why he makes fun of himself]: I don't consider myself to be an essentially lovable person. I run the risk of creating a great deal of

hard feeling against myself because I am extraordinarily bright, and I know it, and there's no secret to the fact that I know it. I find that if I don't take myself seriously, if I'm ready to laugh at myself, I get forgiven an awful lot. And that makes life a little simpler. And secondly, it's a part of security. Often this terrible dignity one experiences, this insistence on never putting yourself in a ridiculous position, exists because you don't dare relax for a moment. You're protecting yourself with this thick shield. I don't fear that looking a little ridiculous now and then is going to alter the essential fact, which is that I am very bright.

Interview, New York/
The Christian Science Monitor, 3-27:(F)1.

Lucille Ball
Actress

5

I have an every-day religion that works for me: Love yourself first and everything else falls into line. Love of self—physical, mental, financial, moral. You have to really love yourself to get anything done in this world.

Interview, Los Angeles/
Los Angeles Herald-Examiner,
10-14:(California Living)36.

Art Buchwald
Newspaper columnist

6

[On his humorous column]: Everyone else had a mother and father. Everyone else lived in a house. Everyone else had love. I didn't have any of those things and I was pretty mad. I was also raised in the Jewish tradition in an area where there weren't many Jewish kids. And if you're Jewish, a lot of the time you get clouted, and one of the traditional defenses of Jewish kids is humor. I discovered early in the game I could make people laugh and, if I did, they liked me. If I was mean, they didn't like me. So to this day, I like to make people laugh

(ART BUCHWALD)

because I get back waves of love. And that's the payoff. It's not the money.

Interview, Washington/
"W": a Fairchild publication, 6-28:8.

Richard Burton
Actor   1

[On his recent divorce]: Of course, I never intend to be married again—but don't put too much emphasis on that; I could change my mind tomorrow. All I have to do is meet some cunning, conniving, gorgeous, glorious creature who'll turn my head around and I'll be lost all over again. There are times when I look forward to that—all those comely creatures in my future. I picture myself as the world's most eligible, glamorous bachelor with nothing but marvelous adventure before me. Then I think a little harder—and I realize that I'm a not-very-good-looking, puffy, paunchy middle-aged man who tends to be a bore a good deal of the time. That's quite depressing and it all saddens me. But what the hell! I've got fame and a good deal of money, and that combination can make even the ugliest duckling seem like a powerful lover. Unfortunately, when I get into bed with a woman these days it's more often than not just to go to sleep.

Interview, New York/
San Francisco Examiner & Chronicle,
7-7:(Datebook)17.

Michael Caine
Actor   2

From the beginning of my career, I wanted to make money. I've spent too long being without it. I don't want it for power, but to buy things. Every suit I buy, I buy three of. I don't wear them all, of course, but they're nice to look at in the closet.

The Dallas Times Herald, 3-17:(Sunday)2.

Prince Charles
Prince of Wales   3

I'm not a rebel by temperament. I don't get a kick out of not doing what is expected of me, or of doing what is not expected of me.

The Christian Science Monitor, 6-13:5.

4

I was asked whether I concentrated on developing or improving my image—as if I was some kind of washing powder, presumably with a special blue whitener. I dare say that I could improve it in some circles by growing my hair to a more fashionable length, being seen in the Playboy Club at frequent intervals and squeezing myself into excruciatingly tight clothes. I have absolutely no idea what my image is, and therefore I intend to go on being myself to the best of my ability.

Before magazine editors, London/
San Francisco Examiner & Chronicle,
11-10:(A)28.

Federico Fellini
Motion picture director   5

Directing a movie is the only thing which carries me away and takes me out of a world of boredom. I don't like to travel; I don't want to change the world; I haven't any hobbies; and I seldom go to the cinema because I'm impatient with the feeling that I'm missing something important which may be happening somewhere outside.

Interview, Rome/
San Francisco Examiner & Chronicle,
2-17:(Datebook)17.

J. Paul Getty
Industrialist   6

Actually, I've never felt rich, because I've always been in business where I was a moderate-sized fellow compared to Exxon, Royal Dutch, Shell, Texaco, Gulf, Standard of California. I'm a small-sized fellow, a small-sized outfit, so I've never had delusions of grandeur ... I've always had a place for every dollar that came in. I've never seen the day where I could say that I felt—rich. Generally, you worry about paying the bills.

Interview, Woking, England/
The New York Times, 2-6:31.

Katharine Graham
Publisher, "The Washington Post"   7

I'm not brilliant, for Chrissake. I'm really sort of a peasant plodding along, kind of doing the best I can. You don't know the eggs I lay along the way—no, I'm not going to list them. I like to leave the opposite opinion.

Interview/Los Angeles Times, 1-27:(4)9.

H. R. Haldeman
*Former Assistant to President of
the United States Richard M. Nixon*

1

[On President Nixon]: This is one you probably won't find credible, but I think his greatest weakness is his softheartedness at the personal level. He's a very tough guy in the abstract. But it is very hard for him to deal with personal problems. He has a very soft heart at the person-to-person human-relationship level . . . It is hard for him to fire people, to reprimand people. He doesn't call people in and chew them out, except for a few of us. His chewing-out was sometimes indirect and delicate, and sometimes that got in our way.

*Before Young Presidents Organization,
Acapulco, Mexico, April 2/
Los Angeles Times, 4-3:(1)12.*

Vladimir Horowitz
Pianist

2

[On why he gives so few public concerts]: I hate planes, trains, hotels and strange beds. If the audience would come to me, I would play every day.

Cleveland/People, 5-27:11.

Henry A. Kissinger
Secretary of State of the United States

3

I would like to think that I will know when to get out [of government]. But very few people have mastered this. And most people are carried out instead of walking out. I have no itch to leave. But I also have no compulsion to stay.

Interview/Newsweek, 12-30:32.

Joseph E. Levine
*Producer; Former president,
Avco Embassy Pictures*

4

[On his recent departure from Avco Embassy Pictures]: I tried retirement for one day, but I couldn't stand it. When I die it's not going to be in a bed, but here [on a podium], on a plane or on some [movie] backlot in Rome.

*News conference, Beverly Hills, Calif./
Los Angeles Herald-Examiner, 8-26:(B)1.*

Alice Roosevelt Longworth
*Daughter of the late President of
the United States Theodore Roosevelt*

5

I don't think I am insensitive or cruel. I laugh; I have a sense of humor; I tease. I must admit a sense of mischief does get hold of me from time to time. I'm a hedonist. I have an appetite for being entertained. Isn't it strange how that upsets people? And I don't mind what I do unless I'm injuring someone in some way.

Interview/The Washington Post, 2-12:(B)3.

John D. MacArthur
*Chairman,
Bankers Life and Casualty Company*

6

I don't think of myself as rich. The company I work for is stinking rich and I happen to own the company. I've always thought the greatest compensation was a day's work well done, not the dollars involved. I certainly didn't have much to start with. I remember my father saying: "Don't be a hog. You can be a pig. Pigs get fat but hogs get slaughtered."

Interview/Nation's Business, July:60.

Makarios III
Exiled President of Cyprus

7

I am satisfied with my life but never with my accomplishments, because life for me should be a continuous struggle for the better. Life is a chain without the last link.

*Interview, Chicago/
Chicago Tribune, 10-29:(1)16.*

Groucho Marx
Comedian

8

I wish I were the lecherous old man I appear to be. Then I would be doing all the things I'm thinking about.

San Francisco Examiner, 3-16:15.

457

Rod McKuen
Poet, Songwriter 1

Being born a bastard, I didn't have to spend my entire life becoming one! That and the fact I had so little formal education—though I wouldn't recommend it for anyone else—were Godsends. I had to really put myself out to find out who I was and what I wanted. I learned everything out of necessity. Like the multiplication tables! One day I found somebody was cheating me. Then I learned—and fast! That's how I became a writer. I had a hard time coming to terms with some things, but when I put them on paper, it was easier. I could stare at them, read them, think them through. I needed to write. And that's how I became a songwriter. There weren't any songs I liked to sing, so I wrote my own. And when they were orchestrated and I didn't like the way they were orchestrated, I learned how to orchestrate.
Interview, Beverly Hills, Calif./
Los Angeles Herald-Examiner, 7-25:(B)1.

Mary Tyler Moore
Actress 2

Basically, I'm a pretty buttoned-up person, and I don't share my innermost feelings with anybody, except my husband. I'm pretty structured. I tend to be ahead of time, and waiting, when I'm working. To pull back from uncomfortable situations. To be reserved. I generally weigh and evaluate social causes, then take a moderate, even conservative, position.
Interview, Studio City, Calif./
The Christian Science Monitor, 6-5:(F)1.

Gunnar Myrdal
Economist 3

I do not look forward to old age and dying. This will not happen with my cooperation.
Interview, Washington/
The Washington Post, 10-21:(B)1.

Rudolf Nureyev
Ballet dancer 4

I do not like the public to know anything about my private and personal life. If I were to reveal what I do or think, then I would have nothing left to call my own. No one needs to know what makes me what I am. Like everyone else, I have many moments of anxiety and loneliness. But when I am tortured, I do not burden others with my problems. I mainly talk to myself, because, you see, I have come to realize that I am my own best listener.
Interview, New York/
The New York Times, 5-5:(2)24.

Oliver Reed
Actor 5

[On his extravagant life-style]: All my life I hadn't been able to buy a bottle of wine, until I started to make the grade. Actors throughout history have been penniless. I have been absolutely destitute in the past, so now [that] I've got it, I respect it. If I need to, I can justify myself completely. I go my way quite happily. I like to be able to choose my friends and buy them drinks or dinner without giving it a second thought. Now I've satisfied my ego and my ambitions. I've stayed in the best hotels; I've done most things. I've got a big house, and horses, and I've got my bird [girl friend]. I've got everything a fellow wants, really. I drive a Rolls, even though I don't need it. But ambition really is simply "getting there." That's what nature provided—the urge and stimulus to win the race. Once you've tasted the fruits of success, it's very easy to go back to fish and chips. My stomach has been trained to eat so much slop that I'd be quite happy without the caviar.
Interview, Dorking, England/
Los Angeles Times, 2-24:(Calendar)22.

Abraham A. Ribicoff
United States Senator, D–Connecticut 6

I'm not a backslapper. I'm not gregarious. I'm not hail-fellow-well-met. But everyone calls me Abe.
The New York Times, 7-30:52.

Harold Robbins
Author 7

The problem is I'm incurably curious. If I'm home and someone rings the doorbell, I've got to know who it is. It's usually the mailman. If Grace [his wife] leaves the house, I have to know where she's going. If Adreana [his daughter] is at home, I want to know what she's doing. If I'm on the yacht and we're expecting guests, I want to know what the hors d'oeuvres will be. Crazy. But I can't help it.

Interview, Los Angeles/
Los Angeles Herald-Examiner, 11-3:(F)4.

Gilbert Roland
Actor

1

My greatest misfortune would have been if I had been an atheist, or a misanthrope, or married for money. Or if I could not make love to a woman. Or had not been with Rodolfo Gaona, Manolete, James Agee, John O'Hara, or had not met the Pope in Rome, or Hemingway, or had not kissed Garbo. That would have been a real misfortune. Or if I had died at 13 when an automobile ran over me, or at 15 from gangrene, or when a prisoner full of marijuana escaped from the Juarez jail wielding a machete went after me. Or if I had not been born. That would have been my greatest misfortune. Once I thought I would like to die in the arms of a beautiful woman. Then in the arena with a fierce Miura bull. Or in the battlefield defending my country. After awhile I changed my mind. Now I do not care. Death is the will of God.

Interview, Beverly Hills, Calif./
Los Angeles Times, 7-14:(Calendar)25.

Marie-Helene (Mrs. Guy de) Rothschild
Wife of the French banker

2

[On the Rothschild name]: It's like a label. People think you have to be some sort of a grand lady. It's boring sometimes, because it cuts you off from people you'd really like to be with. You always have to be nicer, sweeter, better than other people. Some people think Guy must be a pompous, chi-chi kind of man. But he's really very simple and humble. He was brought up with the motto, "One has to be forgiven for having more than others."

The Washington Post, 1-20:(L)2.

Artur Rubinstein
Pianist

3

[On his being 87]: My contemporaries crawl about half-dead. I can still run down the street, see three movies a day, and do all the silly things I did 40 years ago when a pretty girl passes by.

San Francisco Examiner & Chronicle,
5-19:(This World)2.

Eric Sevareid
News commentator,
Columbia Broadcasting System

4

I hope I have not come to believe my own publicity. I often think I'm just plain lucky to have a good job. And I get such diverse mail that I'm not even sure what my image is. I think I know my own shortcomings. I'm not your All-American freckle-faced boy next door. I'm not even a performer type. I can't cajole people or talk to people. I'm just an ordinary writer who reads what he writes.

Interview, Washington/
"W": a Fairchild publication, 6-14:11.

Gloria Swanson
Actress

5

Many people like me because they sense my honesty. I say exactly what I please and always have. I'm no mental sissy. No matter what sort of trouble it may get me in, I always speak my mind.

Interview, Beverly Hills, Calif./
Los Angeles Herald-Examiner, 11-17:(E)1.

Gore Vidal
Author

6

Under this cold exterior, once you break through the ice, you find cold water. There is no warm, wonderful person underneath. I am exactly what I seem. People sometimes fight with me. It usually starts out political and ends up personal. [Norman] Mailer and [Truman] Capote, for instance, are always attacking me. They want to be Numero Uno. But I'm Number 1. I am a highly moral person. Purely moralistic. That doesn't, however, apply to sex. I've

(GORE VIDAL)

never been envious of anyone in my life. But I do go into black despair if someone thinks Norman is a greater writer than I am.

Interview, Washington/
The Washington Post, 11-6:(B)3.

Raquel Welch
Actress
1

If I'm a sex symbol, I'm a modern one. Some of those ladies—Marilyn [Monroe], [Jean] Harlow—never had the advantages of having children. They really denied themselves. I have stability and responsibility that they never had. I'm hard-driving and I have tremendous energy. If I were to go down the drain, my children would pay the penalty. So I'm never going to hit the bottle or attempt suicide, or any of those other things people think about when you mention Hollywood's sex symbols.

There may be smears and smirks about me forever, but that's not my problem.

People, 3-25:56.

Jerry West
Former basketball player,
Los Angeles "Lakers"
2

I really don't ever want to be an adult. I'm 36 and still feel like a kid. I've been playing a kid's game for the past 25 years. I always want to be a kid.

Announcing his retirement from playing
basketball, Los Angeles, Oct. 3/
Los Angeles Herald-Examiner, 10-4:(C)1.

Tennessee Williams
Playwright
3

I have always regarded myself as not successful, because whatever I do falls somewhat short of what I wanted it to be.

Television interview, New Orleans/
"The Dick Cavett Show,"
American Broadcasting Company, 8-22.

George Beall
United States Attorney for Maryland

1

Somewhere along the line there has been an erosion of our sense of right and wrong; that is, we have lost our belief that certain actions are wrong simply because they are wrong, whether or not they violate the statutes. Morality is not relative; ethics do not depend upon the situation.

Before American Bar Association,
Honolulu/The Washington Post, 8-22:(A)20.

Ezra Taft Benson
President, Council of Twelve Apostles,
Church of Jesus Christ of Latter-day Saints
(Mormon); Former Secretary of Agriculture
of the United States

2

There is a type of "broadmindedness" abroad today that tolerates about anything short of outright murder. It isn't broadmindedness at all; it's moral apathy, or maybe moral cowardice.

Quote, 7-7:2.

Ingrid Bergman
Actress

3

I am sure that a woman can exude sex appeal throughout her entire life. I know from experience that many men prefer older women because they are interesting . . . have something to say. They have had a lot of experience of life, whereas a young woman of 20 does not really know very much at all; she has very little to offer other than the simple accident of being young, which is really an act of nature!

The Atlanta Constitution, 9-11:(B)5.

Jacqueline Bisset
Actress

4

I like a more flexible attitude toward beauty, an attitude that implies an awareness of attributes other than physical. Character contributes to beauty. It fortifies a woman as her youth fades. A mode of conduct, a standard of courage, discipline, fortitude and integrity can do a great deal to make a woman beautiful. I am aware that the way I look depends on my attitude and self-discipline. You have to evaluate yourself and know your own qualities. I do not make great strides, I do not make incredible bounds, but I know where I am going and what I want. I will not allow others to put me down.

Interview, Los Angeles/
Los Angeles Times, 5-16:(4)13.

Daniel J. Boorstin
Historian, National Museum of History
and Technology, Washington

5

The only certainty is the unexpected. We need to feel delight and respect for the unpredictable. The future will be full of surprises. Man has to live with a love affair with the unexpected, with infinite and unplumbed experiences.

Interview, Los Angeles/
Los Angeles Times, 5-10:(4)12.

Zbigniew Brzezinski
Director, Research Institute on
Communist Affairs, Columbia University

6

Since World War II, we have developed democratic systems in which . . . our publics have come to expect continuously an annual increase in growth and income—irrespective of social consequences. At the same time, citizenship—the notion of loyalty to society, the notion of occasional subordination of private interests to collective interests—has become increasingly unpopular.

Newsweek, 3-18:45.

Constantine Caramanlis
Premier of Greece   *1*

We are given to the cult of personality; when things go badly we look to some messiah to save us. But in our day there are no messiahs! And if by chance we think we have found one, it will not be long before we destroy him.

The New York Times Magazine, 11-17:62.

Chiao Kuan-hua
Foreign Minister of the People's
Republic of (Communist) China   *2*

The current international situation is characterized by great disorder under heaven. The entire world is amidst intense turbulence and unrest [that] reflect the sharpening of various contradictions and is something independent of man's will. The history of mankind always moves forward amidst turmoil. In our view such turmoil is a good thing, and not a bad thing.

At banquet honoring U.S. Secretary of State
Henry Kissinger, Peking,
Nov. 25/The Washington Post, 11-26:(A)12.

Charles W. Colson
Former Special Counsel to President of
the United States Richard M. Nixon   *3*

Democracy is more than just majority rule. It is the will of the majority but never at the expense of one member of society. The erosion of one man's rights is the erosion of democracy.

At his sentencing for obstruction
of justice, Washington, June 21/
Los Angeles Times, 6-22:(1)12.

Norman Cousins
Editor, "Saturday Review/World" magazine   *4*

Every major problem in the world today calls for a global response, just as technologies of instant communication and travel in space have engendered a global perception, a quality of community, despite all the barricades which persist. Yet the major powers persist in devising means to shore up existing, outdated sovereignties and preconceptions about who is right and who is wrong about the destiny of the world. This is as foolhardy as stocking a great ship with lifeboats that have holes in them. In the midst of debate and maneuvering, we sit in one end of the lifeboat; the other fellow in the other end. And we spend our time and energy on trying to figure out how to make the other fellow's hole bigger—all in the frightening delusion, which many quarters have come to call "national security," that somehow the other end of the boat will sink first, and that maybe we can grab hold of the debris just in time, and float until the rescue. But there will be no rescue. I believe it will be far easier to avoid destroying the lifeboat in the first place than to seek a covenant among ourselves after the deluge has occurred.

Interview, New York/
The Christian Science Monitor, 11-5:5.

Archibald Cox
Professor of Law, Harvard University   *5*

As the scholar does not know the truth he seeks, as he lacks assurance that there is a truth and knows only that by putting one foot before the other, despite false starts and blind alleys, he makes a little progress, so upon our joint human adventure we do not know the goal, we have no proof there is a goal, but can catch glimpses of a bright potential and perhaps can see by reason, mutual trust and forebearance, [that] man can learn to walk a little straighter.

Before graduating class of
Stanford University/
San Francisco Examiner, 7-19:35.

Joan Crawford
Actress   *6*

There hasn't been a single day in my life that I haven't found something new and rewarding. Time, precious time, I never waste because I find living in this world a most extraordinary experience. Every second, every minute of every hour can be exciting and fulfilling. I marvel at every sunrise and am wonderstruck at each sunset. There is beauty and love everywhere for those who seek it and for all who wish to give it.

Interview/The Dallas Times Herald, 7-5:(F)3.

Simone de Beauvoir
Author

1

I think marriage is a very alienating institution, for men as well as for women. I think it's a very dangerous institution—dangerous for men, who find themselves trapped, saddled with a wife and children to support; dangerous for women, who aren't financially independent and end up by depending on men who can throw them out when they are 40; and very dangerous for children, because their parents vent all their frustrations and mutual hatred on them. The very words "conjugal rights" are dreadful. Any institution which solders one person to another, obliging people to sleep together who no longer want to, is a bad one.

Interview, Paris/
The New York Times Magazine, 6-2:22.

Catherine Deneuve
Actress

2

All the doors automatically open for a beautiful woman. I know it's very fashionable for good-looking ladies to say how hard it is to be beautiful, but that's not true; there are times when it depresses and bothers me to see just how easy things are made for a beautiful woman. I am much more conscious of it now that I'm 30 than I was when I was younger. When I'm in a rush, or when I have a problem, people react differently for me. As I say, the doors open; there seem to be no limits—it's unbelievable. It's really the great injustice in the life. of a woman—all this because nature has been kinder to one than to another. We all fall into the trap.

Interview, Paris/People, 9-2:29.

John Denver
Singer

3

What I sing about is what I know. That's where the music comes from. I'm not trying to make life anything that it isn't. What I'm trying to do is communicate what is so about my life. What I feel. Every once in a while, you realize what is so for you, see, and that's what I'm talking about. You don't have to go to Colorado to find out what is so for you. You need

to look inside yourself. Then you find out what the truth is for you. And the moment you find out what your truth is, you are on top of life ... The truth is not what you see. The truth is what you feel about what you see.

Interview, Los Angeles/TV Guide, 11-30:34.

Sam J. Ervin, Jr.
United States Senator, D—North Carolina

4

...I assert that the freedom of the individual is life's most precious value. If it is to endure in our land, we must renew our love for it, exercise eternal vigilance, recur frequently to fundamental principles and make manifest our determination to guard and defend it, cost what it may.

At National Conference on Church
and State, Orlando, Fla.,
Feb. 4/Vital Speeches, 5-15:456.

5

I'm against mandatory retirement. It ought to be left to individuals. It is a shame to assume that all fools are old fools. I've found there are more young fools than old fools. Nature has a way of getting rid of old fools.

Interview/U.S. News & World Report, 5-6:24.

Federico Fellini
Motion picture director

6

In our moments of exultation, woman seems an angelic creature—the good mother, the madonna, the inspiring muse—everything good and holy that exists in this world and the other. In moments of discomfort, when we are desperate, the image of woman changes and she becomes the malignant mother, sin and the devil.

San Francisco Examiner & Chronicle,
4-14:(Datebook)20.

Henry Fonda
Actor

7

Thinking young will solve 80 per cent of your problems. If you think old, pretty soon you'll start creaking around like some old geriatric fuddy-duddy. Include young people in your life. That alone is an elixir.

Quote, 3-24:266.

Jane Fonda
Actress

1

The only thing worthwhile in life is to do everything you can to make things better. Sure, people should laugh and celebrate; but what is there to celebrate if you're not achieving things? And what is there to really achieve except making things better? ... As someone who has been there, I think it's a sad and empty existence to have a life of balls and parties. I have seen too many women destroyed because of that. I spent too much of my own life into that.

Interview/
"W": a Fairchild publication, 11-15:7.

J. William Fulbright
United States Senator, D—Arkansas

2

It is one of the perversities of human nature that people have a far greater capacity for enduring disasters than for preventing them, even when the danger is plain and imminent.

Lecture, Westminster College, Fulton, Mo.,
Nov. 2/The New York Times, 11-4:7.

Fung Yu-lan
Professor of Philosophy, Peking University

3

What is wrong with brain-washing? People regularly wash their faces and take baths so as to keep clean. Why should a person not cleanse his mind of filth?

Interview/The New York Times, 2-8:2.

Indira Gandhi
Prime Minister of India

4

I have many moods but no sense of frustration. I have never felt frustrated, because I find the world is an exciting place, a challenging place. And I think it would be dull without troubles. I do not think any individual or group or country can grow unless it has such challenges.

News conference, New Delhi,
June 15/The New York Times, 6-16:(1)2.

J. Paul Getty
Industrialist

5

I think women like failure. Yes, failure. A man that's very successful very often doesn't have much success with marriage. I think women feel they're more important to a failure. You probably know a number of cases yourself of men considered failures who have very happy marriages. A hard-working, go-ahead sort of fellow generally winds up in the divorce courts.

Interview, Woking, England/
The New York Times, 2-6:58.

Hermione Gingold
Actress

6

Cooking is such a violent art, isn't it? Recipes always seem to begin with something like, "Tear the hearts out of six artichokes," or, "Crush two little garlic cloves." And they use such dreadful language: mash, squeeze, whip, slice open and the like. It's all rather terrifying if you're a humanitarian.

San Francisco Examiner & Chronicle,
12-1:(This World)2.

Francoise Giroud
French Secretary of State for the Condition of Women; Former editor, "L'Express," Paris

7

I always say that nobody's life is reconciled. The human condition is contradiction. And the worst contradiction is not to live the life for which one is made.

Interview, Paris/
The New York Times, 7-24:48.

Barry M. Goldwater
United States Senator, R—Arizona

8

Long ago I learned that very little could be accomplished by talking over matters of serious public concern with people who were in total agreement with your views.

Quote, 2-10:122.

Martha Graham
Dancer

9

[On what is beauty]: That which touches me very deeply. Whether it is symmetrical or not is another matter. Unless something has in it the divine flaw which makes you cry or brings tears to your eyes, it does not have the absolute in it.

*Interview, San Francisco/
San Francisco Examiner & Chronicle,
11-3:(This World)21.*

Ralph Greenson
Psychoanalyst

1

Nothing brings one so abruptly to self-appraisal as a success which one had expected to bring triumph or ecstacy, and instead brings disappointment.

*At program sponsored by Women's Division,
Reiss-Davis Child Study Center, Los Angeles/
Los Angeles Times, 4-4:(W)14.*

Nancy Hanks
*Chairman, National Endowment for the Arts of
the United States*

2

My parents always told me that people will never know how long it takes you to do something. They will only know how well it is done.

The Washington Post, 7-28:(Potomac)25.

Alfred Hitchcock
Motion picture director

3

. . . I do believe that something of us survives after death. The mind survives. The voice certainly survives, in sound waves that may never stop once they enter the world. How long do they go on? Forever. It's like tossing a pebble into the water: The ripples go on and on and on. You say they stop at the shore, and I say there is no shore. The voice of Henry VIII could still be floating around in the air for all we know.

*Interview, New York, April 29/
The Washington Post, 5-1:(B)9.*

Eric Hoffer
Philosopher

4

. . . we kid ourselves if we believe that as we grow older we get better. Life is a slow decline. I don't think my mind is as good as it was 20 years ago. I can't hold as many complex trains of thought in my head at once; my memory is worse. When I sent my first book to a publisher, I only had that single copy; and someone once asked me whether I wasn't afraid that it might get lost in the mails. But I could have reproduced that book by heart; I had it memorized. Today, my judgment may be better, but not my memory. I used to think that the elderly needed routine in order to give them security, but now I know that we need routine simply in order not to forget things. When I take a bath, for example, I am always thinking of something else; and if I hadn't developed a routine long ago, I might get out of the bath wondering whether I had washed under my arms, between my toes, and so forth.

*Interview, San Francisco/
San Francisco Examiner & Chronicle,
7-21:(California Living)38.*

John A. Howard
President, Rockford (Ill.) College

5

I am sometimes inclined to wonder how many people have registered on the significance of the actual meaning of the term "counter-culture." It seems as if the counter-culture often is thought of simply as a handy catch-all designation to apply to those people who are being fractious in one way or another. It is far more than that. The intent of the concept is to defy all the judgments and habits of conduct of the dominant culture. If the accepted practice is for men to wear short hair, then it must be long. If modesty is good, be immodest. If it is assumed women's dress should be different from men's, provide identical clothes. If patriotism is held to be a virtue, scorn it and mock it. If neatness is prized, be slovenly. If premarital chastity and marital fidelity are advocated, opt for sexual freedom. And so on throughout the whole range of the prevailing expectations of society. The counter-culture thrust is, in fact, a systematic rejection of the moral values of the society.

*At Farmington Trust Conference,
Ditchley Park (Oxford), England,
July 12/Vital Speeches, 8-15:666.*

Glenda Jackson
Actress

6

You can't appreciate happiness fully when you have never experienced unhappiness. If you

(GLENDA JACKSON)

are faced with an unpleasant situation, accept it if it can't be changed; do not waste energy on regrets. I do not believe that one should strive to be too sheltered or to try to avoid being vulnerable. Pain is part of growth.

Interview, Los Angeles/
Los Angeles Times, 11-3:(4)11.

Maynard H. Jackson, Jr.
Mayor of Atlanta

1

If a person uses violence to achieve change, he will use violence to keep it. In that situation, those who were once the beneficiaries will become the oppressed.

Dallas/The Dallas Times Herald, 3-24:(I)3.

Danny Kaye
Entertainer

2

When I was young, I wanted to be a doctor because the idea of making people happy appealed to me. Well, I'm not a doctor—but I think I make people happy anyway. When you make someone laugh, you're giving him medicine.

Interview, Beverly Hills, Calif./
The Reader's Digest, December:159.

Kim Il Sung
Premier of North Korea

3

Independence is each nation's right; no nation wants to be subjected by anybody or to allow its dignity to be trampled underfoot. Independence is prerequisite for national welfare and honour, and a nation with an independent spirit alone can achieve genuine independence and prosperity. The exploited and oppressed peoples who had groaned for a long time under imperialist, colonialist tyranny have bravely fought for freedom, liberation and national independence. As a result, ours is now changing into an era in which the oppressed and maltreated peoples are taking their place on the stage of history as masters, whereas the imperialists are destined to fall like the setting sun.

At rally, Pyongyang, North Korea/
International Herald Tribune, 10-9:9.

Henry A. Kissinger
Secretary of State of the United States

4

I think any society needs individuals that symbolize what it stands for. It is difficult to run countries without great figures.

Interview/Newsweek, 12-30:32.

John H. Knowles
President, Rockefeller Foundation

5

I am a born optimist. I sleep well at night. I find my work important. I keep going at it day by day. But I look over the long range, and I would have to say that man's numbers have outstripped his wisdom and that life has cheapened in its abundance.

Interview, New York/
Los Angeles Times, 2-13:(2)7.

6

. . . the basic social unit of any society is the family, no matter how you cut it. Kinship was, always has been and always will be a source of strength at a time of crisis. Any one of us has only a handful of friends who really identify with us. The source of security and succor at a time of need is still your own flesh and blood.

Interview, New York/
Los Angeles Times, 2-13:(2)7.

Bruno Kreisky
Chancellor of Austria

7

The history of the last 50 years has shown that there are [political] movements which resort to harsh and brutal methods in their struggle to assert themselves, yet whose leaders subsequently, after an acceptable compromise has been achieved, acquire considerable moral stature. We should therefore not pass judgment on a movement before it has had a chance to prove its moral and political responsibility.

Before UN General Assembly,
New York, Nov. 11/
The Christian Science Monitor, 11-12:6.

Jerry Lewis
Actor, Comedian

8

[On why the Jerry Lewis character is popular] : He is a 9-year-old kid. He's what everyone would like to be. I've been 9 for 47 years and it's fun. Now, if we can teach some of the adults to feel that way—not to take things so darned seriously—it would be a better world.

Los Angeles Times, 8-26:(1)2.

Alice Roosevelt Longworth
Daughter of the late President of the United States Theodore Roosevelt

1

I have a simple philosophy: Fill what's empty, empty what's full and scratch where it itches.

Quote, 10-20:361.

Bryce MacKasey
Postmaster General of Canada

2

What we're calling a crisis of confidence is really a crisis of values. Without moral values in politics, what price justice?—all is expediency. Without moral values in business, what price humanity?—all is efficiency . . . Without morals in science, what price man?—man is expendable. And without values in education, what price ends?—all is means. Without values to shape ends and means, all is self-interest. There's nothing to hold us together. We all pull in different directions. As values go, so goes civilization.

Before Audit Bureau of Circulation, Chicago, Nov. 7/Vital Speeches, 12-1:122.

Frank E. Manuel
Historian

3

Some of us are beginning to think the unthinkable and conceive of a world society that has virtually banished the past and its culture. Instead of a complex existence that interweaves the three presences of St. Augustine—the presence of present things, the presence of past things, the presence of future things—there would be total saturation with present things only. Such a society might become possessed with the manufacture of novelty to a point where any extension into the past has no meaning for it. Technological change can be so dazzling and so ruthlessly destructive of objects that the past loses visibility. And though we may have access to far more data about preceding centuries than ever before, we may have far less feeling for them, as their buildings and their vehicles and their implements are effectively removed from sight . . . Past history and future Utopia are the only ways I know of wrestling with the finitude of existence. The cutting off of one or the other leaves us with a firefly span of life that is shorn of its significance.

At Milton S. Eisenhower Symposium, Johns Hopkins University/Quote, 6-2:515.

William J. McGill
President, Columbia University

4

It is a truism that morality is a very personal thing. I am always suspicious of public morality. Public morality is like public patriotism— a mask for scoundrels.

Interview, New York/ Los Angeles Times, 4-24:(2)7.

Margaret Mead
Anthropologist

5

If I were planning an ideal society, I would separate the boys and girls from the moment the girls were taller than the boys until the time the boys were taller than the girls.

San Francisco Examiner, 2-21:32.

Gian Carlo Menotti
Composer

6

The older I get, the more bewildered I become. The more I find out about my nature, the more bewildered I am of what's inside me, and of what's inside other people. Finally, I've come to the conclusion that a man only becomes wise when he begins to calculate the approximate depth of his ignorance.

Interview, New York/ The New York Times, 4-14:(2)17.

Henry Miller
Author

7

My philosophy is to live life to the full and joyously. Certainly I have no principles, no

(HENRY MILLER)

ideologies and no morality. Life is the teacher. You must experience everything. Most importantly, the worst. Only when you know the worst can you take what comes along.

Interview, Pacific Palisades, Calif./
Los Angeles Times, 12-8:(Calendar)45.

Garry Moore
Television personality

1

[On fame]: If you're a performer and you can come out of "stardom" or whatever it is you encounter, as I did, with your feet on the ground, you're lucky. There came the day when our little creative morning show [in the 1950s] ... was adjudged a success. Suddenly, there were four guys filling a job where only one had filled it before. Six guys from an advertising agency suddenly showed up. When you dropped your handkerchief, they swooped down and picked it up. You said, "Hey, fellows, I can pick up my own handkerchief!" But in six weeks you were yelling out, "Hey, where are those guys who are supposed to pick up my handkerchief?"

Interview/Los Angeles Times, 8-9:(4)9.

Malcolm Muggeridge
Author

2

It is sometimes difficult to resist the conclusion that Western man has decided to abolish himself, creating his own boredom out of his own affluence, his own vulnerability out of his own strength, his own impotence out of his own erotomania, himself blowing the trumpet that brings down the walls of his own city. And having convinced himself that he is too numerous, laboring with pill and scalpel and syringe to make himself fewer, until at last, having educated himself into imbecility, and polluted and drugged himself into stupefaction, he keels over, a weary, battered old brontosaurus, and becomes extinct.

At International Conference on World
Evangelization, Lausanne, Switzerland,
July 22/Los Angeles Times, 7-23:(1)16.

Roderick Nash
Chairman, environmental studies program,
University of California, Santa Barbara

3

Ideas are the keystone. They leave their mark on the landscape in the same way as chain saws and bulldozers. Machines, after all, are only the agents of a set of ethical precepts sanctioned by the members of a particular society.

San Francisco Examiner & Chronicle,
7-28:(This World)2.

Richard M. Nixon
President of the United States

4

... most civilizations or nations run out their course in about 200 years. The reason is not because they become poor or weak, but because they lost the will to be great. They turned inward, and the division destroyed them.

At Honor America Day rally,
Huntsville, Alabama, Feb. 18/
Los Angeles Times, 2-19:(1)19.

5

Many things are necessary to lead a full, free life, [such as good health and] a fair break in the marketplace. But none of these is more important than the most basic of all individual rights, the right to privacy. A system that fails to respect its citizens' right to privacy fails to respect the citizens themselves.

Radio address to the nation, Washington,
Feb. 23/The New York Times, 2-24:(1)1.

Jesse Owens
Former Olympic track champion

6

How many of you here are fulfilling your dedication to help children to make a better world for mankind? We must teach them respect for their fellow men and how to live with others. These are the things that will go with and sustain and inspire them forever, not the trophies that gather dust.

Before Texas State Teachers Association,
Fort Worth, March 15/
The Dallas Times Herald, 3-17:(A)16.

Paul VI
Pope

1

Hedonism, which becomes the false gospel of so many men and women, is in the long run the philosophy of illusion and death.

Easter address, Vatican City, April 14/The New York Times, 4-15:3.

Gregory Peck
Actor

2

I love the seasons of life, the process of change. I'm fascinated with the pageant of growing older . . . with maturity one gains confidence that there's always another chance to do one's best. I look upon maturity not as a sad sequel to lost youth but as a time of knowing what is really important and enjoying it to the fullest.

Interview, Los Angeles/ Los Angeles Times, 7-21:(Home)33.

Alfred E. Perlman
President, Western Pacific Railroad

3

A person can stay on one job too long. I often say, after you've done a thing for two years, look it over carefully; after you've done it for five years, look at it suspiciously; and after you've done it for 10 years, throw it out and start all over again.

Interview, San Francisco/ The Christian Science Monitor, 11-8:6.

Russell W. Peterson
Chairman, Federal Council on Environmental Quality

4

All of our [developed countries'] planning and all our doing has been based on growing—to work, to produce more goods, to get more GNP per capita, to use more resources. Now people are saying: "Wait a minute, now. There are some other things. I'm not getting satisfaction out of life that I ought to be getting. I'm not getting self-fulfillment or self-actualization." So we have to focus on something else besides GNP per capita . . . I believe one of the reasons people are becoming more and more disenchanted with leaders in every walk of life is

because those leaders are still talking about fulfilling those needs that are already filled, rather than talking about self-fulfillment and self-actualization. What leaders in the world [must do] is to determine where their people are in this hierarchy of needs and then help them fulfill their aspirations to move to ever-higher rungs on that ladder of needs.

Interview, Washington, April 27/ The Washington Post, 4-29:(A)2.

J. B. Priestley
Author, Playwright

5

Being old is like playing a character role. Inside you're just the same, but you have a lot of stuff clamped onto you—various ailments. They won't kill me yet, but they're no joke. You can't walk 20 miles. You're just the same inside. You are doing a character part.

Interview, London/ The New York Times, 4-6:2.

Donald Ratajczak
Director, economic forecasting project, Georgia State University

6

The world has got to slow down its population growth. Ten years ago, India's population growth rate was 2.3 per cent; today it's 2.6 per cent. In Southeast Asia it's three per cent. Anti-population-control people say, "Let's not kill the babies of the poor [by not shipping them food]. Let's not deal genocide to these people." Yet the U.S. has a population growth of seven-tenths of one per cent; in Western Europe it's one-half of one per cent. Who's dealing genocide to whom? . . . Does every person have the right to be fed regardless of the efforts of that country where the problems are? The world is going to answer, "No." The world will say, "Self-sufficiency, yes; bail-out, no" . . . Should you ask the U.S. baker, the farmer and others to lose their livelihoods [and endanger the U.S. economy] because the Indian government did not support its farmers enough and therefore they did not plant as much as they could? If we see a motion in countries toward improvement, we will, I'm sure, move rapidly to bail them out. If they have a program that

(DONALD RATAJCZAK)

promises that within 10 to 15 years they will be self-sufficient, instead of mere body-counts, then we will help them. But that's not what these countries are saying. They are telling us to stop consuming so that they can survive a little bit longer. That's not good enough. It will solve today's problems but only by making them tomorrow's problems for more people. Selective starvation is never a good idea; but the question we face is whether to let people there starve today, or have the people there and some other places starve in 20 years—and everyone starve in 100 years.

Interview/
The Atlanta Constitution, 11-18:(A)13.

Elliot L. Richardson
Former Attorney General of the United States [1]

My view of morality springs from two rather simple propositions. One is that other people are also real. That means that their claims, their interests, desires, aspirations, feelings, are just as important as mine . . . The other thing which is related to this is that none of us as an individual is capable of being described in all our individuality and separate identity except in terms of other people . . . I like to quote, even though to some extent it has become hackneyed, John Donne's lines about "no man is an island." The part I always use most is the sentence which goes, "For I am involved in all mankind." So that leads me to a feeling about all morality and the kinds of things you see. All human wrongs against each other involve a denial of these things. All cheating is an assertion that I'm more important than other people. The willingness to grab more than your share, to let yourself do it, is what you see in padding expense accounts, cheating on insurance claims, accepting kickbacks on engineering commissions, misrepresenting facts on a political issue in order to win votes . . . Every one of them comes down to the same proposition: a willingness to let yourself act on the basis that if you can get away with more for yourself, you will . . . I discovered a long time ago that any-

thing I did like that made me so uncomfortable that it wasn't worth it.

Interview, Washington/
The Christian Science Monitor, 7-8:7.

A. L. Rowse
Author, Scholar, Oxford University, England [2]

Cats are the perfect companion for a writer. Quiet. Affectionate. Independent. Not pestering you to take them out all the time. Doctor Johnson doted on his "Hodge." Colette wrote the most marvelous novel about a cat. T. S. Eliot did a book of cat poems. Matthew Arnold. Victor Hugo. Baudelaire. Mallarme. So many others . . . But you don't really possess a cat. They inhabit your loneliness.

Interview, Oxford, England/
The Christian Science Monitor, 5-28:5B.

Dean Rusk
Professor of International Law, University of Georgia; Former Secretary of State of the United States [3]

Free speech and free press are not based on the notion that everyone is going to tell the truth. From John Milton to Thomas Jefferson, and up to the present time, the right of free speech and free press is based upon the notion that, if everyone is free to say and write what he pleases, then the truth has a better chance to emerge than if these processes were subject to some sort of external control, particularly control by government.

Quote, 6-23:577.

Albert B. Sabin
Medical researcher [4]

. . . I believe that the fate of the entire world—of the relatively affluent as well as of the poverty-stricken, economically undeveloped parts of it—may very well be decided during [the remaining 26 years of this century]. The affluent countries will not be able to isolate themselves from the fate of the rest of the world. During a critical period in the life of this nation [the U.S.] more than 100 years ago, Abraham Lincoln said that this nation could not long survive half slave and half free. In the present era there is, in my judgment, sufficient justification for saying that the world cannot long survive one-third relatively affluent and two-thirds on a collision course with catastrophe. The challenge to all of us—not just the universities—is whether we can succeed in finding ways to use the tremendous store of knowledge already available, plus that which is in our power to acquire, to create a life and a world better by far than any we have yet known, or whether we shall descend to a level of barbarism unequalled in human history. I know that this is strong language, but I am convinced that it is warranted. The history of human civilization is to me a history of the growth of cooperation among ever larger units of human society in order to achieve those survival values which can be realized only through cooperative effort. And yet, with full appreciation of the reality and immensity of the difficulties, the present national and world leaderships seem to me to be largely bogged down in the ruts of "business as usual" in dealing with totally new problems which require totally new approaches and cooperative efforts, both nationally and internationally, on a hitherto unprecedented scale.

At winter convocation,
George Washington University,
Feb. 18/Vital Speeches, 4-15:393.

Jonas Salk
Director, Salk Institute for Biological
Studies, San Diego, California 1

If we could understand *why* nature behaves as it does, it would be of tremendous help to man in shaping a new quality of life for mankind. To me, the quality would correspond analogically to a great painting which is of value because of what is left out as well as what is included.

Interview, La Jolla, Calif./
Los Angeles Times, 9-8:(Home)36.

May Sarton
Author, Poet 2

You make your old age by how you have lived your life. You must prepare for old age.

There are people who are nothing when they are old because they have never been anything at any age. You stay alive by living.

Interview/Publishers Weekly, June 24:16.

William B. Saxbe
Attorney General of the United States 3

Some suggest that old-time truths really are not truths any more. When we hear that, we should ask what the options are. We are either honest or dishonest. We are either moral or immoral. And it really doesn't take much soul-searching to know which is which.

At Ohio State University commencement,
June 6/The Dallas Times Herald, 6-9:(B)2.

Irving S. Shapiro
Chairman, E. I. du Pont de Nemours
& Company 4

The thing you tend to forget is that human ingenuity is a tremendous force. In time, people will come up with solutions [to the world's problems]. Sometimes you run out of time and have severe consequences. But given sufficient time, the human brain can come up with answers . . . The more you live and the more you see problems get solved, the more you become confident in man's ability to solve his problems in due time in ways that can't be anticipated. If you have any respect for history at all, you have to say that man has gradually improved his lot. I refuse to believe that this thing [civilization] runs out and we have to start from scratch. Given the long pull, you will come out on your feet, if you have the will to do it. You can't do it by standing on the sidelines and wringing your hands.

Interview, Wilmington, Del./
Los Angeles Times, 3-28:(2)7.

Jerome L. Singer
Professor of Psychology, Yale University 5

I think that we can learn to use our daydreams much more than we do . . . We can become more aware of some of the more interesting aspects of our personalities. We can play with our fantasies and help the time pass in

(JEROME L. SINGER)

relatively boring situations. We can develop a certain increase in aesthetic sensitivity ... In psychotherapy there's an increasing movement to use the daydream, and the capacity to daydream, as a very central part of the treatment process and to help people overcome their fears through systematic kinds of daydream trips ... Americans, being more action-oriented people, think of themselves as very practical, very mechanically oriented on the whole, and as a result sort of scorn this sort of whimsical quality that these fleeting fantasies have.

Interview, New Haven, Conn., March 21/
Los Angeles Herald-Examiner, 3-24:(A)15.

Maurice F. Strong
Executive Director, United Nations
Environment Program   1

For the first time we have a situation in which the moral, philosophical, spiritual insights of the great religious leaders of the world which used to be thought of as fuzzy-minded idealism—concepts of brotherhood, caring and sharing—now are preconditions for survival.

Interview, United Nations, New York/
The Christian Science Monitor, 12-20:5.

Gloria Swanson
Actress   2

There are no standards any more. Materialism is stressed at the expense of spiritualism. The world is no longer the beautiful place it once was. Negativism and despair have destroyed so much of the beauty. Paris isn't Paris. London isn't London. New York isn't New York. Style, good manners, service, graciousness are things of the past. Everything is breaking down. It's an ugly age.

Interview, Beverly Hills, Calif./
Los Angeles Herald-Examiner, 11-17:(E)1.

Barbara Tuchman
Author, Historian   3

Self-respect or the absence thereof is the key to the judgment of future historians, for they may modify but will not essentially alter our own estimate [of ourselves today]. In the great ages, men see themselves but a little lower than the angels. They are filled with a sense of infinite capacity, prepared to kill giants like David, conquer the world like Alexander, summarize knowledge like Aquinas, or sail the endless loneliness of the enchanted seas, severed from any connection with home. The hero of Greek tragedy is noble; that is the essence of his tragedy. Ours is in the death of a salesman. We see man a victim and as small, without grandeur or pride, whereas even slaves, sculptured by Michelangelo struggling against their bonds, have an indomitable quality no artist today could duplicate because he would not feel it. Ours is an age, judging by its literature, that sees man as the prey of his weakness and on the whole nasty.

At University of California, Berkeley/
The National Observer, 4-13:13.

Jerome B. Wiesner
President,
Massachusetts Institute of Technology   4

The condition of mankind has more or less gotten better throughout history, so if you take the long-term view, you have history on our side. Of course, that doesn't help if we have a 100-year fluctuation of trouble. But beyond that, the kind of problems we are currently wrestling with have solutions. Problems of physical resources, food, energy conservation are matters we can cope with. I think we can build a world that provides a more-than-adequate life for everybody, because the resources, knowledge and technology to do it exist.

Interview, Cambridge, Mass./
Los Angeles Times, 12-12:(2)7.

Duchess of Windsor   5

When you're old, you find that good men are so scarce ... The men are all dead. That's why growing old is so difficult; there are so many more women than men. An extra man is always the rarest of birds ... Of course, it's wonderful to have women friends. American women, especially, tend to develop very close friendships ... much closer, say, than French women. But there's simply nothing like having a man around the house.

Interview, New York/
"W": a Fairchild publication, 5-3:4.

The trouble today is that everybody and everything looks exactly the same. The people wear the same clothes; the buildings all look alike. The newspapers are full of gloom. I think people have quite forgotten how to laugh ...

Interview, Paris/People, 8-12:7.

Religion

George Appleton
Anglican Archbishop of Jerusalem

1

I resemble the patriarch who from his own land steps across the frontier into the unknown, not sure of where he is going, but convinced that he must be on the way. I try to cross the frontier between Christianity and other faiths, see what they have to show me, tell those who hold them what I have found. I come back across my own frontier, enriched by what I have found, and confirmed by the values of my own faith ... Where you learn something of a faith not your own, you have got to relate that to your own belief. I do this. Probably the Jew does also, as do the Moslems and the Buddhists. Thus, in a sense, you never get away from the place where you started.

Interview, Los Angeles/
Los Angeles Times, 5-5:(9)9.

R. Pierce Beaver
Professor Emeritus of Missions,
University of Chicago Divinity School

2

There are thousands in the United States and Canada who think that overseas mission is a thing of the past, a mere vestige of what it once was and now fast vanishing ... [But] now, as was the case in 1870, and indeed in 1812, this on-going sending of representatives and funds in support of Christian programs all around the world is the major "people-to-people movement" in which Americans are involved. It is a vehicle of sharing and cultural exchange which penetrates to the heart of societies and to the most remote corner of nations far more than in any governmental operation ... Mission is big business by any standard.

Los Angeles Herald-Examiner, 2-16:(A)7.

Robert McAfee Brown
Professor of Religion, Stanford University

3

[Saying Christians must be activist, or as he puts it, "subversive," in dealing with today's issues]: Christians have to be subversives in relation to racism, sexism, economic injustice, war—all things found in the world of today. All are being challenged, with demands that they be overturned. Their correction is subversion, and that is what Christian subversion is all about ... It is said that the church is not to be a fomenter, but a reconciler; and that, of course, is what the church is meant to be. We hear, too, that there would be no conflicts within the church until we stir them up, and I wish that that were so. But the trouble with premature appeal for reconciliation is the failure to recognize that conflict is around us all the time, and reconciliation on these terms is phony reconciliation. The wounds of society are all around us. If treated superficially— bandaged without cleaning them out—instead of healing, the infection goes deeper and becomes spread so widely that it can disease the whole body.

At Pasadena (Calif.) Presbyterian Church,
Jan. 13/Los Angeles Times, 1-14:(2)4.

W. Sterling Cary
President, National Council of Churches

4

The role of the church is to be the conscience of the society, not provide the solution for its problems.

News conference, Los Angeles, Feb. 25/
Los Angeles Times, 2-26:(2)6.

Harvey Cox
Professor of Divinity, Harvard University

5

Since the Industrial Revolution or the post-Reformation period, the real religion of the

West hasn't been Christianity at all. It's been growth, the accumulation of wealth, success, competition. The central message of Christianity has been twisted in many ways to support the values of industrial capitalism.

The Christian Science Monitor, 11-12:7.

Robert L. DeWitt, Jr.
Former Episcopal Bishop of Pennsylvania

1

[Explaining his recent participation in the ordaining of 11 women deacons, which has caused controversy in the Church]: [It had been] intended as an act of obedience to the spirit [and] as an act of solidarity with those in whatever institution, in whatever part of the world—of stratum of society—who in their search for freedom, liberation, for dignity, are moved by that same spirit to struggle against sin, to proclaim that victory, to attempt to walk in newness of life. For whatever offense to sensitivities and for whatever abrogation of canonical rights we were responsible, we [he and the other bishops involved] are truly sorry. However, what we did was done with informed conscience and in good faith, and we believe that what we did was right.

Before Episcopalian House of Bishops, Chicago, Aug. 14/The New York Times, 8-15:60.

Avery Dulles
Roman Catholic theologian

2

I think people are turning more toward prayer, spiritual life. While I see no immediate return of the religious boom we had in the 1950s, a very significant number of people today are intensely religious. Consider the charismatic movement, a tremendously deep faith that would be hard to match by what we experienced in the 1950s . . . [In the universities,] any course touching on religion, prayer, mysticism, is bound to be over-subscribed, I have heard . . . I wouldn't be surprised to see strong religious figures emerge again within the next few years, although it wouldn't necessarily be the official leadership. But a great preacher,

should he come forth, could achieve a tremendous following. We don't seem to have them at the moment.

Interview, Los Angeles/ Los Angeles Times, 1-27:(6)4,5.

Roger Etchegaray
Roman Catholic Archbishop of Marseille

3

Many reports strongly emphasize that the church must shift its gaze from itself and toward Christ and man. In fact, the church, bearer of the gospel, appears to have become an obstacle to the gospel. Its reputation is damaged, especially because the church seems to use up all its energy dealing with internal matters. The image of a narcissistic church has nothing attractive about it.

At Synod of Bishops, Rome, Sept. 28/ The New York Times, 9-29:(1)12.

Jay Forrester
Professor of Management, Massachusetts Institute of Technology

4

There is no custodian of [society's] long-term goals unless it be the religious institutions. On religion rests the responsibility for maintaining long-term values and preventing the collapse of operating goals.

Before National Council of Churches officials/The Christian Science Monitor, 11-26:9.

Billy Graham
Evangelist

5

Today's teen-agers are more serious, more aware, more interested in finding their faith. They're turned on. I see more Bible classes and study groups on the campuses. In my day, science was a great god that would make us all happy, but now we are disillusioned by pollution, the bomb and all those other dreadful things; disillusioned with materialism. The young are going into the occult—and Christianity.

Interview/The Washington Post, 6-30:(H)11.

John Cardinal Heenan
Roman Catholic Archbishop of
Westminster (England)

1

The greatest blessing to come from the Vatican Council was ecumenism. Catholics now see that something can be learned from their separated brethren. The churches of tomorrow will, I believe, grow closer together. Christians will never return to the old rivalries and enmities.

Los Angeles Times, 10-16:(1-B)2.

Iakovos (Demetrios A. Coucouzis)
Greek Orthodox Archbishop of
North and South America

2

There is nothing wrong with Christianity. Christianity has failed no one. The institutional church may have failed many. Those who claim that the church has failed would do a great service to their souls if they could re-examine who has failed whom. There are no substitutes for Christianity as there is no substitute for truth.

At the Archdiocese congress, Chicago,
July 1/The New York Times, 7-5:10.

Reggie Jackson
Baseball player, Oakland "Athletics"

3

. . . I realize God gave me talent to make a lot of money. But it's not necessarily the money that's made me happy. It's the solidification of my life that religion has brought me. I've learned that I can be happier and stay successful if I've got something like my faith to tie it all together. If you're at peace in your own mind, you can trust other people and believe in yourself. Man, that's where it's at today. That's when you have a real philosophy of life, when you realize you can touch people and do things with meaning. You must be at peace with yourself before you can do these things. If not, you're only Jonathan Livingston Seagull halfway through the book.

Interview, Oakland, Calif./
Los Angeles Times, 6-26:(3)6.

Spencer W. Kimball
President, Church of Jesus Christ of
Latter-day Saints (Mormon)

4

[On the Mormon policy that forbids blacks from attaining the priesthood]: I do not anticipate any change. If it should be done, the Lord will reveal it, and we believe in revelation and we believe that the leader of the Church is entitled to that revelation and that it would come if it is necessary and if it's proper.

Television interview, Salt Lake City/
The New York Times, 3-15:32.

5

We [the Mormons] stand for cleanliness of life, as no one else does, I think. We teach morality on a very high plane . . . We have to admit that we live in the world. We try to be not of the world, but it's impossible to be entirely unaffected by it. We have some broken homes, some divorces, some immoralities at times. We try to handle it. We teach against these things, and we take action against them. We excommunicate people who are in viciously immoral situations.

Interview, Salt Lake City/
Los Angeles Times, 10-5:(1)24.

John H. Knowles
President, Rockefeller Foundation

6

Based on declining rates of attendance at church, the modern pulpit has failed in its ability to reach the average person about the meaning of life. If God is dead in the minds of people and there is no hereafter, then we are going to have it now and live it up and enjoy it now and don't think about the ultimate tragedy of the life-cycle or the ultimate meaning of the individual life.

Interview, New York/
Los Angeles Times, 2-13:(2)7.

David Kucharsky
Managing editor,
"Christianity Today" magazine

7

I think the biggest theological change in the last 10 to 15 years has occurred in the Roman Catholic Church. It's just a theological free-for-all. If there isn't a common core of belief, then you don't have that influence.

The Washington Post, 5-24:(D)19.

Hans Kung
Theologian

1

It is a fact that we [in the Roman Catholic Church] have more troubles, but we certainly have more freedom. That freedom is likely to remain a highly controversial issue within the ruling circles of the Church. Is such freedom necessary to allow the Church to adjust to the bewildering, stressful changes of the modern world? Or will it perhaps fatally loosen the authoritative ties that have bound the church together for 20 centuries?

Los Angeles Times, 10-16:(1-B)3.

Charles Long
Executive secretary,
World Council of Churches

2

[On the occult phenomenon]: I feel it reflects a new interest in the transcendental ... and it indicates a criticism of the churches for failing to help people deal with the depth of the spiritual longings in man ... This phenomenon will pass as people look more deeply, are not satisfied with superficial interpretations of the difficult. The church can take this opportunity for teaching that God is the one to be trusted, that He has all power to overcome fear and explain powers that seem beyond our control. The emphasis will have to come back anew on the positive nature of God's concern for us.

The Christian Science Monitor, 3-6:(F)1.

Clare Boothe Luce
Former American diplomat and playwright

3

... no man can live and no society can survive for very long without a religion and a faith of some sort that explains man's nature and the meaning of his life and death. I agree entirely with Toynbee that the history of civilization is the history of society's religions. By "religion" I mean any system of thought and belief that "ties things together" and gives a society something which explains to its satisfaction the meaning of life and death, of good and evil, and of man's own nature. Communism was such a religion to many young people in my youth. So, in Germany, was Nazism. It's hard to make a religion of democracy, because it's such a flexible system. Besides, democracy as we know it in the West is the political formulation of our Judeo-Christian ideas about the nature of man. We are bound to lose democracy in proportion as we desert our Judeo-Christian religious beliefs and values. And I'm afraid that may be what is happening now.

Interview/
U.S. News & World Report, 6-24:55.

Abner V. McCall
President, Baylor University

4

The average American does not commit murder, robbery, theft, arson and other crimes against the law because he fears punishment by the state, but because of his religion—his obligation to his God. Remove the influence of religion and we can have law and order only with a police state, with almost unlimited powers.

At Texas Police Association Conference,
Dallas, June 16/
The Dallas Times Herald, 6-18:(B)1.

William J. McGill
President, Columbia University

5

We are passing through a very strange transitional era. It is the case that the hold which traditional religious faith had on young people of earlier generations is clearly beginning to diminish. Ethical strength and morality which came from religious commitments and concepts of moral law are dissolving. You can see that more clearly by looking at what is happening in the churches as they have had to confront the contradictions of modern society. You hear the concerns about moral confusion from people at the Union Theological Seminary here at Columbia or from the elders of the neighboring Jewish Theological Seminary, where they are concerned about the extent to which young Jews are drifting away and being assimilated into modern American pop-culture. Certainly,

(WILLIAM J. McGILL)

it is splitting my own [Roman Catholic] Church down the middle.

Interview, New York/
Los Angeles Times, 4-24:(2)7.

John W. Meister
Director, Council of Theological
Seminaries, United Presbyterian Church
in the U.S.A. 1

There's no doubt we're going to have a spiritual revival, and I think the establishment churches will have a big part in it. In the social excitement of the last 10 years, religion has been sort of beside the point. But now things have changed. I have yet to see a church that isn't experiencing a new vitality of some sort.

U.S. News & World Report, 2-25:53.

Ralph Nader
Lawyer; Consumer advocate 2

There is a pervasive fear [on the part of the church] of offending secular powers—the powers which all too often control the bastions of the political power in this country. There have been a number of impressive developments that have restored the moral authority of the church: its approach to the Vietnam war, its approach to hunger, its approach to civil rights. Now, in a very interesting way, we are awaiting the church's approach to government corruption. Why has it been so tardy?

At seminar sponsored by Southern Baptist
Convention, Houston, March 26/
The Dallas Times Herald, 3-27:(A)1.

Jacob Needleman
Professor of Philosophy,
San Francisco State University;
Editor, "Penguin Metaphysical Library" 3

[On reasons for the current growth in spiritual questing and the search for spiritual values]: [1] The failure of science to live up to its promises. Even 10 years ago, we were thinking of science as the answer, and still many people do. In fact, it creates as many problems as it solves. [2] Disillusionment with the world

view of science, the view of the universe as a non-conscious, non-religious, non-purposive entity which ordinary human intellect can manipulate at will. With the ecological crisis, we're beginning to see that we're much more the conquered than the conquerors. [3] Connected with that, the disruption of patterns of life—such as the family structure—that go back thousands of years. All that, connected with technology. [4] The liberalizing of education. The idea that everybody should be able to learn everything about anything. But you just can't take certain ideas and give them out and expect that people will use and digest them in the right way. [5] In another direction, the tendency of modern religion to have lost contact with its practical, mystical roots. Through them people were able to have experience of the things that the church for the last century has only been talking about. [6] Then modern psychology came along and offered people a practical method to improve their lives. But then psychology's failed. So we're left without science, without religion, without the belief in technology. But we're also left with all these tremendous problems.

The Christian Science Monitor, 11-12:7.

David J. O'Brien
Historian, Holy Cross College,
Worcester, Mass. 4

There never was, is not now and never will be a Christian social order. The flaw of the old Catholic social doctrine was that it presupposed the existence of a mythical Christendom, and thus propagated models of social, political and economic organization derived from doctrine, heedless of the consequences for human freedom and human dignity. Political, social and economic institutions are human creations; none should be endowed with a Christian sanction ... It is possible to say in the name of Christianity that racism, war, social injustice and destitution are evils, social sins ... In no way does an honest recognition of the absence of a specifically Christian model of the good society make the Christian a social relativist, indifferent to crimes against humanity. While there is no specifically Christian understanding of the world as it ought to be, there is a clear commitment to equality, freedom, justice and love, and an imperative to act.

Before National Federation of Priests'
Councils, San Francisco/
Los Angeles Times, 3-23:(1)27.

Paul VI
Pope

1

[Criticizing priests who are interested in personal wealth]: Woe if our priests want to be rich. We must not be like a priest who, in his advancing age, makes himself a balance sheet such as, "I came to Rome without a penny. Now I have a house, an automobile, items of value and a bank account." No, this is not good business.

Before Roman Lenten preachers,
Vatican City, Feb. 25/
Los Angeles Times, 2-26:(1)10.

2

[On atheism]: How can we render sensitive to the values of the gospel a world dominated by an atmosphere marked by the absence of God? How can we make it understood that religion constitutes a positive factor for man and not a deviation of the effort to establish truly human dimensions in the construction of the earthly city? How can we reawaken those spiritual stimuli, that nostalgia for a faith, those seeds of religiousness that are certainly latent even in souls lacking any religious faith?

Before Vatican secretariat for non-believers,
Vatican City, March 15/
Los Angeles Times, 3-17:(3)15.

3

Let us open our eyes. The [Roman Catholic] Church is now, in some aspects, experiencing serious suffering, radical opposition and corrosive dissent ... The world is changing. Everything is in upheaval. Therefore, the Church is in difficulty. In the modern world, religion in general, and especially our religion oriented to the world beyond, does not seem to be able to prosper. It seems, to one who looks at things superficially, a church fated to die or to be extinguished.

Castel Gandolfo, Italy, Sept. 11/
Los Angeles Herald-Examiner, 9-11:(A)3.

John R. Quinn
Roman Catholic Archbishop
of Oklahoma City

4

The only time many young people see a priest or bishop is at the liturgy. If they do not perceive in him on those occasions the qualities [of love, kindness, patience, tolerance] and especially joy and a spirit of faith, they do not believe in the church. They frequently find that the liturgy is celebrated in an impersonal manner, without joy and without any really obvious faith on the part of the celebrant. This does not seem to them to reflect the gospel as they understand it. They recognize the paradox of the joyless herald of the good news and are repelled by it.

Before Synod of Bishops, Oct. 3/
Quote, 11-24:493.

Robert Claflin Rusack
Episcopal Bishop of Los Angeles

5

We [the churches] forgot to feed people's souls. Many parishes became involved every Sunday with the peace movement or with the war resisters up in Canada. Now the church has to begin to minister to the people in the pews who have no one to turn to—the people who are desperate and whose souls need to be saved.

U.S. News & World Report, 2-25:53.

Charles V. Willie
Vice president, House of Deputies,
and member, Executive Council,
Episcopal Church

6

[Criticizing the Episcopal House of Bishops' invalidation of the recent ordination of 11 women deacons]: If you think they [women] are unlearned, we can send them to seminary. If you think they are not holy, we can teach them how to pray. But if you dismiss them from the priesthood simply because they are female, they can do nothing because God Almighty made them that way. By questioning their admission to the priesthood because they are women, you are questioning the judgment of God Almighty.

News conference, Chicago, Aug. 15/
The Washington Post, 8-16:(A)1.

Charles A. Berry
Director of Life Sciences, National
Aeronautics and Space Administration
of the United States   *1*

There is no question in my mind that, when you get away from earth and see it as a small globe from out there in space, it changes the way you perceive things. The astronauts are basically machine-oriented men; they tend to be narrowly focused on their technical capabilities and their technical training. Then suddenly they find themselves looking at the earth in an entirely different way than they ever had an opportunity to do before. Each man has a different way of expressing this new feeling. One turned to parapsychology. For another, it was a deeply religious experience. Others focused on the earth's problems. They realized, after seeing the earth from space, how everything in the universe really is linked together; that people have got to get along better; that the environment must be protected.

Interview, Washington/
U.S. News & World Report, 2-11:63.

Frank Borman
Former American astronaut   *2*

[On his 1968 flight around the moon on *Apollo 8*]: The flight made me more aware of the wonders of the universe, more appreciative of life on earth ... when you view our planet from the desolation of 240,000 miles away, you realize that life is more than transitory.

Interview, Miami/
Los Angeles Times, 4-22:(3)12.

Eugene A. Cernan
American astronaut   *3*

Our *Apollo* spacecraft is far, far more sophisticated and has got a greater capability than their [Soviets'] *Soyuz*. That doesn't say the *Soyuz* is no good—it was just built for a differ-

ent job. The medical profession had a tremendous influence on their space program. It said that the Soviet engineers had to build and design for incapacitated astronauts. So they built a spacecraft in which everything is controlled from the ground or by pre-automated devices. Their spacecraft basically is designed around a philosophy that it doesn't need a man to fly. We built ours with the human being in the loop. Without a human being in *Apollo* it won't work. Because they [the Soviets] don't have a man in the loop, their controls and displays are not very sophisticated. Now, perhaps it's with good reason. Because, politically speaking, their space program, from my way of thinking, had no major over-all goal, like landing on the moon. Their goals were all to be "first": get the first iron ball in orbit; get the first man there; get the first woman; get the first two people up there at the same time; the first multi-man spacecraft. So, politically, they gained some significant first.

Los Angeles Times, 6-8:(1)17.

Edward N. Cole
President, General Motors Corporation   *4*

We need technical specialists who understand and are not afraid to become involved with people, with politics or with social problems. People like that, if they speak out, can have a great influence on the way we put technology to work for mankind. Many people mistrust technology, and they listen to those who question whether the problem that it has caused outweighs the benefits it has brought.

Before Lawrence Institute of Technology
graduates, Detroit/Los Angeles Times, 6-3:(1)2.

Michael Collins
Former American astronaut   *5*

I don't know if I really succeeded in getting across [in his new book on his experiences in space] the strangeness of it. There's just you, hanging there in that deep dark space, with the world going by your shoulder. And I wanted to get across a sense of the fragility of everything— of men's little pink bodies carried in all that fire and metal; of all that complicated machinery, which has to work just right; and of the whole world itself, just that little blue and white globe hanging there in space with that thin envelope of air around it.

Interview, New York/
Publishers Weekly, 8-5:8.

Walter Cronkite
News commentator,
Columbia Broadcasting System
1

I still believe what I originally said, *ad lib,* on the day of the [first] moon landing: that the major achievement of the moon landing is that it proves that we truly have the capability at this stage of man's civilization to do any darn thing we want—the most outlandish or the most practical things. If we have the will and are willing to spend the resources, we can solve any problem on earth: hunger, housing, transportation, disease—anything we want to do. We have the capability, the know-how, the tools, the intelligence. All we lack sometimes is the will. Going to the moon definitely proved that.

Interview, New York/
The Christian Science Monitor, 7-19:14.

2

Dr. Harold Urey, the great astronomer, used to say, when asked if there is life like ours on other planets, that he is certain that somewhere there is a world about the same size, same atmosphere, same people as ours—maybe even with a civilization which precisely parallels ours. There are as many planets and suns out there as there are grains of sand on all the beaches of the world. And you can't tell me that on all the beaches of the world there are not two grains of sand essentially alike.

Interview, New York/
The Christian Science Monitor, 7-19:14.

Frederick B. Dent
Secretary of Commerce of the
United States
3

The priority we give to science and technology will have a direct and corresponding impact on our supply of energy resources, on our economy and on the quality of our lives. To downgrade scientific research and technological development is to decelerate the main engine that gives a dynamic, wealth-generating thrust to our society. This is to say that to be *for* social improvements and *against* technology is, to put it mildly, an illogical posture.

Vital Speeches, 10-1:752.

Peter F. Drucker
Management consultant; Professor of
Social Science and Business Administration,
Claremont (Calif.) College Graduate School
4

Technology is certainly no longer the "Cinderella" of management, which it has been for so long. But it is still to be decided whether it will become the beautiful and beloved bride of the "prince," or instead turn into the fairy-tale's "wicked stepmother." Which way it will go will depend very largely on the business executive and his ability and willingness to manage technology. But which way it will go will also very largely determine which way business will go. For we need new technology, both major "breakthroughs" and the technologically minor but economically important and productive changes to which the headlines rarely pay attention. If business cannot provide them, business will be replaced as a central institution—and will deserve to be replaced. Managing technology is no longer a separate and subsidiary activity that can be left to the "longhairs" in "R and D." It is a central management task.

At New York University, April 4/
Vital Speeches, 5-15:478.

Lawrence Durrell
Author; Visiting Professor of English,
California Institute of Technology
5

I'm very excited to teach literature at a great center of technology like this, because rather

(LAWRENCE DURRELL)

than a vast separation between two cultures, I see science as a force that has greatly altered poetry, literature and our whole understanding of humanism. At nearly the same time, the atom was split and the ego was split—our age takes off from that point. Modern technology has caused a semantic disturbance, a sort of earthquake in syntax; and in my course we're attempting to unravel the apparent obscurity of modern literature. That ought to be easy for these very bright students because it is all rooted in Einstein anyway. We are all by-products of the theory of relativity. Subject and object can no longer be separated in the same way. To the Victorians, the world was a constant that they could observe. But now we know that the very act of observation disturbs the field, changes the object, so that subject-object are fused in an entirely different way. We're getting a sort of telescoped, multiple-car-crash effect in literature and syntax, which reflects the philosophic changes.

Interview, Pasadena, Calif./
Los Angeles Times, 2-12:(4)1.

Loren C. Eisely
Anthropologist, Author
1

People think anthropologists look for some mysterious creature popularly known as the missing link. But in reality the biological history of man, or any other animal, is a whole series of missing links, or rather a succession of genetic changes. The history of man is like a movie that runs for millions of years. We have found only a few stills from that motion picture, and we don't know where many of those stills belong in the evolution of man.

San Francisco Examiner, 3-16:13.

Indira Gandhi
Prime Minister of India
2

No technology is evil in itself. It is the use that nations make of technology which determines its character.

Before Parliament, New Delhi/
The Washington Post, 7-23:(A)15.

Barry M. Goldwater
United States Senator, R—Arizona
3

If I'm convinced of one thing, it is that as a result of inventions flowing from the conquest of space—miniaturizing techniques, the capture of solar energy and such—mankind will make more progress over the next 50 years than it has made since the beginning of time. I pray to be on hand long enough to see some of that.

The Reader's Digest, October:136.

Francois Jacob
Geneticist
4

Science can perfectly well stand up to the fact that there are questions one cannot yet answer, such as how DNA grows. But there are some, even scientists, who cannot get along without a global explanation, and they fall into magic—mysticism, religion, Freud, Marx. It is much easier to explain a storm by the anger of Zeus or Jehovah than by a difference of pressure. Man needs more than reason. The success of religion is that it explained the world in a way that you could love it. Then, what made science explode was that the logic of knowledge did not jibe with religion—it broke the link. But you can't love a flock of electrons. Man needs a unique vision of the world, and there's nothing much to offer him. We have a society that functions on an ethic that is 25 or 30 centuries old, and a science that is brand new; and the two don't fit.

Interview, New York/
The New York Times, 4-11:47.

Christopher C. Kraft
Director, Johnson Space Center,
National Aeronautics and Space
Administration of the United States
5

It's almost incredible to me, frankly, that this country [the U.S.] has the capability to fly a man in space as we do and it's going to be another five or six years before we do it again. There's so much to be gained from having continuous manned vehicles in space that aid us in dealing with all our detailed earth-resources problems. But I guess that's characteristic of the United States. And that's unfortunate . . .

I'm convinced that what the space program is achieving is a necessary part of the country's future, because the solution of the nation's problems has become so complex that it needs all the data, all the techniques, all the new approaches to handling it that we are being provided as a result of the things we have learned [from the] space program.

Interview, Houston/
Los Angeles Times, 2-11:(1)1,12.

Clare Boothe Luce
Former American diplomat and playwright

1

For decades Americans believed that there was nothing wrong with America, or the world, that technology and science couldn't cure. So science gave us all those lovely nuclear bombs, which more perhaps than anything else have turned so much of the American dream into the American nightmare. And the beautiful technology that was going to produce Utopia has, of course, produced some marvelous things—airplanes, TVs, autos—but it has also produced smog, pollution, traffic jams, urban decay and endless weapons of prodigious destructiveness. In my lifetime, science has prolonged the average life span 10 or 15 years, but it has also made it possible for an enemy to wipe out 50 million American lives in a 20-minute nuclear attack. Our faith—which had virtually become a religious faith—in salvation by science and technology probably began to collapse when we realized that we didn't know—we still don't know—how to get the nuclear genie back into the bottle. A great part of our American malaise is that we have lost confidence in our ability to use our own prodigious scientific and technological know-how to our own good. We can plant our flag on the distant moon and send satellites whizzing around Mars. But we can't seem to keep our own rivers and lakes and cities clean. "Is a puzzlement" for everyone.

Interview/U.S. News & World Report, 6-24:53.

Paul Moore, Jr.
Episcopal Bishop of New York

2

The total faith in science and technology as being the final answer to truth and human problems obviously has been badly shattered since World War II, and in the last few years in the U.S. particularly. The energy crisis, inflation, unnecessary wars have built up so that most persons question science as the final answer.

The Christian Science Monitor, 3-6:(F)1.

Richard M. Nixon
President of the United States

3

[On space travel]: Always look to the unknown. Go there, take any risk, make any sacrifice and don't be discouraged because sometimes you may fail . . . There are other worlds out there [in space]—far out . . . we must go because . . . failure to try to find what is there means we've lost something in the spirit of a great nation.

At Lyndon B. Johnson Space Center,
Houston, March 20/
San Francisco Examiner, 3-21:6.

Simon Ramo
Vice chairman, TRW, Inc.

4

Almost everywhere we can apply innovative technology to increase supply, decrease costs and teach us how to provide for our needs with diminished impairment of the environment. By proper technological development we can obtain more oil from land and under the sea and can do so without ruining the environment. We can learn to burn coal more cleanly. We can move faster with nuclear power and find ways to do it that will be safe . . . We have politicians, and engineers, and businessmen—but no accepted professionals for putting it all together. What we need are some interdisciplinary experts who will be looked to for authoritative proposals because of their recognized professional experience and leadership. We need socio-technologists.

Accepting Award of Merit of American
Consulting Engineers Council, Kansas City,
Oct. 22/Los Angeles Times, 10-22:(2)5.

Hyman G. Rickover
Admiral, United States Navy

5

We are so easily pressured by purveyors of technology into permitting so-called progress to

(HYMAN G. RICKOVER)

alter our lives without attempting to control it—as if technology were an irresistible force of nature to which we must submit.

Quote, 5-12:433.

S. Dillon Ripley
Secretary, Smithsonian Institution, Washington 1

The average young American today is accustomed to thinking about computers. His capacity for understanding the computer system of organization is 100 per cent ahead of the average European's. All this is a question of education through environment. It doesn't mean we [Americans] are innately superior beings. Ours is a pluralistic society. The education has been absorbed by all the elements in it. The environment in America is so much more innovative in itself we become more accustomed to thinking in different terms. And ingenuity feeds on itself. Whatever we export [in the way of American scientific ingenuity] we are still ahead. By exporting, we create a climate of continuing demand for our export. But the others never quite catch up, unless the Japanese are going to catch up, but it won't be for another generation, if then.

*Interview, Washington/
Los Angeles Times, 6-26:(2)7.*

Richard W. Roberts
Director, National Bureau of Standards of the United States 2

I believe technology is an inescapable part of man's culture. It always has been; it always will be. We cannot turn it off; we cannot send it away; we can only use it and control it to the best of our ability. The blessings of technology are often complicated by what doctors call adverse side effects. I believe that most of these side effects can be anticipated and their impact greatly reduced ... The voice of science and technology needs to be heard more in the corporate board room, in the city council, and at the highest levels of government. The message must be clear and in lay language, so that non-specialists can understand. The challenges that face us are enormous; our technological potential is equally great. The task of matching the two for the common good is our number one priority. My prediction is: more technology, not less; more technological input to decision-making at all levels; more attention to potential technology hazards; better use of material resources; and more problems of a social-technical nature.

*Before Association.of Home Appliance
Manufacturers, Oct. 18/
Vital Speeches, 11-15:69.*

Stuart Roosa
American astronaut 3

When you're out there as far away as the moon, you can hold your hand up and blot out the earth inside your palm. You begin to think: "There is my planet. It is a beautiful blue and green planet with white, that is, the cloud layers. Space is so black, pitch black." But when you hide the world in your hand, you forget race, politics, differences.

*Cottage Grove, Ore./
The Washington Post, 1-23:(A)8.*

Jonas Salk
Director, Salk Institute for Biological Studies, San Diego, California 4

If a scientist is imaginative, he will make connections between seemingly unrelated facts or systems and suddenly arrive at an insight that is, in effect, an *artistic* expression, because it puts elements together in a transcendental way ... And discovering makes it all explicit. Thus, you witness an artist's work and you say, "That's a great painting." You encounter a conception already arrived at in the mind of a scientist and you say, "What a great idea!" The *expression* of the concept is illuminating, and therefore, in my view, art goes before science.

*Interview, La Jolla, Calif./
Los Angeles Times, 9-8:(Home)36.*

Robert W. Sarnoff
Chairman, RCA Corporation 5

We could drown in a sea of information that our new technology can provide, if we don't gather and organize it properly. I think a great number of us are not fully prepared for the impact of the new technology. We don't really know how to use it yet . . . The only way is an empirical, pragmatic one. We have to be guided by sound advice from scientists who understand this technology—those who design it and know what its function is—and not by promoters or people full of wild theory.

Interview, New York/
Nation's Business, March:49.

Sports

Henry Aaron
Baseball player, Atlanta "Braves" 1

[On his having tied Babe Ruth's home-run record]: I thought that tying the record would mean a lot to me, but it was just another home run. It's a load off my back, but losing the ball game took some of the excitement off it—it only tied the record. When I hit the next one, I'll probably run around the bases backwards.

Cincinnati, April 4/
Los Angeles Herald-Examiner, 4-5:(C)1.

2

[On his having surpassed Babe Ruth's all-time home-run record]: I don't think anyone knows how happy I was to get that home-run thing over with. Not only for myself but also for my teammates. I believe it was almost as tough on them as it was on me. It was hard to concentrate on playing baseball with so many newsmen hanging around night after night. That's why I was so determined to get the two homers I needed to break Ruth's record as quick as I could—in those first few games. I went up to the plate with just one thought in mind—home run. That's no way to play baseball.

Atlanta/The Washington Post, 4-27:(C)3.

3

The big thing about my [recently accomplished all-time home-run] record is that I have stayed healthy for almost all my 21 years [in baseball]. I have been able to play almost every day. When I started, there were eight teams in the league. We played mostly day ball. We didn't travel as much, and there wasn't the pressure from the press, from television. There weren't all the demands on your time. I think there are some great home-run hitters now, but they will have to play 20 years to challenge the

record. I don't think anybody will be able to last that long.

May 16/Los Angeles Times, 5-17:(3)6.

Tommy Aaron
Golfer 4

Golf is mostly a game of failures. If you know you've got to make three birdies on seven holes to tie the tournament, you seldom can do it. The fun is in trying, and not many people really get to try. When you get to where you don't enjoy the challenge, you shouldn't do it any more.

Interview, Las Vegas, Nev./
The Atlanta Constitution, 10-12:(A)4.

Muhammad Ali
Former heavyweight boxing
champion of the world 5

[Saying he didn't watch football's Super Bowl this year]: If somebody like O. J. Simpson was playing, I'd watch. I like quality because *I'm* quality and I appreciate quality. Someone like that does the unbelievable at any moment. But to watch two any-old teams . . . nah.

Los Angeles Times, 1-24:(3)2.

Muhammad Ali
Heavyweight boxing champion of the world 6

[On his just-won victory over George Foreman]: He was humiliated. I did it. I told you he was nothing. Did you listen? I knew all along Foreman didn't like to be hit. It was so clear to me. He just didn't like to be punched . . . I'm a pro. He was an amateur. I was the professional. I hope that the boxing world will finally recognize me as the professor of boxing.

News conference, Kinshasa, Zaire, Oct. 30/
Los Angeles Herald-Examiner, 10-30:(D)2.

Dick Allen
Baseball player, Chicago "White Sox"
1

[On the race horses he owns]: Racing is a great game for all sorts of reasons. I finish a ball game and hear all the alibis. One player says we were robbed by the umpire; another tells me about his marital problems; another has girl-friend problems. I heard all the alibis. You send a horse out there to run—he gives you his all, hangs his head down from exhaustion and never complains. I like that.

Interview, Miami/
Los Angeles Herald-Examiner, 3-31:(B)1.

Bobby Allison
Auto racing driver
2

My goal in racing is to continue to be suc-cessful. In auto racing that's very difficult to do. What more can you do than win the Inter-national Race of Champions? Except that's on Sunday, and on Monday you start all over again.

Los Angeles Times, 11-4:(3)10.

Walter Alston
Baseball manager, Los Angeles "Dodgers"
3

I don't think today's fellows appreciate the chance to play in the big leagues the way they did 20 years ago. They don't ride the buses today, stay in the cheap hotels and eat in the greasy spoons. So in that sense, they don't know what perseverance is all about. But except for more outspokenness and a dislike for rules, they haven't changed much. Years ago there were guys who didn't like to listen and there still are. Same the other way. And money? Well, you can't blame them. The whole society is that way.

Los Angeles Times, 2-22:(3)10.

4

There is not much science to managing. You have to enjoy it. You have to be able to take the disappointments, the grief, the moaning. It's like teaching school: You have to know what player needs a pat on the head and which one should get a good kick in the pants.

The New York Times, 3-17:(5)8.

Sparky Anderson
Baseball manager, Cincinnati "Reds"
5

I can't demand that the guys don't wear beards and moustaches, but I can ask it. If my players don't respect me enough to obey my wishes, I shouldn't be manager. It's not the moustaches and beards in themselves that bother me so much. It's what they represent: the hippie image, defiance of parental au-thority, uncleanliness, even marijuana and dope. I wish that player representatives in the big pro sports would work harder toward improving the public image of the pro athlete instead of concentrating on big salaries. I'm not self-righteous or overly religious. But I think kids are hard enough to control without getting encouragement from their sports heroes. When I was a kid, my mother made me take a bath every day. Some of these guys [in sports today] look as if they haven't had a bath in weeks.

Interview, Tampa, Fla./
Los Angeles Times, 3-24:(3)4.

6

[On baseball managers]: They're a necessary evil. I don't believe a manager ever won a pen-nant. Casey Stengel won all those pennants with the *Yankees*. How many did he win with the Boston *Braves* and the *Mets?* I've never seen a team win a pennant without players ... I think the only thing the manager has to do is keep things within certain boundaries.

Interview, Anaheim, Calif.,
Aug. 6/Los Angeles Times, 8-8:(3)10.

Rick Barry
Basketball player, "Golden State Warriors"
7

Our team just doesn't have a killer instinct—never has in the two years I've been back. Some teams when they get somebody down, can go out and play harder and bury them. There's something missing here ... A lot depends on the organization—whether people have the ability to motivate players. I think the atmo-sphere on this club is much too leisurely, from the top of the organization right on down ... I don't know if it's a lack of discipline exactly. A big business, I think, has to be treated like one,

487

WHAT THEY SAID IN 1974

(RICK BARRY)

and our organization is not run like a business. Because of that, the atmosphere is not right for winning . . . there are never any threats about being treated severely or reprimanded. It's just too casual. It's "the big, happy family." And that's a bunch of baloney. Most teams that play are not big, happy families. They're told to get the job done or they won't be around. Sometimes, you know, you have to have an ax over your head. That's one of the problems in this organization: Everybody's a nice guy. I think to win somebody's got to be a real—you can't print it. I hate to use the cliche, but nice guys finish last. Well, maybe not last, but they don't win. On the *Knicks*, I'm sure Red Holzman is a terror; he's not going to put up with mediocrity. On the *Lakers*, I'm sure Jack Kent Cooke and Bill Sharman raise hell when the team isn't playing right. The atmosphere that prevails in other organizations is lacking in this one.

Interview/Los Angeles Times, 3-27:(3)1.

George Blanda
Football player, Oakland "Raiders"
1

[Criticizing the current NFL player strike]: No owner puts a gun to your head and says you have to play. Once you sign a contract you're obligated to fulfill it. That is why I reported to camp when the contract specified. I don't believe in unions for football players. I don't like the connotation of the word "union" for athletes. I am not against unions for steelworkers or truck-drivers or whatever, but we are not in the same ballpark. The money, the conditions are different. The players have been misled [in the strike].

The Washington Post, 8-25:(D)6.

Lou Brock
Baseball player, St. Louis "Cardinals"
2

If you aim to steal 30 to 40 bases a year, you do it by surprising the other side. But if your goal is 50 to 100 bases, the element of surprise doesn't matter. You go, even though they know you're going to go. Then each steal

becomes a contest, matching your skills against theirs.

Los Angeles Herald-Examiner, 6-13:(C)1.

Paul (Bear) Bryant
Football coach, University of Alabama
3

There are three types of football players. First, there are those who are winners and know they are winners. Then, there are the losers who know they are losers. Then, there are those who are not winners but don't know it. They're the ones for me. They never quit trying. They're the soul of our game.

At Jack Stovall All Sports Clinic,
Anaheim, Calif./Los Angeles Times, 1-29:(3)3.

Steve Busby
Baseball pitcher, Kansas City "Royals"
4

Baseball, to me, is still the national pastime because it is a summer game. I feel that almost all Americans are summer people, that summer is what they think of when they think of their childhood. I think it stirs up an incredible emotion within people.

Interview/The Washington Post, 7-8:(D)8.

Walter Byers
Executive director, National Collegiate
Athletic Association
5

They [those who run professional sports] have no regard of any kind for the welfare of amateur sports and particularly intercollegiate athletics. I scarcely know a professional operator who shows any genuine concern whether interscholastic sports on the high-school or college level are going to be hurt, and, if they are hurt, who is going to make up the deficit. I consider professional operators one of the most selfish breeds ever associated with any form of sports. And it runs right through their entire structure.

Los Angeles Times, 3-22:(3)2.

Robert C. Byrd
United States Senator, D—West Virginia
6

The United States is in the midst of another summer sports happening—the National Football League players' strike. As an isolated event, the strike hardly would be worth noting, since it is extremely difficult to find sympathy for the players earning an average of $32,000 a year when the public-school teachers in our country average only $10,673 annually. But the strike does not stand by itself. It follows . . . an American League baseball game during which the fans, armed with bottles, lead pipes and knives, swarmed onto the field to attack a visiting team; and it comes on the heels of a college recruiting season which many observers believe was the most unethical ever. It is time athletics were viewed in a more proper perspective. It is time we all realized that . . . few things are less vital to our national survival than a fall without NFL football, the outcome of a single baseball game, or the location where high-school athletes choose to continue their athletic training. I enjoy sports as much as anyone. It is both relaxing and entertaining to watch skilled athletes compete. Yet, my enjoyment is blunted when I see athletics given a greater importance than they deserve—and given it, in many cases, at the expense of education.

Before the Senate, Washington/
Los Angeles Times, 8-27:(3)1.

Roy Campanella
Former baseball player, Brooklyn "Dodgers"

1

Pro sports are a tough business—whether you're in baseball, football or something else. But when you're running around the bases after hitting a home run or jumping up and down after a touchdown, a little boy comes to the surface.

San Francisco Examiner & Chronicle,
2-17:(This World)2.

Howard Cosell
Sports commentator,
American Broadcasting Company

2

The most exciting moment [in sports] is still the heavyweight [boxing] championship fight. You get caught up in the scary anticipation of the whole goddamn thing. Those two men are half naked and hitting one another. And every instinct is basic, and every reaction is basic, and

the brutality is basic. The human animal is captured by it. You wonder which man is going to give way to fear. In general, I find boxers possess more wisdom than baseball players. In baseball, the principal level of conversation is last night's sexual conquest.

Interview, New York/
The New York Times Magazine, 9-1:31.

Bob Cousy
Former basketball player and coach

3

It starts with the recruiting system spoiling kids so badly. They're pampered and catered to from the time they're playground players. They have an exaggerated opinion of their role in society. They expect instant exposure, recognition and financial rewards . . . The system has created monsters.

Los Angeles Times, 2-22:(3)10.

4

[On college sports recruiting]: You recruit a kid by licking his boots. Once you've begged like that, there can never be a player-coach relationship. The kid is the boss.

The New York Times, 3-14:46.

5

[When I was an active player,] I played—and my teammates played—for the enjoyment of playing and the thrill of winning. We worked hard in order to win. Today's athlete—in basketball, football or any other sport—has been pampered and catered to and given everything he wants from the time he starts high school. Then, when he gets to the pros, the coach is given 12 millionaires, who care more about their bankbooks than they do about the game, and told to mold them into a selfless team.

New York/
Los Angeles Herald-Examiner, 10-6:(B)7.

Bruce Crampton
Golfer

6

No matter how well you play, you have to get some breaks along the way. It could be something as simple as making a good trap shot to save par, or a saving putt. It needn't be a

(BRUCE CRAMPTON)

long super putt or an eagle or ace. Nothing like that. But *you* know when you've made a good shot, and that's the one person you have to make happy playing on the tour. As far as I'm concerned, the hardest person in the world to convince is myself. When you've made that good shot, your attitude seems to change. Now you start thinking positively instead of negatively, and that's the real secret to winning. However, it's easier said than done. No matter what anyone else says, golf on the tour is more in your mind than in your clubs. Everyone out here can play the game mechanically or they wouldn't be here. The difference in winning and losing boils down to who concentrates the best and gets a few breaks.

*Pebble Beach, Calif./
Los Angeles Times, 1-6:(3)6.*

Larry Csonka
Football player, Miami "Dolphins"
1

[Describing how he feels running with the ball]: You can hear the noise of the clank of equipment and you can see their eyes peering at you through their face masks and through their hands clawing for you. With good blocking, you know you're getting away from them, and even for a few yards that's a great feeling.

The New York Times, 1-20:(5)17.

Bill Curry
*President, National Football League
Players Association*
2

[On the current player strike]: It is important that the fans know we don't have [it] in our minds to destroy the game. When you figure out who has the most to lose, it is not the fans, but the players. Contrary to what some say, we're not a bunch of greedy slobs. We really believe in what we are doing. We just want the same things other people have, a chance to pick where we work.

The New York Times, 7-7:(5)6.

3

[On the current NFL players strike and the emergence of the new World Football League]:

The people love professional football. The fact that so many people are watching the "new league" tells me that times are changing. Our players are on strike, so the people are willing to watch the worst players imaginable to fill in the gaps. This new league is terrible, but the citizens love professional football and here we are.

San Francisco Examiner & Chronicle, 7-21:(C)2.

Mike Curtis
Football player, Baltimore "Colts"
4

[Criticizing the NFL Players Association's demands against management and the threatened player strike]: The union's plea for more individual freedoms is so downright trite it makes me want to throw up—when, in fact, the reason behind most of the 90 demands is greed, greed, greed. Football players make good money. We eat well, live well, drive nice cars and get a vacation six months a year. If we wish, we can work at another profession during these six months, and once we finish our playing careers, we are still young enough to find something else to do.

The Washington Post, 6-28:(D)3.

Al Davis
*Managing general partner,
Oakland "Raiders" football team*
5

Pro football is dictatorial. The hope is that it will be a benevolent dictatorship. We have a commitment to excellence. Within the rules and regulations, the individual [player] must be considered, but it is the group that is most important. Pro football is a vicious struggle to be Number 1. You must have discipline—either self-imposed or, for those who can't do it themselves, it must be done for them. Too many lives are affected by the actions of each individual on or off the field.

San Francisco Examiner & Chronicle, 9-1:(C)3.

Lee Elder
Golfer
6

[On playing golf as guest of Moroccan King Hassan]: I was there last year, and I couldn't quite get used to the custom there of stopping after every five holes to have something to eat and drink. By the time I got to the 18th hole and had had a few wines, I had my choice of hitting any one of three golf balls I saw on the tee.

The Washington Post, 10-27:(D)12.

Tom Fears
Football coach,
Southern California "Sun"

1

When good, evenly matched teams get together on any level of football, WFL, NFL or college, there isn't going to be much scoring. The definition of a good team is one with a good defense, and defense is bound to dominate unless you make some truly extraordinary rules changes. Neither the WFL nor NFL has made the kind of changes this year that would affect the basically defensive nature of the game.

Birmingham, Ala./
Los Angeles Times, 7-12:(3)1.

Pat Fischer
Football player, Washington "Redskins"

2

Football is a big business. The career expectancy makes it difficult to play more than five-six years. One must take into consideration such factors as injuries and coaching changes which affect players more than people realize ... I believe the player should be rewarded for his abbreviated span commensurate with his skills because he's losing out in the business world. What all of us do while we're playing football is to delay our training for our life's work. A man can't play football forever. He's competing with students who have that much more business experience by the time the football player hangs 'em up.

Interview/The Washington Post, 6-20:(D)1.

Gerald R. Ford
Vice President of the United States

3

If I had gone into professional football, the name Jerry Ford might be a household word today. But instead, I had to find a different way to make a living ... And yet, looking back on 25 years in public life, what amazes me most

is not the differences between sports and politics, but the similarities. In both fields you need the same qualities to survive and to succeed—stamina, loyalty, discipline, teamwork and, most of all, a true love of the game ... There is no better place for a political leader to learn the meaning of sportsmanship and honest, whole-hearted, good-humored competition than on the playing field—or even on the bench.

Upon receiving an award from the
Touchdown Club of Columbus, Ohio/
The National Observer, 2-16:13.

Gerald R. Ford
President of the United States

4

I have never seen a [golf] tournament, regardless of how much money or fame or prestige or emotion was involved, that didn't end with the victor extending his hand to the vanquished. The pat on the back, the arm around the shoulder, the praise for what was done right and the sympathetic nod for what wasn't are as much a part of golf as life itself. I would hope that understanding and reconciliation are not limited to the 19th hole alone.

At dedication of World Golf Hall
of Fame, Pinehust, N.C., Sept. 11/
The New York Times, 9-12:28.

George Foreman
Heavyweight boxing champion
of the world

5

I'm not the best fighter; I'm just one of the best. Nobody's the best. Most of the guys in the top 10 all are one of the best. [Joe] Frazier's one of the best: He's got great determination; he's great. [Muhammad] Ali's one of the best: speed, confidence, footwork, talking up a bout. [Ken] Norton, he's one of the best: determination, strength. Jerry Quarry, he's one of the best: great comeback. And there's Ron Lyle: He can land a heavy punch; he's one of the best, too. To me, there's no real champion right now. Like with Norton and me signed for the title now, it's as much his title as mine until the fight's over.

New York/
Los Angeles Herald-Examiner, 1-31:(C)2.

WHAT THEY SAID IN 1974

(GEORGE FOREMAN)

1

I want to be an executioner. I want men to come out of the ring saying that they are sorry they ever heard my name. Fighting is my business and I'm good at it. I won the heavyweight championship by knocking out a truly fine fighter named Joe Frazier. I've heard all I want to hear about [Muhammad] Ali and Frazier. Now I want people to know who George Foreman is. I have a lot of pride in what I do.

San Francisco Examiner, 3-6:52.

A. J. Foyt
Auto racing driver

2

I hear these drivers say, well, they never get scared [during a race] . . . but I've been scared many times. When I hear these guys say they've never been scared, I say they're either a damn liar or a complete idiot . . . Usually that type's never a winner.

'Los Angeles Times, 10-22:(3)1.

Joe Frazier
*Former heavyweight boxing champion
of the world*

3

There are too many people [in sports] who play when they're injured. They just get a shot or take some pain killers and get in there. That can cause permanent damage. In boxing, if you're not right, the doctor won't let you get into the ring. Besides, all those team sports with a lot of contact are rougher than boxing. I'm in there depending on nobody but myself and my opponent in front of me. If I get nailed, it's my own fault. In those other sports, especially football, you're depending on too many other people to do their job. If someone misses a block, you can get creamed, even maimed for life.

Los Angeles Times, 2-10:(3)8.

4

Boxing is a complicated business. A guy can use some help keeping it all straight. If you have good people taking care of you, this can be a great thing to do for a living. If you don't, you can wind up hurt and broke. It shouldn't be that way.

The New York Times, 11-15:42.

Ed Garvey
*Executive director, National Football
League Players' Association*

5

It doesn't follow that he [football commissioner Pete Rozelle] represents the players. He says he represents the owners, the players and the fans. Now, what could be more absurd than to say that when he is selected by the owners and we [players] have no say in who the commissioner is, or what he's paid, or what his contract calls for, that he represents us? If they [owners] don't like what he does, they terminate his employment. They fire him. He says he can do anything he wants to the owners, but the answer is that they can fire him. We can't fire him. So since we have no control over him, obviously he does not represent us. King George tried to say he represented the colonists in this country. When it came to taxing us, he soon found out that he didn't.

*Interview, Washington/
Los Angeles Herald-Examiner, 2-12:(C)3.*

6

[On NFL commissioner Pete Rozelle's fining and placing on probation eight players for violation of NFL drug rules]: Rozelle makes up rules without consulting the players, hires a private police force to enforce those rules, determines who should be investigated, and sits and listens to hearsay evidence and unsupported allegations against players. Rozelle then acts as grand jury, judge and appellate court. Most importantly, he can destroy a person's career by simply stating publicly that the player is guilty. It is McCarthyism at its best.

*Washington, May 1/
Los Angeles Herald-Examiner, 5-1:(D)2.*

7

[Supporting the Federal-court decision that the NFL's player-reserve system violated antitrust laws]: It's the most significant development in the history of professional sports from the point of view of the athlete. One of the reasons we went to training camp without a contract was [this reserve-system] case. We felt if it was successful we would have achieved in court what we wanted in collective bargaining... It won't be a damaging thing to football.

Dec. 20/Los Angeles Times, 12-21:(1)9.

Jim Gilliam
Baseball coach, Los Angeles "Dodgers"

1

There are some great ballplayers, but there aren't any superstars. Superstars you find on the moon.

Los Angeles Times, 8-3:(3)2.

George Halas
President, Chicago "Bears" football team

2

[On the current NFL player strike]: There is a constant refrain in the players union that says, "We just want to be like other people." The simple truth is that pro football players are not just like other people. Other people are not given college scholarships that, in turn, enable them to get football jobs that pay approximately $40,000 annually in salary and benefits for six months of work. The union professes to want to overthrow the system that produces these rewards so that they can get more benefits and more money, which, of course, will then make them even less like other people.

Los Angeles Times, 7-14:(3)3.

Woody Hayes
Football coach, Ohio State University

3

[Comparing football to warfare]: Winners are men who have dedicated their whole lives to winning. The winners of every battle have dedicated themselves to the same two things: killing as many of the other side as possible and saving as many lives on their side as possible. The strategy of football and warfare is similar, but we have different goals.

Quote, 1-13:26.

4

I don't think it's possible to be too intent on winning. If we played for any other reason... we would be totally dishonest. This country is

built on winning and on that alone. Winning is still the most honorable thing a man can do.

News conference, New York, Dec. 10/
The New York Times, 12-11:59.

Bobby Hull
Hockey player, Winnipeg "Jets"

5

[Professional athletes] today get a dollar in their pocket and they think they have the world on a string. They say, "Who, me work? Who, me sweat?" Why should a guy with a half-million dollar contract want to have blood dripping down his face, or sweat, or play with bruises? Hell, they won't even play with bruised feelings now.

Los Angeles Times, 2-22:(3)1.

Lamar Hunt
Owner, Kansas City "Chiefs" football team

6

I am not alarmed about what people call the sports explosion. There is room in sports for more leagues and more teams in all sports. After all, we have 210 million people in the country today compared with 140 million before World War II. That means 50 per cent more people with $5 and $10 to spend for a ticket. Sports has become tremendous theatre. I don't think there is an end in sight to the recreation dollar or recreation time.

Dallas/The Washington Post, 5-30:(E)5.

Robert M. Hutchins
Chairman, Center for the Study
of Democratic Institutions;
Former president, University of Chicago

7

[On his decision, as University of Chicago president in 1939, to eliminate the University's football program]: It was one of the few totally successful things we did. At Chicago, and in the Midwest generally in the 1930s, the emphasis on winning football games tended to preoccupy the constituency—alumni, trustees and students—in a non-educational enterprise that prevented us from getting on with the business of an educational institution. And at the universities where the game is still important, this is still true. Everything that has happened in college football since 1939 has confirmed the wisdom of our course.

Interview, Santa Barbara, Calif./
Los Angeles Times, 10-25:(3)10.

Hale Irwin
Golfer

1

[College] football has been some help to me in golf, but I can't say it had any direct bearing on it—just the idea of competition, a challenge to overcome. To me, a golf course is a series of those situations. Each situation is me and the shot . . . Golf is tougher than football, at least for me. On the football field, you can blow off your emotion by belting someone. In golf, pressure just keeps building up within you and there is no outlet or relief. You must learn to control your emotions, and that's not easy.

Mamaroneck, N.Y., June 16/
The New York Times, 6-17:42.

Reggie Jackson
Baseball player, Oakland "Athletics"

2

I'd rather hit than have sex. To hit is to show strength. It's two against one at the plate, the pitcher and the catcher versus you. When I'm up there, I'm thinking, "Try everything you want. Rub up the ball. Move the fielders around. Throw me hard stuff, soft stuff. Try anything. I'm still going to hit that ball." God, do I love to hit that little round sum-bitch out of the park and make 'em say "Wow!"

Time, 6-3:62.

3

When you've played this game for 10 years, gone to bat 7,000 times and gotten 2,000 hits, do you know what that really means? It means you've gone zero for 5,000!

The Christian Science Monitor, 9-20:11.

Al Kaline
Baseball player, Detroit "Tigers"

4

[On his being made a designated hitter after a career in the outfield] : I'm 39 years old and I

can't field like I did when I was 29. What's the use of embarrassing myself at 39? I can't get to some balls I used to suck up easily. If I was a half-assed outfielder it would be different. I was a good outfielder. It's hard for me to accept mediocrity.

Los Angeles Times, 4-15:(3)2.

Michael Killanin
President, International Olympic Committee

5

. . . 95 per cent of my problems involve national and international politics. It's our [the Olympics'] biggest bugbear . . . I wish we could do away with the news media adding up all the medals each day. It all contributes to that "my country is better than yours" syndrome. I'm trying to cut down all the flags and anthems, but I often find myself in the minority.

Interview, Dublin, Ireland/People, 8-12:32.

6

There is no doubt at all that sport is a common denominator which bridges and crosses all political, national and religious barriers. At the same time with this over-all policy, it must be borne in mind that the Olympic Games are principally for the individual competitor, and one hopes that by the fine example set by the Olympic competitors and champions that the younger generation will take an interest in their personal complete development that is physical, moral and mental. Cynics say that sport possibly leads to more international misunderstanding than anything else, but it is only the exceptions that make the headlines for these pessimists. For the greater part of the time, sport brings people together in a friendly atmosphere with the common interest either in a particular sport or particular continent, area or region.

At Olympic Solidarity Symposium, Teheran/
The New York Times, 12-15:(5)2.

Harmon Killebrew
Baseball player, Minnesota "Twins"

7

To me, hitting is a very unnatural thing. Even though I've always done fairly well at it,

I've always had to work at it. There has to be a relationship between the eye and home plate, and when you lose that relationship, you have the beginnings of a slump. When I go up to the plate, for example, I'm not generally trying to hit a home run, unless the situation dictates it. I'm just trying to hit the ball hard—somewhere. Under those conditions, I know I'm going to get my share of hits.

Interview/
The Christian Science Monitor, 8-28:9.

Billie Jean King
Tennis player

1

The tour has been selling out regularly. After all these years, the girls [women players] are an overnight sensation. Suddenly, people who always thought tennis was a sissy game know exactly how tough it is. I think tennis can rank with football as the favorite national sport in a few years... Sure, our [women's] game is shorter and weaker. That makes you play tougher. I curse myself out all the time. The crowd loves it and it helps me let off steam. Our strokes are far more precise than the ones the men use. They like the big power serve and the strong over-head volleys. I defeated [Bobby] Riggs by playing a man's game. He tried to beat me with a lot of female-style lobs. I think he's probably more entertaining than any other male tennis player in America, because he plays like a woman. He always has. That's why our game is so much fun.

San Francisco/
San Francisco Examiner & Chronicle,
1-20:(C)2.

Evel Knievel
Motorcycle stunt-man

2

Remember Captain Marvel? Well, I'm the comic-book hero in real life. In a phony world, I stand for something simple and direct. I love life, but I know that you have to take chances to make it worth living. People look up to me for that. They wouldn't pay to see just anybody do what I do ... If I wasn't doing this, I'd probably be in jail for something crazy ... be-

cause I always liked to live with a lump in my throat and a knot in my stomach.

Interview/Newsweek, 8-26:78.

Chuck Knox
Football coach, Los Angeles "Rams"

3

Getting the most out of your football players is the real test in coaching, and there is no magic formula. It takes work, a tremendous effort on the part of each coach on the staff. Motivation to me is simply teaching. It's the ability to relate to your players... All the great football coaches I have known have all been excellent teachers. We look at the football field as an extension of the classroom... Our whole approach to our football, every day, is how can we go out there today and make each member of our team a little better than he was yesterday?... I don't think it matters how much technical football you know. You can buy books that are full of Xs and Os. But we are in a people business, and the only thing that counts is when you ask a player to do something, when you demonstrate or try to sell him on a particular technique, how successful are you at getting him to do it? Why is it, if you take two different coaches and give them the same material, one coach is going to go 9-1 and the other will be 6-4? The difference is the ability to motivate.

At Jack Stovall All-Sports Clinic/
Los Angeles Times, 2-20:(3)3.

4

I hear a lot of people say pro players get paid and that's why they should do well. Well, I'll tell you something: When it's fourth and one in the fourth quarter and that monkey is on my big round-eared offensive tackle's back and he's got a little blood up his nose and he's hurting, it doesn't make any difference whether you pay him $1,000 or $5,000 or $50,000. If he's not self-motivated, if he doesn't believe, you can't pay him enough money to make the block ... It has to come from pride and character, and it's the same in high school, college or pro.

Los Angeles, Feb. 20/
Los Angeles Times, 2-21:(3)3.

WHAT THEY SAID IN 1974

Sandy Koufax
Former baseball pitcher,
Los Angeles "Dodgers"

1

Pitching is the art of instilling fear, making a man [the batter] flinch by making him look for the wrong pitch. You're trying to control his instincts.

Los Angeles Times, 9-11:(3)2.

Ray Kroc
Owner, San Diego "Padres" baseball club

2

[On his recent acquisition of the *Padres*]: I'm not interested in making a great amount of money in baseball; that's far down the list. This is a matter of pride and accomplishment. But in America, you know, we have a saying: "If you're so smart, why aren't you rich?" You can't run a business and not make money and call yourself successful. So I want the team to be successful financially. But I don't need the money. If I needed money, the last investment I would make would be in baseball, or any other sport. But you want a winner. A winner means the fans are happy. You're giving them their money's worth. There is a *gemutlichkeit*.

Interview, Fort Lauderdale, Fla./
Los Angeles Times, 2-8:(3)4.

Bowie Kuhn
Commissioner of Baseball

3

Most of us will be here to see major-league baseball on an international basis. Mexico, Venezuela, Cuba, Canada [Toronto], Japan, Puerto Rico and Panama are among the countries not only eager for it but ready for it. Further away, time-wise, in baseball's global plans is Europe, with Holland and Italy the most advanced in interest, knowledge and facilities. Any new federal sports structures in those places, as well as many others, must include a baseball field.

Interview, Hermosillo, Mexico/
Los Angeles Herald-Examiner, 2-4:(C)2.

4

Now is the time for the major leagues to have a black manager ... It's more imminent now than ever. I'm pained that it hasn't happened, especially when there were times in the last few years when I thought it should happen. I can't order anybody to hire anybody, but the two league presidents are working closely with me trying to exert pressure on the clubs. These efforts are being intensified because now is the time to do it. If you push some issues long and unsuccessfully, you eventually undermine your role as commissioner. In this case, I could not function as commissioner if I kept pushing it and lost.

Interview, New York, Aug. 17/
The New York Times, 8-18:(5)1.

Bill Lee
Baseball pitcher, Boston "Red Sox"

5

Everything is so specialized now. Once, baseball was a sport where you were supposed to do a lot of things and be able to put it all together. Now we've got the designated hitter, just prolonging the careers of a lot of guys who can't play any more. Maybe we ought to adopt Little League rules where everybody has to play at least three innings a week.

Interview, Boston, July 28/
The New York Times, 7-30:36.

Ted Lindsay
Former hockey player; Former president,
National Hockey League Players Association

6

I don't care if they bury baseball, football and basketball. But my game is the best game in the world, and I hate to see what the Congress of our country has done by allowing players to play out their option and by allowing all these new leagues. It's become a hockey-player's market instead of management's market, and that's not right. Management should always have the upper hand over the players. Most of these guys today think that hockey owes them something. But it's the other way around. Now this World Hockey Association is the worst thing that ever happened to hockey. Most of these players have no dedication to the game of hockey. They figure they don't owe the sport anything. The WHA has created a situation where management has no authority over an athlete in either league any more. I'm not begrudging any guy his money, but I'm loyal to the NHL. You see, I believe that sports cannot survive unless a club management can exert an almost militaristic atmosphere over its players.

Interview, Chicago/
San Francisco Examiner & Chronicle,
12-15:(C)6.

Whitey Lockman
Baseball manager, Chicago "Cubs"

1

... power is fine as long as it's consistent. We've had power clubs in the past. But if that power cools, you're in trouble, because you keep waiting for the big inning that never comes. Then, if you can't score with speed or finesse, or have given up too much on defense, there's only one way you can go: You have to lose more often than you win.

Scottsdale, Ariz./
The Christian Science Monitor, 3-13:(F)3.

Tom Mack
Football player, Los Angeles "Rams"

2

Fining [of football players] isn't an adult way to discipline professionals. A sportswriter who doesn't do the job might be fired, but he isn't fined. Nobody fines teachers, dentists or truck drivers. It's the same in all businesses and professions—except ours ... [We players are] trying to create more of a business atmosphere in pro football, instead of the "special item" atmosphere of the past. We want to move in the direction of the free market that other businesses have in America. A pro football player is a professional, an adult. Curfew systems, fining systems and the like have no proper place in American businesses and professions.

Interview/Los Angeles Times, 4-1:(3)7.

Arnold Mandell
Football-team psychiatrist,
San Diego "Chargers"

3

Football is like going to war. But in this country [the U.S.], one of the psychological problems coaches face is the parallel growth of football. On one hand our society is questioning war; we don't want to fight. We look for beauty and we try to be friendly. We care about the welfare of others. But there is a contra-

diction with football, which ascribes to a Darwinian theory. It's the survival of the fittest and natural selection. Coaches who are the most successful are ones who can reintroduce that survival dimension to their players. They have to hang a sword over their players' heads and get them off their meanderings.

Interview/Los Angeles Times, 3-28:(3)1.

Mickey Mantle
Former baseball player, New York "Yankees"

4

I am always dreaming about trying to make a comeback. In one dream, I drive up to Yankee Stadium and can't get in. In the background I hear the loudspeaker blaring, "At bat, Number 7, Mickey Mantle." I try to squeeze through a hole, but there I am stuck. It's a terrible feeling.

The New York Times, 1-20:(5)17.

Wellington T. Mara
Owner, New York "Giants" football team

5

[On the NFL Players Association's demands to management which include abolition of the option clause, waiver system, reserve lists, trades, etc.] : It is simply good business to be attentive to the desires of your customer [the fan]. It requires nothing more virtuous than a lively self-interest for anyone in management to feel deep concern when the players' union presents 58 demands, and not one of them proposes to add anything to the structure of professional football or to its salability to the public. Individually and collectively, these demands reflect only one thesis—that the experience of generations is worthless ... that a structure that has evolved through the years should be torn down and replaced by nothing.

The Christian Science Monitor, 4-26:(F)3.

Ed Marinaro
Football player, Minnesota "Vikings"

6

Pro football is dull if you don't like perfection. It's become very systematized. Every man is a star. Every play is worked out like a problem in geometry. Football no longer is the game

(ED MARINARO)

for the physical brute. It's a thinking-man's game.

News conference, New York/
The Christian Science Monitor, 1-25:(F)3.

Mike Marshall
Baseball pitcher, Los Angeles "Dodgers"
1

If I was out there every day worrying strictly about winning, well, I wouldn't be out there. To me, it's all in the competition, the concept, the artistry. Just because I got a guy out on five straight screwballs the last time he was up doesn't mean I'm going to go that way again. That would make it dull. I'll undoubtedly try a new concept to make it more artistic. And when the game's over, you'll see no false sorrow from me. I'll have given my best. That's what it's all about.

News conference, Los Angeles,
March 19/Los Angeles Times, 3-20:(3)8.

Willie Mays
Former baseball player
2

Baseball players are no different than other performers. We're all actors, when you come right down to it, so I always thought I had to put a little acting into the game—you know, make it more interesting for the fans. So, whenever a ball was hit to center field, I'd try to time it right and get under the ball just in time to make the catch. It always made the play look a little more spectacular.

Television interview/
San Francisco Examiner, 6-14:59.

3

. . . baseball is a fun game. When the game began to be a "job," that bothered me. That's why I quit, when it began to be work. In baseball, at a certain age, you have to get out. You can't go back. There is nothing to go back to.

Interview, Atlanta/
The Atlanta Constitution, 10-12:(B)7.

Al McGuire
Basketball coach, Marquette University
4

We have no training rules. The week of a big game . . . we just tell them [the players] to be a little more careful in what they do and how they eat. It's very simple. We just ask that the players not . . . embarrass themselves and we remind them they're representing an institution, as well as themselves. I don't treat them completely like men. If you do that, you get burned. I'm still the dictator—on the court.

Greensboro, N.C./
Los Angeles Times, 3-25:(3)2.

John McKay
Football coach,
University of Southern California
5

I never want my record marred because I got somebody hurt in practice. I know some coaches who get mad or have a fight with their wives—so they hold a scrimmage. Football is a violent contact game, and we don't want to risk injuries in a scrimmage. Some coaches scrimmage to see if a player is tough. If they have coached them half the season and don't know if the player is tough, the coach is an idiot.

At NCAA media seminar,
Colorado Springs, Colo./
Los Angeles Times, 3-18:(3)3.

6

When I'm coaching, I concentrate so hard that I wouldn't be embarrassed if my pants fell down.

Los Angeles Times, 11-4:(3)3.

Dave Meggyesy
Former football player,
St. Louis "Cardinals"
7

[Criticizing football]: More than one-third of the population watched the last Super Bowl. It's nothing more than a war game. National sports, particularly in the colleges and pros, have become national theatres resembling Roman circuses. Athletics is one of the primary systems for how you become socialized—but only for a few. The remainder are the vicarious watchers and beer-drinkers who watch football on television.

*At conference on athletics, Portland, Ore./
Los Angeles Times, 4-8:(3)2.*

Andy Messersmith
Baseball pitcher, Los Angeles "Dodgers"

1

Statistics are overrated. Championships are won in the clubhouse. You hear about team-work from the time you're old enough to pick up a glove, but you don't really appreciate it until you reach this level. You've got to like each other. You've got to play for each other. But first you've got to pull for each other. It's not enough to have it one day, but be thinking of yourself the next. A baseball team is com-posed of 25 temperamental dudes. They've all been stars at one level or another; they all have different emotions. But when they walk into the clubhouse, each of them has to swallow that individualism. Mr. Big has to make sure he's no different than Mr. Small.

*Interview, Daytona Beach, Fla./
Los Angeles Times, 3-15:(3)11.*

James A. Michener
Author

2

I think a nation loses through not having a more varied and vigorous sports program. Sports do something for the spirit of a society. I agree with those who have said the essence of a city is its theatre, its art museum, a hall where its orchestra can play, and stadiums in which large numbers of people can see its sports teams play. The problem of financing these places, including the sports stadiums, is often acute. But a city should worry as much about losing a stadium as losing a library. A city needs pro clubs for every season.

*Interview, Tinicum, Pa./
Los Angeles Times, 11-3:(3)10.*

Gale E. Milkes
*Director, health and recreation department,
Michigan State University*

3

The competitive spirit comes too soon now for most children to handle. This tears down basic values taught at home and destroys valu-able young friendships. What organized sports really does with kids is to break down their own individuality and trim them to fit into a system. It does not help to develop their own personality.

Los Angeles Times, 8-1:(3)2.

Johnny Miller
Golfer

4

They say I don't have any charisma, that I don't show any emotion on the golf course. Well, I don't think you have to. I don't think you have to cut up or tell jokes or anything. I'm just not that kind of guy. Mr. [Ben] Hogan didn't do those things. You don't see [Jack] Nicklaus jumping up in the air and running around the green when he makes a putt. And I don't go "whoop-de-do, look at me" when I make one. Ben Crenshaw doesn't, either. He doesn't have to. But he has charisma. So does Jack. I don't think you have to do all those things to make people want to come see you. I think I'm more like Gene Littler. He's relaxed and easy and just goes about his business. If he makes a bad shot, he just forgets it and goes on to the next one and doesn't throw clubs and yell and scream and jump up and down.

Los Angeles Times, 1-27:(3)7.

5

. . . the time is past when any one man will dominate the game. There are too many good players for that to happen now. I'm not knock-ing Jack [Nicklaus]; not at all. He's still my idol—sort of. He's probably the best player in the world. But I don't think you're going to see Jack winning 50 per cent of his starts any more. There are just too many good young players now . . . There are just too many of them that are too good for any one man to dominate the game completely, the way Jack has and the way Arnold [Palmer] did.

*Mamaroneck, N.Y./
Los Angeles Herald-Examiner, 6-11:(C)2.*

Dick Motta
Basketball coach, Chicago "Bulls"

6

The trouble with pro basketball from a coach's standpoint is that he doesn't have

(DICK MOTTA)

enough control over his own destiny. Too much of it is in the hands of the referees. The officials make the calls and most of the time they are not very consistent. And if I've done a good job, I don't want some official messing it up. I know pretty much what to expect from my own players. After all, it's my system and I'm with them almost every day. I also know what to expect from rival teams, because no club changes that much from year to year. Coaches and players have habits and they usually adhere to them. But too many NBA officials are inconsistent. They often don't call fouls the same way two games in a row. And that can really hurt because your team never knows how to adjust to what is going on. I've been fined for saying things like this before, but I've always believed that it's important to fight for what you think is right.

Interview/
The Christian Science Monitor, 11-4:9.

Merlin Olsen
Football player, Los Angeles "Rams"

1

Exciting plays are largely created by mistakes—whereas the way to win football games is to eliminate mistakes. There is a fundamental conflict in all this that makes winning and excitement hard to reconcile in football—unless you're excited just to win, which most fans are. In the nature of things, when two good teams get together, as in the Super Bowl, it's likely to be a little dull because they got there by concentrating on eliminating mistakes. Losers entertain. Winners win. It's the nature of football.

Interview, Los Angeles/
Los Angeles Times, 12-6:(3)14.

Peter O'Malley
President, Los Angeles "Dodgers"
baseball club

2

If winning isn't everything, it's *almost* everything. Because a winning team makes all the parts of the pleasure-puzzle fit into place. The fans want the best team, the championship team. The fans buy the tickets and support the team. So they're *entitled* to have a winner. When the game is over, and we've lost, the fans are disappointed. But when we've won, they're happy. They've been better entertained. They're satisfied, and that's the way it should be.

Interview, Los Angeles/
Los Angeles Times, 7-14:(Home)27.

3

Life is incredibly hectic. We're all surrounded by pressures. We're all caught up in the traffic jam of living. Why do more than two million people a year come out to our baseball park? Because they'd like to temporarily put aside their problems and sit down outdoors and relax. The game is not obsolete. I think it will be a part of our lives a hundred years from now.

Interview, Los Angeles/
Los Angeles Times, 7-14:(Home)27.

Arnold Palmer
Golfer

4

[On suggestions of enlarging the cups for better putting]: ...enlarging the cups would not be good for golf. Like some of the others, Ben Hogan is full of baloney, too, when he advocates expanding them. Make them eight inches wide, and you'd have the same winners. It's all relative. But I do have a solution: Put a big fence around the hole; then have a trough inside that will funnel the ball into the cup. There's only one thing wrong with that, however—the same guys still will win.

Los Angeles/
Los Angeles Herald-Examiner, 2-16:(B)2.

Ara Parseghian
Football coach, University of Notre Dame

5

The days of the dictatorial coach are over. Players expect you to explain things now. They want to know why. A coach has to be a chaplain, a public-relations man, a disciplinarian, a counsellor, an educator. But I like that. I like it a lot.

Interview, South Bend, Ind./
Los Angeles Times, 11-28:(3)11.

Joe Paterno
Football coach, Pennsylvania State University 1

Athletes are more dedicated than when I played in the '40s. There's more of a year-round commitment to being a good athlete, what with all the work they do in the off-season. Once they're aware you're treating them as individuals, not conning or exploiting them, I think they're more coachable. The few kids who are spoiled I blame on recruiting. Some are overcome by it and get a false sense of their importance to society. But they're a minority.

Los Angeles Times, 2-22:(3)1.

Gaylord Perry
Baseball pitcher, Cleveland "Indians" 2

Primarily, every rule change over the past 10 years has been against pitchers: lowering the mound, the designated hitter ... I've got a kid 6 years old. He likes sports, but I definitely won't let him pitch. There would be too many things against him.

*Tucson, Ariz./
Los Angeles Herald-Examiner, 3-10:(B)5.*

3

[Criticizing a new rule that permits umpires to merely watch a pitch to determine if it is illegal, such as a spitter, greaser, etc.]: Up until this rule, the umpire actually had to find a foreign substance on the ball. Now they don't have to find anything. All they've got to do is think something, think they see a pitch acting in a funny way. Even the best umpires have trouble sometimes telling the difference between a ball and a strike, so how are they supposed to tell the difference between a fork-ball and a spitter, a knuckler and a greaser, a slider and a sweat-ball? Managers have never hesitated to tell umpires what they ought to see. Now they're certainly going to try to tell them what they ought to think. The hollering and crying is going to be terrible. There won't be any time left to play ball.

Los Angeles Times, 4-8:(3)8.

Richard Petty
Auto racing driver 4

... my philosophy about racing hasn't changed: To me the most important race is the one that's coming up. The most important race I've ever won is the last one I won.

*Interview, Darlington, S.C./
Chicago Tribune, 8-30:(3)8.*

5

I don't really know what an athlete is, but by my definition a race driver is an athlete. He has to go five hours with no relief handling a 3,800-pound car with all the physical strength he can muster just to keep it on the road, plus the mental strain of knowing that one mistake and you done busted your dad-gum head. I'll put a race driver above any other athlete because he's got everything on the line. He does it all himself. He's got no teammate. It's a combination of mind and body. There's a machine, the car, but somebody's got to run that dad-gum thing.

Los Angeles Times, 11-6:(3)1.

Gary Player
Golfer 6

[On his winning the Masters Tournament]: I've sacrificed, traveled and exercised as much as any athlete, with the goal of winning great championships like this one. But every shot here is within a fraction of disaster—that's what makes it so great. To work so hard, to accept the challenges and to be rewarded for it—that's the gratification of the Masters.

Quote, 5-26:501.

7

Proper mental attitude is the greatest key to good golf. Every day I try to improve my mind, even in areas not associated with golf. Every day I practice patience. When I think pressure is building up, I slow down. Maybe I walk a little slower, or take more time with what I'm doing. I keep calm and cool and do the very best I can.

*Mamaroneck, N.Y./
The Christian Science Monitor, 6-13:(F)6.*

501

Sam Posey
Auto racing driver

1

When you're driving hard out on the limit and the true love of speed comes over you, you don't want to slow up. It's always the same: The faster you go, the less you care about being able to stop ever.

San Francisco Examiner, 3-25:5.

William Proxmire
United States Senator, D Wisconsin

2

Tax advantages, antitrust exemptions, reserve clauses, some tax-supported stadiums and a cavalier attitude toward labor organizations—these are the benefits enjoyed by the owners of big-time sports enterprises that other businesses just don't have. Thanks to the reserve clause, professional team owners are playing Simon Legrees to the players' Topsy. It keeps players from getting the highest salaries they can in the marketplace, supposedly so that there will be better-balanced leagues for fans to watch. Actually, the reserve clause benefits the owners and creates a second-class group of citizens . . . [Owners] get great competitive advantages from the government, either directly or indirectly, while the fan faces nothing but higher ticket prices and even higher parking, hot-dog and beer prices.

Aug. 27/Los Angeles Times, 8-28:(3)1.

Bob Pulford
Hockey coach, Los Angeles "Kings"

3

Coaching has been a lot more difficult job than I imagined. You have to think about it all your waking hours. You're dealing with 21 different personalities and trying to be fair, yet motivating. It can also be nerve-wracking. You miss the playoffs one year and you have that hanging over your head all summer. But I'm enjoying it. You come into contact with a good cross-section of people and that makes it interesting. And when your team plays well, then it's very satisfying.

Los Angeles Herald-Examiner, 3-13:(D)1.

Lance Rentzel
Football player, Los Angeles "Rams"

4

[On the current NFL player strike]: I sup-

pose it's natural for anyone to start taking things for granted, but it's the one thing a professional football player can't do. We're nothing without the fans . . . That's why this strike is a tragedy. We're only hurting the fans. Sure, the animosity is between the owners and players, but it's the fans who suffer. I think both sides are to blame. The issue could have been settled with constructive negotiation, with determination on both sides. But the whole thing seems to follow the pattern of what's happening nationally. There is just too much striking, too much disdain for reason. It's wrecking the economy. We've lost an appreciation of what we have.

Interview, Long Beach, Calif., July 22/
Los Angeles Times, 7-23:(3)5.

Frank Robinson
Baseball player, California "Angels"

5

[Saying he hasn't been asked to manage a team in the major leagues because he is black]: They make excuses; nothing but excuses. They tell me I haven't managed in the minors, even though I have five years of managing in Puerto Rico. They tell me people wouldn't come to watch a team with a black [manager]. That's nonsense. People will come to watch any team that wins. Baseball owners are prejudiced. They are almost all bigots. Only when I see a black manager will my opinion change.

Interview/Los Angeles Times, 6-25:(3)2.

Frank Robinson
Baseball player and manager-designate,
Cleveland "Indians"

6

[On his being named manager of the *Indians*]: The only reason I'm the first black manager [in major-league baseball] is that I was born black. That's the color I am. I'm not a superman. I'm not a miracle-worker. Your ballplayers determine how good a team you have. I might influence the ballplayers to some extent, but if we have a good team, they deserve the credit. If a ball club fails, I think the manager should be held responsible. I want to be judged by the play on the field.

News conference, Cleveland, Oct. 3/
The New York Times, 10-4:1.

1

[On his being named as the first black manager in major-league baseball]: No, I don't think my presence will cause an increase in black attendance at Cleveland. People come out to see the players. When do you see a manager anyway? When he's out on the field arguing with the umpires, making a fool of himself—you know he can't win—and when he brings out the line-up card.

TV-radio interview/"Face the Nation,"
Columbia Broadcasting System, 10-13.

Pepper Rodgers
Football coach,
Georgia Institute of Technology

2

Football is a fun game, but not unless you win. You can't win without work and a certain element of fear. I don't punish players, I just work them. I care—I really do care—what the players think about me. I want them to like me. But they still have to fear me. I still have to be The Man.

Interview/
The Atlanta Constitution, 8-19:(D)6.

Pete Rose
Baseball player, Cincinnati "Reds"

3

You pick up the paper sometimes and read where a player says, "I can't play for this manager." Makes me laugh. You don't play for the manager; you play for the team. This is who I play for [the *Reds*]. I play for 24 other players, the manager and the trainer—everybody on the team.

Interview, Tampa, Fla./
The Dallas Times Herald, 3-13:(D)2.

4

[On fan rowdyism and fan abuse of players]: We have to face it. People's frustrations seem much greater today than they were, say, 20-25 years ago. Stop and think a minute. What better place for someone to relieve his frustrations than in a baseball park? The ballpark is warm and comfortable. It's outdoors and affords a perfect opportunity for free expression. Where else can a guy walk in and call someone making $100,000 anything he wants, practically to his face, without being answered back?

The Dallas Times Herald, 6-2:(C)3.

5

Playing baseball for a living is like having a license to steal.

Los Angeles Times, 8-5:(3)3.

Carroll Rosenbloom
Owner, Los Angeles "Rams"
football team

6

[On a possible player strike]: . . . we've got to get a season of some kind under way, not only for our [owners'] sake, but for the sake of the players, too. If we let the National [Football] League black out for a whole season, we might find that no one missed us. With the competition you have for the sports dollar today, you don't dare walk off the field.

Los Angeles Herald-Examiner, 6-24:(C)1.

Pete Rozelle
Commissioner of Professional
Football (United States)

7

That for me is where a commissioner really gets his strength: It really comes down to confidence, persuasion in many cases. It's hard to point to a book and say, "It says this, so you've got to do that." It comes down to your ability to persuade people. And if things have been going well and you have been a part of the going-well, you've got a better shot at persuading them . . . For me, personally, I don't view the job as power. The things some people call power I view as an obligation, as responsibility . . . I've had at various times probably every owner in the league upset with me on a given issue.

Interview, New York/
Los Angeles Times, 3-17:(3)1.

Bill Russell
General manager and coach,
Seattle "SuperSonics" basketball
team; Former player

8

[Saying people in basketball tend to take themselves too seriously today]: Sometimes I

WHAT THEY SAID IN 1974

get up and cuss and swear and feel like grabbing one of the guys and smacking him. Then I say, what the hell am I doing? These are grown men out there, half-naked, running up and down throwing a ball around, getting enormous amounts of money for doing it—and I'm getting mad.

At National Press Club, Washington, April 17/Los Angeles Times, 4-18:(3)1.

Tex Schramm
President, Dallas "Cowboys"
football team
1

The way to run a pro club is to stay in contention all the time. Aim to be one of the half-dozen best clubs each season. If you're always in the race, you'll get lucky once in a while and win it all. Football isn't a one-day event like the Indianapolis 500. It's a six-month event. You owe it to yourself and your fans to build a team that can win most of the time every year during the 20-game schedules. The media focuses on one big Sunday in January [the Super Bowl]. But your fans like to win in August and October and December, too. The history of this league is the history of teams that splurged to win the "big one" and then dropped out of sight for years.

Los Angeles Times, 12-21:(3)1.

Omar Sharif
Actor
2

Bridge is better than backgammon, because luck does not enter at all. Bridge is all skill, like chess. But chess is one long problem, while bridge is many small problems. It presents a series of puzzles to solve. Bridge trains the mind and, therefore, is very useful in other walks of life. It requires a very high standard of ethics, and that's good for the world. It keeps people out of mischief. When my son plays bridge, I know he is not smoking pot.

Interview, Paris/ Chicago Tribune, 10-28:(1)20.

Steve Smith
Pole vaulter
3

As a youth, I regarded the Olympics as a pinnacle. When I got there, I saw it was different—50 per cent politics and 50 per cent athletics. In Europe, where you can make $50,000 as an amateur, it makes sense [to be an amateur]. But a gold medal in this country [the U.S.] is worth about as much loose change as I have . . . Pro track is the future of track.

Los Angeles Herald-Examiner, 2-27:(D)3.

Lou Spadia
President, San Francisco "49ers"
football team
4

[On the current NFL player strike]: They [the strikers] don't seem to realize that professional football teams do not show the fantastic profit they all think they do. If the net profit for all the teams in the league is more than $7 million, it would be amazing. Professional football is not a sound business investment for a man who wants to get rich . . . Understand that nobody is pleading poverty with this team. If necessary, increased benefits and salaries can be budgeted. It is the so-called "freedom issues" that I object to. The option clause isn't in there to hurt the players. It's in there to protect the owners from each other . . . There is no way that we could function, with the complete freedom of players to move as they please. It would be the ruination of the sport.

Interview, Goleta, Calif./ San Francisco Examiner & Chronicle, 8-4:(C)2.

Casey Stengel
Former baseball manager, New York "Mets"
5

The *Mets* have been paying me for the past 10 years and people ask me what I do for them. I don't bother them, that's what.

New York/The Washington Post, 1-27:(D)12.

Mike Storen
Commissioner,
American Basketball Association
6

I would like to see us [the ABA] expand if all the elements and all the reasons for expanding are present. If we have good solid ownership, a good arena, a good rental agreement in the arena; if we have dates, if we have a formula that will allow us to stock a team to make it competitive; if we know that the ownership of the franchise is going to establish professional management, if we know that we have enough time to go in and establish a viable franchise instead of going in in September and opening in October—only if we have all those elements will we expand.

Norfolk, Va./The Washington Post, 1-27:(D)4.

Joe Torre
Baseball player, St. Louis "Cardinals"
1

[Saying baseball is more complicated than other sports]: In basketball and hockey, as well as football, the players operate on fixed patterns. They play against the clock. In baseball, it's different. We're at the whims of a thrown or batted ball . . . It's sad that so many of the young people coming up don't understand or appreciate the intricacies of baseball—I mean the way the dyed-in-the-wool baseball fan does. But we play every day, not just once a week; and we are not able to build up to the one big Sunday. If you go 4-for-4 today, you can't let down tomorrow. The demands are always there—day in and day out.

St. Petersburg, Fla./
The Dallas Times Herald, 3-14:(E)1.

Lee Trevino
Golfer
2

Golf is 30 per cent talent and 70 per cent luck. Look at Doug Sanders. He has one of the best games in golf and he's never won a major championship. Arnold Palmer has never won the PGA. Sam Snead never won the U.S. Open. When I won at Muirfield, I chipped in four times from off the green. You can't call that talent. Somebody higher than me told those balls where to go.

Lytham St. Annes, England, July 8/
The Washington Post, 7-9:(D)3.

John V. Tunney
United States Senator, D–California
3

[Supporting a proposed bill that would eliminate the reserve clause in sports]: What we hope to accomplish is to give athletes an opportunity to negotiate with any team wanting to buy their services. Why should we have special rules for athletes not to enjoy the freedom we all have? There is no reason why an athlete should be treated like a child and not sell his services for what they are worth like everyone else . . . There will be some contention and some oxen gored, but that's freedom and the price that has to be paid. Congress must recognize athletes have dignity. I pledge I will do all I can to get this legislation through as a Bill of Rights for athletes. The [team] owners are unified and strong, and the only way the players can be strong is to be unified. I hope there is no [football players] strike. I love football. But it is important for you to have a common purpose and a common goal. If you are unified, you can move mountains.

Before National Football League
Players Association, Chicago, March 3/
The New York Times, 3-4:43.

Al Unser
Auto racing driver
4

[On the effect of the fuel shortage on auto racing]: With the fuel restrictions they've placed on us, all we can do is go out and watch the gas gauge. What we're involved in now is not auto racing—it's an economy run. It's crazy, stupid. We spend $100,000 building a car; we spend another $100,000 buying engines; we spend $50,000 to $75,000 testing to see that we've got a car that will be competitive against all comers. So what does it boil down to? A simple little thing like who can go farther on 280 gallons of fuel?

Los Angeles Times, 3-9:(3)2.

Bobby Unser
Auto racing driver
5

Every driver that's good has to scare himself, constantly, over and over again. You don't ever

505

(BOBBY UNSER)

drive 100 per cent. You drive 105 per cent . . . But if you drive 115 per cent, you're going to crash. Unfortunately, when you're young you do have to go through the experience of going over the limit to find out where it is. That's the reason a car owner hates to get a rookie.

Los Angeles Times, 10-22:(3)1.

Bill van Breda Kolff
Basketball coach, Memphis "Tams"

1

Sometimes when I get up in the morning, I'll stare at myself in the bathroom mirror for several minutes. The hair's grayer, there're a few more lines in the face and my eyes are red. And I look around and I'm standing in another hotel room. I've got to shave and pack and catch another train. And I say to myself: "You're 51 years old and you're still running around with these 20-year-old basketball players." There are times when I'd like to say the hell with it, spend some more time with my family and live in a quieter life. But there's a certain excitement in being a coach, something I'm not sure I could give up. It's exciting to be out on the court, with the fans cheering, talking to the people from the press. It's an ego thing, I guess, but there's glamor in it. I guess I'm still a kid who hasn't grown up.

Interview, Norfolk, Va., January/
San Francisco Examiner & Chronicle,
11-24:(C)6.

Bill Veeck
Former baseball-club owner

2

[Saying many successful baseball managers were not very good players]: They had to learn more about the game to maximize their small ability. The star doesn't have to think; he just walks up and hits the ball or rocks back and throws it. The fringe player has to scheme and connive and study just to hold a job, and in the process he learns more about the game and about people than the star ever does.

The New York Times, 7-28:(5)3.

Wade Walker
Athletic director, University of Oklahoma

3

Athletics is still one of the true free-enterprise areas of the American democracy. It doesn't make any difference what color your skin is or what your social status is, because you just got 11 youngsters out there [in football], nose to nose and toes to toes, and the guy who really wants to qualify can make it. That's the way this country began, and this is still one place where a guy can be rewarded by what he does. And it's not like that in any other area any more.

Interview/The New York Times, 1-16:91.

Tom Weiskopf
Golfer

4

[Criticizing high-money corporate-sponsored tournaments]: There's too much emphasis placed on the dollar. I think we're playing for too much money. When I say we're playing for too much money, I mean to say $500,000 for a golf tournament is ridiculous. Why should a guy make $100,000 in two weeks? . . . I think we need tournaments that have supported the PGA tour. We need tournaments like the San Antonio Open a heck of a lot more than the Mickey Mouse Open or the Dow Jones Open or the Campbell Soup Open. I don't want my grandchildren to come up to me and say, "What did you win in 1972? Was that the Mickey Mouse Open?" I just think these big companies . . . they're with us for only two or three years and it's just like a commercial. It just seems in past history that these big tournaments with these fantastic purses never last. When I first started on the tour in 1965, the Greensboro Open was $60,000. They've increased their purse every year and they'll be with us forever. It's a civic, organized week, something that a whole town looks forward to. It's something that grandfathers tell their grandchildren about.

The New York Times, 1-20:(5)5.

Jerry West
Basketball player, Los Angeles "Lakers"

5

I can see quite a difference from the time I started playing. Because of the importance our society places on sports, many athletes' lives are so much softer. Suddenly, from a pretty good living, guys are commanding huge salaries. We used to stay in some not-so-great hotels. Today, if they don't stay at the best place, have the best equipment and best practice facilities, the athletes are quick to spot it. So in that sense, it's true . . . we're spoiled. And there's no question motivation is lacking. The athlete almost can't help it. Every guy has a lawyer, an agent and a battery of other people working for him. He's an athlete, sure, but he's also an investor, a businessman and so on. But I don't blame the athletes . . . not entirely, anyway. It's the owners who pay the ridiculous prices for franchises, who pay the ridiculous salaries and meet the demands. Then they turn around and charge the public for it. More than anything, it's a reflection of the times we live in.

Los Angeles Times, 2-22:(3)10.

Dick Williams
Baseball manager, California "Angels"

1

I've always gone back to the belief that you don't win—that the other team usually beats itself. That's why I'll continue to emphasize pitching and defense. You get those two things straightened out and the offense will take care of itself.

The Christian Science Monitor, 7-17:9.

Maury Wills
Former baseball player,
Los Angeles "Dodgers"

2

Baseball managers go hard on fundamentals for two weeks of spring training, and then drop it. By mid-season, most players have forgotten everything they learned in March. Some have no idea what the sign is for a pick-off play, if the club had one to start with . . . I suppose that to keep harping on fundamentals at the major-league level sounds ridiculous, but kids come up now after only one or two years in the minors. They don't have the experience. I would devote a half hour prior to all 162 games for a review of the cutoff, the pick-off, the hit-and-run, the steal. It's a matter of minimizing risks in plays that are calculated risks. I've had

people say there wouldn't be enough time for a program like this. But there is. Most players burn up time standing around or playing cards. My feeling is that they'd rather be receiving help . . . I can't think of one player who'd get a passing grade if tested on the rule book. I was able to pull off a number of trick plays because I knew the other guy didn't know the rules. Maybe that knowledge doesn't make you that much of a better player, but it's part of the game, part of our business. A broker has to be aware of government regulations and a baseball player should be aware of the rules.

Interview, Los Angeles/
Los Angeles Times, 1-28:(3)1,7.

Bobby Winkles
Baseball manager, California "Angels"

3

My ideas haven't changed. I still have my players *running* on and off the field, and that includes the pitchers. There's no reason why they should *walk* back and forth to the mound. I keep on my players to run hard on every hit, too. If you're trotting on a base hit and the outfielder juggles the ball, you may not be able to go to second; but if you're running all the way, you may steal yourself an extra base now and then. Running also instills the proper attitude. There's an Olympic event for walking, and as far as I'm concerned that's the only walking you should see in sports.

Interview/
The Christian Science Monitor, 5-3:(F)3.

Charley Winner
Football coach, New York "Jets"

4

Professional football isn't just what we do here at the training center. It's what you do at home at night, too. There has to be a lot of mental preparation off the field. The guy who's highly motivated will spend an hour at home, instead of watching television, preparing himself mentally and going over the things he has to know. It boils down to the individual who is willing to do a little more than is necessary.

Interview, Hempstead, N.Y., Oct. 15/
The New York Times, 10-16:52.

John Wooden
Basketball coach, University of
California, Los Angeles   1

Whenever you lose a game you're going to have your critics. Everyone has their critics. A doctor is criticized for losing a patient. A dentist is criticized for losing a patient's teeth. A salesman is criticized for losing a sale. No coach has a corner on material. No coach has a corner on brains. For every winner, there is a loser. But people sometimes forget that. I've even heard people criticize the Mona Lisa.

Interview, Los Angeles/
Los Angeles Herald-Examiner, 1-3:(C)2.

2

I'm disappointed in the [current] National Football League players' strike. I feel there was a time when labor was at the mercy of management completely. But now I think labor unions have gotten out of hand, in many ways. Unions of professional athletes are asking and demanding too much. I'd always been on the players' side, until the last few years. But things have gotten so outlandish. Who is going to pay for it? The general public—you and I. I hear pro athletes say their careers are short-lived, so they have to get it while they can. What the heck? Do they want to have all the retirement benefits after 5 or 10 years of play? . . . Most people work year 'round with only a month's vacation. How about professional athletes? And so many doors are open to them for income that isn't available to the average person at all. So, frankly, I'm disappointed.

Interview, Los Angeles/
Los Angeles Times, 7-16:(3)5.

Gump Worsley
Hockey goaltender, Minnesota "North Stars"   3

Kids coming up today have no pride. After a loss, they stand around the dressing room laughing. Imagine that? They couldn't care less. All they're concerned about is rushing out and having a few beers.

Los Angeles Times, 2-22:(3)1.

4

A goaltender should have a hard skull, quick hands and skin like a rhinoceros. The skull and hands are for flying pucks; the thick skin will defy the slings and arrows of critical coaches, customers and the news media.

Los Angeles Times, 3-13:(3)1.

Jim Wynn
Baseball player, Los Angeles "Dodgers"   5

What I think I have not learned is to avoid "pressing." Baseball isn't like football, which is played once a week and has a season of only 14 games. You must make yourself realize in baseball that you have 162 chances. You have a bad day, you don't have to wait a week—you can get even the next day. In my estimation, the toughest thing about hitting is selling yourself on this philosophy. You make yourself comfortable at bat, free of worries that you must prove yourself that minute, and you will hit the ball a lot better.

Interview/
Los Angeles Herald-Examiner, 5-15:(D)1.

The Indexes

Index to Subjects

A

H

I

K

L

N

U

V

W